Collins

D0994043

Collins Student World Atlas

Collins
An imprint of HarperCollinsPublishers
77–85 Fulham Palace Road
London
W6 8JB

© HarperCollinsPublishers 2007
Maps © Collins Bartholomew Ltd 2007

First published 2005, reprinted 2005
Second edition 2007
ISBN-10 0-00-723460-0 (HB School edition)
ISBN-13 978-0-00-723460-8 (HB School edition)
ISBN-10 0-00-723462-7 (PB School edition)
ISBN-13 978-0-00-723462-2 (PB School edition)
ISBN-10 0-00-723459-7 (HB Trade edition)
ISBN-13 978-0-00-723459-2 (HB Trade edition)
ISBN-10 0-00-723461-9 (PB Trade edition)
ISBN-13 978-0-00-723461-5 (PB Trade edition)

Imp 001

The contents of this edition of the Collins Student
World Atlas are believed correct at the time of
printing. Nevertheless the publishers can accept
no responsibility for errors or omissions, changes
in the detail given, or for any expense or loss thereby
caused.

Printed and bound in Singapore

British Library Cataloguing in Publication Data.
A catalogue record for this book is available from
the British Library.

All mapping in this atlas is generated from Collins
Bartholomew digital databases. Collins
Bartholomew, the UK's leading independent
geographical information supplier, can provide a
digital, custom, and premium mapping service to
a variety of markets.
For further information:
Tel: +44 (0) 141 306 3752
e-mail: collinsbartholomew@harpercollins.co.uk

visit our websites at: www.collinsbartholomew.com
www.collinseducation.com/atlases

Collins. Do More.
www.collins.co.uk

2 Contents

4 Map types and Satellite images
5 Map projections and Satellite images
6 Latitude and Longitude
7 Map scale

UNITED KINGDOM

8–9 **United Kingdom** Counties
10–11 **United Kingdom** Southeast England
12–13 **United Kingdom** Wales and Southwest England
14–15 **United Kingdom** Northern England
16–17 **United Kingdom** Northern Ireland and Southern Scotland
18–19 **United Kingdom** Northern Scotland
20–21 **United Kingdom** Climate
22 **United Kingdom** Relief
23 **United Kingdom** Rock types
24–25 **United Kingdom** Population and Migration
26–27 **United Kingdom** Economic activity
28 **United Kingdom** Energy
29 **United Kingdom** Tourism
30–31 **United Kingdom** Transport and Communications
32–33 **Greater Manchester**

EUROPE

34–35 **Europe** Relief
35 **Europe** Physical regions, Countries, European Union
36 **Europe** Climate
37 **Europe** Population
38 **Europe** Economic activity
39 **Europe** Tourism
40 **Scandinavia**
41 **Ireland**
42 **Netherlands, Belgium and Luxembourg**
43 **Rotterdam–Europoort**
44 **France**
45 **France** Regions, Population, Energy, Trade
46 **Poland**
47 **Poland** Regions, Population, Minerals and Energy, Conservation
48 **Spain and Portugal**
49 **Spain** Regions, Population, Tourism and Water management
50 **Italy**
51 **Italy** Regions, Earthquakes and Volcanoes
52–53 **Mediterranean Basin**
54–55 **Central Europe**
56–57 **Southeast Europe**
58–59 **Russian Federation**

NORTH AMERICA

60 **North America** Relief, Physical regions
61 **North America** Climate
62–63 **Canada**
63 **North America** Countries
64–65 **United States of America**
66 **United States** Population
67 **United States** Economic activity, Trade
68–69 **San Francisco**
70–71 **Mexico and the Caribbean**

SOUTH AMERICA

72–73 **South America**
72 **South America** Physical regions
73 **South America** Countries
74 **South America** Climate
75 **South America** Land cover
76–77 **Brazil**
76 São Paulo
78 **Brazil** Population
79 **Brazil** Economic activity, Trade
80–81 **Rondônia**

AFRICA

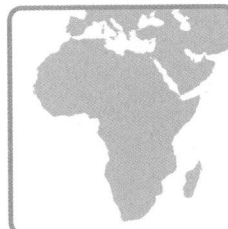

82 **Africa** Relief, Physical regions
83 **Africa** Climate
4–85 **Northern Africa**
84 **Africa** Countries
86 **Southern Africa**
87 **Kenya**
88 **Kenya** Population, Tourism
89 **Kenya** Economic activity, Nairobi, Trade

ASIA

0–91 **Asia** Relief
91 **Asia** Physical regions, Countries
92 **Asia** Climate
93 **Asia** Monsoon
4–95 **Middle East**
94 **Middle East** Oil
6–97 **Pakistan, India, Bangladesh and Myanmar**
97 **Kolkata**
98 **India** Population
99 **India** Tourism, Economic activity, Trade
100 **Bangladesh** Population, Economic activity, Trade
101 **Bangladesh** Rainfall, Flood control
2–103 **China**
4–105 **Southeast Asia**
106 **Japan**
107 **Japan** Economic activity, Population, Energy, Tectonics

OCEANIA

108–109 **Pacific Ocean**
110–111 **Australia and New Zealand**
111 **Australia and New Zealand** Climate
112 **The Arctic Ocean and Antarctica**

WORLD

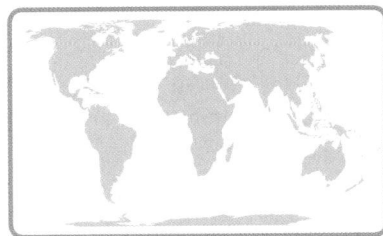

113 **World** International organizations
114–115 **World** Countries, Time zones
116–117 **World** Relief
118–119 **World** Climate, Vegetation
120–121 **World** Tectonics
122–123 **World** Population, Population density, Population change, Urban population
124 **World** Birth rates, Death rates, Infant mortality rate
125 **World** Life expectancy, Literacy, Doctors
126 **World** Human Development Index, Access to safe water, Nutrition
127 **World** HIV/AIDS, Poverty, Aid
128–129 **World** Environmental issues
130 **World** Fuel production, Energy production, Energy consumption
131 **World** Gross National Income, Employment, Trade
132–133 **World** Tourism
134 **World** Communications
135 **World** Air transport
136–143 **World** Statistics

144–168 **Index**

Map Symbols

Symbols are used, in the form of points, lines or areas, on maps to show the location of and information about specific features.
The colour and size of a symbol can give an indication of the type of feature and its relative size.
The meaning of map symbols is explained in a key shown on each page. Symbols used on reference maps are shown below.

Relief and physical features

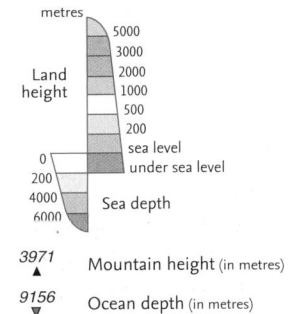

3971 ▲ Mountain height (in metres)
9156 ▼ Ocean depth (in metres)
⬜ Permanent ice (ice cap or glacier)

Water features

〰 River
Intermittent river
Canal
Lake / Reservoir
Intermittent lake
Marsh

Communications

—— Railway
═══ Motorway
—— Road
········· Ferry
⊕ Main airport
✈ Regional airport

Administration

——— International boundary
——— Internal boundary
– – – Disputed boundary
········ Ceasefire line

Settlement

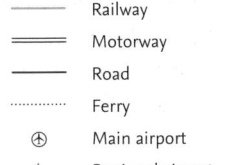 Urban area

National capital	Population classification
■ BUCHAREST	Over 10 000 000
■ ATHENS	1 000 000–10 000 000
☐ SKOPJE	500 000–1 000 000
☐ NICOSIA	100 000–500 000

Other city or town	Population classification
● İstanbul	Over 10 000 000
● İzmir	1 000 000–10 000 000
○ Konya	500 000–1 000 000
○ Split	100 000–500 000
○ Dubrovnik	10 000–100 000
○ Bar	0–10 000

Map Types

Many types of map are included in the atlas to show different information. The type of map, its symbols and colours are carefully selected to show the theme of each map and to make them easy to understand. The main types of map used are explained below.

Extract from page 114

Political maps provide an overview of the size and location of countries in a specific area, such as a continent. Coloured squares indicate national capitals. Coloured circles represent other cities or towns.

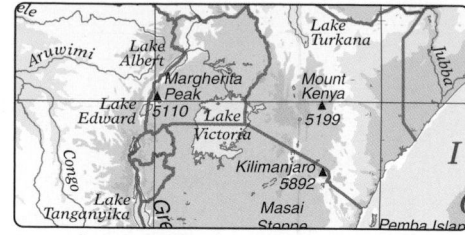

Extract from page 82

Physical or relief maps use colour to show oceans, seas, rivers, lakes, and the height of the land. The names and heights of major landforms are also indicated.

Extract from page 96

Physical/political maps bring together the information provided in the two types of map described left. They show relief and physical features as well as country borders, major cities and towns, roads, railways, and airports.

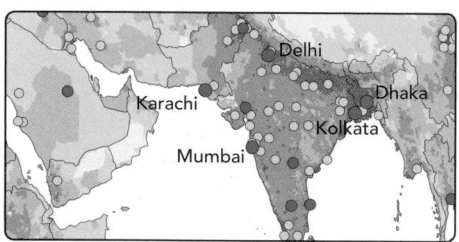

Extract from page 123

Distribution maps use different colours, symbols, or shading to show the location and distribution of natural or man-made features. In this map, symbols indicate the distribution of the world's largest cities.

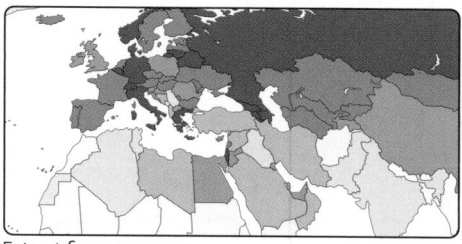

Extract from page 125

Graduated colour maps use colours or shading to show a topic or theme and a measure of its intensity. Generally, the highest values are shaded with the darkest colours. In this map, colours are used to show the number of doctors per 100 000 people.

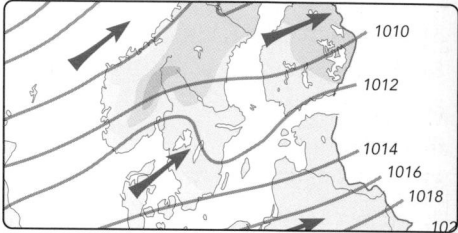

Extract from page 36

Isoline maps use thin lines to show the distribution of a feature. An isoline passes through places of the same value. Isolines may show features such as temperature (isotherm), air pressure (isobar), or height of land (contour). The value of the line is usually written on it. On either side of the line the value will be higher or lower.

Creating Satellite Images

Images captured by a large number of Earth-observing satellites provide unique views of the Earth. The science of gathering and interpreting such images is known as remote sensing. Geographers use images taken from high above the Earth to determine patterns, trends and basic characteristics of the Earth's surface. Satellites are fitted with different kinds of scanners or sensors to gather information about the Earth. The most well known satellites are Landsat and SPOT.

Satellite sensors detect electromagnetic radiation —X-rays, ultraviolet light, visible colours and microwave signals. This data can be processed to provide information on soils, land use, geology, pollution and weather patterns. Colours can be added to this data to help understand the images. In some cases this results in a 'false-colour' image where red areas represent vegetation and built-up areas show as blue/grey. Examples of satellite images are included in this atlas to illustrate geographical themes.

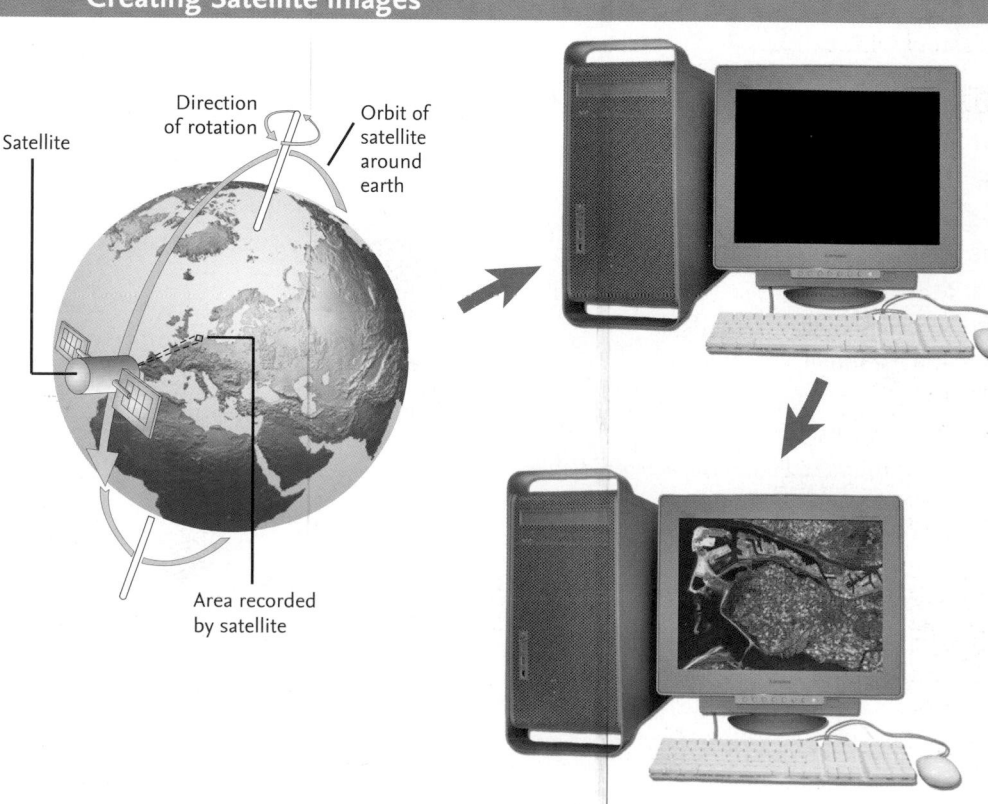

Satellite

Direction of rotation

Orbit of satellite around earth

Area recorded by satellite

Because the Earth is a sphere and maps are flat, map makers (cartographers) have developed different ways of showing the Earth's surface on a flat piece of paper. These methods are called map projections, because they are based on the idea of the Earth's surface being 'projected' onto a piece of paper.

There are many types of map projection, but none of them show the Earth with perfect accuracy. Every map projection must stretch or distort the surface to make it fit onto a flat map. As a result, either shape, area, direction or distance will be distorted. The amount of distortion increases away from the point at which

the globe touches the piece of paper onto which it is projected. Areas of increasing distortion are shown in red on the diagrams below. Map projections are carefully chosen in this atlas to show the area of the Earth's surface as accurately as possible. The three main types of map projection used are explained below.

Cylindrical Projections

 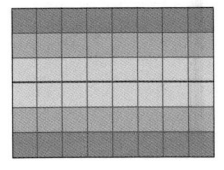

Cylindrical projections are constructed by projecting the surface of the globe or sphere (Earth) onto a cylinder that just touches the outside edges of that globe. Two examples of cylindrical projections are Mercator and Times.

Mercator Projection (see pages 104-105 for an example of this projection)

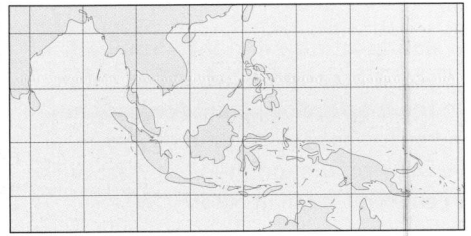

The Mercator cylindrical projection is useful for areas near the equator and to about 15 degrees north or south of the equator, where distortion of shape is minimal. The projection is useful for navigation, since directions are plotted as straight lines.

Conic Projections

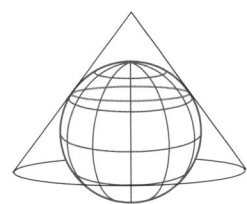 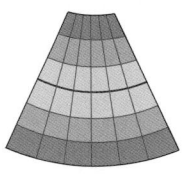

Conic projections are constructed by projecting the surface of a globe or sphere (Earth) onto a cone that just touches the outside edges of that globe. Examples of conic projections are Conic Equidistant and Albers Equal Area Conic.

Conic Equidistant Projection (see pages 58-59 for an example of this projection)

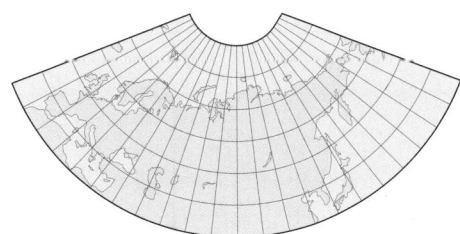

Conic projections are best suited for areas between 30° and 60° north and south of the equator when the east-west distance is greater than the north-south distance (such as Canada and Europe). The meridians are straight and spaced at equal intervals.

Azimuthal Projections

 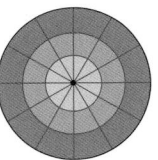

Azimuthal projections are constructed by projecting the surface of the globe or sphere (Earth) onto a flat surface that touches the globe at one point only. Some examples of azimuthal projections are Lambert Azimuthal Equal Area and Polar Stereographic.

Polar Stereographic Projection (see page 112 for an example of this projection)

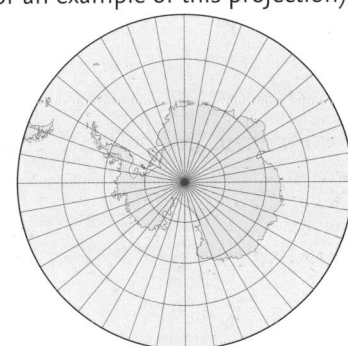

Azimuthal projections are useful for areas that have similar east-west and north-south dimensions such as Antarctica and Australia.

Satellite Images

Land use – Port of Rotterdam

Deforestation – Rondônia

Latitude

Latitude is distance, measured in degrees, north and south of the equator. Lines of latitude circle the globe in an east-west direction. The distance between lines of latitude is always the same. They are also known as parallels of latitude. Because the circumference of Earth gets smaller toward the poles, the lines of latitude are shorter nearer the poles.

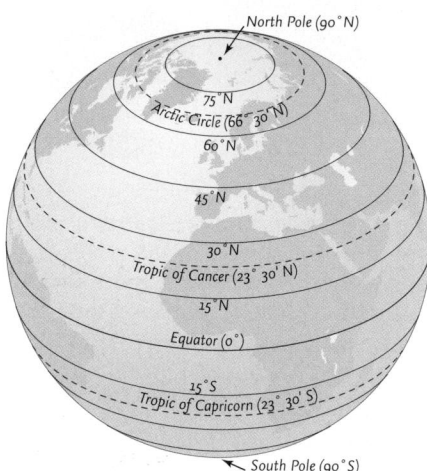

All lines of latitude have numbers between 0° and 90° and a direction, either north or south of the equator. The equator is at 0° latitude. The North Pole is at 90° north and the South Pole is at 90° south. The 'tilt' of Earth has given particular importance to some lines of latitude . They include:

- the Arctic Circle at 66° 30' north
- the Antarctic Circle at 66° 30' south
- the Tropic of Cancer at 23° 30' north
- the Tropic of Capricorn at 23° 30' south

The Equator also divides the Earth into two halves. The northern half, north of the Equator, is the **Northern Hemisphere.** The southern half, south of the Equator, is the **Southern Hemisphere.**

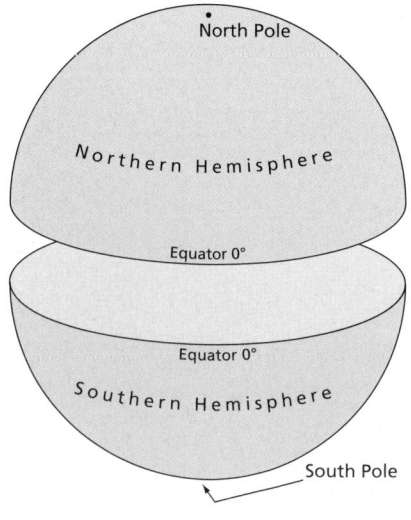

Longitude

Longitude is distance, measured in degrees, east and west of the Greenwich Meridian (prime meridian). Lines of longitude join the poles in a north-south direction. Because the lines join the poles, they are always the same length, but are farthest apart at the equator and closest together at the poles. These lines are also called meridians of longitude.

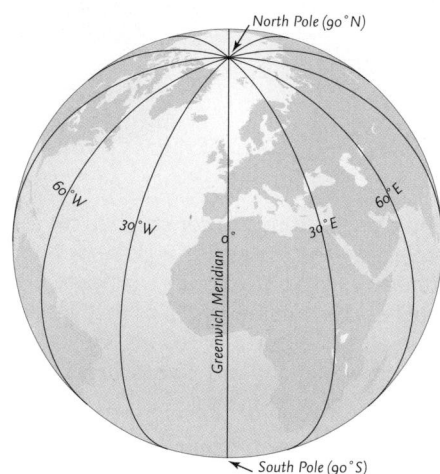

Longitude begins along the Greenwich Meridian (prime meridian), at 0°, in London, England. On the opposite side of Earth is the 180° meridian, which is the International Date Line. To the west of the prime meridian are Canada, the United States, and Brazil; to the east of the prime meridian are Germany, India and China. All lines of longitude have numbers between 0° and 180° and a direction, either east or west of the prime meridian.

The Greenwich Meridian and the International Date Line can also be used to divide the world into two halves. The half to the west of the Greenwich Meridian is the **Western Hemisphere.** The half to the east of the Greenwich Meridian is the **Eastern Hemisphere.**

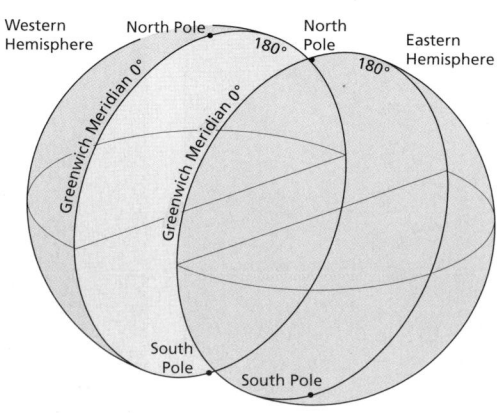

Finding Places

When lines of latitude and longitude are drawn on a map, they form a grid, which looks like a pattern of squares. This pattern is used to find places on a map. Latitude is always stated before longitude (e.g., 42°N 78°W).

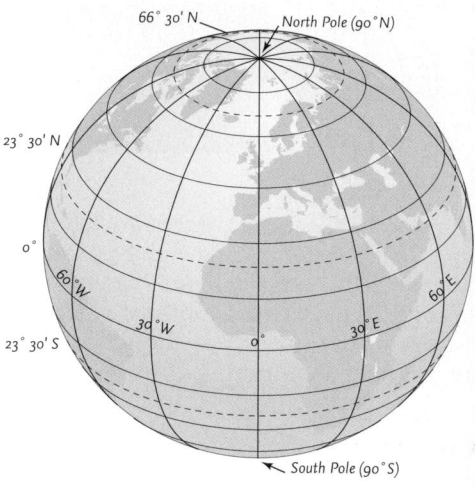

By stating latitude and then longitude of a place, it becomes much easier to find. On the map (below) point A is easy to find as it is exactly latitude 58° North of the Equator and longitude 4° West of the Greenwich Meridian (58°N 4°W).

To be even more accurate in locating a place, each degree of latitude and longitude can also be divided into smaller units called **minutes** ('). There are 60 minutes in each degree. On the map (below) Halkirk is one half (or 30/60ths) of the way past latitude 58°N, and one-half (or 30/60ths) of the way past longitude 3°W. Its latitude is therefore 58 degrees 30 minutes North and its longitude is 3 degrees 30 minutes West. This can be shortened to 58°30'N 3°30'W. Latitude and longitude for all the places and features named on the maps are included in the index.

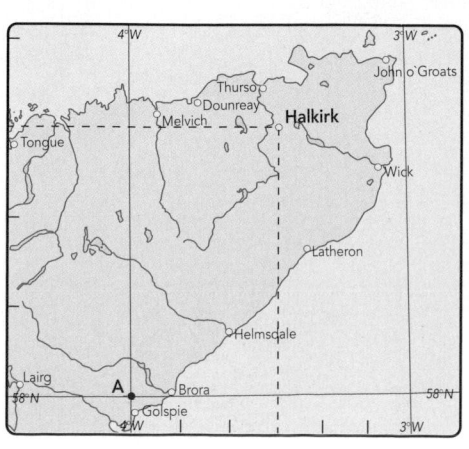

Scale

To draw a map of any part of the world, the area must be reduced, or 'scaled down,' to the size of a page in this atlas, a foldable road map, or a topographic map. The scale of the map indicates the amount by which an area has been reduced.

The scale of a map can also be used to determine the actual distance between two or more places or the actual size of an area on a map. The scale indicates the relationship between distances on the map and distances on the ground.

Scale can be shown
- **using words:** for example, 'one centimetre to one kilometre' (one centimetre on the map represents one kilometre on the ground), or 'one centimetre to 100 kilometres' (one centimetre on the map represents 100 kilometres on the ground).
- **using numbers:** for example, '1 : 100 000 or 1/100 000' (one centimetre on the map represents 100 000 centimetres on the ground), or '1 : 40 000 000 or 1/40 000 000' (one centimetre on the map represents 40 million centimetres on the ground). Normally, the large numbers with centimetres would be converted to metres or kilometres.
- **as a line scale:** for example,

```
0      200      400      600      800 km
```

Scale and Map Information

The scale of a map also determines how much information can be shown on it. As the area shown on a map becomes larger and larger, the amount of detail and the accuracy of the map becomes less and less.

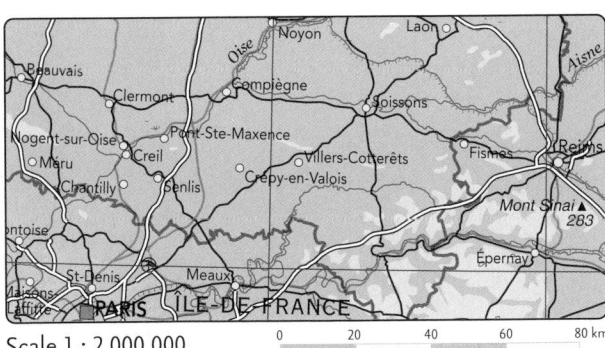

Scale 1 : 2 000 000

```
0      20      40      60      80 km
```

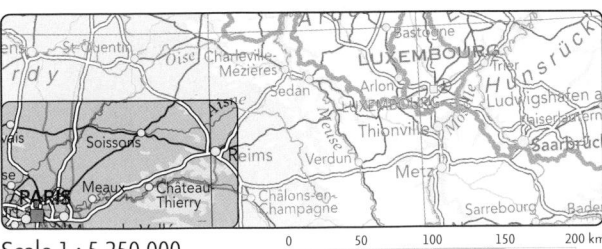

Scale 1 : 5 250 000

```
0      50      100      150      200 km
```

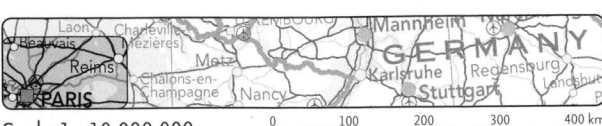

Scale 1 : 10 000 000

```
0      100      200      300      400 km
```

Measuring Distance

The instructions below show you how to determine how far apart places are on the map, then using the line scale, to determine the actual distance on the ground.

To use the line scale to measure the straight-line distance between two places on a map:
1. place the edge of a sheet of paper on the two places on a map,
2. on the paper, place a mark at each of the two places,
3. place the paper on the line scale,
4. measure the distance on the ground using the scale.

To find the distance between Calgary and Regina, line up the edge of a piece of paper between the two places and mark off the distance.

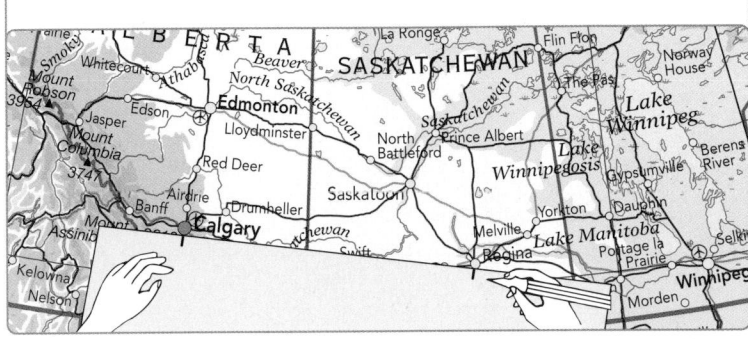

Compare this distance with the marks on the line scale. The straight-line distance between Calgary and Regina is about 650 kilometres.

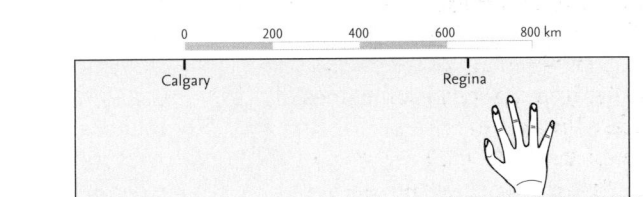

Often, the road or rail distance between two places is greater than the straight-line distance. To measure this distance:

1. place the edge of a sheet of paper on the map and mark off the start point on the paper,
2. move the paper so that its edge follows the bends and curves on the map (Hint: use the tip of your pencil to pin the edge of the paper to the curve as you pivot the paper around each curve),
3. mark off the end point on the sheet of paper,
4. place the paper on the line scale and read the actual distance following a road or railroad.

To find the distance by road between Calgary and Regina, mark off the start point, then twist the paper to follow the curve of the road through Medicine Hat, Swift Current, Moose Jaw, and then into Regina. The actual distance is about 750 kilometres.

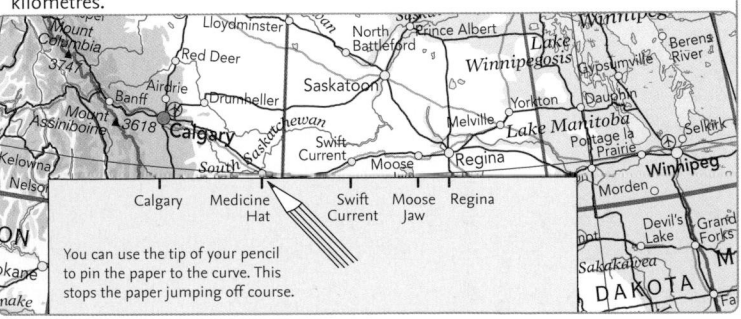

United Kingdom

SCOTLAND

NORTHERN IRELAND

ENGLAND

WALES

IRELAND

Edinburgh

Belfast

Cardiff

London

West Central Scotland

NORTH LANARKSHIRE

Kirkintilloch

GLASGOW CITY

Glasgow

Motherwell

EAST DUNBARTON-SHIRE

Giffnock

EAST RENFREW-SHIRE

WEST DUNBARTON-SHIRE

Dumbarton

RENFREWSHIRE

Paisley

Greenock

INVERCLYDE

East Central Scotland

Haddington

EAST LOTHIAN

Dalkeith

MIDLOTHIAN

Edinburgh

CITY OF EDINBURGH

CLACKMANNAN-SHIRE

Alloa

FALKIRK

Falkirk

Livingston

WEST LOTHIAN

SHETLAND

Lerwick

ORKNEY

Kirkwall

HIGHLAND

Inverness

WESTERN ISLES

Stornoway

Lochgilphead

ARGYLL AND BUTE

MORAY

Elgin

ABERDEEN-SHIRE

Aberdeen

S C O T L A N D

PERTH & KINROSS

Perth

ANGUS

Forfar

DUNDEE

Dundee

FIFE

Glenrothes

STIRLING

Stirling

Falkirk 7

Dumbarton 2

1

Paisley 3

RENFREWSHIRE

Glasgow 4

Hamilton

Kilmarnock

Irvine

NORTH AYRSHIRE

SOUTH LANARKSHIRE

EAST AYRSHIRE

Ayr

SOUTH AYRSHIRE

Alloa

8

9

10

Livingston

Edinburgh

MIDLOTHIAN

Dalkeith

Haddington

EAST LOTHIAN

Mothwell

6

5

SCOTTISH BORDERS

Newtown St Boswells

NORTHUMBERLAND

Ballycastle

MOYLE

Coleraine

SCOTLAND

1. INVERCLYDE
2. WEST DUNBARTONSHIRE
3. EAST RENFREWSHIRE
4. GLASGOW CITY
5. EAST DUNBARTONSHIRE
6. NORTH LANARKSHIRE
7. FALKIRK
8. CLACKMANNANSHIRE
9. WEST LOTHIAN
10. EDINBURGH

NORTHERN IRELAND

1. NEWTOWNABBEY
2. CARRICKFERGUS
3. BELFAST
4. CASTLEREAGH
5. NORTH DOWN

Key

Administration
Boundaries

International

National

Administrative

Settlement

■ Capital city

○ Administrative centre

Scale 1 : 3 000 000

0   25   50   75   100 km

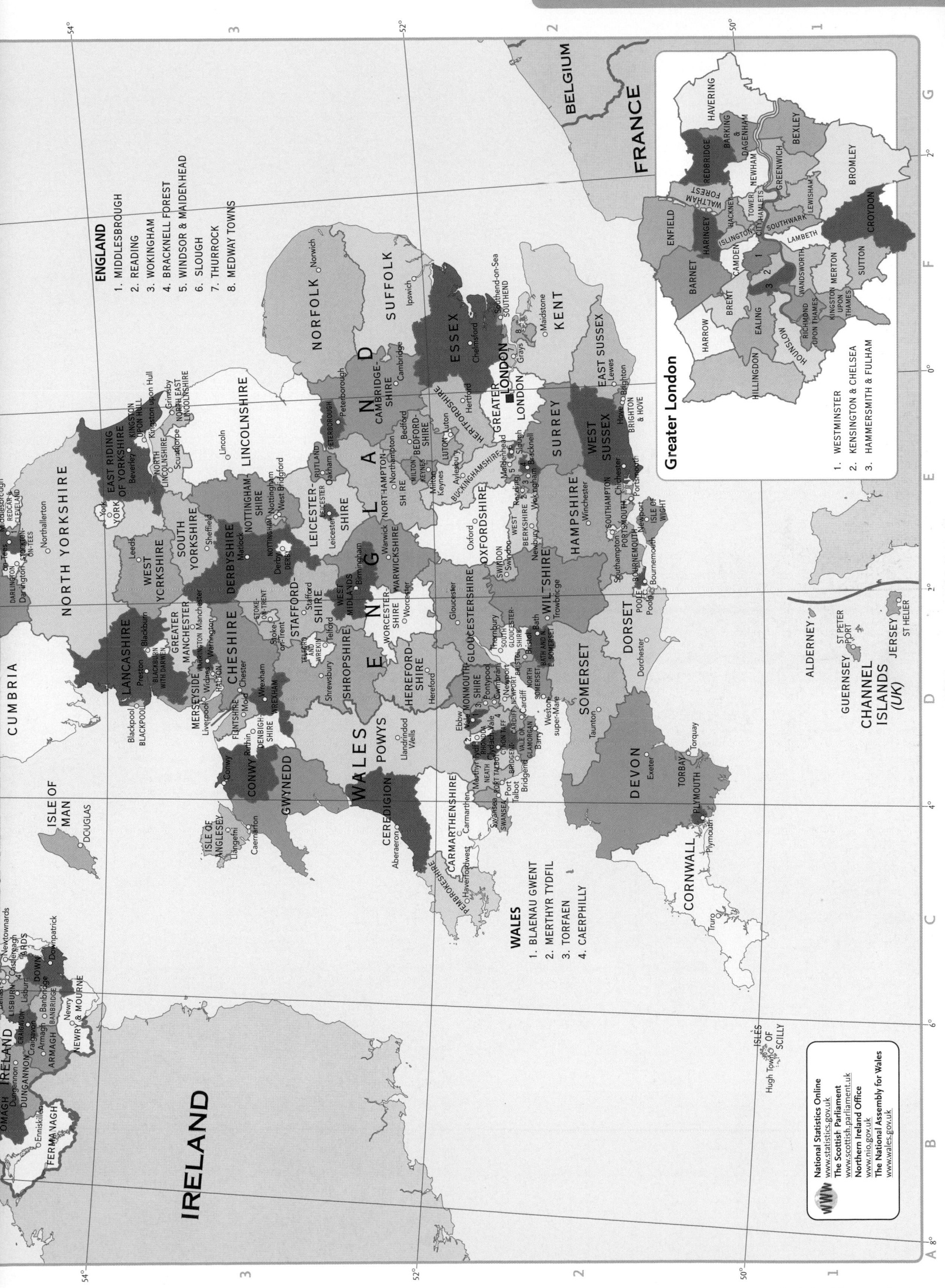

ENGLAND
1. MIDDLESBROUGH
2. READING
3. WOKINGHAM
4. BRACKNELL FOREST
5. WINDSOR & MAIDENHEAD
6. SLOUGH
7. THURROCK
8. MEDWAY TOWNS

WALES
1. BLAENAU GWENT
2. MERTHYR TYDFIL
3. TORFAEN
4. CAERPHILLY

Greater London

1. WESTMINSTER
2. KENSINGTON & CHELSEA
3. HAMMERSMITH & FULHAM

National Statistics Online
www.statistics.gov.uk
The Scottish Parliament
www.scottish.parliament.uk
Northern Ireland Office
www.nio.gov.uk
The National Assembly for Wales
www.wales.gov.uk

Conic Equidistant projection

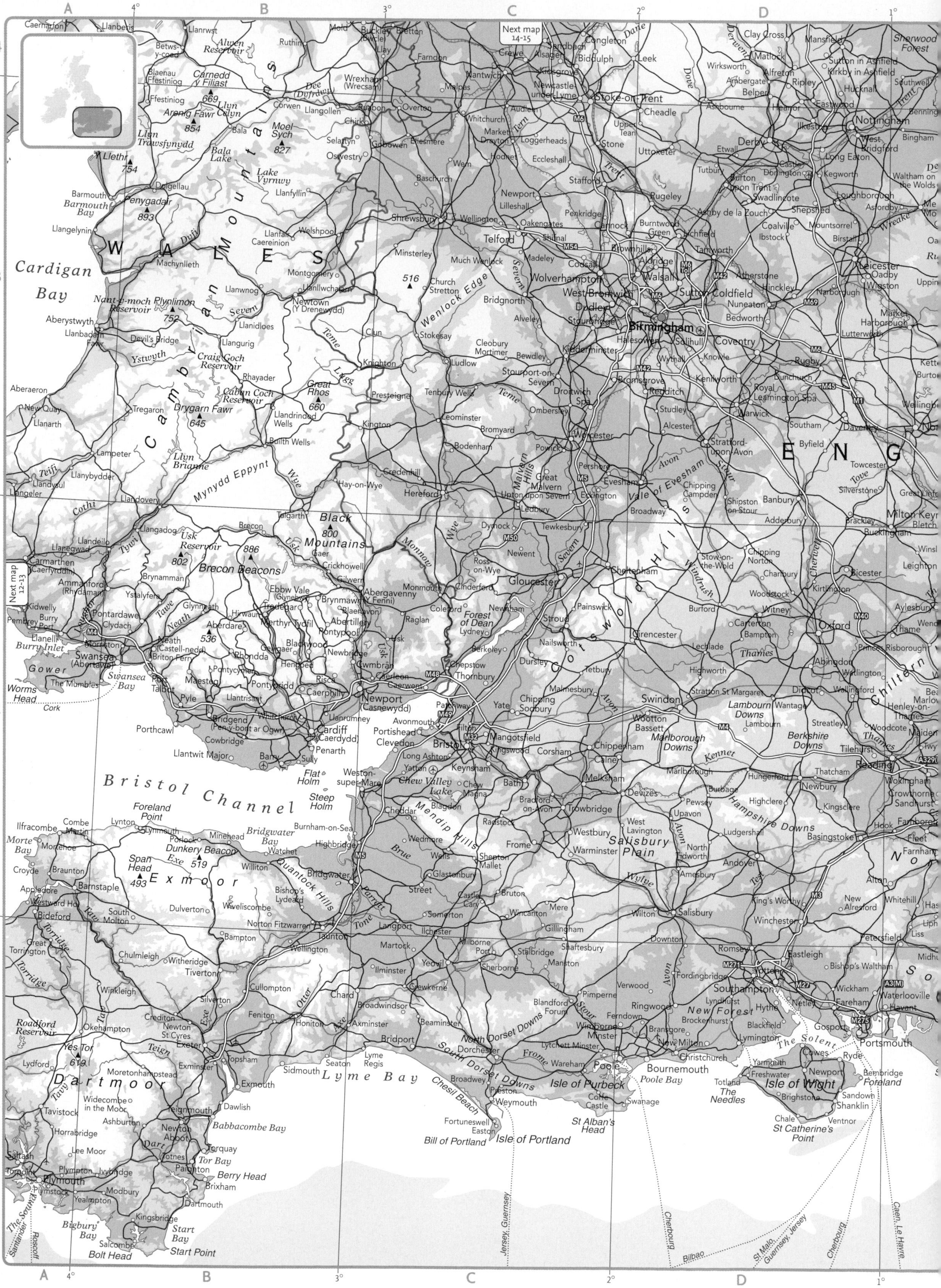

Next map 14-15

Next map 12-13

Cardigan Bay

W A L E S

Cambrian Mountains

Bristol Channel

E N G

Exmoor

Dartmoor

Lyme Bay

New Forest

Isle of Wight

The Solent

Salisbury Plain

Mendip Hills

Cotswold Hills

Chiltern

Brecon Beacons

Black Mountains

Malvern Hills

Lambourn Downs

Berkshire Downs

Marlborough Downs

Hampshire Downs

North Dorset Downs

South Dorset Downs

Isle of Purbeck

Quantock Hills

Birmingham

Wolverhampton

Coventry

Worcester

Gloucester

Swindon

Bristol

Cardiff

Swansea

Newport

Bath

Salisbury

Southampton

Portsmouth

Bournemouth

Poole

Exeter

Plymouth

Oxford

Reading

Stoke-on-Trent

Derby

Nottingham

Leicester

Stratford-upon-Avon

Scale 1 : 1 200 000

0 10 20 30 40 km

Key

Relief and physical features

Relief
metres
1000
500
200
100
sea level
0
50
100
200
under sea level

▲ 1085 Mountain height (in metres)

Water features

~~~ River

~~~ Canal

⬭ Lake / Reservoir

Communications

—— Railway

═══ Motorway

—— Road

····· Car ferry

⊕ Main airport

✈ Regional airport

Administration

Boundaries

━━━ International

—— Internal

Settlement

▨ Urban area

Cities and towns in order of size

National capital   Other city or town

■ LONDON   ● Birmingham

○ Oxford

○ Colchester

◦ Wantage

Conic Equidistant projection

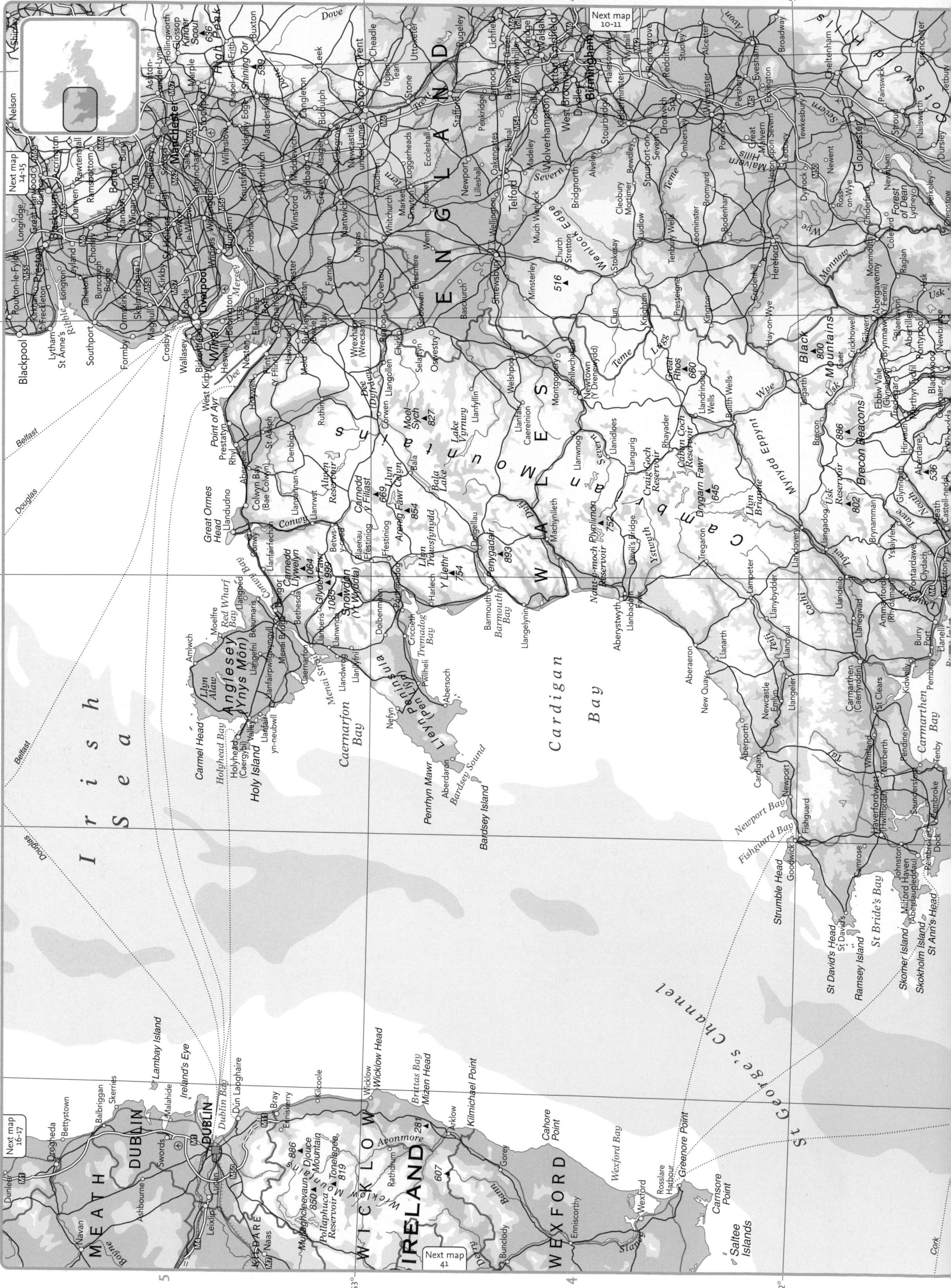

Next map 14-15

Next map 10-11

Nelson

Blackpool
Lytham
St Anne's
Southport
Formby
Crosby
Liverpool
Wallasey
West Kirby
Point of Ayr
Prestatyn
Rhyl
Manchester
Stockport
Macclesfield
Buxton
Kinder Scout
636
Shining Tor
590
Leek
Congleton
Biddulph
Stoke-on-Trent
Newcastle-under-Lyme
Stone
Stafford
Cheadle
Uttoxeter
Rugeley
Lichfield
Cannock
Walsall
West Bromwich
Birmingham
Dudley
Halesowen
Stourbridge
Bromsgrove
Redditch
Droitwich
Kidderminster
Bewdley
Stourport-on-Severn
Bridgnorth
Cleobury Mortimer
Ludlow
Leominster
Bromyard
Tenbury Wells
Hereford
Ross-on-Wye
Gloucester
Newent
Cheltenham
Tewkesbury
Evesham
Broadway
Worcester
Malvern
Great Malvern
Malvern Hills

Wolverhampton
Telford
Wellington
Much Wenlock
Wenlock Edge
Shrewsbury
516
Church Stretton
Stretton
Minsterley
Clun
Knighton
Presteigne
Kington
Hay-on-Wye
Hereford

Whitchurch
Wem
Ellesmere
Oswestry
Welshpool
Montgomery
Newtown (Y Drenewydd)
Llanidloes
Llangurig
Rhayader

ENGLAND

Chester
Frodsham
Runcorn
Widnes
Warrington
Northwich
Winsford
Middlewich
Sandbach
Crewe
Nantwich
Market Drayton

Wrexham (Wrecsam)
Mold (Yr Wyddgrug)
Flint (Y Fflint)
Holywell
Ruthin
Denbigh
St Asaph
Abergele
Colwyn Bay (Bae Colwyn)
Llandudno
Great Ormes Head
Conwy
Llanrwst
Betws-y-Coed
Blaenau Ffestiniog
Llangollen
Corwen
Bala
Bala Lake
Lake Vyrnwy
Llanfyllin
Llanfair Caereinion
Machynlleth
Aberystwyth
Devil's Bridge
Ystwyth

Moel Sych
827
Arenig Fawr
854
Aran Fawddwy
893
Cadair Idris
Dolgellau
Plynlimon (Pumlumon)
752
Nant-y-moch Reservoir
Llanbadarn

WALES (CYMRU)

Mynydd Eppynt
Brecon
Brecon Beacons
886
Llandovery
Llandeilo
Llangadog
Tywi
Black Mountains
800

Snowdonia (Eryri)
Carnedd y Filiast
669
Llyn Celyn
Trawsfynydd
Lake Trawsfynydd
754
Y Llethr
754

Carnedd Llywelyn
1064
Glyder Fawr
999
Snowdon (Yr Wyddfa)
1085
Bethesda
Bangor
Menai Bridge
Beaumaris
Caernarfon
Llanberis
Porthmadog
Criccieth
Pwllheli
Tremadog Bay
Harlech
Barmouth
Barmouth Bay
Llangelynin

Anglesey (Ynys Môn)
Amlwch
Moelfre
Red Wharf Bay
Llangefni
Holyhead (Caergybi)
Holyhead Bay
Holy Island
Carmel Head
Llanfairpwllgwyngyll
Valley
Llanfaelog
Rhosneigr
Aberffraw
Menai Strait
Llanddwyn
Llandwrog
Llyn Alaw

Caernarfon Bay
Llŷn Peninsula
Nefyn
Penrhyn Mawr
Aberdaron
Bardsey Island
Bardsey Sound
Abersoch

Cardigan Bay

Aberdovey
Aberaeron
New Quay
Aberporth
Cardigan
Newcastle Emlyn
Llandysul
Lampeter
Tregaron
Llanarth
Teifi

New Quay
Newport
Newport Bay
Fishguard
Fishguard Bay
Strumble Head
Goodwick
St David's
St David's Head
Ramsey Island
Skomer Island
Skokholm Island
St Bride's Bay
St Ann's Head
Milford Haven (Aberdaugleddau)
Pembroke
Pembroke Dock
Haverfordwest (Hwlffordd)
Narberth
Whitland
St Clears
Carmarthen (Caerfyrddin)
Kidwelly
Burry Port
Llanelli
Pendine
Saundersfoot
Tenby (Dinbych-y-pysgod)

Ammanford (Rhydaman)
Llandybie
Pontardawe
Neath (Castell-nedd)
536
Aberdare
Merthyr Tydfil
Ebbw Vale (Glynebwy)
Abertillery
Blackwood
Pontypool
Abergavenny (Y Fenni)
Crickhowell
Usk
Monmouth (Trefynwy)
Raglan
Chepstow
Forest of Dean
Lydney
Coleford
Cinderford
Newnham
Dursley
Nailsea
Cirencester
Stroud
Painswick

Severn
Wye
Teme
Lugg
Monnow

Irish Sea

Belfast
Douglas

Lambay Island
Ireland's Eye
Howth
Dublin
Dublin Bay
Dún Laoghaire
Bray
Greystones
Wicklow
Wicklow Head
Brittas Bay
Mizen Head
Arklow
Kilmichael Point
Cahore Point
Gorey
Courtown
Wexford
Wexford Bay
Rosslare
Rosslare Harbour
Greenore Point
Carnsore Point
Saltee Islands

WICKLOW
WEXFORD
MEATH
KILDARE
DUBLIN
IRELAND

Navan
Bourne
Drogheda
Balbriggan
Skerries
Bettystown
Dunleer
Ashbourne
Swords
Malahide
Leixlip
Lucan
Naas
Newbridge
Kildare
Athy
Carlow
Enniscorthy
Bunclody
New Ross
Ferns

Lugnaquillia
886
Mullaghcleevaun
850
Tonelagee
819
Djouce Mountain
Pollaphuca Reservoir
Blessington
Avonbeg
Avonmore
Avoca
607
281
Slaney
Barrow

Next map 16-17

Next map 41

St George's Channel

Scale 1 : 1 200 000

0 10 20 30 40 km

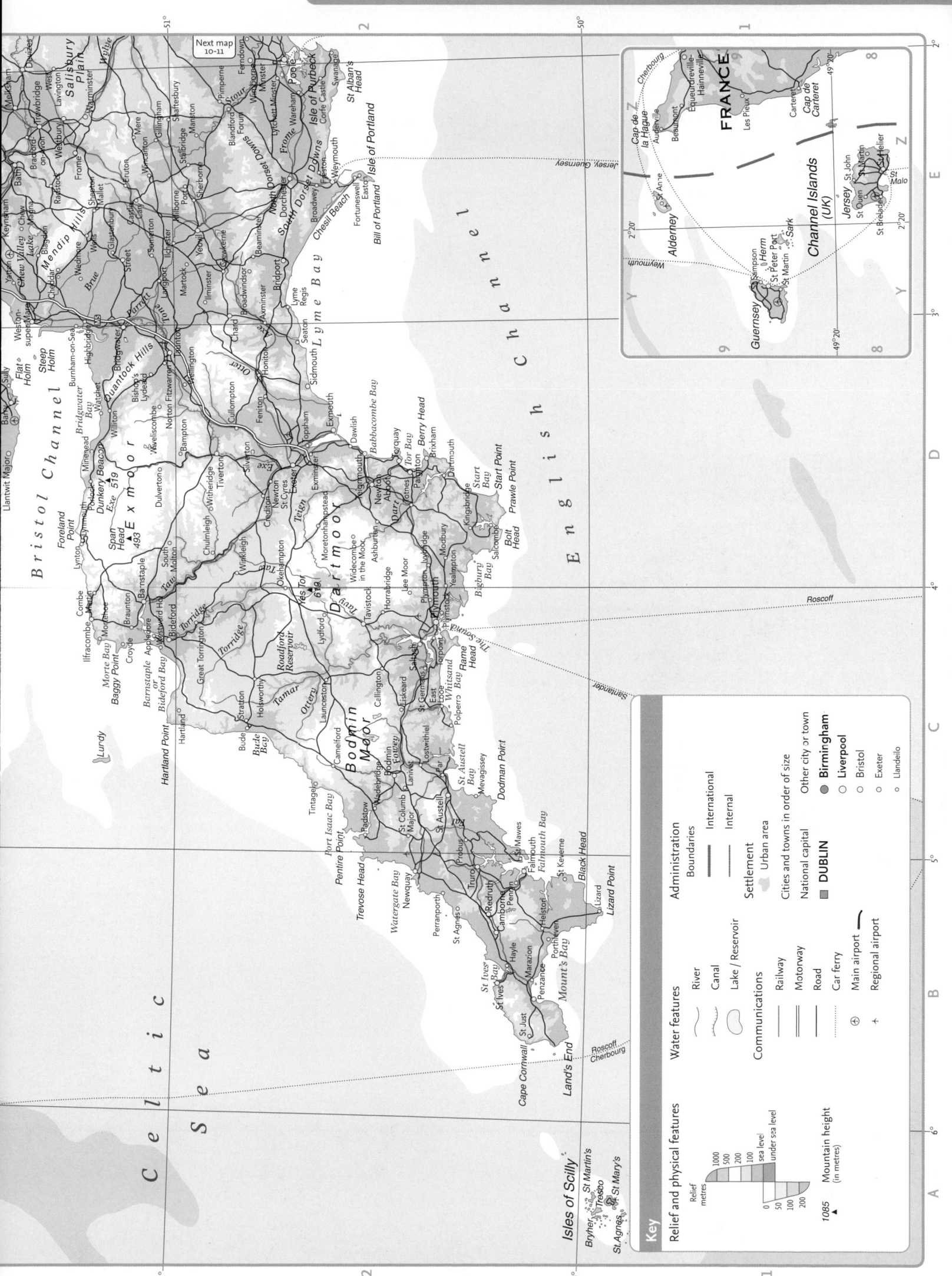

Conic Equidistant projection

Scale 1 : 1 200 000

0   10   20   30   40 km

Key

Relief and physical features

Relief metres

1000
500
200
100
0 sea level
50 under sea level
100
200

▲ 1085 Mountain height (in metres)

Water features

～～ River

～～ Canal

Lake / Reservoir

Communications

Railway

Motorway

Road

Car ferry

⊕ Main airport

✈ Regional airport

Administration

Boundaries

International

Internal

Settlement

Urban area

Cities and towns in order of size

National capital

■ DUBLIN

Other city or town

● Manchester

○ Liverpool

○ Belfast

○ Carlisle

○ Keswick

Conic Equidistant projection

Scale 1 : 1 200 000

0   10   20   30   40 km

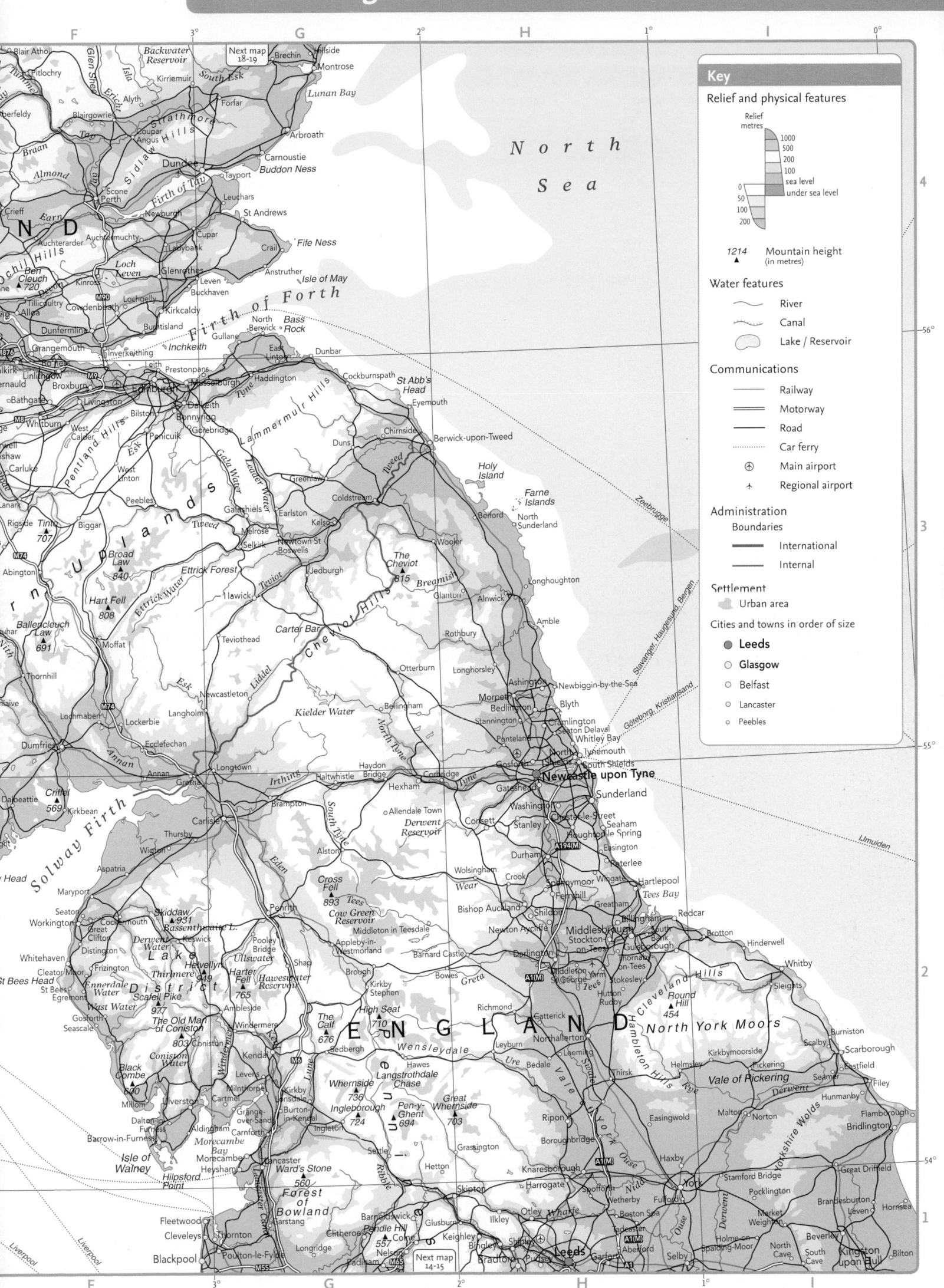

Key

Relief and physical features

Relief
metres
1000
500
200
100
sea level
0
50 under sea level
100
200

▲ 1214 Mountain height (in metres)

Water features

River
Canal
Lake / Reservoir

Communications

Railway
Motorway
Road
Car ferry
⊕ Main airport
✈ Regional airport

Administration

Boundaries
International
Internal

Settlement

Urban area

Cities and towns in order of size

● Leeds
○ Glasgow
○ Belfast
○ Lancaster
○ Peebles

Conic Equidistant projection

Key

Relief and physical features

Relief
metres
1000
500
200
100
0 sea level
50
100 under sea level
200

1344 ▲ Mountain height (in metres)

Water features

~ River
~ Canal
Lake / Reservoir

Communications

Railway
Road
Car ferry
⊕ Main airport
✈ Regional airport

Settlement

Urban area

Cities and towns in order of size
○ Aberdeen
○ Inverness
○ Kirkwall

Cape Wrath

Butt of Lewis
Port Ness

Kinlochbervie
Loch Inchard
Loch Laxford
Foina
915

Flannan Isles

Muirneag
248
Tolsta Head

Handa Island
Scourie

Isle of Lewis

West Loch Roag

Great Bernera

Callanish
Stornoway
Broad Bay
Eye Peninsula

Point of Stoer

Outer Hebrides

Mealasta Island

Loch Langavat

North Harris

Kebock Head

Loch Assynt

Lochinver

Canisp
846

Ben As
9

Scarp
Tirga Mòr
679
Clisham
799

Rubha Coigeach

Summer Isles

Cul Mòr
849

Loch Lurgainn

Taransay

Tarbert

Shiant Islands

Greenstone Point

Rubha Reidh

Ullapool

St Kilda

South Harris
Loch Tarbert
Scalpay

Loch Langavat

Rodel

Gruinard Bay

An Teallach
1062

Beinn Dearg
1084

Pabbay
Berneray
Boreray

Sound of Harris

Rubha Hunish

Gairloch
Gair Loch

Fionn Loch

Loch Maree

Sgurr Mòr
1110

Loch Fannich

North Uist
Lochmaddy

Sound of Monach

L. Dunvegan

Uig

Loch Snizort

L. Torridon

Torridon

W E S T E R
R O S S

Monach Islands

Balivanich

Benbecula

The Storr
719

Rona

Sound of Raasay

Inner Sound

Shieldaig

Loch Monar

Portree

Raasay

Skye

Carn Eighe
1183

Cuillin Hills

Scalpay

Kyle of Lochalsh

Sgurr Alasdair
993
Blaven
928

L. Bracadale

A T L A N T I C

South Uist

A'Chralaig
1120
Loch Cluanie
Glen M

Lochboisdale

Soay

Loch Eishort

Loch Hourn
Loch Quoich
Loch Garry
Loch Loy

O C E A N

Sound of Barra

Eriskay

Canna

Cuillin Sound

Ardvasar

Sound of Sleat

Ladhar Bheinn
1020

Glen Garry

Barra
Vatersay
Castlebay

Rum

Eigg

Arisaig
Mallaig

Sound of Arisaig

Loch Morar

Loch Arkaig

Stob C
Clau

Ben Nevis
1344

Pabbay
Sandray

Mingulay

Muck

Eilean Shona

Sgurr Dhomhnuill
888

Fort William

Loch Shiel

Loch Leven
Glen Coe

Kinloc

Bidean nam Bian
1150

Berneray

Point of Ardnamurchan

Coll

Tobermory

Morvern

Loch Linnhe

Mea
Bhui

Loch Arienas

Mull

Tiree

Next map 16-17

1108
▲

The Minch

Little Minch

Scale 1 : 1 200 000

0 10 20 30 40 km

Herma Ness
Unst
Baltasound

Point of
Fethaland
Isbister
Yell Sound
Yell
Fetlar

Ronas
Hill
450
Out Skerries
Esha Ness
Hillswick
Toft
St Magnus
Bay
Muckle
Roe
Voe
Whalsay
Papa
Stour
Melby
Mainland
Walls
Bressay
Shetland
Islands
Scalloway
Lerwick
Isle of Noss

Foula
Burra
Bergen (& Hanstholm)
(summer only)

Mousa

Sumburgh
Burra

Sumburgh Head

Fair Isle

Mull Head
Papa Westray
North Ronaldsay
Noup Head
The North
Sound
North Ronaldsay Firth
Westray
Eday
Sanday
Westray Firth
Loch
Sound
Brough Head
Rousay
Egilsay
Stronsay
Birsay
Stronsay
Firth
Shapinsay
Orkney Islands
Loch of
Harray
Auskerry
Loch of Stenness
Mainland
Kirkwall
Stromness
Wide Firth
Ward Hill
479
Scapa
Flow
Gritley
Copinsay
Hoy
Flotta
Burray
South
Walls
St Margaret's Hope
South
Ronaldsay
Burwick
Pentland Firth
Brough Ness
Island of
Stroma
Pentland Skerries
Dunnet Head
John o'Groats
Thurso
Bay
Dunnet
Bay
Loch
Heilen
Duncansby Head
Strathy
Point
Dounreay
Thurso
Loch
Watten
Sinclair's Bay
Tongue
Naver
Melvich
Halkirk
Wick
Loch
Loyal
Halladale
C A I T H N E S S
Wick
Klibreck
961
Loch
Rimsdale
Thurso
Latheron
THERLAND
Helmsdale
Lairg
Brora
Helmsdale
Golspie
Bonar Bridge
Brora
Dornoch
Dornoch Firth
Tarbat Ness
Tain
Loch Glass
Balintore
Invergordon
Nigg
Bay
Cromarty
Moray Firth
Lossiemouth
Portknockie
Troup
Head
Fraserburgh
Black Isle
Fortrose
Burghead
Buckie
Portsoy
Macduff
Loch of
Strathbeg
Conon
Bridge
Nairn
Kinloss
Elgin
Cullen
Banff
Crimond
Rattray Head
Beauly Firth
Inverness
Forres
Lossie
Fochabers
Knock
Hill
430
Aberchirder
New
Pitsligo
North Ugie
Moray
Firth
Findhorn
Isla
Keith
Turriff
Mintlaw
Peterhead
Ness
Rothes
Deveron
Boddam
Dufftown
(Charlestown
of Aberlour)
Huntly
Ythan
Cruden Bay
Spey
Strathspey
S T R A T H B O G I E
Grantown-
on-Spey
Bogie
Insch
Oldmeldrum
Ellon
Hills of
Cromdale
Urie
Carn Mòr
804
Inverurie
North Sea
Geal
Charn
821
Avon
Kemnay
Kintore
Don
Don
Dyce
dhliath Mountains
Aviemore
Cairn
Gorm
1245
Westhill
Aberdeen
Carn Dearg
945
Kingussie
Ben Macdui
Cairn Toul
1309
1291
Dee
Aboyne
Banchory
Portlethen
Newtonhill
Newtonmore
Cairngorm Mts
Braemar
Ballater
Mount
Keen
939
Stonehaven
Spey
Dee
Forest of Atholl 1121
Lochnagar
1155
Loch Ericht
Beinn
Dearg
1008
Carn nan
Gabhar
Mayar
928
Inverbervie
Grampian Mountains
Loch
Garry
Laurencekirk
Loch
Errochty
Water of Saughs
Loch
Tummel
Blair Atholl
Backwater
Reservoir
North Esk
Hillside
Brechin
Loch
Rannoch
1083
Schiehallion
Pitlochry
Isla
Kirriemuir
South Esk
Montrose
Tay
Aberfeldy
Alyth
Forfar
Lunan Bay
Lyon
Blairgowrie
Strathmore
Arbroath

Next map
16-17

Conic Equidistant projection

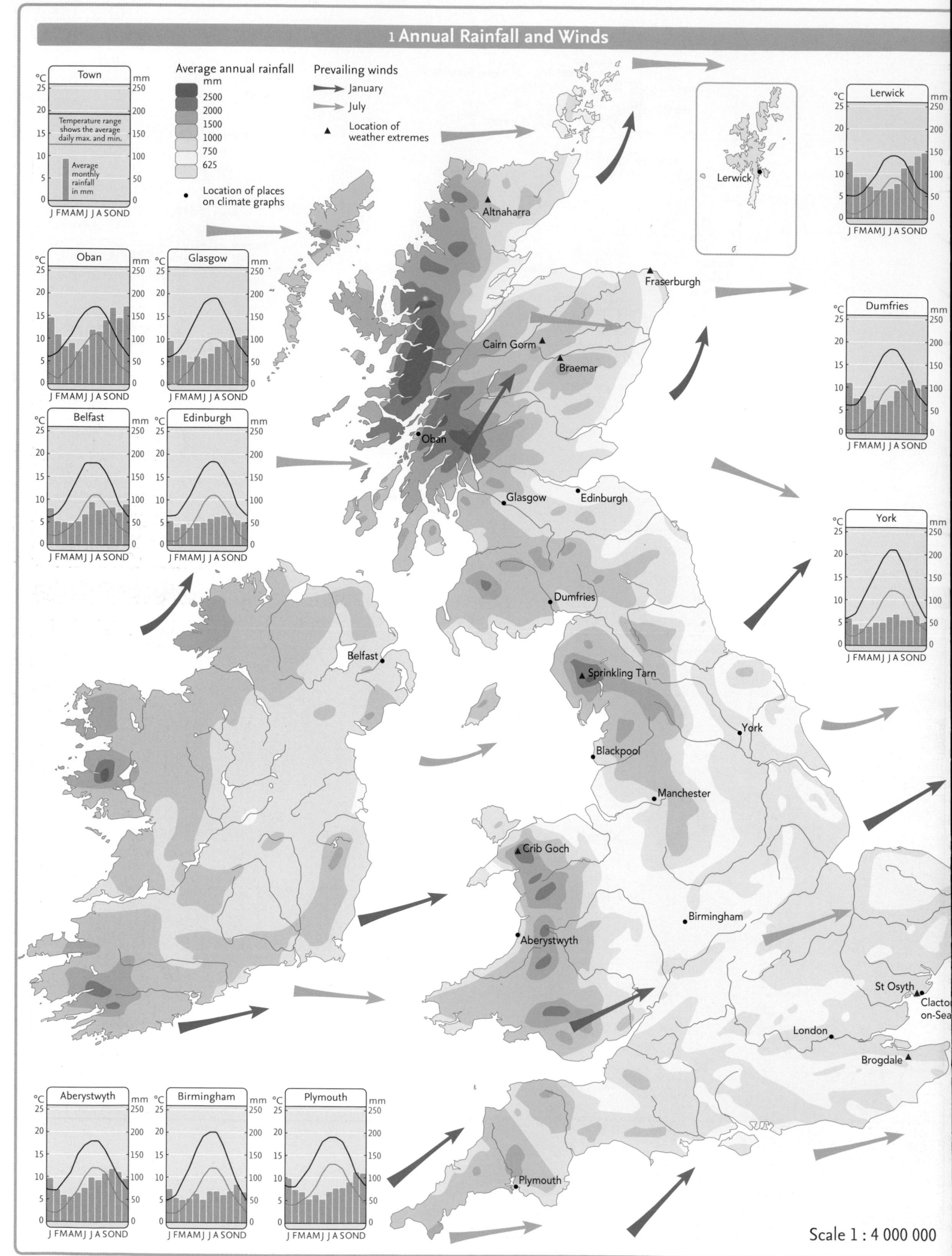

1 Annual Rainfall and Winds

Town

°C / mm

Temperature range shows the average daily max. and min.

Average monthly rainfall in mm

J F M A M J J A S O N D

Average annual rainfall
mm
2500
2000
1500
1000
750
625

• Location of places on climate graphs

Prevailing winds
→ January
→ July
▲ Location of weather extremes

Oban
Glasgow
Belfast
Edinburgh
Lerwick
Dumfries
York
Aberystwyth
Birmingham
Plymouth

Altnaharra
Fraserburgh
Cairn Gorm ▲
Braemar ▲
Oban
Glasgow
Edinburgh
Dumfries
Sprinkling Tarn ▲
Blackpool
York
Manchester
Crib Goch ▲
Birmingham
Aberystwyth
St Osyth ▲
Clacton-on-Sea
London
Brogdale ▲
Plymouth
Belfast
Lerwick

Scale 1 : 4 000 000

2 Temperature and Currents

January

Temperature °C
- 6
- 4
- 2
- 0

Currents
→ Warm
→ Cold

July

Temperature °C
- 16
- 14
- 12
- 10

Currents
→ Warm
→ Cold

Scale 1 : 12 000 000

3 Weather Extremes

Temperature

	Value	Location	Date
Highest	38.5°	Brogdale, Kent	10th August 2003
Lowest	-27.2°	Braemar, Aberdeenshire	10th January 1982 & 11th February 1895
		Altnaharra, Highlands	30th December 1995

Rainfall

	Value	Location	Date
Highest in 1 year	6 528mm	Sprinkling Tarn, Cumbria	1954
Lowest annual average	513mm	St Osyth, Essex	
Highest annual average	4 000mm	Crib Goch, Gwynedd	

Winds

	Value	Location	Date
Strongest low-level gust	123 knots	Fraserburgh, Aberdeenshire	13th February 1989
Strongest high-level gust	150 knots	Cairn Gorm, Highland	20th March 1986

www
Met Office www.metoffice.com
BBC Weather www.bbc.co.uk/weather
UK Climate Impacts Programme www.ukcip.org.uk

4 Climate Statistics

Blackpool (mm 250/200/150/100/50/0) J F M A M J J A S O N D

Manchester (mm 250/200/150/100/50/0) J F M A M J J A S O N D

Clacton-on-Sea (mm 250/200/150/100/50/0) J F M A M J J A S O N D

London (mm 250/200/150/100/50/0) J F M A M J J A S O N D

Aberystwyth	Jan	Feb	Mar	Apr	May	Jun	Jul	Aug	Sep	Oct	Nov	Dec
Temperature - max. (°C)	7	7	9	11	15	17	18	18	16	13	10	8
Temperature - min. (°C)	2	2	3	5	7	10	12	12	11	8	5	4
Rainfall - (mm)	97	72	60	56	65	76	99	93	108	118	111	96

Belfast	Jan	Feb	Mar	Apr	May	Jun	Jul	Aug	Sep	Oct	Nov	Dec
Temperature - max. (°C)	6	7	9	12	15	18	18	18	16	13	9	7
Temperature - min. (°C)	2	2	3	4	6	9	11	11	9	7	4	3
Rainfall - (mm)	80	52	50	48	52	68	94	77	80	83	72	90

Birmingham	Jan	Feb	Mar	Apr	May	Jun	Jul	Aug	Sep	Oct	Nov	Dec
Temperature - max. (°C)	5	6	9	12	16	19	20	20	17	13	9	6
Temperature - min. (°C)	2	2	3	5	7	10	12	12	10	7	5	3
Rainfall - (mm)	74	54	50	53	64	50	69	69	61	69	84	67

Blackpool	Jan	Feb	Mar	Apr	May	Jun	Jul	Aug	Sep	Oct	Nov	Dec
Temperature - max. (°C)	7	7	9	11	15	17	19	19	17	14	10	7
Temperature - min. (°C)	1	1	2	4	7	10	12	12	10	8	4	2
Rainfall - (mm)	78	54	64	51	53	59	61	78	86	93	89	87

Clacton-on-Sea	Jan	Feb	Mar	Apr	May	Jun	Jul	Aug	Sep	Oct	Nov	Dec
Temperature - max. (°C)	6	6	9	11	15	18	20	20	18	15	10	7
Temperature - min. (°C)	2	2	3	5	8	11	13	14	12	9	5	3
Rainfall - (mm)	49	31	43	40	40	45	43	43	48	48	55	50

Dumfries	Jan	Feb	Mar	Apr	May	Jun	Jul	Aug	Sep	Oct	Nov	Dec
Temperature - max. (°C)	6	6	8	11	14	17	19	18	16	13	9	7
Temperature - min. (°C)	1	1	2	3	6	9	11	10	9	6	3	1
Rainfall - (mm)	110	76	81	53	72	63	71	93	104	117	100	107

Edinburgh	Jan	Feb	Mar	Apr	May	Jun	Jul	Aug	Sep	Oct	Nov	Dec
Temperature - max. (°C)	6	7	9	11	14	17	18	18	16	13	9	7
Temperature - min. (°C)	1	1	2	4	6	9	11	11	9	7	3	2
Rainfall - (mm)	54	40	47	39	49	50	59	63	66	63	56	52

Glasgow	Jan	Feb	Mar	Apr	May	Jun	Jul	Aug	Sep	Oct	Nov	Dec
Temperature - max. (°C)	6	7	9	12	15	18	19	19	16	13	9	7
Temperature - min. (°C)	0	0	2	3	6	9	10	10	9	6	2	1
Rainfall - (mm)	96	63	65	50	62	58	68	83	95	98	105	108

Lerwick	Jan	Feb	Mar	Apr	May	Jun	Jul	Aug	Sep	Oct	Nov	Dec
Temperature - max. (°C)	5	5	6	8	10	13	14	14	13	10	7	6
Temperature - min. (°C)	1	1	2	3	5	7	9	9	8	6	3	2
Rainfall - (mm)	127	93	93	72	64	64	67	78	113	119	140	147

London	Jan	Feb	Mar	Apr	May	Jun	Jul	Aug	Sep	Oct	Nov	Dec
Temperature - max. (°C)	8	8	11	13	17	20	23	23	19	15	11	9
Temperature - min. (°C)	2	2	4	5	8	11	14	13	11	8	5	3
Rainfall - (mm)	52	34	42	45	47	53	38	47	57	62	52	54

Manchester	Jan	Feb	Mar	Apr	May	Jun	Jul	Aug	Sep	Oct	Nov	Dec
Temperature - max. (°C)	6	7	9	12	15	18	20	20	17	14	9	7
Temperature - min. (°C)	1	1	3	4	7	10	12	12	10	8	4	2
Rainfall - (mm)	69	50	61	51	61	67	65	79	74	77	78	78

Oban	Jan	Feb	Mar	Apr	May	Jun	Jul	Aug	Sep	Oct	Nov	Dec
Temperature - max. (°C)	6	7	9	11	14	16	17	17	15	12	9	7
Temperature - min. (°C)	2	1	3	4	7	9	11	11	9	7	4	3
Rainfall - (mm)	146	109	83	90	72	87	120	116	141	169	146	172

Plymouth	Jan	Feb	Mar	Apr	May	Jun	Jul	Aug	Sep	Oct	Nov	Dec
Temperature - max. (°C)	8	8	10	12	15	18	19	19	18	15	11	9
Temperature - min. (°C)	4	4	5	6	8	11	13	13	12	9	7	5
Rainfall - (mm)	99	74	69	53	63	53	70	77	78	91	113	110

York	Jan	Feb	Mar	Apr	May	Jun	Jul	Aug	Sep	Oct	Nov	Dec
Temperature - max. (°C)	6	7	10	13	16	19	21	21	18	14	10	7
Temperature - min. (°C)	2	2	3	5	7	10	12	12	11	8	5	4
Rainfall - (mm)	59	46	37	41	50	50	62	68	55	56	65	50

Key

Relief and physical features

Relief
metres

	1000
	500
	200
	100
	sea level
	under sea level
	50
	100
	200

▲ 1344 Mountain height
(in metres)

Water features

〜〜〜 River

〜〜〜 Canal

⬭ Lake / Reservoir

Scale 1 : 4 000 000

0   50   100   150 km

Conic Equidistant project

Sedimentary Rocks

Sediments deposited in layers mainly under water and, through time, compressed into rock.

	Unconsolidated Sands & Shell Banks	< 1 million years old
	Clay	1.225 m. yrs old
	Chalk	70 – 135 m. yrs old
	Oolitic Limestone	135 – 180 m. yrs old
	Carboniferous Limestone	225 – 570 m. yrs old
	Magnesian Limestone	225 – 570 m. yrs old
	Friable Sandstone	70 – 270 m. yrs old
	Hard Sandstone	350 – 570 m. yrs old
	Greywacke and Slate	400 – 570 m. yrs old
	Mixed Hard Sediments including sandstone, shale, mudstone, greywacke, slate and limestone	225 – 570 m. yrs old

Igneous Rocks

Fluid material, from the Earth's interior, solidified on (Extrusive), or beneath (Intrusive), the Earth's surface.

	Extrusive (Volcanic) Lava, Basalt	various ages
	Intrusive Granite etc	various ages

Metamorphic Rocks

Sedimentary, igneous and metamorphic rocks reconstituted by heat and pressure.

	Gneiss, Schist, Quartzite etc	various ages
——	Major fault line	

The Geological Time-scale

Figures represent million years before present

		Pliocene	1.0
		Miocene	11
		Oligocene	25
	CAINOZOIC	Eocene	40
		Palaeocene	60 / 70
		Cretaceous	135
	MEZOZOIC	Jurassic	180
		Triassic	225
		Permian	270
		Carboniferous	350
		Devonian	400
		Silurian	440
	PALAEOZOIC	Ordovician	500
		Cambrian	570
		Pre-Cambrian	

Pleistocene →

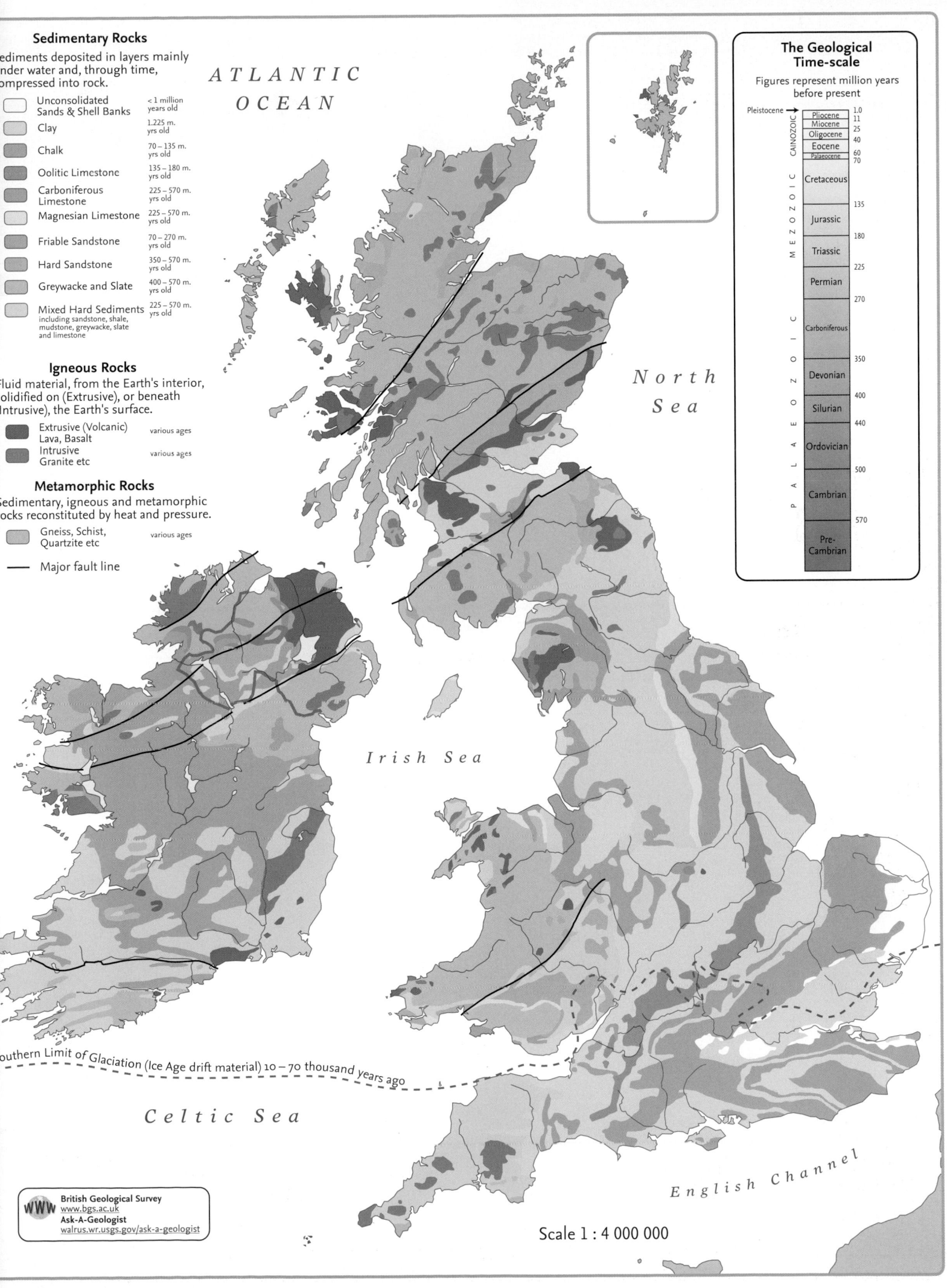

ATLANTIC OCEAN

North Sea

Irish Sea

Southern Limit of Glaciation (Ice Age drift material) 10 – 70 thousand years ago

Celtic Sea

English Channel

Scale 1 : 4 000 000

WWW British Geological Survey
www.bgs.ac.uk
Ask-A-Geologist
walrus.wr.usgs.gov/ask-a-geologist

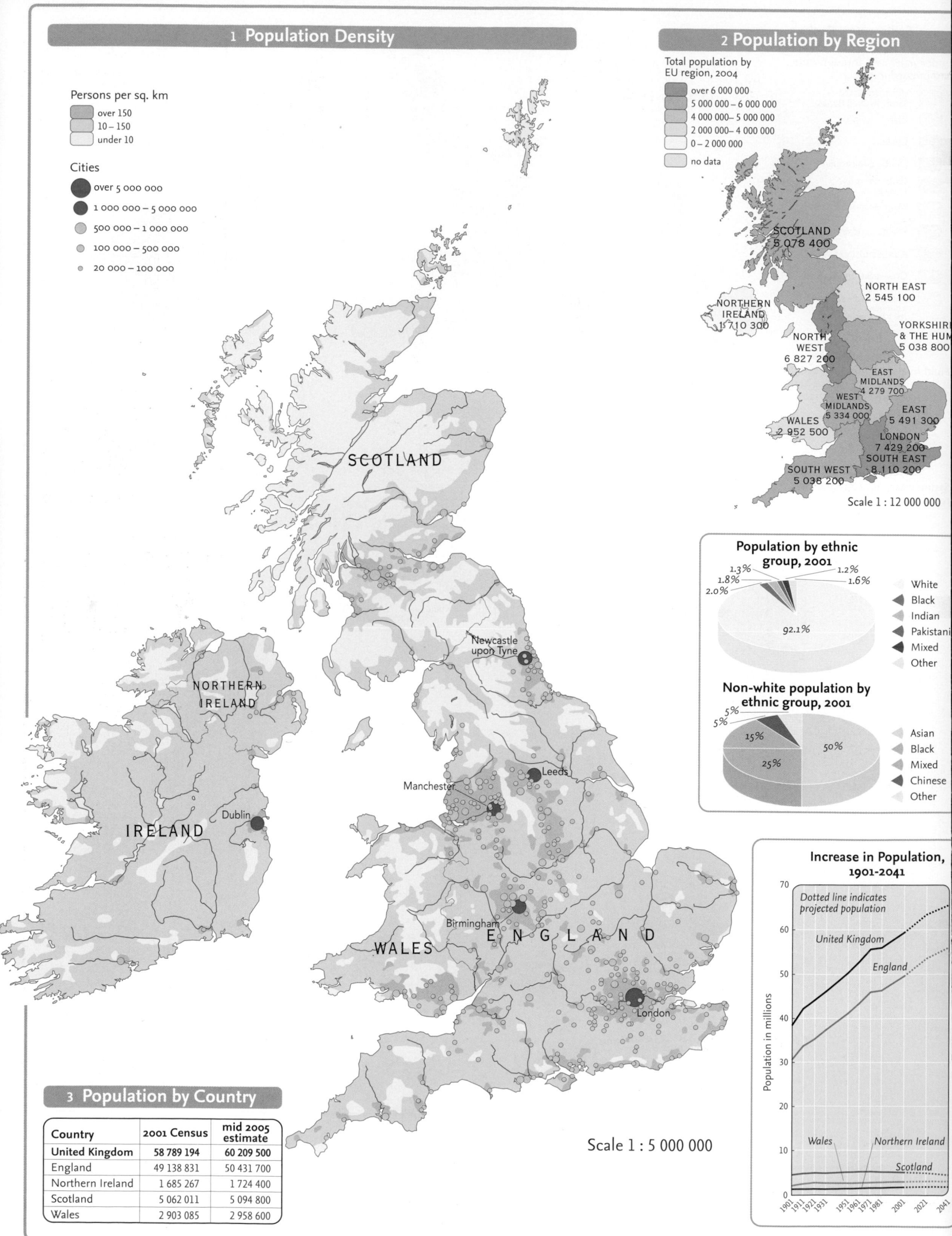

1 Population Density

Persons per sq. km
- over 150
- 10 – 150
- under 10

Cities
- over 5 000 000
- 1 000 000 – 5 000 000
- 500 000 – 1 000 000
- 100 000 – 500 000
- 20 000 – 100 000

Scale 1 : 5 000 000

2 Population by Region

Total population by
EU region, 2004
- over 6 000 000
- 5 000 000 – 6 000 000
- 4 000 000 – 5 000 000
- 2 000 000 – 4 000 000
- 0 – 2 000 000
- no data

SCOTLAND 5 078 400
NORTHERN IRELAND 1 710 300
NORTH EAST 2 545 100
NORTH WEST 6 827 200
YORKSHIRE & THE HUMBER 5 038 800
EAST MIDLANDS 4 279 700
WEST MIDLANDS 5 334 000
WALES 2 952 500
EAST 5 491 300
LONDON 7 429 200
SOUTH EAST 8 110 200
SOUTH WEST 5 038 200

Scale 1 : 12 000 000

Population by ethnic group, 2001

- 1.3%
- 1.2%
- 1.8%
- 1.6%
- 2.0%
- 92.1%

- White
- Black
- Indian
- Pakistani
- Mixed
- Other

Non-white population by ethnic group, 2001

- 5%
- 5%
- 15%
- 50%
- 25%

- Asian
- Black
- Mixed
- Chinese
- Other

Increase in Population, 1901-2041

Dotted line indicates projected population

- United Kingdom
- England
- Wales
- Northern Ireland
- Scotland

Population in millions

3 Population by Country

Country	2001 Census	mid 2005 estimate
United Kingdom	**58 789 194**	**60 209 500**
England	49 138 831	50 431 700
Northern Ireland	1 685 267	1 724 400
Scotland	5 062 011	5 094 800
Wales	2 903 085	2 958 600

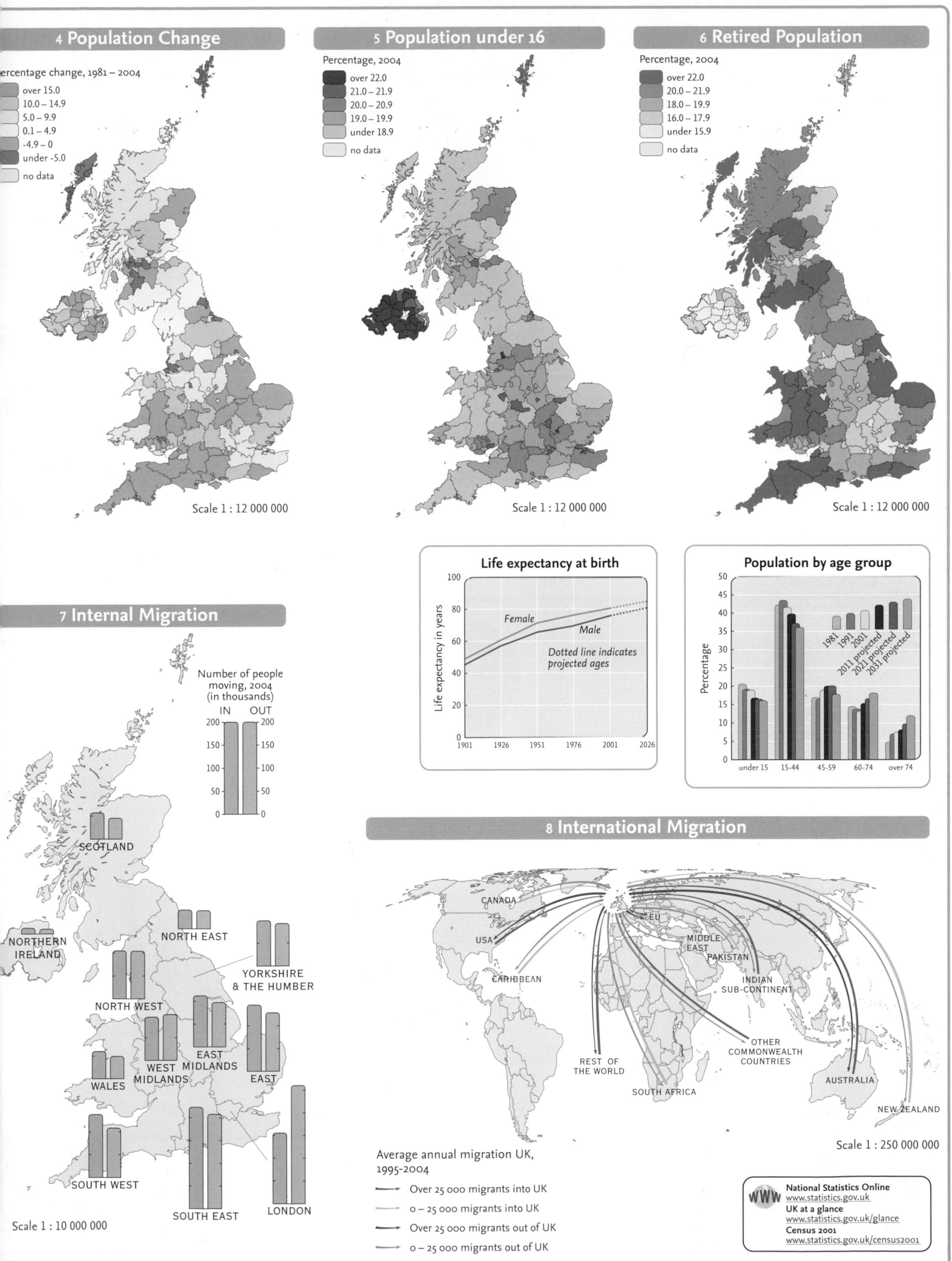

4 Population Change

Percentage change, 1981 – 2004

- over 15.0
- 10.0 – 14.9
- 5.0 – 9.9
- 0.1 – 4.9
- -4.9 – 0
- under -5.0
- no data

Scale 1 : 12 000 000

5 Population under 16

Percentage, 2004

- over 22.0
- 21.0 – 21.9
- 20.0 – 20.9
- 19.0 – 19.9
- under 18.9
- no data

Scale 1 : 12 000 000

6 Retired Population

Percentage, 2004

- over 22.0
- 20.0 – 21.9
- 18.0 – 19.9
- 16.0 – 17.9
- under 15.9
- no data

Scale 1 : 12 000 000

7 Internal Migration

Number of people moving, 2004 (in thousands)

IN OUT
200 — 200
150 — 150
100 — 100
50 — 50
0 — 0

SCOTLAND

NORTHERN IRELAND

NORTH EAST

YORKSHIRE & THE HUMBER

NORTH WEST

EAST MIDLANDS

WEST MIDLANDS

WALES

EAST

SOUTH WEST

SOUTH EAST

LONDON

Scale 1 : 10 000 000

Life expectancy at birth

Life expectancy in years

Female

Male

Dotted line indicates projected ages

1901 1926 1951 1976 2001 2026

Population by age group

Percentage

1981
1991
2001
2011 projected
2021 projected
2031 projected

under 15   15-44   45-59   60-74   over 74

8 International Migration

CANADA

USA

CARIBBEAN

EU

MIDDLE EAST

PAKISTAN

INDIAN SUB-CONTINENT

REST OF THE WORLD

SOUTH AFRICA

OTHER COMMONWEALTH COUNTRIES

AUSTRALIA

NEW ZEALAND

Scale 1 : 250 000 000

Average annual migration UK, 1995-2004

- → Over 25 000 migrants into UK
- → 0 – 25 000 migrants into UK
- → Over 25 000 migrants out of UK
- → 0 – 25 000 migrants out of UK

WWW National Statistics Online
www.statistics.gov.uk
UK at a glance
www.statistics.gov.uk/glance
Census 2001
www.statistics.gov.uk/census2001

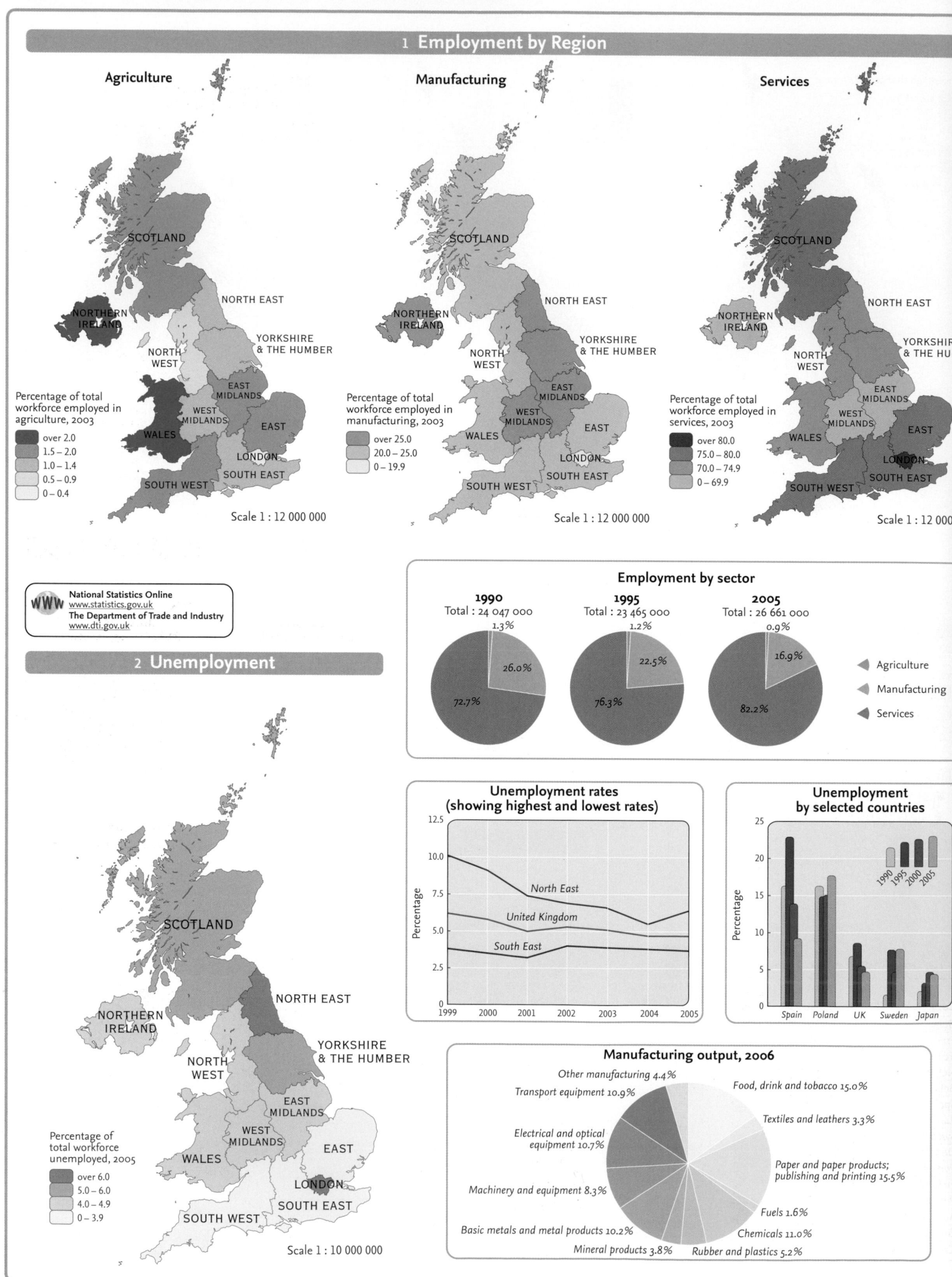

1 Employment by Region

Agriculture

Percentage of total workforce employed in agriculture, 2003

- over 2.0
- 1.5 – 2.0
- 1.0 – 1.4
- 0.5 – 0.9
- 0 – 0.4

Scale 1 : 12 000 000

Manufacturing

Percentage of total workforce employed in manufacturing, 2003

- over 25.0
- 20.0 – 25.0
- 0 – 19.9

Scale 1 : 12 000 000

Services

Percentage of total workforce employed in services, 2003

- over 80.0
- 75.0 – 80.0
- 70.0 – 74.9
- 0 – 69.9

Scale 1 : 12 000 0

WWW National Statistics Online
www.statistics.gov.uk
The Department of Trade and Industry
www.dti.gov.uk

2 Unemployment

Percentage of total workforce unemployed, 2005

- over 6.0
- 5.0 – 6.0
- 4.0 – 4.9
- 0 – 3.9

Scale 1 : 10 000 000

Employment by sector

1990
Total : 24 047 000
1.3%
26.0%
72.7%

1995
Total : 23 465 000
1.2%
22.5%
76.3%

2005
Total : 26 661 000
0.9%
16.9%
82.2%

◄ Agriculture
◄ Manufacturing
◄ Services

Unemployment rates (showing highest and lowest rates)

North East
United Kingdom
South East

Unemployment by selected countries

1990 1995 2000 2005

Spain Poland UK Sweden Japan

Manufacturing output, 2006

- Other manufacturing 4.4%
- Transport equipment 10.9%
- Electrical and optical equipment 10.7%
- Machinery and equipment 8.3%
- Basic metals and metal products 10.2%
- Mineral products 3.8%
- Rubber and plastics 5.2%
- Chemicals 11.0%
- Fuels 1.6%
- Paper and paper products; publishing and printing 15.5%
- Textiles and leathers 3.3%
- Food, drink and tobacco 15.0%

3 Land Use

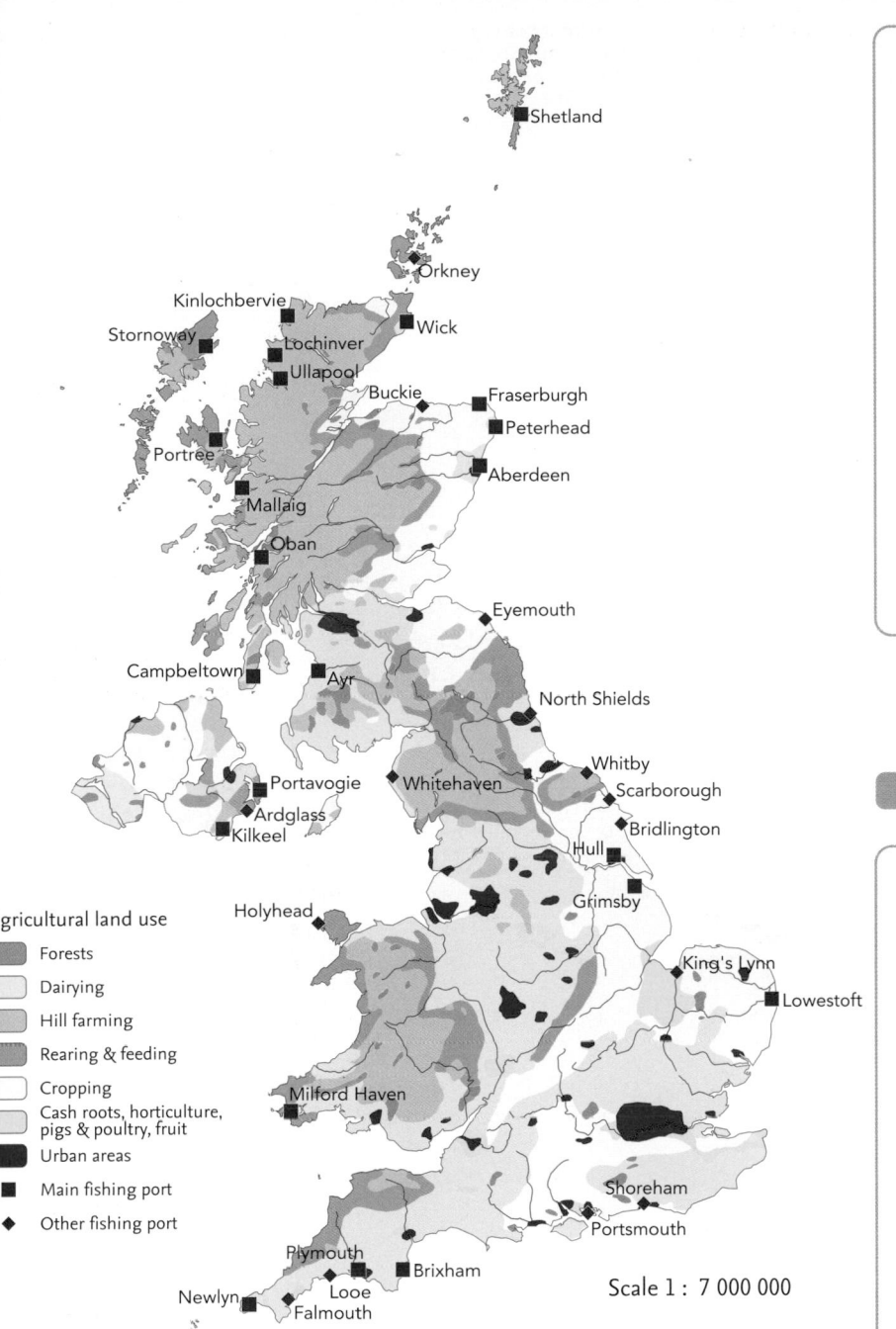

Agricultural land use

- Forests
- Dairying
- Hill farming
- Rearing & feeding
- Cropping
- Cash roots, horticulture, pigs & poultry, fruit
- Urban areas
- ■ Main fishing port
- ◆ Other fishing port

Scale 1 : 7 000 000

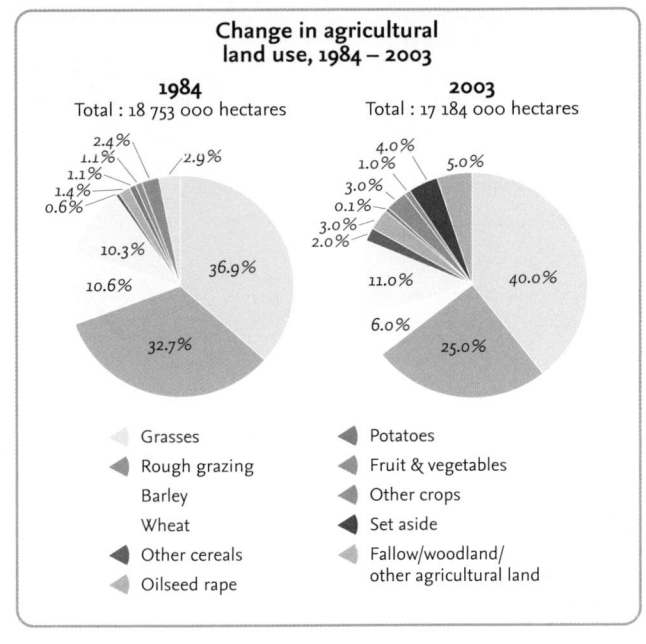

Change in agricultural land use, 1984 – 2003

1984
Total : 18 753 000 hectares

2.4% 1.1% 1.1% 1.4% 0.6% 2.9%
10.3%
10.6%
32.7%
36.9%

2003
Total : 17 184 000 hectares

4.0% 1.0% 3.0% 0.1% 3.0% 2.0% 5.0%
11.0%
6.0%
25.0%
40.0%

- ◅ Grasses
- ◅ Rough grazing
- Barley
- Wheat
- ◅ Other cereals
- ◅ Oilseed rape
- ◅ Potatoes
- ◅ Fruit & vegetables
- ◅ Other crops
- ◅ Set aside
- ◅ Fallow/woodland/ other agricultural land

4 International Trade

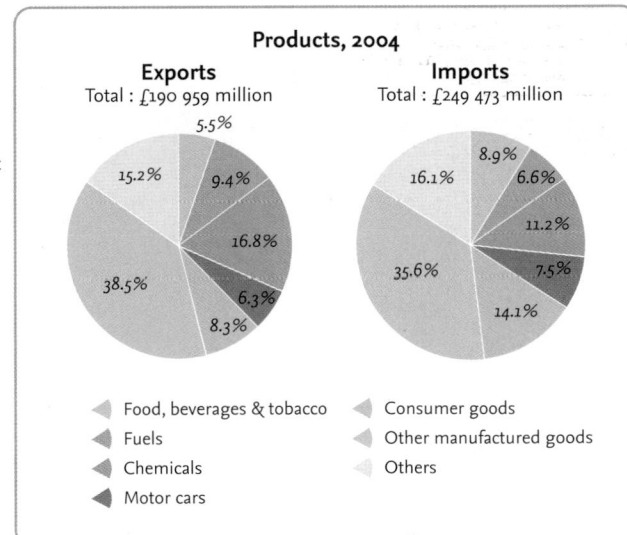

Products, 2004

Exports
Total : £190 959 million

5.5%
15.2% 9.4%
16.8%
38.5% 6.3%
8.3%

Imports
Total : £249 473 million

8.9%
16.1% 6.6%
11.2%
35.6% 7.5%
14.1%

- ◅ Food, beverages & tobacco
- ◅ Fuels
- ◅ Chemicals
- ◅ Motor cars
- ◅ Consumer goods
- ◅ Other manufactured goods
- ◅ Others

UK trade with European Union, 2005

Country	% of total UK exports	% of total UK imports
Germany	10.8	13.0
France	9.3	7.3
Ireland	7.7	3.6
Netherlands	5.9	6.8
Belgium	5.2	4.7
Spain	4.9	3.4
Italy	4.1	4.3
Sweden	2.1	1.8
Denmark	1.1	1.4
Portugal	0.8	0.6
Finland	0.7	0.8
Poland	0.7	0.8
Austria	0.6	0.8
Greece	0.6	0.2
Czech Republic	0.5	0.6

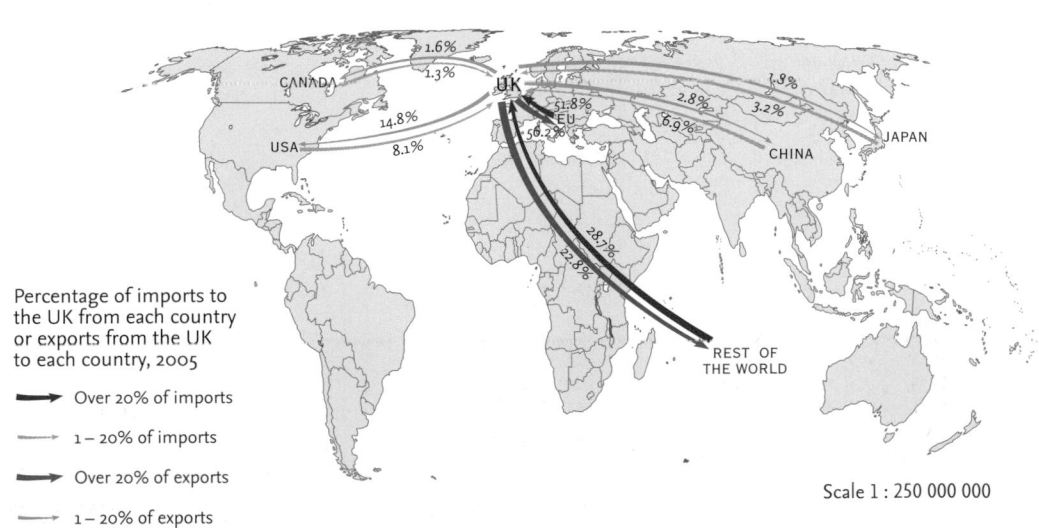

Percentage of imports to the UK from each country or exports from the UK to each country, 2005

- ➤ Over 20% of imports
- → 1 – 20% of imports
- ➤ Over 20% of exports
- → 1 – 20% of exports

Scale 1 : 250 000 000

1 Energy Sources

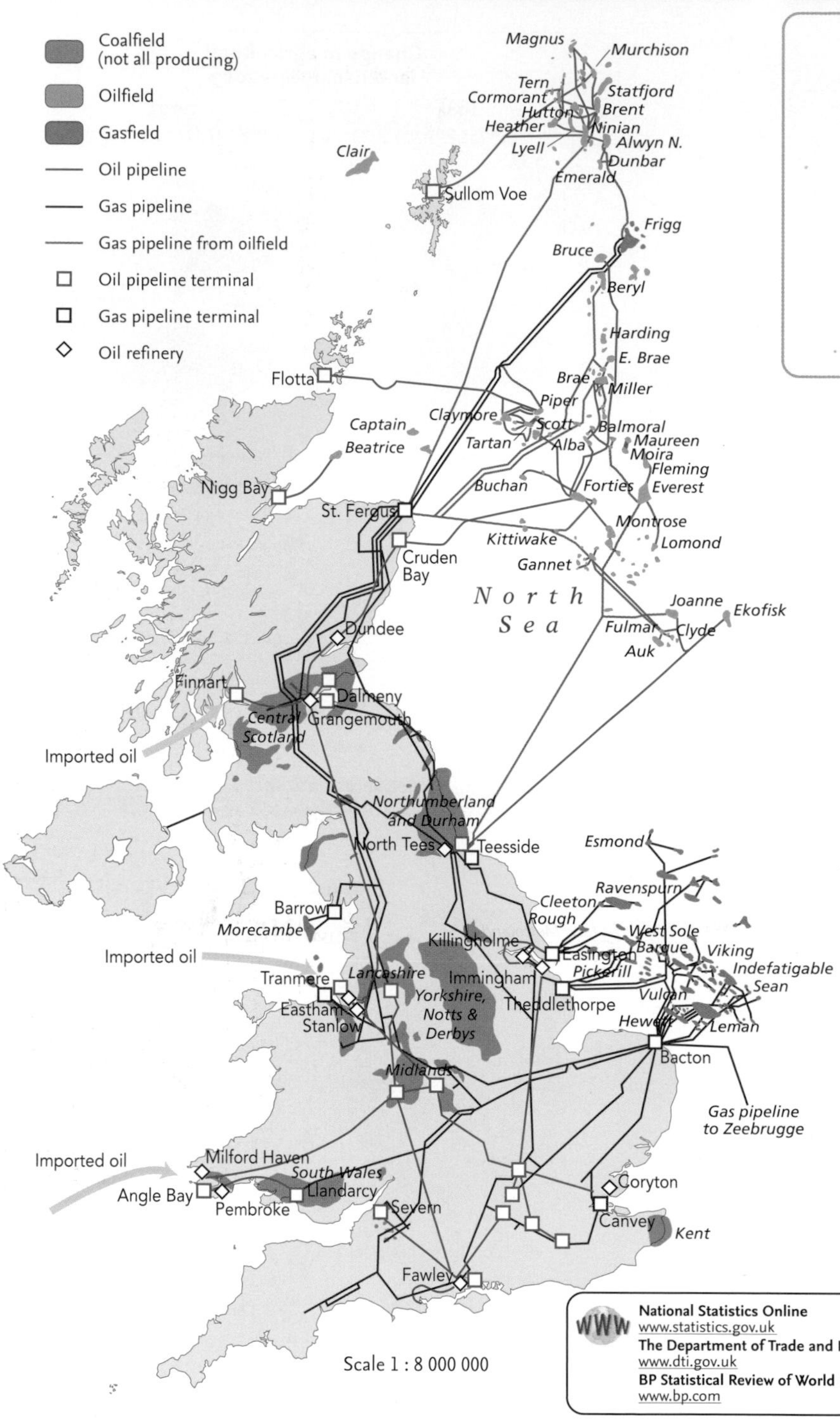

Coalfield (not all producing)
Oilfield
Gasfield
Oil pipeline
Gas pipeline
Gas pipeline from oilfield
☐ Oil pipeline terminal
☐ Gas pipeline terminal
◇ Oil refinery

Magnus
Murchison
Tern
Cormorant
Hutton
Heather
Lyell
Statfjord
Brent
Ninian
Alwyn N.
Dunbar
Emerald
Clair
Sullom Voe
Frigg
Bruce
Beryl
Harding
E. Brae
Brae
Piper
Miller
Claymore
Scott
Balmoral
Captain
Beatrice
Tartan
Alba
Maureen
Moira
Fleming
Everest
Buchan
Forties
Nigg Bay
St. Fergus
Kittiwake
Gannet
Montrose
Lomond
Flotta
Cruden Bay
Joanne
Ekofisk
Fulmar
Clyde
Auk

North Sea

Finnart
Dundee
Dalmeny
Central Scotland
Grangemouth
Imported oil
Northumberland and Durham
North Tees
Teesside
Esmond
Ravenspurn
Barrow
Morecambe
Cleeton
Rough
West Sole
Barque
Viking
Indefatigable
Sean
Imported oil
Tranmere
Lancashire
Killingholme
Easington
Pickerill
Eastham
Stanlow
Immingham
Theddlethorpe
Yorkshire, Notts & Derbys
Vulcan
Hewett
Leman
Midlands
Bacton
Gas pipeline to Zeebrugge
Imported oil
Milford Haven
South Wales
Llandarcy
Coryton
Angle Bay
Pembroke
Severn
Canvey
Kent
Fawley

Scale 1 : 8 000 000

National Statistics Online
www.statistics.gov.uk
The Department of Trade and Industry
www.dti.gov.uk
BP Statistical Review of World Energy
www.bp.com

2 Energy Production

Primary energy consumption, 2005
Total : 227.3 million tonnes oil equivalent

Nuclear 8.1%   Other 0.8%
Coal 17.2%
Oil 36.5%
Natural Gas 37.4%

Power Stations
☐ Pumped storage hydro-electric
☐ Hydro-electric (40MW or over)
☐ Coal powered (1000MW or over)
☐ Combined cycle gas turbine (1000MW or over)
○ Oil powered
○ Oil/gas powered (1000MW or over)
○ Coal/gas powered (1000MW or over)
○ Coal/oil powered (1000MW or over)
△ Nuclear
△ Wind farm
△ Wave
△ Geothermal aquifer

Peterhead
Fasnakyle
Foyers
Fort William
Errochty
Rannoch
Clunie
Cruachan
Lochay
Clachan
Sloy
Longannet
Islay
Cockenzie
Torness
Hunterston B
Ballylumford
Chapelcross
Hartlepool
Teesside
Heysham I
Ferrybridge
Eggborough
Saltend
Heysham II
Fiddler's Ferry
Drax
Wylfa
Connah's Quay
Cottam
Denorwig
West Burton
Ffestiniog
Ratcliffe-on-Soar
Rheidol
Rugeley
Sizewell A
Sizewell B
Oldbury
Barking
Aberthaw B
Didcot A & B
Kingsnorth
Littlebrook
Tilbury B
Hinkley Point B
Southampton
Dungeness B
Fawley
Dungeness A
Indian Queens

Scale 1 : 8 000 000

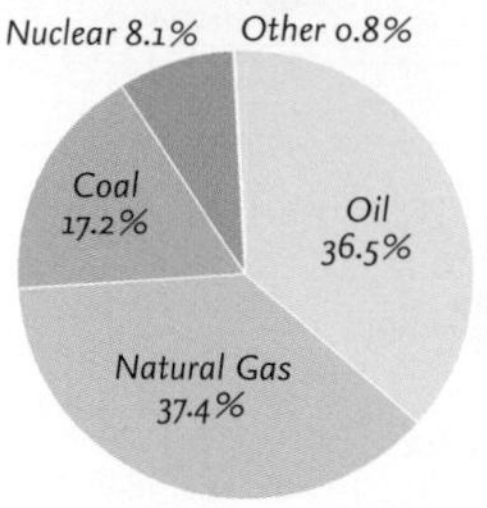

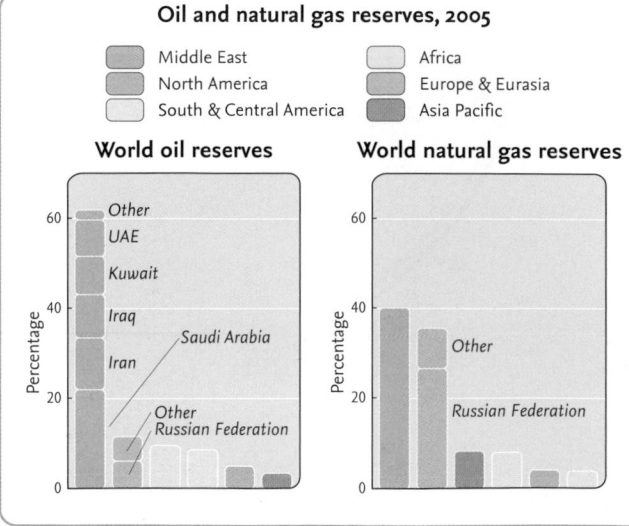

Oil and natural gas reserves, 2005
Middle East
North America
South & Central America
Africa
Europe & Eurasia
Asia Pacific

World oil reserves
Other
UAE
Kuwait
Iraq
Iran
Saudi Arabia
Other
Russian Federation
Percentage

World natural gas reserves
Other
Russian Federation
Percentage

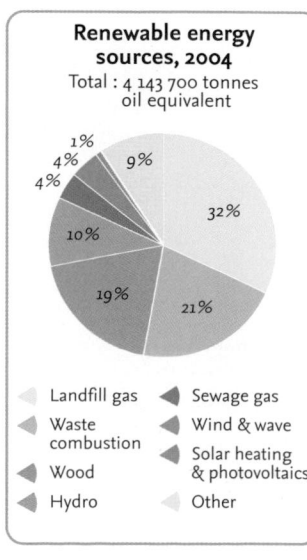

Renewable energy sources, 2004
Total : 4 143 700 tonnes oil equivalent

1%
4%
4%
9%
32%
10%
19%
21%

◁ Landfill gas
◁ Waste combustion
◁ Wood
◁ Hydro
◁ Sewage gas
◁ Wind & wave
◁ Solar heating & photovoltaics
◁ Other

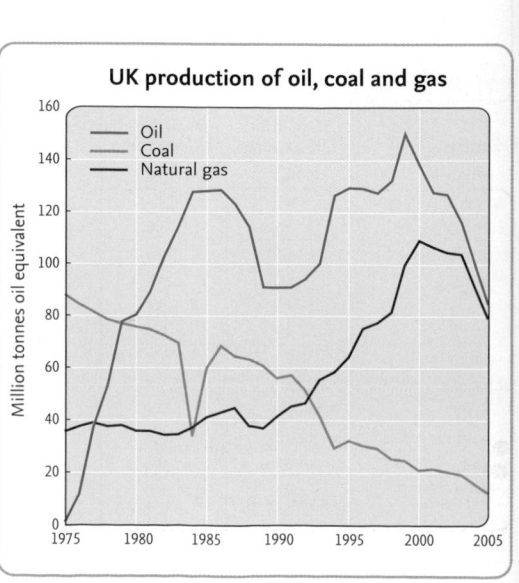

UK production of oil, coal and gas
Oil
Coal
Natural gas
Million tonnes oil equivalent
160
140
120
100
80
60
40
20
0
1975 1980 1985 1990 1995 2000 2005

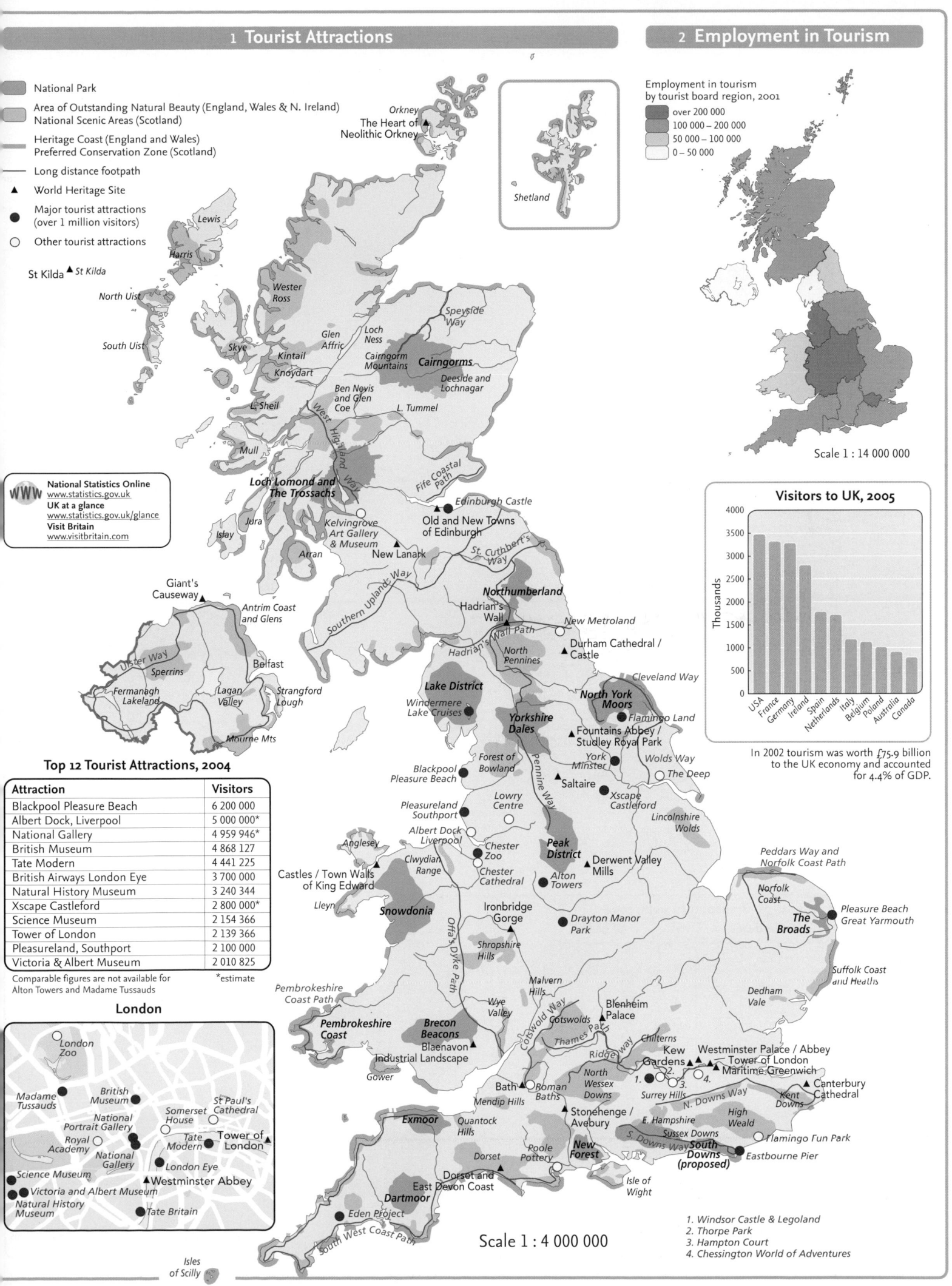

1 Tourist Attractions

National Park

Area of Outstanding Natural Beauty (England, Wales & N. Ireland)
National Scenic Areas (Scotland)

Heritage Coast (England and Wales)
Preferred Conservation Zone (Scotland)

Long distance footpath

▲ World Heritage Site

● Major tourist attractions (over 1 million visitors)

○ Other tourist attractions

St Kilda ▲ St Kilda

WWW National Statistics Online
www.statistics.gov.uk
UK at a glance
www.statistics.gov.uk/glance
Visit Britain
www.visitbritain.com

Top 12 Tourist Attractions, 2004

Attraction	Visitors
Blackpool Pleasure Beach	6 200 000
Albert Dock, Liverpool	5 000 000*
National Gallery	4 959 946*
British Museum	4 868 127
Tate Modern	4 441 225
British Airways London Eye	3 700 000
Natural History Museum	3 240 344
Xscape Castleford	2 800 000*
Science Museum	2 154 366
Tower of London	2 139 366
Pleasureland, Southport	2 100 000
Victoria & Albert Museum	2 010 825

Comparable figures are not available for Alton Towers and Madame Tussauds   *estimate

London

London Zoo, Madame Tussauds, British Museum, National Portrait Gallery, Somerset House, St Paul's Cathedral, Royal Academy, National Gallery, Tate Modern, Tower of London, Science Museum, London Eye, Westminster Abbey, Victoria and Albert Museum, Natural History Museum, Tate Britain

Scale 1 : 4 000 000

1. Windsor Castle & Legoland
2. Thorpe Park
3. Hampton Court
4. Chessington World of Adventures

2 Employment in Tourism

Employment in tourism by tourist board region, 2001

over 200 000
100 000 – 200 000
50 000 – 100 000
0 – 50 000

Scale 1 : 14 000 000

Visitors to UK, 2005

(Thousands)

USA, France, Germany, Ireland, Spain, Netherlands, Italy, Belgium, Poland, Australia, Canada

In 2002 tourism was worth £75.9 billion to the UK economy and accounted for 4.4% of GDP.

1 Road Network

M1 ─── Motorway and number

A1 ─── Linking primary road and number

Scale 1 : 8 000 000

2 Rail Network

─── Inter-city and express routes

---- Channel Tunnel

WWW **UK at a glance**
www.statistics.gov.uk/glanc
Department for Transport
www.dft.gov.uk
Highways Agency
www.highways.gov.uk

Scale 1 : 8 000 000

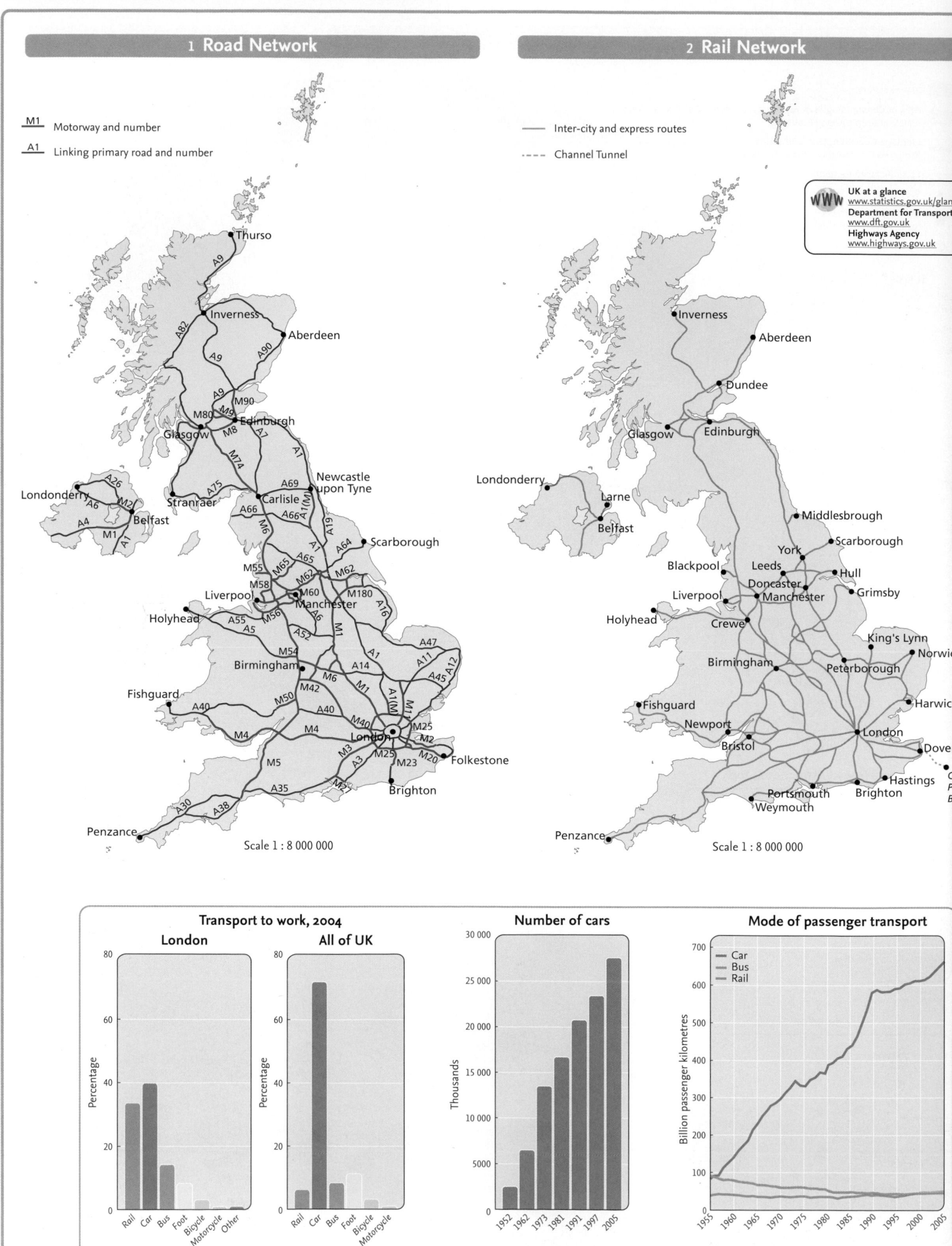

Transport to work, 2004

London

All of UK

Number of cars

Mode of passenger transport

3 Ports and Airports

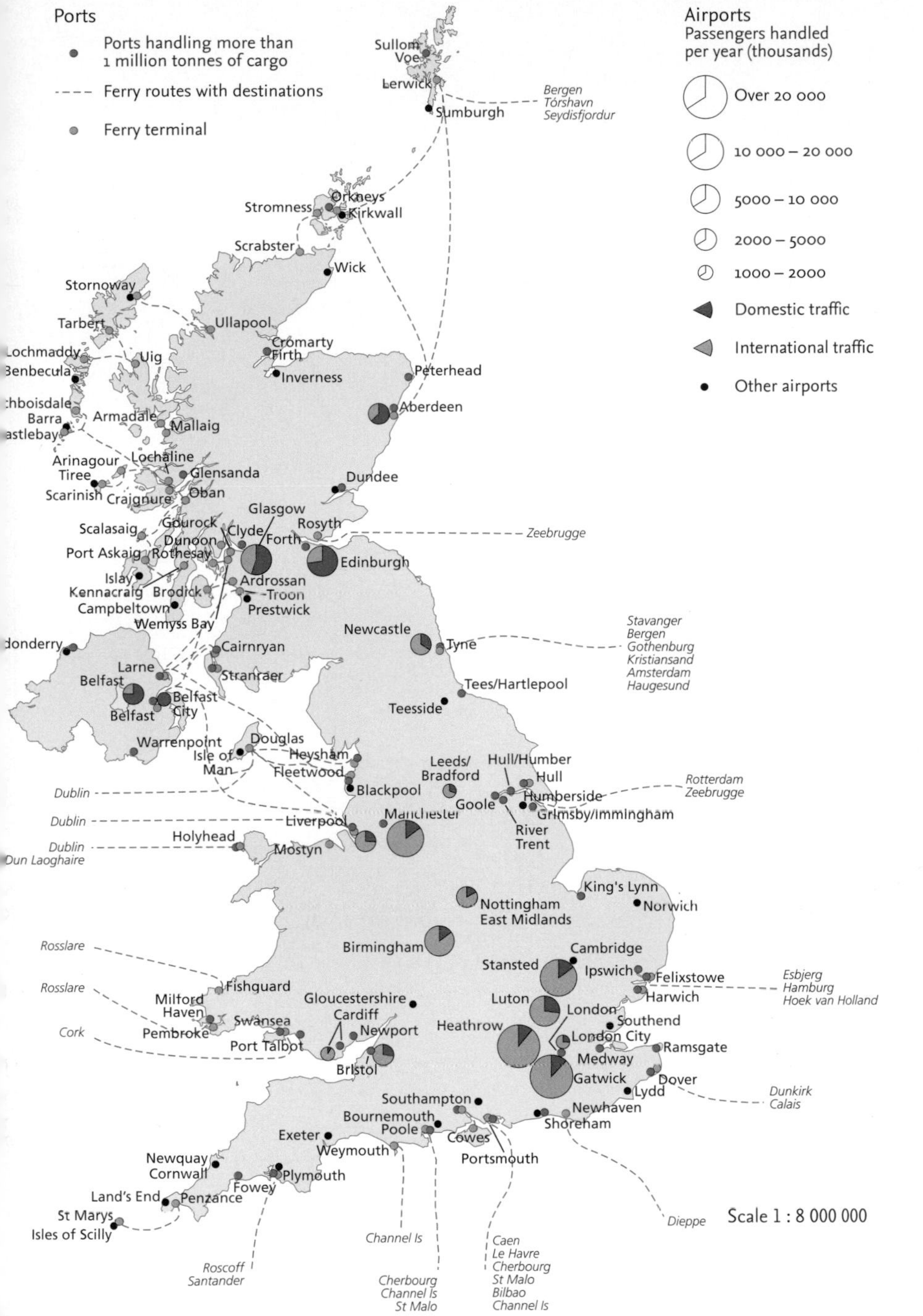

Ports

- Ports handling more than 1 million tonnes of cargo
- - - Ferry routes with destinations
- Ferry terminal

Airports
Passengers handled per year (thousands)

- Over 20 000
- 10 000 – 20 000
- 5000 – 10 000
- 2000 – 5000
- 1000 – 2000
- Domestic traffic
- International traffic
- • Other airports

Sullom Voe
Lerwick
Sumburgh
Bergen
Tórshavn
Seydisfjordur

Stromness
Orkneys
Kirkwall
Scrabster
Wick

Stornoway
Tarbert
Ullapool
Lochmaddy
Benbecula
Uig
Cromarty Firth
Inverness
Peterhead
chboisdale
Barra
Armadale
Mallaig
astlebay
Arinagour
Tiree
Lochaline
Glensanda
Aberdeen
Scarinish
Craignure
Oban
Dundee
Scalasaig
Gourock
Glasgow
Rosyth
Port Askaig
Dunoon
Clyde/Forth
Zeebrugge
Islay
Rothesay
Edinburgh
Kennacraig
Brodick
Ardrossan
Campbeltown
Troon
Wemyss Bay
Prestwick
Newcastle
Stavanger
Bergen
Gothenburg
Kristiansand
Amsterdam
Haugesund
donderry
Cairnryan
Tyne
Larne
Tees/Hartlepool
Belfast
Stranraer
Belfast
Belfast City
Teesside
Warrenpoint
Douglas
Heysham
Isle of Man
Leeds/Bradford
Hull/Humber
Dublin
Fleetwood
Hull
Rotterdam
Zeebrugge
Blackpool
Goole
Humberside
Dublin
Liverpool
Manchester
Grimsby/Immingham
Holyhead
River Trent
Dublin
Mostyn
un Laoghaire
King's Lynn
Nottingham East Midlands
Norwich
Rosslare
Birmingham
Cambridge
Rosslare
Fishguard
Stansted
Ipswich
Felixstowe
Milford Haven
Gloucestershire
Luton
Harwich
Esbjerg
Hamburg
Hoek van Holland
Cork
Swansea
Cardiff
London
Pembroke
Newport
Heathrow
Southend
Port Talbot
London City
Bristol
Gatwick
Medway
Ramsgate
Southampton
Dover
Dunkirk
Calais
Bournemouth
Newhaven
Lydd
Exeter
Poole
Shoreham
Weymouth
Cowes
Newquay
Portsmouth
Cornwall
Fowey
Land's End
Plymouth
Penzance
St Marys
Isles of Scilly
Channel Is
Caen
Le Havre
Cherbourg
St Malo
Bilbao
Channel Is
Dieppe

Roscoff
Santander
Cherbourg
Channel Is
St Malo

Scale 1 : 8 000 000

4 Telecommunications

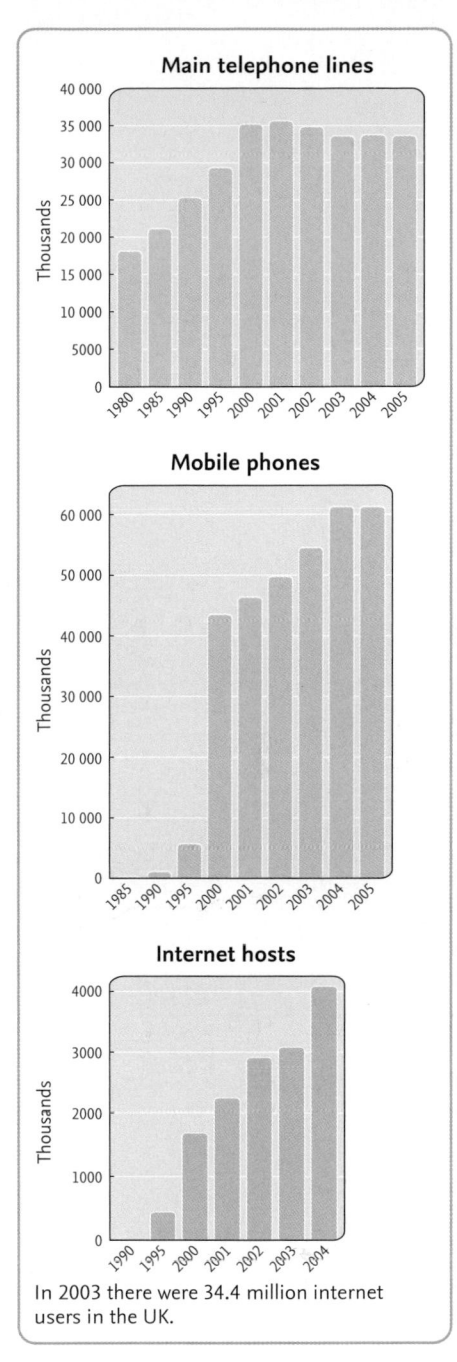

Main telephone lines
(Thousands) 1980–2005

Mobile phones
(Thousands) 1985–2005

Internet hosts
(Thousands) 1990–2004

In 2003 there were 34.4 million internet users in the UK.

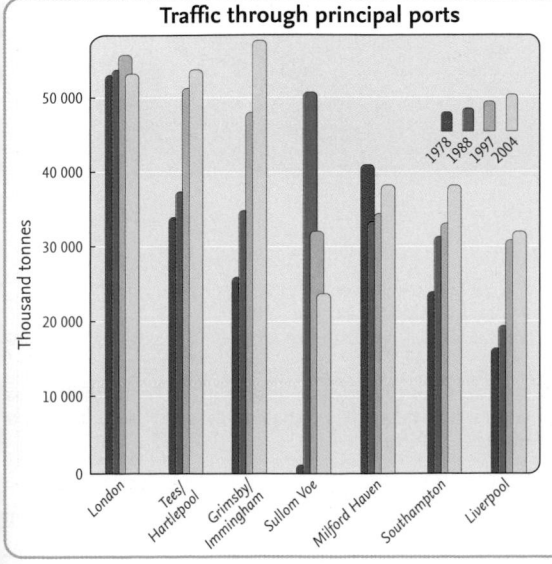

Traffic through principal ports
(Thousand tonnes)
1978, 1988, 1997, 2004
London, Tees/Hartlepool, Grimsby/Immingham, Sullom Voe, Milford Haven, Southampton, Liverpool

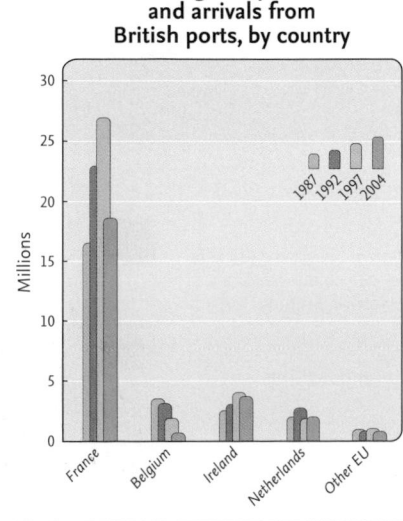

Passenger departures and arrivals from British ports, by country
(Millions)
1987, 1992, 1997, 2004
France, Belgium, Ireland, Netherlands, Other EU

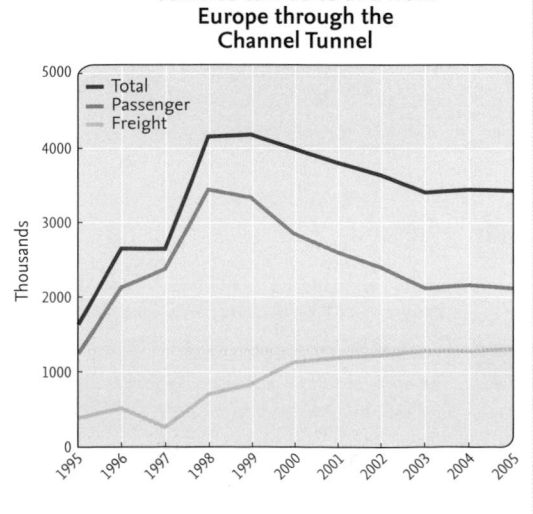

Vehicles carried to and from Europe through the Channel Tunnel
(Thousands) 1995–2005
— Total
— Passenger
— Freight

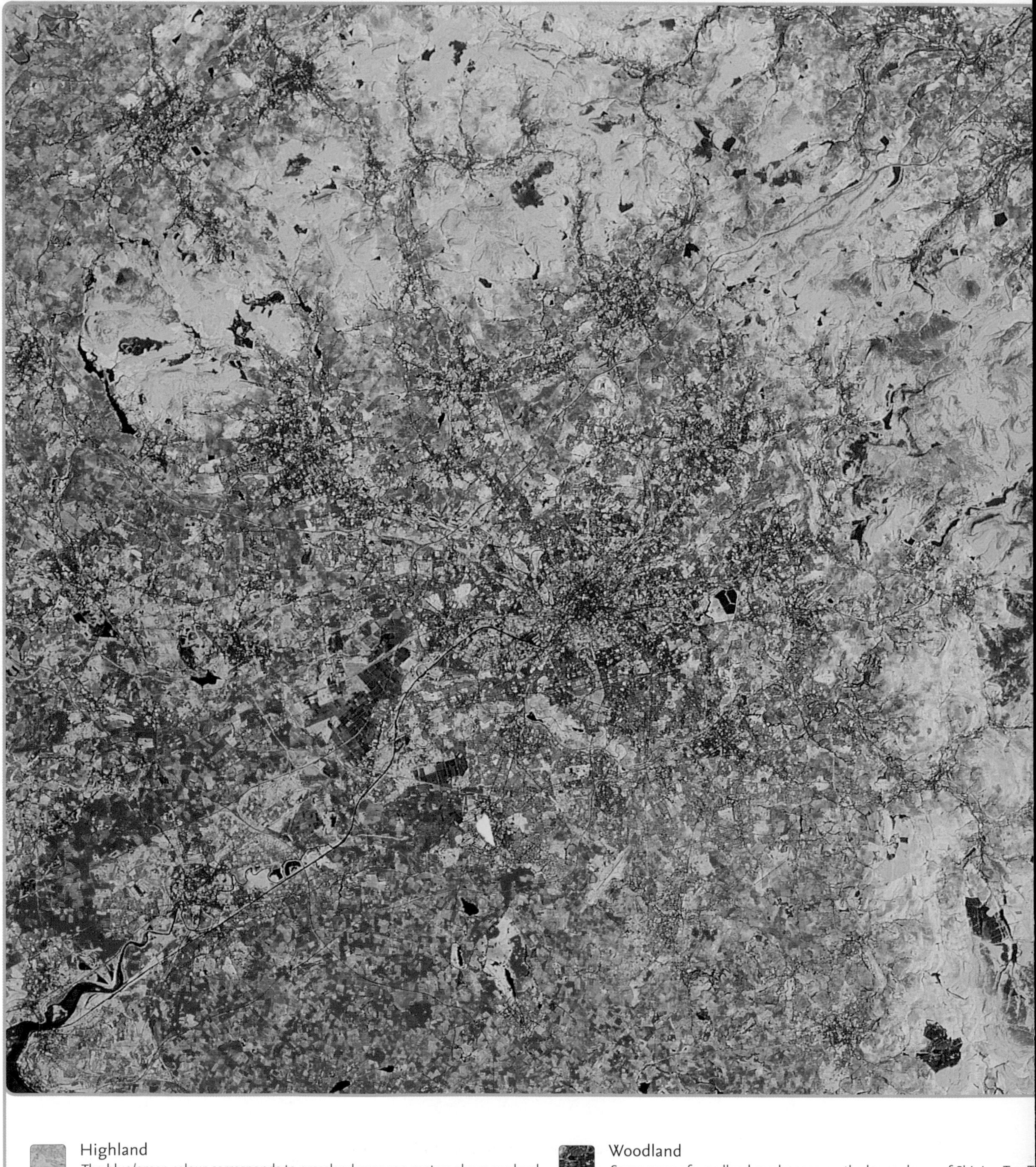

Highland

The blue/green colour corresponds to grassland over 300 metres above sea level on the map opposite. In the higher areas of the Pennines the colour becomes greener as grassland changes to moorland, for example around Shining Tor.

Lowland and arable land

The areas around Manchester appear as shades of orange and red. The cultivated areas near the river Mersey are redder.

Built up area

These areas are dark blue on the satellite image. The largest area is the Manchester urban sprawl. In the top left of the image the built up areas of Blackburn and Accrington stand out from the surrounding farmland.

Woodland

Some areas of woodland can be seen on the lower slopes of Shining Tor. T is also a small area near Alderley Edge.

Reservoir

The small distinctive shape of these can be seen in the Pennines area. Exar are Watergrove Reservoir near Whitworth and Errwood Reservoir south of Whaley Bridge.

Canal

The straight line of the Manchester Ship Canal can be seen running along the winding course of the river Mersey.

Key

Relief and physical features

Relief metres

600
500
400
300
200
100
sea level

633 ▲ Mountain height (in metres)

Woodland

Water features

River

Canal

Lake / Reservoir

Communications

Railway

Motorway

Road

⊕ Main airport

Boundary

Administrative

Settlement

Built-up area

Cities and towns

● over 1 000 000 population

○ 100 000 – 500 000 population

○ under 100 000 population

Scale 1 : 250 000

0 2 4 6 8 10 km

Manchester City Council
www.manchester.gov.uk
Association of Greater Manchester Authorities
www.agma.gov.uk
Destination Manchester
explore.destinationmanchester.com

Cross section from Accrington to Shining Tor

Height in metres

600
500
400
300
200
100
sea level

Accrington   Bury   Manchester city centre   Stockport   Shining Tor

Arctic Circle

Denmark Strait

Jan Mayen

Barents Sea

North Cape
Sørøya

Inarijärvi

Iceland
Húnaflói
Faxaflói
Vestmannaeyjar
Snæfell 1833
Vatnajökull
Fontur

Vesterålen
Loften
Vestfjorden

L a p p l a n d

Ozero
Ekostrovskaya
Imandra

Norwegian Sea

Lulealven

Ozero
Ekostrovskaya

Kemijoki

S c a n d i n a v i a

Umeälven

Indalsälven

Gulf of Bothnia

Lake
Ladoga

A T L A N T I C

O C E A N

Faroe Islands

Åland
Islands

Hiiumaa
Saaremaa

Lake
Peipus

Shetland

Outer Hebrides
Orkney

Ben Nevis
1344

Mälaren

Gulf of Finland

Vänern

Vättern

Gotland

Gulf of
Riga

N o r t h

S e a

Skagerrak

Öland

Malin Head

British
Isles

Donegal Bay

Ireland

Galway Bay

Shannon

Cape Clear

St George's Channel

Irish Sea

P e n n i n e s

Great

Britain

Snowdon
1085

The Wash

Thames

Kattegat

Jutland

Fyn

Zealand

Bornholm

B a l t i c S e a

Pripet
Marshes

Kyyivs'k
Vodoskhovyshche

N o r t h   E u r o p e a n   P

Frisian
Islands

IJsselmeer

Weser

Elbe

Warta

Vistula

Bug

Land's End
Isles of Scilly

English Channel

Channel Islands

Maas

Rhine

Elbe

Oder

Vistula

Dniester

Brittany

Seine

Marne

Ardennes

Moselle

Taunus

Erzgebirge

S u d e t y

C a r p a t h i a n   M t s

Seine

Loire

Vienne

Allier

Saône

Vosges

Rhine

Danube

Bohemian Forest

Inn

Danube

Tisza

B a y   o f

B i s c a y

Cape Finisterre

Puy de Sancy
1895

Gironde

Massif
Central

Rhône

Lake
Geneva

Mont Blanc
4808

A L P S

Lake
Constance

Großglockner
3798

Matterhorn
4478

Lake
Balaton

Hungarian Plain

Mures

Transylvanian Alps

Danube

Morava

Cantabrian Mts

Douro

Duero

Pyrenees

Aneto
3404

Ebro

Gulf of Lions

Côte d'Azur

Po

A p e n n i n e s

D i n a r i c   A l p s

A d r i a t i c   S e a

Balkan Mts

Rhodope
Mts

Gulf of
Genoa

Ligurian
Sea

Corsica

Strait of
Bonifacio

Vesuvius
1281

Mt Olympus
2917

P i n d u s   M t s

Tagus

Gulf of
Gascony

Sierra Morena

Guadalquivir

Cabo de
São Vicente

Golfo de
Valencia

Balearic Is

Ibiza

Minorca

Majorca

Sardinia

Tyrrhenian
Sea

G. of
Taranto

Corfu

Evvoia

Aegean
Sea

Sierra Nevada

Strait of
Gibraltar

M e d i t e r r a n e a n

Sicily

Stromboli

Mount
Etna
3323

I o n i a n
Sea

Zakynthos

C. Passero

Kythira

Dodecan

Naxos

Crete

Haut Atlas

Atlas Mountains

Hauts Plateaux

Atlas Saharien

Gulf of Gabès

Scale 1 : 16 000 000

0   250   500   750   1000 km

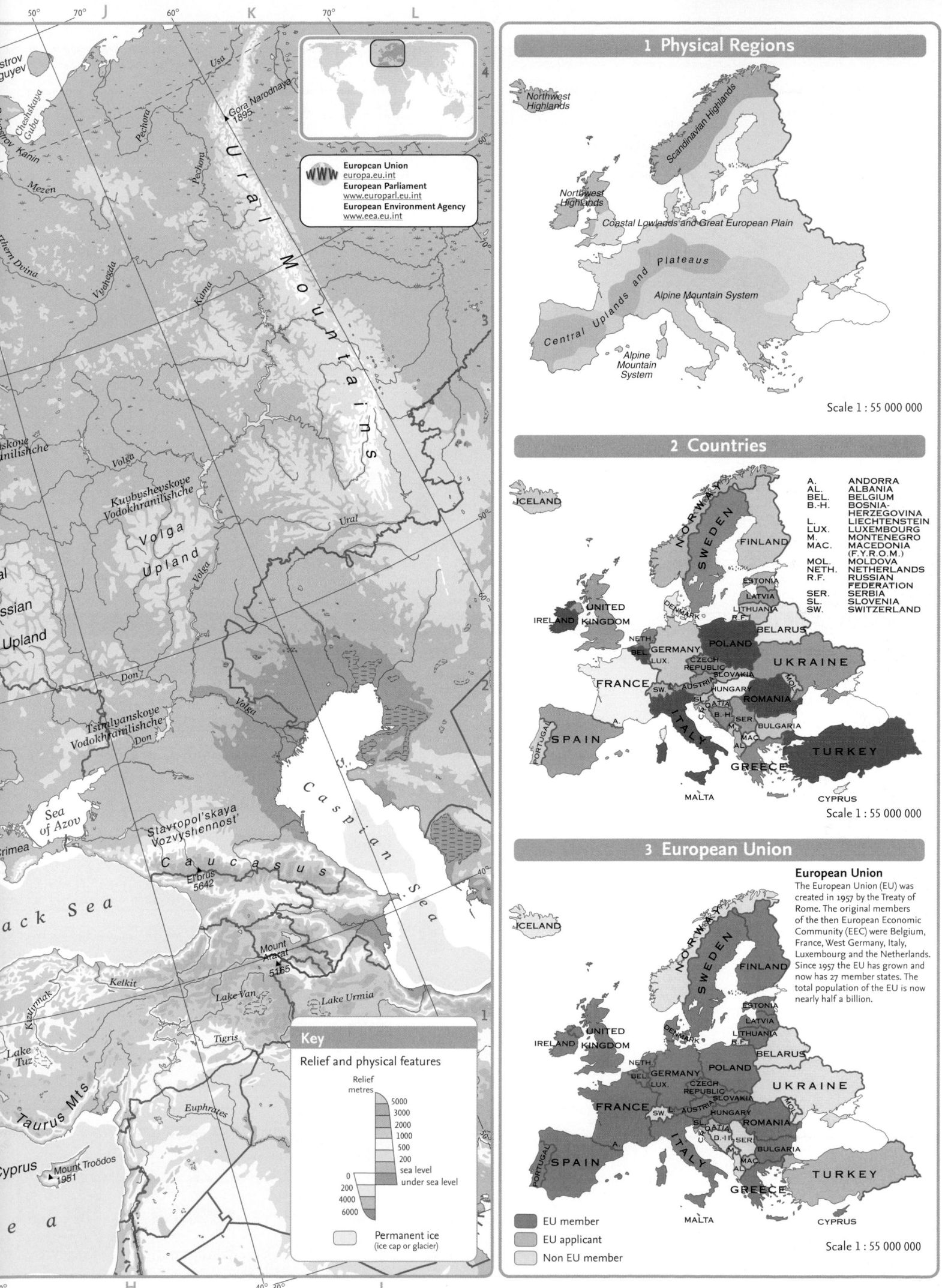

Map labels (main relief map)

Ostrov Kolguyev
Poluostrov Kanin
Cheshskaya Guba
Mezen
Usa
Gora Narodnaya 1895
Pechora
Ural Mountains
Northern Dvina
Vychegda
Kama
Volga
Kuybyshevskoye Vodokhranilishche
Volga Upland
Ural
Russian Upland
Don
Volga
Tsimlyanskoye Vodokhranilishche
Don
Sea of Azov
Crimea
Stavropol'skaya Vozvyshennost'
Caspian Sea
Caucasus
El'brus 5642
Black Sea
Mount Ararat 5165
Kelkit
Lake Van
Lake Urmia
Kızılırmak
Tigris
Lake Tuz
Taurus Mts
Euphrates
Cyprus
Mount Troödos 1951

Inset legend box
www European Union
europa.eu.int
European Parliament
www.europarl.eu.int
European Environment Agency
www.eea.eu.int

1 Physical Regions

Northwest Highlands
Scandinavian Highlands
Northwest Highlands
Coastal Lowlands and Great European Plain
Central Uplands and Plateaus
Alpine Mountain System
Alpine Mountain System

Scale 1 : 55 000 000

2 Countries

A. ANDORRA
AL. ALBANIA
BEL. BELGIUM
B.-H. BOSNIA-HERZEGOVINA
L. LIECHTENSTEIN
LUX. LUXEMBOURG
M. MONTENEGRO
MAC. MACEDONIA (F.Y.R.O.M.)
MOL. MOLDOVA
NETH. NETHERLANDS
R.F. RUSSIAN FEDERATION
SER. SERBIA
SL. SLOVENIA
SW. SWITZERLAND

ICELAND
NORWAY
SWEDEN
FINLAND
ESTONIA
LATVIA
LITHUANIA
R.F.
DENMARK
IRELAND
UNITED KINGDOM
BELARUS
NETH.
BEL.
GERMANY
POLAND
LUX.
CZECH REPUBLIC
SLOVAKIA
UKRAINE
FRANCE
SW. L
AUSTRIA
HUNGARY
MOL.
SL.
CROATIA
ROMANIA
ITALY
U.
B.-H.
SER.
BULGARIA
M.
MAC.
AL.
PORTUGAL
SPAIN
GREECE
TURKEY
MALTA
CYPRUS

Scale 1 : 55 000 000

3 European Union

European Union
The European Union (EU) was created in 1957 by the Treaty of Rome. The original members of the then European Economic Community (EEC) were Belgium, France, West Germany, Italy, Luxembourg and the Netherlands. Since 1957 the EU has grown and now has 27 member states. The total population of the EU is now nearly half a billion.

ICELAND
NORWAY
SWEDEN
FINLAND
ESTONIA
LATVIA
LITHUANIA
R.F.
DENMARK
IRELAND
UNITED KINGDOM
BELARUS
NETH.
BEL.
GERMANY
POLAND
LUX.
CZECH REPUBLIC
SLOVAKIA
UKRAINE
FRANCE
SW. L
AUSTRIA
HUNGARY
MOL.
SL.
CROATIA
ROMANIA
ITALY
U.
B.-H. SER.
M.
BULGARIA
MAC.
AL.
PORTUGAL
SPAIN
GREECE
TURKEY
MALTA
CYPRUS

EU member
EU applicant
Non EU member

Scale 1 : 55 000 000

Key
Relief and physical features

Relief metres
5000
3000
2000
1000
500
200
sea level
0
200
under sea level
4000
6000

Permanent ice (ice cap or glacier)

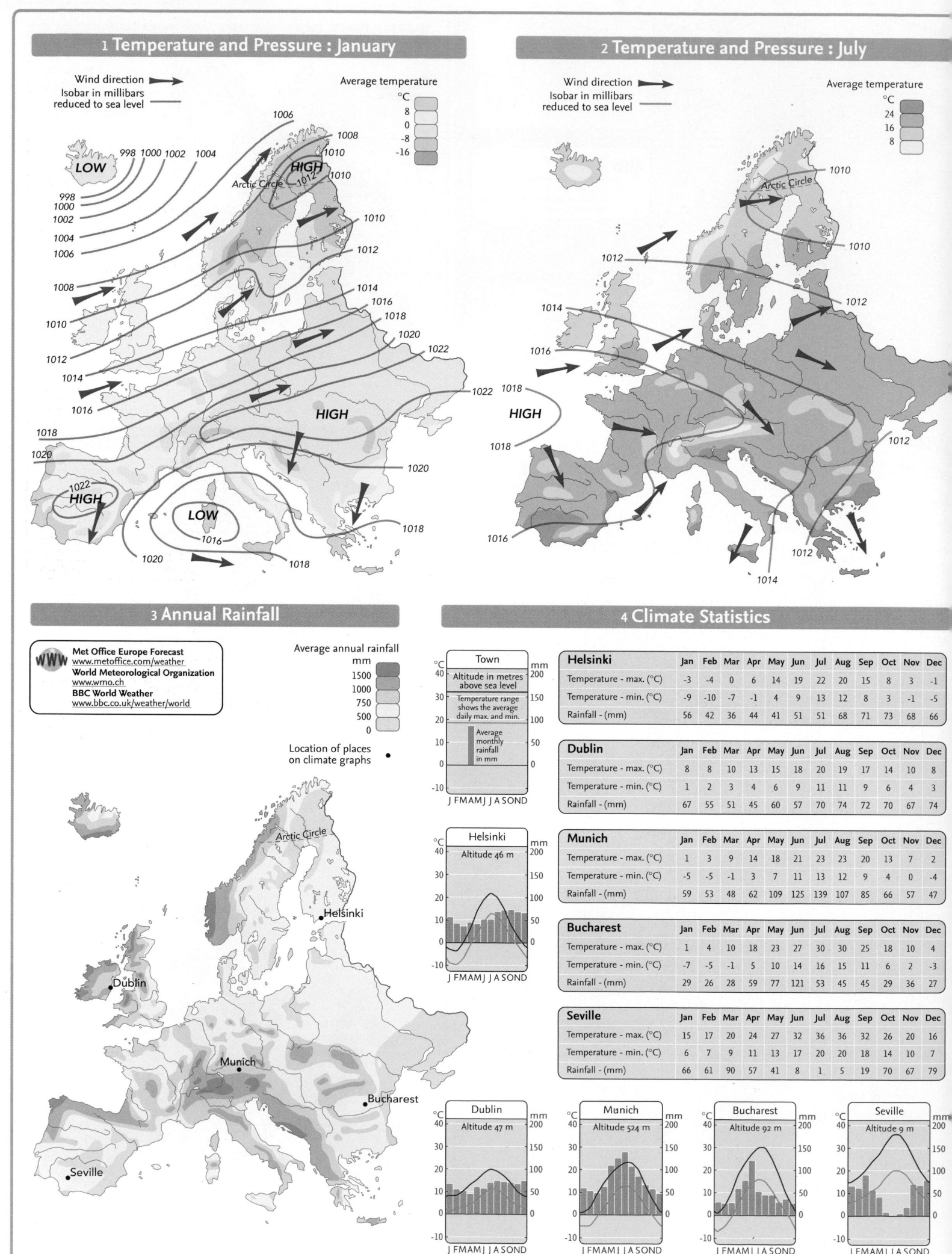

1 Temperature and Pressure : January

Wind direction →
Isobar in millibars reduced to sea level ―

Average temperature
°C
8
0
-8
-16

2 Temperature and Pressure : July

Wind direction →
Isobar in millibars reduced to sea level ―

Average temperature
°C
24
16
8

3 Annual Rainfall

WWW
Met Office Europe Forecast
www.metoffice.com/weather
World Meteorological Organization
www.wmo.ch
BBC World Weather
www.bbc.co.uk/weather/world

Average annual rainfall
mm
1500
1000
750
500
0

Location of places
on climate graphs •

4 Climate Statistics

Town
Altitude in metres above sea level
Temperature range shows the average daily max. and min.
Average monthly rainfall in mm

Helsinki	Jan	Feb	Mar	Apr	May	Jun	Jul	Aug	Sep	Oct	Nov	Dec
Temperature - max. (°C)	-3	-4	0	6	14	19	22	20	15	8	3	-1
Temperature - min. (°C)	-9	-10	-7	-1	4	9	13	12	8	3	-1	-5
Rainfall - (mm)	56	42	36	44	41	51	51	68	71	73	68	66

Dublin	Jan	Feb	Mar	Apr	May	Jun	Jul	Aug	Sep	Oct	Nov	Dec
Temperature - max. (°C)	8	8	10	13	15	18	20	19	17	14	10	8
Temperature - min. (°C)	1	2	3	4	6	9	11	11	9	6	4	3
Rainfall - (mm)	67	55	51	45	60	57	70	74	72	70	67	74

Munich	Jan	Feb	Mar	Apr	May	Jun	Jul	Aug	Sep	Oct	Nov	Dec
Temperature - max. (°C)	1	3	9	14	18	21	23	23	20	13	7	2
Temperature - min. (°C)	-5	-5	-1	3	7	11	13	12	9	4	0	-4
Rainfall - (mm)	59	53	48	62	109	125	139	107	85	66	57	47

Bucharest	Jan	Feb	Mar	Apr	May	Jun	Jul	Aug	Sep	Oct	Nov	Dec
Temperature - max. (°C)	1	4	10	18	23	27	30	30	25	18	10	4
Temperature - min. (°C)	-7	-5	-1	5	10	14	16	15	11	6	2	-3
Rainfall - (mm)	29	26	28	59	77	121	53	45	45	29	36	27

Seville	Jan	Feb	Mar	Apr	May	Jun	Jul	Aug	Sep	Oct	Nov	Dec
Temperature - max. (°C)	15	17	20	24	27	32	36	36	32	26	20	16
Temperature - min. (°C)	6	7	9	11	13	17	20	20	18	14	10	7
Rainfall - (mm)	66	61	90	57	41	8	1	5	19	70	67	79

Helsinki Altitude 46 m

Dublin Altitude 47 m

Munich Altitude 524 m

Bucharest Altitude 92 m

Seville Altitude 9 m

1 Population Density

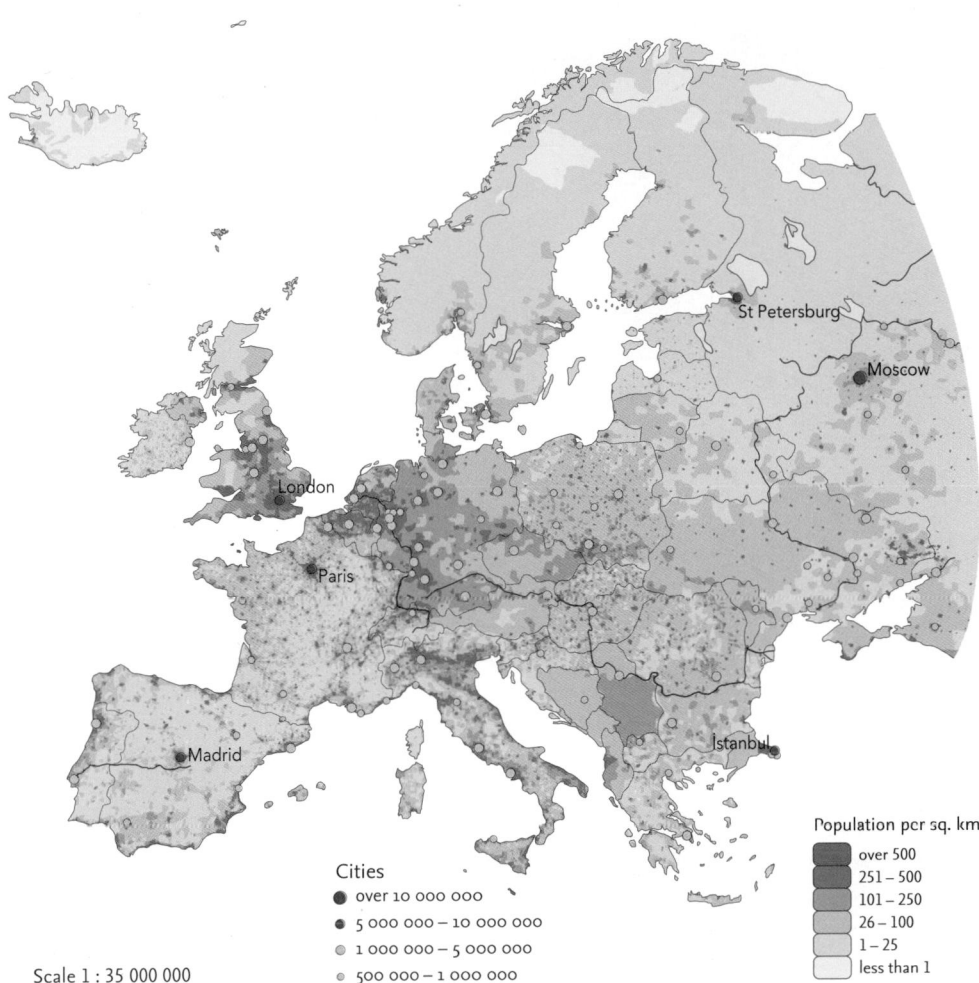

Scale 1 : 35 000 000

Cities
- ● over 10 000 000
- ● 5 000 000 – 10 000 000
- ○ 1 000 000 – 5 000 000
- ○ 500 000 – 1 000 000

Population per sq. km
- over 500
- 251 – 500
- 101 – 250
- 26 – 100
- 1 – 25
- less than 1

2 City Populations

City	Country	Population
Moscow	Russian Federation	10 672 000
Paris	France	9 854 000
İstanbul	Turkey	9 760 000
London	United Kingdom	7 615 000
Essen-Dortmund	Germany	6 566 000
St Petersburg	Russian Federation	5 315 000
Madrid	Spain	5 145 000
Barcelona	Spain	4 424 000
Milan	Italy	4 007 000
Frankfurt am Main	Germany	3 721 000
Berlin	Germany	3 328 000
Dusseldorf	Germany	3 325 000
Athens	Greece	3 238 000
Cologne	Germany	3 084 000
Katowice	Poland	2 914 000
Naples	Italy	2 905 000
Stuttgart	Germany	2 705 000
Hamburg	Germany	2 686 000
Rome	Italy	2 628 000
Kiev	Ukraine	2 623 000
Munich	Germany	2 318 000
Birmingham	United Kingdom	2 215 000
Warsaw	Poland	2 204 000
Manchester	United Kingdom	2 193 000
Vienna	Austria	2 190 000
Lisbon	Portugal	1 977 000
Bucharest	Romania	1 764 000
Stockholm	Sweden	1 729 000
Minsk	Belarus	1 709 000
Budapest	Hungary	1 670 000
Mannheim	Germany	1 625 000

WWW **EUROSTAT**
europa.eu.int/comm/eurostat
United Nations Population Information Network
www.un.org/popin

3 Population under 15

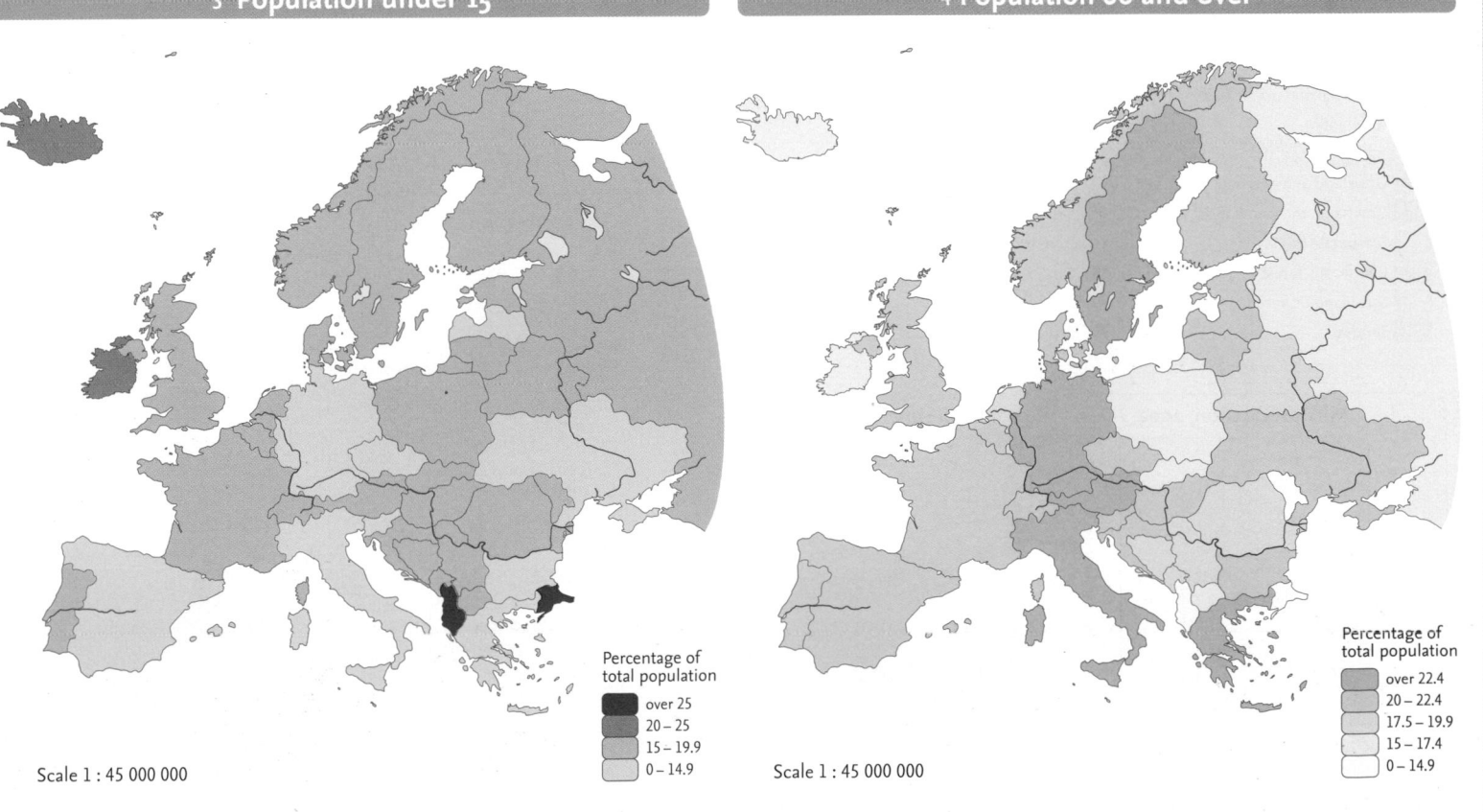

Scale 1 : 45 000 000

Percentage of total population
- over 25
- 20 – 25
- 15 – 19.9
- 0 – 14.9

4 Population 60 and over

Scale 1 : 45 000 000

Percentage of total population
- over 22.4
- 20 – 22.4
- 17.5 – 19.9
- 15 – 17.4
- 0 – 14.9

Economic Activity

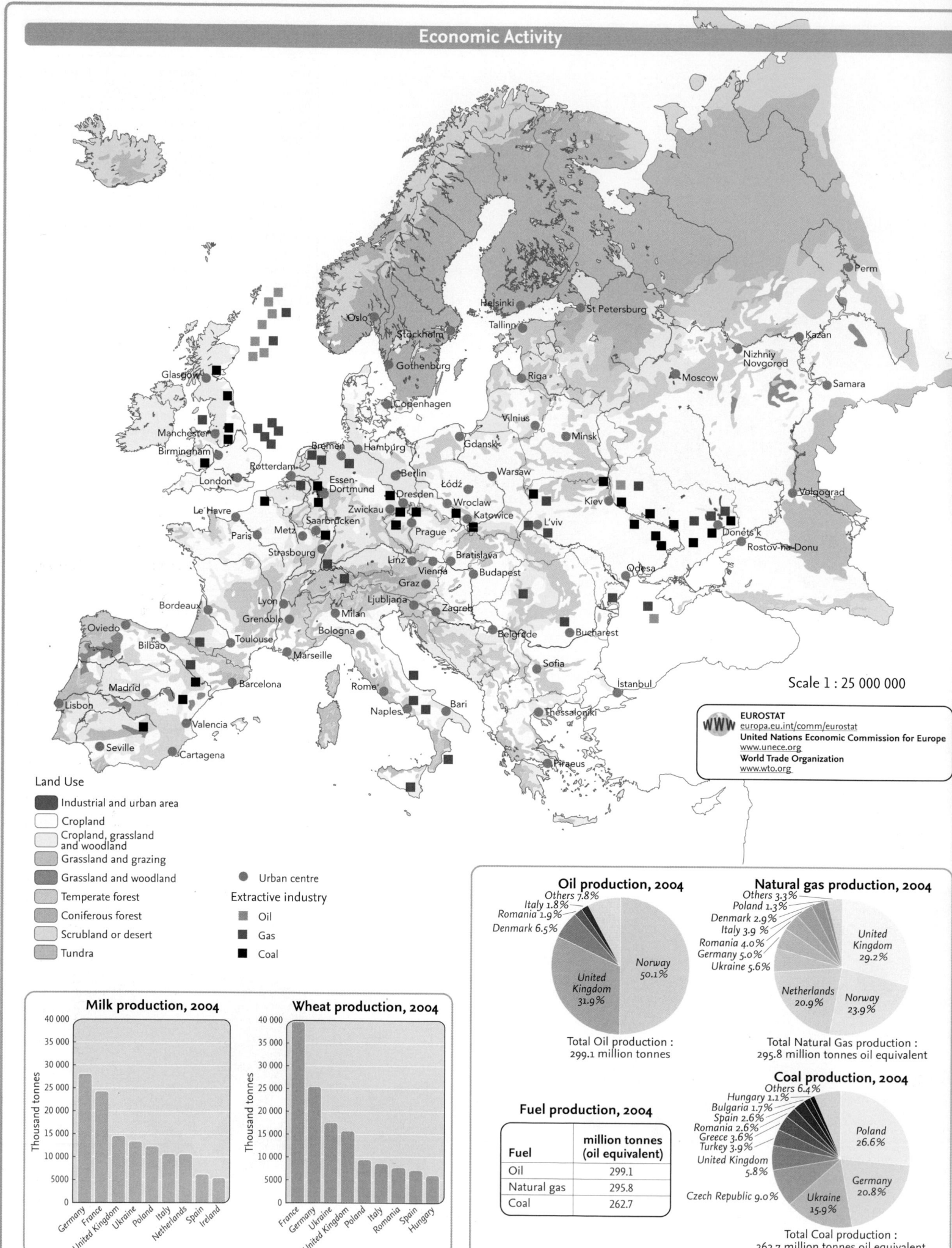

Scale 1 : 25 000 000

EUROSTAT
europa.eu.int/comm/eurostat
United Nations Economic Commission for Europe
www.unece.org
World Trade Organization
www.wto.org

Land Use

- Industrial and urban area
- Cropland
- Cropland, grassland and woodland
- Grassland and grazing
- Grassland and woodland
- Temperate forest
- Coniferous forest
- Scrubland or desert
- Tundra

- Urban centre

Extractive industry
- Oil
- Gas
- Coal

Oil production, 2004

Others 7.8%
Italy 1.8%
Romania 1.9%
Denmark 6.5%
United Kingdom 31.9%
Norway 50.1%

Total Oil production :
299.1 million tonnes

Natural gas production, 2004

Others 3.3%
Poland 1.3%
Denmark 2.9%
Italy 3.9 %
Romania 4.0%
Germany 5.0%
Ukraine 5.6%
United Kingdom 29.2%
Netherlands 20.9%
Norway 23.9%

Total Natural Gas production :
295.8 million tonnes oil equivalent

Coal production, 2004

Others 6.4%
Hungary 1.1%
Bulgaria 1.7%
Spain 2.6%
Romania 2.6%
Greece 3.6%
Turkey 3.9%
United Kingdom 5.8%
Czech Republic 9.0%
Poland 26.6%
Germany 20.8%
Ukraine 15.9%

Total Coal production :
262.7 million tonnes oil equivalent

Fuel production, 2004

Fuel	million tonnes (oil equivalent)
Oil	299.1
Natural gas	295.8
Coal	262.7

Milk production, 2004

Thousand tonnes

Germany, France, United Kingdom, Ukraine, Poland, Italy, Netherlands, Spain, Ireland

Wheat production, 2004

Thousand tonnes

France, Germany, Ukraine, United Kingdom, Poland, Italy, Romania, Spain, Hungary

Tourism

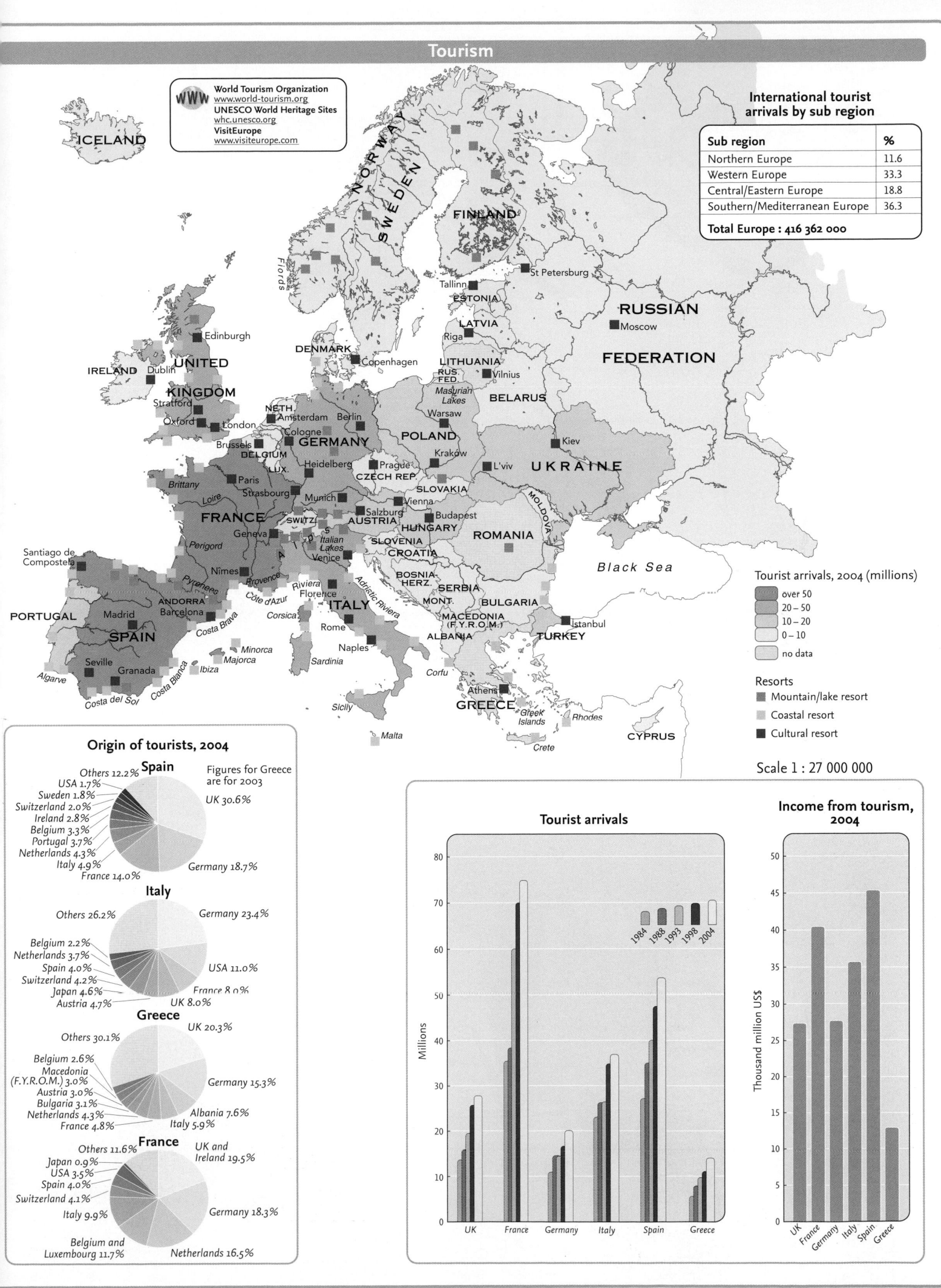

World Tourism Organization
www.world-tourism.org
UNESCO World Heritage Sites
whc.unesco.org
VisitEurope
www.visiteurope.com

International tourist arrivals by sub region

Sub region	%
Northern Europe	11.6
Western Europe	33.3
Central/Eastern Europe	18.8
Southern/Mediterranean Europe	36.3
Total Europe : 416 362 000	

Tourist arrivals, 2004 (millions)
- over 50
- 20 – 50
- 10 – 20
- 0 – 10
- no data

Resorts
- Mountain/lake resort
- Coastal resort
- Cultural resort

Scale 1 : 27 000 000

Origin of tourists, 2004

Spain
Figures for Greece are for 2003
- Others 12.2%
- USA 1.7%
- Sweden 1.8%
- Switzerland 2.0%
- Ireland 2.8%
- Belgium 3.3%
- Portugal 3.7%
- Netherlands 4.3%
- Italy 4.9%
- France 14.0%
- UK 30.6%
- Germany 18.7%

Italy
- Others 26.2%
- Belgium 2.2%
- Netherlands 3.7%
- Spain 4.0%
- Switzerland 4.2%
- Japan 4.6%
- Austria 4.7%
- Germany 23.4%
- USA 11.0%
- France 8.0%
- UK 8.0%

Greece
- Others 30.1%
- Belgium 2.6%
- Macedonia (F.Y.R.O.M.) 3.0%
- Austria 3.0%
- Bulgaria 3.1%
- Netherlands 4.3%
- France 4.8%
- UK 20.3%
- Germany 15.3%
- Albania 7.6%
- Italy 5.9%

France
- Others 11.6%
- Japan 0.9%
- USA 3.5%
- Spain 4.0%
- Switzerland 4.1%
- Italy 9.9%
- Belgium and Luxembourg 11.7%
- UK and Ireland 19.5%
- Germany 18.3%
- Netherlands 16.5%

Tourist arrivals

1984 1988 1993 1998 2004

Millions

UK   France   Germany   Italy   Spain   Greece

Income from tourism, 2004

Thousand million US$

UK   France   Germany   Italy   Spain   Greece

Scale 1 : 7 500 000

0   100   200   300 km

Conic Equidistant project

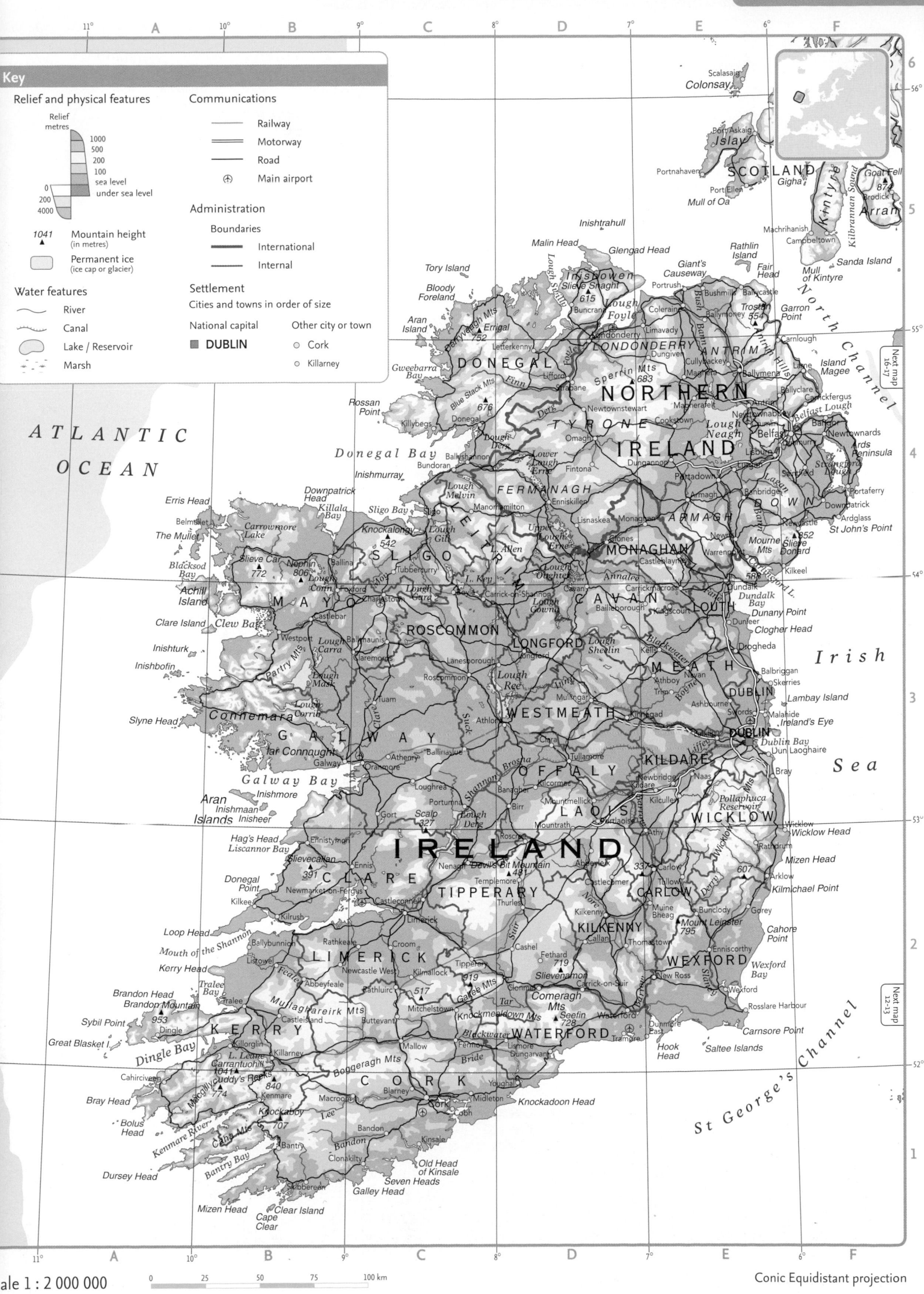

Key

Relief and physical features

Relief metres
1000
500
200
100
sea level
0 sea level
200 under sea level
4000

1041 ▲ Mountain height (in metres)

Permanent ice (ice cap or glacier)

Water features

River
Canal
Lake / Reservoir
Marsh

Communications

Railway
Motorway
Road
✈ Main airport

Administration

Boundaries
International
Internal

Settlement

Cities and towns in order of size

National capital
■ DUBLIN

Other city or town
○ Cork
○ Killarney

Scale 1 : 2 000 000

0   25   50   75   100 km

Conic Equidistant projection

Key

Relief and physical features

Relief
metres

5000
3000
2000
1000
500
200
sea level
0
under sea level
200
4000
6000

818 ▲ Mountain height
(in metres)

Water features

~ River
~ Canal
Lake / Reservoir
Marsh

Communications

— Railway
═ Motorway
— Road
⊕ Main airport

Administration

Boundaries

━━ International
━ Internal

Settlement

Cities and towns in order of size

National capital

■ AMSTERDAM
□ THE HAGUE
▫ LUXEMBOURG

Other city or town

● Rotterdam
○ Saarbrücken
○ Antwerp
○ Leuven

Scale 1 : 2 000 000

0 20 40 60 80 km

Conic Equidistant projecti

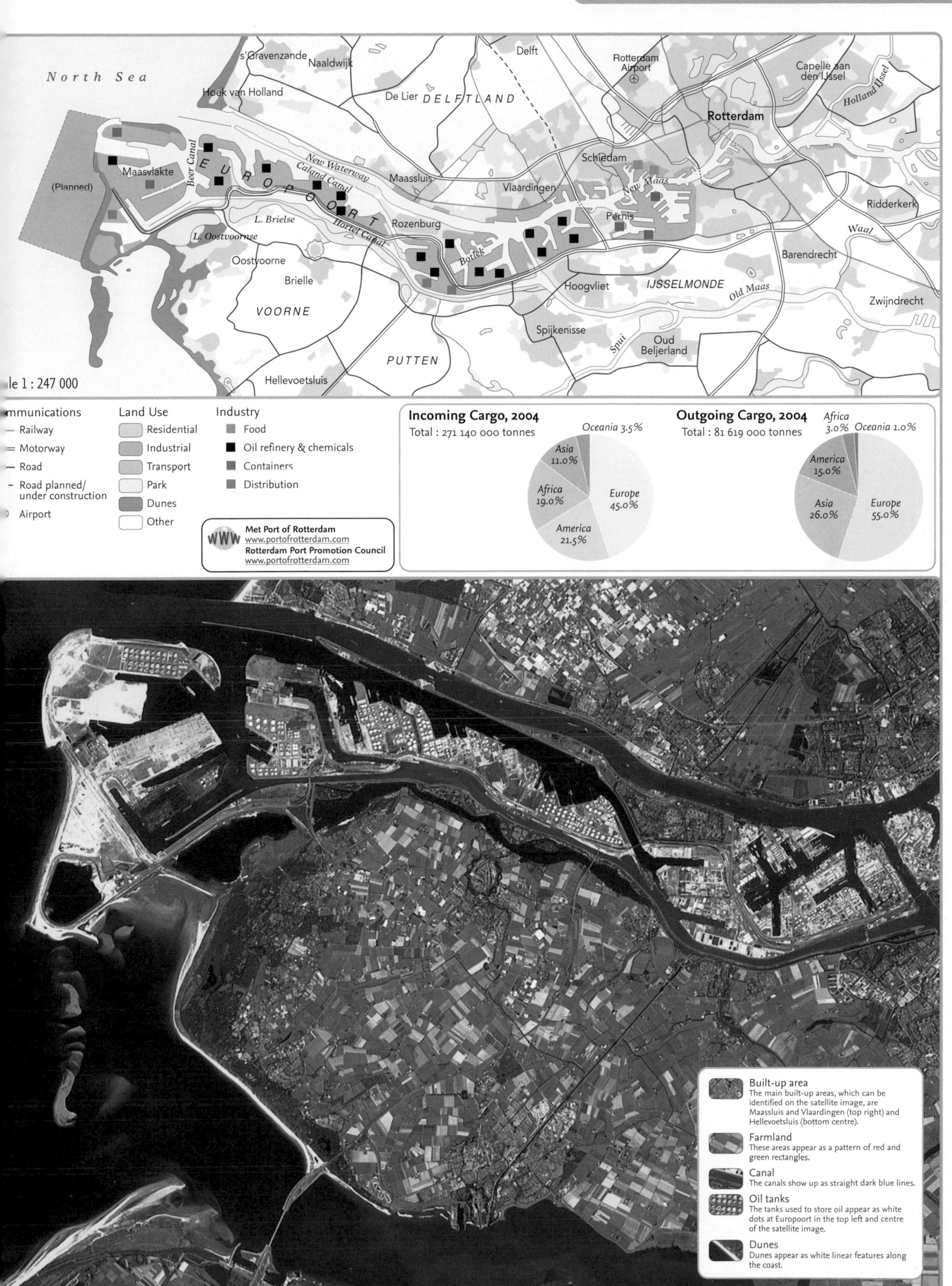

mmunications
— Railway
═ Motorway
— Road
-- Road planned/
   under construction
) Airport

Land Use
| Residential
| Industrial
| Transport
| Park
| Dunes
| Other

Industry
■ Food
■ Oil refinery & chemicals
■ Containers
■ Distribution

WWW Met Port of Rotterdam
www.portofrotterdam.com
Rotterdam Port Promotion Council
www.portofrotterdam.com

Incoming Cargo, 2004
Total : 271 140 000 tonnes

Oceania 3.5%
Asia 11.0%
Africa 19.0%
America 21.5%
Europe 45.0%

Outgoing Cargo, 2004
Total : 81 619 000 tonnes

Africa 3.0% Oceania 1.0%
America 15.0%
Asia 26.0%
Europe 55.0%

Built-up area
The main built-up areas, which can be identified on the satellite image, are Maassluis and Vlaardingen (top right) and Hellevoetsluis (bottom centre).

Farmland
These areas appear as a pattern of red and green rectangles.

Canal
The canals show up as straight dark blue lines.

Oil tanks
The tanks used to store oil appear as white dots at Europoort in the top left and centre of the satellite image.

Dunes
Dunes appear as white linear features along the coast.

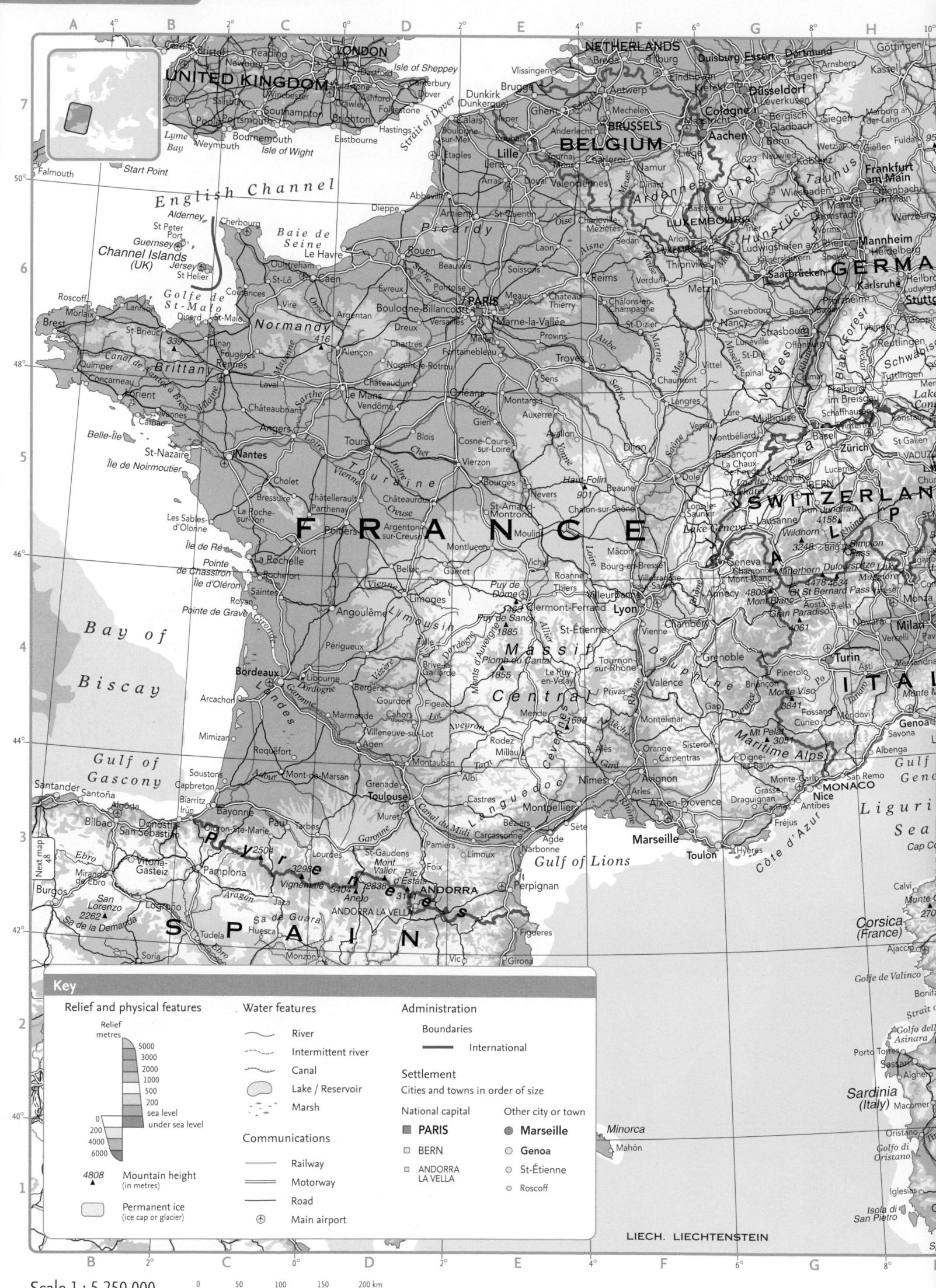

Key

Relief and physical features

Relief
metres
5000
3000
2000
1000
500
200
0 sea level
under sea level
200
4000
6000

4808 ▲ Mountain height
(in metres)

Permanent ice
(ice cap or glacier)

Water features

～ River
～ Intermittent river
～ Canal
Lake / Reservoir
Marsh

Communications

Railway
Motorway
Road
⊕ Main airport

Administration

Boundaries

International

Settlement

Cities and towns in order of size

National capital

■ **PARIS**
□ BERN
□ ANDORRA
  LA VELLA

Other city or town

● **Marseille**
○ **Genoa**
○ St-Étienne
○ Roscoff

Scale 1 : 5 250 000

0   50   100   150   200 km

Lambert Conformal Conic pro

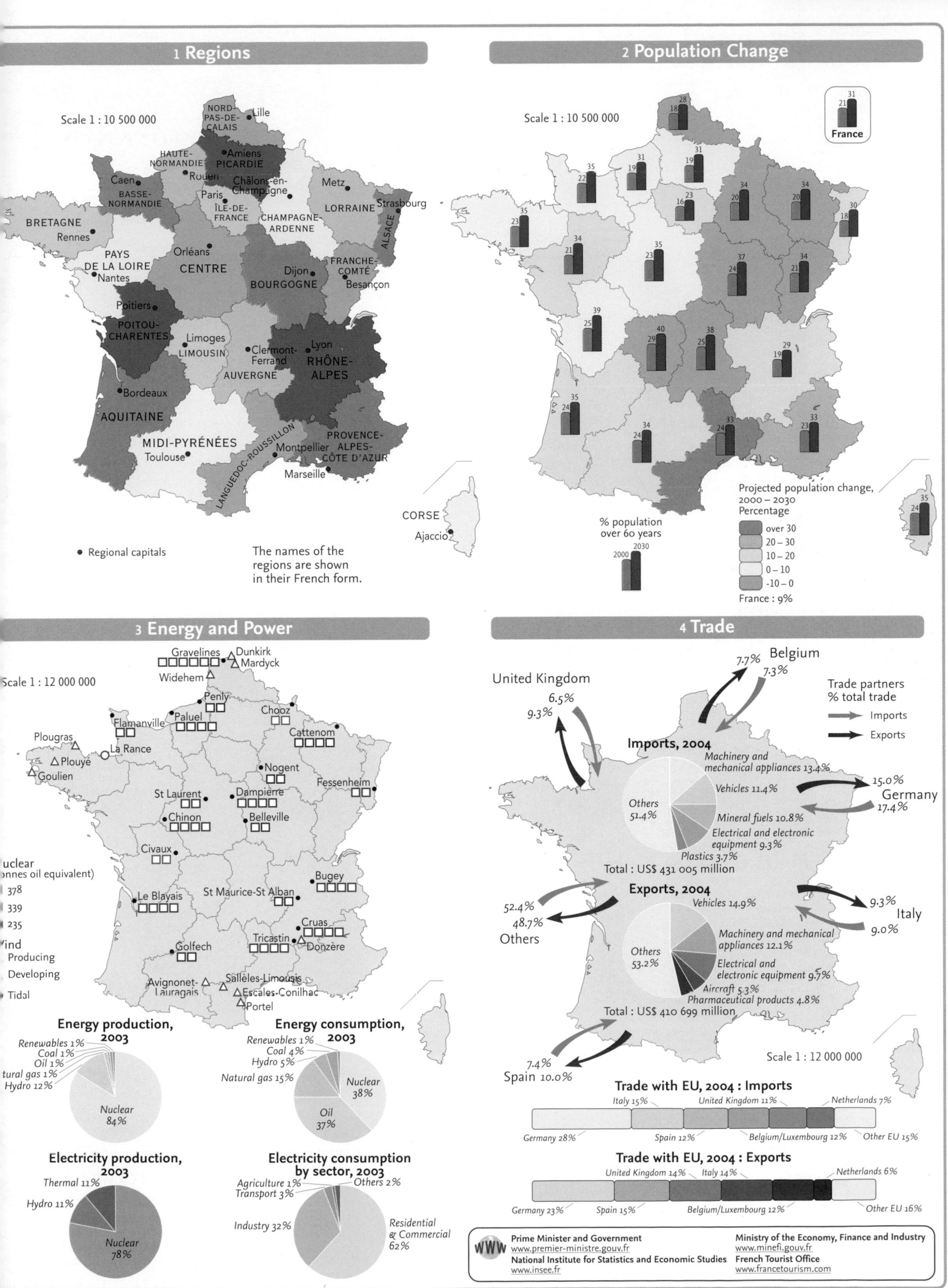

1 Regions

Scale 1 : 10 500 000

NORD-PAS-DE-CALAIS • Lille

HAUTE-NORMANDIE
Amiens
PICARDIE

Caen
BASSE-NORMANDIE
Rouen

Metz
LORRAINE
Strasbourg

Paris
ÎLE-DE-FRANCE

Châlons-en-Champagne
CHAMPAGNE-ARDENNE

ALSACE

BRETAGNE
Rennes

PAYS DE LA LOIRE
Nantes

Orléans
CENTRE

Dijon
BOURGOGNE

FRANCHE-COMTÉ
Besançon

Poitiers
POITOU-CHARENTES

Limoges
LIMOUSIN

Clermont-Ferrand
AUVERGNE

Lyon
RHÔNE-ALPES

Bordeaux

AQUITAINE

LANGUEDOC-ROUSSILLON

MIDI-PYRÉNÉES
Toulouse

Montpellier

PROVENCE-ALPES-CÔTE D'AZUR

Marseille

CORSE
Ajaccio

• Regional capitals

The names of the regions are shown in their French form.

2 Population Change

Scale 1 : 10 500 000

31 21 France

% population over 60 years
2000   2030

Projected population change, 2000 – 2030
Percentage
over 30
20 – 30
10 – 20
0 – 10
-10 – 0
France : 9%

3 Energy and Power

Scale 1 : 12 000 000

Gravelines   Dunkirk
Mardyck
Widehem

Penly
Paluel   Chooz
Flamanville
Cattenom
Plougras
La Rance
Plouyé
Goulien
Nogent
Fessenheim
St Laurent   Dampierre
Chinon   Belleville
Civaux
Bugey
Le Blayais   St Maurice-St Alban
Cruas
Golfech   Tricastin   Donzère
Avignonet-Lauragais   Salleles-Limousis
Escales-Conilhac
Portel

Nuclear
(tonnes oil equivalent)
378
339
235

Wind
Producing
Developing

Tidal

Energy production, 2003
Renewables 1%
Coal 1%
Oil 1%
Natural gas 1%
Hydro 12%
Nuclear 84%

Energy consumption, 2003
Renewables 1%
Coal 4%
Hydro 5%
Natural gas 15%
Nuclear 38%
Oil 37%

Electricity production, 2003
Thermal 11%
Hydro 11%
Nuclear 78%

Electricity consumption by sector, 2003
Agriculture 1%   Others 2%
Transport 3%
Industry 32%
Residential & Commercial 62%

4 Trade

Belgium
7.7%
7.3%

United Kingdom
6.5%
9.3%

Trade partners % total trade
→ Imports
→ Exports

Imports, 2004
Machinery and mechanical appliances 13.4%
Vehicles 11.4%
Others 51.4%
Mineral fuels 10.8%
Electrical and electronic equipment 9.3%
Plastics 3.7%
Total : US$ 431 005 million

15.0%
17.4%
Germany

9.3%
9.0%
Italy

Exports, 2004
Vehicles 14.9%
Others 53.2%
Machinery and mechanical appliances 12.1%
Electrical and electronic equipment 9.5%
Aircraft 5.3%
Pharmaceutical products 4.8%
Total : US$ 410 699 million

52.4%
48.7%
Others

7.4%
Spain 10.0%

Scale 1 : 12 000 000

Trade with EU, 2004 : Imports
Italy 15%   United Kingdom 11%   Netherlands 7%
Germany 28%   Spain 12%   Belgium/Luxembourg 12%   Other EU 15%

Trade with EU, 2004 : Exports
United Kingdom 14%   Italy 14%   Netherlands 6%
Germany 23%   Spain 15%   Belgium/Luxembourg 12%   Other EU 16%

WWW   Prime Minister and Government
www.premier-ministre.gouv.fr
National Institute for Statistics and Economic Studies
www.insee.fr

Ministry of the Economy, Finance and Industry
www.minefi.gouv.fr
French Tourist Office
www.francetourism.com

Scale 1 : 4 000 000

Lambert Conformal Conic proje

1 Regions

- Regional capitals

The names of the
regions are shown
in their Polish form.

Scale 1 : 8 000 000

2 Population

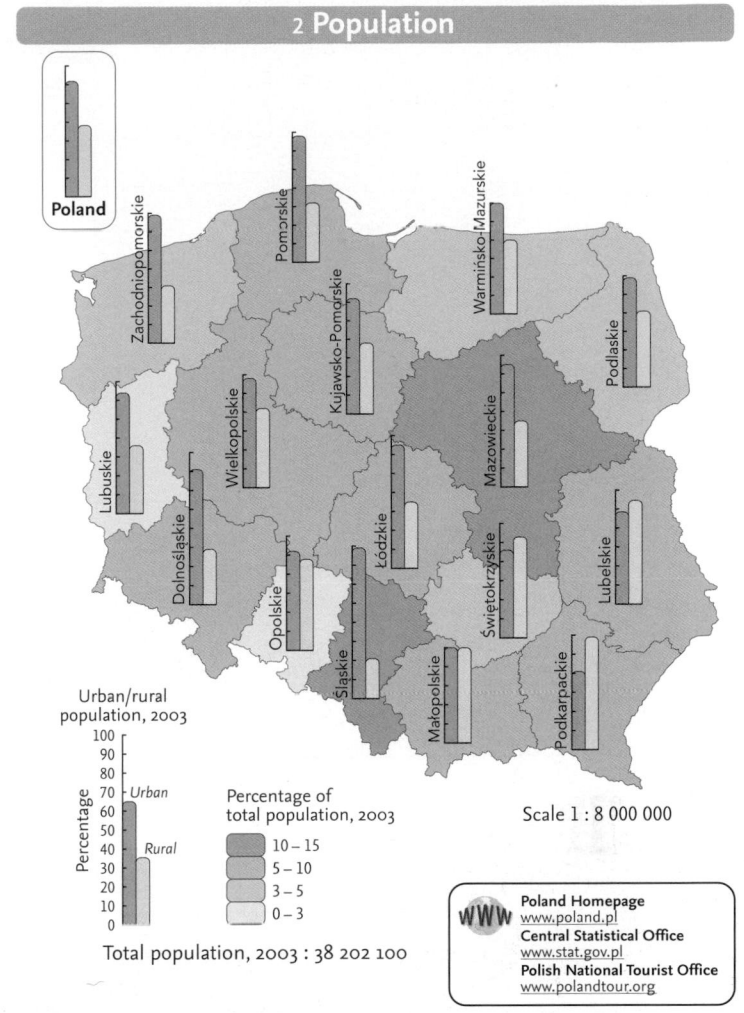

Poland

Urban/rural
population, 2003

Percentage

100
90
80
70   *Urban*
60
50
40   *Rural*
30
20
10
0

Percentage of
total population, 2003

- 10 – 15
- 5 – 10
- 3 – 5
- 0 – 3

Scale 1 : 8 000 000

Total population, 2003 : 38 202 100

WWW   Poland Homepage
www.poland.pl
Central Statistical Office
www.stat.gov.pl
Polish National Tourist Office
www.polandtour.org

3 Minerals and Energy

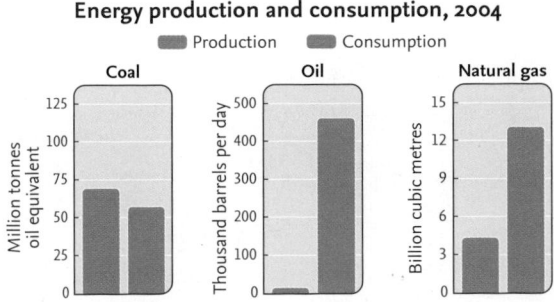

□ Iron and steel
□ Petroleum refinery products
□ Aluminium
□ Nickel
□ Iron ore
○ Coal
○ Crude petroleum
○ Cement
○ Lead
○ Copper
◇ Zinc
◇ Salt
◇ Phosphate
◇ Natural gas
◎ Processing plant or oil refinery

Scale 1 : 8 000 000

Mineral production, 2003

Copper
Zinc
Lead
Aluminium

0   100   200   300   400   500   600
Thousand tonnes

Energy production and consumption, 2004

■ Production   ■ Consumption

Coal

Million tonnes oil equivalent

125
100
75
50
25
0

Oil

Thousand barrels per day

500
400
300
200
100
0

Natural gas

Billion cubic metres

15
12
9
6
3
0

4 Conservation

National parks

▲ Mountain
▲ Highland
▲ Lowland/forest/lake
▲ Coastal

Scale 1 : 8 000 000

World Heritage sites

① Wieliczka Salt Mine
② Cracow's Historic Centre
③ Auschwitz Concentration Camp
④ Belovezhskaya Pushcha / Bialowieza Forest
⑤ Historic Centre of Warsaw
⑥ Old City of Zamosc
⑦ Medieval Town of Torun
⑧ Castle of the Teutonic Order in Malbork
⑨ Kalwaria Zebrzydowska: the Mannerist
    Architectural and Park Landscape
    Complex and Pilgrimage Park
⑩ Churches of Peace in Jawor and Swidnica
⑪ Wooden Churches of Southern Little Poland
⑫ Muskauer Park / Park Muzakowski

Key

Relief and physical features

Relief metres

5000
3000
2000
1000
500
200
sea level
under sea level
0
200
4000
6000

▲ 3482 Mountain height (in metres)

Water features

∼ River
∼ Intermittent river
∼ Canal
Lake / Reservoir
Marsh

Communications

— Railway
═ Motorway
— Road
⊕ Main airport

Administration

Boundaries
— International

Settlement
Cities and towns in order of size

National capital
■ **MADRID**
□ ANDORRA LA VELLA

Other city or
● **Barcelo**
○ Seville
○ Pamplona
○ Benidorm

1 Regions

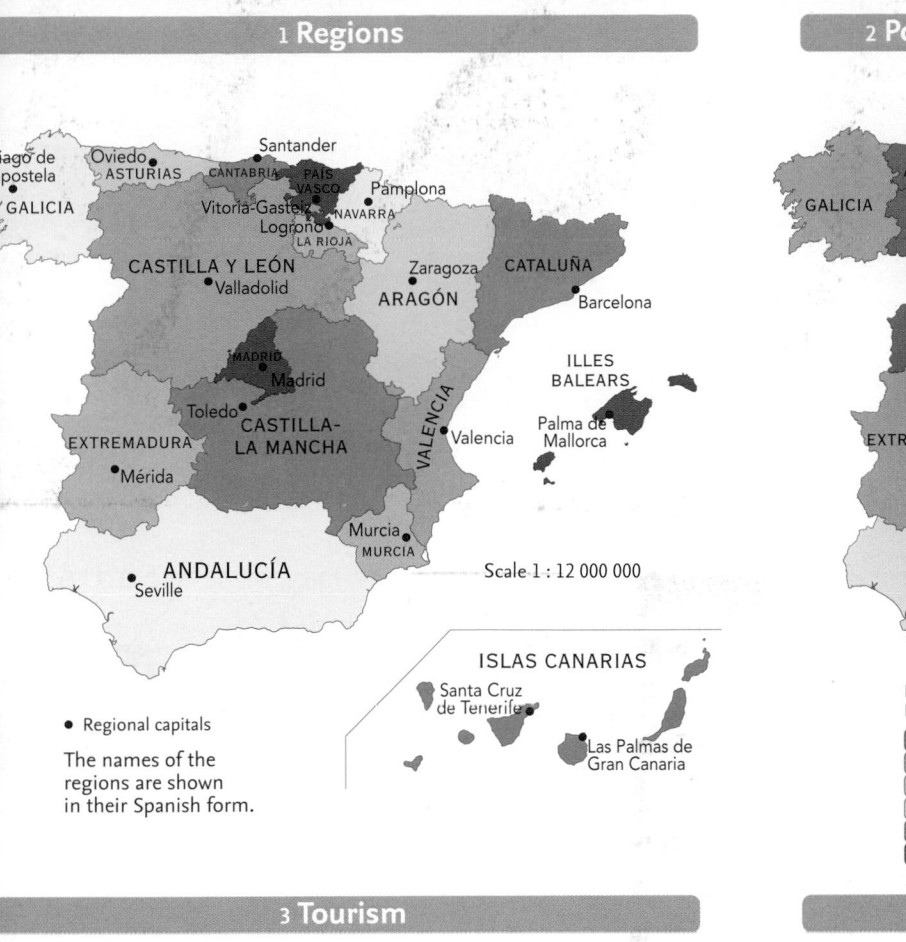

Santiago de Compostela

GALICIA

Oviedo
ASTURIAS
CANTABRIA
Santander
PAÍS VASCO
Vitoria-Gasteiz
Logroño
LA RIOJA
NAVARRA
Pamplona

CASTILLA Y LEÓN
• Valladolid

Zaragoza
ARAGÓN

CATALUÑA
• Barcelona

MADRID
• Madrid

Toledo

CASTILLA-LA MANCHA

EXTREMADURA
• Mérida

VALENCIA
• Valencia

ILLES BALEARS
Palma de Mallorca

Murcia
MURCIA

ANDALUCÍA
• Seville

Scale 1 : 12 000 000

ISLAS CANARIAS
Santa Cruz de Tenerife
Las Palmas de Gran Canaria

• Regional capitals

The names of the regions are shown in their Spanish form.

2 Population Change and Internal Migration

Main population movement, 2002
→ over 10 000 people
→ 5000 – 10 000 people

GALICIA
ASTURIAS
CANTABRIA
PAÍS VASCO
NAVARRA
LA RIOJA

CASTILLA Y LEÓN
ARAGÓN
CATALUÑA

MADRID

EXTREMADURA

CASTILLA-LA MANCHA

VALENCIA

ILLES BALEARS

MURCIA

ANDALUCÍA

Scale 1 : 12 000 000

ISLAS CANARIAS

Population change, 1991 – 2001 Percentage

- 15 – 20
- 10 – 15
- 5 – 10
- 0 – 5
- -2.5 – 0
- -5.0 – -2.5

3 Tourism

A Coruña
1 2 3
4
5
6 Bilbao
7 8 9 Burgos
10 11
Zaragoza
16 36
14
12
13 Barcelona
15
36
17 18
19
20 21
22 23 Madrid
24
Valencia
28
36
Palma de Mallorca
29
30
25 27
26
32 31
Cartagena
36
33 36
34 Seville
35
Cádiz
Málaga

Scale 1 : 12 000 000

Santa Cruz de Tenerife
37
38

Beaches

World Heritage sites
▲ Cultural
● City
■ Natural
▼ Mixed

1 The Route of Santiago de Compostela
2 Santiago de Compostela (Old Town)
3 Roman Walls of Lugo
4 Las Médulas
5 Churches of the Kingdom of the Asturias
6 Altamira Cave
7 Burgos Cathedral
8 Archaeological Site of Atapuerca
9 San Millan Yuso and Suso Monasteries
10 Pyrenees - Mount Perdu
11 Catalan Romanesque Churches of the Vall de Boi
12 Parque Guell, Palacio Guell and Casa Mila, Barcelona
13 The Palau de la Musica Catalana and the Hospital de Sant Pau, Barcelona
14 Poblet Monastery
15 The archaeological ensemble of Tarraco
16 Mudejar Architecture of Aragón
17 Old City of Salamanca
18 Old Town of Segovia, including its aqueduct
19 Old Town of Ávila, including its Extra Muros churches

20 Monastery and Site of the Escorial, Madrid
21 University and Historic Precinct of Alcalá de Henares
22 Historic City of Toledo
23 Aranjuez Cultural Landscape
24 Historic Walled Town of Cuenca
25 Old Town of Cáceres
26 Archaeological Ensemble of Mérida
27 Royal Monastery of Santa Maria de Guadalupe
28 "La Lonja de la Seda" of Valencia
29 Ibiza, Biodiversity and Culture
30 The Palmeral of Elche
31 Renaissance Monumental Ensembles of Úbeda and Baeza
32 Mosque of Córdoba
33 Cathedral, the Alcazar and Archivo de Indias, Seville
34 Doñana National Park
35 Alhambra, Generalife and Albayzin, Granada
36 Rock-Art of the Mediterranean Basin on the Iberian Peninsula
37 San Cristóbal de la Laguna
38 Garajonay National Park

4 Water Management

Oviedo
Santander
I I
III
Ebro
II
Duero
Valladolid
Zaragoza
Barcelona
Madrid
IV
Tagus
Toledo
IX
Guadiana
Júcar
Valencia
V
Segura
VIII
Murcia
Guadalquivir
VI
Seville
VII
Málaga

Scale 1 : 12 000 000

X
XI

▽ Dam
— River basin boundary

☐ River basins
I Northern Basins
II Duero Basin
III Ebro Basin
IV Tagus Basin
V Guadiana Basin
VI Guadalquivir Basin
VII Southern Basins
VIII Segura Basin
IX Júcar Basin
X La Palma
XI Las Palmas

☐ Other areas

WWW **Government** www.la-moncloa.es
National Statistical Institute www.ine.es
Tourism Studies Institute www.iet.tourspain.es

Scale 1 : 5 250 000

0   50   100   150   200 km

Lambert Conformal Conic pro

1 Regions

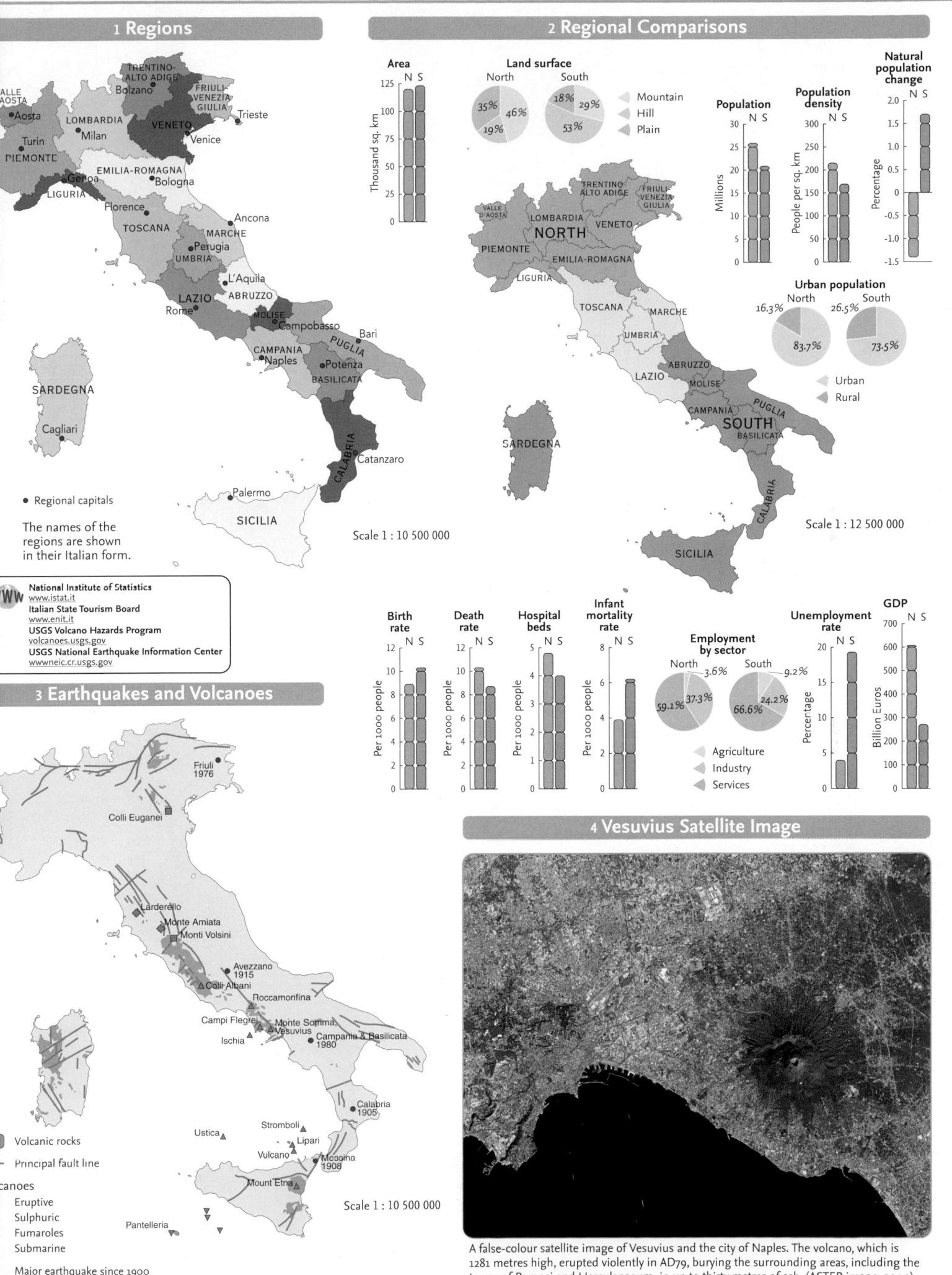

TRENTINO-ALTO ADIGE
Bolzano
VALLE D'AOSTA
Aosta
LOMBARDIA
Milan
Turin
PIEMONTE
VENETO
Venice
FRIULI-VENEZIA GIULIA
Trieste
LIGURIA
Genoa
EMILIA-ROMAGNA
Bologna
Florence
TOSCANA
Ancona
MARCHE
Perugia
UMBRIA
L'Aquila
LAZIO
Rome
ABRUZZO
Campobasso
MOLISE
Bari
CAMPANIA
Naples
PUGLIA
Potenza
BASILICATA
SARDEGNA
Cagliari
CALABRIA
Catanzaro
Palermo
SICILIA

● Regional capitals

The names of the regions are shown in their Italian form.

National Institute of Statistics
www.istat.it
Italian State Tourism Board
www.enit.it
USGS Volcano Hazards Program
volcanoes.usgs.gov
USGS National Earthquake Information Center
wwwneic.cr.usgs.gov

Scale 1 : 10 500 000

3 Earthquakes and Volcanoes

Friuli 1976
Colli Euganei
Larderello
Monte Amiata
Monti Volsini
Avezzano 1915
Colli Albani
Roccamonfina
Campi Flegrei
Monte Somma
Vesuvius
Ischia
Campania & Basilicata 1980
Calabria 1905
Stromboli
Ustica
Lipari
Vulcano
Messina 1908
Mount Etna
Pantelleria

◼ Volcanic rocks
— Principal fault line

Volcanoes
▽ Eruptive
▽ Sulphuric
▽ Fumaroles
▽ Submarine

▲ Major earthquake since 1900 greater than magnitude 6.5

Scale 1 : 10 500 000

2 Regional Comparisons

Area
N S
Thousand sq. km
0–125

Land surface
North: 35%, 46%, 19%
South: 18%, 29%, 53%
◁ Mountain
◁ Hill
◁ Plain

Population
N S
Millions
0–30

Population density
N S
People per sq. km
0–300

Natural population change
N S
Percentage
-1.5 to 2.0

NORTH
VALLE D'AOSTA
PIEMONTE
LOMBARDIA
TRENTINO-ALTO ADIGE
VENETO
FRIULI-VENEZIA GIULIA
LIGURIA
EMILIA-ROMAGNA
TOSCANA
MARCHE
UMBRIA
LAZIO
ABRUZZO
MOLISE
CAMPANIA
PUGLIA
SOUTH
BASILICATA
SARDEGNA
CALABRIA
SICILIA

Scale 1 : 12 500 000

Urban population
North: 16.3%, 83.7%
South: 26.5%, 73.5%
◁ Urban
◁ Rural

Birth rate
N S
Per 1000 people
0–12

Death rate
N S
Per 1000 people
0–12

Hospital beds
N S
Per 1000 people
0–5

Infant mortality rate
N S
Per 1000 people
0–8

Employment by sector
North: 3.6%, 37.3%, 59.1%
South: 9.2%, 24.2%, 66.6%
◁ Agriculture
◁ Industry
◁ Services

Unemployment rate
N S
Percentage
0–20

GDP
N S
Billion Euros
0–700

4 Vesuvius Satellite Image

A false-colour satellite image of Vesuvius and the city of Naples. The volcano, which is 1281 metres high, erupted violently in AD79, burying the surrounding areas, including the towns of Pompei and Herculanaeum, in up to thirty metres of ash. (ASTER image, 2000)

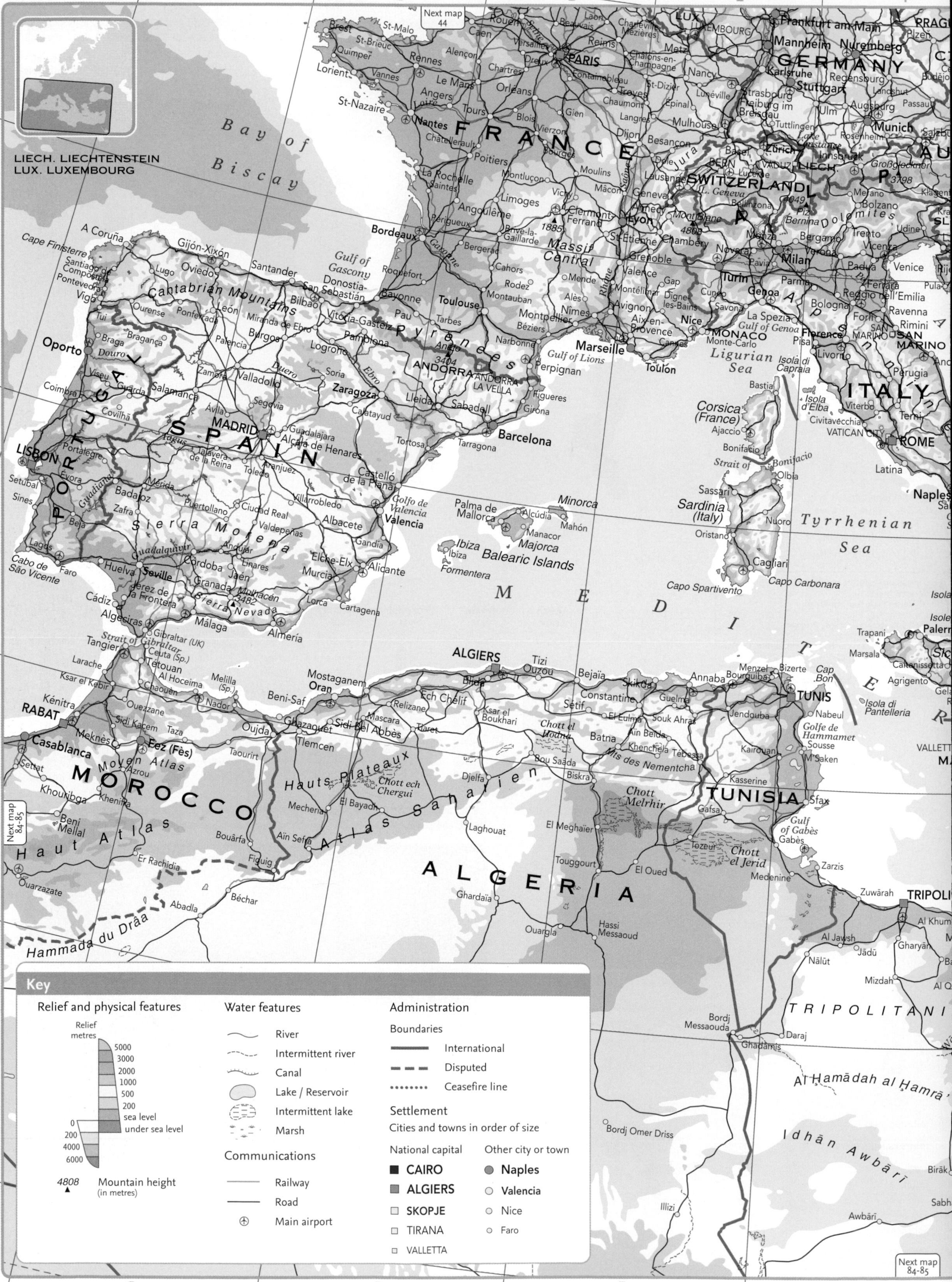

LIECH. LIECHTENSTEIN
LUX. LUXEMBOURG

Next map 44

Bay of Biscay

FRANCE

Brest, St-Malo, Caen, Rouen, Beauvais, Reims, Charleville-Mézières, LUXEMBOURG, Frankfurt am Main, Mannheim, Nuremberg, PRAG, Plzeň

Quimper, St-Brieuc, Rennes, Alençon, Dreux, Versailles, PARIS, Chartres, Châlons-en-champagne, Metz, Nancy, Karlsruhe, Stuttgart, Regensburg, Landshut, Passau

GERMANY

Lorient, Vannes, Le Mans, Orléans, Fontainebleau, Troyes, St-Dizier, Épinal, Lunéville, Strasbourg, Freiburg im Breisgau, Tuttlingen, Ulm, Augsburg, Munich, Salzburg

St-Nazaire, Nantes, Angers, Tours, Blois, Vierzon, Chaumont, Langres, Besançon, Basel, Zürich, Konstanz, Innsbruck, Rosenheim

La Rochelle, Saintes, Poitiers, Châtellerault, Bourges, Moulins, Mâcon, Dijon, L. Geneva, BERN, Luzern, VADUZ, LIECH., Großglockner 3798

A Coruña, Gijón-Xixón, Santander, Bordeaux, Brive-la-Gaillarde, Clermont-Ferrand, Vichy, Lyon, Mont Blanc 4808, Chambéry, Annecy, Geneva, Lausanne, Bellinzona, Bernina 4049, Dolomites, Bolzano, Trento, Udine

Cape Finisterre, Santiago de Compostela, Pontevedra, Vigo, Lugo, Oviedo, León, Cantabrian Mountains, Bilbao, San Sebastián, Bayonne, Pau, Tarbes, Toulouse, Carcassonne, Montauban, Rodez, Mende, Alès, Montélimar, Digne-les-Bains, Grenoble, Valence, Gap, Cuneo, Turin, Pavia, Milan, Verona, Vicenza, Venice

Tui, Ourense, Ponferrada, Miranda de Ebro, Logroño, Pamplona, **Pyrenees** 3404, **ANDORRA**, ANDORRA LA VELLA, Figueres, Perpignan, Narbonne, Béziers, Nîmes, Montpellier, Aix-en-Provence, **Marseille**, Nice, **MONACO**, Monte-Carlo, Cannes, Savona, Genoa, La Spezia, Pisa, **Florence**, Bologna, Forlì, Ravenna, Rimini, Reggio nell'Emilia, Parma, Modena

Oporto, Braga, Bragança, Douro, Zamora, Valladolid, Soria, Zaragoza, Lleida, Sabadell, Girona, Barcelona, **Gulf of Lions**, Toulon, **Ligurian Sea**, **Gulf of Genoa**, SAN MARINO

Viseu, Coimbra, Ávila, **MADRID**, Guadalajara, Alcalá de Henares, Segovia, Catalayud, **Corsica (France)**, Bastia, Isola di Capraia, Perugia, Terni

Covilhã, Portalegre, Tagus, Talavera de la Reina, Toledo, Aranjuez, Tortosa, Tarragona, Ajaccio, Isola d'Elba, Viterbo, Civitavecchia, VATICAN CITY, **ROME**, Latina

LISBON, Évora, Badajoz, Mérida, Ciudad Real, Villarrobledo, Albacete, **Valencia**, Gandía, Bonifacio, Strait of Bonifacio, Olbia, **Naples**

Setúbal, Guadiana, Zafra, Puertollano, Valdepeñas, Elche-Elx, Alicante, Palma de Mallorca, Alcúdia, Minorca, Mahón, **Sardinia (Italy)**, Nuoro, **Tyrrhenian Sea**

Sines, Beja, **Sierra Morena**, Andújar, Murcia, Ibiza, Manacor, Majorca, Oristano

Lagos, Cabo de São Vicente, Faro, Huelva, **Seville**, Córdoba, Linares, Jaén, Mulhacén 3482, **Sierra Nevada**, Lorca, Cartagena, Formentera, **Balearic Islands**, Cagliari, Capo Spartivento, Capo Carbonara

Cádiz, Jerez de la Frontera, Granada, Málaga, Almería, Tangier, Gibraltar (UK), Ceuta (Sp.), Algeciras, Strait of Gibraltar

PORTUGAL / SPAIN

MOROCCO

RABAT, Kénitra, Casablanca, Settat, Khouribga, Beni Mellal, Marrakech, Ouarzazate, Larache, Ksar el Kebir, Tetouan, Al Hoceima, Chaouen, Ouezzane, Meknès, Fez (Fès), Azrou, Moyen Atlas, Khenifra, Haut Atlas, Er Rachidia, Figuig, Abadla, Béchar, Hammada du Drâa

Melilla (Sp.), Nador, Oujda, Taza, Sidi Kacem, Taourirt, Taroudant, Bouârfa, Ain Sefra

ALGIERS, Tizi Ouzou, Blida, Béjaïa, Skikda, Annaba, Menzel Bourguiba, Bizerte, Cap Bon, **TUNIS**, Nabeul, Mostaganem, Oran, Beni-Saf, Relizane, Ech Chélif, Constantine, Guelma, Souk Ahras, Jendouba, Isola di Pantelleria, Golfe de Hammamet, Sousse, M'Saken

Oran, Ghazaouet, Sidi Bel Abbès, Mascara, Tiaret, Ksar el Boukhari, Sétif, El Eulma, Batna, Aïn Beïda, Khenchela, Tébessa, Kairouan, Kasserine, Gafsa, Sfax

Tlemcen, Saïda, Chott el Hodna, Bou Saâda, Biskra, Mts des Nementcha, **TUNISIA**, Chott Melrhir, Gulf of Gabès, Gabès

Hauts Plateaux, Mecheria, El Bayadh, Djelfa, Laghouat, El Meghaïer, Touggourt, Chott el Jerid, Tozeur, Medenine, Zarzis

Chott ech Chergui, **Atlas Saharien**, Ghardaïa, Ouargla, Hassi Messaoud, El Oued, Zuwārah, TRIPOLI

ALGERIA

Bordj Messaouda, Daraj, Ghadamis, Al Jawsh, Gharyān, Nālūt, Mizdah, **TRIPOLITANIA**, Al Hamādah al Hamrā

Bordj Omer Driss, Illizi, Birāk, Sabhā, Awbārī, **Idhān Awbārī**

Scale 1 : 10 000 000

0 100 200 300 400 km

Key

Relief and physical features

Relief metres
5000
3000
2000
1000
500
200
sea level
0
under sea level
200
4000
6000

▲ 4808 Mountain height (in metres)

Water features

~ River
~ Intermittent river
~ Canal
◯ Lake / Reservoir
◯ Intermittent lake
~ Marsh

Communications

— Railway
— Road
⊕ Main airport

Administration

Boundaries
— International
--- Disputed
······ Ceasefire line

Settlement

Cities and towns in order of size

National capital
■ CAIRO
■ ALGIERS
□ SKOPJE
□ TIRANA
□ VALLETTA

Other city or town
● Naples
○ Valencia
○ Nice
○ Faro

Next map 84-85

Next map 84-85

Scale 1 : 5 000 000

0   50   100   150   200 km

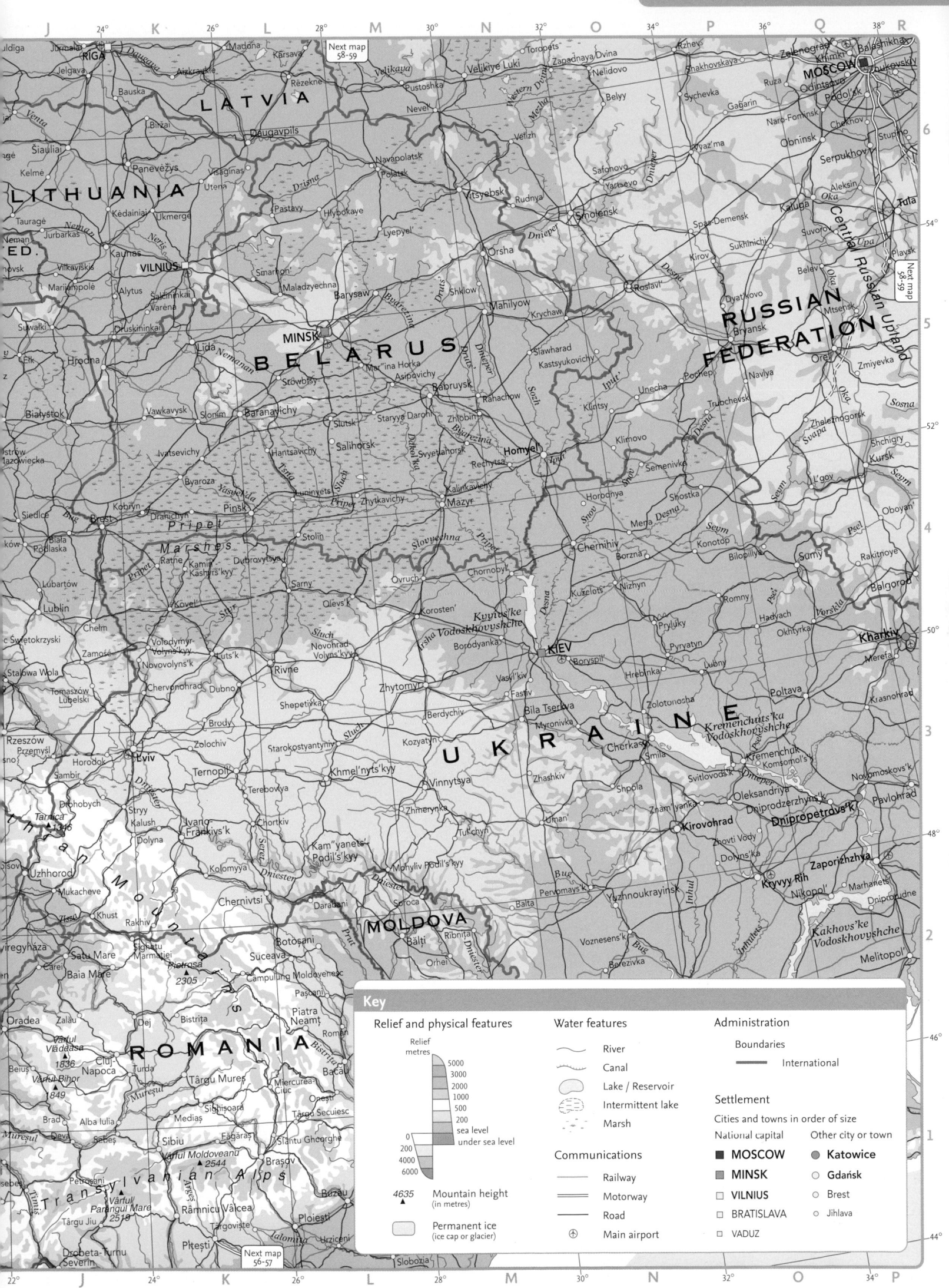

Key

Relief and physical features

Relief metres
5000
3000
2000
1000
500
200
sea level
under sea level
0
200
4000
6000

▲ 4635 Mountain height (in metres)

Permanent ice (ice cap or glacier)

Water features

~ River

~ Canal

Lake / Reservoir

Intermittent lake

Marsh

Communications

Railway

Motorway

Road

⊕ Main airport

Administration

Boundaries

——— International

Settlement

Cities and towns in order of size

National capital

■ MOSCOW

■ MINSK

□ VILNIUS

□ BRATISLAVA

□ VADUZ

Other city or town

● Katowice

○ Gdańsk

○ Brest

○ Jihlava

Conic Equidistant projection

CROATIA
BOSNIA-HERZEGOVINA
SARAJEVO
SERBIA
MONTENEGRO
PODGORICA
BELGRADE
ROMANIA
BUCHAREST
BULGARIA
SOFIA
MACEDONIA (F.Y.R.O.M.)
SKOPJE
ALBANIA
TIRANA
GREECE
ATHENS
ITALY
ZAGREB

Adriatic Sea
Ionian Sea
Ionian Islands
Strait of Otranto
MEDITERRANEAN SEA
Aegean Sea
Krytiko Pelagos
Thrakiko Pelagos
Dardanelles

Nova Mesto, Snežnik 1796, Metlika, Karlovac, Sisak, Virovitica, Pécs, Baja, Szeged, Subotica, Arad, Lipova, Brad, Alba Iulia, Miercurea-Ciuc, Sighișoara, Târgu Secuiesc
Rieka, Ogulin, Una, Kupa, Osijek, Vinkovci, Slavonski Brod, Novi Sad, Zrenjanin, Kikinda, Sombor, Timișoara, Deva, Sebeș, Mediaș, Sibiu, Fāgāraș, Sfântu Gheorghe, Brașov, Focșani
Cres, Pag, Gospić, Vaganski Vrh 1758, Bihać, Prijedor, Bosanska Dubica, Banja Luka, Doboj, Bijeljina, Ruma, Vršac, Reșița, Caransebeș, Lugoj, Vârful Moldoveanu 2544, Petroșani, Târgu Jiu, Vârful Parângul Mare 2519, Ramnicu Vâlcea, Târgoviște, Ploiești
Dugi Otok, Zadar, Knin, Sinj, Jajce, Gornji Vukuf, Zenica, Tuzla, Zvornik, Loznica, Šabac, Požarevac, Orșova, Drobeta-Turnu Severin, Negotin, Craiova, Slatina, Caracal, Pitești, Urziceni
Split, Brač, Hvar, Makarska, Ploćno 2228, Mostar, Foča, Srebrenica, Valjevo, Kragujevac, Užice, Prijepolje, Kruševac, Zaječar, Calafat, Lom, Montana, Vratsa, Corabia, Mägurele, Giurgiu, Ruse
Vis, Korčula, Mljet, Metković, Durmitor Tara 2522, Novi Pazar, Ibar, Kuršumlija, Niš, Pirot, Botevgrad, Pernik, Karlovo, Pleven, Oltu, Veliko Tûrnovo, Razgrad
Dubrovnik, Nikšić, Bijelo Polje, Kosovska Mitrovica, Leskovac, Vranje, Peć, Priština, Musala 2925, Panagyurishte, Kazanluk, Gabrovo, Lovech, Osûm
Cetinje, Maja Jezerce 2694, Lake Scutari, Bar, Prizren, Tetovo, Kumanovo, Kyustendil, Pazardzhik, Plovdiv, Stara Zagora, Sliven, Yambol
Shkodër, Bistra 2650, Gostivar, Veles, Kočani, Blagoevgrad, Asenovgrad, Khaskovo, Dimitrovgrad, Edirne
Lezhë, Peshkopi, Kičevo, Prilep, Strumica, Sandanski, Smolyan, Rhodope Mountains, Kûrdzhali, Komotini, Uzunköprü
Durrës, Elbasan, Ohrid, Lake Ohrid, Lake Prespa, Bitola, Gevgelija, Polykastro, Kilkis, Serres, Drama, Xanthi, Kavala, Keșan
Lushnjë, Berat, Korçë, Florina, Edessa, Kastoria, Veroia, Thessaloniki, Polygyros, Thasos, Alexandroupoli, Samothraki, Gökçeada, Çanakkale
Vlorë, Fier, Gjirokastër, Smolikas 2637, Grevena, Kozani, Katerini, Mt Olympus 2911, Thermaikos Kolpos, Athos 2033, Limnos, Imroz
Sarandë, Kerkyra, Corfu, Ioannina, Igoumenitsa, Trikala, Ossa 1978, Larisa, Agios Efstratios, Lesbos, Mytilini
Preveza, Arta, Karditsa, Pineios, Volos, Voreioi Sporades, Skyros, Psara, Chios
Lefkada, Cephalonia, Mesolongi, Amfissa, Parnassos 2457, Levadeia, Chalkida, Evvoia, Akra Kafireas, Andros, Tinos, Ikaria, Samos
Zakynthos, Patras, Gulf of Corinth, Nea Liosia, Marathonas, Athens, Piraeus, Kea, Syros, Ermoupoli, Kythnos, Cyclades, Paros, Naxos, Dodecanese
Kyparissia, Tripoli, Nafplio, Corinth, Aigina, Agios Dimitrios, Milos, Ios, Amorgos
Pylos, Sparti, Kalamata, Messiniakos Kolpos, Lakonikos Kolpos, Akra Maleas, Thira, Kos
Akra Tainaro, Neapoli, Kythira, Antikythira, Akra Spatha, Kasteli, Chania, Rethymno, Idi 2456, Iraklion, Crete, Agios Nikolaos, Karpathos, Kasos

Key

Relief and physical features

Relief metres
5000
3000
2000
1000
500
200
0 sea level
200 under sea level
4000
6000

3917 ▲ Mountain height (in metres)

Water features
~ River
- - - Intermittent river
~ Canal
Lake / Reservoir
Intermittent lake
Marsh

Communications
Railway
Motorway
Road
⊕ Main airport

Administration
Boundaries
—— International
······· Ceasefire line

Settlement
Cities and towns in order of size

National capital
■ ATHENS
□ SARAJEVO
□ NICOSIA

Other city or town
● İstanbul
○ Konya
○ Split
○ Dubrovnik

Next map 54-55
Next map 50

Scale 1 : 5 000 000
0   50   100   150   200 km

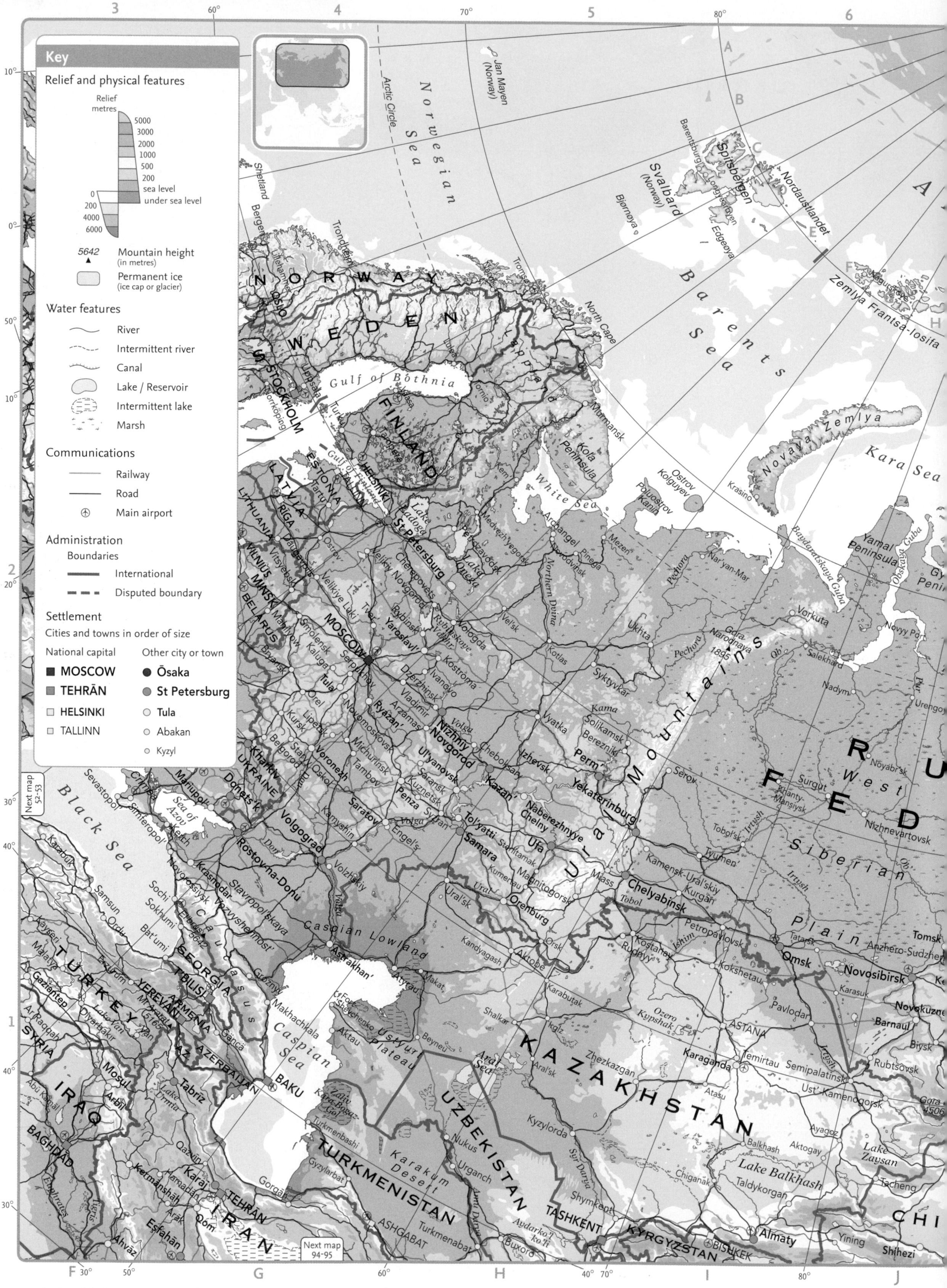

Key

Relief and physical features

Relief
metres

5000
3000
2000
1000
500
200
0 sea level
under sea level
200
4000
6000

▲ 5642 Mountain height
(in metres)

Permanent ice
(ice cap or glacier)

Water features

River

Intermittent river

Canal

Lake / Reservoir

Intermittent lake

Marsh

Communications

Railway

Road

⊕ Main airport

Administration

Boundaries

International

Disputed boundary

Settlement

Cities and towns in order of size

National capital

■ MOSCOW
■ TEHRĀN
□ HELSINKI
□ TALLINN

Other city or town

● Ōsaka
● St Petersburg
○ Tula
○ Abakan
○ Kyzyl

Next map 52–53

Next map 94–95

Scale 1 : 20 000 000

0   200   400   600   800 km

Conic Equidistant projection

Key

Relief and physical features

Relief
metres
5000
3000
2000
1000
500
200
sea level
under sea level
0
200
4000
6000

Permanent ice
(ice cap or glacier)

Physical Regions

Scale 1 : 100 000 000

Arctic Circle
Pacific Ranges
Rocky Mountains
Canadian Shield
Interior Plains and Lowlands
Western Plateaus, Ranges and Basins
Appalachian Highlands
Coastal Lowlands
Tropic of Cancer
Central American Highlands
Caribbean Islands

Scale 1 : 40 000 000

0   500   1000   1500   2000 km

Lambert Azimuthal Equal Area projection

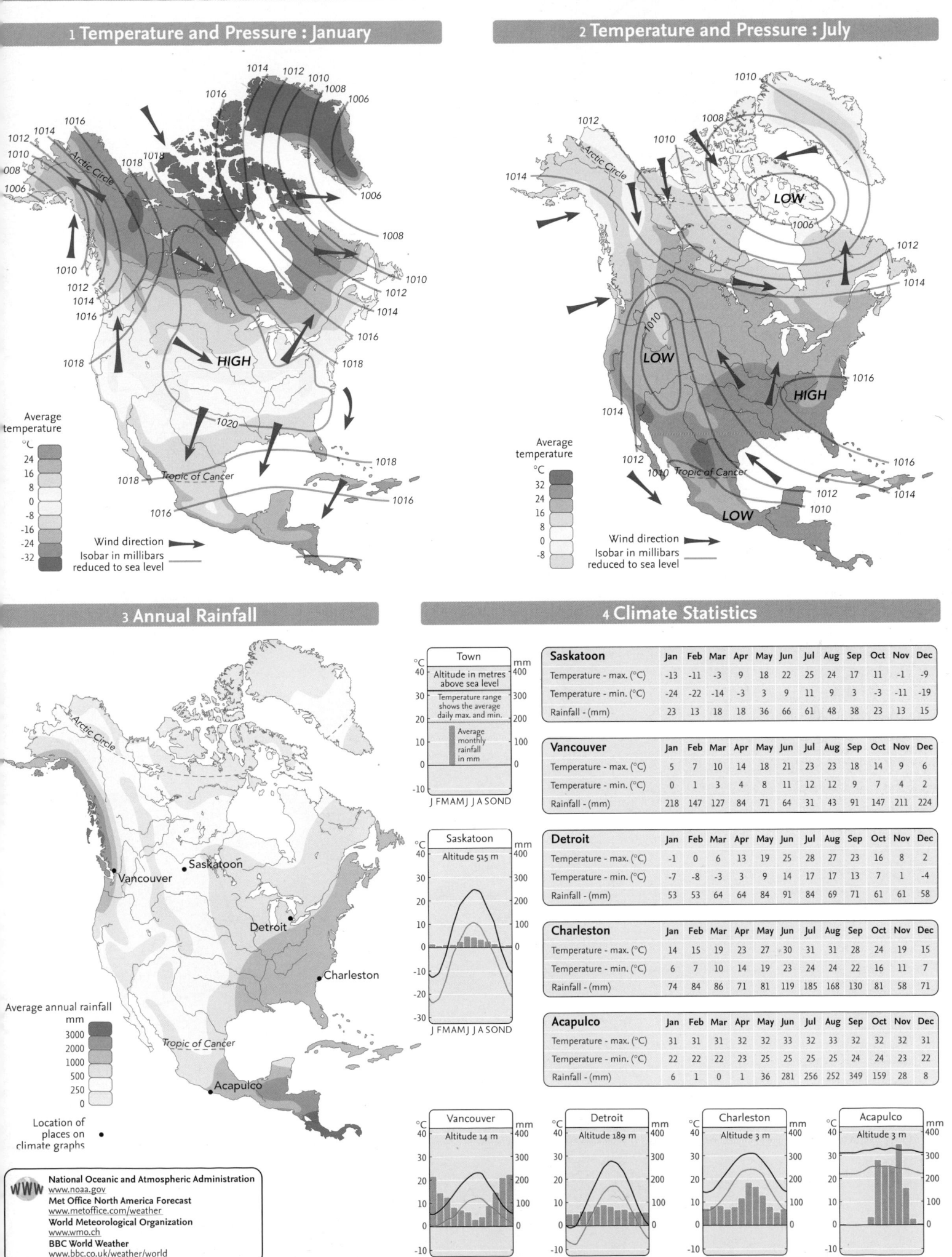

1 Temperature and Pressure : January

Average temperature
°C
24
16
8
0
-8
-16
-24
-32

Wind direction

Isobar in millibars reduced to sea level

2 Temperature and Pressure : July

Average temperature
°C
32
24
16
8
0
-8

Wind direction

Isobar in millibars reduced to sea level

3 Annual Rainfall

Average annual rainfall
mm
3000
2000
1000
500
250
0

Location of places on climate graphs ●

www National Oceanic and Atmospheric Administration
www.noaa.gov
Met Office North America Forecast
www.metoffice.com/weather
World Meteorological Organization
www.wmo.ch
BBC World Weather
www.bbc.co.uk/weather/world

4 Climate Statistics

Town
°C / mm
Altitude in metres above sea level
Temperature range shows the average daily max. and min.
Average monthly rainfall in mm

Saskatoon	Jan	Feb	Mar	Apr	May	Jun	Jul	Aug	Sep	Oct	Nov	Dec
Temperature - max. (°C)	-13	-11	-3	9	18	22	25	24	17	11	-1	-9
Temperature - min. (°C)	-24	-22	-14	-3	3	9	11	9	3	-3	-11	-19
Rainfall - (mm)	23	13	18	18	36	66	61	48	38	23	13	15

Vancouver	Jan	Feb	Mar	Apr	May	Jun	Jul	Aug	Sep	Oct	Nov	Dec
Temperature - max. (°C)	5	7	10	14	18	21	23	23	18	14	9	6
Temperature - min. (°C)	0	1	3	4	8	11	12	12	9	7	4	2
Rainfall - (mm)	218	147	127	84	71	64	31	43	91	147	211	224

Detroit	Jan	Feb	Mar	Apr	May	Jun	Jul	Aug	Sep	Oct	Nov	Dec
Temperature - max. (°C)	-1	0	6	13	19	25	28	27	23	16	8	2
Temperature - min. (°C)	-7	-8	-3	3	9	14	17	17	13	7	1	-4
Rainfall - (mm)	53	53	64	64	84	91	84	69	71	61	61	58

Charleston	Jan	Feb	Mar	Apr	May	Jun	Jul	Aug	Sep	Oct	Nov	Dec
Temperature - max. (°C)	14	15	19	23	27	30	31	31	28	24	19	15
Temperature - min. (°C)	6	7	10	14	19	23	24	24	22	16	11	7
Rainfall - (mm)	74	84	86	71	81	119	185	168	130	81	58	71

Acapulco	Jan	Feb	Mar	Apr	May	Jun	Jul	Aug	Sep	Oct	Nov	Dec
Temperature - max. (°C)	31	31	31	32	32	33	32	33	32	32	32	31
Temperature - min. (°C)	22	22	22	23	25	25	25	25	24	24	23	22
Rainfall - (mm)	6	1	0	1	36	281	256	252	349	159	28	8

Saskatoon — Altitude 515 m
Vancouver — Altitude 14 m
Detroit — Altitude 189 m
Charleston — Altitude 3 m
Acapulco — Altitude 3 m

ale 1 : 80 000 000

0   800   1600   2400   3200 km

Bonne projection

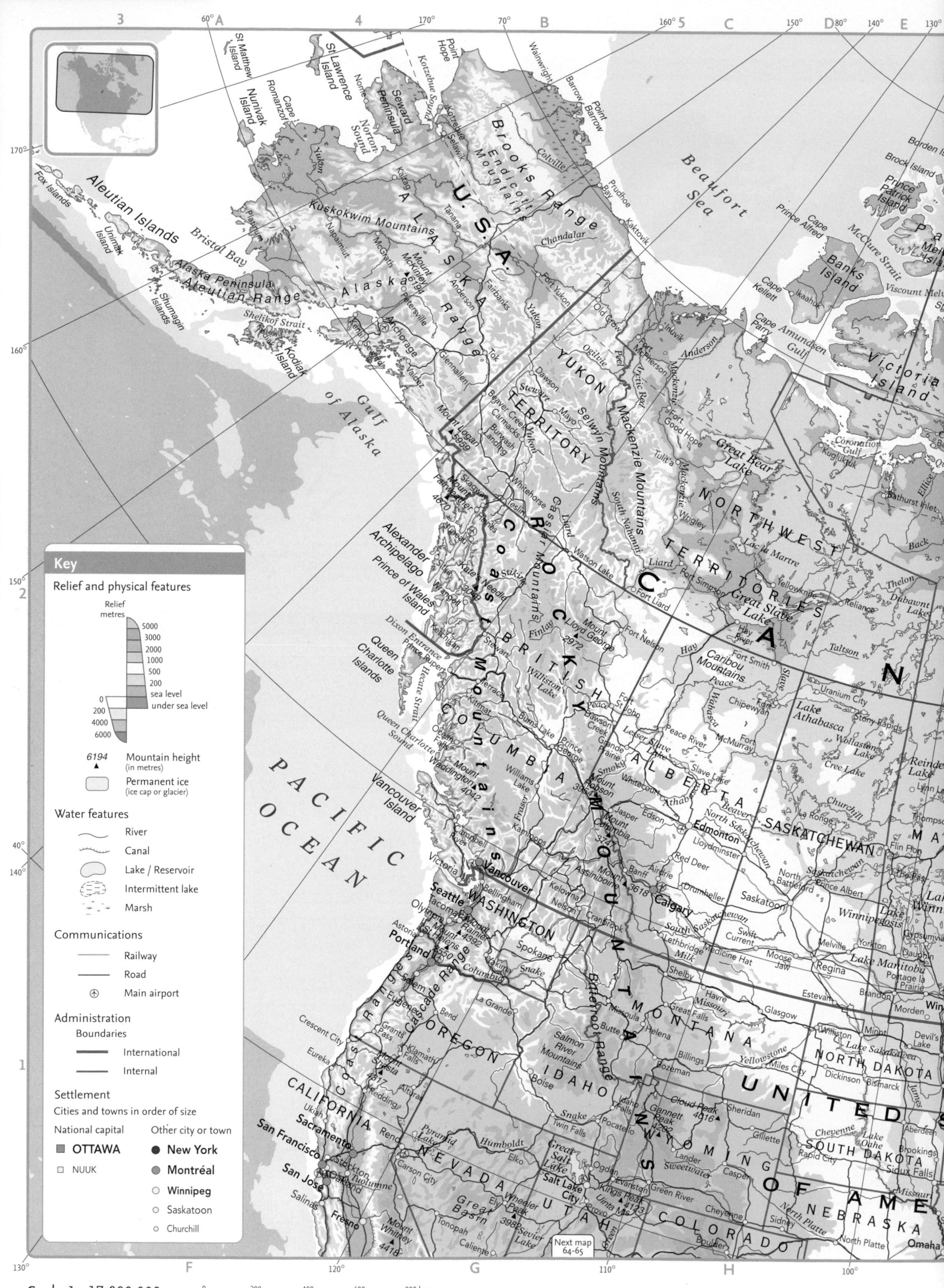

Scale 1 : 17 000 000

0   200   400   600   800 km

Map labels and geographic features:

I 90° J 80° K 70° L 60° M 50° N 40° O 80° 30° P 520° Q 70° 10° 4 R 60°

British Empire Range
Axel Heiberg Island
Amund Ringnes Island
Ellesmere Island
Nares Strait
Cape Parry
Thule
Cape York
Melville Bay
Upernavik

GREENLAND (Denmark)

Kong Christian IX Land

Baffin Bay

Devon Island
Cornwallis Island
Resolute
Lancaster Sound
Somerset Island
Brodeur Peninsula
Arctic Bay
Bylot Island
Borden Peninsula
Mittimatalik
Gulf of Boothia
Baffin Island
Clyde River
Home Bay
Qasigiannguit
Disko
Saqqaq
Sisimiut
Maniitsoq

Davis Strait

Prince of Wales
Melville Peninsula
Hall Beach
Prince Charles Island
Penny Icecap
Pangnirtung
Cape Dyer
NUUK (Godthåb)
Cumberland Sound
Paamiut

Repulse Bay
Foxe Basin
Nettilling Lake
Amadjuak Lake
Iqaluit
Frobisher Bay

Labrador Sea

Southampton Island
Coral Harbour
Coats Island
Foxe Channel
Foxe Peninsula
Resolution Island

Akpatok Island
Cape Chidley

ATLANTIC OCEAN

Mansel Island
Fisher Strait

D A

NEWFOUNDLAND AND LABRADOR

Péninsule d'Ungava
Kangiqsujuaq
Ungava Bay
Kangiqsualujjuaq

Hudson Strait

Salluit
Ottawa Islands
Puvirnituq
Inukjuak
Rivière aux Feuilles
Kuujjuaq
George
Rivière à la Baleine
Nain
Hopedale
Cape Harrison

Hudson Bay

Belcher Islands

Cape Henrietta Maria
Fort Severn
Caniapiscau
Smallwood Reservoir
Labrador
Schefferville
Churchill
Happy Valley-Goose Bay
Port Hope Simpson
St Anthony
Strait of Belle Isle

James Bay
Réservoir La Grande 2
Chisasibi
Réservoir La Grande 3
Réservoir La Grande 4
Lac à l'Eau Claire
Lac Caniapiscau
Petit Mécatina

Wînisk
Big Trout Lake
Akimiski Island
Fort Albany
Eastmain
Waskaganish
Lac Mistassini
Mistassini
Gagnon
Réservoir Manicouagan
Sept-Îles
Labrador City
Wabush

Grand Falls-Windsor
Gander
Bonavista
St John's
Newfoundland
Cape Race

ONTARIO
Sioux Lookout
Moosonee
Moose
Missinaibi
Chibougamau
Lac Evans
QUÉBEC
Île d'Anticosti
Corner Brook
Channel-Port-aux-Basques
St Pierre and Miquelon (France)
Cape Breton Island

Lake Nipigon
Nipigon
Kapuskasing
Groundhog
Timmins
Réservoir Gouin
Amos
Val-d'Or
Baie-Comeau
Pén. de Gaspé
Gaspé
Gulf of St Lawrence
St Lawrence
P.E.I.
Charlottetown
Sydney
Sable Island

Thunder Bay
Isle Royale
Chapleau
Kirkland Lake
Roberval
Jonquière
Chicoutimi
Rimouski
Rivière-du-Loup
Edmundston
NEW BRUNSWICK
Fredericton
Moncton
Truro
NOVA SCOTIA
Halifax

Lake Superior
Sault Sainte Marie
Sudbury
North Bay
Ottawa
Trois-Rivières
Québec
Presque Isle
Saint John
Bay of Fundy
Cape Sable

Duluth
Marquette
Escanaba
Georgian Bay
Parry Sound
OTTAWA
Peterborough
Kingston
Sherbrooke
MAINE
Mount Washington 1918
VER.
N.H.
Augusta
Bangor
Portland
Yarmouth

Lake Huron
Barrie
Oshawa
Burlington
Concord
Cape Cod

Minneapolis
Eau Claire
Green Bay
Traverse City
Bay City
Flint
Toronto
Hamilton
Lake Ontario
Rochester
Syracuse
Albany
Springfield
Hartford
MASS.
Boston
Providence

WISCONSIN
La Crosse
MICHIGAN
Grand Rapids
Buffalo
London
NEW YORK
Long Island

Milwaukee
Cedar Rapids
Rockford
Des Moines
Chicago
Gary
South Bend
Detroit
Toledo
Akron
Cleveland
PENN.
Scranton
Allentown
Trenton
New York
Lake Michigan
Lake Erie

Next map 64-65

I 90° J K 80° L 70° M 60°

90° J 80° K 70° L 60° M

Lambert Conformal Conic projection

CO.   CONNECTICUT
MASS. MASSACHUSETTS
N.H.   NEW HAMPSHIRE
P.E.I. PRINCE EDWARD ISLAND
PENN. PENNSYLVANIA
R.I.   RHODE ISLAND
VER.   VERMONT

PACIFIC OCEAN

BRITISH COLUMBIA
ALBERTA
SASKATCHEWAN
CANADA
MANITOBA

WASHINGTON
OREGON
IDAHO
MONTANA
NORTH DAKOTA
SOUTH DAKOTA
NEBRASKA
WYOMING
NEVADA
UTAH
COLORADO
KANSAS
CALIFORNIA
ARIZONA
NEW MEXICO
OKLAHOMA
TEXAS

UNITED STATES OF AMERICA

BAJA CALIFORNIA
BAJA CALIFORNIA SUR
SONORA
CHIHUAHUA
COAHUILA
NUEVO LEON
SINALOA
DURANGO
ZACATECAS
SAN LUIS POTOSI
TAMAULIPAS
MEXICO

Gulf of California

Vancouver Island
Vancouver
Victoria
Seattle
Tacoma
Olympia
Portland
Salem
Eugene
Coos Bay
Cape Blanco
Crescent City
Eureka
Point Arena
Sacramento
San Francisco
San Jose
Oakland
Stockton
Salinas
Fresno
Bakersfield
Santa Barbara
Los Angeles
Long Beach
Pasadena
Riverside
Santa Ana
Oceanside
San Diego
Tijuana
Ensenada
Mexicali

Calgary
Saskatoon
Regina
Moose Jaw
Swift Current
Medicine Hat
Lethbridge
Shelby
Great Falls
Havre
Helena
Bozeman
Billings
Missoula
Butte
Dillon
Boise
Idaho Falls
Pocatello
Twin Falls
Salt Lake City
Ogden
Provo
Denver
Aurora
Boulder
Colorado Springs
Pueblo
Santa Fe
Albuquerque
Las Cruces
El Paso
Ciudad Juárez
Phoenix
Tucson
Flagstaff
Las Vegas
Reno
Carson City
Tonopah

Rocky Mountains
Sierra Nevada
Cascade Range
Coast Ranges
Great Basin
Colorado Plateau
Great Salt Lake
Death Valley
Grand Canyon
Mount Whitney 4418
Mount Shasta 4317
Mount Rainier 4392
Mount St Helens 2550
Mount Hood 3427
Gannett Peak 4202
Kings Peak 4123
Mount Elbert 4398
Mount Peale 3877
Wheeler Peak 3982
Humphreys Peak 3851
Cloud Peak 4016
Baldy Peak 3476
Wheeler Peak 4011

Monterrey
Reynosa
Nuevo Laredo
Laredo
Torreón
Mazatlán
Culiacán
Durango
Chihuahua

Tropic of Cancer

Scale 1 : 12 000 000

0 150 300 450 600 km

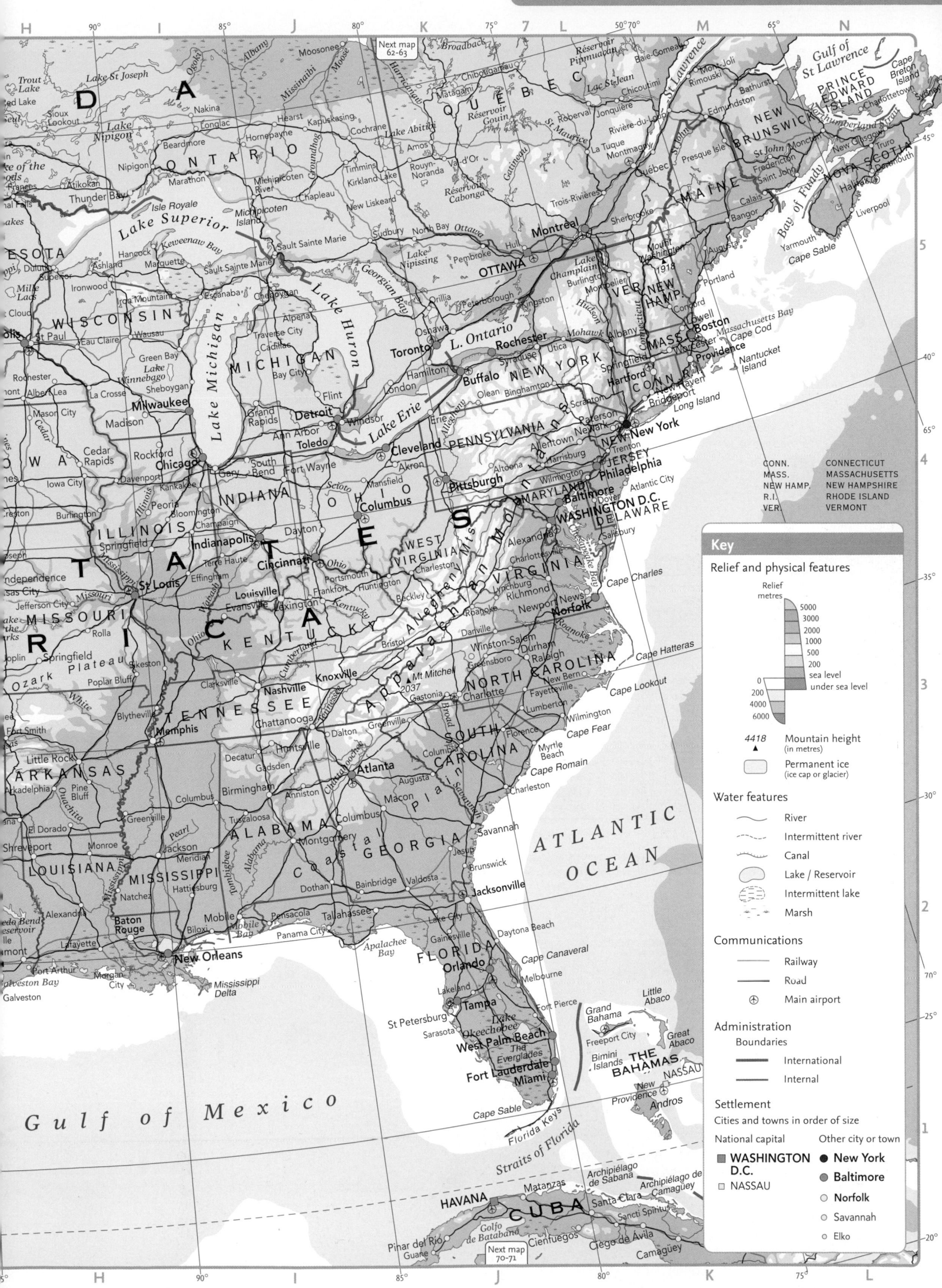

Key

Relief and physical features

Relief metres

5000
3000
2000
1000
500
200
0 sea level
200 under sea level
4000
6000

4418 ▲ Mountain height (in metres)

Permanent ice (ice cap or glacier)

Water features

River
Intermittent river
Canal
Lake / Reservoir
Intermittent lake
Marsh

Communications

Railway
Road
⊕ Main airport

Administration

Boundaries
International
Internal

Settlement

Cities and towns in order of size

National capital

■ WASHINGTON D.C.
□ NASSAU

Other city or town

● New York
● Baltimore
○ Norfolk
○ Savannah
○ Elko

CONN.   CONNECTICUT
MASS.   MASSACHUSETTS
NEW HAMP.   NEW HAMPSHIRE
R.I.   RHODE ISLAND
VER.   VERMONT

Lambert Conformal Conic projection

1 Population Density

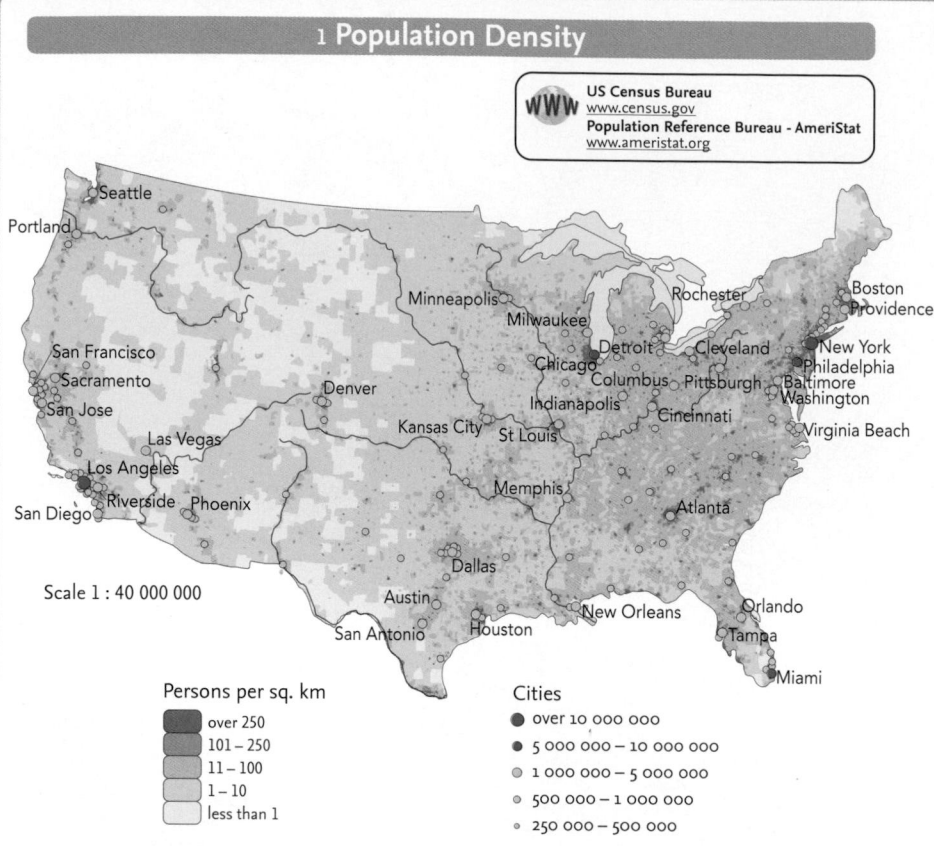

US Census Bureau
www.census.gov
Population Reference Bureau - AmeriStat
www.ameristat.org

Scale 1 : 40 000 000

Persons per sq. km
- over 250
- 101 – 250
- 11 – 100
- 1 – 10
- less than 1

Cities
- over 10 000 000
- 5 000 000 – 10 000 000
- 1 000 000 – 5 000 000
- 500 000 – 1 000 000
- 250 000 – 500 000

2 State Comparisons

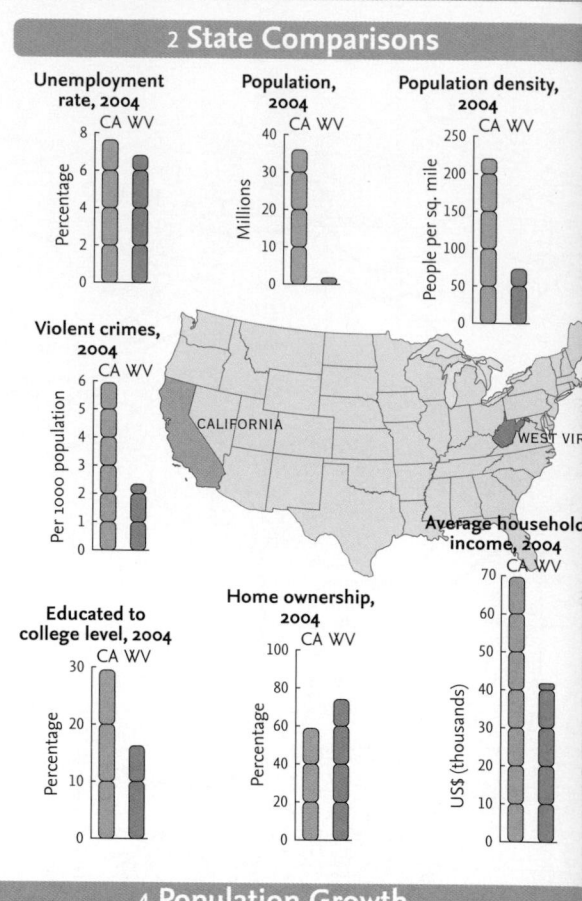

Unemployment rate, 2004 — CA WV
Population, 2004 — CA WV
Population density, 2004 — CA WV
Violent crimes, 2004 — CA WV
Average household income, 2004 — CA WV
Educated to college level, 2004 — CA WV
Home ownership, 2004 — CA WV

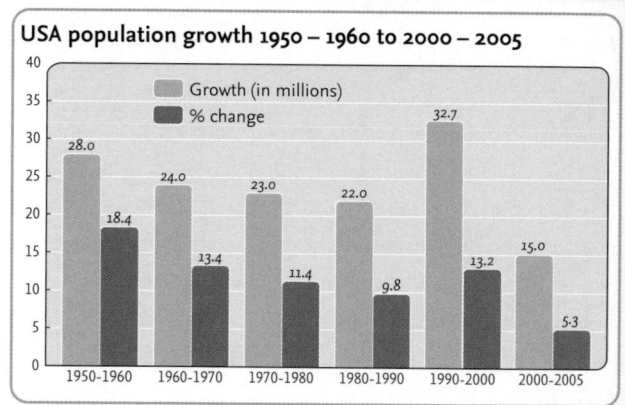

3 Main Urban Agglomerations

Urban agglomeration	1980	1990	2000	2005 (projected)
New York	15 601 150	16 086 000	17 846 000	18 498 000
Los Angeles	9 512 100	10 883 000	11 814 000	12 146 000
Chicago	7 216 000	7 374 000	8 333 000	8 711 000
Miami	3 122 000	3 969 000	4 946 000	5 380 000
Philadelphia	4 540 000	4 725 000	5 160 000	5 325 000
Dallas	2 468 000	3 219 000	4 172 000	4 612 000
Boston	3 281 000	3 428 000	4 049 000	4 313 000
Atlanta	1 625 000	2 184 000	3 542 000	4 284 000
Houston	2 424 000	2 922 000	3 849 000	4 283 000
Washington	2 777 000	3 376 000	3 949 000	4 190 000
Detroit	3 807 000	3 703 000	3 909 000	3 980 000
San Francisco	2 656 000	2 961 000	3 236 000	3 342 000
San Diego	1 718 000	2 356 000	2 683 000	2 818 000

4 Population Growth

USA population growth 1950 – 1960 to 2000 – 2005

- Growth (in millions)
- % change

1950-1960: 28.0 / 18.4
1960-1970: 24.0 / 13.4
1970-1980: 23.0 / 11.4
1980-1990: 22.0 / 9.8
1990-2000: 32.7 / 13.2
2000-2005: 15.0 / 5.3

5 Population Change

Midwest 2.4%
Northeast 2.0%
West 8.1%
South 7.3%

Population change, 2000 – 2005
Percentage
- over 20
- 10 – 20
- 5 – 9.9
- 0 – 4.9
- -5 – -0.1

Scale 1 : 40 000 000

6 Immigration

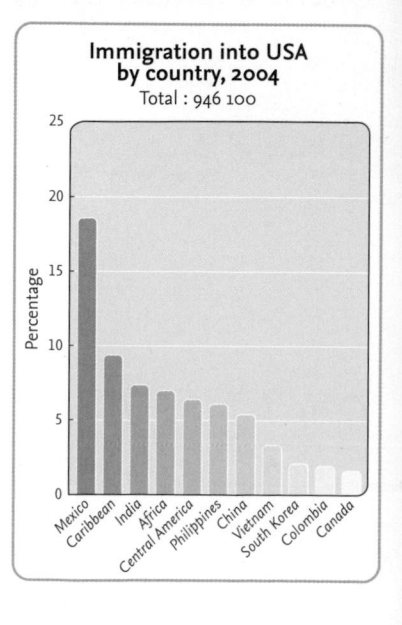

Immigration into USA by country, 2004
Total : 946 100

Mexico, Caribbean, India, Africa, Central America, Philippines, China, Vietnam, South Korea, Colombia, Canada

7 Economic Activity

Seattle

Minneapolis/St Paul
Milwaukee   Detroit
Chicago
Buffalo
Cleveland
New York

n Francisco/Oakland
ilicon
alley

Indianapolis
Pittsburgh
Philadelphia

Kansas City
St Louis
Baltimore

Los Angeles
Washington

Dallas
Birmingham
Atlanta

Houston
New Orleans

Miami

Scale 1 : 40 000 000

- Major industrial centre

Manufacturing industry
- Metal working
- Oil refinery
- Shipbuilding
- Aircraft manufacturing
- Car manufacturing
- Mechanical engineering

- Electrical engineering
- Publishing / Paper
- Chemicals
- Textiles
- Food processing

Service industry
- Banking and finance
- Tourism

8 Silicon Valley

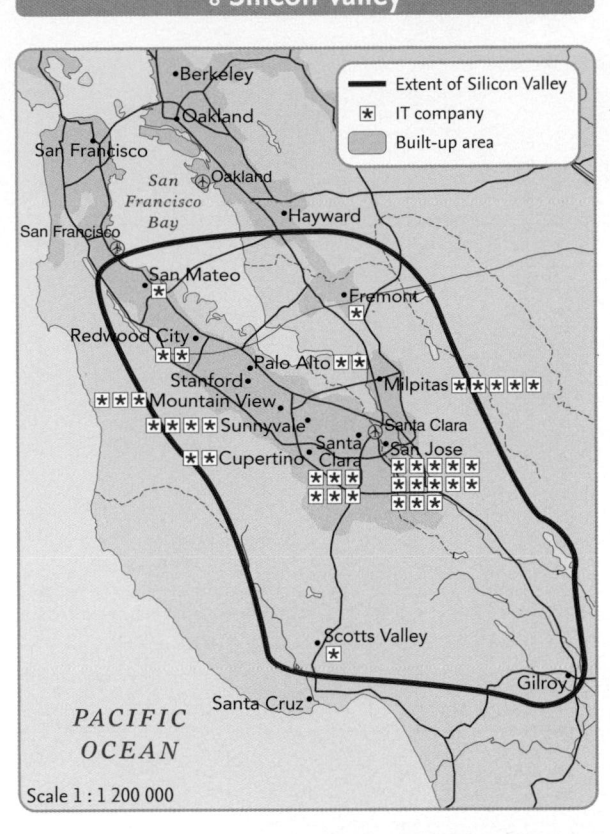

Berkeley
Oakland
San Francisco
San Francisco Bay
Oakland
Hayward
San Francisco
San Mateo
Fremont
Redwood City
Palo Alto
Stanford
Milpitas
Mountain View
Sunnyvale
Santa Clara
San Jose
Cupertino
Santa Clara
Scotts Valley
Santa Cruz
Gilroy

PACIFIC OCEAN

Scale 1 : 1 200 000

— Extent of Silicon Valley
⊛ IT company
▨ Built-up area

Department of Commerce
www.commerce.gov
US Trade and Development Agency
www.tda.gov
UN Commodity Trade Statistics
unstats.un.org/unsd/comtrade

9 Trade

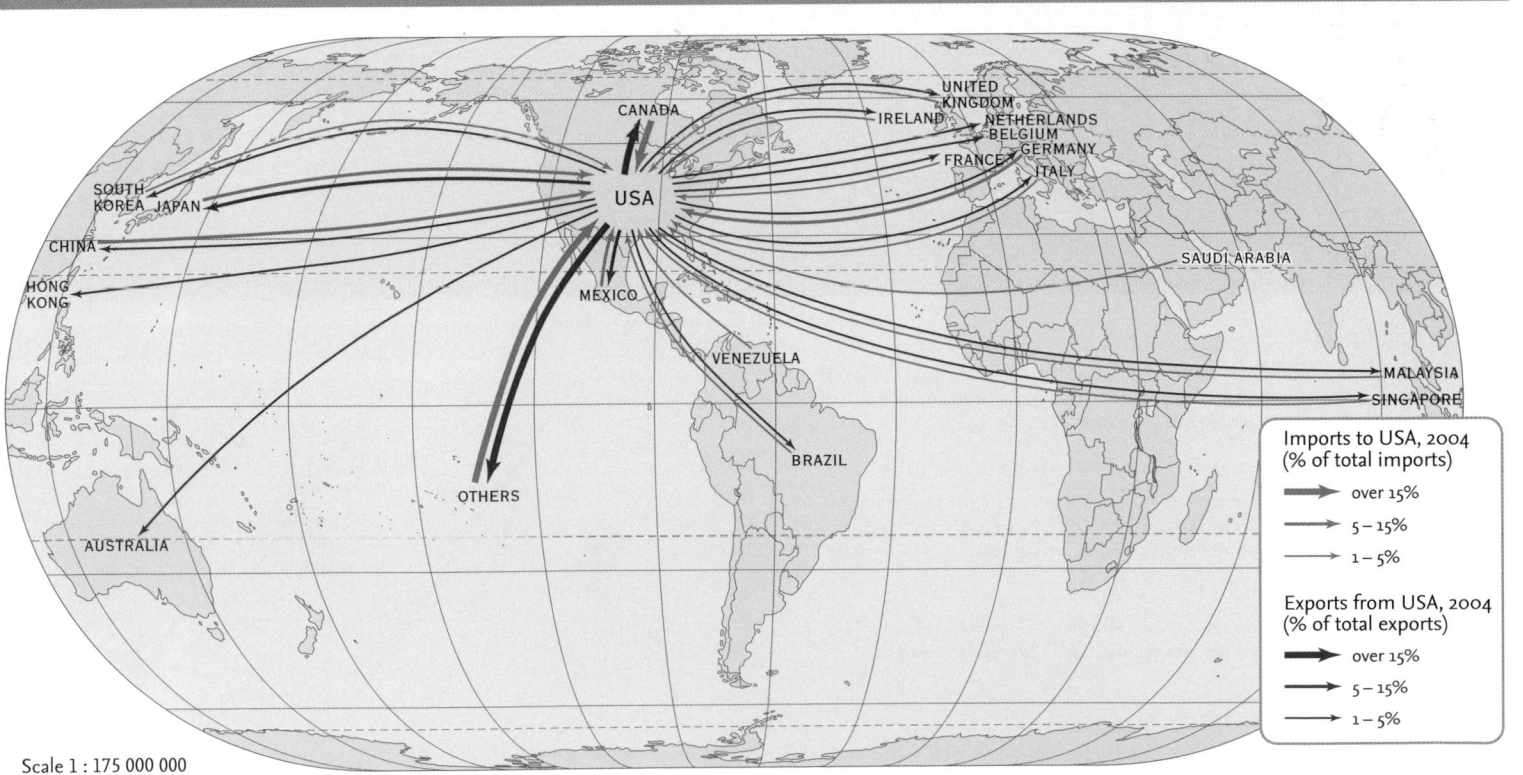

CANADA
UNITED KINGDOM
IRELAND
NETHERLANDS
BELGIUM
GERMANY
FRANCE
ITALY
SOUTH KOREA   JAPAN
USA
CHINA
SAUDI ARABIA
HONG KONG
MEXICO
MALAYSIA
SINGAPORE
VENEZUELA
BRAZIL
OTHERS
AUSTRALIA

Imports to USA, 2004 (% of total imports)
→ over 15%
→ 5 – 15%
→ 1 – 5%

Exports from USA, 2004 (% of total exports)
→ over 15%
→ 5 – 15%
→ 1 – 5%

Scale 1 : 175 000 000

Import commodities, 2004

Mineral fuels 14%   Vehicles 13%
Others 47%
Machinery and mechanical appliances 14%   Electrical and electronic equipment 12%

Total : US$ 1 525 268 million

Export commodities, 2004

Machinery and mechanical appliances 18%   Vehicles 9%   Aircraft 5%
Others 46%
Electrical and electronic equipment 15%   Optical and technical apparatus 7%

Total : US$ 817 906 million

Built-up area

The built up area shown as blue/green on the satellite image surrounds San Francisco Bay and extends south to San Jose. Three bridges link the main built up areas across San Francisco Bay.

Woodland

Areas of dense woodland cover much of the Santa Cruz Mountains to the west of the San Andreas Fault Zone. Other areas of woodland are found on the ridges to the east of San Francisco Bay.

Marsh / Salt Marsh

Areas of dark green on the satellite image represent marshland in the Coyote Creek area and salt marshes between the San Mateo and Dumbarton Bridges.

Reservoir / lake

Lakes and reservoirs stand out from the surrounding land. Good examples are the Upper San Leandro Reservoir east of Piedmont and the San Andreas Lake which lies along the fault line.

Airport

A grey blue colour shows San Francisco International Airport as a flat rectangular strip of land jutting out into the bay.

Main fault line

Fault Lines in the San Francisco Bay Region

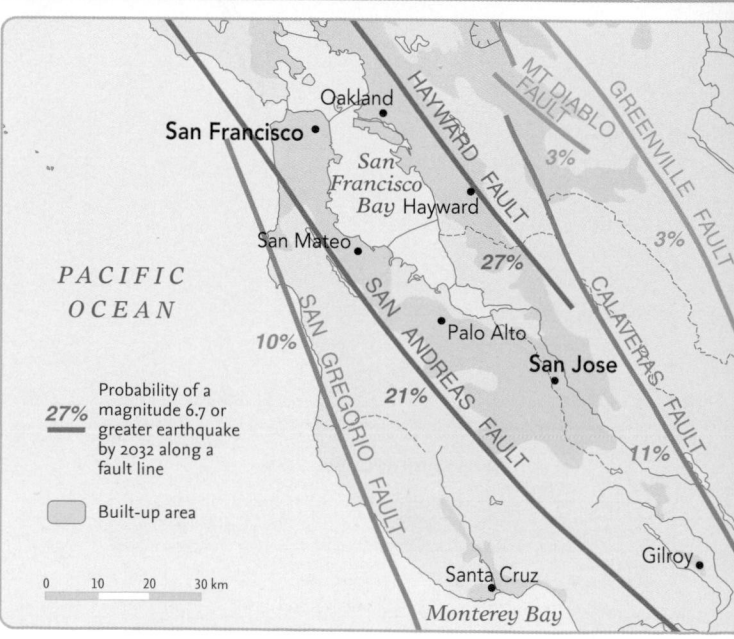

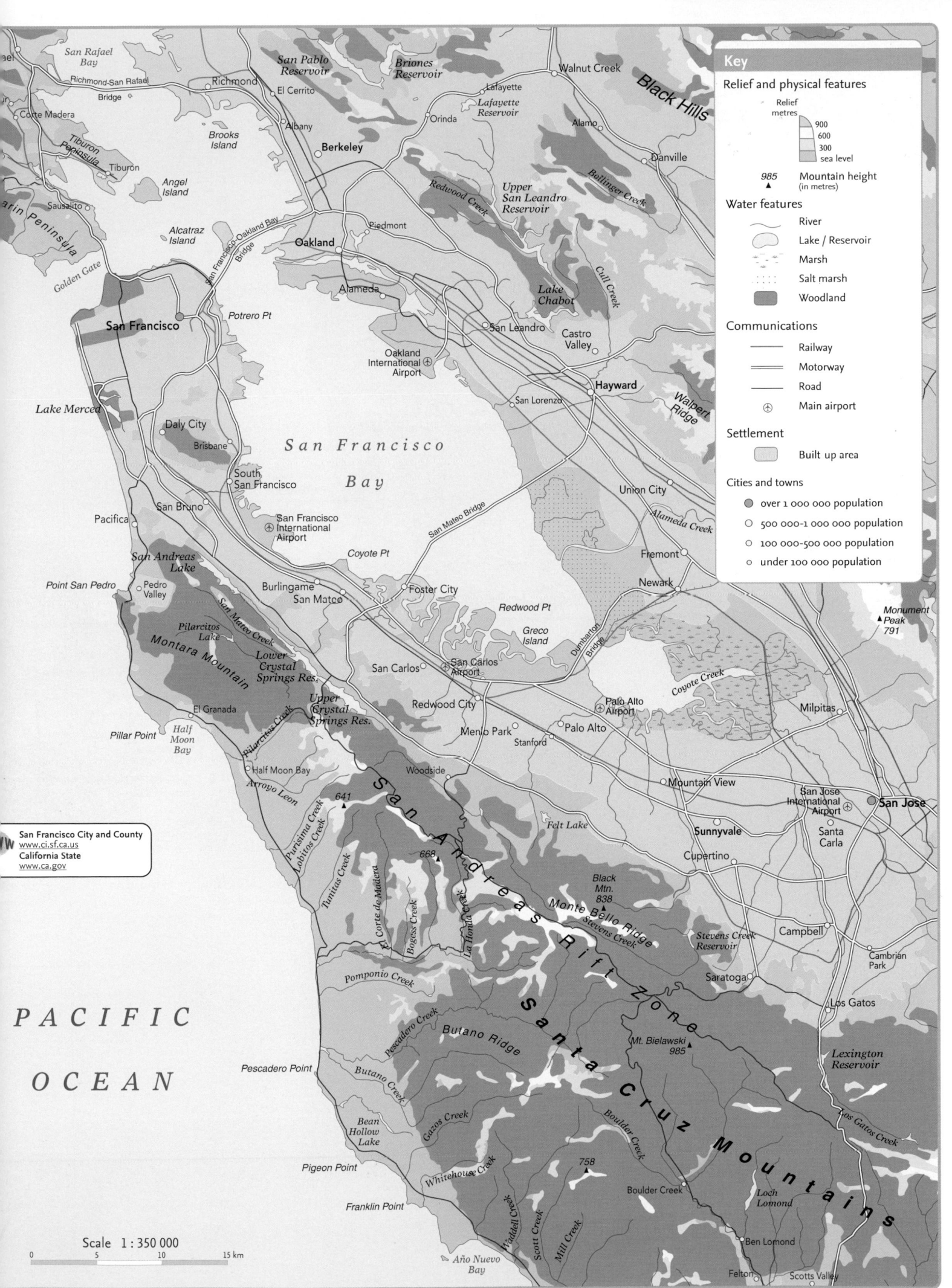

Key

Relief and physical features

Relief
metres
900
600
300
sea level

985 ▲ Mountain height
(in metres)

Water features

River
Lake / Reservoir
Marsh
Salt marsh
Woodland

Communications

Railway
Motorway
Road
⊕ Main airport

Settlement

Built up area

Cities and towns

● over 1 000 000 population
○ 500 000-1 000 000 population
○ 100 000-500 000 population
○ under 100 000 population

San Francisco City and County
www.ci.sf.ca.us
California State
www.ca.gov

Scale 1 : 350 000
0   5   10   15 km

PACIFIC
OCEAN

Key

Relief and physical features

Relief metres

5000
3000
2000
1000
500
200
sea level
under sea level
0
200
4000
6000

5493 ▲ Mountain height (in metres)

Water features

〜 River
〜 Intermittent river
〰 Canal
⬭ Lake / Reservoir
⬭ Intermittent lake
Marsh

Communications

—— Railway
—— Road
⊕ Main airport

Administration

Boundaries

—— International
—— Internal

Settlement

Cities and towns in order of size

National capital

■ **MÉXICO CITY**
■ **BOGOTÁ**
□ **KINGSTON**
□ NASSAU
□ CASTRIES

Other city or town

● **Monterrey**
○ **Chihuahua**
○ Oaxaca
○ Zacatecas

Mexican States numbered on map
1. AGUASCALIENTES
2. DISTRITO FEDERAL
3. TLAXCALA

Scale 1 : 13 500 000

0   200   400   600   800 km

ATLANTIC

OCEAN

SOUTH CAROLINA

Dalton
Greenville
Florence
Lumberton
Columbia
Wilmington
Atlanta
Augusta
Myrtle
Beach
Macon
Cape Fear
Columbus
Cape Romain
mery
Charleston
Savannah
GEORGIA
Jesup
Brunswick
Bainbridge
Valdosta
Tallahassee
Lake City
Jacksonville

FLORIDA
Gainesville
Daytona Beach
Apalachee
Bay
Orlando
Cape Canaveral
Lakeland
Melbourne
Tampa
St Petersburg
Fort
Sarasota
Pierce
Lake
Okeechobee
West Palm Beach
Fort Lauderdale
Miami
Cape Sable
Florida Keys

Bermuda
(UK)
Hamilton

Grand
Bahama
Little Abaco
Freeport City
Great Abaco
Bimini
Islands
Eleuthera
New
Providence
NASSAU
THE BAHAMAS
Cat Island
Andros
San Salvador
Exuma
Cays
Rum Cay
Straits of Florida
Great Exuma
Long I.
Crooked I. Pass.
Crooked Island

Tropic of Cancer

HAVANA
Matanzas
CUBA
Archipiélago
de Sabana
Pinar del Río
Santa Clara
Archipiélago
de Camagüey
Mayaguana
**Turks and
Caicos Islands
(UK)**
Guane
Golfo
de Batabanó
Cienfuegos
Sancti Spíritus
Ciego de Ávila
Acklins
Island
Caicos
Islands
bo
Isla de la
Juventud
Archipiélago
de los Canarreos
Camagüey
Holguín
Little Inagua Island
Grand Turk
Turks Islands
nío
Archipiélago
de los Jardines
de la Reina
Las Tunas
Golfo de
Guacanayabo
Bayamo
Baracoa
Great
Inagua
Hispaniola
Leeward Islands

Little Cayman
Cabo Cruz
Sa Maestra
1994
Santiago
de Cuba
Guantánamo
Port-de-Paix
Cap-Haitien
Santiago
San
Juan
Virgin Is
(UK)
Anegada
(UK)
Anguilla (UK)
Grand Cayman
Cayman
Brac
Pico
Turquino
Gonaives
Pico
Duarte
3175
**SANTO
DOMINGO**
Mayagüez
Virgin Is
(USA)
St-Martin
Sint
St-Barthélemy (Fr.)
Cayman Islands
(UK)
Montego Bay
HAITI
**PORT-AU-
PRINCE**
Maarten
(Neth.)
Barbuda
**ANTIGUA AND
BARBUDA**
JAMAICA
KINGSTON
Jérémie
Les
Cayes
Jacmel
**DOMINICAN
REPUBLIC**
Ponce
**PUERTO
RICO
(USA)**
Isla
Mona
ST JOHN'S
Antigua
Montserrat
(UK)
Guadeloupe (Fr.)
Marie-Galante (Fr.)
**ST KITTS
AND NEVIS**
Isla Beata
Cabo Beata
Mona Passage
Basse-Terre
DOMINICA
ROSEAU
Windward Passage
C
a
r
i
b
b
e
a
n
Sea
Martinique
(Fr.)
Fort-de-
France
ST LUCIA
CASTRIES

Laguna de
Caratasca
Cayos Miskitos
Netherlands
Antilles
Isla
Blanquilla
(Ven.)
GRENADA
ST GEORGE'S
KINGSTOWN
BRIDGETOWN
**ST VINCENT AND
THE GRENADINES**
BARBADOS

Coco
rd Isabella
Punta Gallinas
Aruba
(Neth.)
Bonaire
Isla Orchila
(Ven.)
Tobago
Rio Grande
Isla de Providencia
(Colombia)
Punta
de Perlas
Islas del Maíz
(Nic.)
Península
de la Guajira
Curaçao
Islas
Los Roques
(Ven.)
Isla de
Margarita
**TRINIDAD
& TOBAGO**
Punta
de Mosquito
Isla de San Andrés
(Colombia)
Ríohacha
Santa
Marta
Maicao
Punto Fijo
Coro
Maiquetía
Isla La
Tortuga
Pen. de Paria
Güiria
Cumaná
PORT OF SPAIN
Trinidad
NICARAGUA
Lake Nicaragua
San Juan
Barranquilla
Valledupar
Golfo de
Venezuela
CARACAS
Barcelona
Maturín
Cartagena
Maracaibo
Barquisimeto
Maracay
Zaraza
COSTA RICA
SAN JOSÉ
Panama Canal
Cabimas
Valencia
Maracay
El Tigre
Orinoco
Delta
Chirripó
3819
Golfo de los
Mosquitos
Colón
Golfo de
Morrosquillo
Sincelejo
Lake
Maracaibo
Valera
Acarigua
San Fernando
de Apure
Ciudad
Guayana
El Callao
Bahía
de Coronado
PANAMA
**PANAMA
CITY**
Aguadulce
Montería
Mérida
Pico
Bolívar
5007
Barinas
Guanare
Orinoco
Embalse
de Guri
Península
de Osa
David
La Palma
Turbo
Bucaramanga
Cúcuta
San Cristóbal
VENEZUELA
Ciudad Bolívar
La Paragua
Golfo de
Chiriquí
Península
de Azuero
Punta Mala
Gulf of
Panama
Cerro Yaví
2285
La Gran
Sabana
Isla de Coiba
Golfo de
Cupica
Medellín
Sierra Nevada
del Cocuy
5493
Meta
Guiana
Highland
Quibdó
Tunja
Pakaraima Mountains
Manizales
Pereira
Armenia
Ibagué
BOGOTÁ
Villavicencio
Guaviare
Orinoco
Sa Parima
Buenaventura
Palmira
Neiva
Cali
COLOMBIA
Tumaco
Florencia
Pico da
Neblina
3014
BRAZIL

Equator

Next map
76-77

Next map
72-73

Lambert Conformal Conic projection

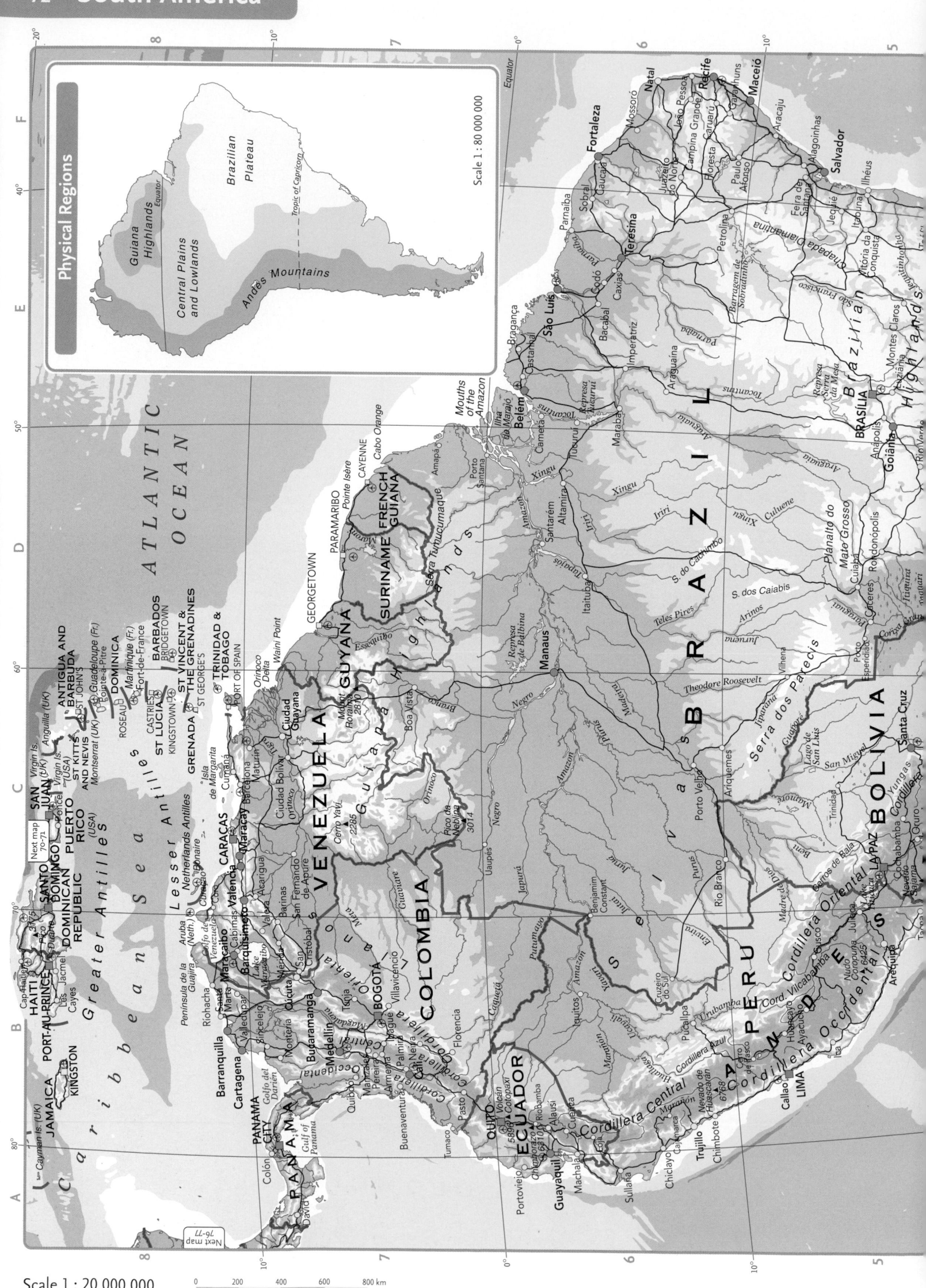

Physical Regions

Guiana Highlands

Equator

Brazilian Plateau

Central Plains and Lowlands

Tropic of Capricorn

Andes Mountains

Scale 1 : 80 000 000

ATLANTIC OCEAN

Caribbean Sea

Greater Antilles

Lesser Antilles

Netherlands Antilles

Cayman Is. (UK)
JAMAICA
KINGSTON
Cap-Haïtien
HAITI
PORT-AU-PRINCE
Les Cayes
Jacmel
Duarte
SANTO DOMINGO
DOMINICAN REPUBLIC
SAN JUAN
Virgin Is. (UK)
Anguilla (UK)
Virgin Is. (USA)
PUERTO RICO (USA)
PONCE
ANTIGUA AND BARBUDA
ST JOHN'S
ST KITTS AND NEVIS
Montserrat (UK)
Guadeloupe (Fr.)
Pointe-à-Pitre
DOMINICA
ROSEAU
Martinique (Fr.)
Fort-de-France
ST LUCIA
CASTRIES
BARBADOS
BRIDGETOWN
ST VINCENT & THE GRENADINES
KINGSTOWN
GRENADA
ST GEORGE'S
TRINIDAD & TOBAGO
PORT OF SPAIN

PANAMA
PANAMA CITY
Colón
David
Gulf of Panama
Golfo del Darién

COLOMBIA
Barranquilla
Cartagena
Santa Marta
Valledupar
Riohacha
Península de la Guajira
Sincelejo
Montería
Cúcuta
Bucaramanga
Medellín
Quibdó
Manizales
Pereira
Armenia
Ibagué
BOGOTÁ
Villavicencio
Buenaventura
Cali
Palmira
Neiva
Popayán
Pasto
Tumaco
Florencia
Cordillera Occidental
Cordillera Central
Cordillera Oriental

VENEZUELA
Maracaibo
Lake Maracaibo
Cabimas
Maracay
Valencia
CARACAS
Barquisimeto
Barcelona
Cumaná
Maturín
Ciudad Bolívar
Ciudad Guayana
San Fernando
San Cristóbal
Barinas
Acarigua
Valera
Mérida
Isla de Margarita
Orinoco
Orinoco Delta
Cerro Yaví
Mount Roraima 2810
Pico da Neblina 3014

GUYANA
GEORGETOWN
Essequibo
Waini Point

SURINAME
PARAMARIBO
Serra Tumucumaque

FRENCH GUIANA
CAYENNE
Pointe Isère
Cabo Orange
Maroni

Mouths of the Amazon

Guiana Highlands

ECUADOR
QUITO
Portoviejo
Guayaquil
Machala
Cuenca
Riobamba
Ambato
Alausí
Volcán Cotopaxi 5897
Chimborazo 6310

PERU
LIMA
Callao
Trujillo
Chiclayo
Chimbote
Sullana
Piura
Cajamarca
Iquitos
Pucallpa
Huánuco
Cusco
Arequipa
Ayacucho
Huancayo
Ica
Nevado de Huascarán 6768
Nudo Coropuna 6425
Cordillera Occidental
Cordillera Central
Cordillera Oriental

BOLIVIA
LA PAZ
Santa Cruz
Cochabamba
Trinidad
Lago de San Luis
Lago de Poopó
Lake Titicaca
Cordillera Oriental

BRAZIL
BRASÍLIA
Fortaleza
Recife
Maceió
Salvador
Natal
João Pessoa
Campina Grande
Caruaru
Aracaju
Ilhéus
Teresina
São Luís
Belém
Manaus
Santarém
Altamira
Marabá
Imperatriz
Araguaína
Mossoró
Sobral
Parnaíba
Caxias
Bacabal
Bragança
Castanhal
Cametá
Porto Santana
Amapá
Macapá
Ilha de Marajó
Boa Vista
Porto Velho
Ariquemes
Vilhena
Rio Branco
Cruzeiro do Sul
Benjamin Constant
Feira de Santana
Vitória da Conquista
Jequié
Itabuna
Itaberaba
Montes Claros
Anápolis
Goiânia
Rondonópolis
Cáceres
Cuiabá
Petrolina
Floresta
Paulo Afonso
Alagoinhas
Barreiras
Juazeiro do Norte
Gafanhuns
Araripina
Theodore Roosevelt
Negro
Amazon
Xingu
Tapajós
Iriri
Teles Pires
Arinos
Juruena
Jiparaná
Madeira
Purus
Juruá
Javari
Putumayo
Caquetá
Japurá
Içá
Napo
Marañón
Ucayali
Huallaga
Madre de Dios
Beni
Mamoré
Guaporé
Paraguai
Serra dos Parecis
Serra dos Caiabis
Serra do Cachimbo
Planalto do Mato Grosso
Brazilian Highlands
Chapada Diamantina
Espinhaço
São Francisco
Tocantins
Araguaia
Represa de Tucuruí
Represa de Sobradinho
Represa de Balbina
Represa de Serra da Mesa

Equator

Next map 70–71

Next map 76–77

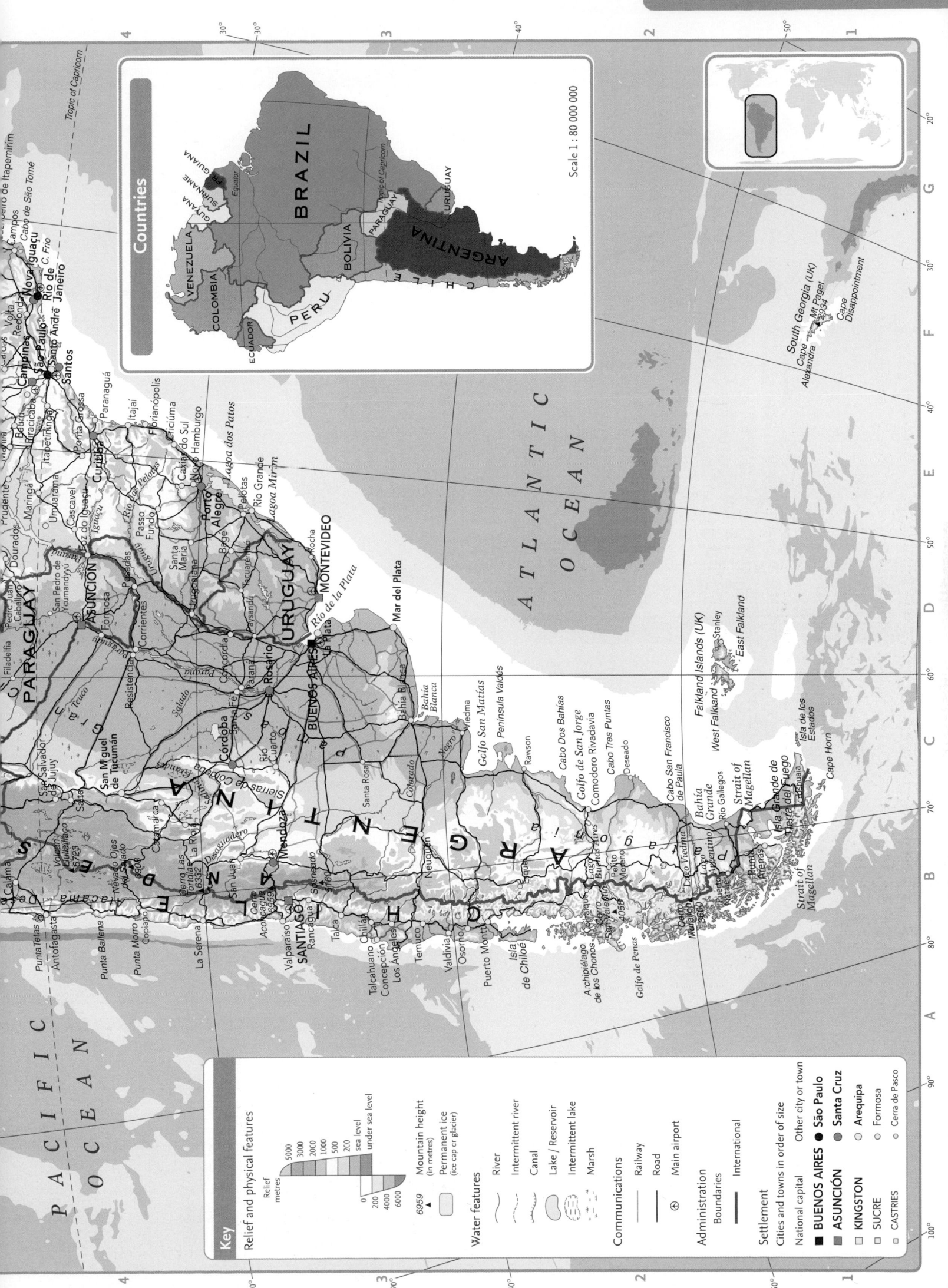

Key

Relief and physical features

Relief
metres

5000
3000
2000
1000
500
200
sea level
under sea level

200
4000
6000

6959 ▲ Mountain height
(in metres)

Permanent ice
(ice cap or glacier)

Water features

〜 River

Intermittent river

Canal

Lake / Reservoir

Intermittent lake

Marsh

Communications

—— Railway

—— Road

⊕ Main airport

Administration

Boundaries

International

Settlement

Cities and towns in order of size

National capital   Other city or town

■ BUENOS AIRES   ● São Paulo

● ASUNCIÓN   ● Santa Cruz

□ KINGSTON   ○ Arequipa

□ SUCRE   ○ Formosa

□ CASTRIES   ○ Cerro de Pasco

Countries

Scale 1 : 80 000 000

VENEZUELA
GUYANA
SURINAME
FRENCH GUIANA
COLOMBIA
ECUADOR
PERU
BRAZIL
BOLIVIA
PARAGUAY
CHILE
URUGUAY
ARGENTINA

PACIFIC OCEAN

ATLANTIC OCEAN

Tropic of Capricorn

PARAGUAY
ASUNCIÓN
URUGUAY
MONTEVIDEO
BUENOS AIRES
La Plata
Mar del Plata
Río de la Plata

ARGENTINA

CHILE
SANTIAGO
Valparaíso

Cerro Aconcagua 6959 ▲

Cerro Ojos del Salado 6908

Mendoza
Córdoba
Rosario
Santa Fe

San Miguel de Tucumán

Falkland Islands (UK)
West Falkland
East Falkland
Stanley

Bahía Blanca
Bahía Grande
Golfo San Matías
Golfo de San Jorge
Península Valdés
Cabo Dos Bahías
Cabo Tres Puntas
Cabo San Francisco de Paula

Comodoro Rivadavia
Deseado
Río Gallegos

Strait of Magellan
Tierra del Fuego
Isla de los Estados
Cape Horn
Ushuaia
Punta Arenas

Cerro Murallón 3600

Lago Buenos Aires
Lago Viedma
Lago Argentino

Perito Moreno

Neuquén
Viedma
Rawson
Santa Rosa

Río Colorado
Río Negro

A'rchipiélago de los Chonos
Golfo de Penas
Isla de Chiloé
Puerto Montt
Osorno
Valdivia
Temuco
Los Ángeles
Concepción
Talcahuano
Chillán
Talca
Rancagua

Antofagasta
Punta Tetas
Punta Ballena
Punta Morro
Copiapó
La Serena

Volcán Llullaillaco 6723
Cerro Las Tórtolas 6332
San Juan
La Rioja
Catamarca
Santiago del Estero

Salta
San Salvador de Jujuy
Calama

Filadelfia
San Pedro de Ycumandyyú
Pedro Juan Caballero
Concepción
Corrientes
Resistencia
Formosa
Posadas

Lagoa dos Patos
Lagoa Mirim
Rio Grande
Pelotas
Porto Alegre
Novo Hamburgo
Caxias do Sul
Passo Fundo
Santa Maria
Rocha

Curitiba
Florianópolis
Itajaí
Criciúma
Paranaguá
Ponta Grossa
Cascavel
Foz do Iguaçu
Maringá
Paranaguá

São Paulo
Santo André
Santos
Campinas
Piracicaba
Itapetininga
Rio de Janeiro
Nova Iguaçu
Volta Redonda
Campos
Cabo de São Tomé
C. Frio
Ribeiro de Itapemirim
Cabo de Itapemirim

South Georgia (UK)
Cape Aleksandra
Mt Paget 2934
Cape Disappointment

Lambert Azimuthal Equal Area projection

1 Temperature and Pressure : January

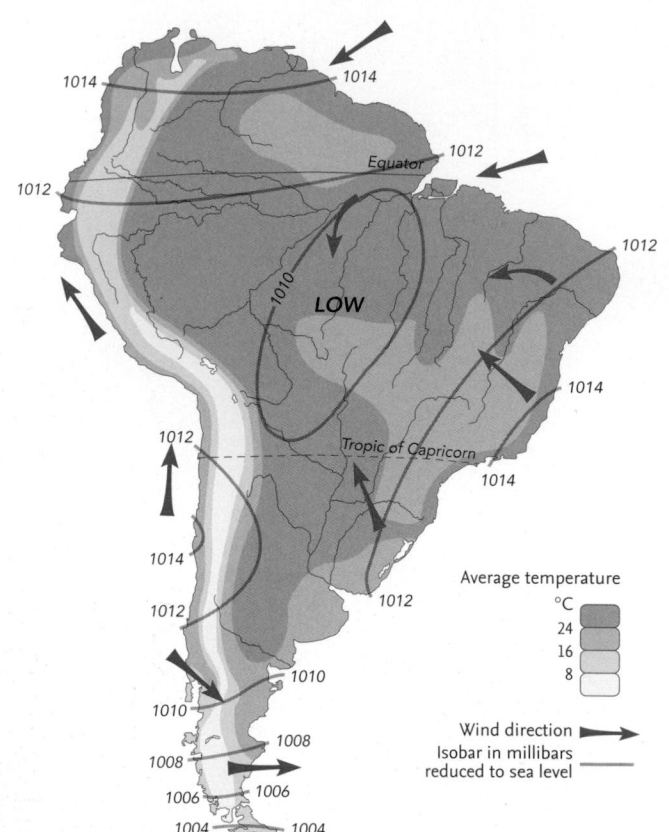

1014 · 1014 · 1012 · Equator · 1012 · 1012 · 1012 · 1010 · **LOW** · Tropic of Capricorn · 1014 · 1014 · 1014 · 1012 · 1012 · 1010 · 1010 · 1008 · 1008 · 1006 · 1006 · 1004 · 1004

Average temperature
°C
24
16
8

Wind direction
Isobar in millibars
reduced to sea level

2 Temperature and Pressure : July

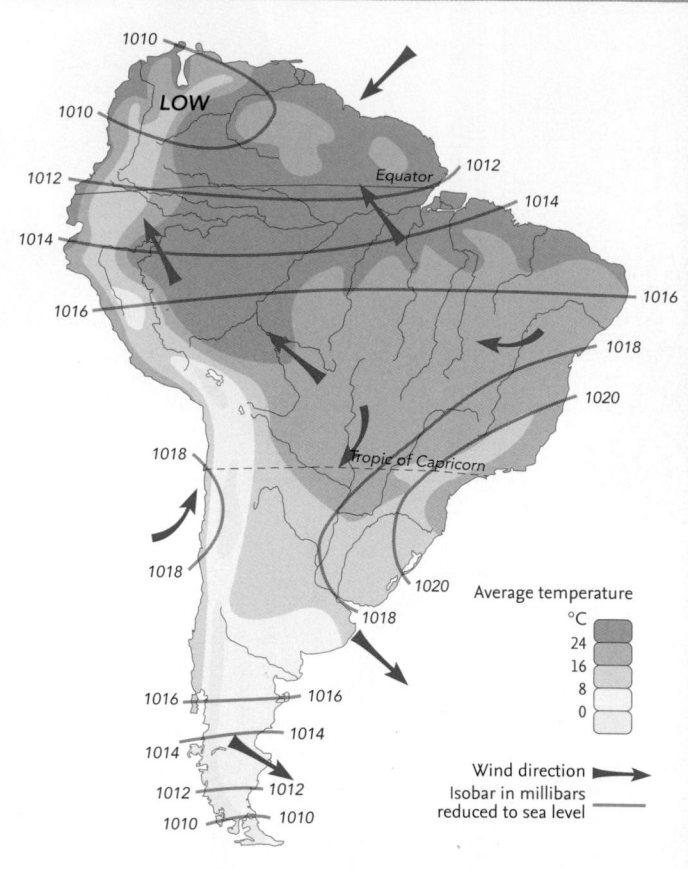

1010 · 1010 · **LOW** · 1012 · 1014 · Equator · 1012 · 1014 · 1016 · 1016 · 1018 · 1020 · Tropic of Capricorn · 1018 · 1018 · 1020 · 1016 · 1016 · 1014 · 1014 · 1012 · 1012 · 1010 · 1010

Average temperature
°C
24
16
8
0

Wind direction
Isobar in millibars
reduced to sea level

3 Annual Rainfall

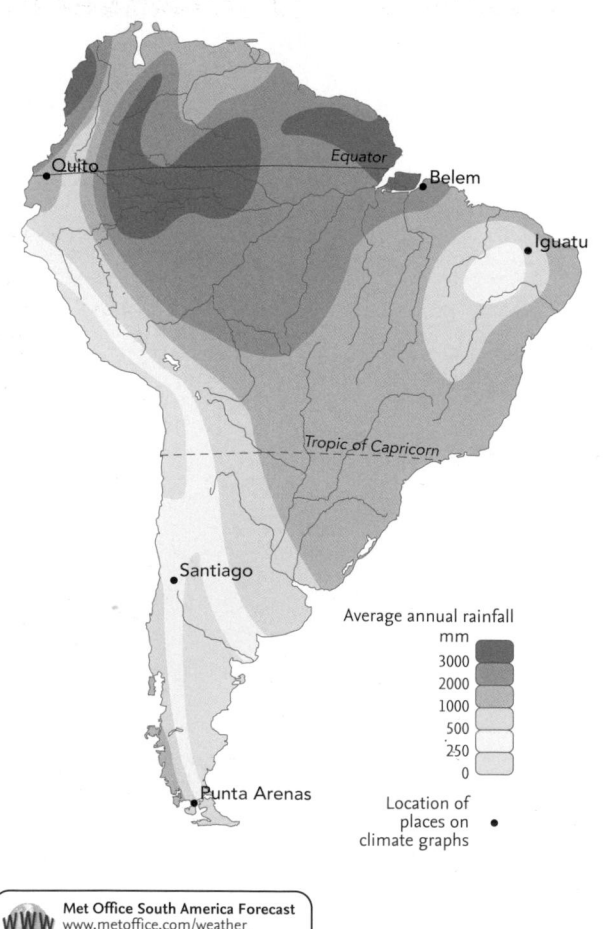

Quito · Equator · Belem · Iguatu · Tropic of Capricorn · Santiago · Punta Arenas

Average annual rainfall
mm
3000
2000
1000
500
250
0

Location of
places on
climate graphs

Met Office South America Forecast
www.metoffice.com/weather
World Meteorological Organization
www.wmo.ch
BBC World Weather
www.bbc.co.uk/weather/world

4 Climate Statistics

Town
°C 40 30 20 10 0 -10
mm 400 300 200 100 0
Altitude in metres above sea level
Temperature range shows the average daily max. and min.
Average monthly rainfall in mm
J F M A M J J A S O N D

Quito
°C 40 30 20 10 0 -10
mm 400 300 200 100 0
Altitude 2879 m
J F M A M J J A S O N D

Quito	Jan	Feb	Mar	Apr	May	Jun	Jul	Aug	Sep	Oct	Nov	Dec
Temperature - max. (°C)	22	22	22	21	21	22	22	23	23	22	22	22
Temperature - min. (°C)	8	8	8	8	8	7	7	7	8	8	7	8
Rainfall - (mm)	99	112	142	175	137	43	20	31	69	112	97	79

Belem	Jan	Feb	Mar	Apr	May	Jun	Jul	Aug	Sep	Oct	Nov	Dec
Temperature - max. (°C)	31	30	31	31	31	31	31	31	32	32	32	32
Temperature - min. (°C)	22	22	23	23	23	22	22	22	22	22	22	22
Rainfall - (mm)	318	358	358	320	259	170	150	112	89	84	66	155

Iguatu	Jan	Feb	Mar	Apr	May	Jun	Jul	Aug	Sep	Oct	Nov	Dec
Temperature - max. (°C)	34	33	32	31	31	31	32	32	35	36	36	36
Temperature - min. (°C)	23	23	23	23	22	22	21	21	22	23	23	23
Rainfall - (mm)	89	173	185	160	61	61	36	5	18	18	10	33

Santiago	Jan	Feb	Mar	Apr	May	Jun	Jul	Aug	Sep	Oct	Nov	Dec
Temperature - max. (°C)	29	29	27	23	18	14	15	17	19	22	26	28
Temperature - min. (°C)	12	11	9	7	5	3	3	4	6	7	9	11
Rainfall - (mm)	3	3	5	13	64	84	76	56	31	15	8	5

Punta Arenas	Jan	Feb	Mar	Apr	May	Jun	Jul	Aug	Sep	Oct	Nov	Dec
Temperature - max. (°C)	14	14	12	10	7	5	4	6	8	11	12	14
Temperature - min. (°C)	7	7	5	4	2	1	-1	1	2	3	4	6
Rainfall - (mm)	38	23	33	36	33	41	28	31	23	28	18	36

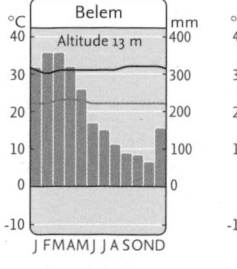

Belem
°C 40 30 20 10 0 -10
mm 400 300 200 100 0
Altitude 13 m
J F M A M J J A S O N D

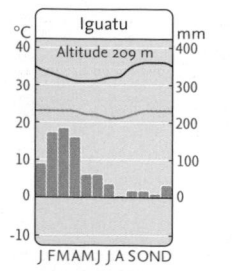

Iguatu
°C 40 30 20 10 0 -10
mm 400 300 200 100 0
Altitude 209 m
J F M A M J J A S O N D

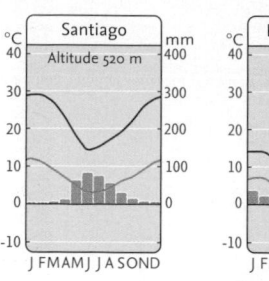

Santiago
°C 40 30 20 10 0 -10
mm 400 300 200 100 0
Altitude 520 m
J F M A M J J A S O N D

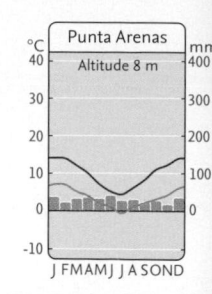

Punta Arenas
°C 40 30 20 10 0 -10
mm 400 300 200 100 0
Altitude 8 m
J F M A M J J A S O N D

Scale 1 : 70 000 000

0 1000 2000 3000 km

Lambert Azimuthal Equal Area project

1 Land Cover

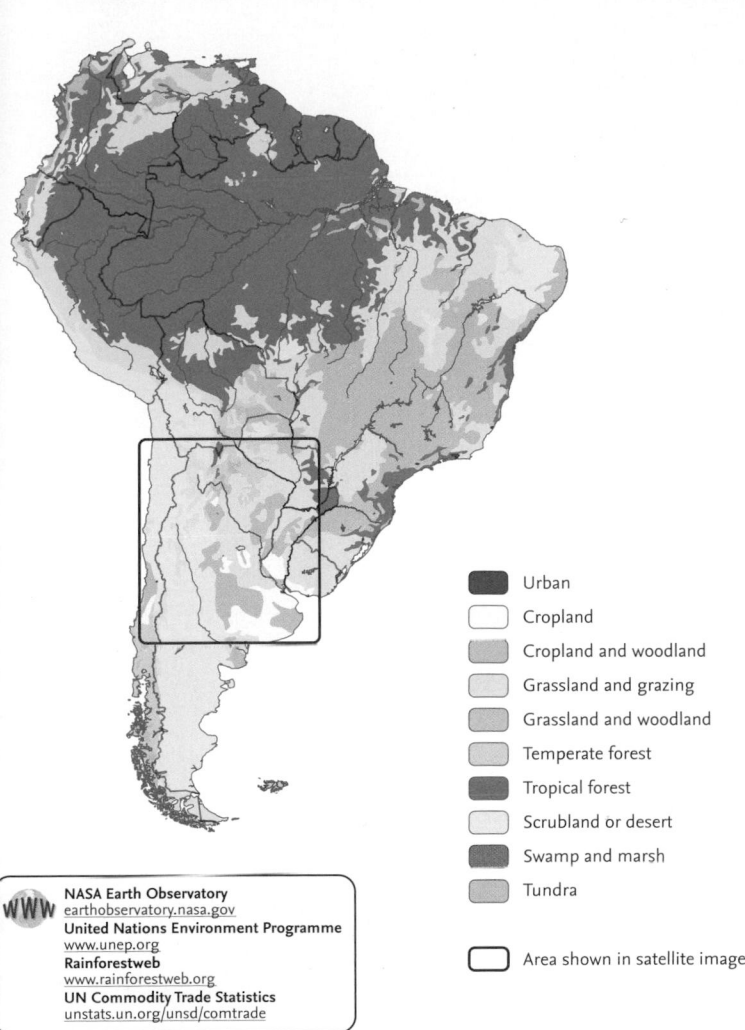

The highest mountains, the Andes, run along the left hand side of this true colour image. The range narrows in the south where a strip of snow can be seen on the highest peaks. Green featureless areas are the vast wetlands of Argentina and Paraguay. In the east the Uruguay river flows along the border between Argentina and Uruguay and into the Rio de La Plata. Sediment dumped by both the Uruguay and Paraná river shows as a murky brown colour in the bay.

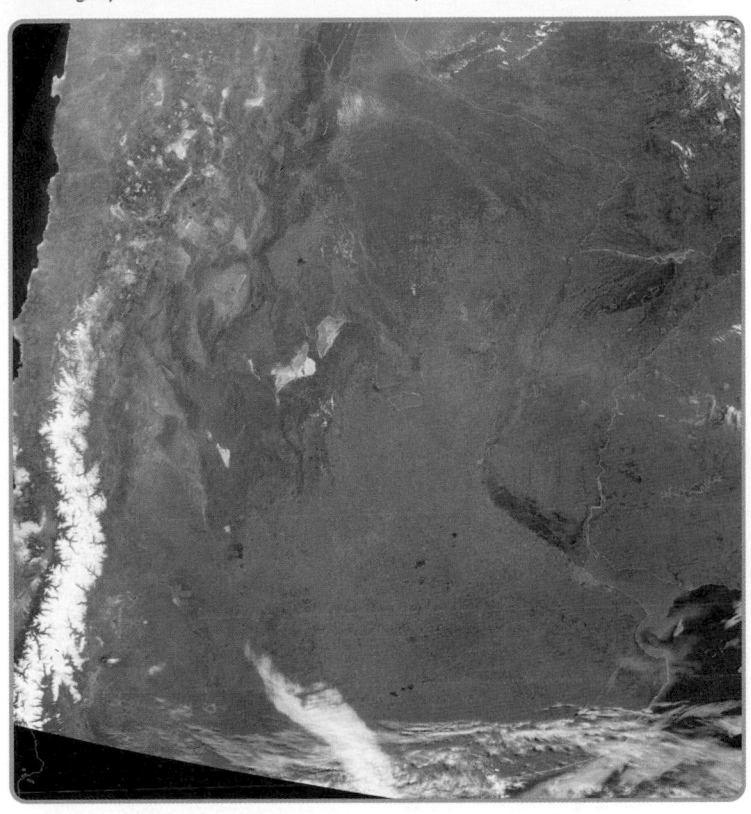

Legend:
- Urban
- Cropland
- Cropland and woodland
- Grassland and grazing
- Grassland and woodland
- Temperate forest
- Tropical forest
- Scrubland or desert
- Swamp and marsh
- Tundra

☐ Area shown in satellite image

WWW NASA Earth Observatory
earthobservatory.nasa.gov
United Nations Environment Programme
www.unep.org
Rainforestweb
www.rainforestweb.org
UN Commodity Trade Statistics
unstats.un.org/unsd/comtrade

2 Population

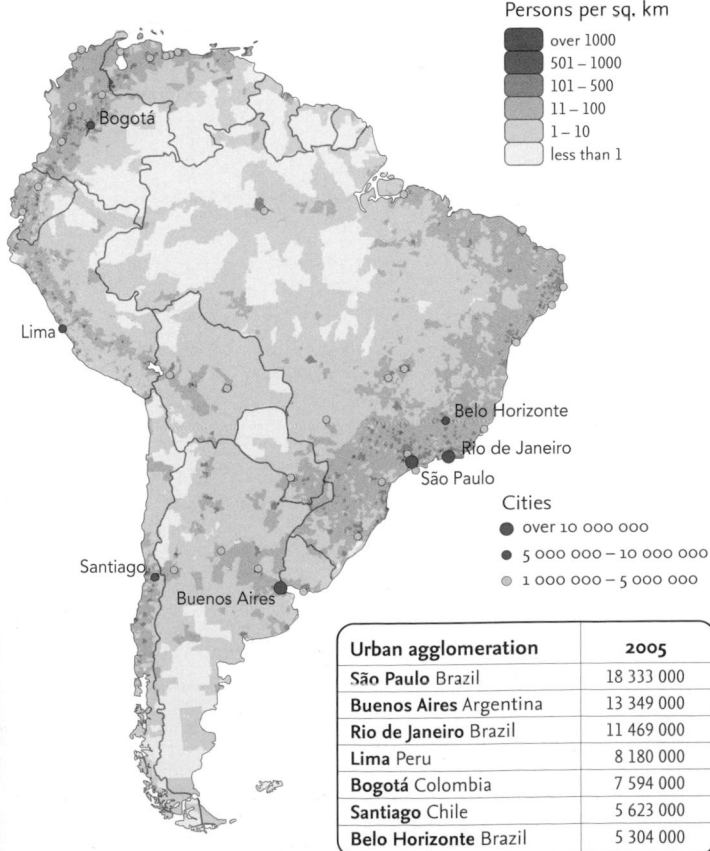

Persons per sq. km
- over 1000
- 501 – 1000
- 101 – 500
- 11 – 100
- 1 – 10
- less than 1

Cities
- ● over 10 000 000
- ● 5 000 000 – 10 000 000
- ◉ 1 000 000 – 5 000 000

Urban agglomeration	2005
São Paulo Brazil	18 333 000
Buenos Aires Argentina	13 349 000
Rio de Janeiro Brazil	11 469 000
Lima Peru	8 180 000
Bogotá Colombia	7 594 000
Santiago Chile	5 623 000
Belo Horizonte Brazil	5 304 000

3 Trade

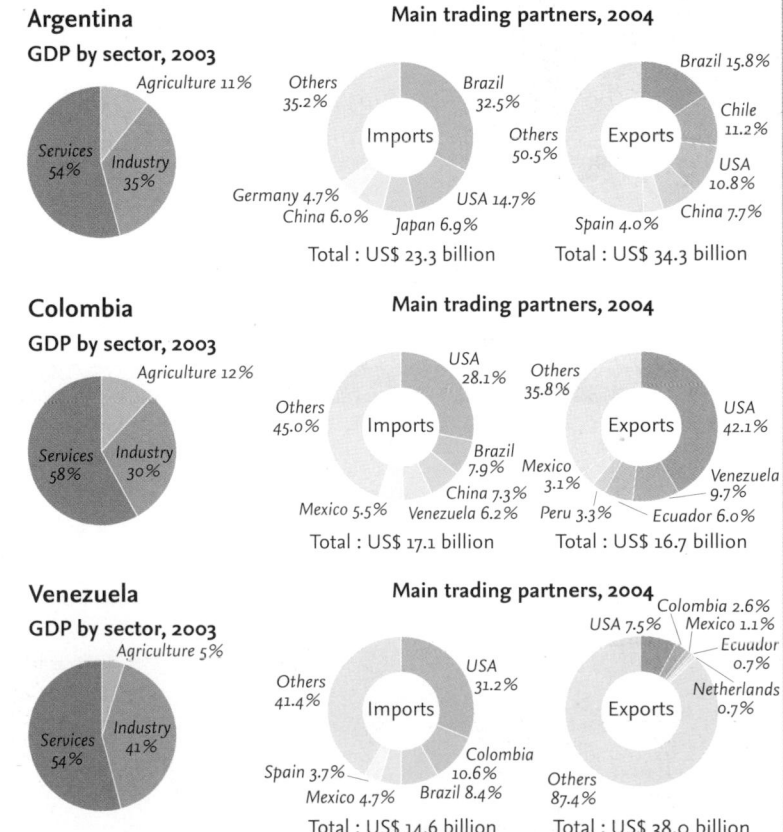

Argentina
GDP by sector, 2003
- Agriculture 11%
- Services 54%
- Industry 35%

Main trading partners, 2004

Imports:
- Others 35.2%
- Brazil 32.5%
- Germany 4.7%
- China 6.0%
- Japan 6.9%
- USA 14.7%

Total : US$ 23.3 billion

Exports:
- Brazil 15.8%
- Chile 11.2%
- USA 10.8%
- China 7.7%
- Spain 4.0%
- Others 50.5%

Total : US$ 34.3 billion

Colombia
GDP by sector, 2003
- Agriculture 12%
- Services 58%
- Industry 30%

Main trading partners, 2004

Imports:
- USA 28.1%
- Others 45.0%
- Brazil 7.9%
- China 7.3%
- Venezuela 6.2%
- Mexico 5.5%

Total : US$ 17.1 billion

Exports:
- Others 35.8%
- USA 42.1%
- Venezuela 9.7%
- Ecuador 6.0%
- Peru 3.3%
- Mexico 3.1%

Total : US$ 16.7 billion

Venezuela
GDP by sector, 2003
- Agriculture 5%
- Services 54%
- Industry 41%

Main trading partners, 2004

Imports:
- Others 41.4%
- USA 31.2%
- Colombia 10.6%
- Brazil 8.4%
- Mexico 4.7%
- Spain 3.7%

Total : US$ 14.6 billion

Exports:
- USA 7.5%
- Colombia 2.6%
- Mexico 1.1%
- Ecuador 0.7%
- Netherlands 0.7%
- Others 87.4%

Total : US$ 38.0 billion

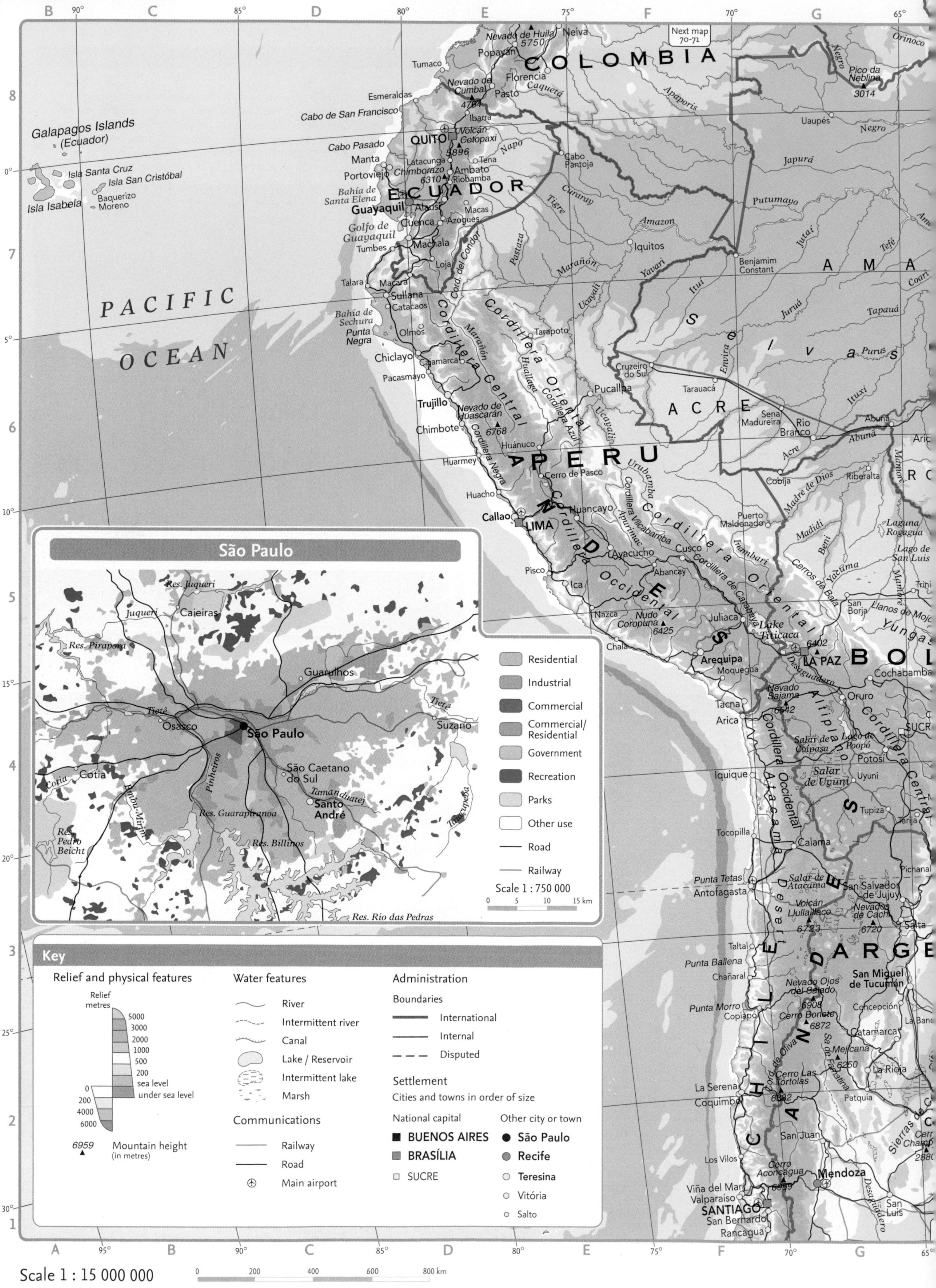

PACIFIC

OCEAN

Galapagos Islands
(Ecuador)

Isla Santa Cruz
Isla San Cristóbal
Isla Isabela
Baquerizo
Moreno

COLOMBIA

Neiva
Nevado de Huila
5750
Popayán
Tumaco
Florencia
Caquetá
Esmeraldas
Pasto
Cabo de San Francisco
Nevado de
Cumbal
Ibarra
4764
Cabo Pasado
Volcán
Cotopaxi
QUITO
Manta
5896
Napo
Portoviejo
Latacunga
Tena
Chimborazo
Ambato
Bahía de
6310
Riobamba
Santa Elena
ECUADOR
Macas
Guayaquil
Alausi
Golfo de
Cuenca
Azogues
Guayaquil
Machala
Tumbes
Loja

PERU

Talara
Macará
Suliana
Catacaos
Cord. del Cóndor
Bahía de
Sechura
Olmos
Punta
Negra
Chiclayo
Cajamarca
Pacasmayo
Trujillo
Nevado de
Huascarán
Chimbote
6768
Huánuco
Huarmey
Cerro de Pasco
Huacho
Huancayo
Callao
LIMA
Ayacucho
Pisco
Cusco
Ica
Abancay
Nazca
Nudo
Coropuna
6425
Chala
Juliaca
Arequipa
Lake
Titicaca
Moquegua
6402
Tacna
Arica

Orinoco
Negro
Pico da
Neblina
3014
Uaupés
Negro
Apaporis
Japurá
Putumayo
AMA
Iquitos
Amazon
Jutaí
Teté
Benjamim
Constant
Tefé
Curaray
Tigre
Marañón
Yavari
Juruá
Itui
Purus
Cruzeiro
do Sul
ACRE
Tarauacá
Sena
Madureira
Rio
Branco
Abuná
Acre
Cobija
Madre de Dios
Riberalta
Puerto
Maldonado
Madidi
Beni
Cerros de Bata
Llanos de Mojo
San
Borja
Laguna
Rogagua
Lago de
San Luis
Yungas
BOL
LA PAZ
Cochabamba
Oruro
Nevado
Sajama
6542
SUCR
Altipla
Salar de
Coipasa
Lago de
Poopó
Potosí
Salar
de Uyuni
Uyuni
Tupiza
Tarija

PACIFIC
Iquique
Tocopilla
Cordillera de Atacama
Punta Tetas
Antofagasta
Salar de
Atacama
San Salvador
de Jujuy
Pichanal
Nevados
de Cachi
6720
Salta
Punta Ballena
Volcán
Llullaillaco
6723
Taltal
Chañaral
DARGE
San Miguel
de Tucumán
Punta Morro
Nevado Ojos
del Salado
6908
Concepción
Copiapó
Cerro Bonete
6872
Catamarca
La Serena
Cerro Las
Tortolas
6250
La Rioja
Coquimbo
6882
Patquía
Sierras de
Los Vilos
San Juan
Cerro
Aconcagua
Champ
6959
Mendoza
Viña del Mar
Valparaíso
SANTIAGO
San Bernardo
Rancagua
San
Luis

São Paulo

Res. Juqueri
Juqueri
Caieiras
Res. Pirapora
Guarulhos
Tietê
Tietê
Osasco
São Paulo
Suzano
Cotia
Pinheiros
São Caetano
do Sul
Embu-Mirim
Tamanduateí
Santo
André
Res. Guarapiranga
Res. Billings
Res.
Pedro
Beicht
Res. Rio das Pedras

	Residential
	Industrial
	Commercial
	Commercial/ Residential
	Government
	Recreation
	Parks
	Other use
——	Road
——	Railway

Scale 1 : 750 000

0   5   10   15 km

Next map
70-71

Key

Relief and physical features

Relief
metres
5000
3000
2000
1000
500
200
0   sea level
200   under sea level
4000
6000

6959   Mountain height
▲   (in metres)

Water features

River
Intermittent river
Canal
Lake / Reservoir
Intermittent lake
Marsh

Communications

Railway
Road
⊕   Main airport

Administration

Boundaries

———   International
———   Internal
- - -   Disputed

Settlement

Cities and towns in order of size

National capital
■ **BUENOS AIRES**
■ **BRASÍLIA**
□ SUCRE

Other city or town
● São Paulo
● Recife
○ Teresina
○ Vitória
○ Salto

Scale 1 : 15 000 000

0   200   400   600   800 km

Lambert Azimuthal Equal Area projection

1 Population Density

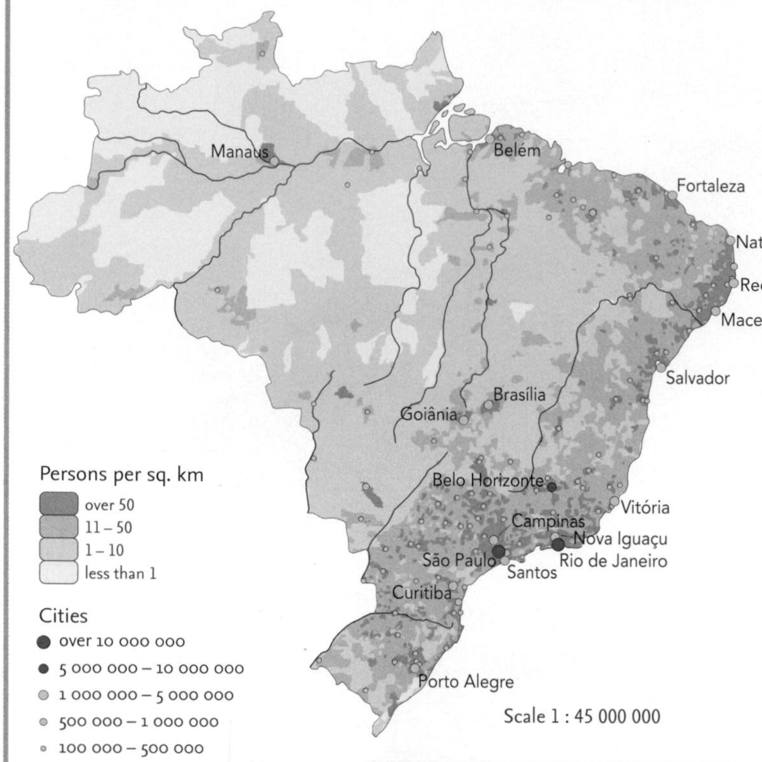

Manaus
Belém
Fortaleza
Natal
Recife
Maceió
Salvador
Brasília
Goiânia
Belo Horizonte
Vitória
Campinas
Nova Iguaçu
São Paulo
Rio de Janeiro
Santos
Curitiba
Porto Alegre

Persons per sq. km
- over 50
- 11 – 50
- 1 – 10
- less than 1

Cities
- over 10 000 000
- 5 000 000 – 10 000 000
- 1 000 000 – 5 000 000
- 500 000 – 1 000 000
- 100 000 – 500 000

Scale 1 : 45 000 000

www Brazilian Institute of Geography and Statistics
www.ibge.gov.br

2 Population Structure

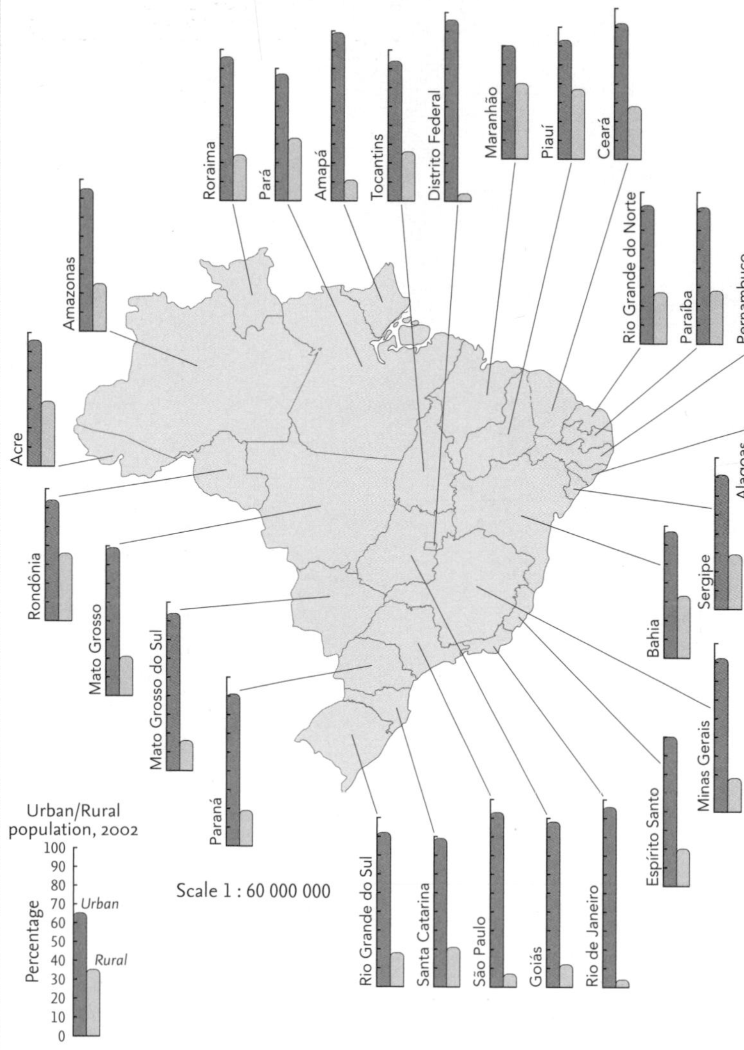

Roraima, Pará, Amapá, Tocantins, Distrito Federal, Maranhão, Piauí, Ceará, Rio Grande do Norte, Paraíba, Pernambuco, Amazonas, Acre, Rondônia, Mato Grosso, Mato Grosso do Sul, Paraná, Rio Grande do Sul, Santa Catarina, São Paulo, Goiás, Rio de Janeiro, Espírito Santo, Minas Gerais, Bahia, Sergipe, Alagoas

Urban/Rural population, 2002

Percentage: 100, 90, 80, 70, 60, 50, 40, 30, 20, 10, 0

Urban
Rural

Scale 1 : 60 000 000

Brazil urban population, 2002 (% of total): 82%

3 Main Urban Agglomerations

Urban agglomeration	1980	1995	2005 (projected)
São Paulo	12 497 000	16 417 000	18 333 000
Rio de Janeiro	8 741 000	9 888 000	11 469 000
Belo Horizonte	2 588 000	3 899 000	5 304 000
Porto Alegre	2 273 000	3 349 000	3 795 000
Recife	2 337 000	3 168 000	3 527 000
Brasília	1 162 000	1 778 000	3 341 000
Salvador	1 754 000	2 819 000	3 331 000
Fortaleza	1 569 000	2 660 000	3 261 000
Curitiba	1 427 000	2 270 000	2 871 000
Campinas	926 000	1 607 000	2 640 000
Belém	992 000	1 574 000	2 097 000
Goiânia	707 000	1 006 000	1 878 000

4 Rio de Janeiro Urban Land Use

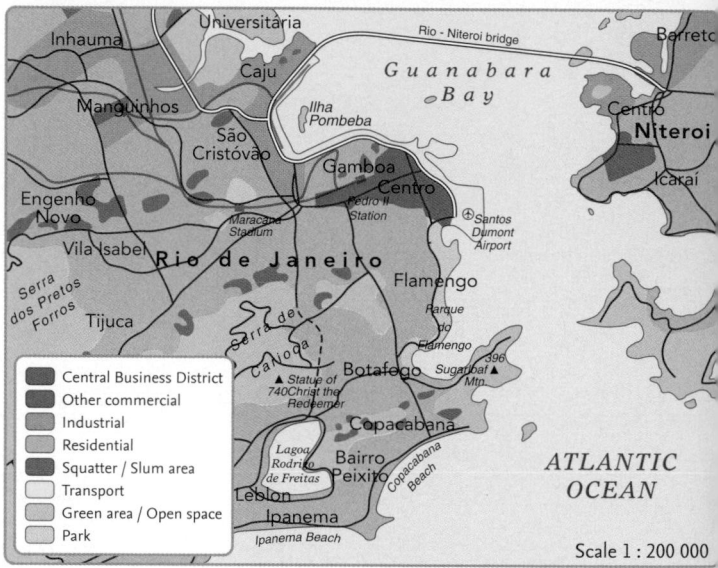

Universitária, Inhaúma, Rio - Niterói bridge, Barreto, Caju, Guanabara Bay, Manguinhos, Ilha Pombeba, Centro, Niterói, São Cristóvão, Gamboa, Icaraí, Engenho Novo, Pedro II Station, Santos Dumont Airport, Vila Isabel, Maracanã Stadium, Rio de Janeiro, Flamengo, Serra dos Pretos Forros, Serra da Carioca, Parque do Flamengo, Tijuca, Statue of Christ the Redeemer, Botafogo, Sugarloaf Mtn., Copacabana, Lagoa Rodrigo de Freitas, Bairro Peixoto, Copacabana Beach, ATLANTIC OCEAN, Leblon, Ipanema, Ipanema Beach

- Central Business District
- Other commercial
- Industrial
- Residential
- Squatter / Slum area
- Transport
- Green area / Open space
- Park

Scale 1 : 200 000

5 Internal Migration

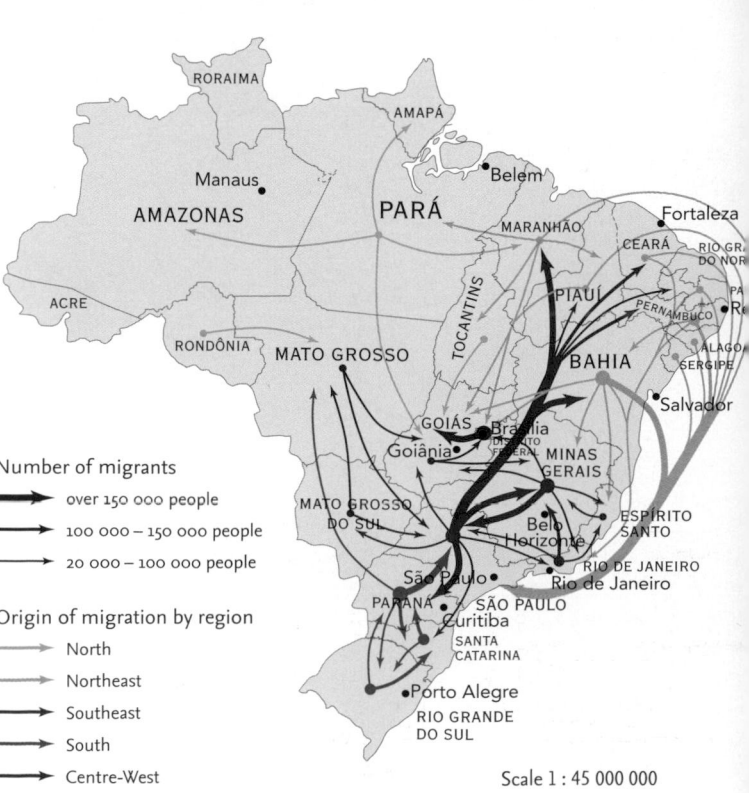

RORAIMA, AMAPÁ, Manaus, Belém, AMAZONAS, PARÁ, Fortaleza, MARANHÃO, CEARÁ, RIO GRANDE DO NORTE, ACRE, TOCANTINS, PIAUÍ, PERNAMBUCO, RONDÔNIA, MATO GROSSO, BAHIA, ALAGOAS, SERGIPE, Salvador, GOIÁS, Brasília, Goiânia, MINAS GERAIS, MATO GROSSO DO SUL, Belo Horizonte, ESPÍRITO SANTO, São Paulo, RIO DE JANEIRO, Rio de Janeiro, PARANÁ, SÃO PAULO, Curitiba, SANTA CATARINA, Porto Alegre, RIO GRANDE DO SUL

Number of migrants
- over 150 000 people
- 100 000 – 150 000 people
- 20 000 – 100 000 people

Origin of migration by region
- North
- Northeast
- Southeast
- South
- Centre-West

Scale 1 : 45 000 000

6 Regional Comparisons

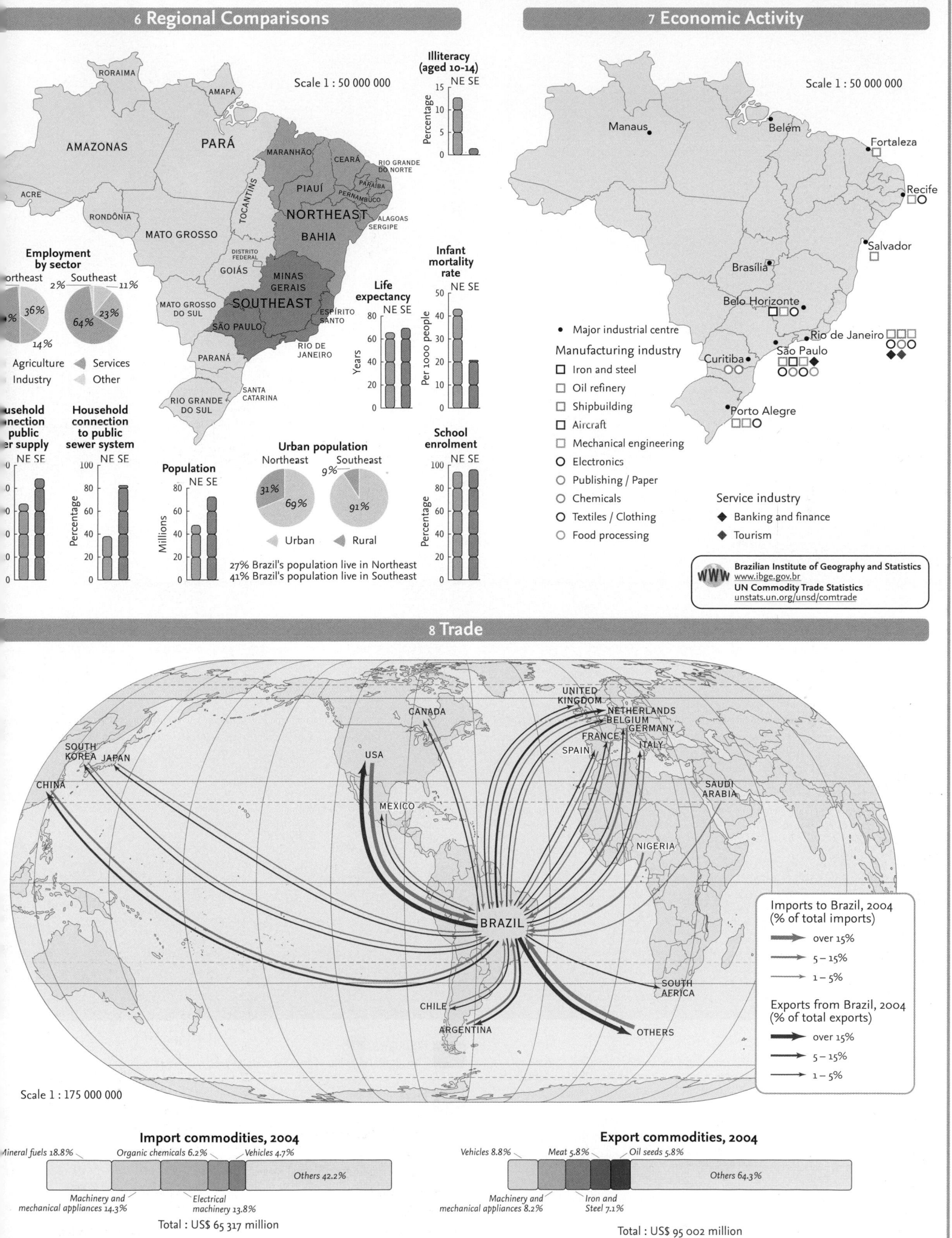

Scale 1 : 50 000 000

RORAIMA
AMAPÁ
AMAZONAS
PARÁ
MARANHÃO
CEARÁ
RIO GRANDE DO NORTE
ACRE
RONDÔNIA
PIAUÍ
PARAÍBA
PERNAMBUCO
TOCANTINS
NORTHEAST
MATO GROSSO
BAHIA
ALAGOAS
SERGIPE
DISTRITO FEDERAL
GOIÁS
MINAS GERAIS
MATO GROSSO DO SUL
SOUTHEAST
ESPÍRITO SANTO
SÃO PAULO
RIO DE JANEIRO
PARANÁ
SANTA CATARINA
RIO GRANDE DO SUL

Illiteracy (aged 10-14) NE SE

Infant mortality rate NE SE

Life expectancy NE SE

School enrolment NE SE

Employment by sector
Northeast 2% Southeast 11%
36% 64% 23%
14%
Agriculture — Services
Industry — Other

Household connection to public water supply NE SE

Household connection to public sewer system NE SE

Population NE SE
Millions

Urban population
Northeast 31% 69%
Southeast 9% 91%
◁ Urban   ▷ Rural

27% Brazil's population live in Northeast
41% Brazil's population live in Southeast

7 Economic Activity

Scale 1 : 50 000 000

Manaus
Belém
Fortaleza
Recife
Salvador
Brasília
Belo Horizonte
Rio de Janeiro
Curitiba
São Paulo
Porto Alegre

- Major industrial centre
Manufacturing industry
□ Iron and steel
□ Oil refinery
□ Shipbuilding
□ Aircraft
□ Mechanical engineering
○ Electronics
○ Publishing / Paper
○ Chemicals
○ Textiles / Clothing
○ Food processing

Service industry
◆ Banking and finance
◆ Tourism

www **Brazilian Institute of Geography and Statistics**
www.ibge.gov.br
UN Commodity Trade Statistics
unstats.un.org/unsd/comtrade

8 Trade

SOUTH KOREA
JAPAN
CHINA
CANADA
USA
MEXICO
UNITED KINGDOM
NETHERLANDS
BELGIUM
GERMANY
FRANCE
ITALY
SPAIN
SAUDI ARABIA
NIGERIA
BRAZIL
CHILE
ARGENTINA
SOUTH AFRICA
OTHERS

Imports to Brazil, 2004 (% of total imports)
→ over 15%
→ 5 – 15%
→ 1 – 5%

Exports from Brazil, 2004 (% of total exports)
→ over 15%
→ 5 – 15%
→ 1 – 5%

Scale 1 : 175 000 000

Import commodities, 2004
Mineral fuels 18.8%   Organic chemicals 6.2%   Vehicles 4.7%   Others 42.2%
Machinery and mechanical appliances 14.3%   Electrical machinery 13.8%
Total : US$ 65 317 million

Export commodities, 2004
Vehicles 8.8%   Meat 5.8%   Oil seeds 5.8%   Others 64.3%
Machinery and mechanical appliances 8.2%   Iron and Steel 7.1%
Total : US$ 95 002 million

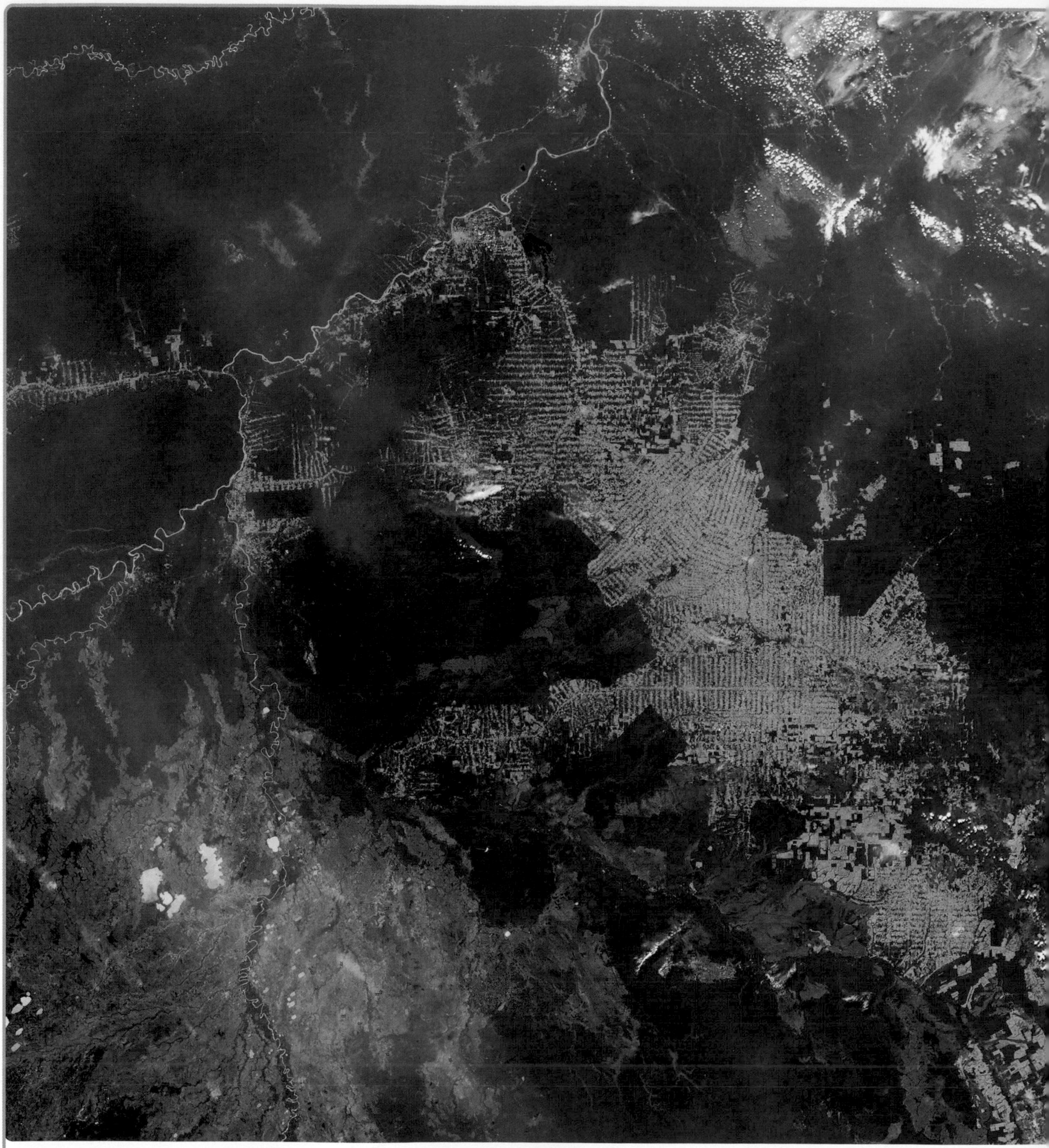

Deforested areas
Yellowish green coloured lines mark land cleared of forest for commercial logging. Most of the deforestation has taken place in Rondônia state which covers most of the right hand side of the image.

Forest
Areas of forest appear deep green on the image. Left of centre the forests of the Pando region of Bolivia remain undisturbed.

Rivers
The course of the Madeira river is clearly visible where it flows through forest, top centre.

Highland
The highland areas of the Serra dos Parecis, in Rondônia state, appear dark brow

Fires
Numerous smoke plumes from forest fires suggest the practice of slash and burr farming is still underway.

Water bodies
Deep reservoirs are almost black in the image, however the outlines of shallower lagoons on the Bolivian side of the border show clearly in pale green.

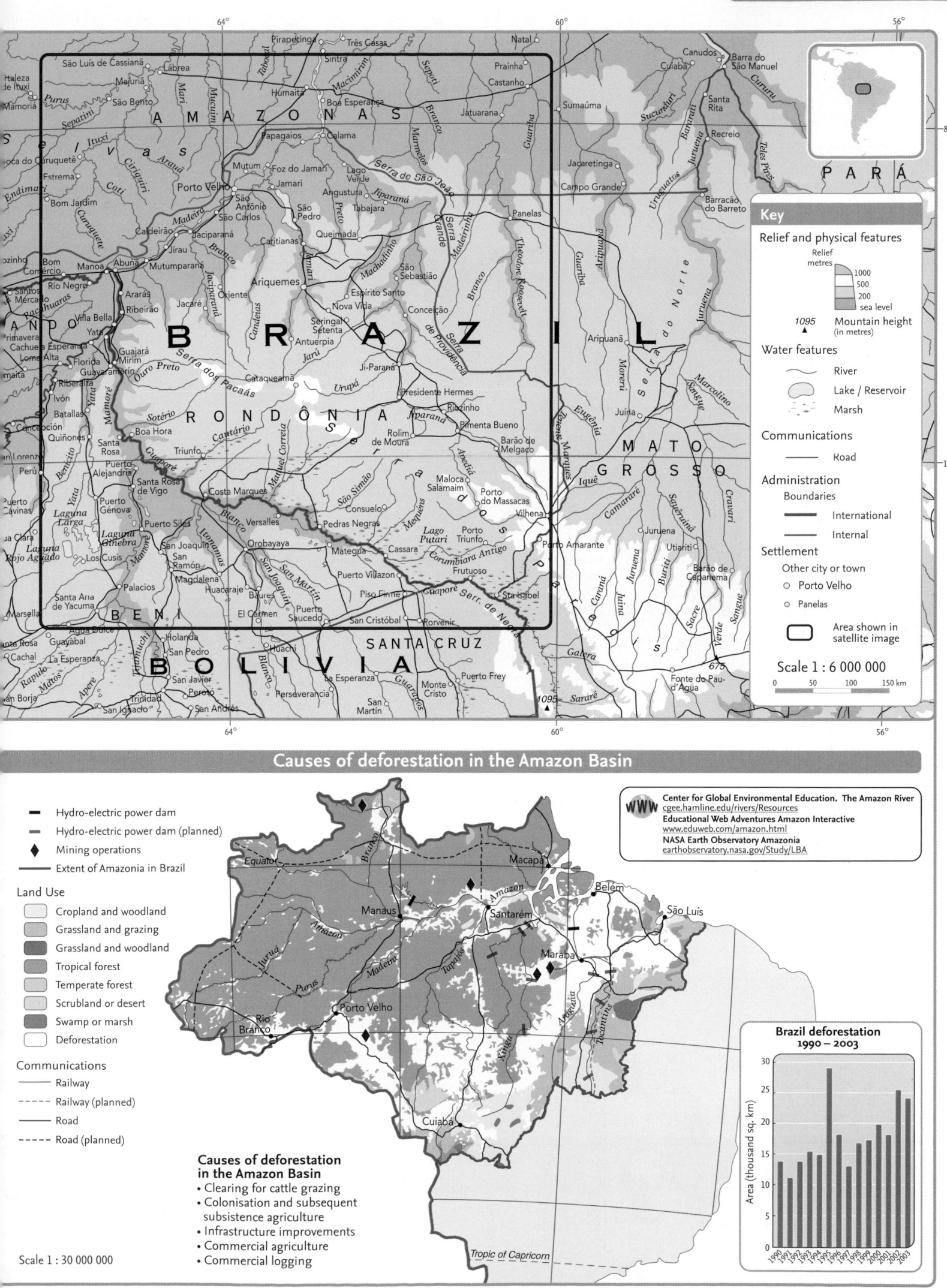

Causes of deforestation in the Amazon Basin

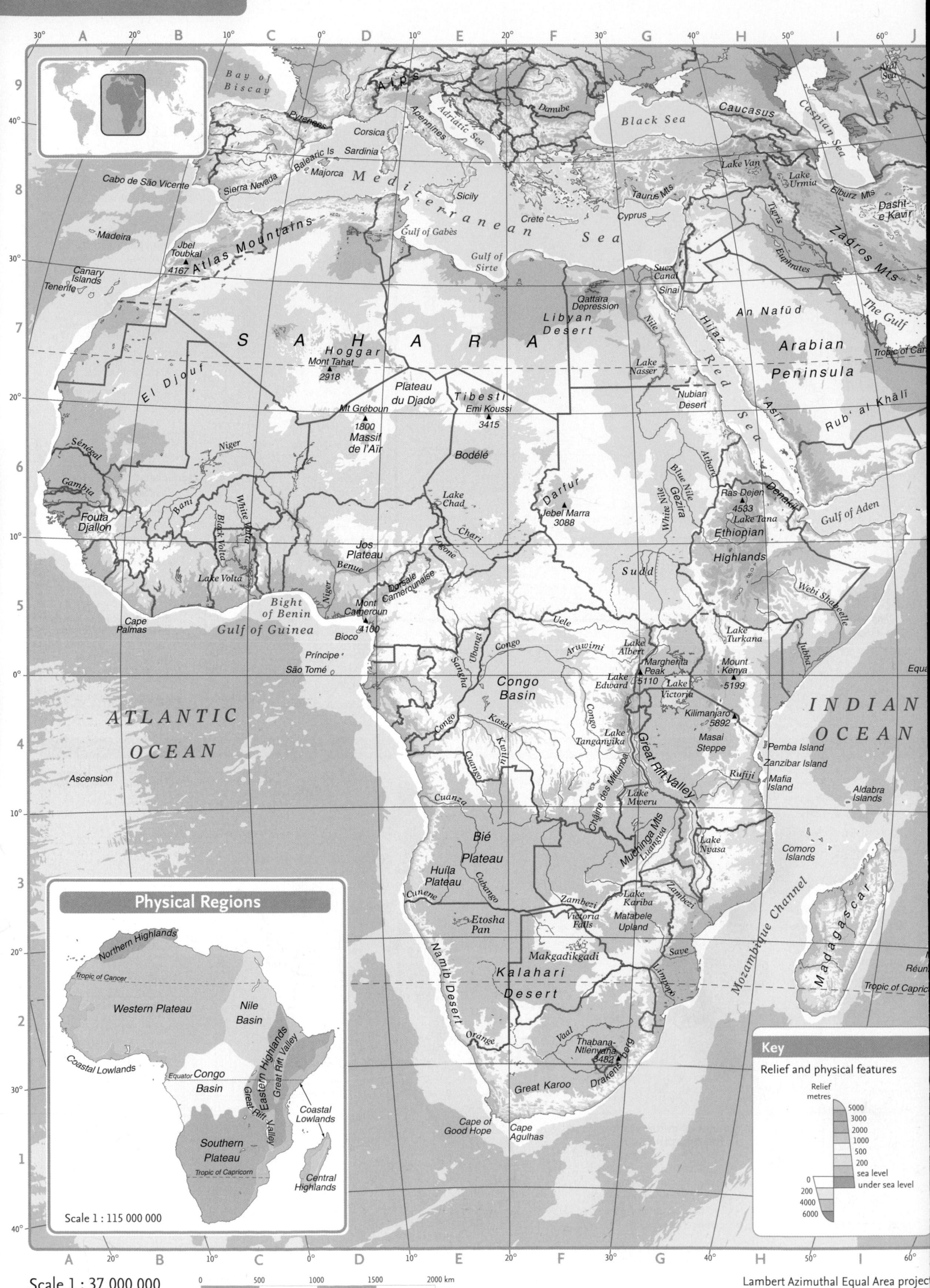

Physical Regions

Northern Highlands

Tropic of Cancer

Western Plateau

Nile Basin

Coastal Lowlands

Equator Congo Basin

Great Rift Valley

Eastern Highlands

Coastal Lowlands

Southern Plateau

Tropic of Capricorn

Central Highlands

Scale 1 : 115 000 000

Key

Relief and physical features

Relief
metres

5000
3000
2000
1000
500
200
sea level
under sea level

0
200
4000
6000

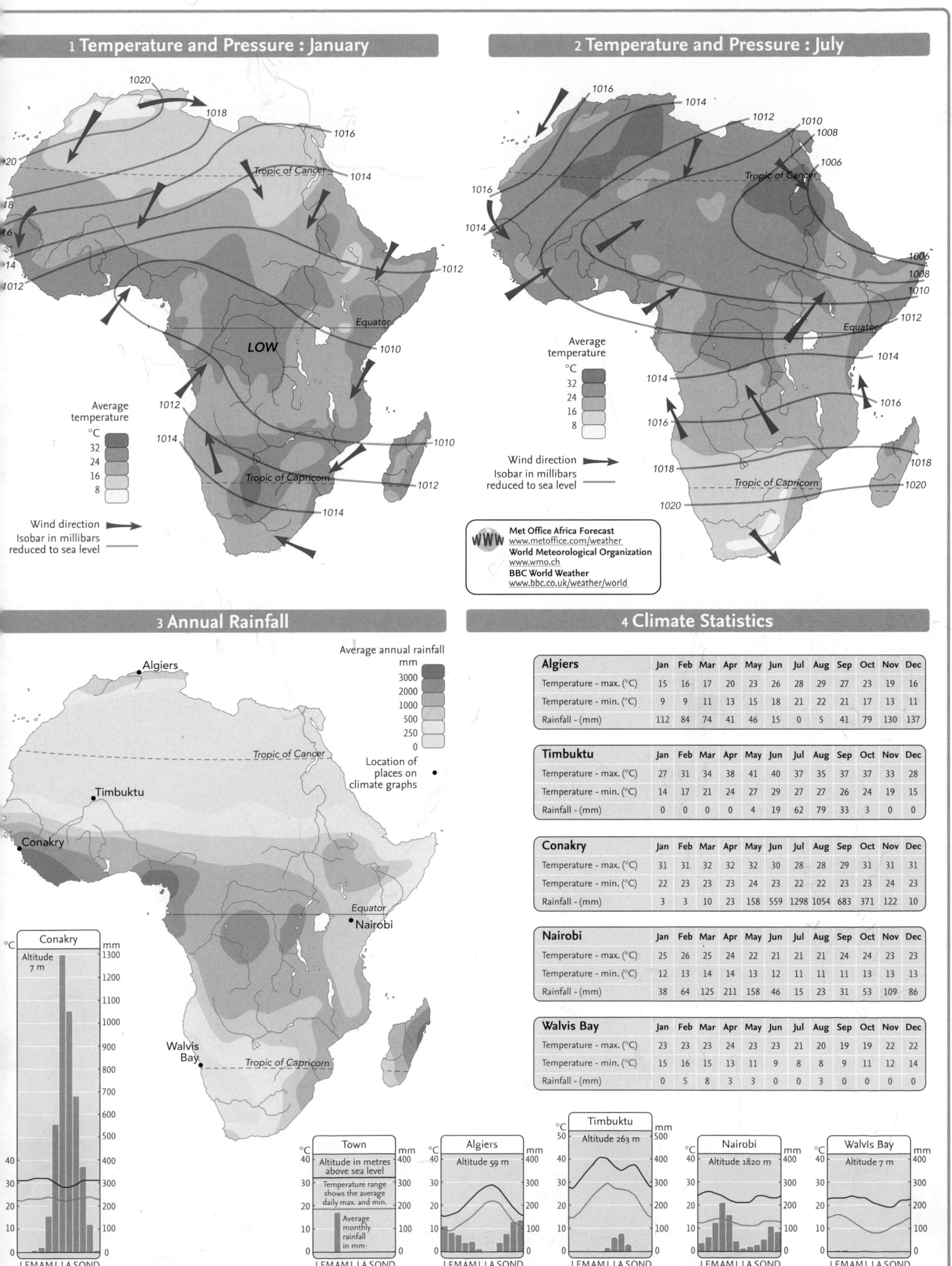

1 Temperature and Pressure : January

Average temperature
°C
32
24
16
8

Wind direction →
Isobar in millibars reduced to sea level ——

2 Temperature and Pressure : July

Average temperature
°C
32
24
16
8

Wind direction →
Isobar in millibars reduced to sea level ——

Met Office Africa Forecast
www.metoffice.com/weather
World Meteorological Organization
www.wmo.ch
BBC World Weather
www.bbc.co.uk/weather/world

3 Annual Rainfall

Average annual rainfall
mm
3000
2000
1000
500
250
0

Location of places on climate graphs •

Conakry
Altitude 7 m

4 Climate Statistics

Algiers	Jan	Feb	Mar	Apr	May	Jun	Jul	Aug	Sep	Oct	Nov	Dec
Temperature - max. (°C)	15	16	17	20	23	26	28	29	27	23	19	16
Temperature - min. (°C)	9	9	11	13	15	18	21	22	21	17	13	11
Rainfall - (mm)	112	84	74	41	46	15	0	5	41	79	130	137

Timbuktu	Jan	Feb	Mar	Apr	May	Jun	Jul	Aug	Sep	Oct	Nov	Dec
Temperature - max. (°C)	27	31	34	38	41	40	37	35	37	37	33	28
Temperature - min. (°C)	14	17	21	24	27	29	27	27	26	24	19	15
Rainfall - (mm)	0	0	0	0	4	19	62	79	33	3	0	0

Conakry	Jan	Feb	Mar	Apr	May	Jun	Jul	Aug	Sep	Oct	Nov	Dec
Temperature - max. (°C)	31	31	32	32	32	30	28	28	29	31	31	31
Temperature - min. (°C)	22	23	23	23	24	23	22	22	23	23	24	23
Rainfall - (mm)	3	3	10	23	158	559	1298	1054	683	371	122	10

Nairobi	Jan	Feb	Mar	Apr	May	Jun	Jul	Aug	Sep	Oct	Nov	Dec
Temperature - max. (°C)	25	26	25	24	22	21	21	21	24	24	23	23
Temperature - min. (°C)	12	13	14	14	13	12	11	11	11	13	13	13
Rainfall - (mm)	38	64	125	211	158	46	15	23	31	53	109	86

Walvis Bay	Jan	Feb	Mar	Apr	May	Jun	Jul	Aug	Sep	Oct	Nov	Dec
Temperature - max. (°C)	23	23	23	24	23	23	21	20	19	19	22	22
Temperature - min. (°C)	15	16	15	13	11	9	8	8	9	11	12	14
Rainfall - (mm)	0	5	8	3	3	0	0	3	0	0	0	0

Town
Altitude in metres above sea level
Temperature range shows the average daily max. and min.
Average monthly rainfall in mm·

Algiers
Altitude 59 m

Timbuktu
Altitude 263 m

Nairobi
Altitude 1820 m

Walvis Bay
Altitude 7 m

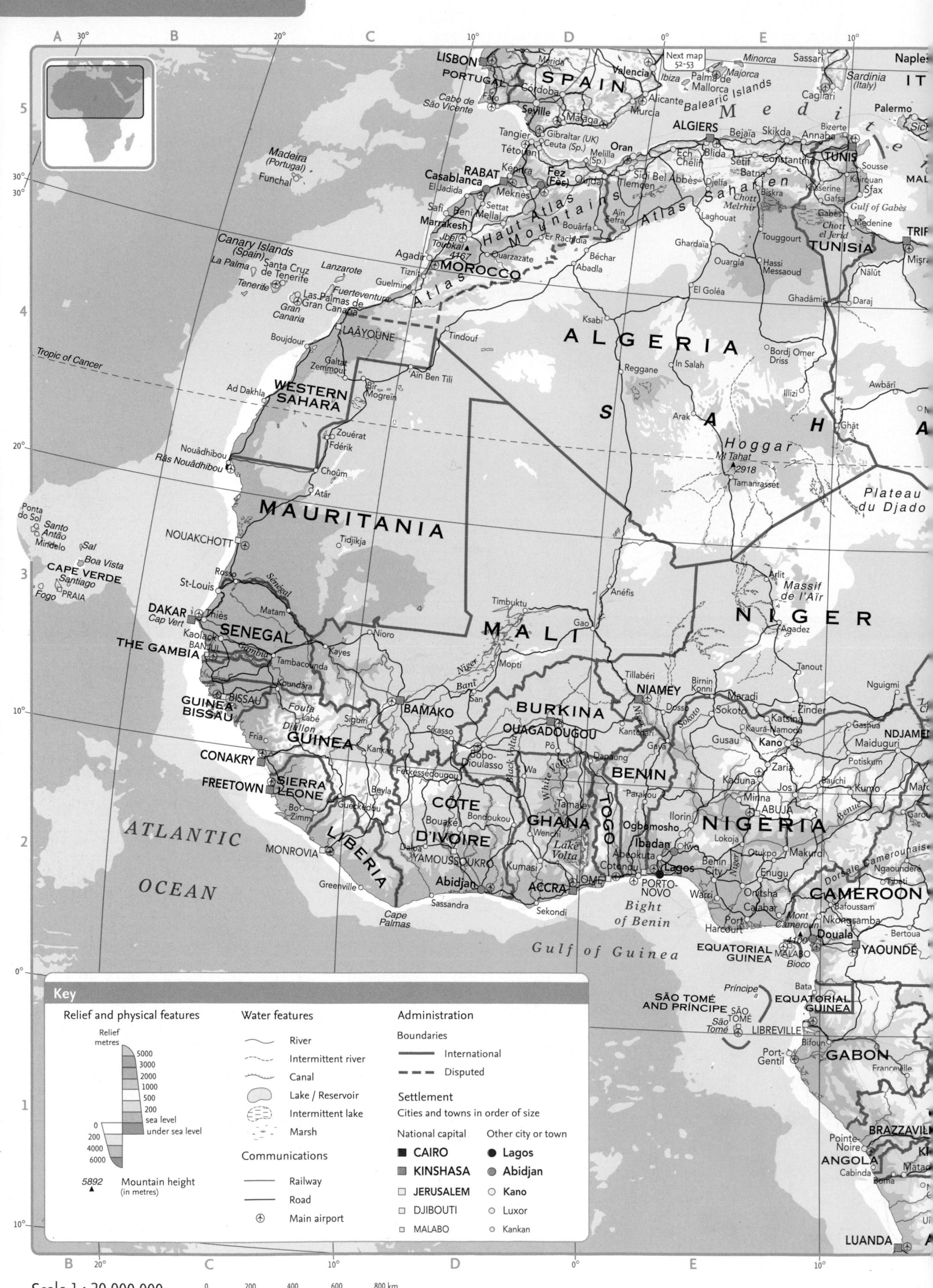

Key

Relief and physical features

Relief
metres
5000
3000
2000
1000
500
200
sea level
0
under sea level
200
4000
6000

5892 Mountain height
(in metres)

Communications

Railway

Road

⊕ Main airport

Water features

～ River

～ Intermittent river

～ Canal

◯ Lake / Reservoir

◯ Intermittent lake

◯ Marsh

Administration

Boundaries

— International

--- Disputed

Settlement

Cities and towns in order of size

National capital

■ CAIRO
■ KINSHASA
□ JERUSALEM
□ DJIBOUTI
□ MALABO

Other city or town

● Lagos
● Abidjan
◯ Kano
◯ Luxor
◯ Kankan

Scale 1 : 20 000 000

0   200   400   600   800 km

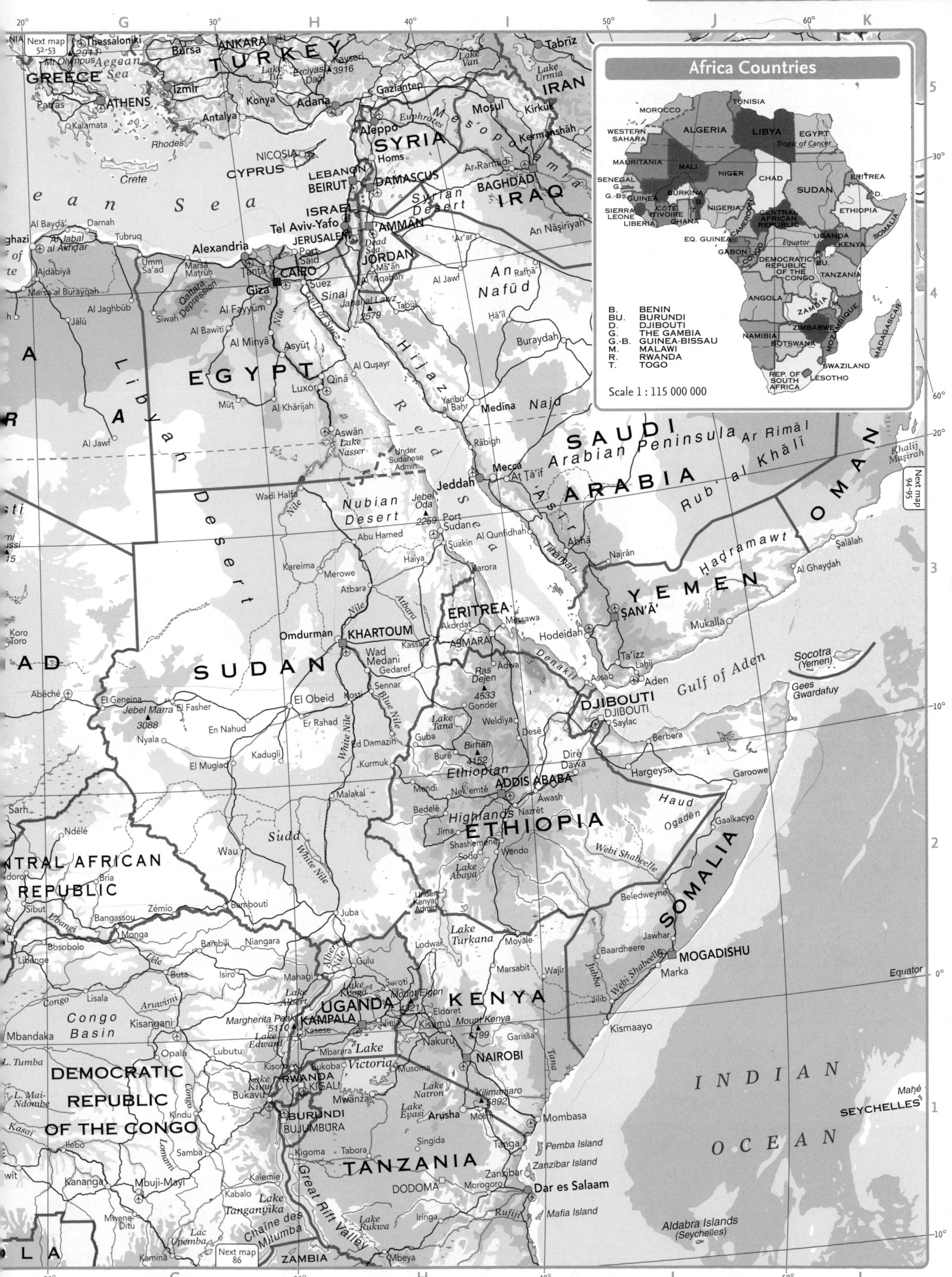

Africa Countries

MOROCCO
TUNISIA
WESTERN SAHARA
ALGERIA
LIBYA
EGYPT
MAURITANIA
MALI
NIGER
CHAD
SUDAN
ERITREA
SENEGAL
G.
BURKINA
D.
G.-B.
GUINEA
B.
NIGERIA
CÔTE D'IVOIRE
ETHIOPIA
SIERRA LEONE
LIBERIA
GHANA
CAMEROON
CENTRAL AFRICAN REPUBLIC
UGANDA
EQ. GUINEA
KENYA
SOMALIA
GABON
CONGO
DEMOCRATIC REPUBLIC OF THE CONGO
R.
BU.
TANZANIA
ANGOLA
ZAMBIA
M.
MOZAMBIQUE
NAMIBIA
ZIMBABWE
MADAGASCAR
BOTSWANA
SWAZILAND
REP. OF SOUTH AFRICA
LESOTHO
Tropic of Cancer
Equator

B.   BENIN
BU.   BURUNDI
D.   DJIBOUTI
G.   THE GAMBIA
G.-B. GUINEA-BISSAU
M.   MALAWI
R.   RWANDA
T.   TOGO

Scale 1 : 115 000 000

Lambert Azimuthal Equal Area projection

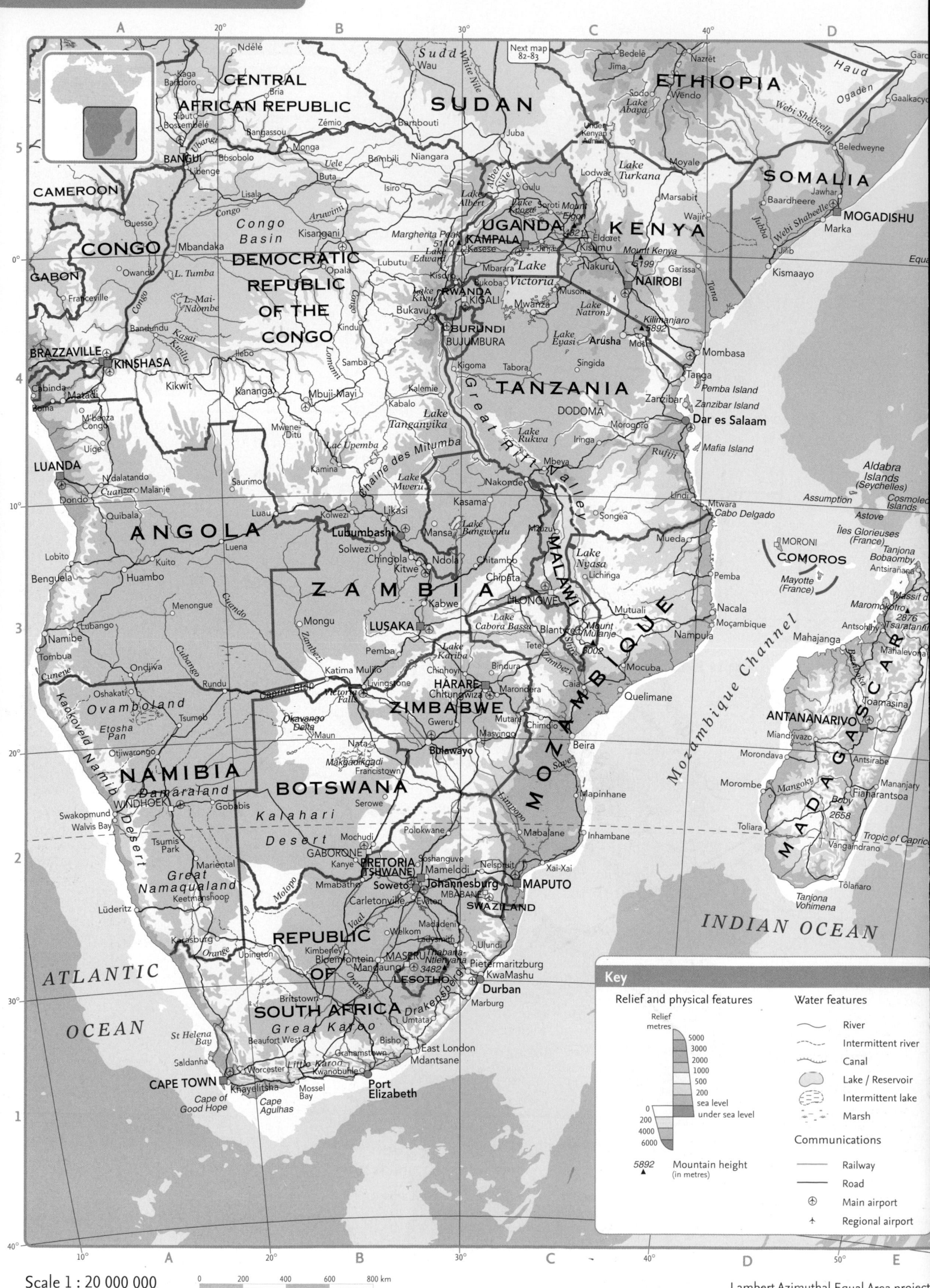

Key

Relief and physical features

Relief
metres

5000
3000
2000
1000
500
200
sea level
0
under sea level
200
4000
6000

▲ 5892 Mountain height
(in metres)

Water features

～～ River

--- Intermittent river

Canal

Lake / Reservoir

Intermittent lake

Marsh

Communications

Railway

Road

⊕ Main airport

↟ Regional airport

Scale 1 : 20 000 000

0   200   400   600   800 km

Lambert Azimuthal Equal Area projection

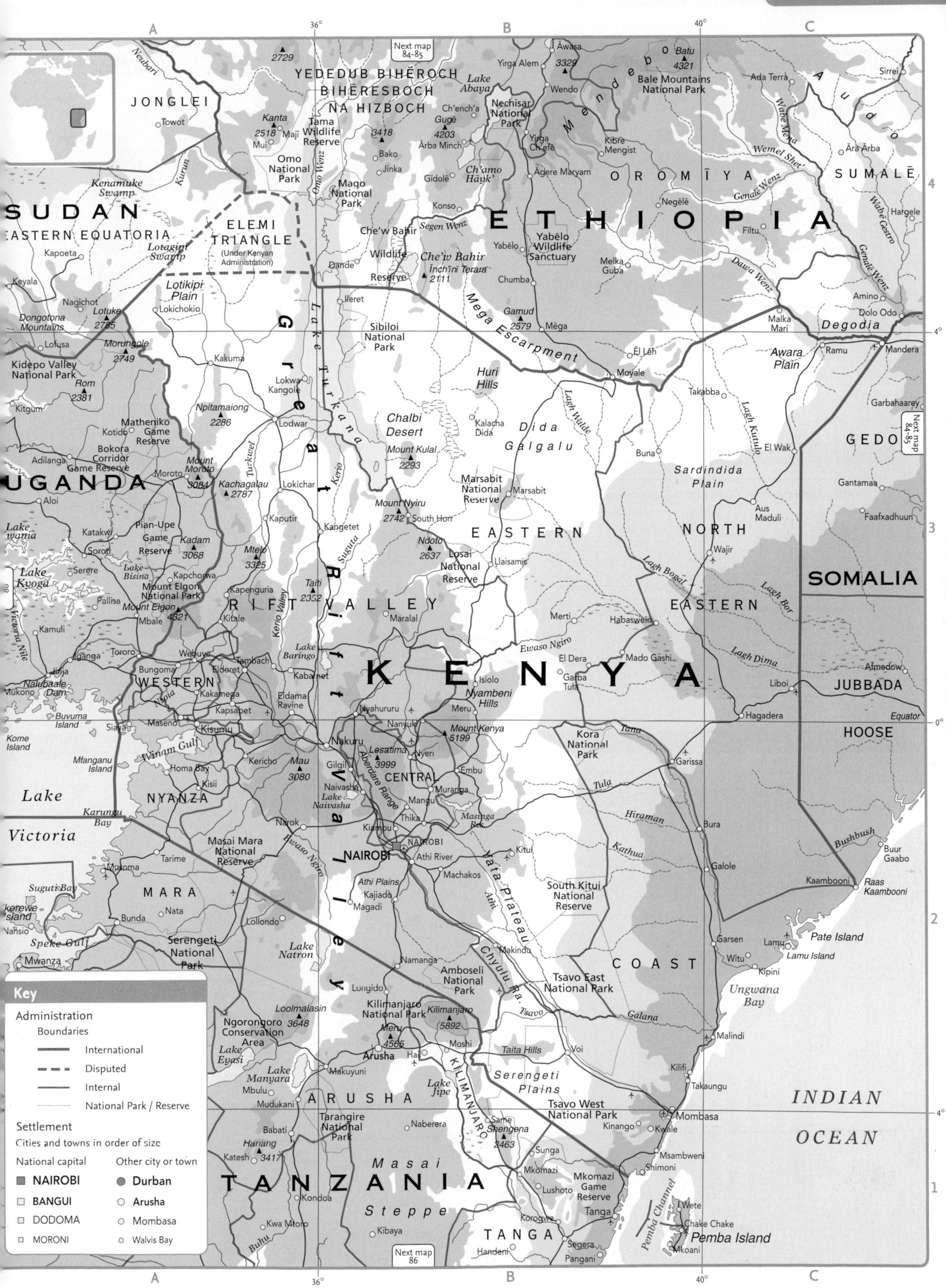

SUDAN

JONGLEI

EASTERN EQUATORIA

YEDEDUB BIHEROCH
BIHERESBOCH
NA HIZBOCH

ELEMI
TRIANGLE
(Under Kenyan
Administration)

ETHIOPIA

OROMIYA

SUMALE

UGANDA

KENYA

EASTERN

RIFT VALLEY

WESTERN

CENTRAL

NYANZA

Lake
Victoria

MARA

NAIROBI

NORTH

EASTERN

SOMALIA

GEDO

JUBBADA

HOOSE

COAST

TANZANIA

TANGA

ARUSHA

INDIAN

OCEAN

Pemba Island

Key

Administration

Boundaries

International

Disputed

Internal

National Park / Reserve

Settlement

Cities and towns in order of size

National capital   Other city or town

■ NAIROBI   ● Durban

□ BANGUI   ○ Arusha

□ DODOMA   ○ Mombasa

□ MORONI   ○ Walvis Bay

Scale 1 : 5 000 000

0   50   100   150   200 km

1 Population Density

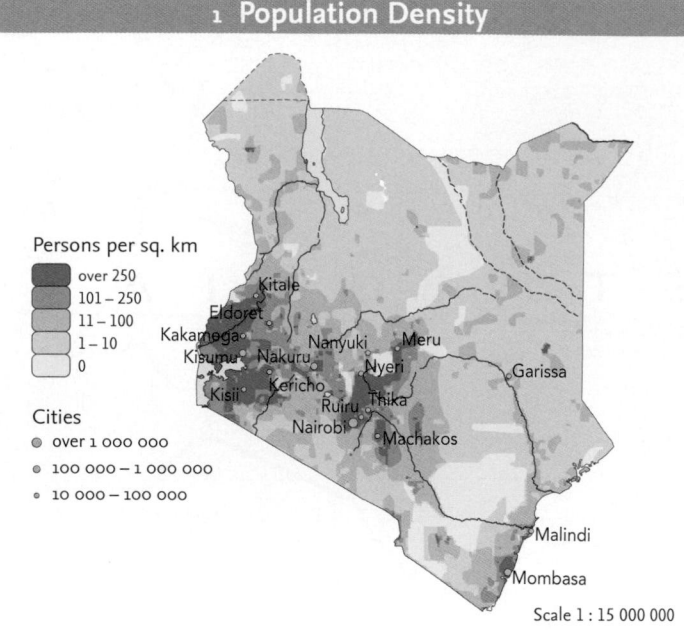

Persons per sq. km
- over 250
- 101 – 250
- 11 – 100
- 1 – 10
- 0

Cities
- over 1 000 000
- 100 000 – 1 000 000
- 10 000 – 100 000

Scale 1 : 15 000 000

2 Population Change

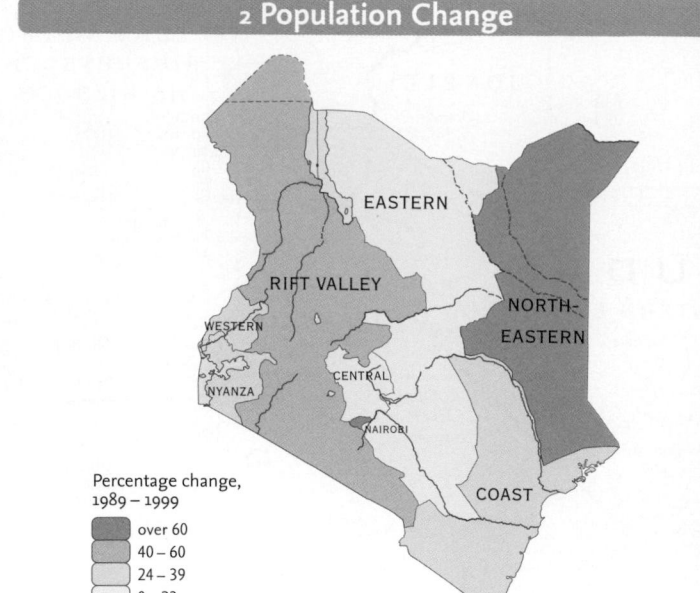

Percentage change,
1989 – 1999
- over 60
- 40 – 60
- 24 – 39
- 0 – 23

Scale 1 : 15 000 000

3 Urban Agglomerations

Urban agglomeration	1969 census	1989 census	1999 census
Nairobi	509 286	1 324 570	2 143 254
Mombasa	247 073	461 753	665 018
Kisumu	32 431	192 733	322 734
Nakuru	47 151	163 927	219 366
Eldoret	18 196	111 882	167 016

WWW
Government of Kenya
http://www.kenya.go.ke/
Kenya Tourist Board
www.magicalkenya.com
Central Bureau of Statistics
www.cbs.go.ke

4 Population Growth

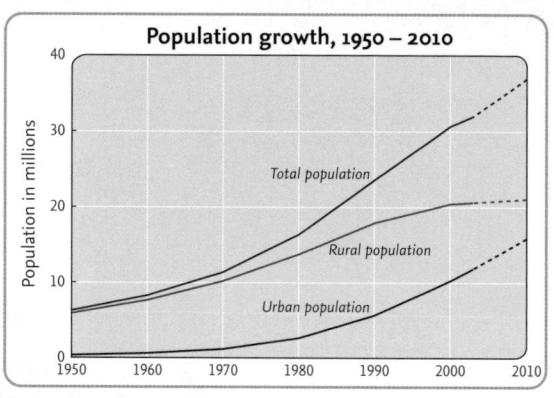

Population growth, 1950 – 2010

Total population

Rural population

Urban population

5 Tourism

Origin of tourists, 2004

- Europe
- North America
- Africa
- Asia
- Other

9%
5%
8%
9%
9%
69%

Total : 1 132 000

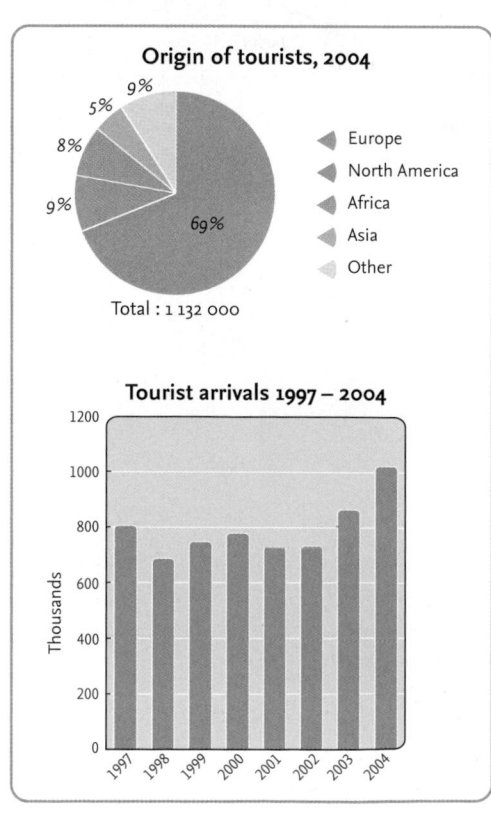

Tourist arrivals 1997 – 2004

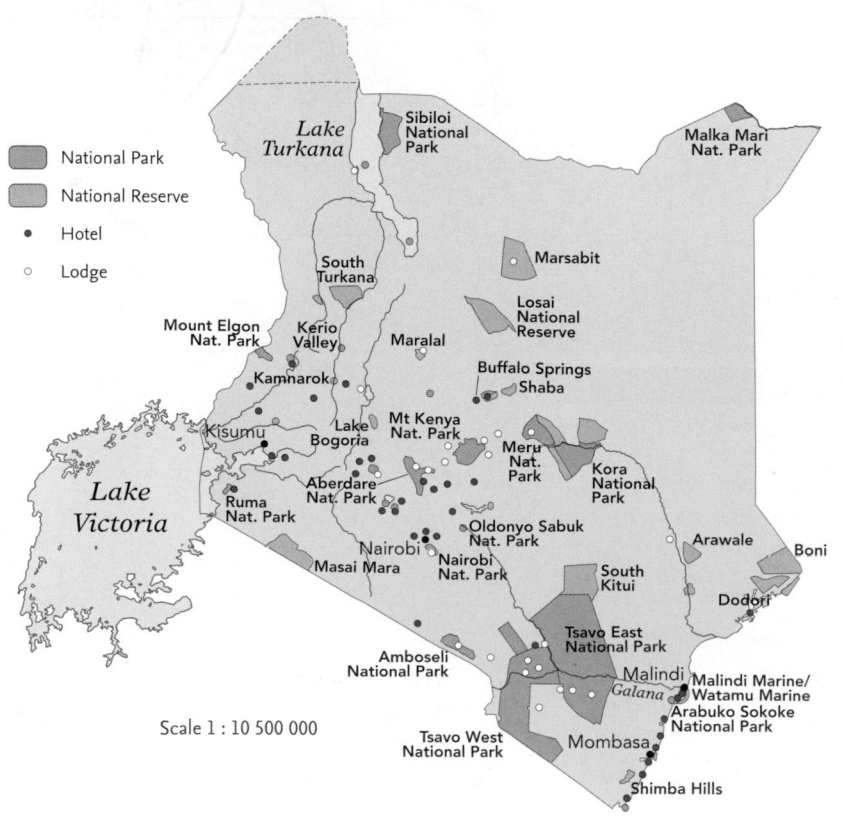

- National Park
- National Reserve
- Hotel
- Lodge

Scale 1 : 10 500 000

6 Economic Activity

SUGAR CANE
Kisumu
COFFEE
Nairobi
COCONUTS — Lamu
Malindi
FRUIT
Mombasa

Scale 1 : 15 000 000

• Major industrial centre

Manufacturing
☐ Iron and steel
☐ Oil refinery
☐ Shipbuilding
☐ Motor vehicles
☐ Mechanical engineering
○ Publishing / paper
○ Chemicals
○ Textiles
○ Food processing
○ Fish processing

Crops
▬ Cash crop producing area

7 Nairobi

Karura Forest
Nairobi River
Railway Station
City Centre
Ngong Road Forest
Wilson Aerodrome
Jomo Kenyatta International Airport
Nairobi National Park
Athi River

Scale 1 : 150 000

Residential
Industrial
Commercial
Transport
Government
Recreation
Other use
Agriculture
— City boundary
— Road
— Railway

WWW Nairobi City Council
www.nairobicity.org
Ministry of Trade and Industry
www.tradeandindustry.go.ke
UN Commodity Trade Statistics
unstats.un.org/unsd/comtrade

8 Trade

USA
UNITED KINGDOM
NETHERLANDS
GERMANY
FRANCE
EGYPT
SAUDI ARABIA
UAE
BAHRAIN
PAKISTAN
INDIA
CHINA
JAPAN
UGANDA
RWANDA
KENYA
TANZANIA
SOUTH AFRICA
OTHERS

Imports to Kenya, 2004 (% of total imports)
→ over 15%
→ 5 – 15%
→ 2.5 – 5%

Exports from Kenya, 2004 (% of total exports)
→ over 15%
→ 5 – 15%
→ 2.5 – 5%

Scale 1 : 175 000 000

Import commodities, 2004
Mineral fuels 24% | Iron and Steel 6% | Electrical and electronic equipment 6%
Others 48%
Machinery and mechanical appliances 8% | Vehicles 8%
Total US$: 4563 million

Export commodities, 2004
Mineral fuels 23% | Fruit and vegetables 6%
Others 40%
Coffee, tea and spices 21% | Live plants 10%
Total US$: 2683 million

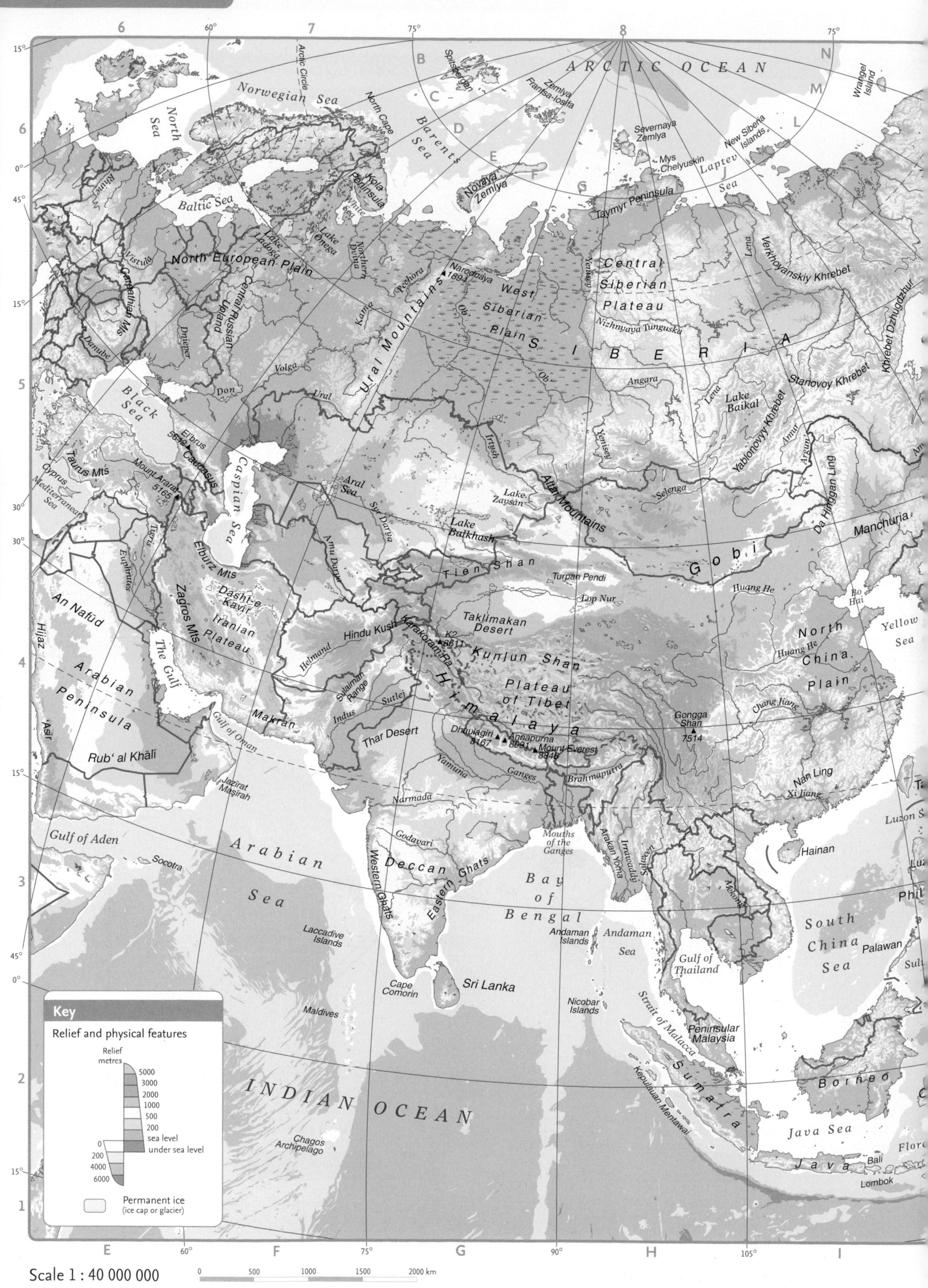

Key

Relief and physical features

Relief
metres
5000
3000
2000
1000
500
200
sea level
0
under sea level
200
4000
6000

Permanent ice
(ice cap or glacier)

Scale 1 : 40 000 000

0   500   1000   1500   2000 km

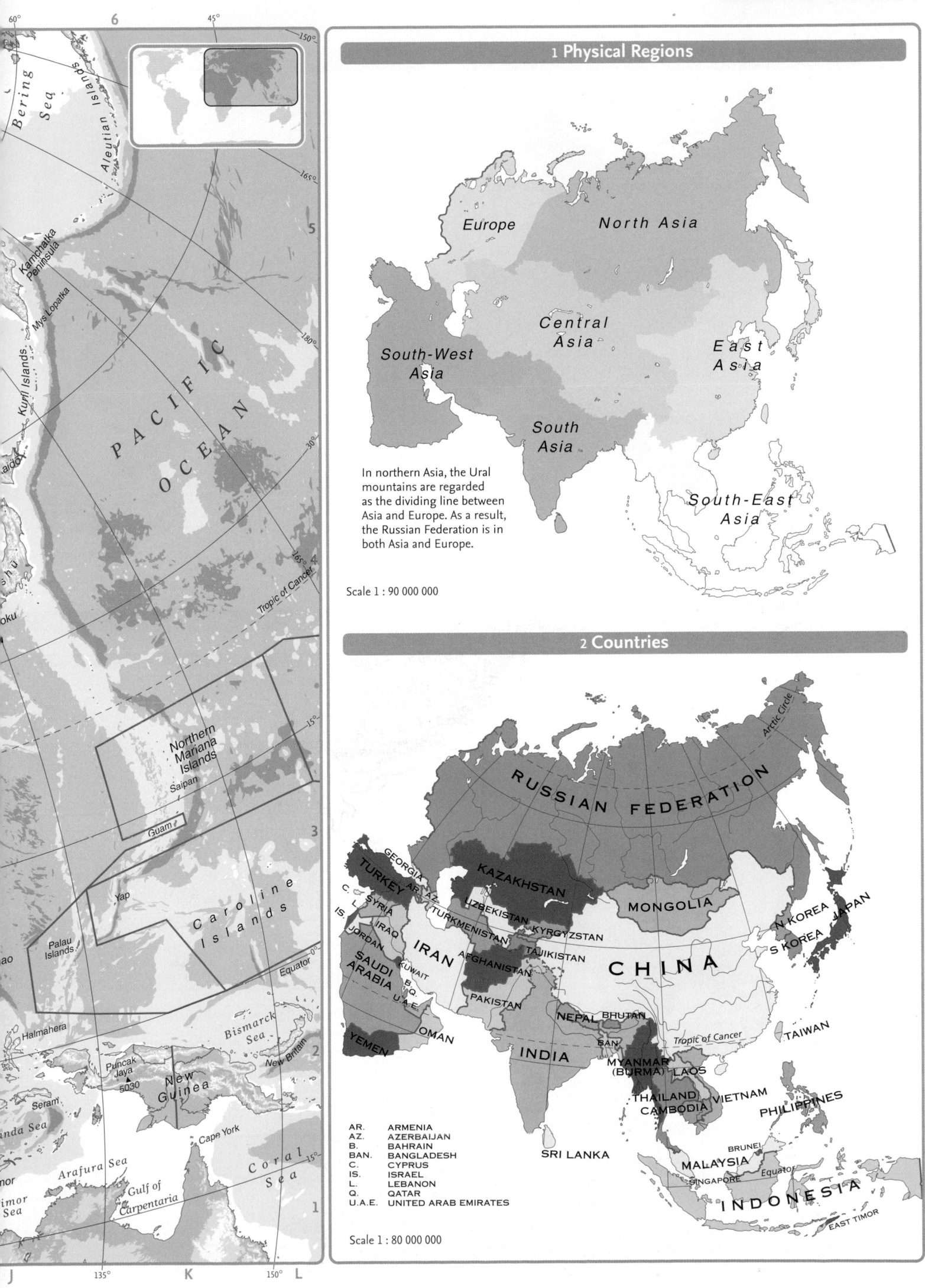

1 Physical Regions

In northern Asia, the Ural mountains are regarded as the dividing line between Asia and Europe. As a result, the Russian Federation is in both Asia and Europe.

Scale 1 : 90 000 000

2 Countries

AR.   ARMENIA
AZ.   AZERBAIJAN
B.   BAHRAIN
BAN.   BANGLADESH
C.   CYPRUS
IS.   ISRAEL
L.   LEBANON
Q.   QATAR
U.A.E. UNITED ARAB EMIRATES

Scale 1 : 80 000 000

Lambert Azimuthal Equal Area projection

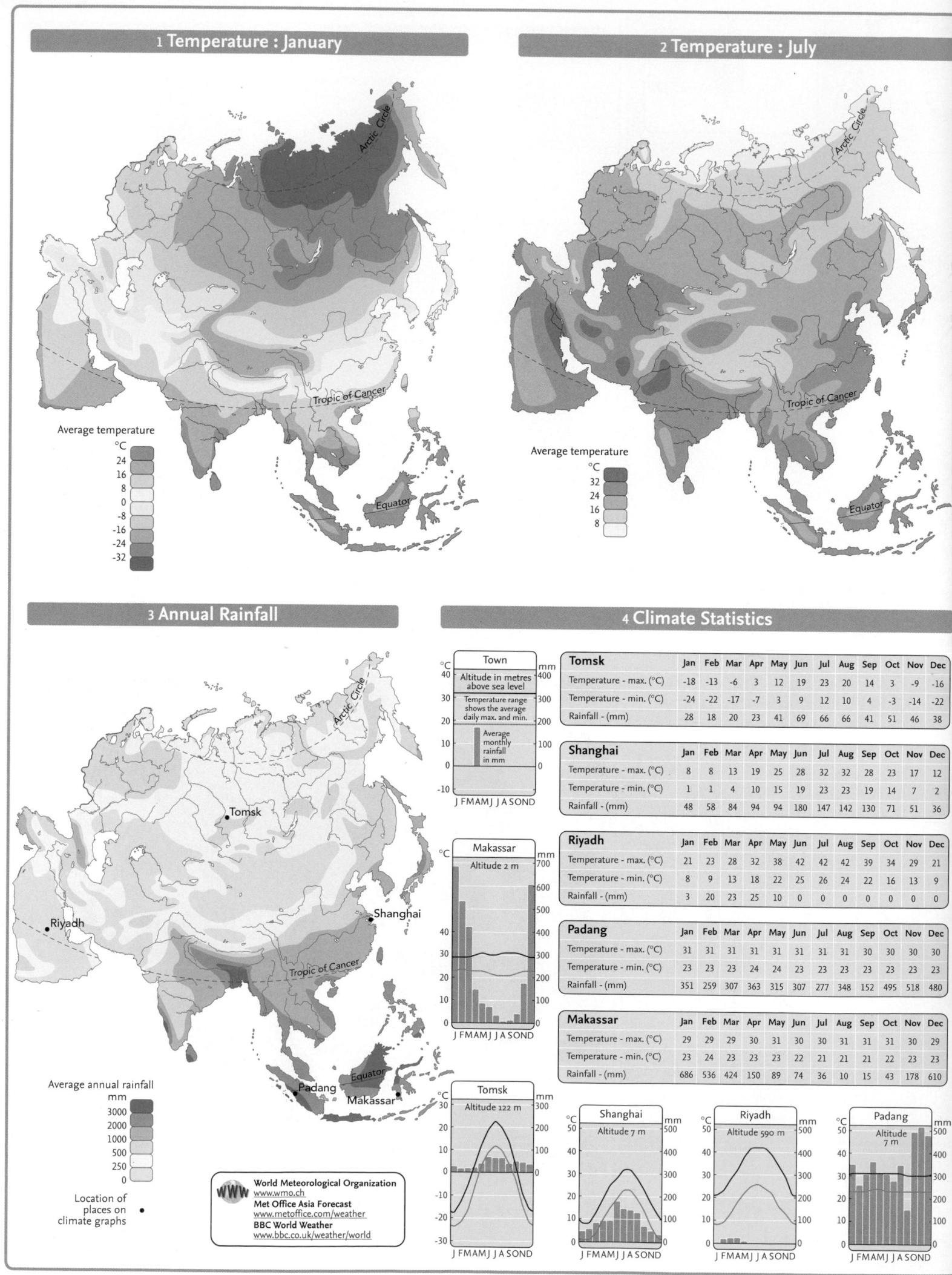

1 Temperature : January

Average temperature
°C
24
16
8
0
-8
-16
-24
-32

2 Temperature : July

Average temperature
°C
32
24
16
8

3 Annual Rainfall

Average annual rainfall
mm
3000
2000
1000
500
250
0

Location of
places on
climate graphs   •

World Meteorological Organization
www.wmo.ch
Met Office Asia Forecast
www.metoffice.com/weather
BBC World Weather
www.bbc.co.uk/weather/world

4 Climate Statistics

Tomsk	Jan	Feb	Mar	Apr	May	Jun	Jul	Aug	Sep	Oct	Nov	Dec
Temperature - max. (°C)	-18	-13	-6	3	12	19	23	20	14	3	-9	-16
Temperature - min. (°C)	-24	-22	-17	-7	3	9	12	10	4	-3	-14	-22
Rainfall - (mm)	28	18	20	23	41	69	66	66	41	51	46	38

Shanghai	Jan	Feb	Mar	Apr	May	Jun	Jul	Aug	Sep	Oct	Nov	Dec
Temperature - max. (°C)	8	8	13	19	25	28	32	32	28	23	17	12
Temperature - min. (°C)	1	1	4	10	15	19	23	23	19	14	7	2
Rainfall - (mm)	48	58	84	94	94	180	147	142	130	71	51	36

Riyadh	Jan	Feb	Mar	Apr	May	Jun	Jul	Aug	Sep	Oct	Nov	Dec
Temperature - max. (°C)	21	23	28	32	38	42	42	42	39	34	29	21
Temperature - min. (°C)	8	9	13	18	22	25	26	24	22	16	13	9
Rainfall - (mm)	3	20	23	25	10	0	0	0	0	0	0	0

Padang	Jan	Feb	Mar	Apr	May	Jun	Jul	Aug	Sep	Oct	Nov	Dec
Temperature - max. (°C)	31	31	31	31	31	31	31	31	30	30	30	30
Temperature - min. (°C)	23	23	23	24	24	23	23	23	23	23	23	23
Rainfall - (mm)	351	259	307	363	315	307	277	348	152	495	518	480

Makassar	Jan	Feb	Mar	Apr	May	Jun	Jul	Aug	Sep	Oct	Nov	Dec
Temperature - max. (°C)	29	29	29	30	31	30	30	31	31	31	30	29
Temperature - min. (°C)	23	24	23	23	23	22	21	21	21	22	23	23
Rainfall - (mm)	686	536	424	150	89	74	36	10	15	43	178	610

Town
°C / mm
40 / 400
Altitude in metres
above sea level
30 / 300
Temperature range
shows the average
daily max. and min.
20 / 200
Average
monthly
rainfall
in mm
10 / 100
0 / 0
-10
J F M A M J J A S O N D

Makassar
Altitude 2 m
°C / mm
700 / 600 / 500 / 400 / 300 / 200 / 100 / 0
J F M A M J J A S O N D

Tomsk
Altitude 122 m
°C / mm
30 / 300
20 / 200
10 / 100
0 / 0
-10
-20
-30
J F M A M J J A S O N D

Shanghai
Altitude 7 m
°C / mm
50 / 500
40 / 400
30 / 300
20 / 200
10 / 100
0 / 0
J F M A M J J A S O N D

Riyadh
Altitude 590 m
°C / mm
50 / 500
40 / 400
30 / 300
20 / 200
10 / 100
0 / 0
J F M A M J J A S O N D

Padang
Altitude 7 m
°C / mm
50 / 500
40 / 400
30 / 300
20 / 200
10 / 100
0 / 0
J F M A M J J A S O N D

Scale 1 : 100 000 000

0   1000   2000   3000   4000 km

Lambert Azimuthal Equal Area project

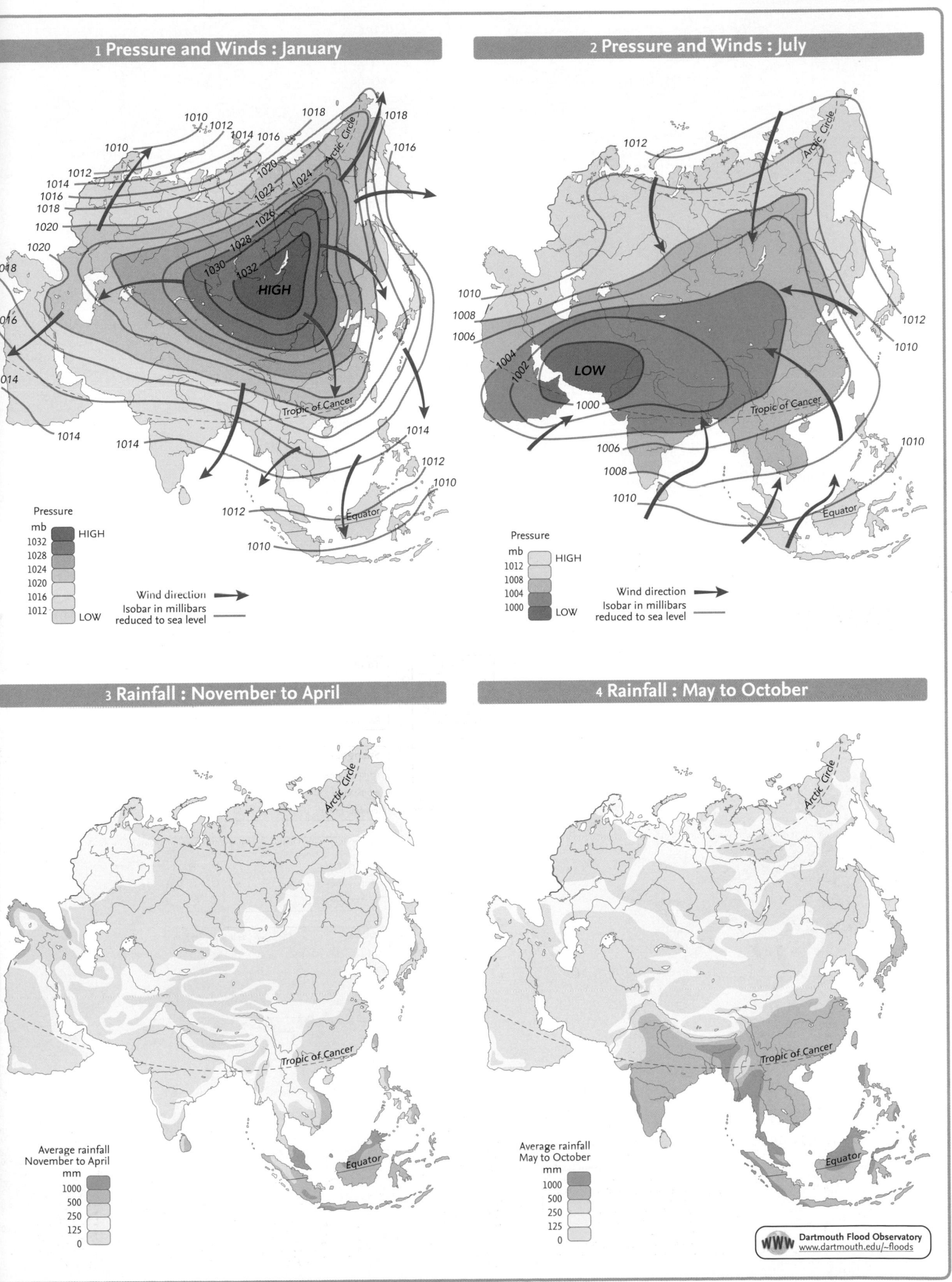

1 Pressure and Winds : January

1010 1012 1014 1016 1018 1018
1010
1012 1020 1016
1014 1022 1024
1016 1026
1018 1028
1020 1030
1020 1032
018 **HIGH**
016
014 Tropic of Cancer
1014
1014 1014
1012
1012
1010
1012 Equator
1010

Pressure
mb
1032 HIGH
1028
1024
1020
1016
1012 LOW

Wind direction
Isobar in millibars
reduced to sea level

2 Pressure and Winds : July

1012
Arctic Circle
1010
1008 1012
1006 1010
1004
1002 **LOW**
1000 Tropic of Cancer
1006
1008
1010 Equator
1010

Pressure
mb
1012 HIGH
1008
1004
1000 LOW

Wind direction
Isobar in millibars
reduced to sea level

3 Rainfall : November to April

Arctic Circle

Tropic of Cancer

Equator

Average rainfall
November to April
mm
1000
500
250
125
0

4 Rainfall : May to October

Arctic Circle

Tropic of Cancer

Equator

Average rainfall
May to October
mm
1000
500
250
125
0

WWW Dartmouth Flood Observatory
www.dartmouth.edu/~floods

cale 1 : 100 000 000   0   1000   2000   3000   4000 km

Lambert Azimuthal Equal Area projection

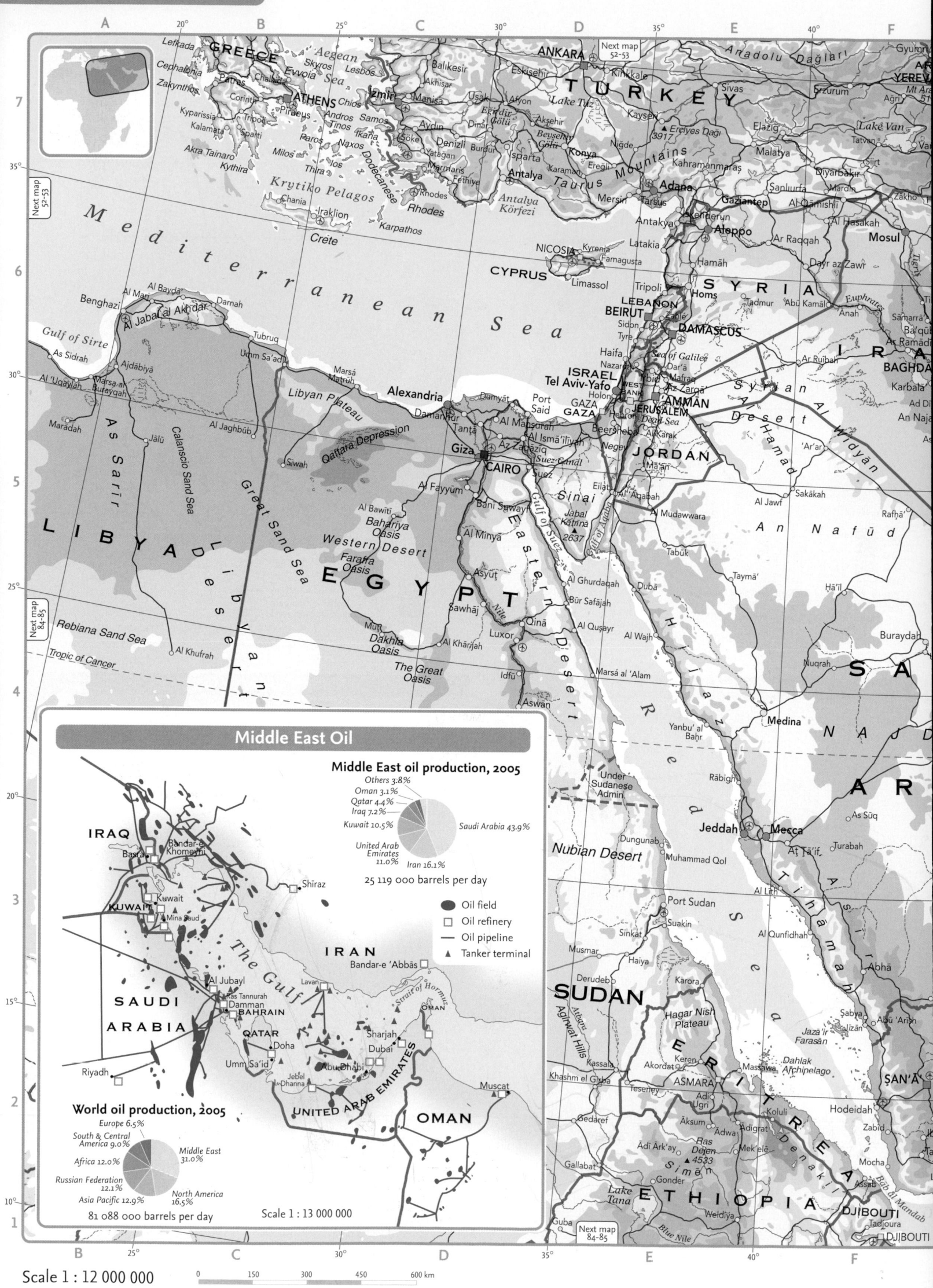

Middle East Oil

Middle East oil production, 2005

Others 3.8%
Oman 3.1%
Qatar 4.4%
Iraq 7.2%
Kuwait 10.5%
Saudi Arabia 43.9%
United Arab Emirates 11.0%
Iran 16.1%

25 119 000 barrels per day

- ⬭ Oil field
- ☐ Oil refinery
- — Oil pipeline
- ▲ Tanker terminal

World oil production, 2005

Europe 6.5%
South & Central America 9.0%
Africa 12.0%
Russian Federation 12.1%
Asia Pacific 12.9%
Middle East 31.0%
North America 16.5%

81 088 000 barrels per day

Scale 1 : 13 000 000

Scale 1 : 12 000 000

0   150   300   450   600 km

Karakum Desert

TURKMENISTAN

UZBEKISTAN

DUSHANBE TAJIKISTAN

Pamir

Hindu Kush

AFGHANISTAN

PAKISTAN

INDIA

IRAN

Caspian Sea

Elburz Mountains

Dasht-e Kavir

Dasht-e Lut

Dasht-e Margow

Dasht-e Arbu Lut

Zagros Mountains

The Gulf

KUWAIT

BAHRAIN MANAMA

QATAR DOHA

UNITED ARAB EMIRATES

ABU DHABI

Strait of Hormuz

Gulf of Oman

OMAN

MUSCAT

Makran

Ar Rimal

Rub' al Khālī

O M A N

Arabian Sea

Khalij Maşīrah

Jazīrat Maşīrah

Gulf of Aden

Socotra (Yemen)

Hadramawt

Selected cities / towns: BAKU, RBAIJAN, Al Bayramli, Salyan, Lānkārān, Āstārā, Aher, Sarāb, Ardabīl, Mīāneh, Tabrīz, Rasht, Bandar-e Anzali, Lāhījān, Zanjān, Qazvīn, Karaj, TEHRĀN, Qom, Kāshān, Arāk, Borūjerd, Malāyer, Hamadān, Nahāvand, Esfahān, Najafābād, Yazd, Shiraz, Ahvāz, Abādān, Basra, KUWAIT, RIYADH, Dammām, Dhahran, Abqaiq, Al Hufūf

Turkmenbashi, Nebitdag, Cheleken, Gumdag, Gyzylarbat, Bakharden, ASHGABAT, Bojnvrd, Gonbad-e Kavus, Gorgān, Mashhad, Neyshābūr, Sabzevār, Damghan, Semnān, Ferdows, Tabas, Bīrjand, Qāyen, Kermān, Zāhedān, Bandar-e 'Abbās, Mīnāb, Jāsk, Chābahār, Gwadar, Pasni, Jiwani, Turbat, Mashhad

Turkmenabat, Qarshi, Buxoro, Termiz, Mazar-e Sharīf, Sheberghān, KĀBUL, Peshawar, ISLAMABAD, Rawalpindi, Herat, Kandahār, Quetta, Multan, Faisalabad

DUSHANBE, Kūlob, Khorugh, Feyzābad, Chitral, Gilgit

Mountain heights: 5601 (Qolleh-ye Damāvand), 5426, 4074, 4432 (Kūh-e Dīnār), 4420, 4425

Albers Conic Equal Area projection

Next map 58-59
Next map 96-97

Key

Relief and physical features

Relief metres

5000
3000
2000
1000
500
200
0 sea level
under sea level
200
4000
6000

▲ 5601 Mountain height (in metres)

Permanent ice (ice cap or glacier)

Water features

River

Intermittent river

Lake / Reservoir

Intermittent lake

Marsh

Communications

Railway

Road

⊕ Main airport

Administration

Boundaries

International

Disputed

Ceasefire line

Settlement

Cities and towns in order of size

National capital

■ CAIRO
■ BAGHDĀD
□ KUWAIT
□ ASMARA

Other city or town

● Adana
○ Medina
○ Port Sudan
○ Kerma

WWW Organization of the Petroleum Exporting Countries www.opec.org
World Energy Council www.worldenergy.org
BP Statistical Review of World Energy www.bp.com

Key

Relief and physical features

Relief metres
5000
3000
2000
1000
500
200
0 sea level
under sea level
200
4000
6000

8848 ▲ Mountain height (in metres)

Permanent ice (ice cap or glacier)

Water features

River
Intermittent river
Canal
Lake / Reservoir
Intermittent lake
Marsh

Communications

Railway
Road
⊕ Main airport

Administration

Boundaries
International
Disputed
Internal
Ceasefire line

Settlement

Cities and towns in order of size

National capital
■ DHAKA
■ BANGKOK
□ ISLAMABAD
□ KATHMANDU
□ THIMPHU

Other city or town
● Mumbai
● Jaipur
○ Ranchi
○ Jammu
○ Ghazni

Scale 1 : 15 000 000

0   200   400   600   800 km

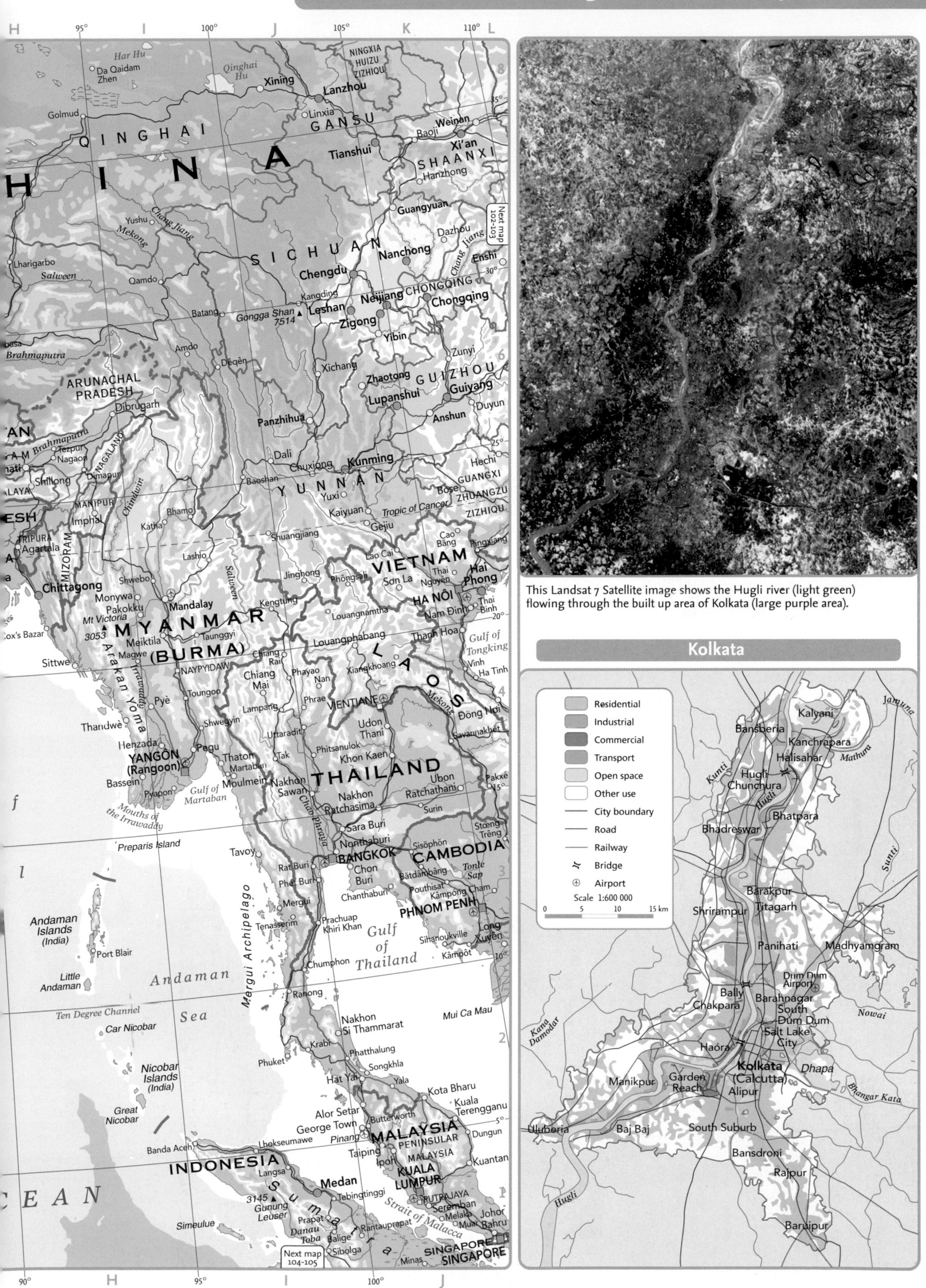

This Landsat 7 Satellite image shows the Hugli river (light green) flowing through the built up area of Kolkata (large purple area).

Kolkata

Residential
Industrial
Commercial
Transport
Open space
Other use
City boundary
Road
Railway
Bridge
Airport
Scale 1:600 000

Lambert Azimuthal Equal Area projection

1 Population Density

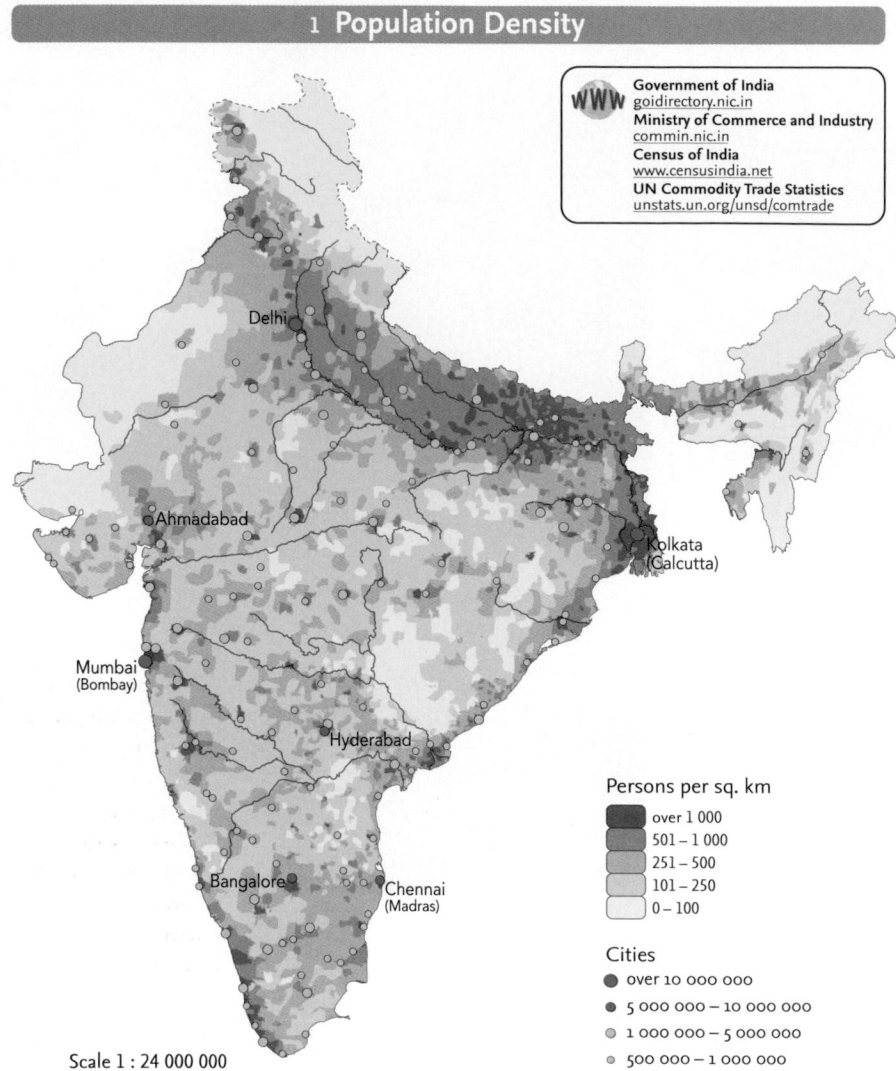

www Government of India
goidirectory.nic.in
Ministry of Commerce and Industry
commin.nic.in
Census of India
www.censusindia.net
UN Commodity Trade Statistics
unstats.un.org/unsd/comtrade

Delhi
Ahmadabad
Kolkata (Calcutta)
Mumbai (Bombay)
Hyderabad
Bangalore
Chennai (Madras)

Persons per sq. km
- over 1 000
- 501 – 1 000
- 251 – 500
- 101 – 250
- 0 – 100

Cities
- over 10 000 000
- 5 000 000 – 10 000 000
- 1 000 000 – 5 000 000
- 500 000 – 1 000 000

Scale 1 : 24 000 000

2 Million Cities

Million city	2005 (projected)
Mumbai (Bombay)	18 337 000
Delhi	15 335 000
Kolkata (Calcutta)	14 299 000
Chennai (Madras)	6 915 000
Bangalore	6 533 000
Hyderabad	6 146 000
Ahmadabad	5 171 000
Pune	4 485 000
Surat	3 672 000
Kanpur	3 040 000
Jaipur	2 796 000
Lucknow	2 589 000
Nagpur	2 359 000
Patna	2 066 000
Indore	1 942 000
Vadodara	1 686 000
Bhopal	1 667 000
Coimbatore	1 628 000
Ludhiana	1 583 000
Visakhapatnam	1 468 000
Kochi	1 461 000
Nashik	1 408 000
Meerut	1 340 000
Faridabad	1 331 000
Varanasi	1 300 000
Ghaziabad	1 277 000
Asansol	1 272 000
Jamshedpur	1 246 000
Madurai	1 245 000
Jabalpur	1 234 000
Rajkot	1 205 000
Dhanbad	1 195 000
Allahabad	1 153 000
Amritsar	1 121 000
Srinagar	1 093 000
Vijayawada	1 093 000
Aurangabad	1 065 000
Durg-Bhilainagar	1 049 000
Solapur	1 012 000

3 Population Change

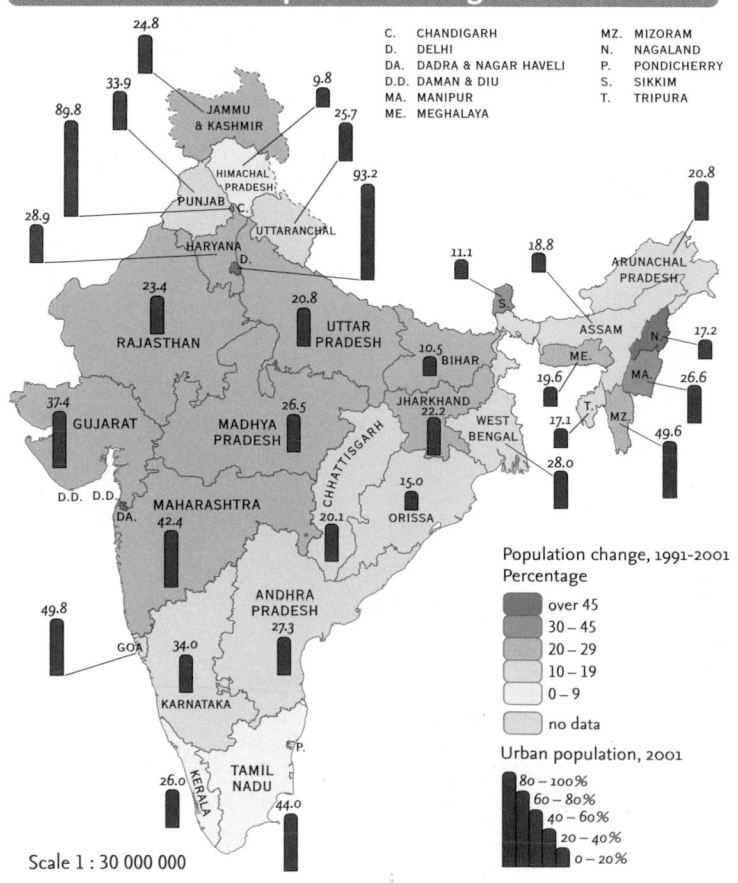

C.	CHANDIGARH	MZ.	MIZORAM
D.	DELHI	N.	NAGALAND
DA.	DADRA & NAGAR HAVELI	P.	PONDICHERRY
D.D.	DAMAN & DIU	S.	SIKKIM
MA.	MANIPUR	T.	TRIPURA
ME.	MEGHALAYA		

Population change, 1991-2001
Percentage
- over 45
- 30 – 45
- 20 – 29
- 10 – 19
- 0 – 9
- no data

Urban population, 2001
- 80 – 100%
- 60 – 80%
- 40 – 60%
- 20 – 40%
- 0 – 20%

Scale 1 : 30 000 000

4 Literacy

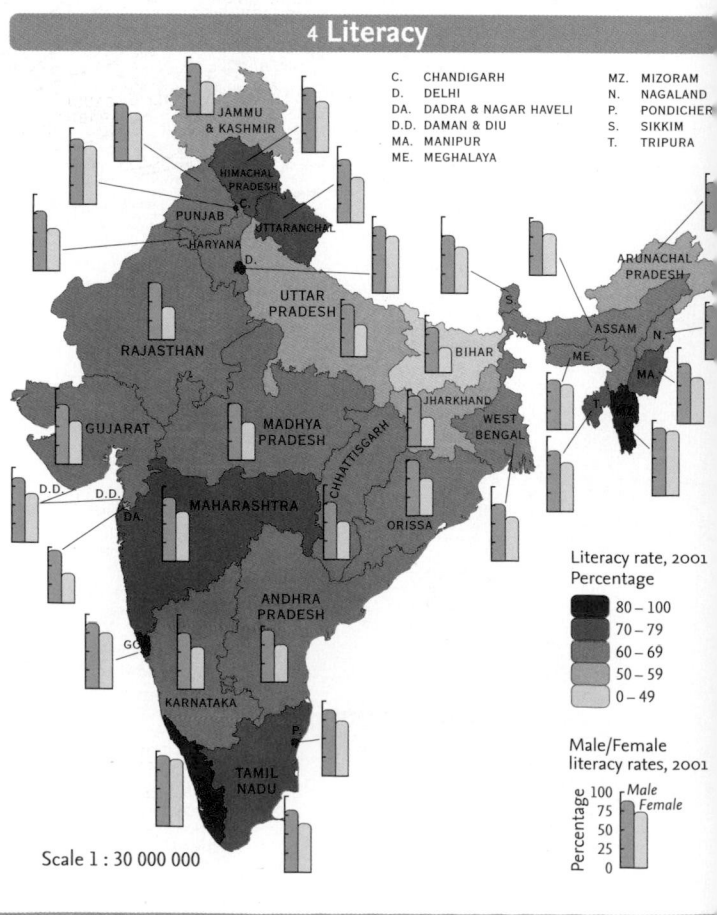

C.	CHANDIGARH	MZ.	MIZORAM
D.	DELHI	N.	NAGALAND
DA.	DADRA & NAGAR HAVELI	P.	PONDICHERRY
D.D.	DAMAN & DIU	S.	SIKKIM
MA.	MANIPUR	T.	TRIPURA
ME.	MEGHALAYA		

Literacy rate, 2001
Percentage
- 80 – 100
- 70 – 79
- 60 – 69
- 50 – 59
- 0 – 49

**Male/Female
literacy rates, 2001**
Percentage 100 / 75 / 50 / 25 / 0
Male / Female

Scale 1 : 30 000 000

5 Tourism

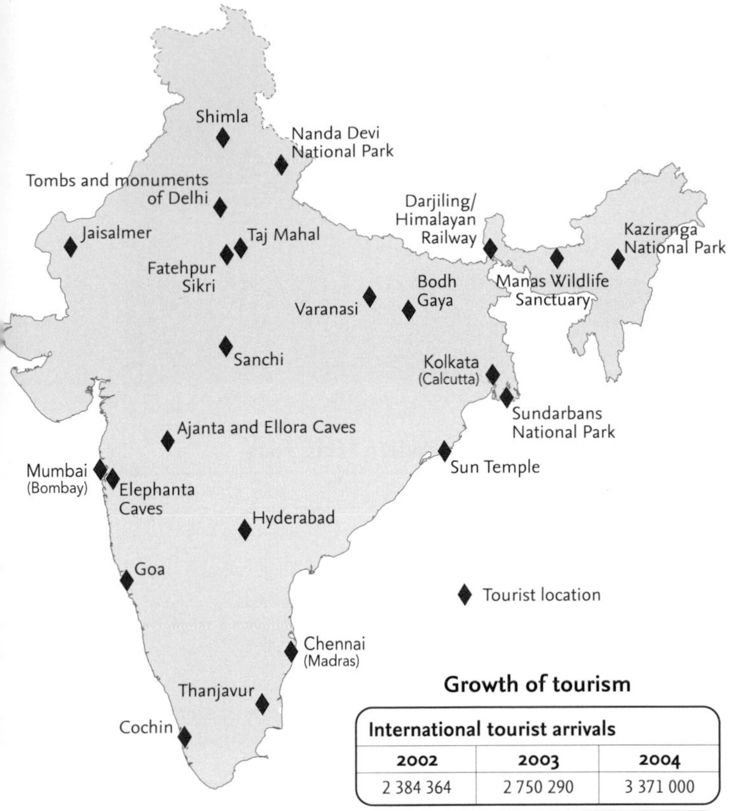

Shimla

Nanda Devi
National Park

Tombs and monuments
of Delhi

Darjiling/
Himalayan
Railway

Kaziranga
National Park

Jaisalmer

Taj Mahal

Fatehpur
Sikri

Manas Wildlife
Sanctuary

Bodh
Gaya

Varanasi

Sanchi

Kolkata
(Calcutta)

Ajanta and Ellora Caves

Sundarbans
National Park

Mumbai
(Bombay)

Sun Temple

Elephanta
Caves

Hyderabad

Goa

Chennai
(Madras)

Thanjavur

Cochin

◆ Tourist location

Growth of tourism

International tourist arrivals		
2002	2003	2004
2 384 364	2 750 290	3 371 000

Tourist receipts US$		
2002	2003	2004
2 923 000 000	3 602 880 000	4 769 000 000

Scale 1 : 30 000 000

6 Economic Activity

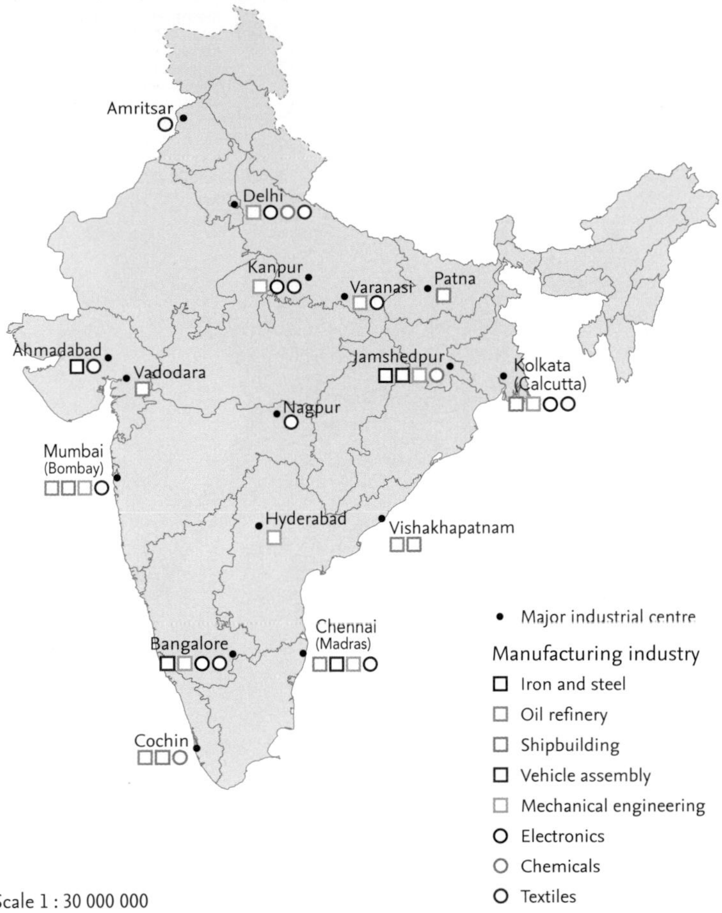

Amritsar

Delhi

Kanpur

Varanasi

Patna

Ahmadabad

Vadodara

Jamshedpur

Kolkata
(Calcutta)

Nagpur

Mumbai
(Bombay)

Hyderabad

Vishakhapatnam

Bangalore

Chennai
(Madras)

Cochin

● Major industrial centre

Manufacturing industry

☐ Iron and steel

☐ Oil refinery

☐ Shipbuilding

☐ Vehicle assembly

☐ Mechanical engineering

○ Electronics

○ Chemicals

○ Textiles

Scale 1 : 30 000 000

7 Trade

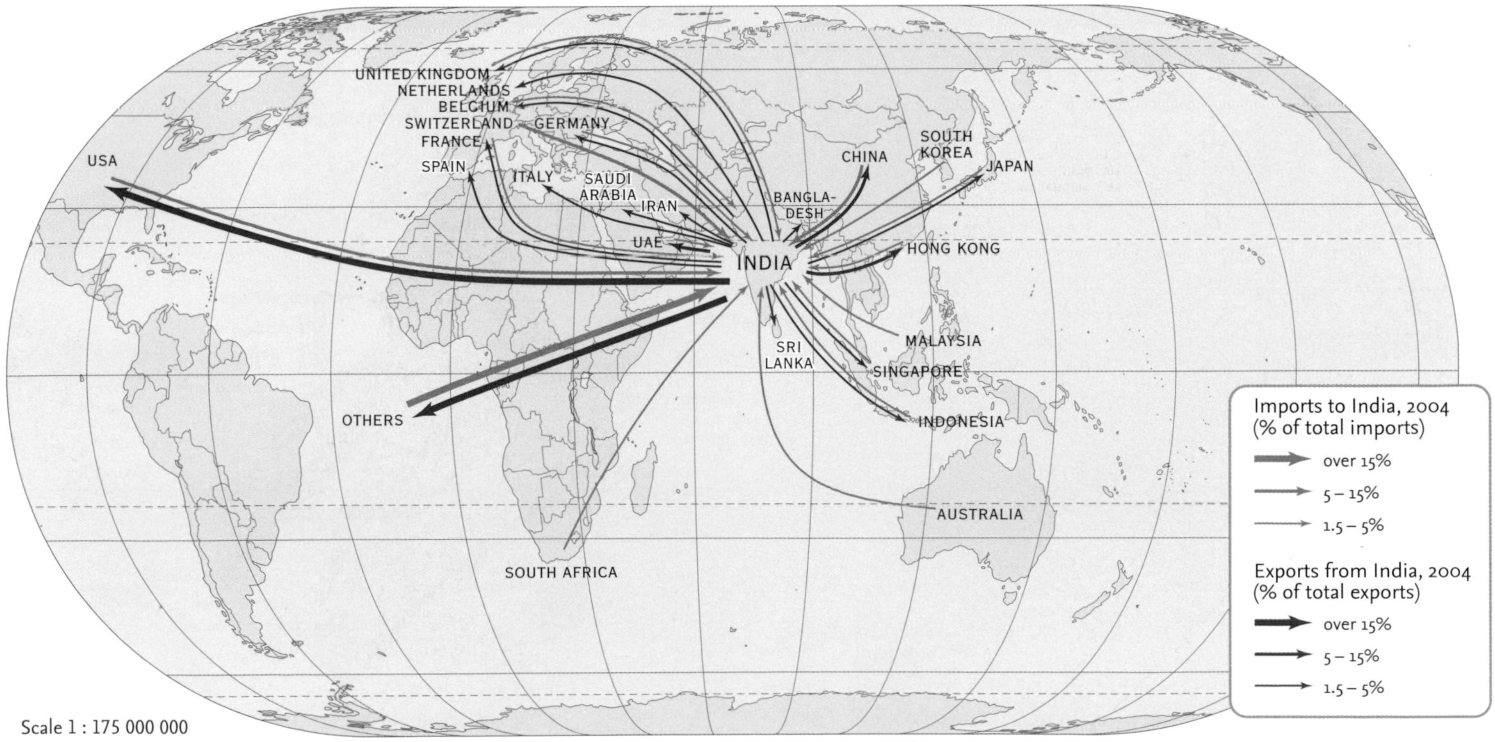

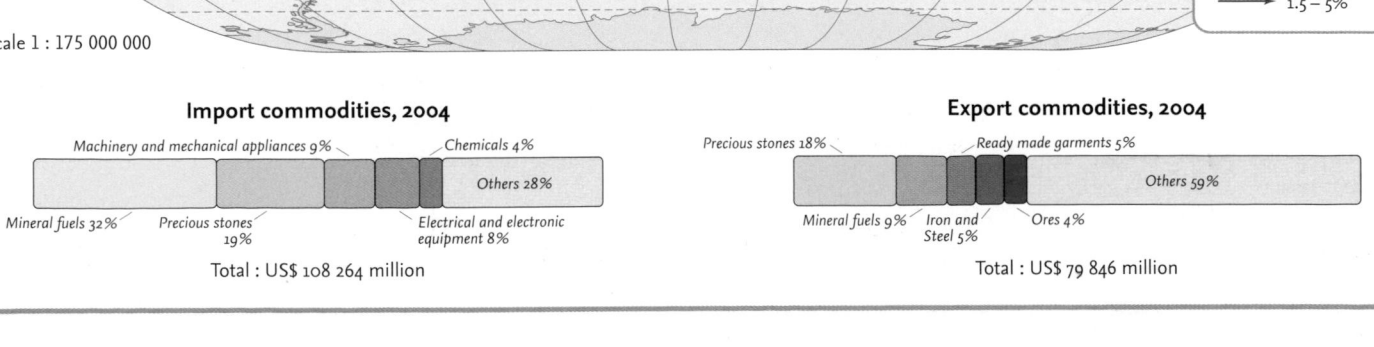

UNITED KINGDOM
NETHERLANDS
BELGIUM
SWITZERLAND GERMANY
FRANCE
SPAIN

ITALY
SAUDI
ARABIA
IRAN
UAE

USA

CHINA

SOUTH
KOREA

JAPAN

BANGLA-
DESH

INDIA

HONG KONG

SRI
LANKA

MALAYSIA

SINGAPORE

OTHERS

INDONESIA

AUSTRALIA

SOUTH AFRICA

**Imports to India, 2004
(% of total imports)**

→ over 15%

→ 5 – 15%

→ 1.5 – 5%

**Exports from India, 2004
(% of total exports)**

→ over 15%

→ 5 – 15%

→ 1.5 – 5%

Scale 1 : 175 000 000

Import commodities, 2004

Machinery and mechanical appliances 9%

Chemicals 4%

Others 28%

Mineral fuels 32%

Precious stones
19%

Electrical and electronic
equipment 8%

Total : US$ 108 264 million

Export commodities, 2004

Precious stones 18%

Ready made garments 5%

Others 59%

Mineral fuels 9%

Iron and
Steel 5%

Ores 4%

Total : US$ 79 846 million

1 Population Density

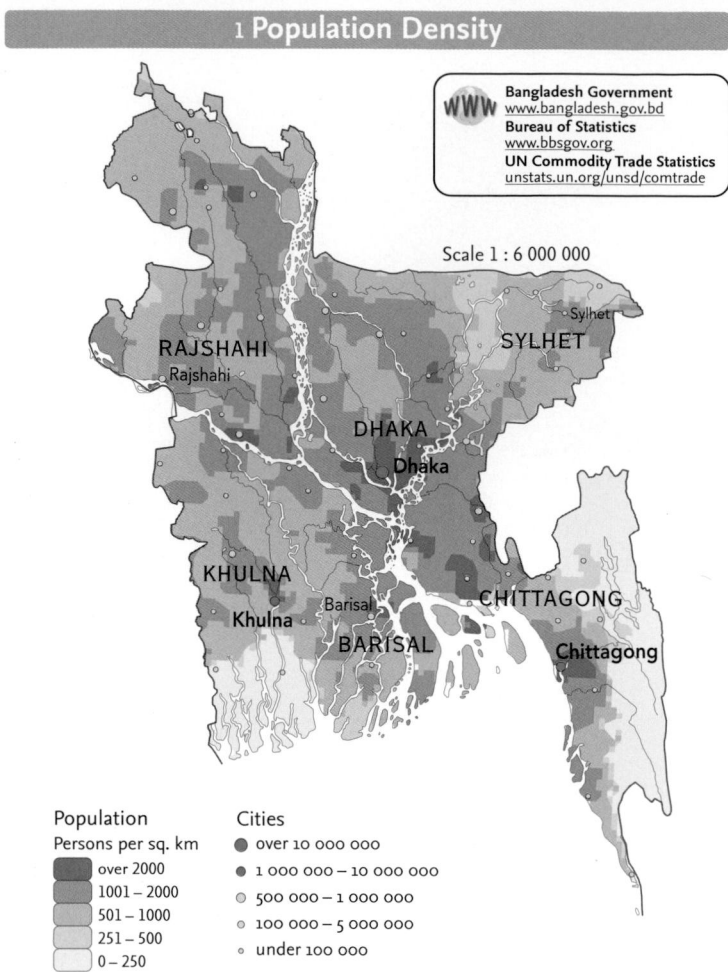

Bangladesh Government
www.bangladesh.gov.bd
Bureau of Statistics
www.bbsgov.org
UN Commodity Trade Statistics
unstats.un.org/unsd/comtrade

Scale 1 : 6 000 000

Population
Persons per sq. km
	over 2000
	1001 – 2000
	501 – 1000
	251 – 500
	0 – 250

Cities
● over 10 000 000
● 1 000 000 – 10 000 000
◉ 500 000 – 1 000 000
○ 100 000 – 5 000 000
○ under 100 000

2 Population Growth

Estimated
Projected

Population (millions)

Bangladesh Facts, 2003

Life expectancy at birth (years)	62
Adult literacy rate (percentage)	41
Infant mortality rate (per 1000 live births)	46
Population density (people per square kilometre)	1061
Urban population (percentage)	24

3 Main Urban Agglomerations

Urban agglomeration	1991 census	1998 estimate	2005 projection
Dhaka	6 105 160	10 979 000	15 921 000
Chittagong	2 040 663	2 906 000	4 468 000
Khulna	877 388	1 229 000	1 731 000

4 Economic Activity

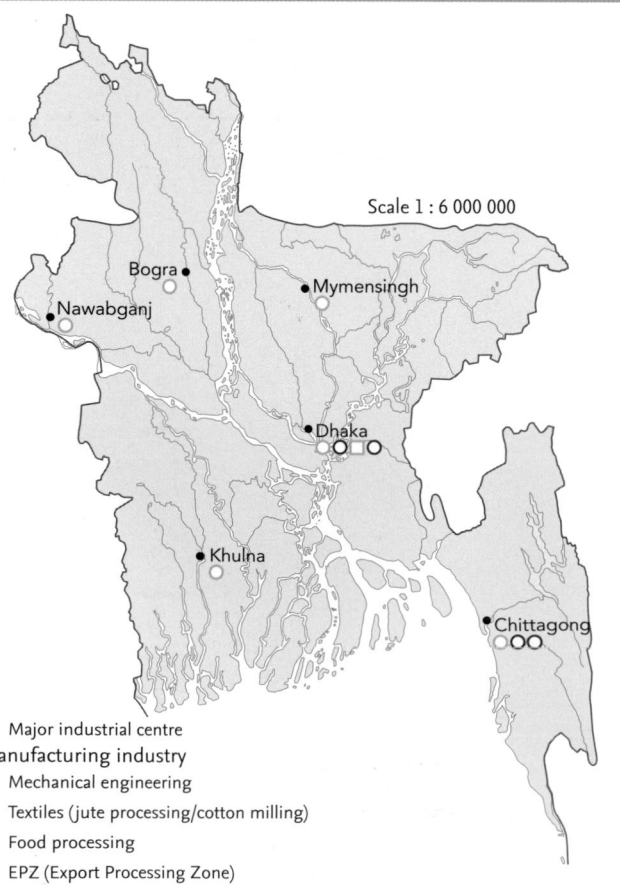

Scale 1 : 6 000 000

● Major industrial centre
Manufacturing industry
☐ Mechanical engineering
○ Textiles (jute processing/cotton milling)
◌ Food processing
○ EPZ (Export Processing Zone)
EPZ's are industrial zones set up to
promote rapid economic growth.

5 Trade

Partners, 2004

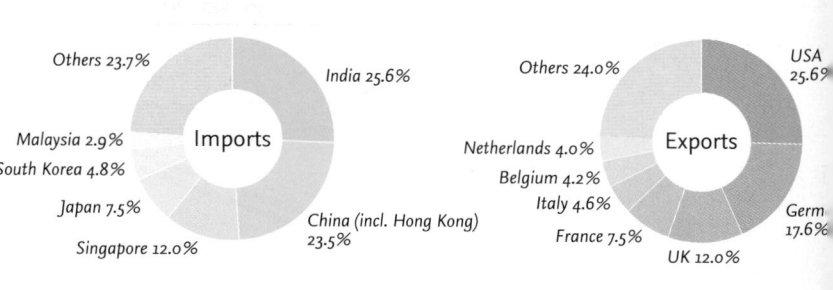

Imports
Others 23.7%
India 25.6%
Malaysia 2.9%
South Korea 4.8%
Japan 7.5%
Singapore 12.0%
China (incl. Hong Kong) 23.5%

Exports
Others 24.0%
USA 25.6%
Netherlands 4.0%
Belgium 4.2%
Italy 4.6%
France 7.5%
UK 12.0%
Germ 17.6%

Products, 2004

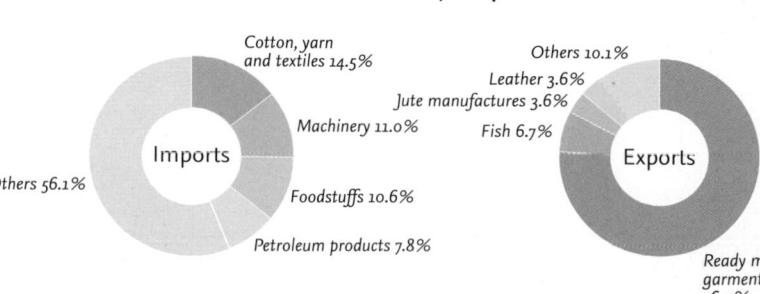

Imports
Cotton, yarn and textiles 14.5%
Machinery 11.0%
Foodstuffs 10.6%
Petroleum products 7.8%
Others 56.1%

Exports
Others 10.1%
Leather 3.6%
Jute manufactures 3.6%
Fish 6.7%
Ready made garments 76.0%

Total : US$ 8537 million

Total : US$ 5797 million

6 Satellite Image

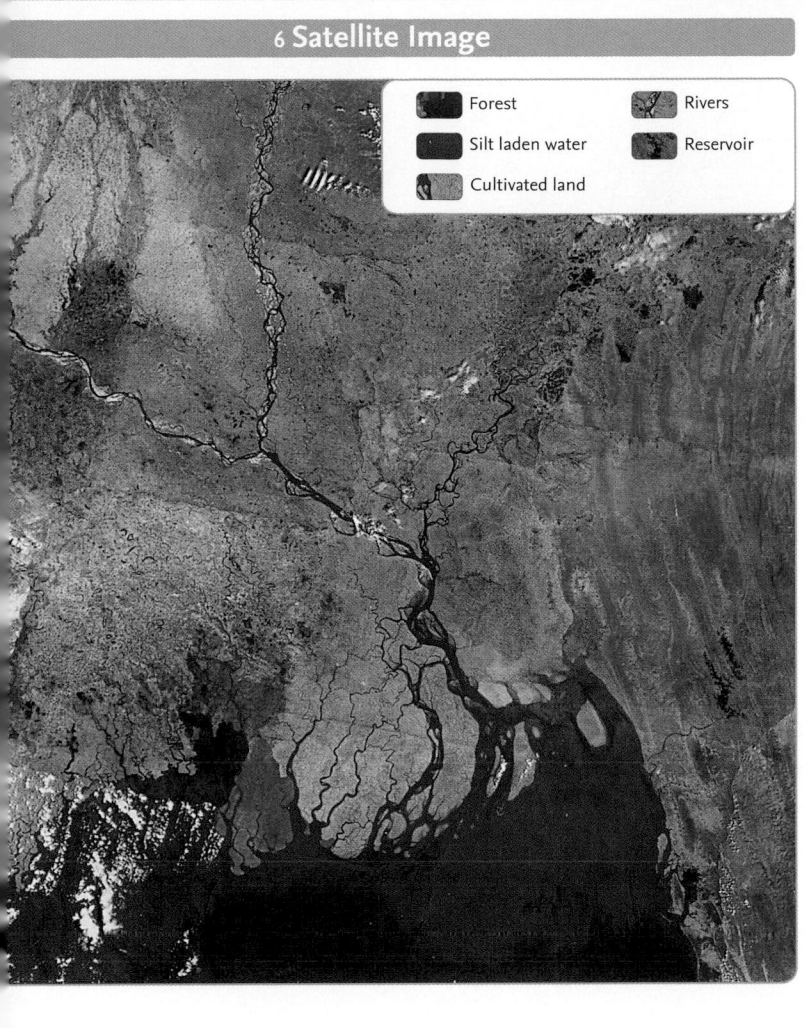

■ Forest		▨ Rivers	
■ Silt laden water		▨ Reservoir	
▨ Cultivated land			

7 Bangladesh

Relief metres
3000
2000
1000
500
200
0
200 sea level

Scale 1 : 6 000 000

8 Annual Rainfall

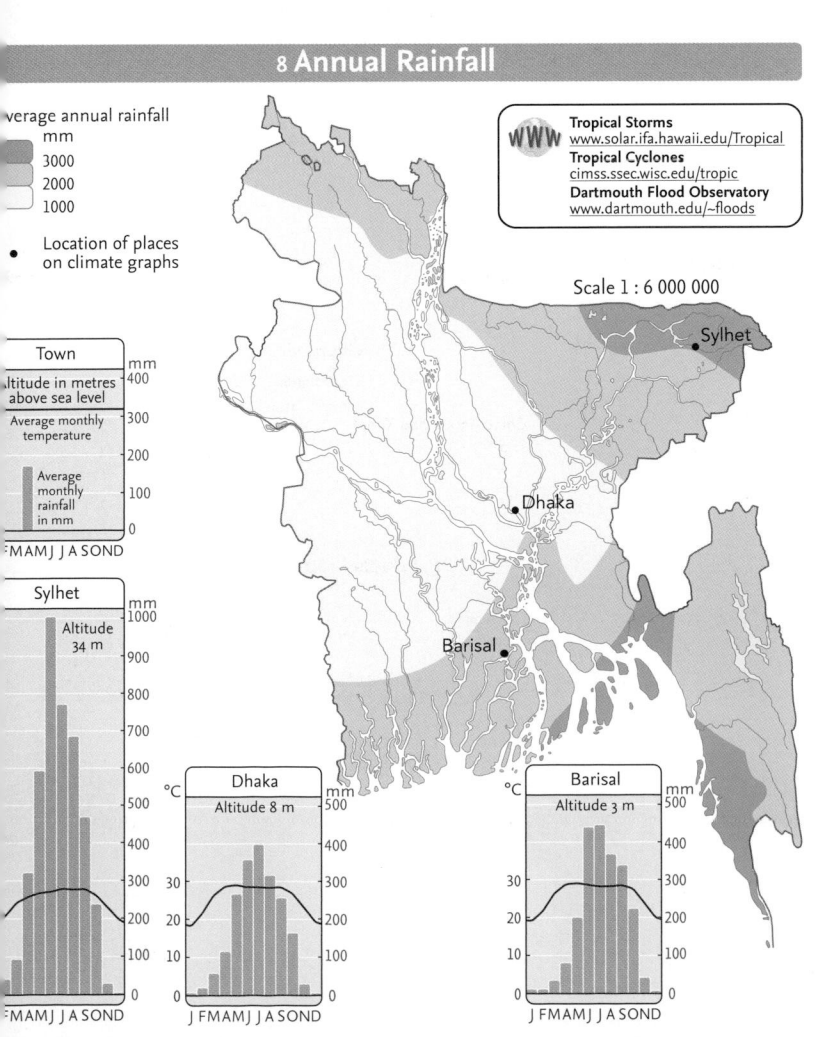

Average annual rainfall
mm
3000
2000
1000

• Location of places
on climate graphs

WWW Tropical Storms
www.solar.ifa.hawaii.edu/Tropical
Tropical Cyclones
cimss.ssec.wisc.edu/tropic
Dartmouth Flood Observatory
www.dartmouth.edu/~floods

Scale 1 : 6 000 000

Town
Altitude in metres above sea level
Average monthly temperature
Average monthly rainfall in mm

mm
400
300
200
100
0
J F M A M J J A S O N D

Sylhet
Altitude 34 m
mm
1000
900
800
700
600
500
400
300
200
100
0
J F M A M J J A S O N D

Dhaka
Altitude 8 m
°C
30
20
10
0
mm
500
400
300
200
100
0
J F M A M J J A S O N D

Barisal
Altitude 3 m
°C
30
20
10
0
mm
500
400
300
200
100
0
J F M A M J J A S O N D

9 Flood Control Projects

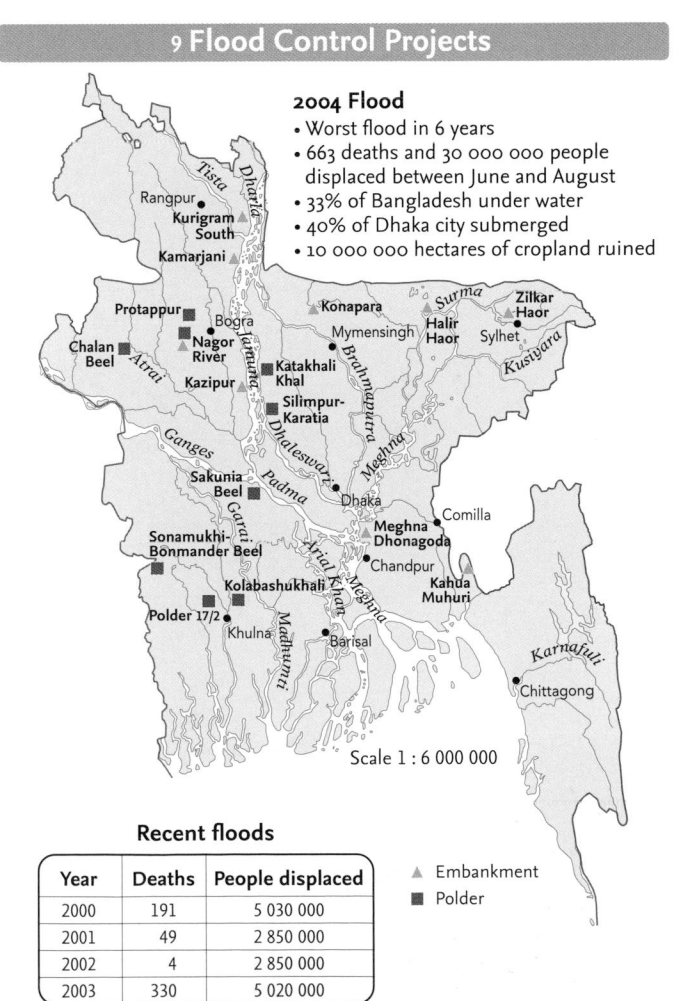

2004 Flood
• Worst flood in 6 years
• 663 deaths and 30 000 000 people
  displaced between June and August
• 33% of Bangladesh under water
• 40% of Dhaka city submerged
• 10 000 000 hectares of cropland ruined

Scale 1 : 6 000 000

▲ Embankment
■ Polder

Recent floods

Year	Deaths	People displaced
2000	191	5 030 000
2001	49	2 850 000
2002	4	2 850 000
2003	330	5 020 000

Key

Relief and physical features

Relief
metres
5000
3000
2000
1000
500
200
sea level
under sea level
200
4000
6000

▲ 8848　Mountain height
(in metres)

Permanent ice
(ice cap or glacier)

Water features

～～　River

～～　Intermittent river

～～　Canal

　　　Lake / Reservoir

　　　Intermittent lake

　　　Marsh

Communications

―――　Railway

―――　Road

⊕　Main airport

Administration

Boundaries

―――　International

―――　Disputed

―――　Internal

‥‥‥　Ceasefire line

Settlement

Cities and towns in order of size

National capital

■ BEIJING　　● Mumbai

■ SEOUL　　　● Yantai

□ BISHKEK　　○ Anshun

□ KATHMANDU　○ Bikaner

□ THIMPHU　　○ Lhasa

Other city or town

Scale 1 : 15 000 000

0　　200　　400　　600　　800 km

Conic Equidistant projection

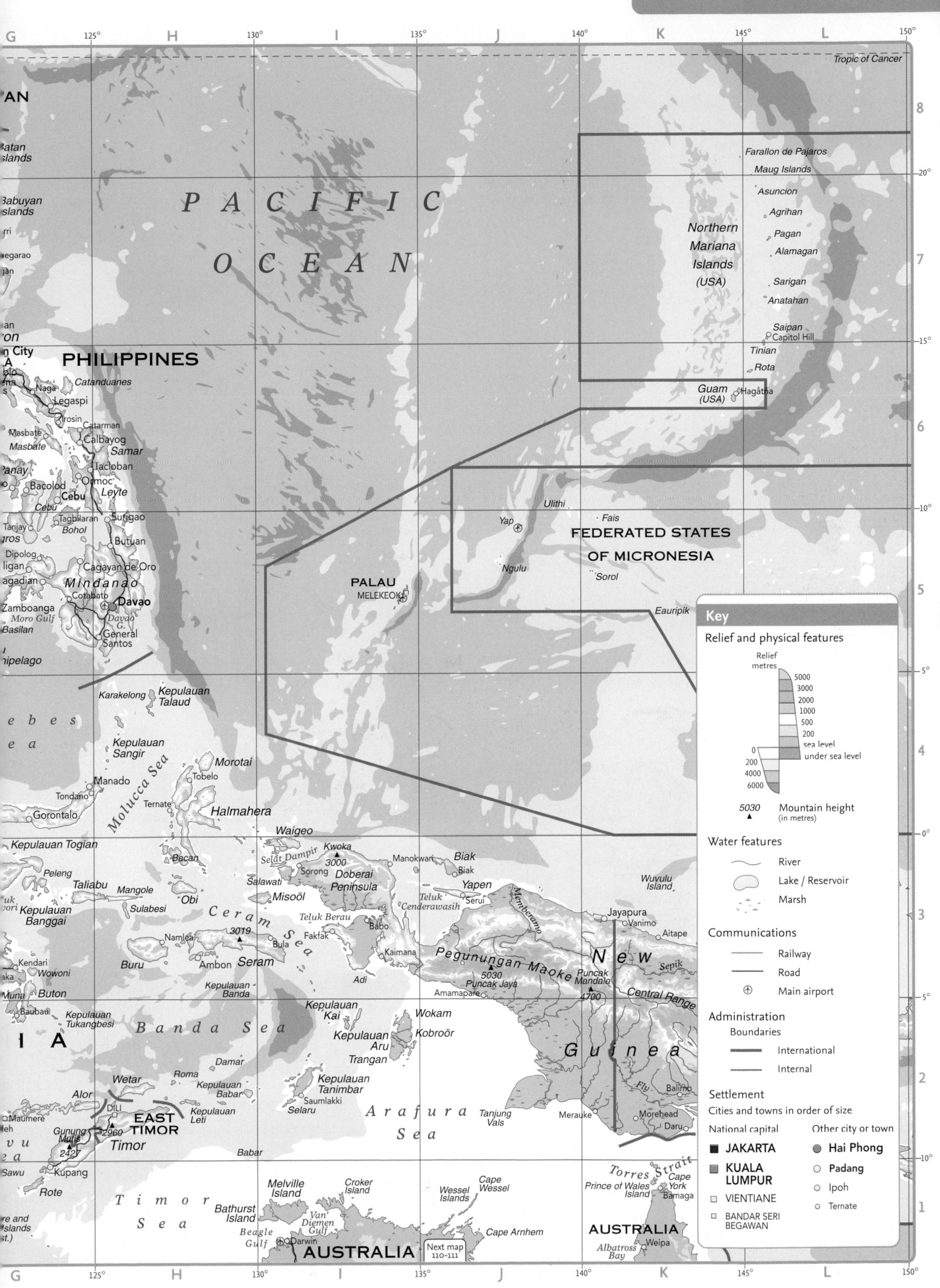

G   125°   H   130°   I   135°   J   140°   K   145°   L   150°

Tropic of Cancer

AN

Batan
Islands

PACIFIC

OCEAN

Farallon de Pajaros
Maug Islands
Asuncion
Agrihan
Pagan
Northern
Mariana
Islands
(USA)
Alamagan
Sarigan
Anatahan
Saipan
Capitol Hill
Tinian
Rota

PHILIPPINES

Catanduanes
Naga Legaspi
Irosin
Catarman
Calbayog
Samar
Tacloban
Ormoc *Leyte*
Cebu
Tagbilaran Surigao
Bohol
Dipolog
Cagayan de Oro
Butuan
Mindanao
Cotabato
Davao
Davao G.
General
Santos
Zamboanga
Moro Gulf
Basilan
Masbate
Masbate
Panay
Bacolod
Cebu

Guam
(USA) Hagåtña

Ulithi
Fais
Yap
FEDERATED STATES
Ngulu
OF MICRONESIA
Sorol
PALAU
MELEKEOK
Eauripik

Karakelong *Kepulauan*
Talaud

e b e s
s e a

Kepulauan
Sangir

Manado
Tondano
Gorontalo
Molucca Sea Ternate
Morotai
Tobelo
Halmahera
Waigeo
Selat Dampir Kwoka
Sorong ▲3000
Manokwari
Biak
Biak
Yapen
Serui
Teluk
Cenderawasih
Wuvulu
Island
Jayapura
Vanimo
Aitape

Kepulauan Togian
Peleng
Taliabu *Mangole*
Obi
Sulabesi
Ceram Sea
Misoöl
Salawati
Doberai
Peninsula
Teluk Berau
Babo
Fakfak
Kaimana
Memberamo
New
Kepulauan
Banggai
Namlea ▲3019
Bula
Ambon *Seram*
Adi
Pegunungan Maoke
5030
Puncak Jaya
Amamapare
Puncak
Mandala
4700
Sepik
Central Range
Guinea

Buru

Kendari
Wowoni
Muna *Buton*
Kepulauan
Tukangbesi
Baubau *Kepulauan*
Kai
Wokam
Kobroör
Banda Sea
Kepulauan
Aru
Trangan

Damar
Wetar
Roma
Alor
Kepulauan
Babar
Kepulauan
Tanimbar
Saumlakki
Kepulauan
Selaru
Leti
Arafura
Sea
Tanjung
Vals
Merauke
Morehead
Daru

DILI
EAST
TIMOR
Maumere
Gunung
Mutis ▲2960
▲2427
Timor
Kupang
Babar

Sawu
Rote

Melville
Island
Croker
Island
Wessel
Islands
Cape
Wessel
Prince of Wales
Island
Cape
York
Bamaga
Timor
Sea
Bathurst
Island
Van
Diemen
Gulf
Beagle
Gulf
Darwin
AUSTRALIA

Next map
110-111

Torres Strait
Fly
Balimo

AUSTRALIA
Albatross
Bay
Weipa
Cape Arnhem

Key

Relief and physical features

Relief
metres

5000
3000
2000
1000
500
200
sea level
0
under sea level
200
4000
6000

5030 ▲ Mountain height
(in metres)

Water features

〜 River

Lake / Reservoir

Marsh

Communications

Railway

Road

⊕ Main airport

Administration

Boundaries

International

Internal

Settlement

Cities and towns in order of size

National capital   Other city or town

■ JAKARTA   ● Hai Phong

■ KUALA
LUMPUR   ○ Padang

□ VIENTIANE   ○ Ipoh

□ BANDAR SERI
BEGAWAN   ▫ Ternate

G   125°   H   130°   I   135°   J   140°   K   145°   L   150°

Mercator projection

A 130° **B** 135° **C** 140° **D** 145° **E**

HEILONGJIANG

Dongfanghong

Qitaihe
Hulin
Next map
58–59

Linkou

Mudan

Jixi

Mishan

Iman

Suifenhe

Lesozavodsk

Sikhote-Alin

Amgu

Sakhalin

La Pérouse Strait

Sea of
Okhotsk

Wakkanai

Monbetsu

Abashiri

Ostro
Kunas

Yuzh
Kuri

CHINA

Jiaohe

Dunhua

Wangqing

Yanji

Tumen

Hunchun

Helong

JILIN

Baotou Shan
2750

Fusong

Changbai

Hyesan

NORTH
KOREA

Puksubaek-san
2522

Pukch'ŏng

Hamhŭng

Kimch'aek

Ch'ŏngjin

Najin

Unggi

Lake
Khanka

Spassk-Dal'niy

Ussuri

RUSSIAN
FEDERATION

Ussuriysk

Vladivostok

Nakhodka

Zaliv
Petra Velikogo

Rudnaya Pristan'

Dal'negorsk

Hokkaidō

Asahikawa

Asahi-dake
2290

Kitami

Bibai

Yubari

Hidaka-sammyaku

Otaru

Sapporo

Ishikari-
wan

Yakumo

Mori

Muroran

Tomakomai

Samani

Obihiro

Kushiro

Nemuro

Hakodate

Tsugaru-kaikyō

Goshogawara

Mutsu

Aomori

Hirosaki

Towada

Hachinohe

Noshiro

Ōdate

Akita

Morioka

Miyako

Ōmono

Hanamaki

Kamaishi

Sea
of
Japan
(East Sea)

Sado-ga-
shima

Ryōtsu

Sakata

Ichinoseki

Kesennuma

Ishinomaki

SOUTH
KOREA

Ch'unch'ŏn

Kangnŭng

Ulchin

Ullŭng-do

Next map
102–103

Andong

P'ohang

Taegu

Masan

Pusan

Chinju

Korea Strait

Tsushima

Higashi-suidō

Iki

Masuda

Matsue

Tottori

Suzu

Nanao

Toyama-
wan

Takaoka

Toyama

Kanazawa

Komatsu

Fukui

Tsuruga

Maizuru

Wakasa-
wan

Yamagata

Tendo

Niigata

Nagaoka

Kashiwazaki

Jōetsu

Matsumoto

Nagano

Ueda

Fukushima

Aizu-wakamatsu

Kōriyama

Iwaki

Sendai

Utsunomiya

Maebashi

Ōyama

Hitachi

Mito

Tsuchiura

Chōshi

JAPAN

Honshū

Shirane-san
3192

Kōfu

Fuji-san
3776

TŌKYŌ

Urawa

Sakura

Chiba

Kawasaki

Yokohama

Numazu

Shizuoka

O-shima

Izu-shotō

Chūgoku-sanchi

Okayama

Ōgaki

Gifu

Nagoya

Toyota

Suzuka

Tsu

Matsusaka

Ise

PACIFIC

OCEAN

Hiroshima

Shimonoseki

Kita-Kyūshū

Fukuoka

Sasebo

Ōmuta

Kurume

Ōita

Nagasaki

Kumamoto

Nobeoka

Kagoshima

Miyazaki

Kuju-san
1788

Kōbe

Ōsaka

Sakai

Kyōto

Biwa-ko

Wakayama

Kii-suidō

Shingū

Hamamatsu

Seto-
naikai

Takamatsu

Tokushima

Shikoku-sanchi
1981

Kōchi

Matsuyama

Uwajima

Ōwatahama

Shikoku

Ōsumi-kaikyō

Ōsumi-
shotō

Tanega-shima

Yaku-shima

Tokara-rettō

Amami-
Ō-shima

Key		
Relief and physical features	**Water features**	**Administration**

Relief and physical features

Relief
metres

5000
3000
2000
1000
500
200
0 sea level
under sea level
200
4000
6000

3776 ▲ Mountain height
(in metres)

Water features

〜 River

⬭ Lake / Reservoir

Marsh

Communications

Railway

Road

⊕ Main airport

Administration

Boundaries

International

Internal

Disputed

Settlement

Cities and towns in order of size

National capital

■ TŌKYŌ

Other city or town

● Ōsaka

● Yokohama

○ Hamamatsu

○ Morioka

○ Yakumo

Scale 1 : 7 500 000

0 100 200 300 400 km

Albers Equal Area Conic project

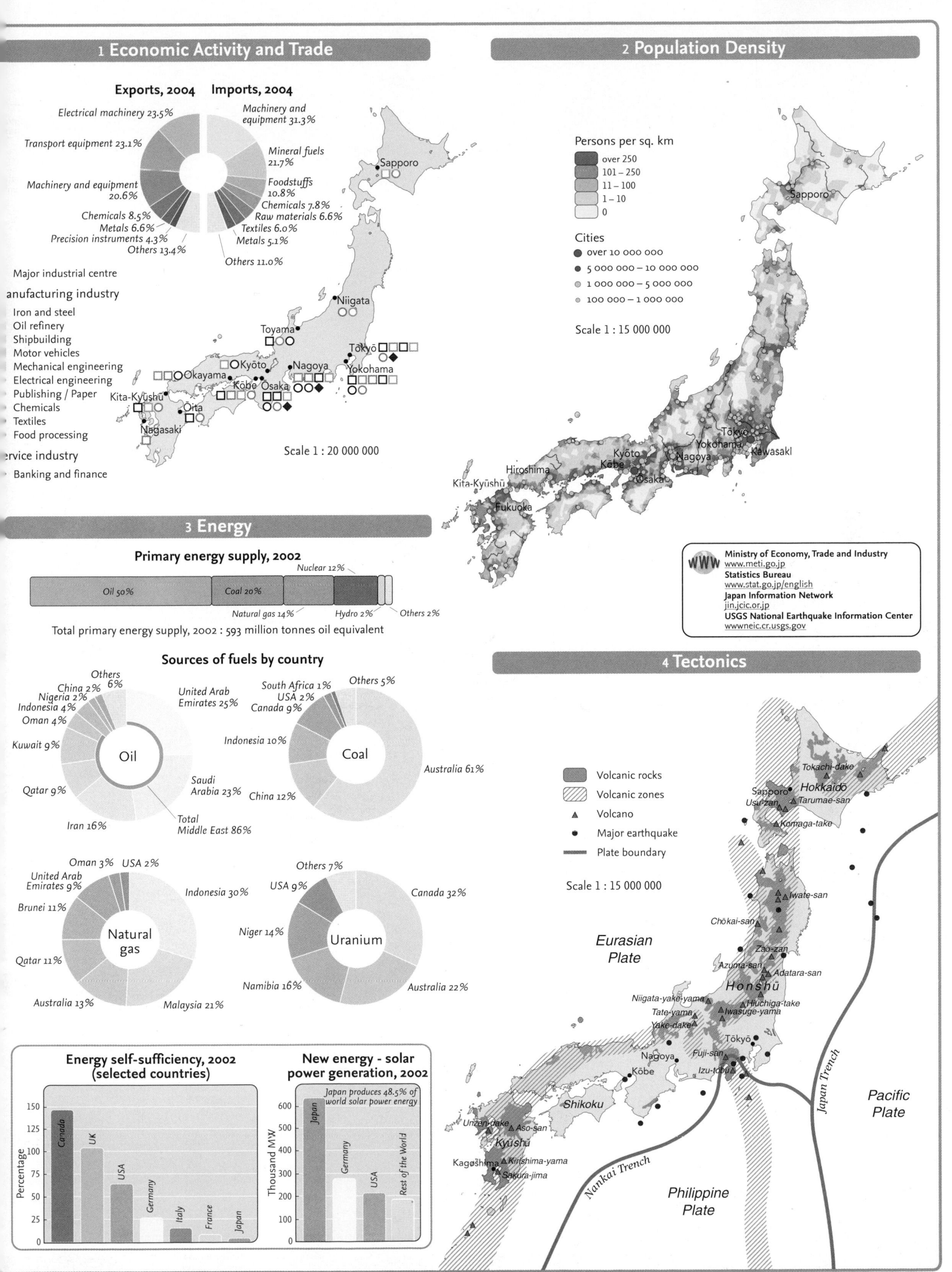

1 Economic Activity and Trade

Exports, 2004   Imports, 2004

Exports, 2004
- Electrical machinery 23.5%
- Transport equipment 23.1%
- Machinery and equipment 20.6%
- Chemicals 8.5%
- Metals 6.6%
- Precision instruments 4.3%
- Others 13.4%

Imports, 2004
- Machinery and equipment 31.3%
- Mineral fuels 21.7%
- Foodstuffs 10.8%
- Chemicals 7.8%
- Raw materials 6.6%
- Textiles 6.0%
- Metals 5.1%
- Others 11.0%

■ Major industrial centre

Manufacturing industry
- Iron and steel
- Oil refinery
- Shipbuilding
- Motor vehicles
- Mechanical engineering
- Electrical engineering
- Publishing / Paper
- Chemicals
- Textiles
- Food processing

Service industry
- Banking and finance

Sapporo
Niigata
Toyama
Tōkyō
Kyōto
Nagoya
Yokohama
Okayama
Kōbe Ōsaka
Kita-Kyūshū
Ōita
Nagasaki

Scale 1 : 20 000 000

2 Population Density

Persons per sq. km
- over 250
- 101 – 250
- 11 – 100
- 1 – 10
- 0

Cities
- over 10 000 000
- 5 000 000 – 10 000 000
- 1 000 000 – 5 000 000
- 100 000 – 1 000 000

Scale 1 : 15 000 000

Sapporo
Niigata
Tōkyō
Yokohama
Kawasaki
Kyōto
Nagoya
Kōbe
Ōsaka
Hiroshima
Kita-Kyūshū
Fukuoka

Ministry of Economy, Trade and Industry
www.meti.go.jp
Statistics Bureau
www.stat.go.jp/english
Japan Information Network
jin.jcic.or.jp
USGS National Earthquake Information Center
wwwneic.cr.usgs.gov

3 Energy

Primary energy supply, 2002

| Oil 50% | Coal 20% | Natural gas 14% | Nuclear 12% | Hydro 2% | Others 2% |

Total primary energy supply, 2002 : 593 million tonnes oil equivalent

Sources of fuels by country

Oil
- Others 6%
- China 2%
- Nigeria 2%
- Indonesia 4%
- Oman 4%
- Kuwait 9%
- Qatar 9%
- Iran 16%
- United Arab Emirates 25%
- Saudi Arabia 23%
- Total Middle East 86%

Coal
- South Africa 1%
- USA 2%
- Canada 9%
- Others 5%
- Indonesia 10%
- China 12%
- Australia 61%

Natural gas
- Oman 3%
- USA 2%
- United Arab Emirates 9%
- Brunei 11%
- Qatar 11%
- Australia 13%
- Malaysia 21%
- Indonesia 30%

Uranium
- Others 7%
- USA 9%
- Niger 14%
- Namibia 16%
- Australia 22%
- Canada 32%

Energy self-sufficiency, 2002 (selected countries)

Percentage
- Canada
- UK
- USA
- Germany
- Italy
- France
- Japan

New energy - solar power generation, 2002

Thousand MW

Japan produces 48.5% of world solar power energy

- Japan
- Germany
- USA
- Rest of the World

4 Tectonics

- Volcanic rocks
- Volcanic zones
- ▲ Volcano
- ● Major earthquake
- — Plate boundary

Scale 1 : 15 000 000

Eurasian Plate
Pacific Plate
Philippine Plate

Hokkaidō
Tokachi-dake
Sapporo
Usu-zan
Tarumae-san
Komaga-take
Iwate-san
Chōkai-san
Zaō-zan
Azuma-san
Adatara-san
Honshū
Niigata-yake-yama
Tate-yama
Hiuchiga-take
Iwasuge-yama
Yake-dake
Tōkyō
Nagoya
Fuji-san
Kōbe
Izu-tōbu
Shikoku
Unzan-dake
Aso-san
Kyūshū
Kagoshima
Kirishima-yama
Sakura-jima
Japan Trench
Nankai Trench

Key

Relief and physical features

Relief metres

5000
3000
2000
1000
500
200
sea level
under sea level
0
200
4000
6000

6959 ▲ Mountain height (in metres)

10920 ▽ Ocean depth (in metres)

Water features

River
Intermittent river
Canal
Lake / Reservoir
Intermittent lake
Marsh

Administration

Boundaries

International
Disputed

Settlement

Cities and towns in order of size

National capital

■ MEXICO CITY
■ BANGKOK
□ KINGSTON
□ CANBERRA
□ VAIAKU

Other city or town

● Los Angeles
● Adelaide
○ Honolulu

CANADA

Peace

Lake Winnipeg

Rocky Mountains

Gulf of Alaska

Kodiak Island

Queen Charlotte Islands

Coast Mountains

Vancouver
Vancouver Island
Seattle

Cascade Range

Columbia

Tufts Abyssal Plain

UNITED STATES OF AMERICA

Sierra Nevada

San Francisco

Mt Whitney 4418 ▲

Los Angeles
San Diego

Colorado

Guadalupe (Mexico)

Baja California

Gulf of California

MEXICO

Gulf of Mexico

Yucatán Channel

HAVANA

CUBA

Greater Antilles

DOMINICAN REPUBLIC

SANTO DOMINGO

PORT-AU-PRINCE

HAITI

PUERTO RICO (USA)

ANTIGUA AND BARBUDA

DOMINICA

Lesser Antilles

Guadalajara

MEXICO CITY

Volcán Popocatépetl 5452 ▲

BELIZE
BELMOPAN

JAMAICA
KINGSTON

ST LUCIA
BARBADOS

GUATEMALA
GUATEMALA CITY
SAN SALVADOR
EL SALVADOR 6662 ▲

HONDURAS
TEGUCIGALPA

NICARAGUA
MANAGUA

ST VINCENT AND THE GRENADINES

GRENADA

TRINIDAD AND TOBAGO

Caribbean Sea

Venezuelan Basin

SAN JOSÉ

COSTA RICA

PANAMA CITY

PANAMA

CARACAS

VENEZUELA

Llanos

Orinoco

GEORGETOWN

PARAMARIBO

GUYANA

SURINAME

FRENCH GUIANA

Medellín

Isla de Coco (Costa Rica)

Isla de Malpelo (Colombia)

Cocos Ridge

BOGOTÁ

COLOMBIA

QUITO

Galapagos Islands (Ecuador)

ECUADOR
Chimborazo 6310 ▲

Equator

Belem

BRAZIL

Negro

Amazon

Marañón

selvas

Madeira

Tapajós

Nevado de Huascarán 6768 ▲

PERU

6601 ▲

LIMA

Xingu

Araguaia

Tocantins

5470 ▽

Nazca Ridge (Southwest Peru Ridge)

L. Titicaca

LA PAZ

BOLIVIA

SUCRE

BRASÍLIA

PARAGUAY

Paraguay

Belo Horizonte

Abrolhos Bank

8170 ▽

Atacama Desert

Nevado Ojos del Salado 6908 ▲

Gran Chaco

ASUNCIÓN

Santos Plateau

San Félix (Chile)
San Ambrosio (Chile)

Chile Basin

Cerro Aconcagua 6959 ▲

ARGENTINA

Paraná

Rio de Janeiro

São Paulo

Isla Sala y Gómez (Chile)

Easter Island (Chile)

Archipiélago Juan Fernández (Chile)

Cerro Aconcagua
5282 ▲

SANTIAGO

Pampas

BUENOS AIRES

URUGUAY

Porto Alegre

MONTEVIDEO

Tropic of Capricorn

Roggeveen Basin

Challenger Fracture Zone

Mornington Abyssal Plain

Patagonia

Golfo San Matías

Golfo San Jorge

Argentine Rise

PACIFIC OCEAN

Pacific-Antarctic Ridge

Southeast Pacific Basin

Isla Grande de Tierra del Fuego

Str. of Magellan

Cape Horn

Falkland Islands (UK)

4325 ▽

5230 ▽

PACIFIC

OCEAN

Pacific Basin

East Pacific Rise

Gallego Rise

Galapagos Rise

Tiki Basin

4385

East Pacific Rise

Îles du Désappointement

Marquesas Islands

Nuku Hiva
Hiva Oa

Rangiroa
Raroia

Tuamotu Islands

French Polynesia (Fr)

Tahiti
Papeete

Society Islands

Moruroa

Groupe Actéon

Îles Gambier

Pitcairn Islands (UK)

Pitcairn Island
Henderson Island
Ducie Island

Rurutu
Tubuai

Raivavae

Tubuai Islands

Rapa

Vostok Island

Caroline Island

Malden Island

KIRIBATI

Kiritimati

Hawaii

Maui

Honolulu

6217 ▽

7022 ▽

5420 ▽

4359 ▽

Lambert Azimuthal Equal Area projection

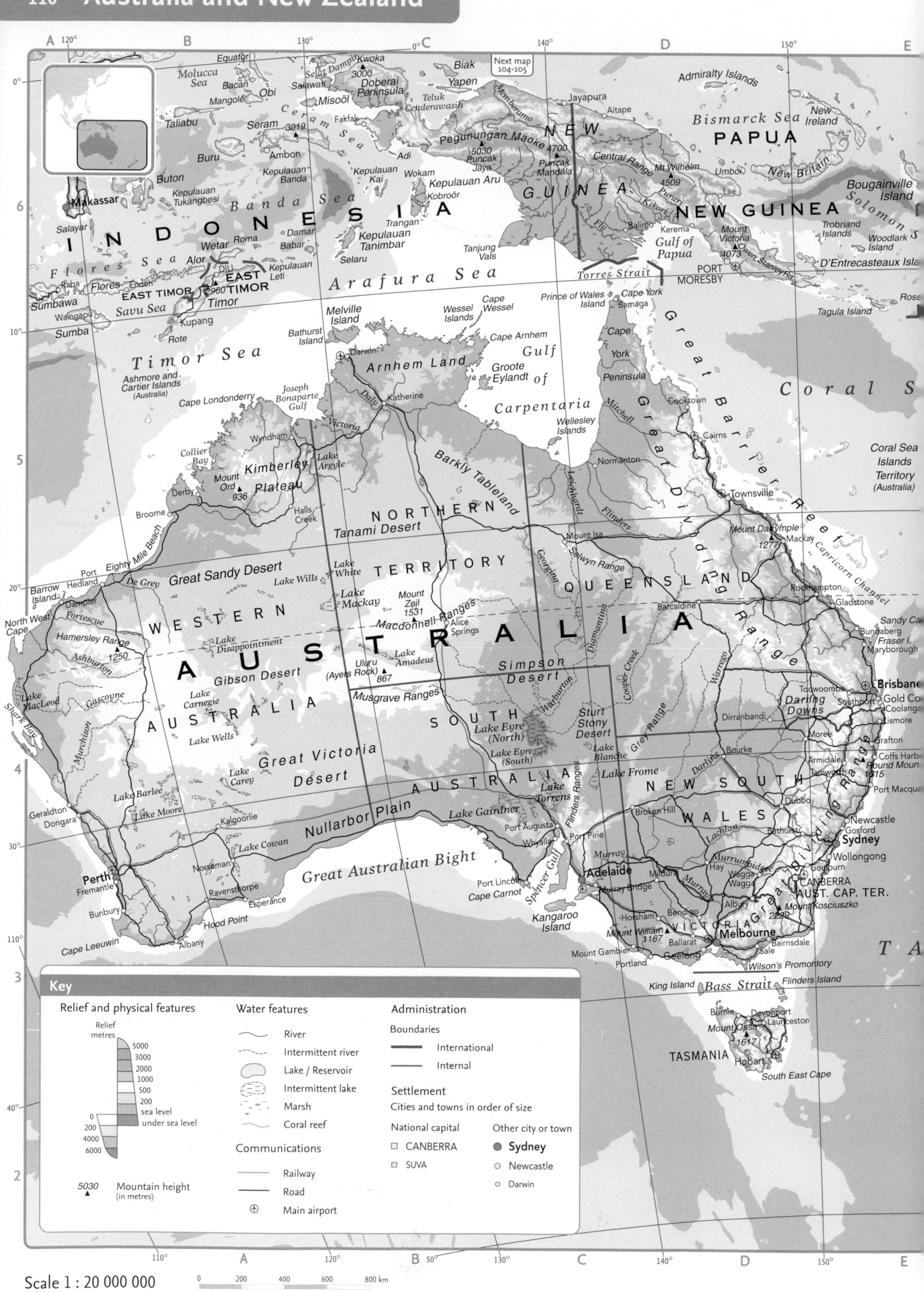

Key

Relief and physical features

Relief metres
- 5000
- 3000
- 2000
- 1000
- 500
- 200
- 0 sea level
- 200 under sea level
- 4000
- 6000

▲ 5030 Mountain height (in metres)

Water features

~ River
- - Intermittent river
- Lake / Reservoir
- Intermittent lake
- Marsh
- Coral reef

Communications

— Railway
— Road
⊕ Main airport

Administration

Boundaries
— International
— Internal

Settlement
Cities and towns in order of size

National capital
- □ CANBERRA
- □ SUVA

Other city or town
- ● **Sydney**
- ○ Newcastle
- ○ Darwin

Scale 1 : 20 000 000

0   200   400   600   800 km

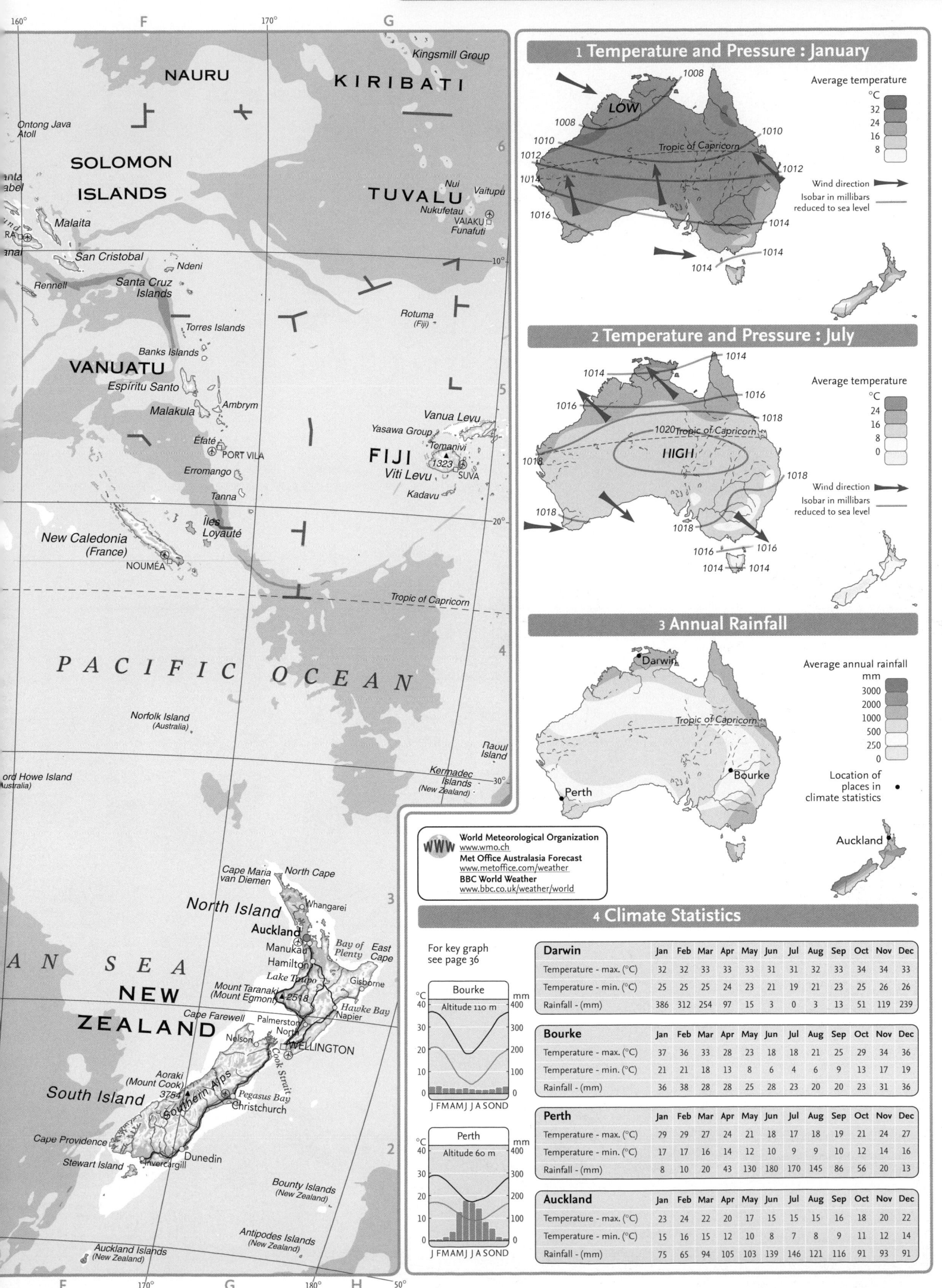

NAURU

KIRIBATI

Kingsmill Group

SOLOMON
ISLANDS

TUVALU

*Ontong Java
Atoll*

Malaita

San Cristobal
Ndeni
*Santa Cruz
Islands*
Rennell

Nui
Vaitupu
Nukufetau
VAIAKU □
Funafuti

*Rotuma
(Fiji)*

Torres Islands
Banks Islands

VANUATU

Espíritu Santo
Malakula
Ambrym
Éfaté ⊕ PORT VILA
Erromango
Tanna

Vanua Levu
Yasawa Group
Tomanivi
1323
FIJI
Viti Levu   SUVA
Kadavu

New Caledonia
(France)
*Îles
Loyauté*
NOUMÉA □

PACIFIC   OCEAN

*Norfolk Island
(Australia)*

*Raoul
Island*
*Kermadec
Islands
(New Zealand)*

*ord Howe Island
Australia)*

TASMAN   SEA

NEW
ZEALAND

North Island
Whangarei
Auckland ⊕
Manukau
Hamilton   *Bay of   East
Plenty   Cape*
Lake Taupo   *Gisborne*
*Mount Taranaki
(Mount Egmont)* △2518
Cape Farewell   *Hawke Bay*
Palmerston   Napier
Nelson   North
WELLINGTON
Cook Strait

*Aoraki
(Mount Cook)*
3754   *Pegasus Bay*
South Island   Southern Alps   *Christchurch*

Cape Providence
Stewart Island   *Dunedin*
Invercargill

*Bounty Islands
(New Zealand)*

*Antipodes Islands
(New Zealand)*

*Auckland Islands
(New Zealand)*

*Cape Maria
van Diemen*   *North Cape*

1 Temperature and Pressure : January

1008   LOW   1008
1008   1010
1010   *Tropic of Capricorn*   1012
1012   1014
1014   1016   1014
1016   1014   1014

Average temperature
°C
32
24
16
8

Wind direction ►
Isobar in millibars
reduced to sea level

2 Temperature and Pressure : July

1014   1014
1014   1016
1016   1018
1018   *Tropic of Capricorn*
1020
1018   HIGH   1018
1018   1018
1018   1016
1016
1014   1014

Average temperature
°C
24
16
8
0

Wind direction ►
Isobar in millibars
reduced to sea level

3 Annual Rainfall

Darwin

Tropic of Capricorn

Bourke
Perth

Average annual rainfall
mm
3000
2000
1000
500
250
0

● Location of
places in
climate statistics

Auckland

WWW   World Meteorological Organization
www.wmo.ch
Met Office Australasia Forecast
www.metoffice.com/weather
BBC World Weather
www.bbc.co.uk/weather/world

4 Climate Statistics

For key graph
see page 36

Bourke
°C   mm
40   400
30   300
20   200
10   100
0
J F M A M J J A S O N D
Altitude 110 m

Perth
°C   mm
40   400
30   300
20   200
10   100
0
J F M A M J J A S O N D
Altitude 60 m

Darwin	Jan	Feb	Mar	Apr	May	Jun	Jul	Aug	Sep	Oct	Nov	Dec
Temperature - max. (°C)	32	32	33	33	33	31	31	32	33	34	34	33
Temperature - min. (°C)	25	25	25	24	23	21	19	21	23	25	26	26
Rainfall - (mm)	386	312	254	97	15	3	0	3	13	51	119	239

Bourke	Jan	Feb	Mar	Apr	May	Jun	Jul	Aug	Sep	Oct	Nov	Dec
Temperature - max. (°C)	37	36	33	28	23	18	18	21	25	29	34	36
Temperature - min. (°C)	21	21	18	13	8	6	4	6	9	13	17	19
Rainfall - (mm)	36	38	28	25	24	22	20	20	23	23	31	36

Perth	Jan	Feb	Mar	Apr	May	Jun	Jul	Aug	Sep	Oct	Nov	Dec
Temperature - max. (°C)	29	29	27	24	21	18	17	18	19	21	24	27
Temperature - min. (°C)	17	17	16	14	12	10	9	9	10	12	14	16
Rainfall - (mm)	8	10	20	43	130	180	170	145	86	56	20	13

Auckland	Jan	Feb	Mar	Apr	May	Jun	Jul	Aug	Sep	Oct	Nov	Dec
Temperature - max. (°C)	23	24	22	20	17	15	15	15	16	18	20	22
Temperature - min. (°C)	15	16	15	12	10	8	7	8	9	11	12	14
Rainfall - (mm)	75	65	94	105	103	139	146	121	116	91	93	91

Lambert Azimuthal Equal Area projection

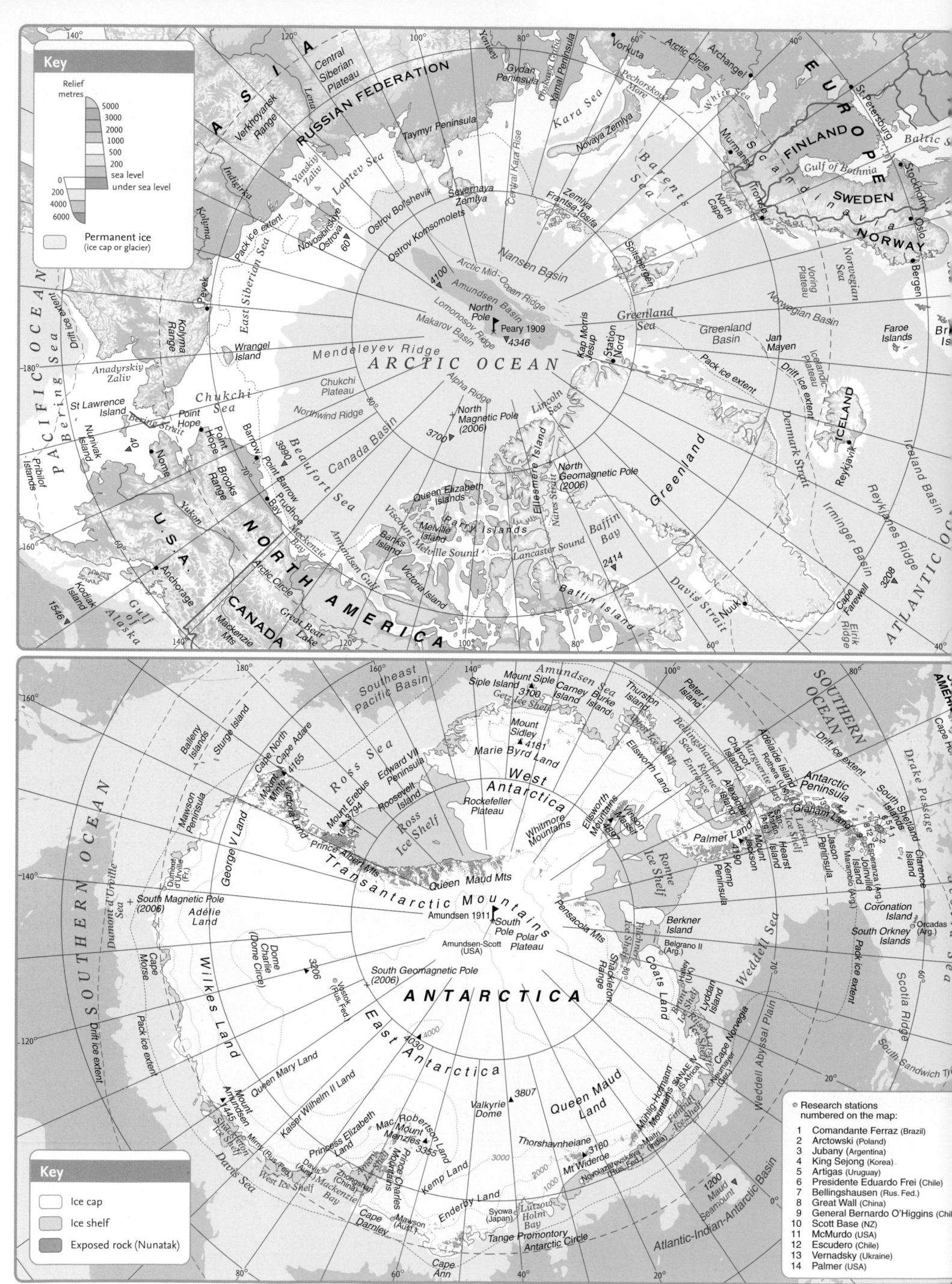

Key

Relief
metres

5000
3000
2000
1000
500
200
0 sea level
under sea level
200
4000
6000

Permanent ice
(ice cap or glacier)

Key

Ice cap

Ice shelf

Exposed rock (Nunatak)

Research stations
numbered on the map:

1   Comandante Ferraz (Brazil)
2   Arctowski (Poland)
3   Jubany (Argentina)
4   King Sejong (Korea)
5   Artigas (Uruguay)
6   Presidente Eduardo Frei (Chile)
7   Bellingshausen (Rus. Fed.)
8   Great Wall (China)
9   General Bernardo O'Higgins (Chile)
10 Scott Base (NZ)
11 McMurdo (USA)
12 Escudero (Chile)
13 Vernadsky (Ukraine)
14 Palmer (USA)

Scale 1 : 36 000 000

0   500   1000   1500 km

Polar Stereographic project

1 International Organizations - Political

Commonweath of Nations

NATO North Atlantic Treaty Organization

OAS Organization of American States

Arab League

African Union

ASEAN Association of Southeast Asian Nations

Pacific Islands Forum

No major political international organization

Cook Is.
Fed. States of Micronesia
Fiji
Kiribati
Marshall Is.
Nauru
Niue
Palau
Samoa
Solomon Is.
Tonga
Tuvalu
Vanuatu

Cyprus
Luxembourg
Malta

Belize

Cape Verde
The Gambia
São Tomé & Principe

Bahrain
Qatar

West Bank
Gaza
Maldives

Comoros
Mauritius
Seychelles

Brunei
Singapore

Antigua & Barbuda
The Bahamas
Barbados
Dominica
Grenada
Jamaica
St Kitts and Nevis
St Lucia
St Vincent & the Grenadines
Trinidad & Tobago

WWW United Nations www.un.org Commonwealth www.thecommonwealth.org

Headquarters of major International Organizations

City	Organisation	Abbreviation
Addis Ababa Ethiopia	African Union	AU
Bangui Central African Republic	Economic and Monetary Community of Central Africa	EMCCA
Brussels Belgium	North Atlantic Treaty Organization	NATO
Brussels Belgium	European Union	EU
Cairo Egypt	Arab League	
Colombo Sri Lanka	Colombo Plan	
Gaborone Botswana	Southern African Development Community	SADC
Geneva Switzerland	World Trade Organization	WTO
Geneva Switzerland	World Health Organization	WHO
Georgetown Guyana	Caribbean Community	CARICOM
Jakarta Indonesia	Association of Southeast Asian Nations	ASEAN
Lima Peru	Andean Community	
Lomé Togo	Economic Community of West African States	ECOWAS
London UK	Commonwealth of Nations	
Montevideo Uruguay	Latin American Integration Association	LAIA
New York USA	United Nations	UN
Paris France	Organisation for Economic Co-operation and Development	OECD
Singapore Singapore	Asia-Pacific Economic Cooperation	APEC
Suva Fiji	Pacific Islands Forum	
Vienna Austria	Organization of Petroleum Exporting Countries	OPEC
Washington DC USA	Organization of American States	OAS

United Nations Factfile

Established:	24th October 1945
Headquarters:	New York, USA
Purpose:	Maintain international peace and security. Develop friendly relations among nations. Help to solve international, economic, social, cultural and humanitarian problems. Help to promote respect for human rights. To be a centre for harmonizing the actions of nations in attaining these ends.
Structure:	The 6 principal organs of the UN are: General Assembly, Security Council, Economic and Social Council, Trusteeship Council, International Court of Justice, Secretariat
Members:	There are 191 members. Vatican City is the only non member country.

2 International Organizations - Economic

Colombo Plan

OPEC Organization of Petroleum Exporting Countries

OECD Organisation for Economic Co-operation and Development

EU European Union

CARICOM Caribbean Community

LAIA Latin American Integration Association

APEC Asia-Pacific Economic Cooperation

Andean Community

ECOWAS Economic Community of West African States

EMCCA Economic and Monetary Community of Central Africa

SADC Southern African Development Community

No major economic international organisation

Canada, United States and Mexico constitute the North American Free Trade Agreement (NAFTA).

Luxembourg

Malta

Cape Verde

Qatar

Brunei

Maldives
Singapore

Mauritius

Fiji

Antigua & Barbuda
The Bahamas
Barbados
Dominica
Grenada
Jamaica
Montserrat
St Kitts and Nevis
St Lucia
St Vincent & the Grenadines
Trinidad & Tobago

Eckert IV projection

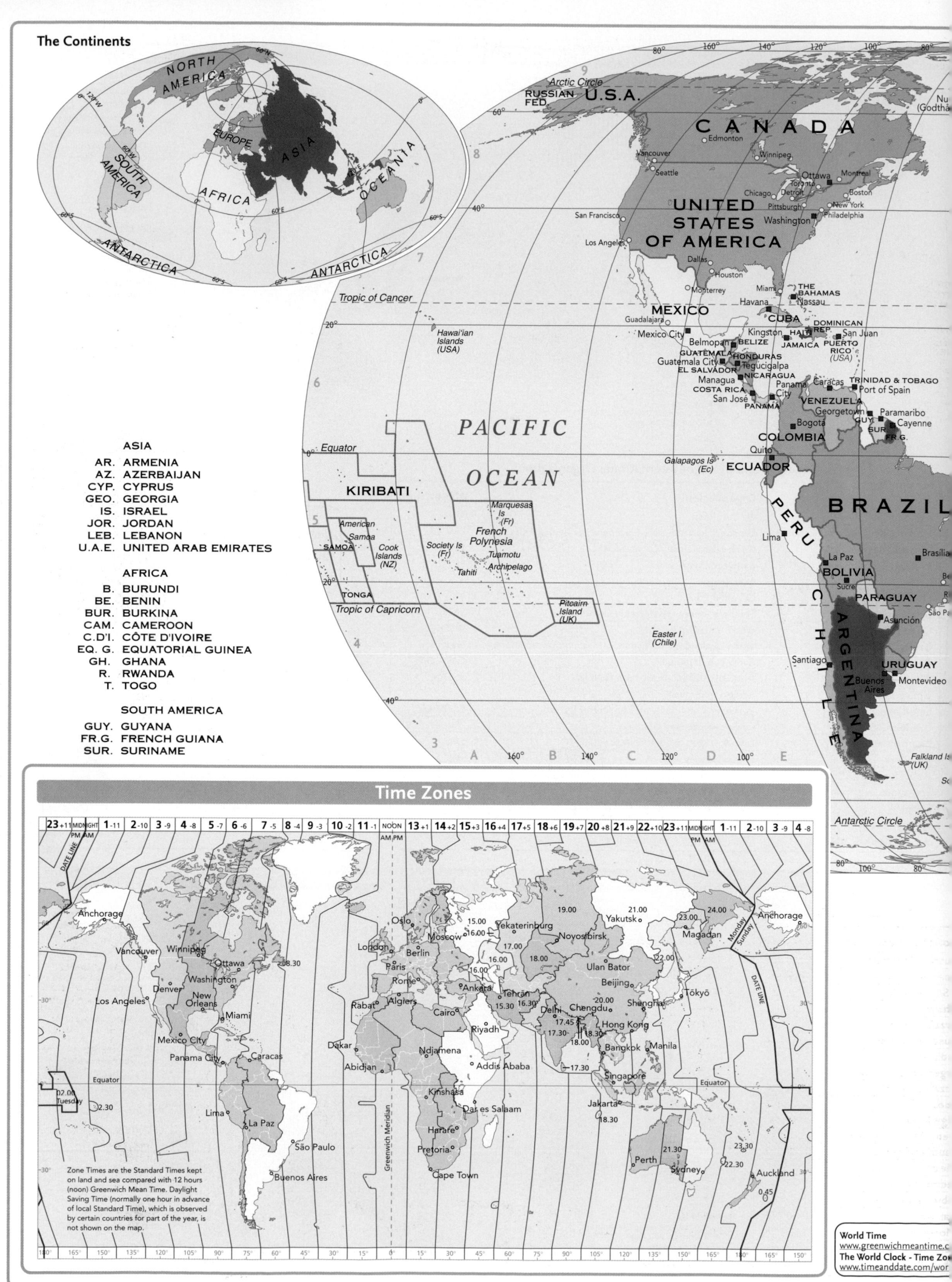

The Continents

NORTH AMERICA
SOUTH AMERICA
EUROPE
ASIA
AFRICA
OCEANIA
ANTARCTICA

ASIA
AR. ARMENIA
AZ. AZERBAIJAN
CYP. CYPRUS
GEO. GEORGIA
IS. ISRAEL
JOR. JORDAN
LEB. LEBANON
U.A.E. UNITED ARAB EMIRATES

AFRICA
B. BURUNDI
BE. BENIN
BUR. BURKINA
CAM. CAMEROON
C.D'I. CÔTE D'IVOIRE
EQ. G. EQUATORIAL GUINEA
GH. GHANA
R. RWANDA
T. TOGO

SOUTH AMERICA
GUY. GUYANA
FR.G. FRENCH GUIANA
SUR. SURINAME

Time Zones

Zone Times are the Standard Times kept on land and sea compared with 12 hours (noon) Greenwich Mean Time. Daylight Saving Time (normally one hour in advance of local Standard Time), which is observed by certain countries for part of the year, is not shown on the map.

World Time
www.greenwichmeantime.c
The World Clock - Time Zo
www.timeanddate.com/wor

Scale 1 : 93 000 000

0   1000   2000   3000   4000 km

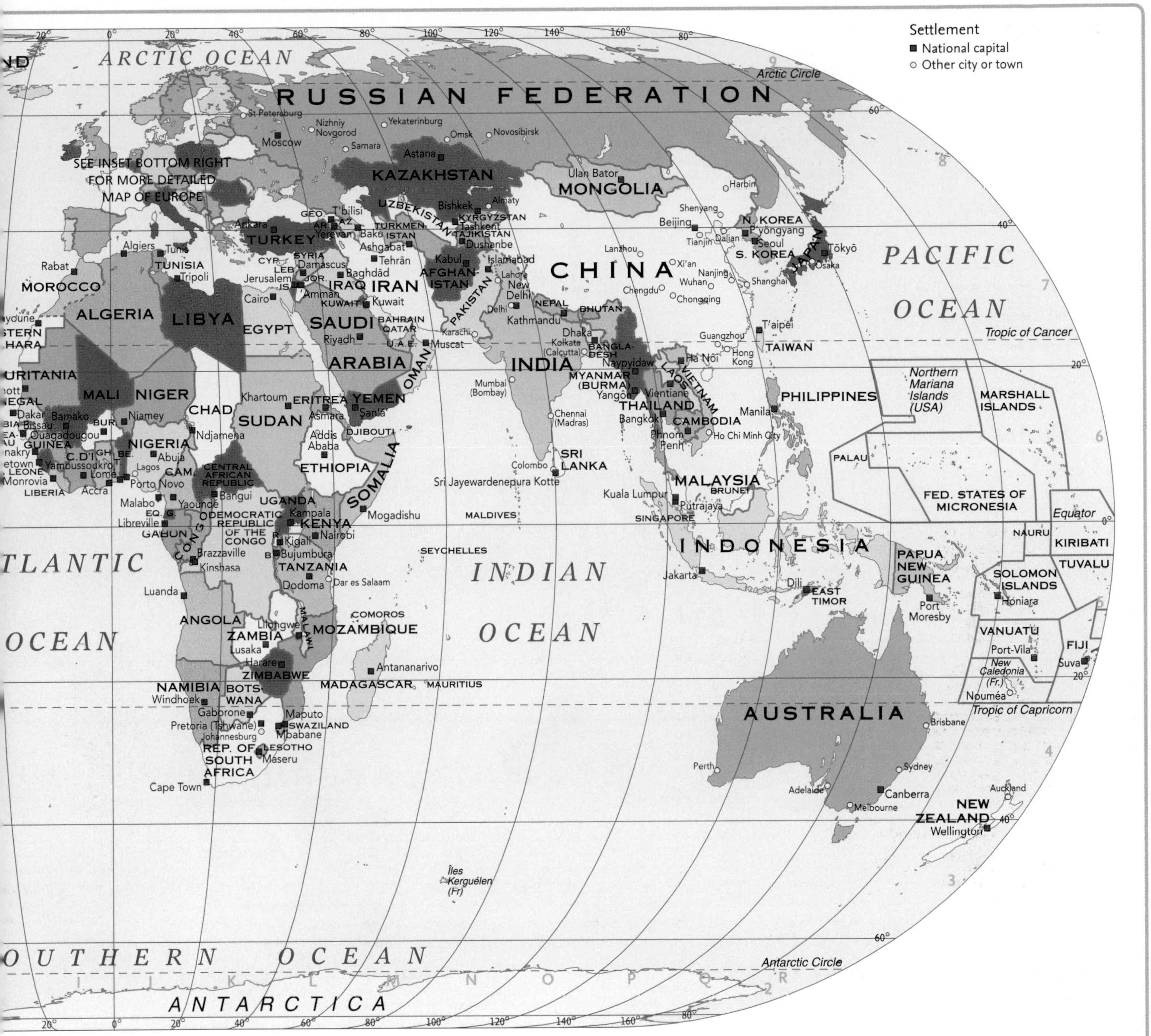

Settlement
- ■ National capital
- ○ Other city or town

Largest countries

Country and continent	Area (sq km)
Russian Federation Asia	17 075 400
Canada N America	9 984 670
USA N America	9 826 635
China Asia	9 584 492
Brazil S America	8 514 879
Australia Oceania	7 692 024
India Asia	3 064 898
Argentina S America	2 766 889
Kazakhstan Asia	2 717 300
Sudan Africa	2 505 813
Algeria Africa	2 381 741
Dem. Rep. Congo Africa	2 345 410
Saudi Arabia Asia	2 200 000
Mexico N America	1 972 545
Indonesia Asia	1 919 445
Libya Africa	1 759 540
Iran Asia	1 648 000
Mongolia Asia	1 565 000
Peru S America	1 285 216
Chad Africa	1 284 000

Largest capitals

Capital and country	Population
Tokyo Japan	35 327 000
Mexico City Mexico	19 013 000
Buenos Aires Argentina	13 349 000
Jakarta Indonesia	13 194 000
Dhaka Bangladesh	12 560 000
Karachi Pakistan	11 819 000
Cairo Egypt	11 146 000
Beijing China	10 849 000
Manila Philippines	10 677 000
Moscow Russian Federation	10 672 000
Paris France	9 854 000
Seoul South Korea	9 592 000
Lima Peru	8 180 000
London United Kingdom	7 615 000
Tehran Iran	7 352 000
Bangkok Thailand	6 604 000
Baghdad Iraq	5 910 000
Kinshasa Dem. Rep. Congo	5 717 000
Santiago Chile	5 623 000
Riyadh Saudi Arabia	5 514 000

Europe Countries

- A. ANDORRA
- AL. ALBANIA
- BEL. BELGIUM
- B.-H. BOSNIA-HERZEGOVENA
- CR. CROATIA
- L. LIECHTENSTEIN
- LUX. LUXEMBOURG
- M. MONTENEGRO
- MAC. MACEDONIA
- MOL. MOLDOVA
- NETH. NETHERLANDS
- R.F. RUSSIAN FEDERATION
- SER. SERBIA
- SL. SLOVENIA
- SW. SWITZERLAND

Eckert IV projection

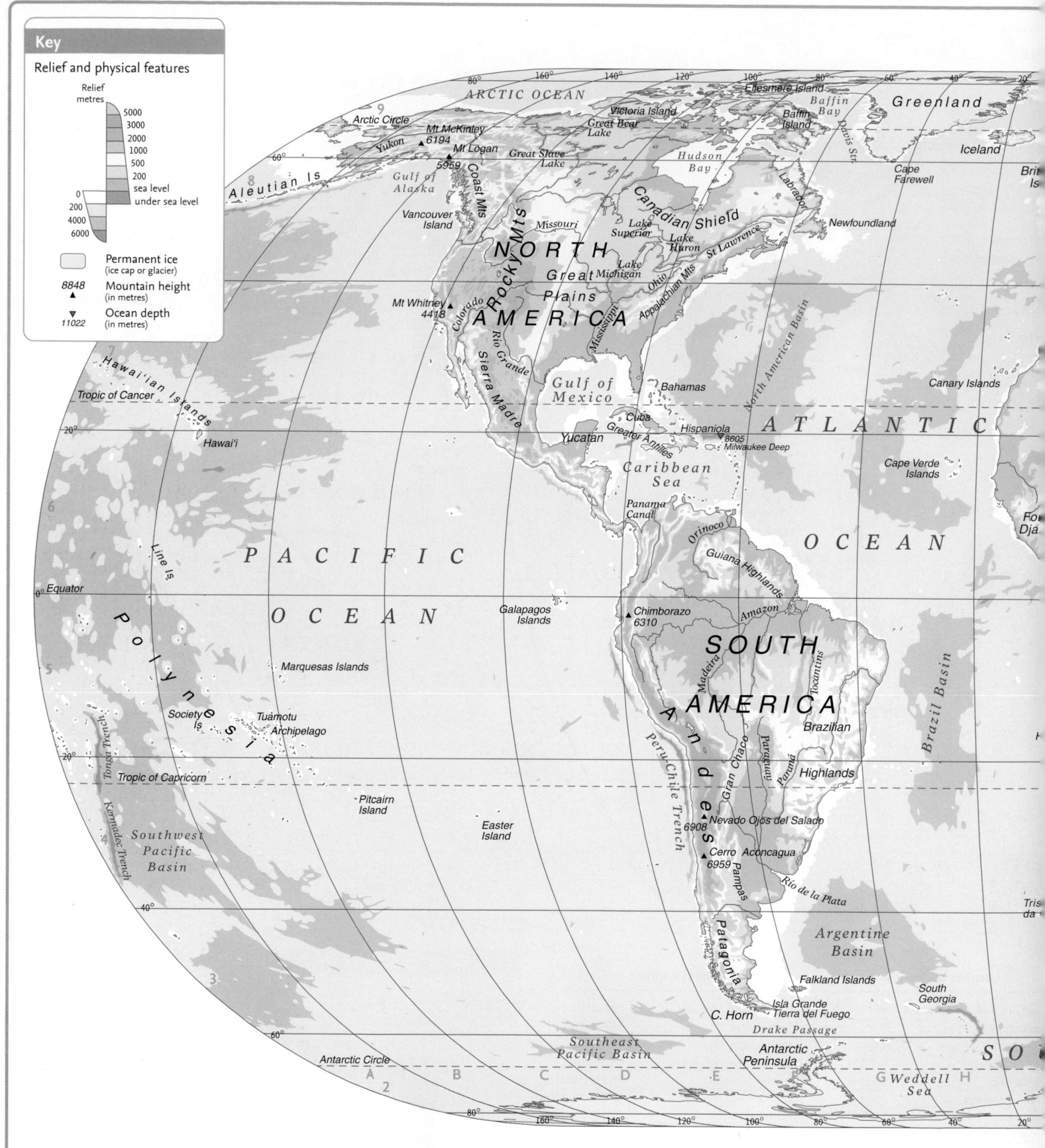

Key

Relief and physical features

Relief
metres
5000
3000
2000
1000
500
200
0 sea level
under sea level
200
4000
6000

Permanent ice (ice cap or glacier)

8848 ▲ Mountain height (in metres)

11022 ▼ Ocean depth (in metres)

Mountain heights	metres
Mt Everest (Nepal/China)	8848
K2 (Jammu & Kashmir/China)	8611
Kangchenjunga (Nepal/India)	8586
Dhaulagiri (Nepal)	8167
Annapurna (Nepal)	8091
Cerro Aconcagua (Argentina)	6959
Nevado Ojos del Salado (Arg./Chile)	6908
Chimborazo (Ecuador)	6310
Mt McKinley (USA)	6194
Mt Logan (Canada)	5959

Island areas	sq km
Greenland	2 175 600
New Guinea	808 510
Borneo	745 561
Madagascar	587 040
Baffin Island	507 451
Sumatra	473 606
Honshū	227 414
Great Britain	218 476
Victoria Island	217 291
Ellesmere Island	196 236

Continents	sq k
Asia	45 036 4
Africa	30 343 5
North America	24 680 3
South America	17 815 4
Antarctica	12 093 0
Europe	9 908 5
Oceania	8 923 0

Scale 1 : 80 000 000

0   800   1600   2400   3200 km

Oceans	sq km
Pacific Ocean	166 241 000
Atlantic Ocean	86 557 000
Indian Ocean	73 427 000
Arctic Ocean	9 485 000

Lake areas	sq km
Caspian Sea	371 000
Lake Superior	82 100
Lake Victoria	68 800
Lake Huron	59 600
Lake Michigan	57 800
Lake Tanganyika	32 900
Great Bear Lake	31 328
Lake Baikal	30 500
Lake Nyasa	30 044

River lengths	km
Nile (Africa)	6695
Amazon (S. America)	6516
Chang Jiang (Asia)	6380
Mississippi-Missouri (N. America)	5969
Ob'-Irtysh (Asia)	5568
Yenisey-Angara-Selenga (Asia)	5500
Huang He (Asia)	5464
Congo (Africa)	4667
Río de la Plata-Paraná (S. America)	4500
Mekong (Asia)	4425

Eckert IV projection

1 Climatic Regions and Ocean Currents

Climatic regions

- Ice cap
- Tundra climate, warmest month below 10°C
- Sub-arctic, rainy climate with severe cold winters and less than 4 months over 10°C
- Continental climate, rainy with warmest month below 22°C
- Continental climate, rainy with warmest month above 22°C
- Temperate, rainy climate with mild winter, coolest month above 0°C
- Wet subtropical, coolest month above 0°C, warmest month above 22°C
- Mediterranean, rainy with mild wet winter, dry summer
- Semi-arid, dry climate
- Desert climate
- Rainy tropical climate with no winter, coolest month above 18°C
- Rainy tropical climate, constantly wet throughout the year

Ocean currents

- → Cold
- → Warm
- → Seasonal

WWW
World Meteorological Organization
www.wmo.ch
Met Office
www.metoffice.com/weather
United Nations Environment Programme
www.unep.org
World Conservation Monitoring Centre
www.unep-wcmc.org
World Resources Institute Earthtrends
earthtrends.wri.org

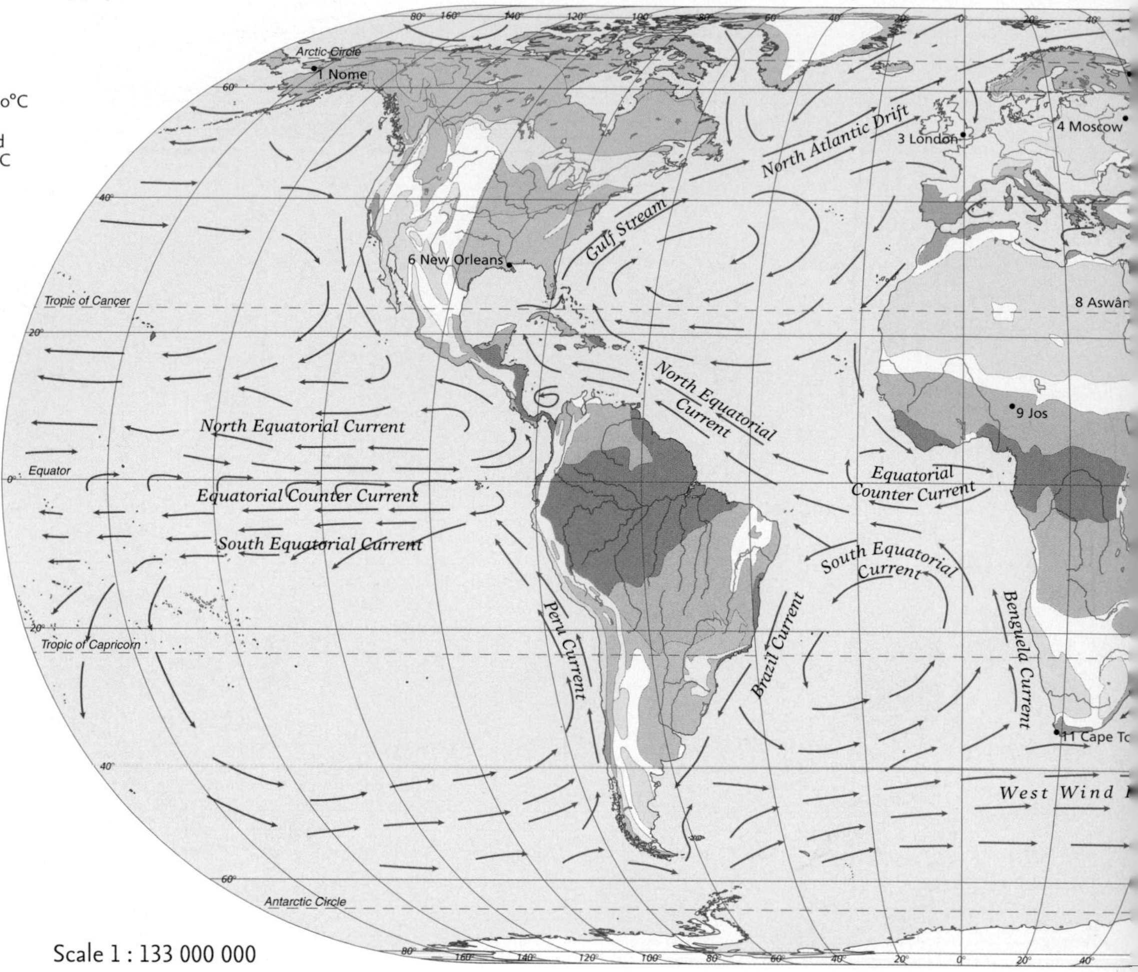

Scale 1 : 133 000 000

3 Tropical Storms

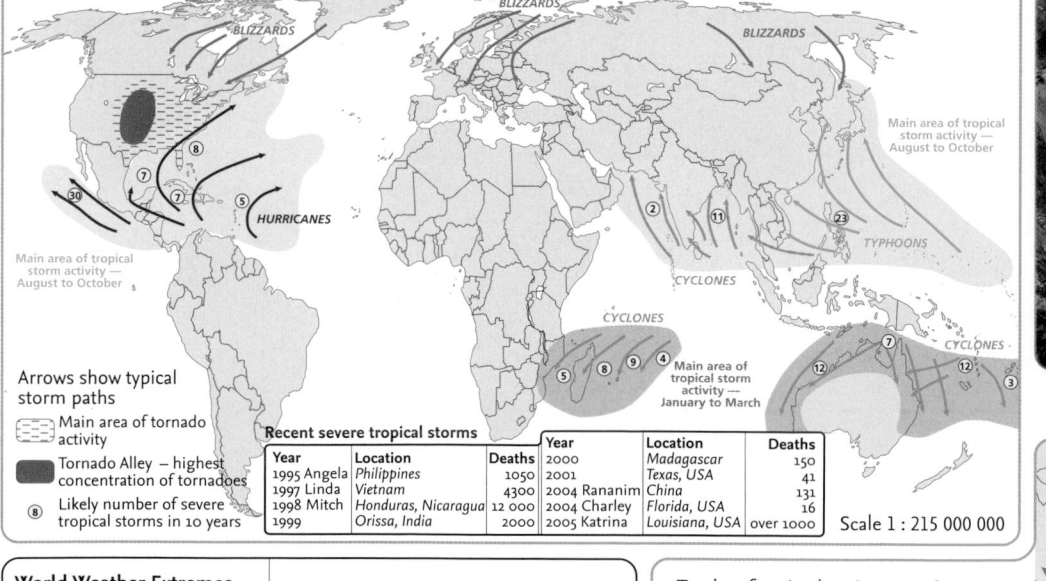

Arrows show typical storm paths
- Main area of tornado activity
- Tornado Alley – highest concentration of tornadoes
- ⑧ Likely number of severe tropical storms in 10 years

Hurricane Katrina, September 2005

Recent severe tropical storms					
Year	Location	Deaths	Year	Location	Deaths
1995 Angela	Philippines	1050	2000	Madagascar	150
1997 Linda	Vietnam	4300	2001	Texas, USA	41
1998 Mitch	Honduras, Nicaragua	12 000	2004 Rananim	China	131
1999	Orissa, India	2000	2004 Charley	Florida, USA	16
			2005 Katrina	Louisiana, USA	over 1000

Scale 1 : 215 000 000

World Weather Extremes	
Hottest place - Annual mean	34.4°C Dalol, Ethiopia
Driest place - Annual mean	0.1 mm Atacama Desert, Chile
Most sunshine - Annual mean	90% Yuma, Arizona, USA (4000 hours)
Least sunshine	Nil for 182 days each year, South Pole
Coldest place - Annual mean	-56.6°C Plateau Station, Antarctica
Wettest place - Annual mean	11 873 mm Meghalaya, India
Most rainy days	Up to 350 per year Mount Waialeale, Hawaii, USA
Greatest snowfall	31 102 mm Mount Rainier, Washington, USA (19th February 1971 - 18th February 1972)
Windiest place	322 km per hour in gales, Commonwealth Bay, Antarctica

Tracks of major hurricanes 1980-2005

- → Allen 1980
- → Gilbert 1988
- → Andrew 1992
- → Gordon 1994
- → Fran 1996
- → Mitch 1998
- → Floyd 1999
- → Isabel 2003
- → Charley 2004
- → Katrina 2005
- → Rita 2005

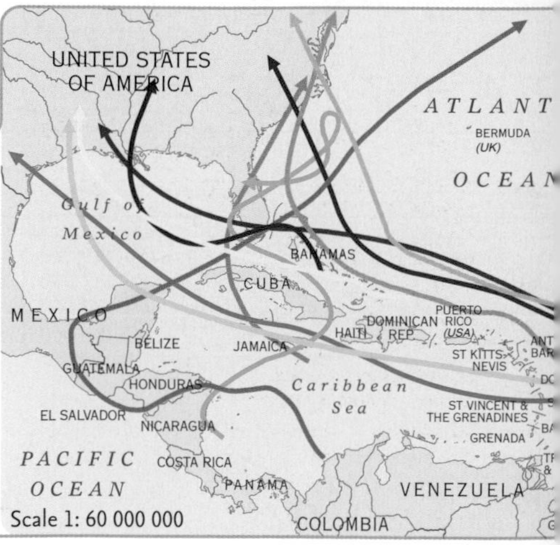

Scale 1: 60 000 000

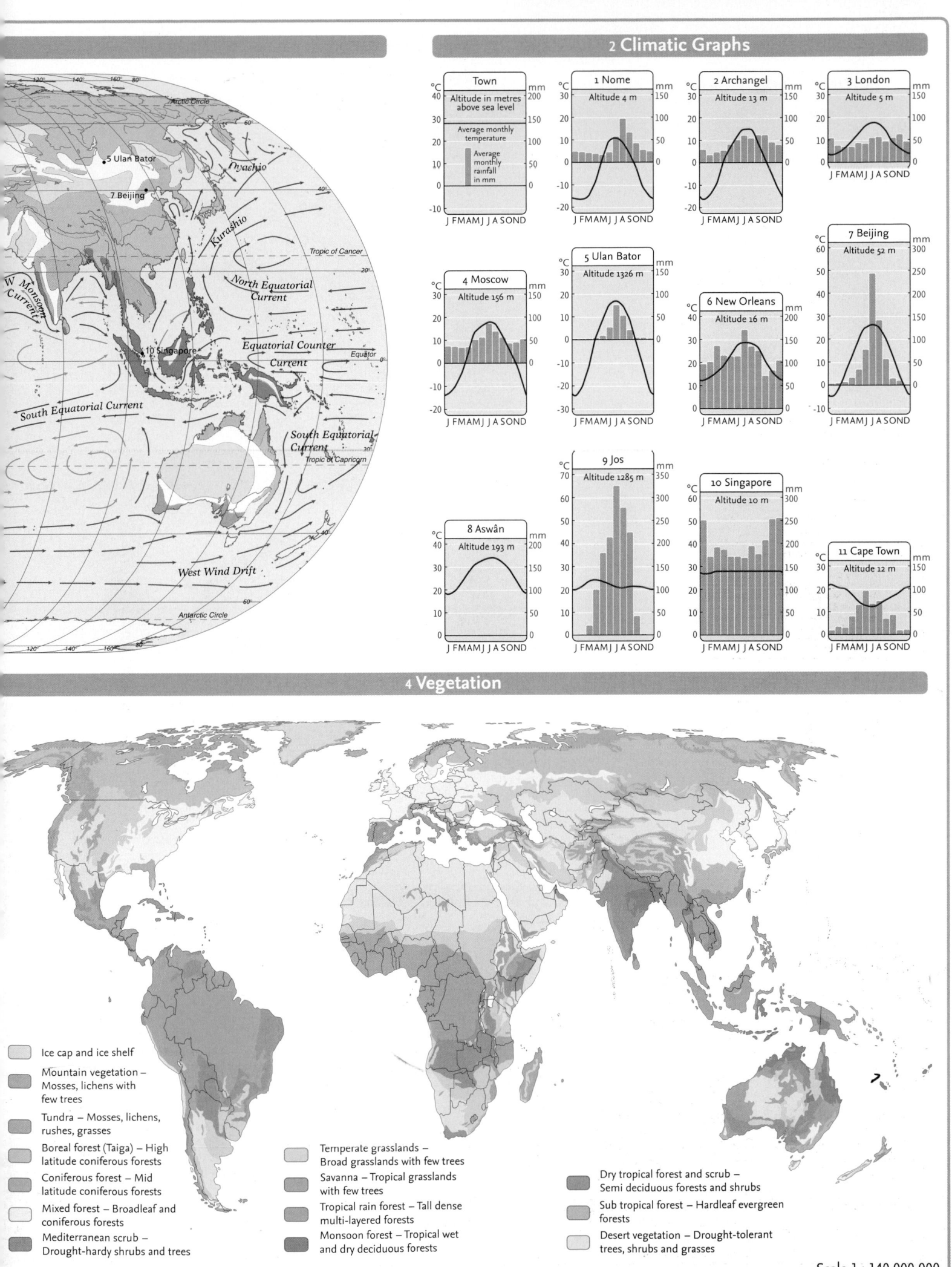

2 Climatic Graphs

Town
- Altitude in metres above sea level
- Average monthly temperature
- Average monthly rainfall in mm

1 Nome — Altitude 4 m

2 Archangel — Altitude 13 m

3 London — Altitude 5 m

4 Moscow — Altitude 156 m

5 Ulan Bator — Altitude 1326 m

6 New Orleans — Altitude 16 m

7 Beijing — Altitude 52 m

8 Aswân — Altitude 193 m

9 Jos — Altitude 1285 m

10 Singapore — Altitude 10 m

11 Cape Town — Altitude 12 m

4 Vegetation

- Ice cap and ice shelf
- Mountain vegetation – Mosses, lichens with few trees
- Tundra – Mosses, lichens, rushes, grasses
- Boreal forest (Taiga) – High latitude coniferous forests
- Coniferous forest – Mid latitude coniferous forests
- Mixed forest – Broadleaf and coniferous forests
- Mediterranean scrub – Drought-hardy shrubs and trees
- Temperate grasslands – Broad grasslands with few trees
- Savanna – Tropical grasslands with few trees
- Tropical rain forest – Tall dense multi-layered forests
- Monsoon forest – Tropical wet and dry deciduous forests
- Dry tropical forest and scrub – Semi deciduous forests and shrubs
- Sub tropical forest – Hardleaf evergreen forests
- Desert vegetation – Drought-tolerant trees, shrubs and grasses

Scale 1 : 140 000 000

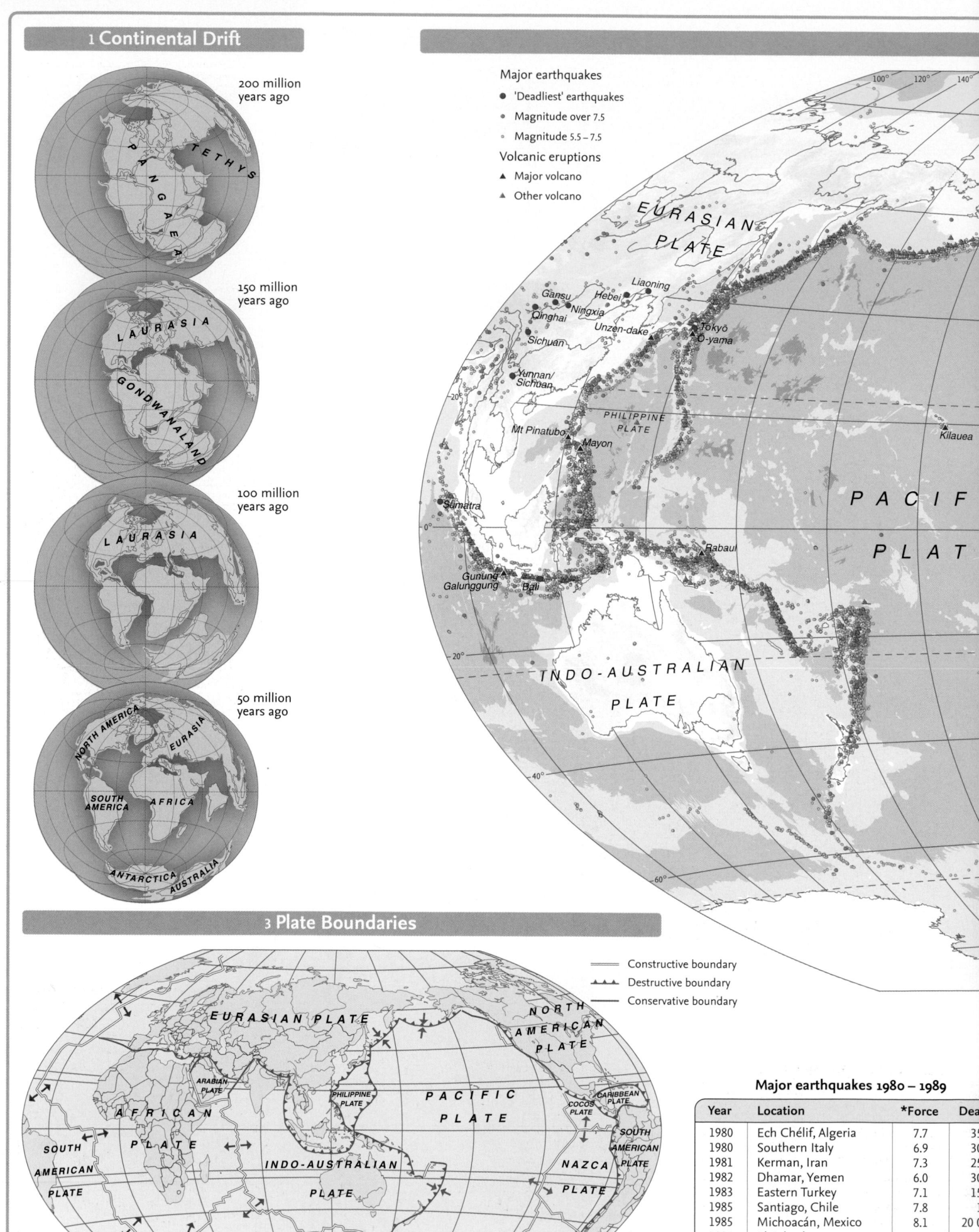

1 Continental Drift

200 million
years ago

150 million
years ago

100 million
years ago

50 million
years ago

Major earthquakes
- 'Deadliest' earthquakes
- Magnitude over 7.5
- Magnitude 5.5 – 7.5

Volcanic eruptions
- ▲ Major volcano
- ▲ Other volcano

3 Plate Boundaries

——— Constructive boundary
▲▲▲ Destructive boundary
——— Conservative boundary

→ Direction of movement

Major earthquakes 1980 – 1989

Year	Location	*Force	Death
1980	Ech Chélif, Algeria	7.7	350
1980	Southern Italy	6.9	300
1981	Kerman, Iran	7.3	250
1982	Dhamar, Yemen	6.0	300
1983	Eastern Turkey	7.1	150
1985	Santiago, Chile	7.8	17
1985	Michoacán, Mexico	8.1	20 00
1986	El Salvador	7.5	100
1987	Ecuador	7.0	200
1988	Yunnan, China	7.6	100
1988	Spitak, Armenia	6.9	25 00
1988	Nepal / India	6.9	100

2 Earthquakes and Volcanoes

WWW USGS Volcano Hazards Program
volcanoes.usgs.gov
USGS National Earthquake Information Center
wwwneic.cr.usgs.gov
British Geological Survey
www.bgs.ac.uk

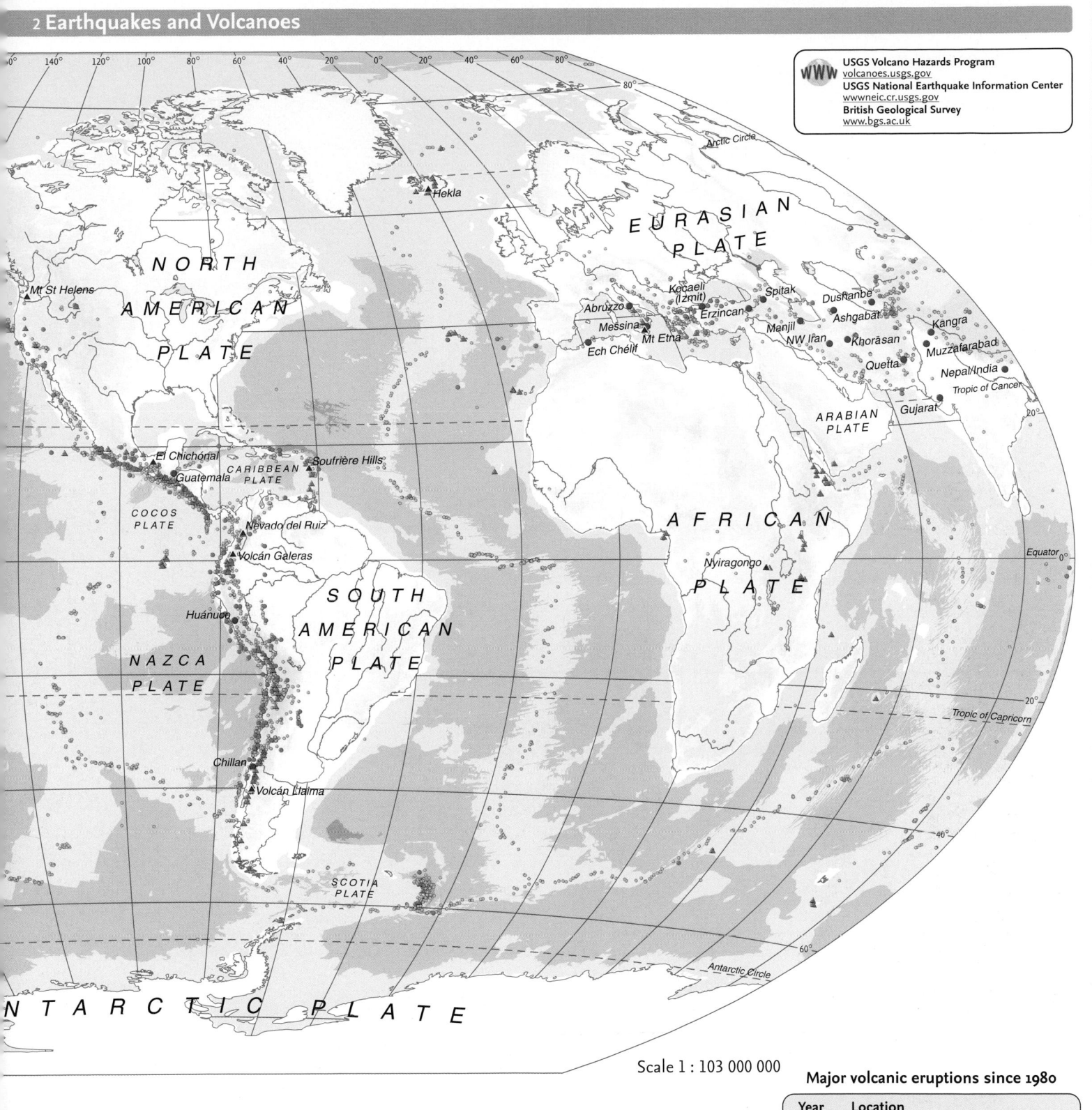

Scale 1 : 103 000 000

Major earthquakes 1990 – 1996

Year	Location	*Force	Deaths
1990	Manjil, Iran	7.7	50 000
1990	Luzon, Philippines	7.7	1600
1991	Georgia	7.1	114
1991	Uttar Pradesh, India	6.1	1600
1992	Flores, Indonesia	7.5	2500
1992	Erzincan, Turkey	6.8	500
1992	Cairo, Egypt	5.9	550
1993	Northern Japan	7.8	185
1993	Maharashtra, India	6.4	9748
1994	Kuril Islands, Japan	8.3	10
1995	Kōbe, Japan	7.2	5502
1995	Sakhalin, Russian Fed.	7.6	2500
1996	Yunnan, China	7.0	251

Major earthquakes 1997 – 2005

Year	Location	*Force	Deaths
1997	Quae'n, Iran	7.1	2400
1998	Papua New Guinea		2183
1999	İzmit, Turkey	7.4	17 118
1999	Chi-Chi, Taiwan		2400
2001	Gujarat, India	6.9	20 085
2002	Hindu Kush, Afghanistan	6.0	1000
2003	Boumerdes, Algeria	5.8	2266
2003	Bam, Iran	6.6	26 271
2004	Sumatra, Indonesia	9.0	283 106
2005	Northern Sumatra, Indonesia	8.7	1313
2005	Muzzafarabad, Pakistan	7.6	80 361

* Earthquake force measured on the Richter scale

Major volcanic eruptions since 1980

Year	Location
1980	Mount St Helens, USA
1982	El Chichónal, Mexico
1982	Gunung Galunggung, Indonesia
1983	Kilauea, Hawaii
1983	Ō-yama, Japan
1985	Nevado del Ruiz, Colombia
1986	Lake Nyos, Cameroon
1991	Hekla, Iceland
1991	Mount Pinatubo, Philippines
1991	Unzen-dake, Japan
1993	Mayon, Philippines
1993	Volcán Galeras, Colombia
1994	Volcán Llaima, Chile
1994	Rabaul, PNG
1997	Soufrière Hills, Montserrat
2000	Hekla, Iceland
2001	Mt Etna, Italy
2002	Nyiragongo, Dem. Rep. of the Congo

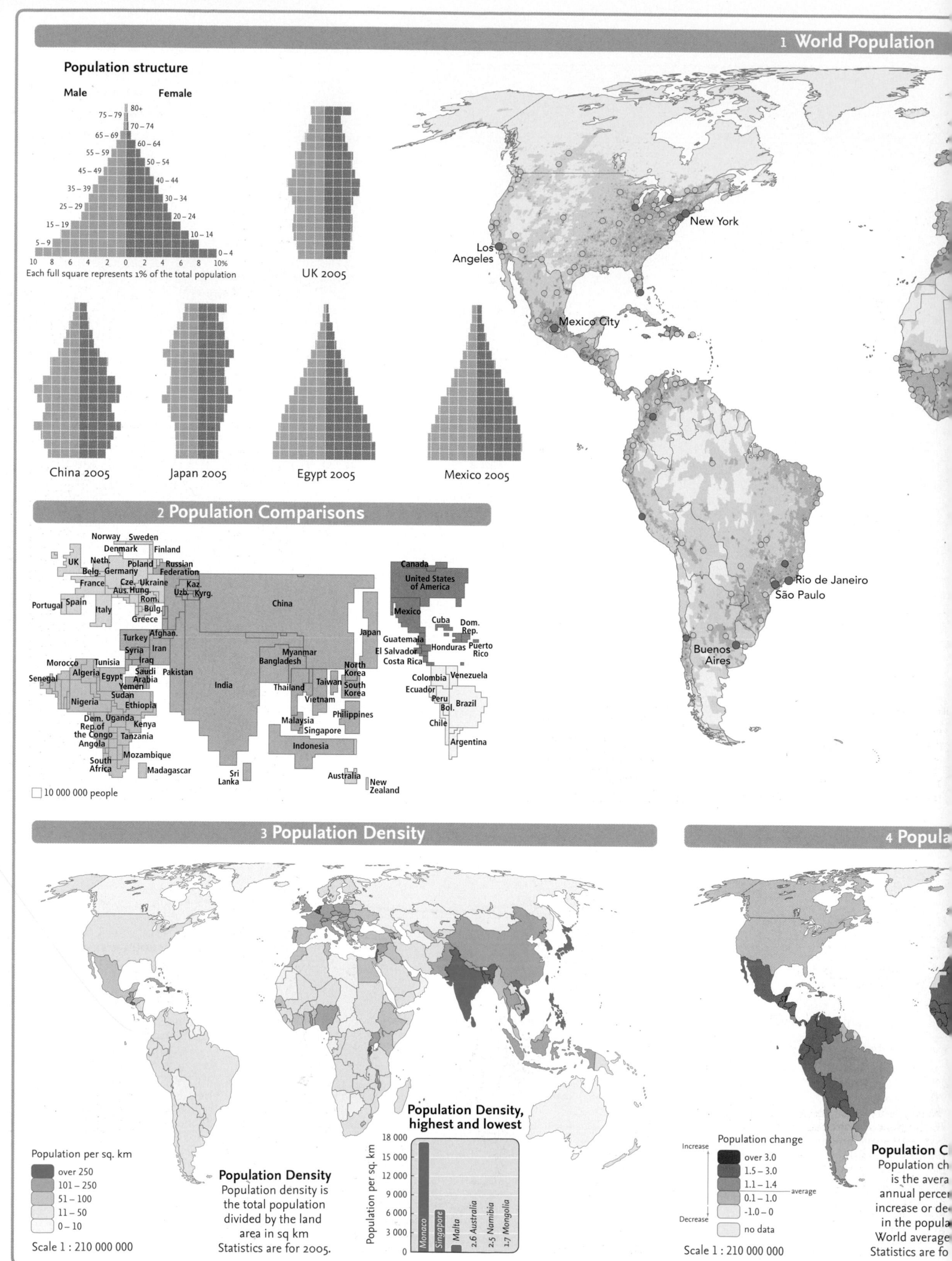

1 World Population

Population structure

Male | Female

75 – 79 | 80+ | 70 – 74
65 – 69 | 60 – 64
55 – 59 | 50 – 54
45 – 49 | 40 – 44
35 – 39 | 30 – 34
25 – 29 | 20 – 24
15 – 19 | 10 – 14
5 – 9 | 0 – 4

10 8 6 4 2 0 2 4 6 8 10%

Each full square represents 1% of the total population

UK 2005

China 2005   Japan 2005   Egypt 2005   Mexico 2005

2 Population Comparisons

Norway Sweden
Denmark Finland
UK Neth. Poland Russian
Belg. Germany Federation
France Cze. Ukraine Kaz.
Aus. Hung. Uzb. Kyrg.
Portugal Spain Rom.
Italy Bulg.
Greece
China
Turkey Afghan.
Syria Iran
Morocco Tunisia Iraq
Algeria Egypt Saudi Pakistan
Senegal Yemen Arabia
Sudan
Nigeria Ethiopia
Dem. Uganda
Rep.of Kenya
the Congo Tanzania
Angola
Mozambique
South
Africa Madagascar

India
Myanmar
Bangladesh
Thailand
Vietnam
Malaysia
Singapore
Indonesia
Sri
Lanka

Japan
North
Korea
Taiwan South
Korea
Philippines

Australia New
Zealand

Canada
United States
of America
Mexico
Cuba Dom.
Rep.
Guatemala Honduras Puerto
El Salvador Rico
Costa Rica
Colombia Venezuela
Ecuador
Peru Brazil
Bol.
Chile
Argentina

☐ 10 000 000 people

3 Population Density

Population per sq. km

- over 250
- 101 – 250
- 51 – 100
- 11 – 50
- 0 – 10

Scale 1 : 210 000 000

Population Density
Population density is
the total population
divided by the land
area in sq km
Statistics are for 2005.

**Population Density,
highest and lowest**

Population per sq. km

18 000
15 000
12 000
9 000
6 000
3 000
0

Monaco
Singapore
Malta
2.6 Australia
2.5 Namibia
1.7 Mongolia

4 Popula

Population change

Increase
- over 3.0
- 1.5 – 3.0
- 1.1 – 1.4 average
- 0.1 – 1.0
Decrease
- -1.0 – 0
- no data

Scale 1 : 210 000 000

Population C
Population ch
is the avera
annual percer
increase or de
in the popula
World averag
Statistics are fo

New York
Los
Angeles
Mexico City
Rio de Janeiro
São Paulo
Buenos
Aires

Largest countries by population, 2005

Country and continent	Population
China Asia	1 323 345 000
India Asia	1 103 371 000
United States of America N America	298 213 000
Indonesia Asia	222 781 000
Brazil S America	186 405 000
Pakistan Asia	157 935 000
Russian Federation Asia/Europe	143 202 000
Bangladesh Asia	141 822 000
Nigeria Africa	131 530 000
Japan Asia	128 085 000
Mexico N America	107 029 000
Vietnam Asia	84 238 000
Philippines Asia	83 054 000
Germany Europe	82 689 000
Ethiopia Africa	77 431 000
Egypt Africa	74 033 000
Turkey Asia	73 193 000
Iran Asia	69 515 000
Thailand Asia	64 233 000
France Europe	60 496 000

Largest urban agglomerations, 2005

Urban agglomeration and country	Population
Tōkyō Japan	35 327 000
Mexico City Mexico	19 013 000
New York United States of America	18 498 000
Mumbai India	18 336 000
São Paulo Brazil	18 333 000
Delhi India	15 334 000
Kolkata India	14 299 000
Buenos Aires Argentina	13 349 000
Jakarta Indonesia	13 194 000
Shanghai China	12 665 000
Dhaka Bangladesh	12 560 000
Los Angeles United States of America	12 146 000
Karachi Pakistan	11 819 000
Rio de Janeiro Brazil	11 469 000
Ōsaka-Kōbe Japan	11 286 000
Cairo Egypt	11 146 000
Lagos Nigeria	11 135 000
Beijing China	10 849 000
Manila Philippines	10 677 000
Moscow Russian Federation	10 672 000

ation per sq. km

over 1000
501 – 1000
101 – 500
11 – 100
1 – 10
less than 1

Cities
● over 10 000 000
● 5 000 000 – 10 000 000
○ 1 000 000 – 5 000 000

WWW United Nations Statistics Division
unstats.un.org
UN Population Information Network
www.un.org/popin
Population Reference Bureau
www.popnet.org
World Bank
www.worldbank.org

Scale 1 : 100 000 000

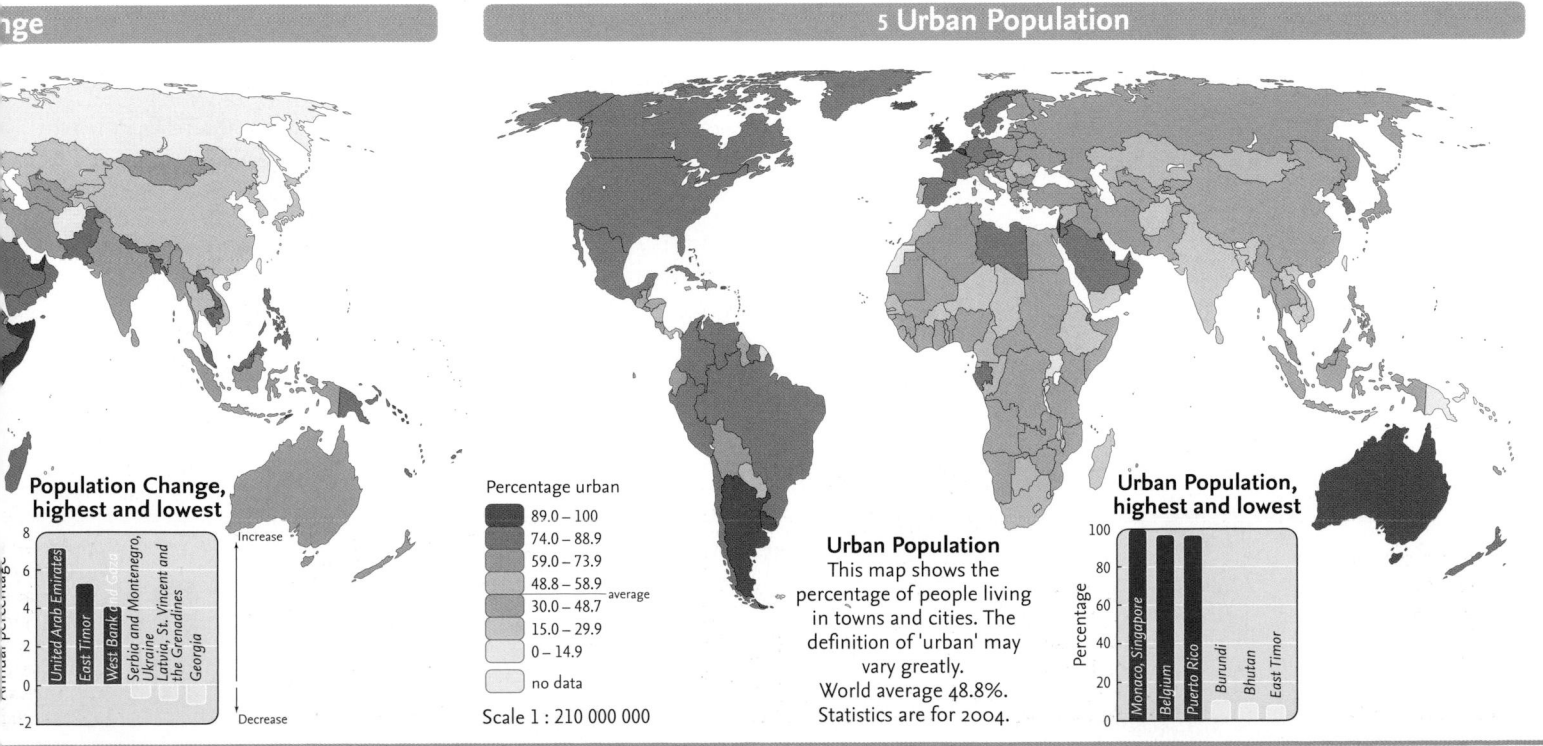

ge

5 Urban Population

Population Change, highest and lowest

United Arab Emirates
East Timor
West Bank and Gaza

Serbia and Montenegro,
Ukraine
Latvia, St. Vincent and
the Grenadines
Georgia

Increase

average

Decrease

Percentage urban

89.0 – 100
74.0 – 88.9
59.0 – 73.9
48.8 – 58.9
30.0 – 48.7
15.0 – 29.9
0 – 14.9
no data

average

Urban Population
This map shows the
percentage of people living
in towns and cities. The
definition of 'urban' may
vary greatly.
World average 48.8%.
Statistics are for 2004.

Scale 1 : 210 000 000

Urban Population, highest and lowest

Monaco, Singapore
Belgium
Puerto Rico

Burundi
Bhutan
East Timor

Percentage

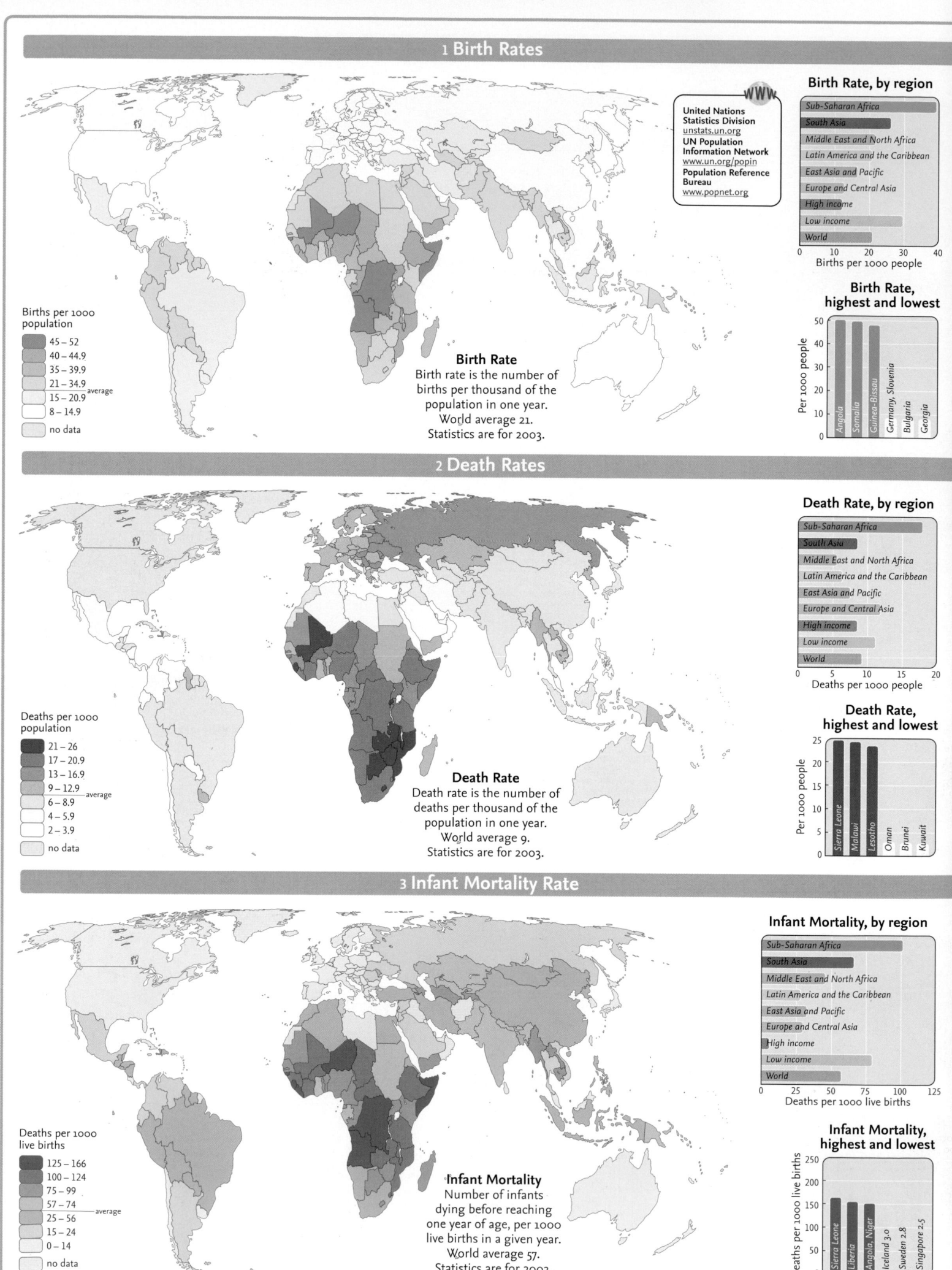

1 Birth Rates

United Nations
Statistics Division
unstats.un.org
**UN Population
Information Network**
www.un.org/popin
**Population Reference
Bureau**
www.popnet.org

**Births per 1000
population**

- 45 – 52
- 40 – 44.9
- 35 – 39.9
- 21 – 34.9
- 15 – 20.9 average
- 8 – 14.9
- no data

Birth Rate
Birth rate is the number of
births per thousand of the
population in one year.
World average 21.
Statistics are for 2003.

Birth Rate, by region

Sub-Saharan Africa
South Asia
Middle East and North Africa
Latin America and the Caribbean
East Asia and Pacific
Europe and Central Asia
High income
Low income
World

0   10   20   30   40
Births per 1000 people

**Birth Rate,
highest and lowest**

Per 1000 people — Angola, Somalia, Guinea-Bissau, Germany, Slovenia, Bulgaria, Georgia

2 Death Rates

**Deaths per 1000
population**

- 21 – 26
- 17 – 20.9
- 13 – 16.9
- 9 – 12.9 average
- 6 – 8.9
- 4 – 5.9
- 2 – 3.9
- no data

Death Rate
Death rate is the number of
deaths per thousand of the
population in one year.
World average 9.
Statistics are for 2003.

Death Rate, by region

Sub-Saharan Africa
South Asia
Middle East and North Africa
Latin America and the Caribbean
East Asia and Pacific
Europe and Central Asia
High income
Low income
World

0   5   10   15   20
Deaths per 1000 people

**Death Rate,
highest and lowest**

Per 1000 people — Sierra Leone, Malawi, Lesotho, Oman, Brunei, Kuwait

3 Infant Mortality Rate

**Deaths per 1000
live births**

- 125 – 166
- 100 – 124
- 75 – 99
- 57 – 74 average
- 25 – 56
- 15 – 24
- 0 – 14
- no data

Infant Mortality
Number of infants
dying before reaching
one year of age, per 1000
live births in a given year.
World average 57.
Statistics are for 2003.

Infant Mortality, by region

Sub-Saharan Africa
South Asia
Middle East and North Africa
Latin America and the Caribbean
East Asia and Pacific
Europe and Central Asia
High income
Low income
World

0   25   50   75   100   125
Deaths per 1000 live births

**Infant Mortality,
highest and lowest**

Deaths per 1000 live births — Sierra Leone, Liberia, Angola, Niger, Iceland 3.0, Sweden 2.8, Singapore 2.5

Scale 1 : 190 000 000

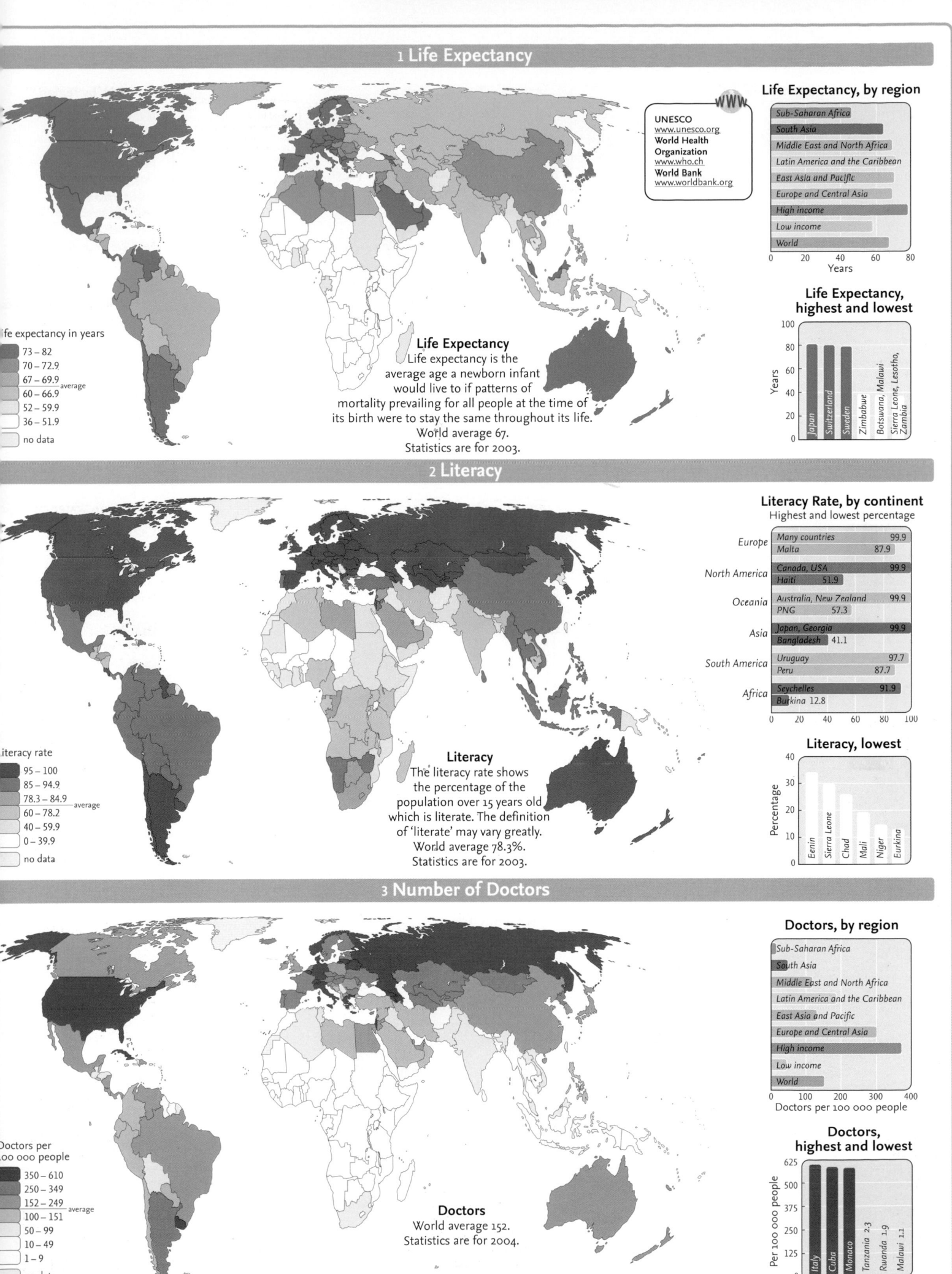

1 Life Expectancy

UNESCO
www.unesco.org
World Health Organization
www.who.ch
World Bank
www.worldbank.org

Life Expectancy, by region

Sub-Saharan Africa
South Asia
Middle East and North Africa
Latin America and the Caribbean
East Asia and Pacific
Europe and Central Asia
High income
Low income
World

0   20   40   60   80
Years

Life Expectancy
Life expectancy is the average age a newborn infant would live to if patterns of mortality prevailing for all people at the time of its birth were to stay the same throughout its life. World average 67. Statistics are for 2003.

Life Expectancy, highest and lowest

Years — 100, 80, 60, 40, 20, 0
Japan, Switzerland, Sweden, Zimbabwe, Botswana, Malawi, Sierra Leone, Lesotho, Zambia

Life expectancy in years
- 73 – 82
- 70 – 72.9
- 67 – 69.9 average
- 60 – 66.9
- 52 – 59.9
- 36 – 51.9
- no data

2 Literacy

Literacy
The literacy rate shows the percentage of the population over 15 years old which is literate. The definition of 'literate' may vary greatly. World average 78.3%. Statistics are for 2003.

Literacy rate
- 95 – 100
- 85 – 94.9
- 78.3 – 84.9 average
- 60 – 78.2
- 40 – 59.9
- 0 – 39.9
- no data

Literacy Rate, by continent
Highest and lowest percentage

Europe	Many countries	99.9
	Malta	87.9
North America	Canada, USA	99.9
	Haiti	51.9
Oceania	Australia, New Zealand	99.9
	PNG	57.3
Asia	Japan, Georgia	99.9
	Bangladesh	41.1
South America	Uruguay	97.7
	Peru	87.7
Africa	Seychelles	91.9
	Burkina	12.8

0   20   40   60   80   100

Literacy, lowest

Percentage — 40, 30, 20, 10, 0
Benin, Sierra Leone, Chad, Mali, Niger, Burkina

3 Number of Doctors

Doctors
World average 152. Statistics are for 2004.

Doctors per 100 000 people
- 350 – 610
- 250 – 349
- 152 – 249 average
- 100 – 151
- 50 – 99
- 10 – 49
- 1 – 9
- no data

Doctors, by region

Sub-Saharan Africa
South Asia
Middle East and North Africa
Latin America and the Caribbean
East Asia and Pacific
Europe and Central Asia
High income
Low income
World

0   100   200   300   400
Doctors per 100 000 people

Doctors, highest and lowest

Per 100 000 people — 625, 500, 375, 250, 125, 0
Italy, Cuba, Monaco, Tanzania 2.3, Rwanda 1.9, Malawi 1.1

Eckert IV projection

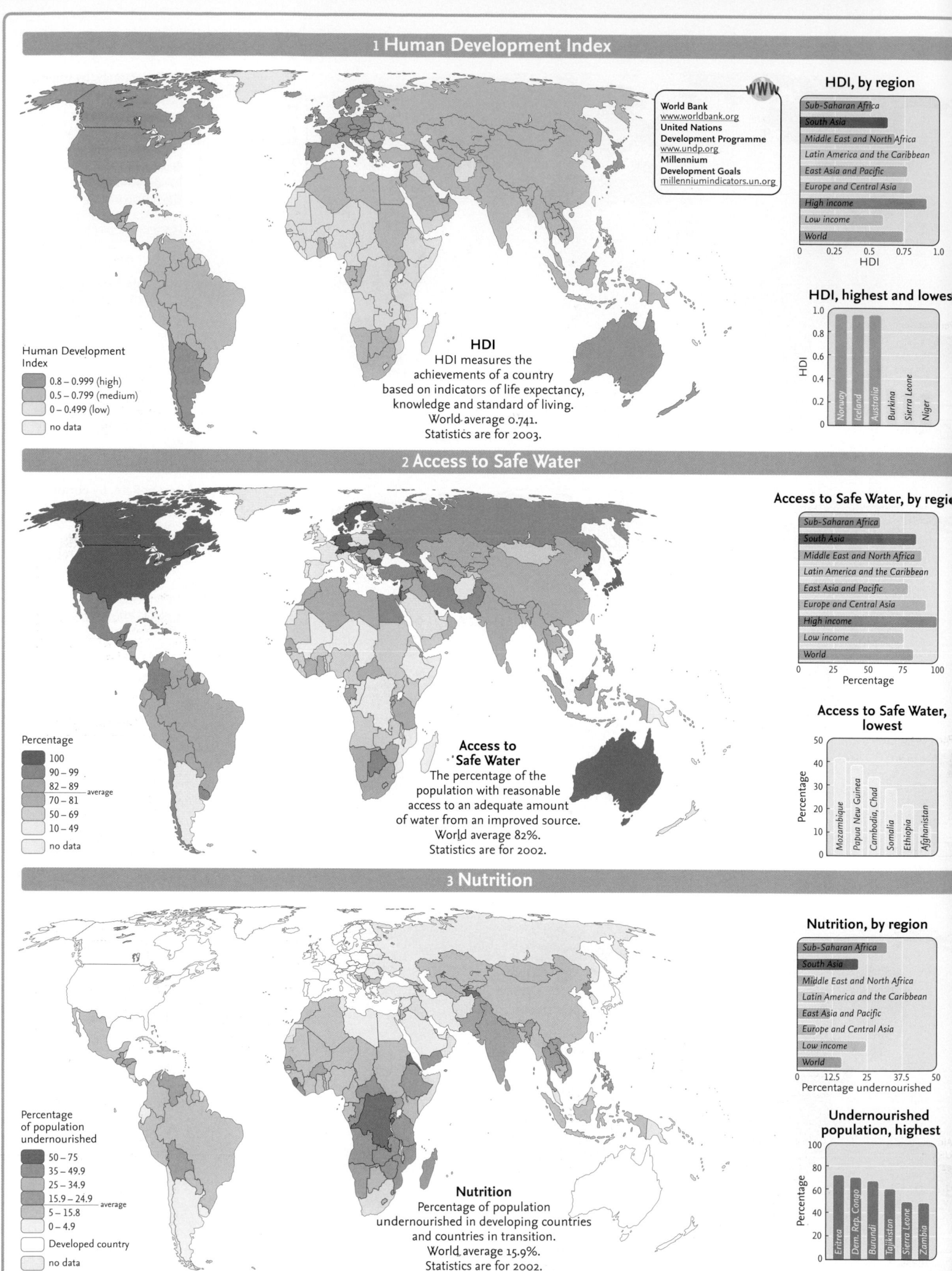

1 Human Development Index

World Bank
www.worldbank.org
United Nations
Development Programme
www.undp.org
Millennium
Development Goals
millenniumindicators.un.org

HDI, by region

Sub-Saharan Africa
South Asia
Middle East and North Africa
Latin America and the Caribbean
East Asia and Pacific
Europe and Central Asia
High income
Low income
World

0   0.25   0.5   0.75   1.0
HDI

HDI, highest and lowest

1.0
0.8
0.6
0.4
0.2
0

HDI

Norway Iceland Australia Burkina Sierra Leone Niger

HDI
HDI measures the achievements of a country based on indicators of life expectancy, knowledge and standard of living.
World average 0.741.
Statistics are for 2003.

Human Development Index
0.8 – 0.999 (high)
0.5 – 0.799 (medium)
0 – 0.499 (low)
no data

2 Access to Safe Water

Access to Safe Water, by region

Sub-Saharan Africa
South Asia
Middle East and North Africa
Latin America and the Caribbean
East Asia and Pacific
Europe and Central Asia
High income
Low income
World

0   25   50   75   100
Percentage

Access to Safe Water, lowest

50
40
30
20
10
0

Percentage

Mozambique Papua New Guinea Cambodia, Chad Somalia Ethiopia Afghanistan

Access to Safe Water
The percentage of the population with reasonable access to an adequate amount of water from an improved source.
World average 82%.
Statistics are for 2002.

Percentage
100
90 – 99
82 – 89 average
70 – 81
50 – 69
10 – 49
no data

3 Nutrition

Nutrition, by region

Sub-Saharan Africa
South Asia
Middle East and North Africa
Latin America and the Caribbean
East Asia and Pacific
Europe and Central Asia
Low income
World

0   12.5   25   37.5   50
Percentage undernourished

Undernourished population, highest

100
80
60
40
20
0

Percentage

Eritrea Dem. Rep. Congo Burundi Tajikistan Sierra Leone Zambia

Nutrition
Percentage of population undernourished in developing countries and countries in transition.
World average 15.9%.
Statistics are for 2002.

Percentage of population undernourished
50 – 75
35 – 49.9
25 – 34.9
15.9 – 24.9 average
5 – 15.8
0 – 4.9
Developed country
no data

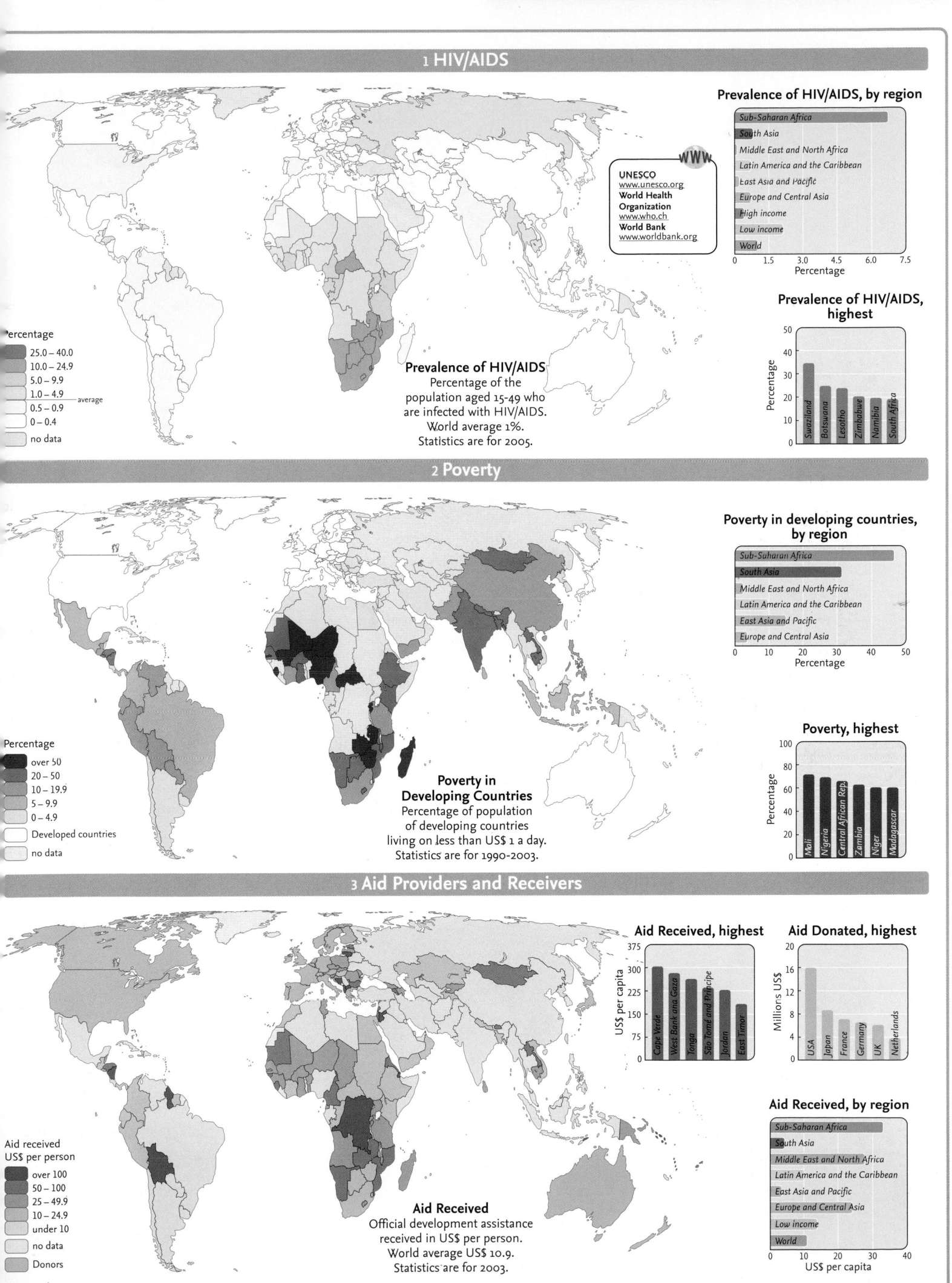

1 HIV/AIDS

Prevalence of HIV/AIDS, by region

Sub-Saharan Africa
South Asia
Middle East and North Africa
Latin America and the Caribbean
East Asia and Pacific
Europe and Central Asia
High income
Low income
World

0   1.5   3.0   4.5   6.0   7.5
Percentage

Prevalence of HIV/AIDS, highest

Percentage — Swaziland, Botswana, Lesotho, Zimbabwe, Namibia, South Africa

UNESCO
www.unesco.org
World Health
Organization
www.who.ch
World Bank
www.worldbank.org

Prevalence of HIV/AIDS
Percentage of the population aged 15-49 who are infected with HIV/AIDS. World average 1%. Statistics are for 2005.

Percentage
- 25.0 – 40.0
- 10.0 – 24.9
- 5.0 – 9.9
- 1.0 – 4.9 — average
- 0.5 – 0.9
- 0 – 0.4
- no data

2 Poverty

Poverty in developing countries, by region

Sub-Saharan Africa
South Asia
Middle East and North Africa
Latin America and the Caribbean
East Asia and Pacific
Europe and Central Asia

0   10   20   30   40   50
Percentage

Poverty, highest

Percentage — Mali, Nigeria, Central African Rep., Zambia, Niger, Madagascar

Poverty in Developing Countries
Percentage of population of developing countries living on less than US$ 1 a day. Statistics are for 1990-2003.

Percentage
- over 50
- 20 – 50
- 10 – 19.9
- 5 – 9.9
- 0 – 4.9
- Developed countries
- no data

3 Aid Providers and Receivers

Aid Received, highest

US$ per capita — Cape Verde, West Bank and Gaza, Tonga, São Tomé and Príncipe, Jordan, East Timor

Aid Donated, highest

Millions US$ — USA, Japan, France, Germany, UK, Netherlands

Aid Received, by region

Sub-Saharan Africa
South Asia
Middle East and North Africa
Latin America and the Caribbean
East Asia and Pacific
Europe and Central Asia
Low income
World

0   10   20   30   40
US$ per capita

Aid Received
Official development assistance received in US$ per person. World average US$ 10.9. Statistics are for 2003.

Aid received US$ per person
- over 100
- 50 – 100
- 25 – 49.9
- 10 – 24.9
- under 10
- no data
- Donors

ale 1 : 190 000 000

Eckert IV projection

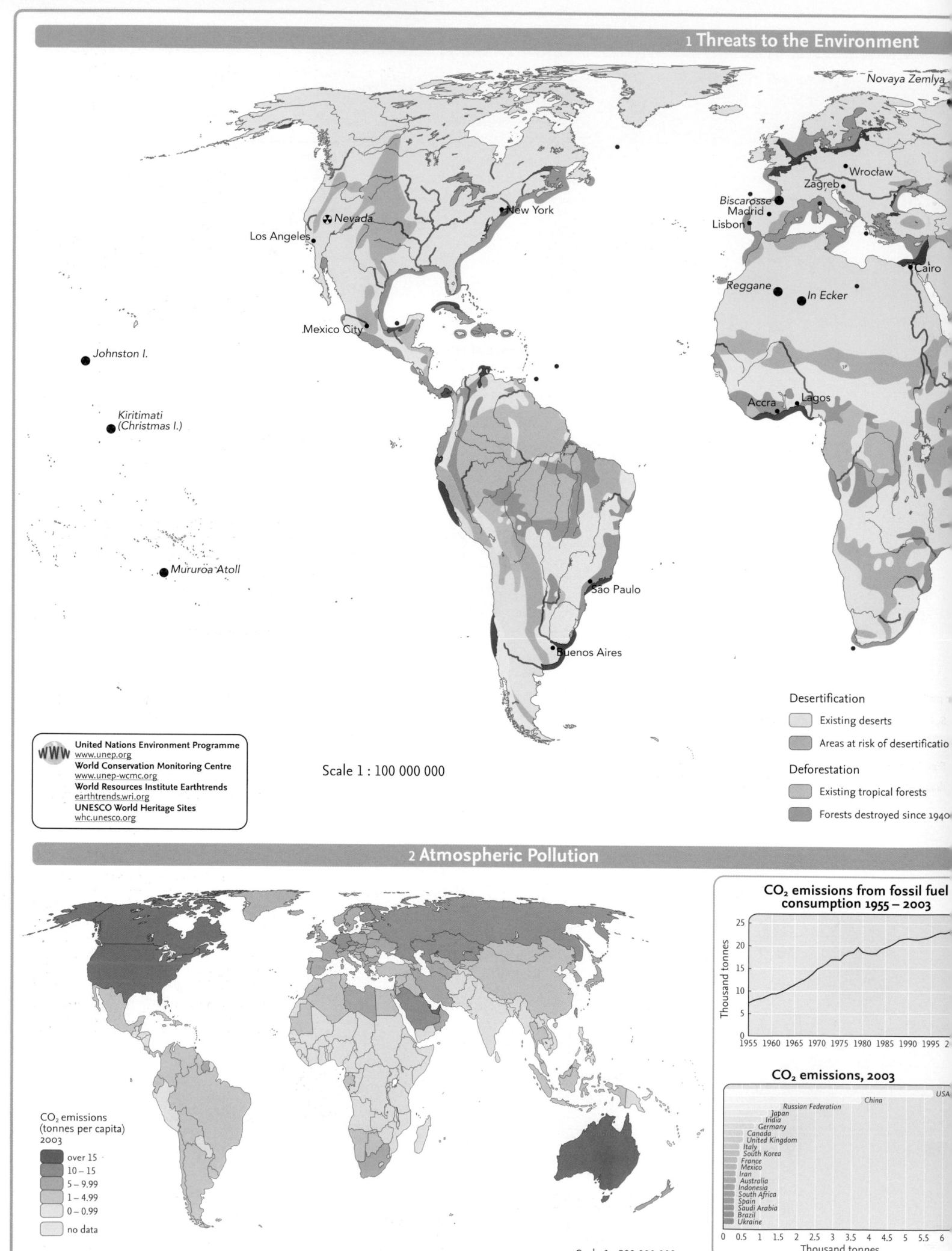

1 Threats to the Environment

Novaya Zemlya

Wrocław

Zagreb

Biscarosse
Madrid

Lisbon

Cairo

Reggane · In Ecker

Accra · Lagos

New York

· Nevada

Los Angeles

Mexico City

Johnston I.

Kiritimati
(Christmas I.)

Mururoa Atoll

Sao Paulo

Buenos Aires

United Nations Environment Programme
www.unep.org
World Conservation Monitoring Centre
www.unep-wcmc.org
World Resources Institute Earthtrends
earthtrends.wri.org
UNESCO World Heritage Sites
whc.unesco.org

Scale 1 : 100 000 000

Desertification

Existing deserts

Areas at risk of desertificatio

Deforestation

Existing tropical forests

Forests destroyed since 1940

2 Atmospheric Pollution

**CO₂ emissions from fossil fuel
consumption 1955 – 2003**

Thousand tonnes

25
20
15
10
5
0

1955 1960 1965 1970 1975 1980 1985 1990 1995 2

**CO₂ emissions
(tonnes per capita)
2003**

over 15
10 – 15
5 – 9.99
1 – 4.99
0 – 0.99
no data

CO₂ emissions, 2003

USA
China
Russian Federation
Japan
India
Germany
Canada
United Kingdom
Italy
South Korea
France
Mexico
Iran
Australia
Indonesia
South Africa
Spain
Saudi Arabia
Brazil
Ukraine

0   0.5   1   1.5   2   2.5   3   3.5   4   4.5   5   5.5   6
Thousand tonnes

Scale 1 : 200 000 000

pollution

- Severe coastal pollution
- Persistent coastal pollution
- Significant oil spill
- River pollution

☢ Current nuclear test site

● Former nuclear test site

• Major city with air pollution.
  Problem due to industry and
  vehicle exhaust

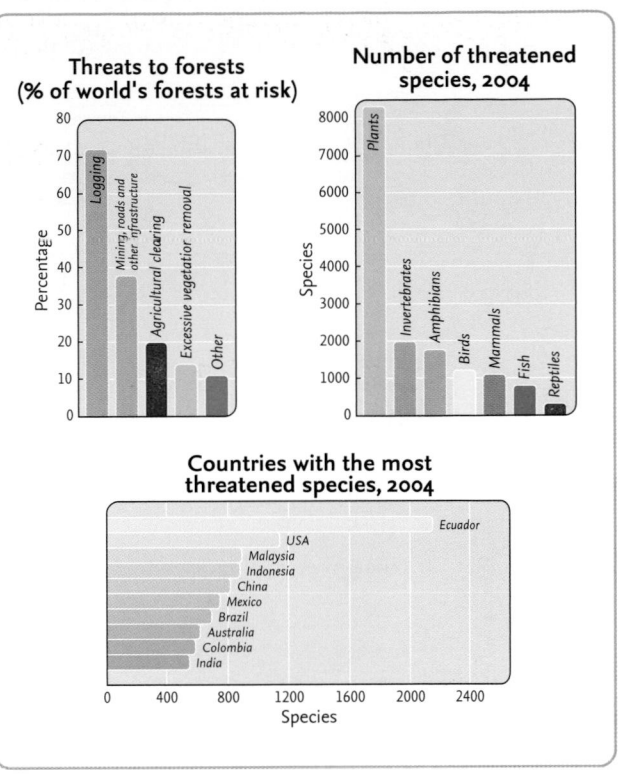

Threats to forests
(% of world's forests at risk)

Logging / Mining, roads and other infrastructure / Agricultural clearing / Excessive vegetation removal / Other

Number of threatened species, 2004

Plants / Invertebrates / Amphibians / Birds / Mammals / Fish / Reptiles

Countries with the most threatened species, 2004

USA / Ecuador / Malaysia / Indonesia / China / Mexico / Brazil / Australia / Colombia / India

Species

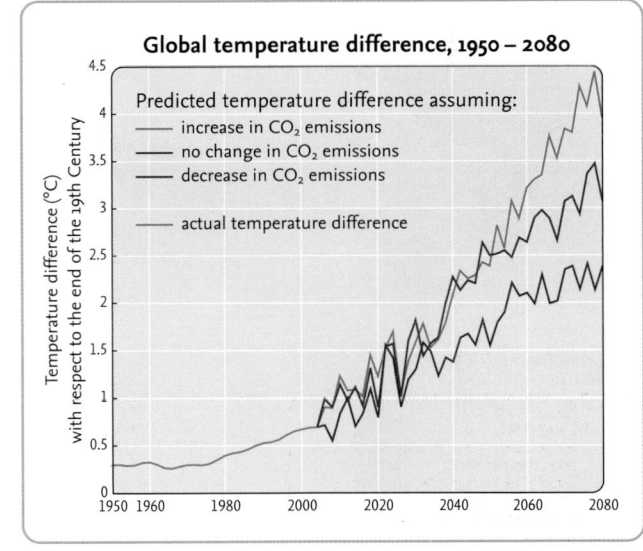

Global temperature difference, 1950 – 2080

Predicted temperature difference assuming:
— increase in CO_2 emissions
— no change in CO_2 emissions
— decrease in CO_2 emissions
— actual temperature difference

3 Forest and Coral Reefs at Risk

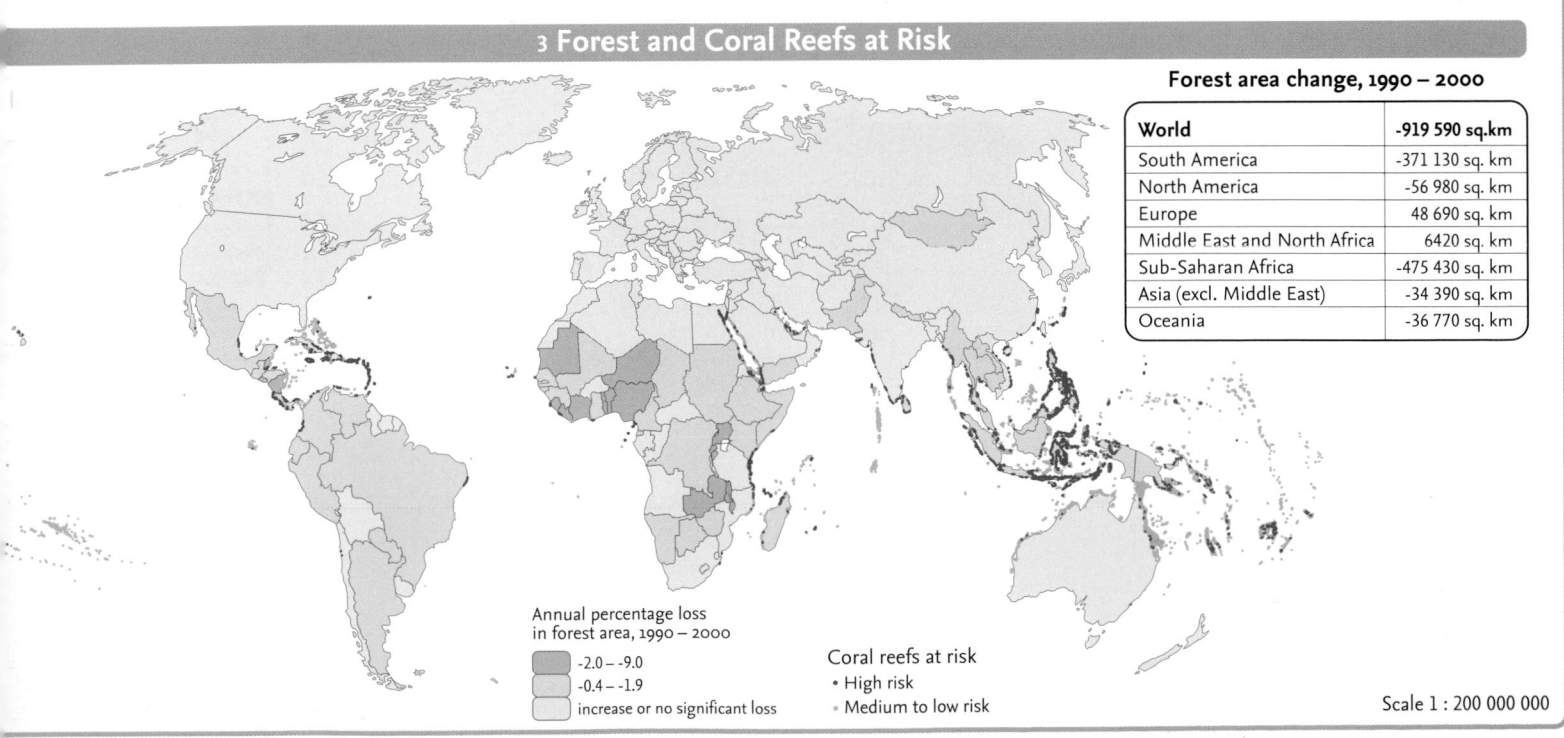

Annual percentage loss
in forest area, 1990 – 2000

- -2.0 – -9.0
- -0.4 – -1.9
- increase or no significant loss

Coral reefs at risk
- High risk
- Medium to low risk

Forest area change, 1990 – 2000

World	-919 590 sq.km
South America	-371 130 sq. km
North America	-56 980 sq. km
Europe	48 690 sq. km
Middle East and North Africa	6420 sq. km
Sub-Saharan Africa	-475 430 sq. km
Asia (excl. Middle East)	-34 390 sq. km
Oceania	-36 770 sq. km

Scale 1 : 200 000 000

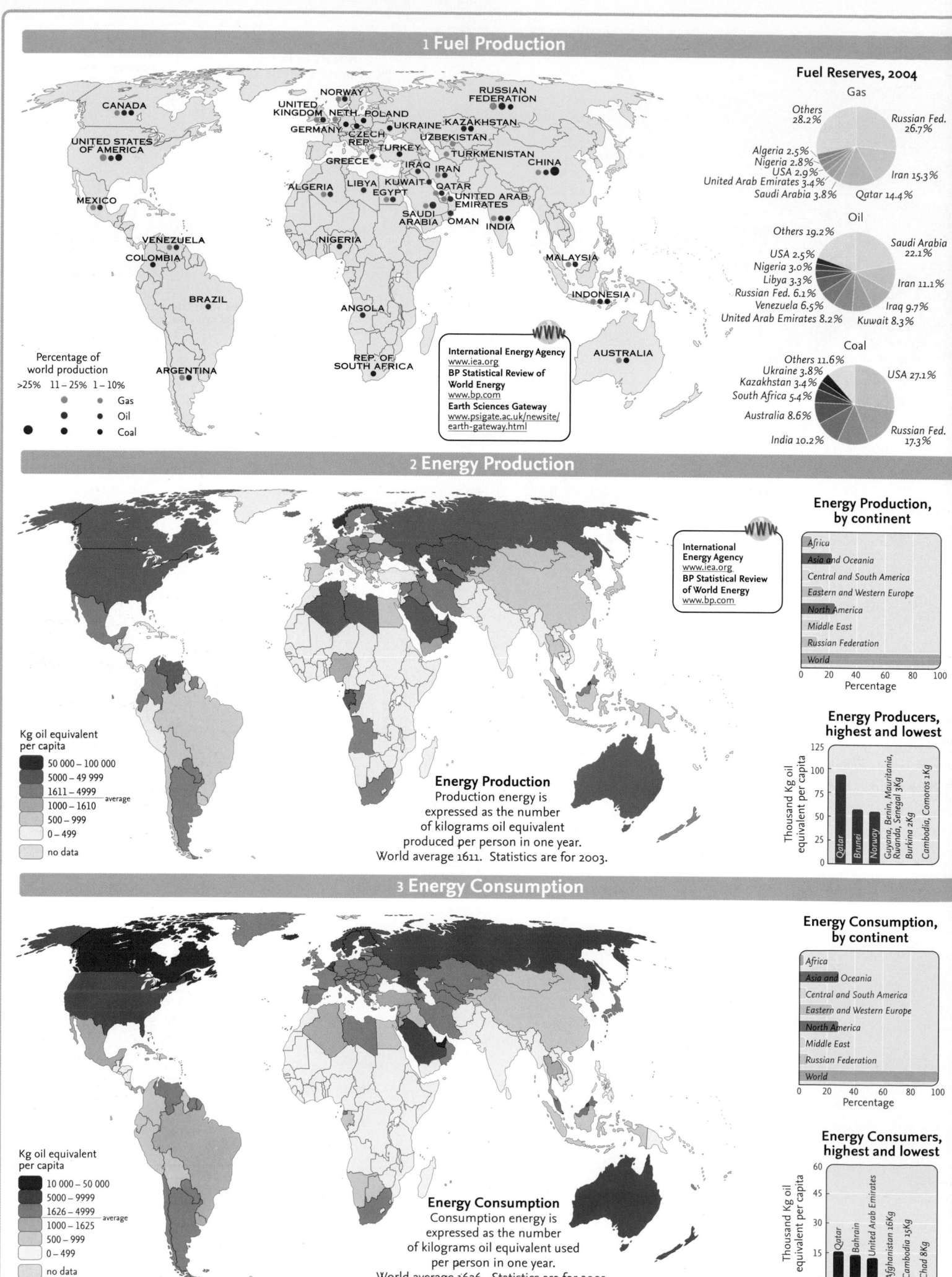

1 Fuel Production

Fuel Reserves, 2004

Gas

Others 28.2%
Russian Fed. 26.7%
Iran 15.3%
Qatar 14.4%
Saudi Arabia 3.8%
United Arab Emirates 3.4%
USA 2.9%
Nigeria 2.8%
Algeria 2.5%

Oil

Others 19.2%
Saudi Arabia 22.1%
USA 2.5%
Nigeria 3.0%
Libya 3.3%
Russian Fed. 6.1%
Venezuela 6.5%
United Arab Emirates 8.2%
Iran 11.1%
Iraq 9.7%
Kuwait 8.3%

Coal

Others 11.6%
Ukraine 3.8%
Kazakhstan 3.4%
South Africa 5.4%
Australia 8.6%
India 10.2%
USA 27.1%
Russian Fed. 17.3%

Percentage of world production

>25%   11 – 25%   1 – 10%

Gas
Oil
Coal

International Energy Agency
www.iea.org
BP Statistical Review of World Energy
www.bp.com
Earth Sciences Gateway
www.psigate.ac.uk/newsite/earth-gateway.html

2 Energy Production

Energy Production, by continent

Africa
Asia and Oceania
Central and South America
Eastern and Western Europe
North America
Middle East
Russian Federation
World

0   20   40   60   80   100
Percentage

Energy Producers, highest and lowest

Thousand Kg oil equivalent per capita

125
100
75
50
25
0

Qatar
Brunei
Norway
Guyana, Benin, Mauritania, Rwanda, Senegal 3Kg
Burkina 2kg
Cambodia, Comoros 1Kg

International Energy Agency
www.iea.org
BP Statistical Review of World Energy
www.bp.com

Kg oil equivalent per capita

50 000 – 100 000
5000 – 49 999
1611 – 4999   average
1000 – 1610
500 – 999
0 – 499
no data

Energy Production
Production energy is expressed as the number of kilograms oil equivalent produced per person in one year. World average 1611. Statistics are for 2003.

3 Energy Consumption

Energy Consumption, by continent

Africa
Asia and Oceania
Central and South America
Eastern and Western Europe
North America
Middle East
Russian Federation
World

0   20   40   60   80   100
Percentage

Energy Consumers, highest and lowest

Thousand Kg oil equivalent per capita

60
45
30
15
0

Qatar
Bahrain
United Arab Emirates
Afghanistan 16Kg
Cambodia 15Kg
Chad 8Kg

Kg oil equivalent per capita

10 000 – 50 000
5000 – 9999
1626 – 4999   average
1000 – 1625
500 – 999
0 – 499
no data

Energy Consumption
Consumption energy is expressed as the number of kilograms oil equivalent used per person in one year. World average 1626. Statistics are for 2003.

Scale 1 : 190 000 000

Eckert IV project

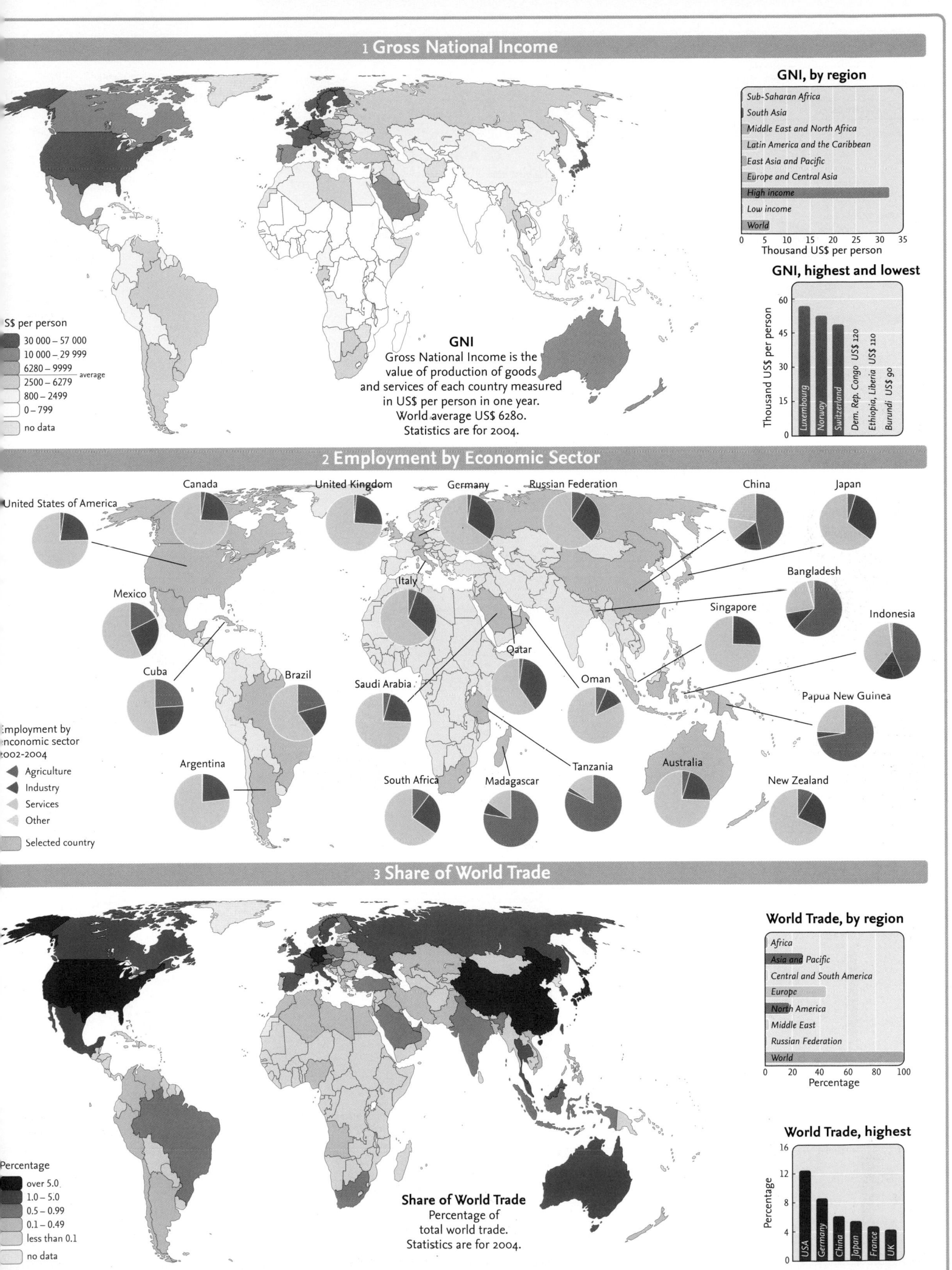

1 Gross National Income

S$ per person
- 30 000 – 57 000
- 10 000 – 29 999
- 6280 – 9999 — average
- 2500 – 6279
- 800 – 2499
- 0 – 799
- no data

GNI
Gross National Income is the value of production of goods and services of each country measured in US$ per person in one year. World average US$ 6280. Statistics are for 2004.

GNI, by region
- Sub-Saharan Africa
- South Asia
- Middle East and North Africa
- Latin America and the Caribbean
- East Asia and Pacific
- Europe and Central Asia
- High income
- Low income
- World

0 5 10 15 20 25 30 35
Thousand US$ per person

GNI, highest and lowest
Thousand US$ per person
60, 45, 15, 0

Luxembourg
Norway
Switzerland
Dem. Rep. Congo US$ 120
Ethiopia, Liberia US$ 110
Burundi US$ 90

2 Employment by Economic Sector

United States of America · Canada · United Kingdom · Germany · Russian Federation · China · Japan
Mexico · Italy · Bangladesh · Singapore · Indonesia
Cuba · Brazil · Qatar · Oman · Papua New Guinea
Saudi Arabia · Argentina · South Africa · Madagascar · Tanzania · Australia · New Zealand

Employment by economic sector 2002-2004
- Agriculture
- Industry
- Services
- Other

Selected country

3 Share of World Trade

Percentage
- over 5.0
- 1.0 – 5.0
- 0.5 – 0.99
- 0.1 – 0.49
- less than 0.1
- no data

Share of World Trade
Percentage of total world trade. Statistics are for 2004.

World Trade, by region
- Africa
- Asia and Pacific
- Central and South America
- Europe
- North America
- Middle East
- Russian Federation
- World

0 20 40 60 80 100
Percentage

World Trade, highest
Percentage
16, 12, 8, 4, 0

USA
Germany
China
Japan
France
UK

Eckert IV projection

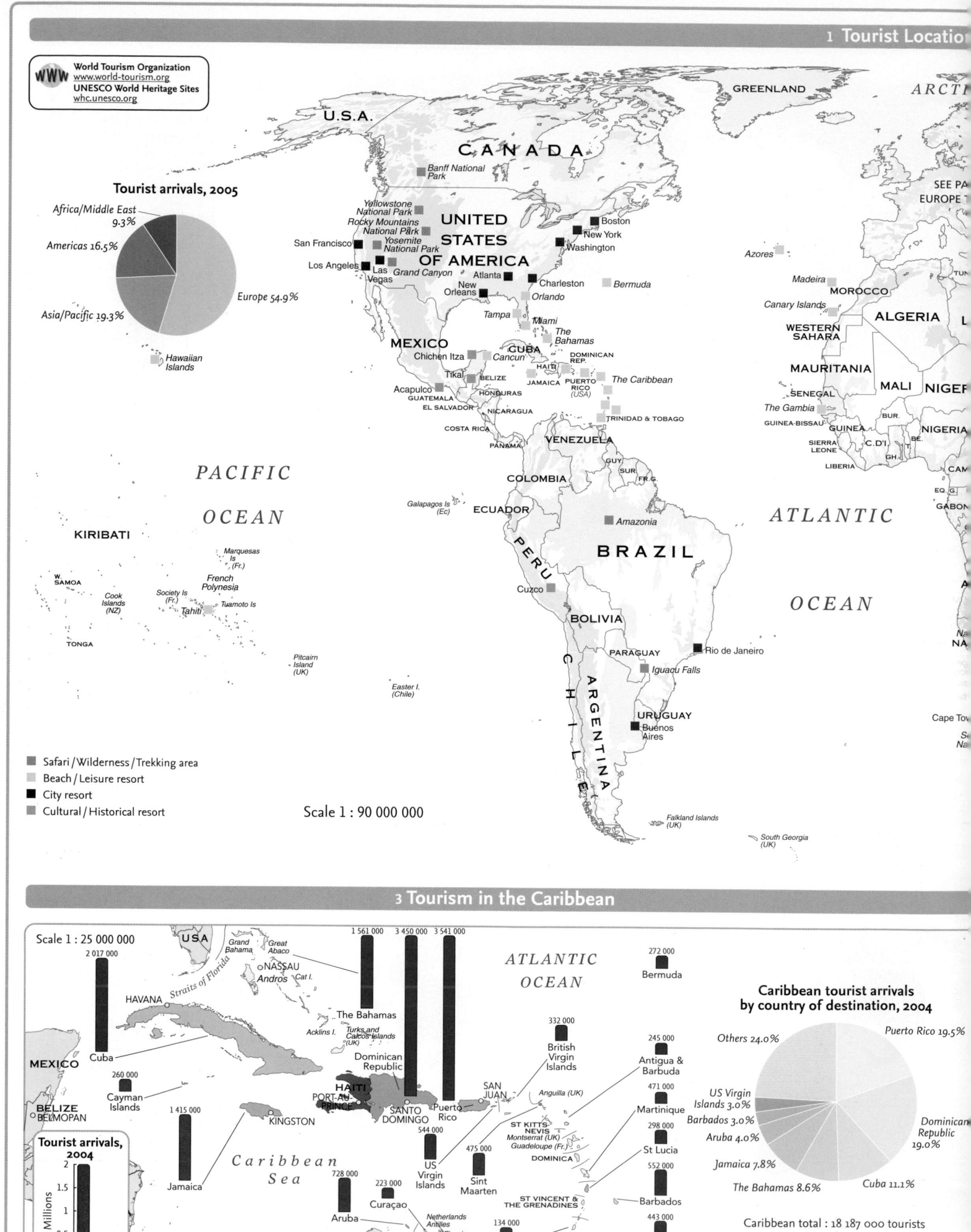

WWW World Tourism Organization
www.world-tourism.org
UNESCO World Heritage Sites
whc.unesco.org

Tourist arrivals, 2005

- Africa/Middle East 9.3%
- Americas 16.5%
- Asia/Pacific 19.3%
- Europe 54.9%

Safari / Wilderness / Trekking area
Beach / Leisure resort
City resort
Cultural / Historical resort

Scale 1 : 90 000 000

3 Tourism in the Caribbean

Scale 1 : 25 000 000

Tourist arrivals, 2004

Millions
2
1.5
1
0.5
0

- 2 017 000 Cuba
- 260 000 Cayman Islands
- 1 415 000 Jamaica
- 1 561 000 The Bahamas
- 3 450 000 Dominican Republic
- 3 541 000 Puerto Rico
- 272 000 Bermuda
- 332 000 British Virgin Islands
- 245 000 Antigua & Barbuda
- 471 000 Martinique
- 298 000 St Lucia
- 552 000 Barbados
- 544 000 US Virgin Islands
- 475 000 Sint Maarten
- 728 000 Aruba
- 223 000 Curaçao
- 134 000 Grenada
- 443 000 Trinidad & Tobago

Caribbean tourist arrivals by country of destination, 2004

- Others 24.0%
- Puerto Rico 19.5%
- US Virgin Islands 3.0%
- Barbados 3.0%
- Aruba 4.0%
- Jamaica 7.8%
- The Bahamas 8.6%
- Cuba 11.1%
- Dominican Republic 19.0%

Caribbean total : 18 187 000 tourists

2 International Tourist Arrivals

Africa

(bar chart, Millions, 1991–2020, with "projected" bars for 2010 and 2020)

Americas

(bar chart, Millions 0–400, 1991–2020, with "projected" bars for 2010 and 2020)

Asia/Pacific

(bar chart, Millions 0–500, 1991–2020, with "projected" bars for 2010 and 2020)

Europe

(bar chart, Millions 0–800, 1991–2020, with "projected" bars for 2010 and 2020)

(Map of Asia, Indian Ocean, Pacific Ocean, Australia and New Zealand with labelled countries and tourist destinations: RUSSIAN FEDERATION, KAZAKHSTAN, MONGOLIA, CHINA, Beijing, Great Wall, Xi'an, N. KOREA, S. KOREA, JAPAN, Tōkyō, Shanghai, Hong Kong, TAIWAN, INDIA, Agra/Taj Mahal, Jaipur, NEPAL, BHUTAN, BANGLADESH, MYANMAR (BURMA), Chiang Mai, LAOS, VIETNAM, THAILAND, Bangkok, CAMBODIA, Koh Samui, Phuket, Goa, Sri Lanka, Maldives, MALAYSIA, Mt Kinabalu, BRUNEI, Singapore, INDONESIA, Bali, EAST TIMOR, PHILIPPINES, PALAU, Northern Marianas (USA), MARSHALL ISLANDS, FED. STATES OF MICRONESIA, NAURU, KIRIBATI, TUVALU, SOLOMON ISLANDS, PAPUA NEW GUINEA, VANUATU, New Caledonia (Fr.), Fiji, AUSTRALIA, Great Barrier Reef Marine Park, Uluru, Gold Coast, Blue Mountains, NEW ZEALAND, North Island, South Island, Seychelles, Comoros, Mauritius, Reunion, MADAGASCAR, MOZAMBIQUE, Kariba, East African National Parks, Mombasa, KENYA, TANZANIA, SOMALIA, ETHIOPIA, YEMEN, SAUDI ARABIA, Abu Dhabi, U.A.E., OMAN, IRAN, AFGHANISTAN, PAKISTAN, UZBEKISTAN, TURKMENISTAN, TAJIKISTAN, KYRGYZSTAN, Aleppo, Petra, Pyramids, Kerguelen (Fr.))

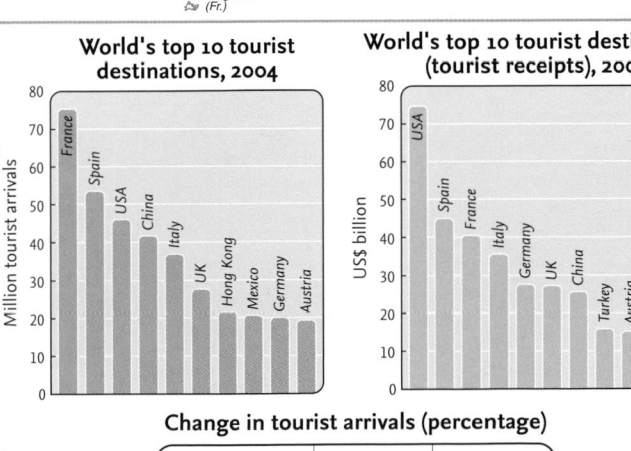

World's top 10 tourist destinations, 2004

(bar chart, Million tourist arrivals 0–80: France, Spain, USA, China, Italy, UK, Hong Kong, Mexico, Germany, Austria)

World's top 10 tourist destinations (tourist receipts), 2004

(bar chart, US$ billion 0–80: USA, Spain, France, Italy, Germany, UK, China, Turkey, Austria, Australia)

Change in tourist arrivals (percentage)

Country	2003/2002	2004/2003
France	-2.6	0.1
Spain	-0.9	3.4
USA	-5.4	11.8
China	-10.4	26.7
Italy	-0.5	-6.4
UK	2.2	12.3
Hong Kong	-6.2	40.4
Mexico	-5.1	10.5
Germany	2.4	9.5
Austria	2.5	1.5

4 Tourism in the Future

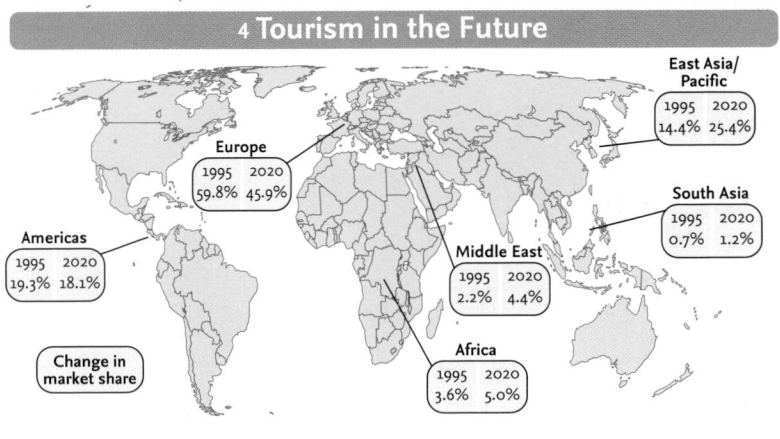

East Asia/Pacific
1995 14.4% 2020 25.4%

South Asia
1995 0.7% 2020 1.2%

Europe
1995 59.8% 2020 45.9%

Americas
1995 19.3% 2020 18.1%

Middle East
1995 2.2% 2020 4.4%

Africa
1995 3.6% 2020 5.0%

Change in market share

Tourist arrivals forecast 1995-2020 (millions)

	1995	2010	2020	Average annual growth rate (%)
World	565.4	1006.4	1561.1	4.1
Africa	20.2	47.0	77.3	5.5
Americas	108.9	190.4	282.3	3.9
East Asia/Pacific	81.4	195.2	397.2	6.5
Europe	338.4	527.3	717.0	3.0
Middle East	12.4	35.9	68.5	7.1
South Asia	4.2	10.6	18.8	6.2

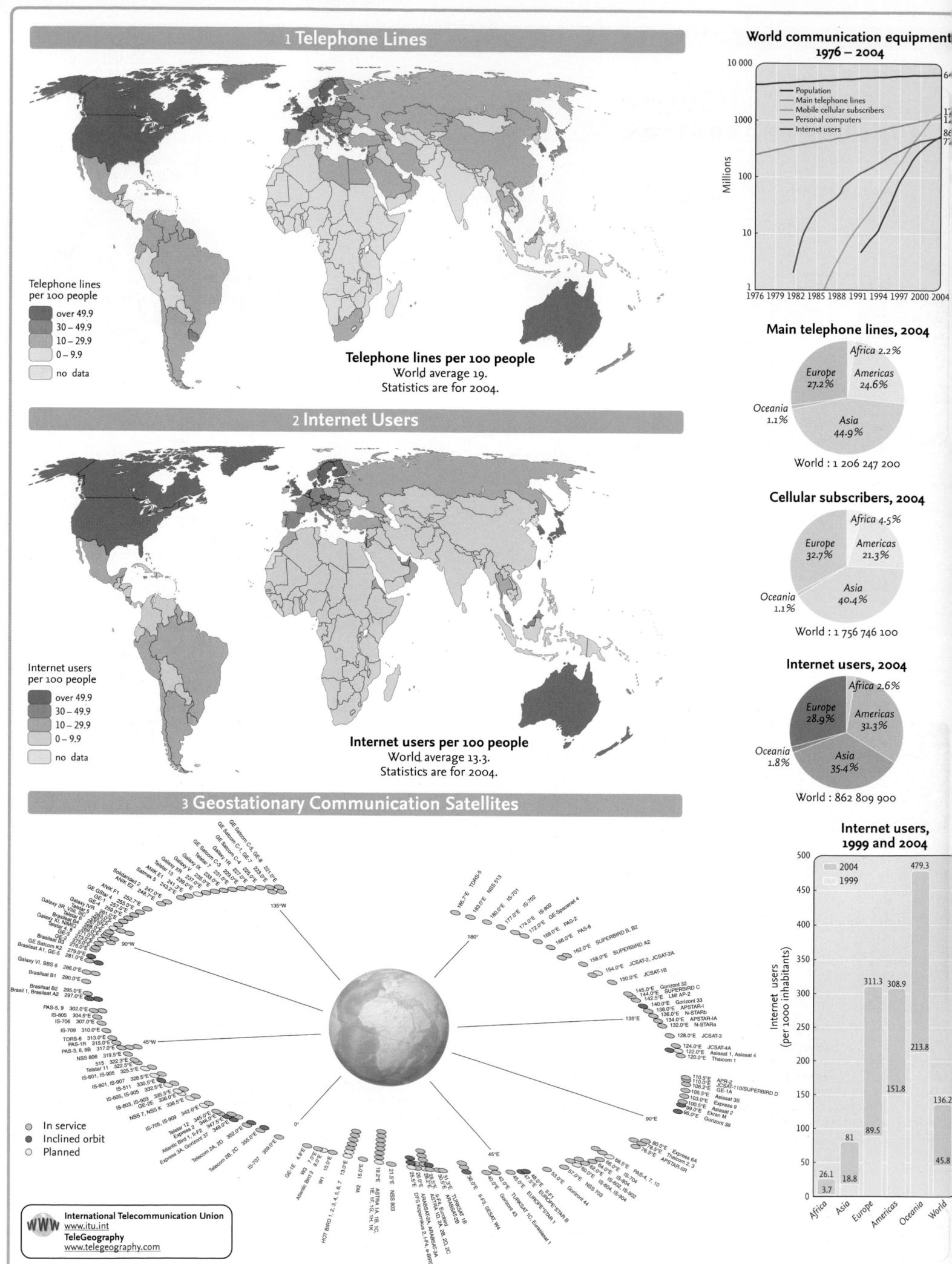

1 Telephone Lines

Telephone lines per 100 people

Telephone lines per 100 people
- over 49.9
- 30 – 49.9
- 10 – 29.9
- 0 – 9.9
- no data

Telephone lines per 100 people
World average 19.
Statistics are for 2004.

2 Internet Users

Internet users per 100 people
- over 49.9
- 30 – 49.9
- 10 – 29.9
- 0 – 9.9
- no data

Internet users per 100 people
World average 13.3.
Statistics are for 2004.

3 Geostationary Communication Satellites

- In service
- Inclined orbit
- Planned

International Telecommunication Union
www.itu.int
TeleGeography
www.telegeography.com

World communication equipment 1976 – 2004

- Population
- Main telephone lines
- Mobile cellular subscribers
- Personal computers
- Internet users

Main telephone lines, 2004

Africa 2.2%
Europe 27.2%
Americas 24.6%
Oceania 1.1%
Asia 44.9%

World : 1 206 247 200

Cellular subscribers, 2004

Africa 4.5%
Europe 32.7%
Americas 21.3%
Oceania 1.1%
Asia 40.4%

World : 1 756 746 100

Internet users, 2004

Africa 2.6%
Europe 28.9%
Americas 31.3%
Oceania 1.8%
Asia 35.4%

World : 862 809 900

Internet users, 1999 and 2004

- 2004
- 1999

Internet users (per 1000 inhabitants)

	Africa	Asia	Europe	Americas	Oceania	World
2004	26.1	81	311.3	308.9	479.3	136.2
1999	3.7	18.8	89.5	151.8	213.8	45.8

Scale 1 : 210 000 000

Eckert IV project

1 Air Transport

Top 20 busiest airports, 2004

	Airport	Passengers carried
1	Atlanta	83 606 583
2	Chicago	75 533 822
3	London Heathrow	67 344 054
4	Tōkyō Haneda	62 291 405
5	Los Angeles	60 688 609
6	Dallas/ Fort Worth	59 412 217
7	Paris	51 260 363
8	Frankfurt	51 098 271
9	Amsterdam	42 541 180
10	Denver	42 393 766
11	Las Vegas	41 441 531
12	Phoenix	39 504 898
13	Madrid	38 704 731
14	Bangkok	37 960 169
15	New York	37 518 143
16	Minneapolis/St Paul	36 713 173
17	Hong Kong	36 711 920
18	Houston	36 506 116
19	Detroit	35 187 517
20	Beijing	34 883 190

Passengers carried in millions

- over 100
- 25 – 100
- 10 – 25
- 1 – 10
- less than 1
- no data
- ● Main airport
- • Other airport
- — Main air route

Passengers carried
Air passengers carried include both domestic and international aircraft passengers. Statistics are for 2003.

Scale 1 : 260 000 000

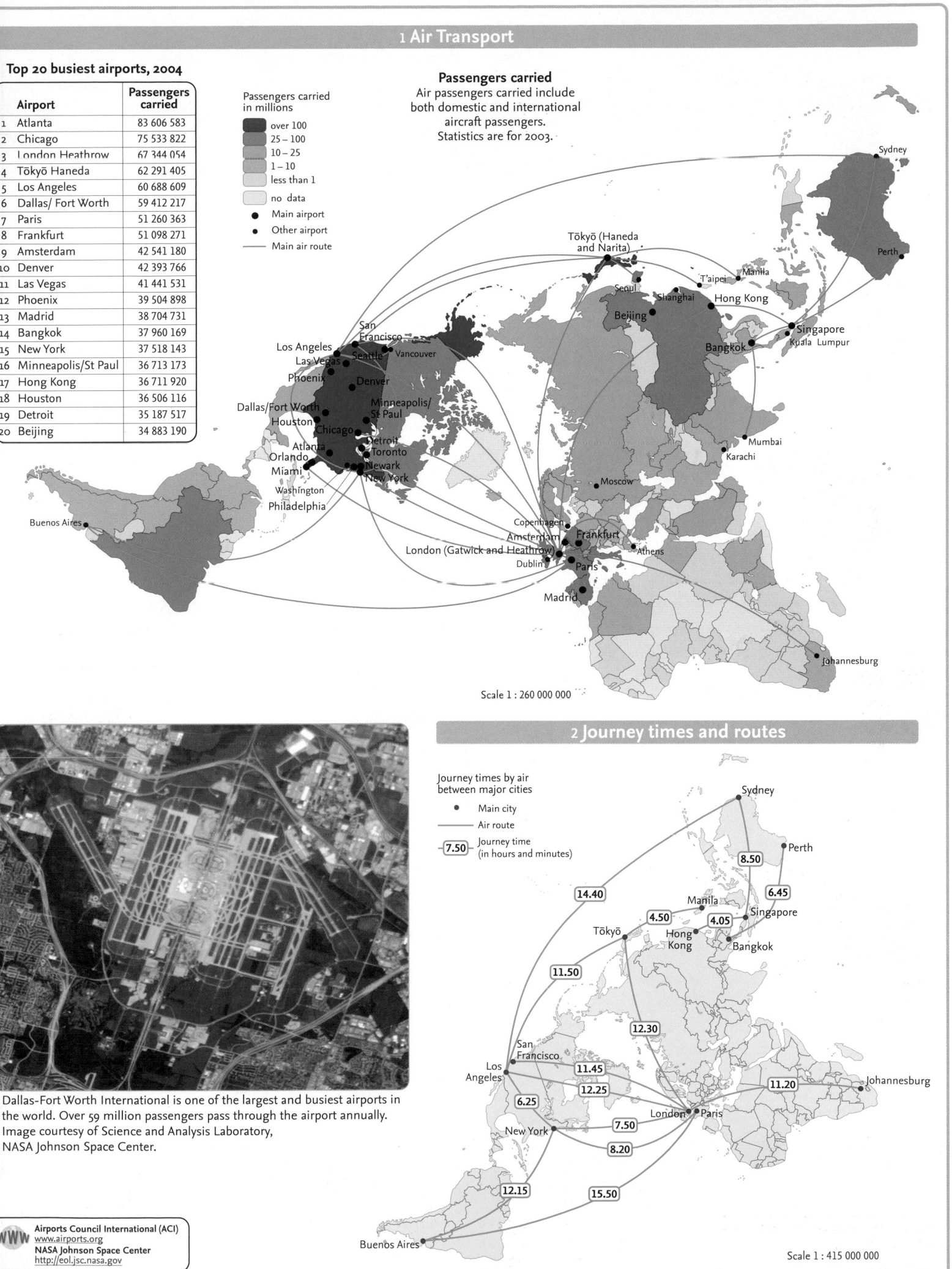

Dallas-Fort Worth International is one of the largest and busiest airports in the world. Over 59 million passengers pass through the airport annually. Image courtesy of Science and Analysis Laboratory, NASA Johnson Space Center.

WWW Airports Council International (ACI)
www.airports.org
NASA Johnson Space Center
http://eol.jsc.nasa.gov

2 Journey times and routes

Journey times by air between major cities
- ● Main city
- — Air route
- ⌐7.50⌐ Journey time (in hours and minutes)

Scale 1 : 415 000 000

Fuller projection

Flag	Country	Capital city	Population total 2005	Density persons per sq km 2005	Birth rate per 1000 population 2003	Death rate per 1000 population 2003	Life expectancy in years 2003	Population change annual % per annum 2004	Urba popula % 200
	Afghanistan	Kābul	29 863 000	46	49	21	43	3.9	23
	Albania	Tirana	3 130 000	109	17	6	74	0.6	44
	Algeria	Algiers	32 854 000	14	22	5	71	1.7	59
	Andorra	Andorra la Vella	67 000	144	...	...	...	...	92
	Angola	Luanda	15 941 000	13	50	19	47	3.2	37
	Antigua & Barbuda	St John`s	81 000	183	18	5	75	2.7	38
	Argentina	Buenos Aires	38 747 000	14	18	8	75	0.8	90
	Armenia	Yerevan	3 016 000	101	9	8	75	-0.2	64
	Australia	Canberra	20 155 000	3	13	7	80	1.2	92
	Austria	Vienna	8 189 000	98	10	10	79	0.3	66
	Azerbaijan	Baku	8 411 000	97	16	7	65	0.6	50
	Bahamas, The	Nassau	323 000	23	18	8	70	0.8	90
	Bahrain	Manama	727 000	1 052	21	4	73	1.9	90
	Bangladesh	Dhaka	141 822 000	985	28	8	62	1.7	25
	Barbados	Bridgetown	270 000	628	14	8	75	0.4	52
	Belarus	Minsk	9 755 000	47	9	14	68	-0.5	71
	Belgium	Brussels	10 419 000	341	11	10	78	0.3	97
	Belize	Belmopan	270 000	12	27	4	71	3.2	49
	Benin	Porto-Novo	8 439 000	75	38	13	53	2.5	45
	Bhutan	Thimphu	2 163 000	46	35	9	64	2.5	9
	Bolivia	La Paz/Sucre	9 182 000	8	29	8	64	1.9	64
	Bosnia & Herzegovina	Sarajevo	3 907 000	76	12	8	74	0.0	45
	Botswana	Gaborone	1 765 000	3	29	23	38	0.3	52
	Brazil	Brasília	186 405 000	22	19	7	69	1.2	84
	Brunei	Bandar Seri Begawan	374 000	65	18	3	77	1.4	77
	Bulgaria	Sofia	7 726 000	70	8	14	72	-0.6	70
	Burkina	Ouagadougou	13 228 000	48	43	19	43	2.3	18
	Burundi	Bujumbura	7 548 000	271	38	20	42	1.9	10
	Cambodia	Phnom Penh	14 071 000	78	29	12	54	1.7	19
	Cameroon	Yaoundé	16 322 000	34	35	16	48	1.9	52
	Canada	Ottawa	32 268 000	3	11	7	79	0.9	81
	Cape Verde	Praia	507 000	126	30	5	69	2.5	57
	Central African Republic	Bangui	4 038 000	6	35	20	42	1.7	43
	Chad	Ndjamena	9 749 000	8	45	16	48	2.8	25
	Chile	Santiago	16 295 000	22	17	5	76	1.1	87
	China	Beijing	1 323 345 000	138	15	8	71	0.6	40
	Colombia	Bogotá	45 600 000	40	22	5	72	1.6	77
	Comoros	Moroni	798 000	429	32	8	62	2.4	36
	Congo	Brazzaville	3 999 000	12	44	14	52	2.6	54
	Congo, Dem. Rep. of the	Kinshasa	57 549 000	25	45	18	45	3.0	32
	Costa Rica	San José	4 327 000	85	17	4	79	1.4	61
	Côte d'Ivoire	Yamoussoukro	18 154 000	56	37	17	45	1.8	45
	Croatia	Zagreb	4 551 000	80	10	12	74	1.4	59
	Cuba	Havana	11 269 000	102	13	8	77	0.3	76
	Cyprus	Nicosia	835 000	90	13	8	78	0.7	69
	Czech Republic	Prague	10 220 000	130	9	11	75	-0.2	74
	Denmark	Copenhagen	5 431 000	126	12	11	77	0.2	86
	Djibouti	Djibouti	793 000	34	36	20	43	1.4	84

Land		Education and Health			Development		Communications			Country	Time Zones
Area km	Forest 'ooo sq km 2005	Adult literacy % 2003	Doctors per 100 000 population 2004	Food intake calories per capita per day 2000-2002	Energy consumption million tonnes oil equivalent 2003	GNI per capita US$ 2004	Telephone lines per 100 population 2004	Cell phones per 100 population 2004	Internet users per 1000 population 2004		+ or - GMT
652 225	9	...	19	...	0.5	...	0.2	2.4	1.0	Afghanistan	+4½
28 748	8	98.7	139	2 860	2.4	2 080	8.3	39.5	23.5	Albania	+1
381 741	23	69.8	85	2 990	33.3	2 280	7.1	14.5	26.1	Algeria	+1
465	< 1	...	259	...	...	...	52.3	93.4	164.2	Andorra	+1
246 700	591	66.8	8	2 040	3.4	1 030	0.7	6.7	12.2	Angola	+1
442	< 1	85.8	17	2 340	0.2	10 000	49.4	70.1	259.7	Antigua & Barbuda	-4
766 889	330	97.2	301	3 070	66.8	3 720	22.8	35.4	161.0	Argentina	-3
29 800	3	99.4	353	2 190	4.3	1 120	15.3	5.4	39.5	Armenia	+5
692 024	1 637	99.9	249	3 090	128.5	26 900	58.6	82.8	652.8	Australia	+8 to +10½
83 855	39	99.9	324	3 740	36.4	32 300	46.2	97.4	475.2	Austria	+1
86 600	9	98.8	354	2 480	15.9	950	12.3	17.4	48.9	Azerbaijan	+4
13 939	5	95.5	106	2 750	1.2	15 100	44.1	58.7	293.4	Bahamas, The	-5
691	...	87.7	160	...	10.2	12 410	26.7	90.6	213.0	Bahrain	+3
143 998	9	41.1	23	2 190	15.4	440	0.6	2.0	2.2	Bangladesh	+6
430	< 1	99.7	121	3 060	0.6	9 270	50.1	73.9	553.5	Barbados	-4
207 600	79	99.6	450	3 010	30.8	2 120	32.2	22.7	249.8	Belarus	+3
30 520	7	99.9	418	3 580	67.0	31 030	46.4	88.3	406.2	Belgium	+1
22 965	17	76.9	105	2 840	0.3	3 940	12.9	35.1	134.1	Belize	-6
112 620	24	33.6	6	2 520	0.6	530	1.0	5.3	13.8	Benin	+1
46 620	32	47.0	5	...	0.5	760	3.9	2.5	25.6	Bhutan	+6
098 581	587	86.5	73	2 250	4.7	960	7.0	20.1	39.0	Bolivia	-4
51 130	22	94.6	134	2 760	5.5	2 040	24.0	34.0	58.1	Bosnia & Herzegovina	+1
581 370	119	78.9	29	2 160	1.3	4 340	8.0	32.9	35.0	Botswana	+2
514 879	4 777	88.4	206	3 010	220.8	3 090	23.5	36.3	121.8	Brazil	-2 to -5
5 765	3	92.7	101	2 860	2.4	...	25.6	56.3	153.0	Brunei	+8
110 994	36	98.2	338	2 800	22.2	2 740	35.1	60.9	159.0	Bulgaria	+2
274 200	68	12.8	4	2 410	0.4	360	0.6	3.0	4.0	Burkina	GMT
27 835	2	58.9	5	1 640	0.2	90	0.3	1.4	3.5	Burundi	+2
181 000	104	73.6	16	2 060	0.2	320	0.3	6.0	2.8	Cambodia	+7
475 442	212	67.9	7	2 260	1.9	800	0.6	9.4	10.2	Cameroon	+1
984 670	3 101	99.9	209	3 560	337.1	28 390	64.3	46.7	623.6	Canada	-3½ to -8
4 033	1	75.7	17	3 210	0.1	1 770	15.6	13.9	53.0	Cape Verde	-1
622 436	228	48.6	4	1 980	0.1	310	0.3	1.5	2.3	Central African Republic	+1
284 000	119	25.5	3	2 150	0.1	260	0.2	1.4	4.0	Chad	+1
756 945	161	95.7	109	2 850	27.6	4 910	21.5	62.1	279.0	Chile	-4
562 000	1 973	90.9	164	2 960	1 137.1	1 290	24.0	25.8	72.3	China	+8
141 748	607	94.2	135	2 580	28.8	2 000	17.1	23.0	89.4	Colombia	-5
1 862	< 1	56.2	7	1 750	< 0.1	530	1.7	1.2	10.1	Comoros	+3
342 000	225	82.8	25	2 090	0.4	770	0.4	10.1	9.4	Congo	+1
345 410	1 336	65.3	7	1 630	2.0	120	< 0.1	3.5	0.9	Congo, Dem. Rep. of the	+1 to +2
51 100	24	95.8	172	2 860	4.3	4 670	31.6	21.7	235.4	Costa Rica	-6
322 463	104	48.1	9	2 620	2.5	770	1.4	9.1	14.4	Côte d'Ivoire	GMT
56 538	21	98.1	237	2 770	9.0	6 590	42.7	63.6	295.1	Croatia	+1
110 860	27	96.9	591	3 000	11.8	...	6.8	0.7	13.2	Cuba	-4
9 251	2	96.8	298	3 250	2.8	17 580	51.8	79.4	369.3	Cyprus	+2
78 864	26	99.9	343	3 120	43.5	9 150	33.6	105.6	499.7	Czech Republic	+1
43 075	5	99.9	366	3 410	22.2	40 650	64.5	95.5	604.1	Denmark	+1
23 200	< 1	65.5	13	...	0.7	1 030	1.6	5.1	13.2	Djibouti	+3

no data available

Flag	Key Information		Population						
	Country	Capital city	Population total 2005	Density persons per sq km 2005	Birth rate per 1000 population 2003	Death rate per 1000 population 2003	Life expectancy in years 2003	Population change annual % per annum 2004	Urb popula % 200
	Dominica	Roseau	79 000	105	18	6	77	0.3	72
	Dominican Republic	Santo Domingo	8 895 000	184	22	7	67	1.4	60
	East Timor	Dili	947 000	64	46	8	62	5.3	8
	Ecuador	Quito	13 228 000	49	22	6	71	1.6	62
	Egypt	Cairo	74 033 000	74	24	6	69	1.7	42
	El Salvador	San Salvador	6 881 000	327	25	6	70	1.9	60
	Equatorial Guinea	Malabo	504 000	18	40	15	52	2.4	49
	Eritrea	Asmara	4 401 000	37	37	13	51	2.0	20
	Estonia	Tallinn	1 330 000	29	10	13	71	-0.6	70
	Ethiopia	Addis Ababa	77 431 000	68	40	20	42	1.9	16
	Fiji	Suva	848 000	46	22	5	70	1.5	53
	Finland	Helsinki	5 249 000	16	11	9	78	0.1	61
	France	Paris	60 496 000	111	13	9	79	0.4	77
	Gabon	Libreville	1 384 000	5	35	15	53	2.1	84
	Gambia, The	Banjul	1 517 000	134	36	14	53	1.9	26
	Georgia	T'bilisi	4 474 000	64	8	10	74	-1.0	52
	Germany	Berlin	82 689 000	232	9	10	78	0.1	88
	Ghana	Accra	22 113 000	93	31	13	54	1.8	46
	Greece	Athens	11 120 000	84	9	9	78	0.4	61
	Grenada	St George's	103 000	272	24	7	73	1.1	42
	Guatemala	Guatemala City	12 599 000	116	33	6	66	2.6	47
	Guinea	Conakry	9 402 000	38	37	17	46	2.1	36
	Guinea-Bissau	Bissau	1 586 000	44	49	20	46	2.9	35
	Guyana	Georgetown	751 000	3	22	10	62	0.4	38
	Haiti	Port–au–Prince	8 528 000	307	32	14	52	1.8	38
	Honduras	Tegucigalpa	7 205 000	64	29	6	66	2.5	46
	Hungary	Budapest	10 098 000	109	10	13	73	-0.6	66
	Iceland	Reykjavík	295 000	3	14	6	80	0.3	93
	India	New Delhi	1 103 371 000	360	24	8	63	1.4	29
	Indonesia	Jakarta	222 781 000	116	21	7	67	1.3	47
	Iran	Tehrān	69 515 000	42	18	6	69	1.3	67
	Iraq	Baghdād	28 807 000	66	29	8	63	2.7	68
	Ireland	Dublin	4 148 000	59	16	7	78	0.6	60
	Israel	*Jerusalem	6 725 000	324	20	6	79	1.6	92
	Italy	Rome	58 093 000	193	9	10	80	-0.1	68
	Jamaica	Kingston	2 651 000	241	19	6	76	0.8	52
	Japan	Tōkyō	128 085 000	339	9	8	82	0.1	66
	Jordan	'Ammān	5 703 000	64	28	4	72	2.5	79
	Kazakhstan	Astana	14 825 000	5	15	10	61	0.5	56
	Kenya	Nairobi	34 256 000	59	34	17	45	1.7	41
	Kiribati	Bairiki	99 000	138	27	7	63	1.5	49
	Kuwait	Kuwait	2 687 000	151	20	3	77	2.6	96
	Kyrgyzstan	Bishkek	5 264 000	27	19		65	0.9	34
	Laos	Vientiane	5 924 000	25	35	12	55	2.3	21
	Latvia	Rīga	2 307 000	36	9	14	71	-0.8	66
	Lebanon	Beirut	3 577 000	342	19	6	71	1.2	88
	Lesotho	Maseru	1 795 000	59	33	24	37	0.9	18
	Liberia	Monrovia	3 283 000	29	43	20	47	2.2	47

* Jerusalem - not internationally recognised.

Land		Education and Health			Development		Communications				
Area q km	Forest 'ooo sq km 2005	Adult literacy % 2003	Doctors per 100 000 population 2004	Food intake calories per capita per day 2000-2002	Energy consumption million tonnes oil equivalent 2003	GNI per capita US$ 2004	Telephone lines per 100 population 2004	Cell phones per 100 population 2004	Internet users per 1000 population 2004	Country	Time Zones + or - GMT
750	< 1	88.0	49	2 750	< 0.1	3 650	29.4	58.7	287.5	Dominica	-4
48 442	14	87.7	188	2 320	7.3	2 080	10.7	28.8	91.0	Dominican Republic	-4
14 874	8	58.6	...	...	...	550	...	...	...	East Timor	+9
272 045	109	91.0	148	2 740	9.7	2 180	12.2	26.9	47.3	Ecuador	-5
000 250	1	55.6	212	3 340	58.1	1 310	13.5	10.9	55.7	Egypt	+2
21 041	3	79.7	127	2 550	3.0	2 350	13.4	27.7	88.8	El Salvador	-6
28 051	16	84.2	25	...	1.2	...	1.8	11.0	9.9	Equatorial Guinea	+1
117 400	16	56.7	3	1 520	0.2	180	0.9	0.5	11.8	Eritrea	+3
45 200	23	99.8	316	2 990	5.6	7 010	34.0	96.0	512.2	Estonia	+2
133 880	130	41.5	3	1 840	1.9	110	0.6	0.3	1.6	Ethiopia	+3
18 330	10	92.9	34	2 890	0.7	2 690	12.4	16.8	72.0	Fiji	+12
338 145	225	99.9	311	3 120	30.5	32 790	45.4	95.6	630.0	Finland	+2
543 965	156	99.9	329	3 630	281.0	30 090	56.0	73.7	413.7	France	+1
267 667	218	71.0	29	2 610	1.0	3 940	2.9	36.2	29.6	Gabon	+1
11 295	5	37.8	4	2 270	0.1	290	2.9	12.0	33.5	Gambia, The	GMT
69 700	28	99.9	391	2 280	3.5	1 040	13.5	16.6	34.6	Georgia	+4
357 022	111	99.9	362	3 470	356.0	30 120	66.2	86.4	426.7	Germany	+1
238 537	55	54.1	9	2 620	3.1	380	1.5	7.9	17.2	Ghana	GMT
131 957	38	91.0	440	3 690	35.6	16 610	57.8	84.8	178.1	Greece	+2
378	< 1	96.0	50	...	0.1	3 760	31.8	42.1	169.0	Grenada	-4
108 890	39	69.1	90	2 190	4.3	2 130	8.9	25.0	59.7	Guatemala	-6
245 857	67	41.0	9	2 380	0.6	460	0.3	2.0	5.9	Guinea	GMT
36 125	21	39.6	17	2 100	0.1	160	0.8	3.2	19.9	Guinea-Bissau	GMT
214 969	151	96.5	48	2 710	0.6	990	13.4	13.6	189.0	Guyana	-4
27 750	1	51.9	25	2 080	0.7	390	1.7	4.9	60.9	Haiti	-5
112 088	46	80.0	83	2 350	2.5	1 030	5.6	10.1	31.8	Honduras	-6
93 030	20	99.3	316	3 470	26.9	8 270	35.4	86.4	267.4	Hungary	+1
102 820	< 1	99.9	347	3 220	3.5	38 620	65.0	99.0	770.0	Iceland	GMT
064 898	677	61.0	51	2 420	350.8	620	4.1	4.4	32.4	India	+5½
919 445	885	87.9	16	2 910	118.0	1 140	4.5	13.5	65.2	Indonesia	+7 to +9
648 000	111	77.0	105	3 070	151.0	2 300	22.0	6.2	78.8	Iran	3½
438 317	8	...	54	...	24.4	23 290	4.0	2.2	1.4	Iraq	+3
70 282	7	99.9	237	3 660	15.2	34 280	49.9	93.5	296.3	Ireland	GMT
20 770	2	96.9	391	3 640	22.3	17 380	43.7	105.3	466.3	Israel	+2
301 245	100	98.5	606	3 690	199.1	26 120	44.8	108.2	497.8	Italy	+1
10 991	3	87.6	85	2 670	3.8	2 900	14.6	82.2	398.7	Jamaica	-5
377 727	249	99.9	201	2 780	560.5	37 180	46.0	71.6	502.0	Japan	+9
89 206	1	89.9	205	2 670	6.0	2 140	11.0	28.4	106.9	Jordan	+2
2 717 300	33	99.5	330	2 550	52.2	2 260	16.2	17.9	26.0	Kazakhstan	+4 to +6
582 646	35	73.6	13	2 110	3.8	460	0.9	7.9	46.3	Kenya	+3
717	< 1	...	30	...	< 0.1	970	5.1	0.7	23.5	Kiribati	+12 to +14
17 818	< 1	82.9	153	3 050	23.5	17 970	19.5	78.3	235.0	Kuwait	+3
198 500	9	98.7	268	2 950	4.6	400	8.2	5.2	51.6	Kyrgyzstan	+5
236 800	161	68.7	59	2 290	1.2	390	1.3	3.5	3.6	Laos	+7
63 700	29	99.7	291	2 960	3.9	5 460	28.5	67.2	354.3	Latvia	+2
10 452	1	86.5	325	3 160	5.7	4 980	17.8	25.0	169.0	Lebanon	+2
30 355	< 1	81.4	5	2 620	0.2	740	2.1	8.8	23.9	Lesotho	+2
111 369	32	...	2	1 990	0.2	110	0.2	2.7	...	Liberia	GMT

no data available

Flag	Country	Capital city	Population total 2005	Density persons per sq km 2005	Birth rate per 1000 population 2003	Death rate per 1000 population 2003	Life expectancy in years 2003	Population change annual % per annum 2004	Urban popula % 200
	Libya	Tripoli	5 853 000	3	27	4	73	2.0	87
	Liechtenstein	Vaduz	35 000	219	...	...	...	0.9	22
	Lithuania	Vilnius	3 431 000	53	9	12	72	-0.4	67
	Luxembourg	Luxembourg	465 000	180	12	9	78	0.4	92
	Macedonia (FYROM)[1]	Skopje	2 034 000	79	14	9	74	0.6	60
	Madagascar	Antananarivo	18 606 000	32	38	12	56	2.6	27
	Malawi	Lilongwe	12 884 000	109	44	25	38	2.0	17
	Malaysia	Kuala Lumpur/Putrajaya	25 347 000	76	21	5	73	1.7	64
	Maldives	Male	329 000	1 104	29	7	70	2.2	29
	Mali	Bamako	13 518 000	11	48	23	41	2.4	33
	Malta	Valletta	402 000	1 272	10	8	79	0.5	92
	Marshall Islands	Delap-Uliga-Djarrit	62 000	343	...	...	65	0.0	67
	Mauritania	Nouakchott	3 069 000	3	34	15	51	2.0	63
	Mauritius	Port Louis	1 245 000	610	16	7	72	1.0	44
	Mexico	Mexico City	107 029 000	54	19	5	74	1.5	76
	Micronesia, Fed. States of	Palikir	110 000	157	25	5	69	1.8	30
	Moldova	Chişinău	4 206 000	125	11	13	67	-0.5	46
	Monaco	Monaco-Ville	35 000	17 500	...	...	...	...	100
	Mongolia	Ulan Bator	2 646 000	2	22	6	66	1.4	57
	Montenegro	Podgorica	620 145	45	11[2]	14[2]	73[2]	-0.7[2]	52[2]
	Morocco	Rabat	31 478 000	70	22	...	69	1.6	58
	Mozambique	Maputo	19 792 000	25	40	21	41	1.8	37
	Myanmar (Burma)	Naypyidaw/ Yangôn	50 519 000	75	23	11	57	1.1	30
	Namibia	Windhoek	2 031 000	2	35	21	40	0.9	33
	Nepal	Kathmandu	27 133 000	184	31	10	60	2.1	15
	Netherlands	Amsterdam/The Hague	16 299 000	393	12	9	79	0.2	66
	New Zealand	Wellington	4 028 000	15	14	7	79	1.3	86
	Nicaragua	Managua	5 487 000	42	29	5	69	2.2	58
	Niger	Niamey	13 957 000	11	48	19	46	2.8	23
	Nigeria	Abuja	131 530 000	142	43	18	45	2.4	48
	North Korea	P'yŏngyang	22 488 000	187	17	11	63	0.6	61
	Norway	Oslo	4 620 000	14	12	9	79	0.4	80
	Oman	Muscat	2 567 000	8	26	3	74	2.3	78
	Pakistan	Islamabad	157 935 000	196	32	8	64	2.4	35
	Panama	Panama City	3 232 000	42	20	5	75	1.5	58
	Papua New Guinea	Port Moresby	5 887 000	13	33	10	57	2.2	13
	Paraguay	Asunción	6 158 000	15	30	5	71	2.4	58
	Peru	Lima	27 968 000	22	22	6	70	1.5	74
	Philippines	Manila	83 054 000	277	25	6	70	1.8	62
	Poland	Warsaw	38 530 000	123	9	9	75	-0.1	62
	Portugal	Lisbon	10 495 000	118	11	10	76	0.7	55
	Qatar	Doha	813 000	71	14	4	75	2.1	92
	Romania	Bucharest	21 711 000	91	10	Population	70	-0.3	55
	Russian Federation	Moscow	143 202 000	8	10	15	66	-0.4	73
	Rwanda	Kigali	9 038 000	343	43	22	40	2.8	20
	St Kitts & Nevis	Basseterre	43 000	165	17	11	72	0.6	32
	St Lucia	Castries	161 000	261	17	6	74	1.9	31
	St Vincent & the Grenadines	Kingstown	119 000	306	18	6	73	-0.8	59

[1] FYROM - Former Yugoslav Republic of Macedonia.

[2] Statistics are for Serbia & Montenegro.

Land		Education and Health			Development		Communications				
Area sq km	Forest '000 sq km 2005	Adult literacy % 2003	Doctors per 100 000 population 2004	Food intake calories per capita per day 2000-2002	Energy consumption million tonnes oil equivalent 2003	GNI per capita US$ 2004	Telephone lines per 100 population 2004	Cell phones per 100 population 2004	Internet users per 1000 population 2004	Country	Time Zones + or - GMT
759 540	2	81.7	129	3 320	18.1	4 450	13.6	4.2	36.2	Libya	+2
160	< 1	...	...	...	...	...	...	...	...	Liechtenstein	+1
65 200	21	99.6	403	3 360	10.9	5 740	23.8	99.3	280.9	Lithuania	+2
2 586	1	99.9	255	3 590	4.5	56 230	79.8	138.2	590.0	Luxembourg	+1
25 713	9	96.1	219	2 640	2.8	2 350	25.2	47.7	77.0	Macedonia (FYROM)[1]	+1
587 041	128	70.6	9	2 060	0.9	300	0.3	1.9	5.0	Madagascar	+3
118 484	34	64.1	1	2 150	0.6	170	0.8	1.8	3.7	Malawi	+2
332 965	209	88.7	70	2 890	57.8	4 650	17.4	57.1	386.2	Malaysia	+8
298	< 1	97.2	78	...	0.2	2 510	9.6	34.5	57.9	Maldives	+5
240 140	126	19.0	4	2 200	0.4	360	0.7	3.6	4.5	Mali	GMT
316	...	87.9	293	3 540	1.0	12 250	51.6	76.5	752.5	Malta	+1
181	...	...	47	...	...	2 370	8.3	1.1	35.1	Marshall Islands	+12
030 700	3	51.2	14	2 780	1.3	420	1.3	17.5	4.7	Mauritania	GMT
2 040	< 1	84.3	85	2 960	1.3	4 640	28.7	41.4	146.0	Mauritius	+4
972 545	642	90.3	171	3 160	169.8	6 770	17.2	36.6	133.8	Mexico	-6 to -8
701	1	...	60	...	...	1 990	10.8	11.5	108.1	Micronesia, F. S. of	+10 to +11
33 700	3	96.2	269	2 720	4.3	710	20.3	18.5	95.2	Moldova	+2
2	< 1	...	586	...	...	...	...	...	...	Monaco	+1
565 000	103	97.8	267	2 240	2.4	590	5.6	16.3	76.0	Mongolia	+8
13 812	27[2]	...	...	2 660[2]	19.2[2]	2 620[2]	32.9[2]	58.0[2]	186.1[2]	Montenegro	+1
446 550	44	50.7	48	3 040	12.4	1 520	4.4	31.2	117.1	Morocco	GMT
799 380	193	46.5	2	2 030	4.2	250	0.4	3.7	7.3	Mozambique	+2
676 577	322	89.7	30	2 880	4.6	...	0.8	0.2	1.2	Myanmar (Burma)	+6½
824 292	77	85.0	30	2 270	1.3	2 370	6.4	14.2	37.3	Namibia	+2
147 181	36	48.6	5	2 440	1.6	260	1.7	0.5	4.8	Nepal	5¾
41 526	4	99.9	329	3 350	100.5	31 700	48.4	91.2	616.3	Netherlands	+1
270 534	83	99.9	223	3 220	21.9	20 310	46.1	77.5	526.3	New Zealand	+12 to +12¾
130 000	52	76.7	164	2 280	1.6	790	3.8	13.0	22.0	Nicaragua	-6
267 000	13	14.4	3	2 130	0.4	230	0.2	1.2	1.9	Niger	+1
923 768	111	66.8	27	2 700	24.6	390	0.8	7.2	13.9	Nigeria	+1
120 538	62	...	297	2 140	22.0	...	4.1	...	...	North Korea	+9
323 878	94	99.9	356	3 420	44.5	52 030	47.2	103.6	393.7	Norway	+1
309 500	< 1	74.4	126	...	9.8	7 890	10.1	33.3	101.4	Oman	+4
803 940	19	48.7	66	2 430	47.7	600	3.0	3.3	13.1	Pakistan	+5
77 082	43	91.9	168	2 240	5.0	4 450	11.9	27.0	94.6	Panama	-5
462 840	294	57.3	5	...	1.2	580	1.1	0.4	29.1	Papua New Guinea	+10
406 752	185	91.6	117	2 560	10.6	1 170	4.7	29.4	24.9	Paraguay	-4
1 285 216	687	87.7	117	2 550	14.2	2 360	7.4	14.8	116.1	Peru	-5
300 000	72	92.6	116	2 380	31.3	1 170	4.2	39.9	53.2	Philippines	+8
312 683	92	99.7	220	3 380	91.2	6 090	31.9	59.9	233.5	Poland	+1
88 940	38	92.5	324	3 750	27.9	14 350	40.3	98.4	280.3	Portugal	GMT
11 437	...	89.2	221	...	12.4	...	25.7	65.9	221.8	Qatar	+3
237 500	64	97.3	189	3 410	42.1	2 920	20.3	47.1	207.6	Romania	+2
7 075 400	8 088	99.4	417	3 000	726.6	3 410	27.5	51.6	111.0	Russian Federation	+2 to +12
26 338	5	64.0	2	2 050	0.3	220	0.3	1.6	4.5	Rwanda	+2
261	< 1	97.8	118	2 640	< 0.1	7 600	50.0	20.0	214.1	St Kitts & Nevis	-4
616	< 1	90.1	518	2 940	0.1	4 310	32.0	62.0	366.7	St Lucia	-4
389	< 1	88.1	88	2 530	0.1	3 650	27.3	59.5	66.1	St Vincent & the Grenadines	-4

no data available

Flag	Key Information		Population						
	Country	Capital city	Population total 2005	Density persons per sq km 2005	Birth rate per 1000 population 2003	Death rate per 1000 population 2003	Life expectancy in years 2003	Population change annual % per annum 2004	Urba popula % 200/
	Samoa	Apia	185 000	65	29	6	70	0.6	22
	San Marino	San Marino	28 000	459	...	...	...	...	89
	São Tomé & Príncipe	São Tomé	157 000	163	31	9	66	2.0	38
	Saudi Arabia	Riyadh	24 573 000	11	31	4	73	3.0	88
	Senegal	Dakar	11 658 000	59	34	13	52	2.1	50
	Serbia	Belgrade	9 379 437	106	11*	14*	73*	-0.7*	52*
	Seychelles	Victoria	81 000	178	19	7	73	1.3	50
	Sierra Leone	Freetown	5 525 000	77	44	25	37	1.8	40
	Singapore	Singapore	4 326 000	6 770	11	5	78	2.0	100
	Slovakia	Bratislava	5 401 000	110	10	10	73	0.0	58
	Slovenia	Ljubljana	1 967 000	97	9	10	76	0.0	51
	Solomon Islands	Honiara	478 000	17	38	4	70	3.1	17
	Somalia	Mogadishu	8 228 000	13	50	18	47	3.2	35
	South Africa, Republic of	Pretoria/Cape Town	47 432 000	39	25	20	46	1.1	57
	South Korea	Seoul	47 817 000	482	12	7	74	0.5	81
	Spain	Madrid	43 064 000	85	10	9	80	0.4	77
	Sri Lanka	Sri Jayewardenepura Kotte	20 743 000	316	19	6	74	1.1	21
	Sudan	Khartoum	36 233 000	14	33	10	59	2.4	40
	Suriname	Paramaribo	449 000	3	21	6	70	1.1	77
	Swaziland	Mbabane	1 032 000	59	35	19	43	1.3	24
	Sweden	Stockholm	9 041 000	20	11	10	80	0.3	83
	Switzerland	Bern	7 252 000	176	10	9	81	0.4	68
	Syria	Damascus	19 043 000	103	29	4	71	2.3	50
	Taiwan	T'aipei	22 858 000	632	...	...	...	...	...
	Tajikistan	Dushanbe	6 507 000	45	22	7	66	0.7	25
	Tanzania	Dodoma	38 329 000	41	38	18	43	1.9	37
	Thailand	Bangkok	64 233 000	125	15	8	69	0.6	32
	Togo	Lomé	6 145 000	108	35	15	50	2.1	36
	Tonga	Nuku'alofa	102 000	136	23	8	72	0.3	34
	Trinidad & Tobago	Port of Spain	1 305 000	254	16	7	72	0.8	76
	Tunisia	Tunis	10 102 000	62	17	6	73	1.2	64
	Turkey	Ankara	73 193 000	94	21	7	69	1.4	67
	Turkmenistan	Ashgabat	4 833 000	10	22	8	65	1.4	46
	Tuvalu	Vaiaku	10 000	400	...	...	...	1.2	...
	Uganda	Kampala	28 816 000	120	44	18	43	2.5	12
	Ukraine	Kiev	46 481 000	77	9	15	68	-0.7	67
	United Arab Emirates	Abu Dhabi	4 496 000	58	17	4	75	7.4	85
	United Kingdom	London	59 668 000	245	12	10	78	0.1	89
	United States of America	Washington	298 213 000	30	14	8	77	0.9	80
	Uruguay	Montevideo	3 463 000	20	16	9	75	0.6	93
	Uzbekistan	Tashkent	26 593 000	59	20	6	67	1.3	37
	Vanuatu	Port Vila	211 000	17	32	5	69	2.3	23
	Vatican City	Vatican City	552	1 104	...	...	...	...	...
	Venezuela	Caracas	26 749 000	29	23	5	74	1.7	88
	Vietnam	Ha Nôi	84 238 000	256	18	6	70	1.0	26
	Yemen	Şan'ā'	20 975 000	40	41	10	58	3.0	26
	Zambia	Lusaka	11 668 000	16	38	23	37	1.4	36
	Zimbabwe	Harare	13 010 000	33	29	22	39	0.4	35

* Statistics are for Serbia & Montenegro.

Land		Education and Health			Development		Communications			Country	Time Zones + or - GMT
Area km	Forest '000 sq km 2005	Adult literacy % 2003	Doctors per 100 000 population 2004	Food intake calories per capita per day 2000-2002	Energy consumption million tonnes oil equivalent 2003	GNI per capita US$ 2004	Telephone lines per 100 population 2004	Cell phones per 100 population 2004	Internet users per 1000 population 2004		
2 831	2	98.7	70	2 900	0.1	1 860	7.3	5.8	33.3	Samoa	-11
61	...	...	251	...	...	...	...	...	...	San Marino	+1
964	< 1	83.1	47	2 390	< 0.1	370	4.6	5.0	122.0	São Tomé & Príncipe	GMT
200 000	27	79.4	140	2 840	142.3	10 430	14.8	36.8	63.6	Saudi Arabia	+3
196 720	87	39.3	8	2 280	1.6	670	2.4	10.9	46.6	Senegal	GMT
88 361	27*	...	...	2 660*	19.2*	2 620*	32.9*	58.0*	186.1*	Serbia	+1
455	< 1	91.9	132	2 450	0.4	8 090	26.2	60.8	246.9	Seychelles	+4
71 740	28	29.6	7	1 930	0.3	200	0.5	2.3	1.9	Sierra Leone	GMT
639	< 1	92.5	140	...	43.9	24 220	43.2	89.5	561.2	Singapore	+8
49 035	19	99.6	325	2 880	20.0	6 480	23.2	79.4	422.7	Slovakia	+1
20 251	13	99.7	219	3 010	7.7	14 810	40.7	100.5	479.6	Slovenia	+1
28 370	22	76.6	13	2 240	0.1	550	1.3	0.2	6.1	Solomon Islands	+11
637 657	71	...	4	...	0.3	...	1.7	4.2	1.3	Somalia	+3
219 090	92	82.4	69	2 920	122.5	3 630	10.4	43.1	78.9	South Africa, Republic of	+2
99 274	63	97.9	181	3 060	215.8	13 980	55.3	76.1	656.8	South Korea	+9
504 782	179	97.7	320	3 360	154.3	21 210	41.5	89.5	331.8	Spain	+1
65 610	19	90.4	43	2 390	4.9	1 010	5.1	11.4	14.4	Sri Lanka	+5½
505 813	675	59.0	16	2 260	3.5	530	3.0	3.0	33.0	Sudan	+3
163 820	148	88.0	45	2 630	1.0	2 250	18.6	48.5	68.3	Suriname	-3
17 364	5	79.2	18	2 360	0.5	1 660	4.4	10.4	33.2	Swaziland	+2
449 964	275	99.9	305	3 140	52.0	35 770	71.5	108.5	754.6	Sweden	+1
41 293	12	99.9	352	3 470	31.9	48 230	71.0	84.6	472.0	Switzerland	+1
185 180	5	82.9	140	3 040	22.7	1 190	14.6	12.9	43.9	Syria	+2
36 179	...	...	...	...	104.4	...	59.6	100.3	538.1	Taiwan	+8
143 100	4	99.5	218	1 840	6.4	280	3.8	2.1	0.8	Tajikistan	+5
945 087	353	69.4	2	1 960	1.9	330	0.4	4.4	8.8	Tanzania	+3
513 115	145	92.6	30	2 450	78.1	2 540	11.0	44.2	112.5	Thailand	+7
56 785	4	53.0	6	2 300	0.5	380	1.2	9.4	44.1	Togo	GMT
748	< 1	98.9	34	...	< 0.1	1 830	11.3	16.4	30.1	Tonga	+13
5 130	2	98.5	79	2 730	13.3	8 580	24.6	49.8	122.4	Trinidad & Tobago	-4
164 150	11	74.3	70	3 270	8.6	2 630	12.1	35.9	84.0	Tunisia	+1
779 452	102	88.3	124	3 360	83.3	3 750	26.5	48.0	141.3	Turkey	+2
488 100	41	98.8	317	2 720	18.5	1 340	7.7	1.0	7.3	Turkmenistan	+5
25	< 1	...	...	...	...	...	...	...	...	Tuvalu	+12
241 038	36	68.9	5	2 360	0.9	270	0.3	4.4	7.5	Uganda	+3
603 700	96	99.4	297	2 980	156.4	1 260	25.2	28.5	77.9	Ukraine	+2
77 700	3	77.3	202	3 200	54.2	20 080	27.3	84.7	318.5	United Arab Emirates	+4
243 609	28	99.9	166	3 400	245.9	33 940	56.4	102.2	628.8	United Kingdom	GMT
826 635	3 031	99.9	549	3 790	2 471.1	41 400	60.6	62.1	630.0	United States	-5 to -10
176 215	15	97.7	365	2 830	4.2	3 950	30.9	18.5	209.8	Uruguay	-3
447 400	33	99.3	289	2 270	53.5	460	6.7	2.1	33.2	Uzbekistan	+5
12 190	4	74.0	11	2 570	< 0.1	1 340	3.2	4.9	35.2	Vanuatu	+11
0.5	< 1	...	...	...	...	...	...	...	...	Vatican City	+1
912 050	477	93.0	194	2 350	72.9	4 020	12.8	32.2	88.4	Venezuela	-4
329 565	129	90.3	53	2 530	24.6	550	12.3	6.0	71.2	Vietnam	+7
527 968	5	49.0	22	2 040	3.9	570	3.9	5.2	8.7	Yemen	+3
752 614	425	67.9	7	1 900	2.7	450	0.8	4.3	21.1	Zambia	+2
390 759	175	90.0	6	2 020	4.7	890	2.7	3.6	69.0	Zimbabwe	+2

... no data available   * Statistics are for Serbia & Montenegro.

How to use the Index

All the names on the maps in this atlas, except some of those on the special topic maps, are included in the index.

The names are arranged in **alphabetical order.** Where the name has more than one word the separate words are considered as one to decide the position of the name in the index:

Thetford
The Trossachs
The Wash
The Weald
Thiers
Thiès

Where there is more than one place with the same name, the country name is used to decide the order:

London Canada
London England

If both places are in the same country, the county or state name is also used:

Avon *r.* Bristol England
Avon *r.* Dorset England

Each entry in the index starts with the name of the place or feature, followed by the name of the country or region in which it is located. This is followed by the number of the most appropriate page on which the name appears, usually the largest scale map. Next comes the alphanumeric reference followed by the latitude and longitude.

Names of physical features such as rivers, capes, mountains etc are followed by a description. The descriptions are usually shortened to one or two letters, these abbreviations are keyed below. Town names are followed by a description only when the name may be confused with that of a physical feature:

Big Spring *town*

To help to distinguish the different parts of each entry, different styles of type are used:

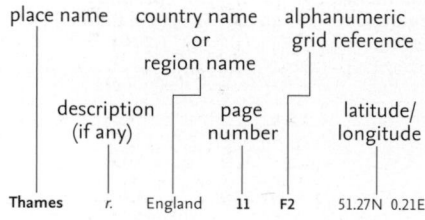

place name	country name or region name	alphanumeric grid reference
description (if any)	page number	latitude/ longitude

| **Thames** | *r.* | England | 11 | F2 | 51.27N 0.21E |

To use the **alphanumeric grid reference** to find a feature on the map, first find the correct page and then look at the coloured letters printed outside the frame along the top, bottom and sides of the map.
When you have found the correct letter and number follow the grid boxes up and along until you find the correct grid box in which the feature appears. You must then search the grid box until you find the name of the feature.

The **latitude and longitude reference** gives a more exact description of the position of the feature.

Page 6 of the atlas describes lines of latitude and lines of longitude, and explains how they are numbered and divided into degrees and minutes. Each name in the index has a different latitude and longitude reference, so the feature can be located accurately. The lines of latitude and lines of longitude shown on each map are numbered in degrees. These numbers are printed in black along the top, bottom and sides of the map frame.

The drawing above shows part of the map on page 41 and the lines of latitude and lines of longitude.

The index entry for Wexford is given as follows

Wexford Ireland **41 E2** 52.20N 6.28W

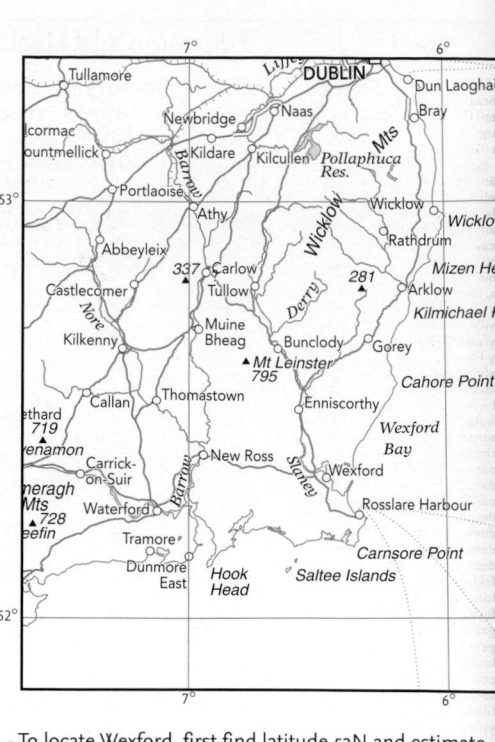

To locate Wexford, first find latitude 52N and estimate 20 minutes north from 52 degrees to find 52.20N, then find longitude 6W and estimate 28 minutes west from 6 degrees to find 6.28W. The symbol for the town of Wexford is where latitude 52.20N and longitude 6.28W meet.

On maps at a smaller scale than the map of Ireland, it is not possible to show every line of latitude and longitude. Only every 5 or 10 degrees of latitude and longitude may be shown. On these maps you must estimate the degrees and minutes to find the exact location of a feature.

Abbreviations

A. and B	Argyll and Bute	*hd*	headland	Orkn.	Orkney
Afgh.	Afghanistan	*i.*	island	Oxon.	Oxfordshire
Ala.	Alabama	Ill.	Illinois	Pacific Oc.	Pacific Ocean
Ang.	Angus	I. o. W.	Isle of Wight	P. and K.	Perth and Kinross
b.	bay	*is*	islands	P'boro.	Peterborough
Baja Calif.	Baja California	*l.*	lake	Pem.	Pembrokeshire
Bangl.	Bangladesh	La.	Louisiana	*pen.*	peninsula
Bos.-Herz.	Bosnia-Herzegovina	Lancs.	Lancashire	P.N.G.	Papua New Guinea
Brist.	Bristol	Leics.	Leicestershire	*pt*	point
c.	cape	Lincs.	Lincolnshire	*r.*	river
Cambs.	Cambridgeshire	Lux.	Luxembourg	*r. mouth*	river mouth
C.A.R.	Central African Republic	Man.	Manitoba	*resr*	reservoir
Colo.	Colorado	Mass.	Massachusetts	Rus. Fed.	Russian Federation
Corn.	Cornwall	Me.	Maine	S. Africa	South Africa
Cumb.	Cumbria	Mich.	Michigan	S. America	South America
Czech Rep.	Czech Republic	Minn.	Minnesota	S. Atlantic Oc.	South Atlantic Ocean
d.	internal division e.g. county, state	Miss.	Mississippi	S. C.	South Carolina
		Mo.	Missouri	S. China Sea	South China Sea
Del.	Delaware	Mor.	Moray	Shetl.	Shetland
Dem. Rep. Congo	Democratic Republic of the Congo	*mt.*	mountain	S. Korea	South Korea
		mts	mountains	Som.	Somerset
Derbys.	Derbyshire	N. Africa	North Africa	Southern Oc.	Southern Ocean
des.	desert	N. America	North America	S. Pacific Oc.	South Pacific Ocean
Dev.	Devon	N. Atlantic Oc.	North Atlantic Ocean	*str.*	strait
Dom. Rep.	Dominican Republic	*nat. park*	National Park	Suff.	Suffolk
Don.	Donegal	*nature res.*	Nature Reserve	Switz.	Switzerland
Dor.	Dorset	N. C.	North Carolina	T. and W.	Tyne and Wear
Dur.	Durham	Neth.	Netherlands	Tel. Wre.	Telford and Wrekin
Equat. Guinea	Equatorial Guinea	Neth. Antilles	Netherlands Antilles	Tex.	Texas
Ess.	Essex	Nev.	Nevada	Tipp.	Tipperary
est.	estuary	New.	Newport	U.A.E.	United Arab Emirates
E. Sussex	East Sussex	Nfld. and Lab.	Newfoundland and Labrador	U.K.	United Kingdom
E. Yorks.	East Riding of Yorkshire	N. Korea	North Korea	U.S.A.	United States of America
f.	physical feature, e.g. valley, plain, geographic area	N. M.	New Mexico	Va.	Virginia
		N. Mariana Is	Northern Marianas Islands	*vol.*	volcano
Falk.	Falkirk	Norf.	Norfolk	Vt.	Vermont
for.	forest	Northum.	Northumberland	Water.	Waterford
g.	gulf	Notts.	Nottinghamshire	Warwicks.	Warwickshire
Ga.	Georgia	N. Pacific Oc.	North Pacific Ocean	Wick.	Wicklow
Glos.	Gloucestershire	N. Y.	New York	W. Isles	Western Isles
Hants.	Hampshire	Oh.	Ohio	W. Va.	West Virginia
High.	Highland	Oreg.	Oregon	Wyo.	Wyoming

France 11 H2 ....51.00N 2.07E
raa Denmark 40 B1 ....55.02N 9.25E
rg Germany 54 B4 ....50.46N 6.05E
rg Denmark 40 B2 ....57.03N 9.55E
Germany 54 D3 ....48.50N 10.06E
Belgium 42 D3 ....50.56N 4.03E
in Iran 95 G6 ....30.20N 48.15E
sh Iran 95 H6 ....31.08N 52.36E
a Algeria 84 D5 ....31.00N 2.43W
n Rus. Fed. 59 K3 ....53.42N 91.25E
cay Peru 76 F5 ....13.39S 72.52W
ū Iran 95 H6 ....31.06N 53.13E
iri Japan 106 D4 ....44.01N 144.15E
, Lake Ethiopia 85 H2 ....6.19N 37.53E
Rus. Fed. 52 G8 ....52.40N 90.06E
ville France 44 D7 ....50.06N 1.50E
feale Ireland 41 B2 ....52.23N 9.18W
y Head Scotland 17 F2 ....54.46N 3.58W
eix Ireland 41 D2 ....51.55N 8.44E
tabad Pakistan 95 L6 ....34.13N 73.17E
é Chad 85 G3 ....13.50N 20.49E
uta Nigeria 84 E2 ....7.07N 3.18E
eron Wales 12 C4 ....52.15N 4.15W
hirder Scotland 19 G2 ....57.34N 2.38W
are Wales 12 D3 ....51.43N 3.27W
are Range mts Kenya 87 B2 ....0.21S 36.19E
aron Scotland 19 G2 ....52.48N 4.43W
deen Scotland 19 G2 ....57.09N 2.06W
deen Scotland 8 D5 ....57.10N 2.11W
deen U.S.A. 64 G6 ....45.28N 98.31W
deenshire d. Scotland 8 D5 ....57.21N 2.32W
eldy Scotland 19 F1 ....56.37N 3.52W
ford England 15 F2 ....53.50N 1.21W
oyle Scotland 16 E4 ....56.11N 4.23W
gavenny Wales 12 D3 ....51.49N 3.01W
gele Wales 12 D5 ....53.17N 3.35W
our Scotland 19 F2 ....57.29N 3.13W
porth Wales 12 C4 ....52.08N 4.33W
soch Wales 12 C4 ....52.50N 4.30W
tillery Scotland 17 F2 ....51.44N 3.08W
rstwyth Wales 12 C4 ....52.25N 4.05W
Saudi Arabia 94 F3 ....18.14N 42.27E
an Côte d'Ivoire 84 D2 ....5.21N 4.02W
ne U.S.A. 64 G3 ....32.26N 99.45W
gdon England 10 D2 ....51.40N 1.17W
gton Scotland 17 F3 ....55.30N 3.41W
bi, Lake Canada 65 J6 ....48.55N 80.01W
ne Scotland 19 G2 ....57.05N 2.47W
q Saudi Arabia 95 G5 ....25.56N 49.42E
hos Bank f. S. Atlantic Oc. 109 R4 ....19.28S 38.59W
Arïsh Saudi Arabia 94 F3 ....16.59N 42.45E
Dhabi U.A.E. 95 H4 ....24.28N 54.20E
Hamed Sudan 85 H3 ....19.30N 33.74E
a Nigeria 84 E2 ....9.06N 7.19E
Kamäl Syria 94 F6 ....34.26N 40.56E
a r. Bolivia 76 F6 ....9.43S 65.20W
iã Brazil 76 G6 ....9.44S 65.20W
Nujaym Libya 53 G3 ....30.28N 15.27E
Sunbul Egypt 94 D4 ....22.26N 31.39E
d Sudan 94 C2 ....13.46N 26.26E
ñiza Spain 48 A5 ....42.13N 8.16W
oneta Mexico 70 C5 ....22.30N 105.25W
ulco Mexico 70 E5 ....16.55N 99.52W
gua Venezuela 72 C7 ....9.33N 69.11W
a Ghana 84 D2 ....5.35N 0.14W
ington England 15 E2 ....53.35N 2.22W
eloös r. Greece 56 D4 ....38.20N 21.06E
ll Island Ireland 41 A3 ....53.56N 10.00W
insk Rus. Fed. 59 K3 ....56.17N 90.34E
ralaig mt. Scotland 18 D2 ....57.11N 5.09W
ns Island Bahamas 71 J5 ....22.18N 74.08W
England 11 G3 ....52.38N 1.33E
ncagua, Cerro mt. Argentina 73 B3 ....32.38S 70.01W
oruña Spain 48 A5 ....43.22N 8.23W
d. Brazil 76 F6 ....9.06S 70.25W
r. Brazil 76 G5 ....10.07S 67.52W
on, Groupe is French Polynesia 109 K4 ....21.20S 135.57W
Spain 48 C4 ....41.33N 4.51W
a r. Spain 48 C4
m's Peak Sri Lanka 96 F2 ....6.49N 80.28E
na Turkey 57 H6 ....36.59N 35.19E
pazarı Turkey 57 I5 ....40.47N 30.23E
Terra Ethiopia 87 C4 ....6.37N 40.56E
r. Italy 50 C6 ....45.08N 9.53E
Dahnä' des. Saudi Arabia 95 G5 ....20.40N 46.52E
Dakhla Western Sahara 84 C4 ....23.42N 15.56W
erbury England 10 D3 ....52.01N 1.19W
Dir'iyah Saudi Arabia 95 G4 ....24.45N 46.34E
Ababa Ethiopia 85 H2 ....9.01N 38.45E
Diwaniyah Iraq 94 F5 ....31.59N 44.57E
aide Australia 110 C3 ....34.56S 138.40E
n Yemen 94 F2 ....12.49N 44.59E
, Gulf of Somalia/Yemen 85 I3 ....11.44N 45.16E
i. Indonesia 105 I3 ....4.15S 133.27E
Ärk'ay Ethiopia 94 E2 ....13.24N 38.03E
grat Ethiopia 94 E2 ....14.16N 39.29E
anga Uganda 87 A3 ....2.43N 33.28E
Ugri Eritrea 94 E2 ....14.52N 38.48E
aman Turkey 57 M3 ....37.46N 38.17E
miralty Islands P.N.G. 110 D6 ....1.44S 146.17E
ur r. France 44 D3 ....43.32N 1.31W
atic Sea Europe 50 E6 ....44.19N 13.24E
a Ethiopia 85 H3 ....14.09N 38.52E
rick le Street England 15 F2 ....53.34N 1.12W
cha r. Rus. Fed. 59 O4 ....66.42N 136.32E
ean Sea Greece/Turkey 56 F4 ....39.00N 24.51E
hanistan Asia 95 K6 ....33.53N 65.52E
adow Somalia 87 C3 ....0.32N 42.04E
ca 82
a Turkey 57 I4 ....38.46N 30.33E
dez Niger 84 E3 ....16.57N 7.59E
dir Morocco 84 C5 ....30.27N 9.37W
no r. Japan 106 C3 ....37.58N 139.02E
rtala India 97 H5 ....23.50N 91.16E
e France 44 E3 ....43.18N 3.28E
France 44 D4 ....44.12N 0.38E
re Maryam Ethiopia 87 B4 ....5.38N 38.13E
os Dimitrios Greece 56 E3 ....37.49N 23.51E
os Efstratios i. Greece 56 F3 ....39.30N 25.01E
os Konstantinos Greece 56 E4 ....38.45N 22.51E
os Nikolaos Greece 56 F2 ....35.12N 25.43E
wat Hills Sudan 94 E1 ....16.26N 35.03E
a India 96 E6 ....27.09N 78.02E
Turkey 94 F2 ....39.43N 43.04E
gento Italy 50 E2 ....37.18N 13.35E
dulce Panama 71 H2 ....8.12N 80.33W
ascalientes Mexico 70 D5 ....21.51N 102.12W
ascalientes Mexico 70 D5 ....21.57N 102.11W
ilar de Campóo Spain 48 C5 ....42.47N 4.14W
las Spain 48 E2 ....37.25N 1.35W

Agulhas, Cape S. Africa 86 B1 ....34.50S 20.03E
Ahar Iran 95 G7 ....38.27N 47.02E
Ahaus Germany 42 G5 ....52.05N 7.01E
Ahmadabad India 96 D5 ....23.03N 72.37E
Ahmadpur East Pakistan 96 D6 ....29.10N 71.22E
Ahväz Iran 95 G6 ....31.15N 48.40E
Aigialousa Cyprus 57 K2 ....35.31N 34.11E
Aigina i. Greece 56 E3 ....37.41N 23.31E
Ailsa Craig i. Scotland 16 D3 ....55.15N 5.06W
Aïn Beïda Algeria 52 E4 ....35.47N 7.25E
'Aïn Ben Tili Mauritania 84 D4 ....25.58N 9.31W
Aïn Sefra Algeria 84 D5 ....32.42N 0.35W
Aïr, Massif de l' mts Niger 84 E3 ....18.46N 8.15E
Airdrie Canada 62 G3 ....51.17N 114.01W
Airdrie Scotland 17 F3 ....55.52N 3.58W
Aisne r. France 44 E6 ....49.26N 2.51E
Aitape P.N.G. 105 K3 ....3.09S 142.22E
Aitutaki i. Cook Is 109 J4 ....18.52S 159.44W
Aix-en-Provence France 44 F3 ....43.32N 5.27E
Aizkraukle Latvia 55 K7 ....56.36N 25.15E
Aizu-wakamatsu Japan 106 C3 ....37.29N 139.56E
Ajaccio France 44 H2 ....41.55N 8.44E
Ajdābiyā Libya 85 G5 ....30.45N 20.13E
Akçakale Turkey 57 M3 ....36.43N 38.57E
Akdağmadeni Turkey 57 K4 ....39.39N 35.54E
Akhdar, Al Jabal al mts Libya 53 H3 ....31.46N 20.46E
Akhdar, Jabal mts Oman 95 I4 ....23.22N 57.00E
Akhisar Turkey 57 G4 ....38.55N 27.50E
Akimiski Island Canada 63 J3 ....53.08N 81.17W
Akita Japan 106 D3 ....39.43N 140.07E
Akkajaure l. Sweden 40 D4 ....67.41N 17.29E
Aknoul Morocco 48 D1 ....34.38N 3.51W
Akpatok Island Canada 63 L4 ....60.24N 67.45W
Akranes Iceland 40 X2 ....64.19N 22.05W
Akron U.S.A. 65 J5 ....41.07N 81.33W
Aksai Chin Asia 96 E8 ....35.08N 79.11E
Aksaray Turkey 57 K4 ....38.23N 34.02E
Akşehir Turkey 57 I4 ....38.21N 31.24E
Aksu China 102 E6 ....41.06N 80.21E
Aksum Ethiopia 94 E2 ....14.07N 38.46E
Aktau Kazakhstan 58 G2 ....43.39N 51.12E
Aktobe Kazakhstan 58 G3 ....50.13N 57.10E
Aktogay Kazakhstan 58 I2 ....47.06N 79.42E
Akureyri Iceland 40 Y2 ....65.41N 18.07W
Alabama d. U.S.A. 65 I3 ....32.41N 86.42W
Alabama r. U.S.A. 65 I3 ....31.09N 87.57W
Alagoas d. Brazil 77 M6 ....9.33S 36.46W
Alagoinhas Brazil 77 M5 ....12.07S 38.17W
Alagón r. Spain 48 B3 ....39.57N 6.03W
Alahärma Finland 40 E3 ....63.15N 22.50E
Al Ahmadi Kuwait 95 G5 ....29.04N 48.02E
Alakol, Ozero l. Kazakhstan 102 E7 ....46.03N 81.30E
Alakurtti Rus. Fed. 40 G4 ....66.58N 30.20E
Alamagan i. N. Mariana Is 105 L7 ....17.35N 145.52E
Åland Islands Finland 40 D3 ....60.28N 19.53E
Al 'Aqabah Jordan 94 E5 ....29.31N 35.01E
Al Artāwīyah Saudi Arabia 95 G5 ....26.30N 45.21E
Alaşehir Turkey 57 H4 ....38.21N 28.30E
Alaska d. U.S.A. 62 D4 ....63.41N 143.45W
Alaska, Gulf of U.S.A. 62 D3 ....58.10N 147.57W
Alaska Peninsula U.S.A. 62 C3 ....55.18N 162.25W
Alaska Range mts U.S.A. 62 D4 ....63.19N 148.01W
Alausí Ecuador 76 E7 ....2.10S 78.52W
Alavus Finland 40 E3 ....62.35N 23.37E
Alaw, Llyn resr Wales 12 C5 ....53.21N 4.25W
Albacete Spain 48 E3 ....39.00N 1.50W
Alba Iulia Romania 56 E8 ....46.05N 23.36E
Albania Europe 56 C5 ....41.56N 19.34E
Albany Australia 110 A3 ....34.58S 117.54E
Albany r. Canada 63 J3 ....52.08N 81.59W
Albany U.S.A. 65 L5 ....42.40N 73.46W
Albatross Bay Australia 105 K1 ....12.41S 141.44E
Al Bawiti Egypt 85 G4 ....28.21N 28.50E
Al Baydā' Libya 85 G5 ....32.44N 21.44E
Albenga Italy 50 C6 ....44.03N 8.13E
Alberche r. Spain 48 C3 ....39.58N 4.46W
Albert France 42 B2 ....49.59N 2.39E
Albert, Lake Dem. Rep. Congo/Uganda 86 C5 ....1.43N 30.52E
Alberta d. Canada 62 G3 ....52.45N 113.59W
Albert Lea U.S.A. 65 H5 ....43.39N 93.22W
Albert Nile r. Sudan/Uganda 85 H2 ....3.36N 32.02E
Albi France 44 E3 ....43.56N 2.08E
Al Biyādh f. Saudi Arabia 95 G4 ....20.57N 46.14E
Alborán, Isla de i. Spain 48 D1 ....35.57N 3.02W
Albuquerque U.S.A. 64 E4 ....35.07N 106.38W
Al Buraymī Oman 95 I4 ....24.14N 55.46E
Albury Australia 110 D3 ....36.03S 146.54E
Alcalá de Henares Spain 48 D4 ....40.29N 3.21W
Alcalá la Real Spain 48 D2 ....37.28N 3.55W
Alcañiz Spain 48 E4 ....41.03N 0.07W
Alcázar de San Juan Spain 48 D3 ....39.23N 3.11W
Alcester England 10 D3 ....52.13N 1.52W
Alcoy-Alcoi Spain 48 E3 ....38.42N 0.27W
Alcúdia Spain 48 G3 ....39.52N 3.08E
Aldabra Islands Seychelles 85 I1 ....9.16S 46.30E
Aldan Rus. Fed. 59 N3 ....58.36N 125.25E
Aldan r. Rus. Fed. 59 N4 ....63.32N 128.46E
Aldbrough England 15 G2 ....53.50N 0.07W
Aldeburgh England 11 G3 ....52.09N 1.36E
Alderley Edge England 15 E2 ....53.18N 2.14W
Alderney i. Channel Is 13 Z9 ....49.42N 2.15W
Aldershot England 10 E2 ....51.15N 0.45W
Aldingham England 14 D3 ....54.08N 3.06W
Aldridge England 10 D3 ....52.36N 1.55W
Aleksandrovsk-Sakhalinskiy Rus. Fed. 59 P3 ....51.08N 142.21E
Aleksin Rus. Fed. 55 Q6 ....54.31N 37.05E
Alençon France 44 D6 ....48.26N 0.06E
Aleppo Syria 94 E7 ....36.12N 37.09E
Alès France 44 F4 ....44.08N 4.05E
Aleşd Romania 46 F1 ....47.03N 22.22E
Alessandria Italy 50 C6 ....44.55N 8.38E
Ålesund Norway 40 A3 ....62.28N 6.12E
Aleutian Basin f. Bering Sea 108 H9 ....57.54N 179.12E
Aleutian Islands U.S.A. 62 A3 ....52.00N 176.15W
Aleutian Range mts U.S.A. 62 C3 ....58.10N 159.17W
Aleutian Trench f. N. Pacific Oc. 108 I9 ....49.44N 178.54W
Alexander Archipelago is U.S.A. 62 E3 ....57.59N 137.31E
Alexandra, Cape S. Atlantic Oc. 73 F1 ....54.05S 37.56W
Alexandria Egypt 85 G5 ....31.13N 29.56E
Alexandria Romania 56 F6 ....43.58N 25.20E
Alexandria Scotland 16 E3 ....55.59N 4.35W
Alexandria La. U.S.A. 65 H3 ....31.17N 92.28W
Alexandria Va. U.S.A. 65 K4 ....38.48N 77.05W
Alexandroupoli Greece 56 F5 ....40.51N 25.53E
Aleysk Rus. Fed. 102 E8 ....52.30N 82.51E
Al Fayyūm Egypt 85 H4 ....29.18N 30.51E
Alford England 15 H2 ....53.16N 0.11E
Alfreton England 15 F2 ....53.06N 1.23W
Algarve f. Portugal 48 A2 ....37.16N 8.07W
Algeciras Spain 48 C2 ....36.07N 5.27W
Algeria Africa 84 E4 ....30.15N 3.31E
Al Ghaydah Yemen 95 H3 ....16.14N 52.13E
Al Ghurdaqah Egypt 53 J2 ....27.12N 33.48E

Al Ghwaybiyah Saudi Arabia 95 G5 ....25.14N 49.43E
Algiers Algeria 84 E5 ....36.46N 3.04E
Algorta Spain 48 D5 ....43.21N 2.59W
Al Hasakah Syria 94 F7 ....36.30N 40.44E
Al Hibāk des. Saudi Arabia 95 H3 ....19.30N 52.27E
Al Hoceima Morocco 52 C4 ....35.15N 3.56W
Al Hufūf Saudi Arabia 95 G5 ....25.22N 49.35E
Aliağa Turkey 56 G4 ....38.47N 26.58E
Aliakmonas r. Greece 56 E5 ....40.28N 22.38E
Äli Bayramlı Azerbaijan 95 G7 ....39.56N 48.56E
Alicante Spain 48 E3 ....38.21N 0.28W
Alice Springs town Australia 110 C4 ....23.42S 133.52E
Alingsås Sweden 40 C2 ....57.56N 12.33E
Al Ismā'īlīyah Egypt 53 J3 ....30.35N 32.17E
Al Jaghbūb Libya 85 G4 ....29.43N 24.31E
Al Jahrah Kuwait 95 G5 ....29.20N 47.41E
Al Jawf Libya 85 G4 ....24.14N 23.24E
Al Jawf Saudi Arabia 94 E5 ....29.47N 39.55E
Al Jawsh Libya 52 F3 ....32.01N 11.42E
Al Jubayl Saudi Arabia 95 G5 ....27.02N 49.38E
Al Karak Jordan 94 E5 ....31.10N 35.42E
Al Khāburah Oman 95 I4 ....23.58N 57.06E
Al Khārijah Egypt 85 H4 ....25.24N 30.33E
Al Khasab Oman 95 I5 ....26.11N 56.14E
Al Khums Libya 52 F3 ....32.35N 14.22E
Alkmaar Neth. 42 D5 ....52.38N 4.45E
Al Kūt Iraq 95 G6 ....32.31N 45.47E
Allahabad India 96 F6 ....25.28N 81.52E
Allakh-Yun' Rus. Fed. 59 O4 ....61.05N 138.03E
Allegheny r. U.S.A. 65 K5 ....40.27N 79.59W
Allegheny Mountains U.S.A. 65 J4 ....36.46N 82.22W
Allen, Lough l. Ireland 41 C4 ....54.09N 8.03W
Allendale Town England 15 E3 ....54.54N 2.15W
Allentown U.S.A. 65 K5 ....40.37N 75.30W
Alleppey India 96 E2 ....9.30N 76.21E
Aller r. Germany 54 C5 ....52.57N 9.11E
Allinge-Sandvig Denmark 46 B5 ....55.16N 14.49E
Al Lith Saudi Arabia 94 F4 ....20.10N 40.16E
Alloa Scotland 17 F4 ....56.07N 3.47W
Almansa Spain 48 E3 ....38.52N 1.05W
Al Mansūrah Egypt 53 J3 ....31.02N 31.23E
Almanzor mt. Spain 48 C4 ....40.15N 5.18W
Al Marj Libya 53 H3 ....32.29N 20.50E
Almaty Kazakhstan 58 I2 ....43.16N 77.01E
Almeirim Brazil 77 J7 ....1.30S 52.35W
Almelo Neth. 42 F5 ....52.21N 6.40E
Almendra, Embalse de resr Spain 48 B4 ....41.17N 6.14W
Almería Spain 48 D2 ....36.50N 2.27W
Almina, Punta pt Spain 48 C1 ....35.54N 5.16W
Al Minyā Egypt 85 H4 ....28.05N 30.45E
Almodôvar Portugal 48 A2 ....37.31N 8.04W
Almond r. Scotland 17 F4 ....56.25N 3.28W
Al Mudawwara Jordan 94 E5 ....29.19N 36.02E
Almuñécar Spain 48 D2 ....36.44N 3.41W
Alnmouth England 15 F4 ....55.25N 1.42W
Alnwick England 15 F4 ....55.25N 1.42W
Alofi Niue 108 I4 ....19.03S 169.54W
Alor i. Indonesia 105 G2 ....8.17S 124.45E
Alor Setar Malaysia 104 C5 ....6.08N 100.22E
Alpena U.S.A. 65 J6 ....45.03N 83.27W
Alpine U.S.A. 64 F3 ....30.18N 103.35W
Alps mts Europe 52 F6 ....46.00N 7.30E
Al Qa'āmīyāt f. Saudi Arabia 95 G3 ....17.59N 47.47E
Al Qaddāhiyah Libya 52 G3 ....31.22N 15.12E
Al Qāmishlī Syria 94 F7 ....37.03N 41.13E
Al Qaryatayn Syria 57 L2 ....34.13N 37.14E
Al Qunfidhah Saudi Arabia 94 F3 ....19.09N 41.04E
Al Qusayr Egypt 85 H4 ....26.07N 34.13E
Alsace d. France 42 G1 ....48.22N 7.24E
Alsager England 15 E2 ....53.06N 2.18W
Alston England 15 E3 ....54.49N 2.26W
Altaelva r. Norway 40 F5 ....69.57N 23.20E
Altai Mountains Asia 102 F7 ....48.55N 87.16E
Altamira Brazil 77 J7 ....3.14S 52.14W
Altamura Italy 50 G4 ....40.49N 16.34E
Altay China 102 F7 ....47.48N 88.10E
Altay Mongolia 102 H7 ....46.18N 96.15E
Altiplano f. Bolivia 76 G4 ....16.24S 69.39W
Altiplano Mexicano mts N. America 60 I5 ....24.00N 105.00W
Alton England 10 E2 ....51.09N 0.58W
Altoona U.S.A. 65 K5 ....40.30N 78.24W
Altötting Germany 54 F3 ....48.14N 12.41E
Altrincham England 15 E2 ....53.23N 2.21W
Altun Shan mts China 102 F5 ....37.45N 86.38E
Alturas U.S.A. 64 B5 ....41.30N 120.31W
Al 'Uqaylah Libya 53 G3 ....30.13N 19.12E
Al 'Uwaynāt Libya 53 G3 ....21.46N 24.51E
Älvdalen Sweden 40 C3 ....61.13N 14.04E
Alveley England 10 C3 ....52.27N 2.21W
Älvsbyn Sweden 40 E4 ....65.40N 21.00E
Al Wajh Saudi Arabia 94 E5 ....26.17N 36.25E
Alwen Reservoir Wales 12 D5 ....53.05N 3.35W
Al Widyān f. Iraq/Saudi Arabia 94 F6 ....32.09N 40.22E
Alyth Scotland 19 F1 ....56.38N 3.14W
Alytus Lithuania 46 G5 ....54.23N 24.03E
Amadeus, Lake Australia 110 C4 ....24.50S 131.09E
Amadjuak Lake Canada 63 K4 ....64.57N 71.09W
Amadora Portugal 48 A3 ....38.46N 9.14W
Åmål Sweden 40 C2 ....59.03N 12.44E
Amamapare Indonesia 105 J3 ....4.54S 136.58E
Amami-Ō-shima i. Japan 106 A1 ....28.13N 129.08E
Amapá Brazil 77 J8 ....2.02N 50.50W
Amapá d. Brazil 77 J8 ....1.29N 51.50W
Amarillo U.S.A. 64 F4 ....35.15N 101.50W
Amasya Turkey 57 K5 ....40.39N 35.50E
Amazon r. S. America 72 D7 ....0.01N 50.37W
Amazon, Mouths of the Brazil 77 K8 ....0.41N 49.28W
Amazonas d. Brazil 76 G7 ....4.38S 65.10W
Ambarchik Rus. Fed. 59 R4 ....69.35N 162.13E
Ambato Ecuador 76 E7 ....1.16S 78.39W
Ambergate England 15 F2 ....53.04N 1.29W
Ambergris Cay f. Belize 70 G4 ....18.08N 87.52W
Amble England 15 F4 ....55.20N 1.35W
Ambleside England 14 E3 ....54.26N 2.58W
Ambon Indonesia 105 H3 ....3.43S 128.11E
Amboseli National Park Kenya 87 B2 ....2.37S 37.14E
Ambrym i. Vanuatu 111 F5 ....16.12S 168.13E
American Samoa is S. Pacific Oc. 108 I5 ....12.00S 170.00W
Amersfoort Neth. 42 E5 ....52.09N 5.23E
Amersham England 10 E2 ....51.41N 0.36W
Amesbury England 10 D2 ....51.10N 1.47W
Amfissa Greece 56 E3 ....38.32N 22.22E
Amga Rus. Fed. 59 O4 ....60.51N 131.57E
Amgu Rus. Fed. 106 C5 ....45.46N 137.32E
Amgun' r. Rus. Fed. 59 O3 ....53.01N 139.38E
Amiens France 44 E6 ....49.54N 2.18E
Amino Ethiopia 87 C4 ....4.21N 41.51E
Amlwch Wales 12 C5 ....53.25N 4.21W
'Ammān Jordan 94 E6 ....31.57N 35.56E
Ammanford Wales 12 D3 ....51.48N 3.59W
Amol Iran 95 H7 ....36.27N 52.20E
Amorgos i. Greece 56 F3 ....36.49N 25.54E
Amos Canada 63 K2 ....48.34N 78.08W

Ampthill England 11 E3 ....52.02N 0.30W
Amravati India 96 E5 ....20.56N 77.51E
Amritsar India 96 D7 ....31.34N 74.56E
Amstelveen Neth. 42 D5 ....52.19N 4.52E
Amsterdam Neth. 42 D5 ....52.23N 4.54E
Amstetten Austria 54 F3 ....48.08N 14.52E
Amu Darya r. Asia 58 H2 ....43.50N 59.00E
Amund Ringnes Island Canada 63 I5 ....78.17N 96.35W
Amundsen Gulf Canada 62 F5 ....70.25N 121.26W
Amuntai Indonesia 104 F3 ....2.25S 115.13E
Amur r. Rus. Fed. 59 P3 ....53.17N 140.37E
Anabar r. Rus. Fed. 59 M5 ....73.13N 113.31E
Anadolu Dağları mts Turkey 57 L5 ....40.59N 36.11E
Anadyr' Rus. Fed. 59 S4 ....64.44N 177.20E
Anadyrskiy Zaliv b. Rus. Fed. 59 T4 ....63.56N 177.42W
'Ānah Iraq 94 F6 ....34.25N 41.56E
Anambas, Kepulauan is Indonesia 104 D4 ....3.17N 105.55E
Anamur Turkey 57 J3 ....36.06N 32.50E
Anapa Rus. Fed. 57 L7 ....44.54N 37.20E
Anápolis Brazil 77 J5 ....16.20S 48.55W
Anatahan i. N. Mariana Is 105 L7 ....16.21N 145.42E
Anatolia f. Turkey 57 J4 ....38.58N 33.19E
Anchorage U.S.A. 62 D4 ....61.12N 149.52W
Ancona Italy 50 E5 ....43.37N 13.31E
Andalsnes Norway 40 A3 ....62.34N 7.42E
Andaman Islands India 97 H3 ....12.46N 93.17E
Andaman Sea Indian Oc. 97 I3 ....11.33N 95.19E
Anderlecht Belgium 42 D3 ....50.49N 4.18E
Andermatt Switz. 54 C2 ....46.38N 8.36E
Anderson r. Canada 62 F4 ....69.41N 128.56W
Anderson U.S.A. 65 I5 ....64.22N 149.12W
Andes mts S. America 73 B6 ....9.10S 77.03W
Andfjorden str. Norway 40 D5 ....68.53S 16.04E
Andhra Pradesh d. India 96 E4 ....16.03N 79.11E
Andkhvoy Afgh. 95 K7 ....36.59N 65.08E
Andong S. Korea 106 A3 ....36.33N 128.43E
Andorra Europe 48 F5 ....42.32N 1.35E
Andorra la Vella Andorra 48 F5 ....42.31N 1.32E
Andover England 10 D2 ....51.12N 1.29W
Andøya i. Norway 40 C5 ....69.11N 15.48E
Andreas Isle of Man 14 C3 ....54.22N 4.27W
Andria Italy 50 G4 ....41.14N 16.18E
Andros i. Bahamas 71 I5 ....24.25N 78.09W
Andros i. Greece 56 F3 ....37.53N 24.57E
Andújar Spain 48 C3 ....38.02N 4.03W
Anéfis Mali 84 E3 ....18.02N 0.32E
Anegada i. Virgin Is (U.K.) 71 L4 ....18.44N 64.19W
Aneto mt. Spain 48 F5 ....42.38N 0.39E
Angara r. Rus. Fed. 59 K3 ....58.05N 92.59E
Angarsk Rus. Fed. 103 I8 ....52.24N 103.45E
Ånge Sweden 40 C3 ....62.32N 15.40E
Ángel de la Guarda, Isla i. Mexico 70 B6 ....29.25N 113.24W
Ängelholm Sweden 40 C2 ....56.15N 12.52E
Angers France 44 C5 ....47.28N 0.33W
Anglesey i. Wales 12 C5 ....53.18N 4.23W
Angola Africa 86 A3 ....11.40S 17.34E
Angola Basin f. Atlantic Oc. 117 J5 ....15.00S 0.00E
Angoulême France 44 D4 ....45.39N 0.10E
Angren Uzbekistan 102 C6 ....41.02N 70.07E
Anguilla i. Central America 71 L4 ....18.14N 63.02W
Angus d. Scotland 8 D5 ....56.43N 2.45W
Anhui d. China 103 L4 ....32.10N 117.07E
Anlaby England 15 G2 ....53.45N 0.26W
Annaba Algeria 84 E5 ....36.54N 7.46E
An Nabk Syria 57 L2 ....34.01N 36.44E
An Nafud des. Saudi Arabia 94 F5 ....28.28N 41.17E
An Najaf Iraq 94 F6 ....31.59N 44.20E
Annalee r. Ireland 41 D4 ....54.02N 7.23W
Annalong Northern Ireland 16 D2 ....54.06N 5.54W
Annan Scotland 17 F2 ....54.59N 3.15W
Annan r. Scotland 17 F2 ....54.59N 3.16W
Annapurna mt. Nepal 96 F6 ....28.34N 83.49E
Ann Arbor U.S.A. 65 J5 ....42.17N 83.45W
An Nāsirīyah Iraq 95 G6 ....31.01N 46.14E
An Nawfalīyah Libya 53 G3 ....30.51N 17.52E
Annecy France 44 G4 ....45.54N 6.08E
Anniston U.S.A. 65 I3 ....33.39N 85.43W
An Nu'ayrīyah Saudi Arabia 95 G5 ....27.29N 48.26E
An Nuşayrīyah, Jabal mts Syria 57 L2 ....35.15N 36.05E
Ansbach Germany 54 D3 ....49.18N 10.36E
Anshan China 103 M6 ....41.05N 123.02E
Anshun China 103 J3 ....26.15N 105.57E
Anstruther Scotland 17 G4 ....56.13N 2.42W
Antakya Turkey 57 L3 ....36.11N 36.07E
Antalya Turkey 57 I3 ....36.53N 30.41E
Antalya Körfezi g. Turkey 57 I3 ....36.40N 30.58E
Antananarivo Madagascar 86 D3 ....18.54S 47.33E
Antarctica 112
Antarctic Peninsula f. Antarctica 116 F2 ....65.00S 64.00W
An Teallach mt. Scotland 18 D2 ....57.48N 5.16W
Antequera Spain 48 C2 ....37.02N 4.33W
Antibes France 44 G3 ....43.35N 7.07E
Anticosti, Île d' i. Canada 63 L2 ....49.27N 62.59W
Antigua i. Antigua 71 L4 ....17.02N 61.43W
Antigua and Barbuda Central America 71 L4 ....17.20N 61.20W
Antikythira i. Greece 56 E2 ....35.52N 23.20E
Antofagasta Chile 73 B4 ....23.37S 70.22W
Antipodes Islands New Zealand 111 G2 ....49.39S 178.44E
Antrim Northern Ireland 16 C2 ....54.43N 6.12W
Antrim d. Northern Ireland 9 B4 ....54.43N 6.16W
Antrim f. Northern Ireland 41 C4 ....54.59N 6.22W
Antrim Hills Northern Ireland 16 C3 ....55.05N 6.16W
Antsirabe Madagascar 86 D3 ....19.53S 47.03E
Antsirañana Madagascar 86 D3 ....12.19S 49.17E
Antsohihy Madagascar 86 D3 ....14.53S 47.59E
Antwerp Belgium 42 D4 ....51.12N 4.26E
Antwerpen d. Belgium 42 D4 ....51.17N 4.46E
Anxi China 102 H6 ....40.27N 95.48E
Anyang China 103 K5 ....36.04N 114.22E
Anzhero-Sudzhensk Rus. Fed. 58 J3 ....56.08N 86.01E
Aomori Japan 106 D4 ....40.49N 140.45E
Aoraki mt. New Zealand 111 G2 ....43.37S 170.08E
Aosta Italy 50 B6 ....45.44N 7.20E
Apa r. Brazil 77 I3 ....22.07S 57.57W
Apalachee Bay U.S.A. 65 J2 ....29.59N 84.06W
Apaporis r. Colombia 76 G7 ....1.04S 69.26W
Aparri Phil. 105 G7 ....18.21N 121.40E
Apatity Rus. Fed. 40 H4 ....67.34N 33.23E
Apeldoorn Neth. 42 E5 ....52.12N 5.58E
Apennines mts Italy 50 D6 ....44.37N 9.47E
Apia Samoa 108 I5 ....13.50S 171.44W
Aporé r. Brazil 77 J4 ....19.25S 50.59W
Apostolos Andreas, Cape Cyprus 57 K2 ....35.41N 34.35E
Appalachian Mountains U.S.A. 65 J4 ....36.08N 83.01W
Appleby-in-Westmorland England 15 E3 ....54.35N 2.29W
Appledore England 13 C2 ....51.03N 4.12W
Apucarana Brazil 77 J3 ....23.34S 51.27W
Apurímac r. Peru 76 F5 ....12.16S 73.54W
Aqaba, Gulf of Asia 94 D5 ....29.19N 34.54E
Ära Ärba Ethiopia 87 C4 ....5.53N 41.26E
Arabian Peninsula Asia 85 I4 ....24.00N 45.00E
Arabian Sea Indian Oc. 90 F4 ....18.08N 66.38E
Aracaju Brazil 77 M5 ....10.52S 37.03W

Aracati Brazil 77 M7 ....4.33S 37.42W
Araçatuba Brazil 77 J3 ....21.12S 50.22W
Aracena, Sierra de *hills* Spain 48 B2 ....37.51N 7.07W
Arad Romania 56 D8 ....46.11N 21.21E
Arafura Sea Australia/Indonesia 110 C6 ....9.04S 132.58E
Aragón r. Spain 48 E5 ....42.13N 1.45W
Araguaia r. Brazil 77 K6 ....5.24S 48.41W
Araguaína Brazil 77 K6 ....7.20S 48.15W
Araguari Brazil 77 K4 ....18.38S 48.09W
Arak Algeria 84 E4 ....25.18N 3.39E
Arāk Iran 95 G6 ....34.05N 49.42E
Arakan Yoma *mts* Myanmar 97 H5 ....20.18N 94.07E
Aral Sea Kazakhstan/Uzbekistan 58 H2 ....45.07N 60.05E
Aral'sk Kazakhstan 58 H2 ....46.46N 61.43E
Aranda de Duero Spain 48 D4 ....41.41N 3.40W
Aran Island Ireland 41 C4 ....54.59N 8.35W
Aran Islands Ireland 41 B3 ....53.07N 9.44W
Aranjuez Spain 48 D4 ....40.02N 3.36W
Arapgir Turkey 57 M4 ....39.02N 38.29E
Arapiraca Brazil 77 M6 ....9.44S 36.37W
Arapis, Akra *pt* Greece 56 F5 ....40.27N 24.00E
'Ar'ar Saudi Arabia 94 F6 ....30.58N 40.58E
Araraquara Brazil 77 K3 ....21.47S 48.06W
Ararat, Mount Turkey 58 F1 ....39.45N 44.15E
Ārba Minch Ethiopia 87 B4 ....5.59N 37.32E
Arbīl Iraq 94 F7 ....36.11N 44.01E
Arboga Sweden 40 D2 ....59.23N 15.51E
Arbroath Scotland 17 G4 ....56.34N 2.35W
Arbu Lut, Dasht-e *des.* Afgh. 95 J5 ....29.57N 63.56E
Arcachon France 44 C4 ....44.40N 1.10W
Archangel Rus. Fed. 64.33N 40.33E
Arctic Bay *town* Canada 63 J5 ....72.55N 85.10W
Arctic Ocean 112
Arctic Red r. Canada 62 E4 ....67.27N 133.44W
Ardabīl Iran 95 G7 ....38.14N 48.15E
Ardas r. Greece 56 G5 ....41.40N 26.30E
Ardèche r. France 44 F4 ....44.16N 4.39E
Ardennes f. Belgium 42 D2 ....49.56N 4.52E
Ardestān Iran 95 H6 ....33.20N 52.21E
Ardglass Northern Ireland 16 D2 ....54.15N 5.36W
Ardila r. Portugal 48 B3 ....38.10N 7.28W
Ardnamurchan, Point of Scotland 18 C1 ....56.43N 6.13W
Ardrishaig Scotland 16 D4 ....56.01N 5.27W
Ardrossan Scotland 16 E3 ....55.39N 4.49W
Ards d. Northern Ireland 9 C4 ....54.28N 5.37W
Ards Peninsula Northern Ireland 16 D2 ....54.30N 5.25W
Ardvasar Scotland 18 D2 ....57.03N 5.55W
Arena, Point U.S.A. 64 B4 ....38.57N 123.44W
Arendal Norway 40 B2 ....58.27N 8.46E
Arenig Fawr *hill* Wales 12 D4 ....52.55N 3.45W
Arequipa Peru 76 F4 ....16.23S 71.32W
Arezzo Italy 50 D5 ....43.27N 11.53E
Arganda Spain 48 D4 ....40.18N 3.25W
Argentan France 44 C3 ....48.45N 0.01W
Argentina S. America 73 C3 ....35.00S 68.00W
Argentine Rise f. S. Atlantic Oc. 109 Q3 ....39.32S 53.02W
Argentino, Lago l. Argentina 73 B1 ....50.20S 72.51W
Argenton-sur-Creuse France 44 D5 ....46.36N 1.31E
Argeş r. Romania 56 G7 ....44.04N 26.37E
Argun' r. China/Rus. Fed. 103 M8 ....53.18N 121.20E
Argyle, Lake Australia 110 B5 ....16.37S 128.41E
Argyll f. Scotland 16 D4 ....56.08N 5.19W
Argyll and Bute d. Scotland 8 C4 ....55.46N 5.25W
Århus Denmark 40 B2 ....56.09N 10.12E
Arica Chile 72 B5 ....18.29S 70.20W
Arienas, Loch l. Scotland 16 D4 ....56.35N 5.46W
Arinos r. Brazil 77 I5 ....10.25S 58.13W
Aripuanã r. Brazil 77 H6 ....5.07S 60.22W
Ariquemes Brazil 76 H6 ....9.59S 63.05W
Arisaig Scotland 18 D1 ....56.55N 5.50W
Arisaig, Sound of *str.* Scotland 18 D1 ....56.51N 5.56W
Arizona d. U.S.A. 64 D3 ....34.11N 111.37W
Arkadelphia U.S.A. 65 H3 ....34.09N 93.03W
Arkaig, Loch l. Scotland 18 D1 ....56.58N 5.13W
Arkansas d. U.S.A. 65 H4 ....35.49N 92.00W
Arkansas r. U.S.A. 65 H3 ....33.49N 91.08W
Arkansas City U.S.A. 64 G4 ....37.04N 97.03W
Arklow Ireland 41 E2 ....52.48N 6.10W
Arkona, Kap c. Germany 54 E6 ....54.41N 13.27E
Arles France 44 F3 ....43.41N 4.38E
Arlit Niger 84 E3 ....18.42N 7.21E
Arlon Belgium 42 E2 ....49.41N 5.49E
Armagh Northern Ireland 16 C2 ....54.20N 6.39W
Armagh d. Northern Ireland 9 B4 ....54.19N 6.39W
Armagh f. Northern Ireland 41 E4 ....54.18N 6.39W
Armant Egypt 53 J2 ....25.37N 32.32E
Armavir Rus. Fed. 53 L6 ....45.01N 41.06E
Armenia Asia 58 F2 ....40.26N 44.30E
Armenia Colombia 72 B7 ....4.30N 75.39W
Armidale Australia 110 E3 ....30.32S 151.41E
Armyans'k Ukraine 57 J8 ....46.07N 33.41E
Arnauti, Cape Cyprus 57 J2 ....35.06N 32.16E
Arnhem Neth. 42 E4 ....51.59N 5.55E
Arnhem, Cape Australia 110 C5 ....12.19S 136.58E
Arnhem Land f. Australia 110 C5 ....13.26S 133.57E
Arno r. Italy 50 D5 ....43.41N 10.16E
Arnsberg Germany 54 C4 ....51.23N 8.04E
Ar Ramādī Iraq 94 F6 ....33.23N 43.16E
Arran i. Scotland 16 D3 ....55.35N 5.20W
Ar Raqqah Syria 94 E7 ....35.57N 39.01E
Arras France 44 E7 ....50.17N 2.46E
Arrecife Canary Islands 48 Z2 ....28.57N 13.33W
Arriagá Mexico 70 F4 ....16.16N 93.52W
Arrieta Canary Islands 48 Z2 ....29.08N 13.28W
Ar Rimāl f. Saudi Arabia 95 H4 ....21.43N 52.53E
Arrochar Scotland 16 E4 ....56.12N 4.44W
Ar Ruṭbah Iraq 94 F6 ....33.01N 40.11E
Arta Greece 56 E4 ....39.10N 20.59E
Artesia U.S.A. 64 F3 ....32.52N 104.25W
Artigas Uruguay 77 I1 ....30.24S 56.29W
Artois f. France 42 A3 ....50.40N 1.55E
Artois, Collines de l' *hills* France 11 G1 ......50.33N 1.54E
Artsyz Ukraine 57 H7 ....45.59N 29.27E
Aru, Kepulauan is Indonesia 105 I2 ....6.09S 134.05E
Aruba i. Central America 71 K3 ....12.30N 69.56W
Arunachal Pradesh d. India 97 H6 ....27.28N 92.48E
Arundel England 11 E1 ....50.51N 0.33W
Arusha Tanzania 86 C4 ....3.22S 36.37E
Arusha d. Tanzania 87 B2 ....3.30S 36.00E
Aruwimi r. Dem. Rep. Congo 86 B5 ....1.14N 23.38E
Arvayheer Mongolia 103 I7 ....46.08N 102.47E
Arviat Canada 63 I4 ....61.12N 94.09W
Arvidsjaur Sweden 40 D4 ....65.35N 19.12E
Arvika Sweden 40 C2 ....59.39N 12.37E
Arzamas Rus. Fed. 58 F3 ....55.23N 43.49E
Asad, Buḩayrat al r. Syria 57 M3 ....36.05N 38.03E
Asahi-dake vol. Japan 106 D4 ....43.41N 142.54E
Asahikawa Japan 106 D4 ....43.46N 142.22E
Asansol India 96 G5 ....23.41N 87.01E
Ascension Island Atlantic Oc. 82 B4 ....8.00S 14.00W
Ascoli Piceno Italy 50 E5 ....42.52N 13.33E
Åsele Sweden 40 D4 ....64.10N 17.22E
Asenovgrad Bulgaria 56 F6 ....42.00N 24.52E
Asfordby England 10 E3 ....52.46N 0.57W

Ashbourne England 15 F2 ....53.01N 1.44W
Ashbourne Ireland 41 E3 ....53.31N 6.23W
Ashburton watercourse Australia 110 A4 ......21.43S 114.54E
Ashburton England 13 D2 ....50.31N 3.45W
Ashby de la Zouch England 10 D3 ....52.45N 1.28W
Ashford England 11 F2 ....51.09N 0.53E
Ashgabat Turkmenistan 58 G1 ....37.53N 58.21E
Ashington England 15 F4 ....55.11N 1.34W
Ashland U.S.A. 65 H6 ....46.35N 90.53W
Ashmore and Cartier Islands Australia 110 B5 ..12.38S 122.40E
Ashmyany Belarus 46 G5 ....54.25N 25.56E
Ash Shiḩr Yemen 95 G2 ....14.49N 49.45E
Ashton-under-Lyne England 15 E2 ....53.30N 2.06W
Asia 90
Asilah Morocco 48 B1 ....35.28N 6.02W
Asinara, Golfo dell' b. Italy 50 C4 ....40.59N 8.31E
'Asīr f. Saudi Arabia 94 F4 ....20.53N 40.14E
Askern England 15 F2 ....53.37N 1.09W
Askim Norway 40 B2 ....59.35N 11.10E
Asmara Eritrea 85 H3 ....15.20N 38.56E
Åsnen l. Sweden 40 C2 ....56.37N 14.50E
Aspang-Markt Austria 54 G2 ....47.33N 16.05E
Aspatria England 14 D3 ....54.46N 3.20W
Aspen U.S.A. 64 E4 ....39.11N 106.49W
Assab Eritrea 85 I3 ....12.59N 42.43E
Assam d. India 97 H6 ....26.14N 91.22E
As Samāwah Iraq 94 G6 ....31.15N 45.19E
As Sarīr f. Libya 53 H2 ....27.02N 21.36E
Assen Neth. 42 F6 ....53.00N 6.33E
As Sidrah Libya 53 G3 ....30.38N 18.18E
Assiniboine, Mount Canada 62 G3 ....50.57N 115.34W
As Sulaymānīyah Iraq 95 G7 ....35.32N 45.27E
Assumption i. Seychelles 86 D4 ....9.30S 47.20E
As Sūq Saudi Arabia 94 F4 ....21.57N 41.59E
Assynt, Loch l. Scotland 18 D3 ....58.11N 5.05W
Astana Kazakhstan 58 I3 ....51.09N 71.27E
Āstārā Iran 95 G7 ....38.27N 48.52E
Asti Italy 50 C6 ....44.54N 8.13E
Astorga Spain 48 B5 ....42.28N 6.03W
Astoria U.S.A. 64 B6 ....46.08N 123.46W
Astove i. Seychelles 86 D4 ....10.05S 47.40E
Astrakhan' Rus. Fed. 58 F2 ....46.20N 48.03E
Astravyets Belarus 46 G5 ....54.36N 25.56E
Asuncion i. N. Mariana Is 105 L7 ....19.40N 145.25E
Asunción Paraguay 77 I2 ....25.16S 57.39W
Aswān Egypt 85 H4 ....24.02N 32.56E
Asyūṭ Egypt 85 H4 ....27.07N 31.08E
Atacama, Salar de l. Chile 76 G3 ....23.23S 68.18W
Atacama Desert Chile 73 C4 ....26.13S 69.39W
Atafu i. Tokelau 108 I5 ....8.33S 172.30W
Atâr Mauritania 84 C4 ....20.32N 13.03W
Atasu Kazakhstan 58 I2 ....48.42N 71.37E
Atatürk Baraji resr Turkey 57 M3 ....37.28N 38.26E
Atbara Sudan 85 H3 ....17.43N 33.55E
Atbara r. Sudan 85 H3 ....17.40N 33.58E
Ath Belgium 42 C3 ....50.38N 3.47E
Athabasca r. Canada 62 G3 ....58.28N 111.09W
Athabasca, Lake Canada 62 H3 ....59.17N 109.24W
Athboy Ireland 41 E3 ....53.37N 6.55W
Athenry Ireland 41 C3 ....53.18N 8.45W
Athens Greece 56 F3 ....37.59N 23.43E
Atherstone England 10 D3 ....52.35N 1.33W
Athi r. Kenya 87 B2 ....2.57S 38.31E
Athi Plains f. Kenya 87 B2 ....1.30S 36.50E
Athi River town Kenya 87 B2 ....1.27S 36.58E
Athlone Ireland 41 D3 ....53.25N 7.57W
Atholl, Forest of Scotland 19 E1 ....56.51N 4.10W
Athos mt. Greece 56 F5 ....40.10N 24.19E
Athy Ireland 41 E2 ....52.59N 6.59W
Ati Chad 85 F3 ....13.14N 18.20E
Atikokan Canada 65 H6 ....48.45N 91.37W
Atiu i. Cook Is 109 J4 ....19.59S 158.07W
Atlanta U.S.A. 65 J3 ....33.46N 84.22W
Atlantic City U.S.A. 65 L4 ....39.21N 74.26W
Atlantic Ocean 116 G7
Atlas Mountains Africa 84 D5 ....30.13N 7.41W
Atlas Saharien mts Algeria 84 E5 ....32.41N 0.20E
Aṭ Ṭā'if Saudi Arabia 94 F4 ....21.15N 40.20E
Attleborough England 11 G3 ....52.31N 1.01E
Atyrau Kazakhstan 58 G2 ....47.08N 51.56E
Aube r. France 44 E6 ....48.34N 3.43E
Auchterarder Scotland 17 F4 ....56.18N 3.42W
Auchtermuchty Scotland 17 F4 ....56.18N 3.14W
Auckland New Zealand 111 G3 ....36.52S 174.46E
Auckland Islands New Zealand 111 F1 ....50.43S 166.12E
Auderville France 13 Z9 ....49.43N 1.55W
Audlem England 10 C3 ....52.59N 2.31W
Audo mts Ethiopia 87 C4 ....6.46N 41.15E
Audruicq France 11 H1 ....50.52N 2.05E
Aughton England 15 F2 ....53.22N 1.19W
Augsburg Germany 54 D3 ....48.22N 10.52E
Augusta Ga. U.S.A. 65 J3 ....33.28N 82.02W
Augusta Me. U.S.A. 65 M5 ....44.19N 69.46W
Aulnoye-Aymeries France 42 C3 ....50.12N 3.51E
Aurangabad India 96 E4 ....19.53N 75.24E
Aurich Germany 42 G6 ....53.28N 7.30E
Aurora U.S.A. 64 F4 ....39.43N 104.53W
Auskerry i. Scotland 19 G4 ....59.02N 2.33W
Aus Maduli Kenya 87 C3 ....2.16N 40.36E
Austin U.S.A. 64 G3 ....30.16N 97.42W
Australia Oceania 110 B4 ....27.17S 129.18E
Australian Capital Territory d. Australia 110 D3 ..35.27S 148.52E
Austria Europe 54 F2 ....47.12N 13.26E
Authie r. France 11 G1 ....50.22N 1.37E
Auvergne, Monts d' mts France 44 E4 ....45.45N 2.59E
Auxerre France 44 E5 ....47.48N 3.35E
Avallon France 44 E5 ....47.30N 3.54E
Avanos Turkey 57 K4 ....38.43N 34.51E
Avarua Cook Is 109 J4 ....21.13S 159.46W
Aveiro Portugal 48 A4 ....40.39N 8.38W
Avellino Italy 50 F4 ....40.55N 14.48E
Avesta Sweden 40 D3 ....60.09N 16.10E
Aveyron r. France 44 D4 ....44.05N 1.16E
Avezzano Italy 50 E5 ....42.02N 13.25E
Aviemore Scotland 19 F2 ....57.12N 3.49W
Avignon France 44 F3 ....43.57N 4.49E
Ávila Spain 48 C4 ....40.40N 4.41W
Avilés Spain 48 C5 ....43.33N 5.54W
Avon r. Brist. England 10 C2 ....51.29N 2.40W
Avon r. Dor. England 10 D1 ....50.44N 1.46W
Avon r. Glos. England 10 C3 ....52.00N 2.10W
Avon r. Scotland 19 F2 ....57.25N 3.22W
Avonmore r. Ireland 12 A4 ....52.48N 6.08W
Avonmouth England 10 C2 ....51.30N 2.42W
Awara Plain f. Kenya 87 C3 ....3.39N 40.54E
Āwasa Ethiopia 87 B4 ....6.57N 38.28E
Āwash Ethiopia 87 C4 ....8.59N 40.16E
Awbārī Libya 84 F4 ....26.34N 12.46E
Awbārī, Idhān des. Libya 52 F2 ....27.23N 10.25E
Awe, Loch l. Scotland 16 D4 ....56.16N 5.14W
Axe r. England 13 D2 ....50.43N 3.04W
Axel Heiberg Island Canada 63 I5 ....79.47N 91.17W
Axminster England 10 C1 ....50.47N 2.59W

Ayacucho Peru 76 F5 ....13.10S 74.13W
Ayagoz Kazakhstan 58 J2 ....47.56N 80.23E
Ayan Rus. Fed. 59 O3 ....56.26N 138.12E
Aydarko'l ko'li l. Uzbekistan 58 H2 ....41.02N 66.33E
Aydın Turkey 57 G3 ....37.50N 27.49E
Ayers Rock hill Australia 110 C4 ....25.20S 131.05E
Aylesbury England 10 E2 ....51.49N 0.48W
Aylesham England 11 G2 ....51.14N 1.12E
Aylsham England 11 G3 ....52.48N 1.15E
Ayr Scotland 16 E3 ....55.28N 4.38W
Ayr r. Scotland 16 E3 ....55.28N 4.38W
Ayr, Point of Wales 12 D5 ....53.21N 3.18W
Ayre, Point of Isle of Man 14 C3 ....54.25N 4.22W
Ayvalık Turkey 56 G4 ....39.17N 26.41E
Azerbaijan Asia 58 F1 ....40.23N 48.09E
Azogues Ecuador 76 E7 ....2.44S 78.50W
Azov Rus. Fed. 53 L6 ....47.06N 39.25E
Azov, Sea of Rus. Fed./Ukraine 58 E2 ....46.03N 36.47E
Azrou Morocco 52 B3 ....33.26N 5.11W
Azuero, Península de pen. Panama 71 H2 .....7.39N 80.41W
Azul, Cordillera mts Peru 76 E6 ....8.31S 75.56W
Azul Argentina 73 D3 ....36.45S 59.50W
Az Zaqāzīq Egypt 53 J3 ....30.35N 31.30E
Az Zarqā' Jordan 94 E6 ....32.04N 36.05E

B

Baardheere Somalia 85 I2 ....2.19N 42.18E
Bāba, Kūh-e mts Afgh. 95 K6 ....34.48N 68.27E
Babadag Romania 57 H7 ....44.54N 28.42E
Babaeski Turkey 56 G5 ....41.26N 27.06E
Bāb al Mandab str. Africa/Asia 94 F2 ....12.21N 43.26E
Babar i. Indonesia 105 H2 ....7.57S 129.51E
Babati Tanzania 87 A1 ....4.15S 35.44E
Babbacombe Bay England 13 D2 ....50.31N 3.28W
Babia Góra mt. Poland 46 D2 ....49.35N 19.32E
Babo Indonesia 105 I3 ....2.35S 133.21E
Babruysk Belarus 55 M5 ....53.09N 29.14E
Bab-Termas hill Morocco 48 D1 ....34.29N 3.53W
Babuyan Islands Phil. 105 G7 ....19.13N 121.59E
Bacabal Brazil 77 L7 ....4.16S 44.47W
Bacan i. Indonesia 105 H3 ....0.44S 127.35E
Bacău Romania 55 L2 ....46.34N 26.54E
Back r. Canada 63 I4 ....66.32N 95.51W
Backwater Reservoir Scotland 19 F1 ....56.44N 3.13W
Bac Liêu Vietnam 104 D5 ....9.15N 105.45E
Bacolod Phil. 105 G6 ....10.37N 122.57E
Badajoz Spain 48 B3 ....38.53N 6.57W
Baden Austria 50 G8 ....48.00N 16.15E
Baden-Baden Germany 54 C3 ....48.45N 8.15E
Bad Neuenahr-Ahrweiler Germany 42 G3 .....50.33N 7.07E
Badulla Sri Lanka 96 F2 ....7.00N 81.01E
Baffin Bay sea Canada/Greenland 63 L5 .....72.51N 66.20W
Baffin Island Canada 63 L4 ....64.57N 68.47W
Bafoussam Cameroon 84 F2 ....5.26N 10.26E
Bāfq Iran 95 I6 ....31.34N 55.21E
Bafra Turkey 57 K5 ....41.34N 35.55E
Bāft Iran 95 I5 ....29.14N 56.36E
Bagé Brazil 77 J1 ....31.20S 54.06W
Baggy Point England 13 C3 ....51.08N 4.16W
Baghdād Iraq 94 F6 ....33.18N 44.22E
Baghlān Afgh. 95 K7 ....36.11N 68.47E
Bagrationovsk Rus. Fed. 46 E5 ....54.23N 20.38E
Bahariya Oasis Egypt 94 C5 ....27.56N 28.51E
Bahawalpur Pakistan 96 D6 ....29.23N 71.45E
Bahia d. Brazil 77 L5 ....14.28S 40.45W
Bahía, Islas de la is Honduras 71 G4 ....16.13N 86.56W
Bahía Blanca Argentina 73 C3 ....38.43S 62.18W
Bahía Negra Paraguay 77 I3 ....20.11S 58.10W
Bahrain Asia 95 H5 ....26.29N 50.51E
Baia Mare Romania 55 J2 ....47.39N 23.35E
Baicheng China 103 M7 ....45.29N 122.50E
Baie-Comeau Canada 63 L2 ....49.13N 68.10W
Baikal, Lake Rus. Fed. 59 L3 ....52.37N 107.12E
Bailieborough Ireland 41 E3 ....53.55N 6.58W
Bain r. England 15 G2 ....53.05N 0.12W
Bainbridge U.S.A. 65 J3 ....30.54N 84.40W
Bairiki Kiribati 108 H6 ....1.21N 172.57E
Bairnsdale Australia 110 D3 ....37.51S 147.37E
Baiyuda Desert Sudan 94 D3 ....18.03N 32.59E
Baja Hungary 54 H2 ....46.12N 18.57E
Baja California d. Mexico 70 A6 ....29.49N 115.07W
Baja California r. Mexico 70 B6 ....30.40N 115.41W
Baja California Sur d. Mexico 70 B6 ....25.19N 112.09W
Baker, Mount vol. U.S.A. 64 B6 ....48.46N 121.47W
Baker Island N. Pacific Oc. 108 I5 ....0.13N 176.28W
Baker Lake Canada 63 I4 ....64.09N 95.23W
Bakersfield U.S.A. 64 C4 ....35.22N 118.59W
Bakharden Turkmenistan 95 I7 ....38.27N 57.24E
Bakhtegan, Daryācheh-ye l. Iran 95 H5 ......29.18N 53.52E
Bakırköy Turkey 57 H5 ....40.58N 28.51E
Bako Ethiopia 87 B4 ....5.49N 36.37E
Baku Azerbaijan 58 F2 ....40.22N 49.50E
Bala Wales 12 D4 ....52.55N 3.36W
Bala, Cerros de mts Bolivia 76 G5 ....13.49S 68.25W
Balabac Strait Malaysia/Phil. 104 F5 ....7.36N 116.45E
Bala Lake Wales 12 D4 ....52.52N 3.39W
Bālā Morghāb Afgh. 95 J7 ....35.35N 63.21E
Balashikha Rus. Fed. 55 Q6 ....55.49N 37.57E
Balaton, Lake Hungary 54 G2 ....46.46N 17.32E
Balbina, Represa de resr Brazil 77 I7 ....1.34S 59.27W
Balbriggan Ireland 41 E3 ....53.36N 6.11W
Baldock England 11 E2 ....51.59N 0.11W
Baldy Peak U.S.A. 64 E3 ....33.54N 109.34W
Balearic Islands Spain 48 F3 ....39.28N 1.30E
Baleia, Ponta da pt Brazil 77 M4 ....17.41S 39.09W
Baleine, Rivière à la r. Canada 63 L3 ....57.57N 67.37W
Bale Mountains National Park Ethiopia 87 B4 ..7.01N 39.41E
Baleshwar India 96 G5 ....21.30N 86.56E
Balestrieri, Punta mt. Italy 50 C4 ....40.51N 9.10E
Bali i. Indonesia 104 E2 ....8.41S 114.55E
Balige Indonesia 104 B3 ....2.20N 99.03E
Balıkesir Turkey 57 G4 ....39.38N 27.52E
Balikpapan Indonesia 104 F3 ....1.12S 116.49E
Balimo P.N.G. 105 K2 ....7.59S 143.01E
Balintore Scotland 19 F2 ....57.45N 3.54W
Bali Sea Indonesia 104 E2 ....7.31S 114.31E
Balivanich Scotland 18 B2 ....57.28N 7.22W
Balkan Mountains Bulgaria/Serbia 56 E6 .....43.23N 22.47E
Balkhash Kazakhstan 58 I2 ....46.50N 74.59E
Balkhash, Lake Kazakhstan 58 I2 ....45.30N 73.51E
Ballagan Point Ireland 16 C1 ....53.59N 6.06W
Ballantrae Scotland 16 D3 ....55.06N 5.00W
Ballater Scotland 19 F2 ....57.03N 3.02W
Ballena, Punta pt Chile 73 B4 ....25.47S 70.47W
Ballencleuch Law hill Scotland 17 F3 ....55.20N 3.41W
Ballina Ireland 41 B4 ....54.07N 9.10W
Ballinasloe Ireland 41 C3 ....53.20N 8.13W
Ballybay Ireland 16 C2 ....54.07N 6.54W
Ballybunnion Ireland 41 B2 ....52.31N 9.40W
Ballycastle Northern Ireland 16 C3 ....55.12N 6.14W
Ballyclare Northern Ireland 16 D2 ....54.45N 5.59W

Ballyhaunis Ireland 41 C3 ....53.46N 8
Ballymena Northern Ireland 16 C2 ....54.52N 6
Ballymena d. Northern Ireland 8 B4 ....54.53N 6
Ballymoney Northern Ireland 16 C3 ....55.04N 6
Ballymoney d. Northern Ireland 8 B4 ....54.58N 6
Ballynahinch Northern Ireland 16 D2 ....54.24N 5
Ballyquintin Point Northern Ireland 16 D2 ...54.19N 5
Ballyshannon Ireland 41 C4 ....54.30N 8
Balochistan f. Pakistan 96 B6 ....27.30N 6
Balsas Brazil 77 K6 ....7.31S 46
Balsas r. Mexico 70 D4 ....17.57N 10
Balta Ukraine 55 M2 ....47.56N 2
Baltasound Scotland 19 I5 ....60.46N 0
Bălți Moldova 55 L2 ....47.47N 2
Baltic Sea g. Europe 40 D1 ....55.28N 1
Baltimore U.S.A. 65 K4 ....39.17N 76
Baltiysk Rus. Fed. 46 D5 ....54.39N 1
Bam Iran 95 I5 ....29.07N 5
Bamaga Australia 110 D5 ....10.53S 14
Bamako Mali 84 D3 ....12.38N 7
Bamberg Germany 54 D3 ....49.54N 10
Bambili Dem. Rep. Congo 86 B5 ....3.38N 2
Bambouti C.A.R. 85 G2 ....5.22N 2
Bāmiān Afgh. 95 K6 ....34.52N 6
Bampton Dev. England 13 D2 ....50.59N 3
Bampton Oxon. England 10 D2 ....51.43N 1
Banaba i. Kiribati 108 H5 ....0.49S 16
Bañados del Izozog f. Bolivia 77 H4 ....18.20S 61
Banagher Ireland 41 D3 ....53.11N 7
Bananal, Ilha do i. Brazil 77 J5 ....11.26S 50
Banaz Turkey 57 H4 ....38.44N 2
Banbridge Northern Ireland 16 C2 ....54.21N 6
Banbridge d. Northern Ireland 9 B4 ....54.20N 6
Banbury England 10 D3 ....52.04N 1
Banchory Scotland 19 G2 ....57.03N 2
Banda, Kepulauan is Indonesia 105 H3 ......4.33S 12
Banda Aceh Indonesia 104 B5 ....5.30N 9
Bandar-e 'Abbās Iran 95 I5 ....27.11N 5
Bandar-e Anzalī Iran 95 G7 ....37.26N 4
Bandar-e Lengeh Iran 95 H5 ....26.34N 5
Bandar-e Torkeman Iran 95 H7 ....36.54N 5
Bandar Lampung Indonesia 104 D2 ....5.27S 10
Bandar Seri Begawan Brunei 104 E4 ....4.57N 11
Banda Sea Indonesia 105 I2 ....5.40S 13
Bandeiras, Pico de mt. Brazil 77 L3 ....20.26S 41
Bandırma Turkey 57 G5 ....40.21N 2
Bandon Ireland 41 C1 ....51.45N 8
Bandon r. Ireland 41 C1 ....51.45N 8
Bandundu Dem. Rep. Congo 86 A4 ....3.17S 1
Bandung Indonesia 104 D2 ....6.56S 10
Banff Canada 62 G3 ....51.11N 11
Banff Scotland 19 G2 ....57.40N 2
Bangalore India 96 E3 ....12.57N 7
Bangassou C.A.R. 85 G2 ....4.44N 2
Banggai, Kepulauan is Indonesia 105 G3 ....1.59S 12
Bangka i. Indonesia 104 D3 ....2.07S 10
Bangkok Thailand 104 C6 ....13.44N 10
Bangladesh Asia 97 H5 ....23.47N 8
Bangor Northern Ireland 16 D2 ....54.39N 5
Bangor U.S.A. 65 M5 ....44.48N 68.
Bangor Wales 12 C5 ....53.14N 4.
Bangui C.A.R. 85 F2 ....4.20N 18
Bangweulu, Lake Zambia 86 B3 ....11.13S 29
Bani r. Mali 84 D3 ....14.30N 4.
Banī Mazār Egypt 53 J2 ....28.29N 30
Banī Suwayf Egypt 53 J2 ....29.05N 31
Banī Walīd Libya 52 F3 ....31.47N 14
Bāniyās Syria 57 K2 ....35.11N 35
Banja Luka Bos.-Herz. 56 B7 ....44.46N 17
Banjarmasin Indonesia 104 E3 ....3.23S 114
Banjul Gambia 84 C3 ....13.27N 16.
Banks Island Canada 62 F5 ....73.06N 121
Banks Islands Vanuatu 111 F5 ....13.55S 167
Banmi Pakistan 96 L6 ....33.00N 70
Bann r. Northern Ireland 16 C3 ....55.09N 6.
Bann r. Ireland 12 A4 ....52.33N 6.
Bantry Ireland 41 B1 ....51.41N 9.
Bantry Bay Ireland 41 B1 ....51.41N 9.
Baoding China 103 L5 ....38.46N 115
Baoji China 103 J4 ....34.21N 107
Baoshan China 103 H3 ....25.07N 99
Baotou China 103 K6 ....40.31N 110
Baoshan Shan mt. China/N. Korea 106 A4 ...41.57N 128
Ba'qūbah Iraq 94 F6 ....33.42N 44
Baquerizo Moreno Ecuador 76 C7 ....0.54S 89.
Bar Montenegro 56 C6 ....42.05N 19
Bara Sudan 94 D2 ....13.40N 30
Baracoa Cuba 71 J5 ....20.21N 74.
Baranavichy Belarus 55 L5 ....53.08N 26.
Baranıs Egypt 53 K1 ....23.55 35.
Barbacena Brazil 77 L3 ....21.13S 43.
Barbados Central America 71 M3 ....13.09N 59.
Barbuda i. Antigua 71 L4 ....17.39N 61.
Barcaldine Australia 110 D4 ....23.32S 145
Barcelona Spain 48 G4 ....41.25N 2.
Barcelona Venezuela 72 C8 ....10.06N 64.
Barcelos Brazil 76 H7 ....0.58S 62.
Bárðarbunga mt. Iceland 40 Y2 ....64.38N 17.
Bardejov Slovakia 46 E2 ....49.18N 21.
Bardney England 15 G2 ....53.13N 0.
Bardsey Island Wales 12 C4 ....52.45N 4.
Bardsey Sound str. Wales 12 C4 ....52.47N 4.
Bareilly India 96 E6 ....28.22N 79.
Barentsburg Svalbard 58 C5 ....77.49N 14.
Barents Sea Arctic Oc. 58 F5 ....75.18N 42.
Barham England 11 G2 ....51.12N 1.
Barinas Venezuela 72 B7 ....8.34N 70.
Baringo, Lake Kenya 87 B3 ....0.33N 36.
Barisan, Pegunungan mts Indonesia 104 C3 ..1.12S 100.
Barkly Tableland f. Australia 110 C5 ....18.06S 135.
Bârlad Romania 56 G8 ....46.13N 27.
Barmer India 96 D6 ....25.44N 71.
Barmouth Wales 12 C4 ....52.43N 4.
Barmouth Bay Wales 12 C4 ....52.43N 4.
Barnard Castle England 15 F3 ....54.33N 1.
Barnaul Rus. Fed. 58 J3 ....53.22N 83.
Barnet England 11 E2 ....51.38N 0.
Barnoldswick England 15 E2 ....53.55N 2.
Barnsley England 15 F2 ....53.33N 1.
Barnstaple England 13 C3 ....51.05N 4.
Barnstaple or Bideford Bay England 13 C3 ...51.05N 4.
Barquisimeto Venezuela 72 C8 ....10.03N 69.
Barra i. Scotland 18 B1 ....56.59N 7.
Barra do Corda Brazil 77 K6 ....5.29S 45.
Barra do Garças Brazil 77 J4 ....15.52S 52.
Barranquilla Colombia 72 B8 ....10.59N 74.
Barreiras Brazil 77 L5 ....12.07S 44.
Barretos Brazil 77 K3 ....20.35S 48.
Barrhead Scotland 16 E3 ....55.48N 4.
Barrow r. Ireland 41 E2 ....52.23N 6.

w U.S.A. 62 C5 ....71.18N 156.43W
w, Point U.S.A. 62 C5 ....71.23N 156.22W
w-in-Furness England 14 D3 ....54.07N 3.13W
w Island Australia 110 A4 ....20.49S 115.22E
Wales 17 J5 ....51.24N 3.17W
ow U.S.A. 64 C3 ....34.54N 117.01W
Turkey 57 J5 ....41.38N 32.21E
n-upon-Humber England 15 G2 ......53.41N 0.27W
szyce Poland 46 E5 ....54.15N 20.49E
n-Urt Mongolia 103 K7 ......46.31N 113.22E
aw Belarus 55 M6 ....54.14N 28.31E
urch England 10 C3 ....52.47N 2.51W
Switz. 50 B7 ....47.33N 7.35E
an i. Phil. 105 H5 ....6.32N 121.52E
don England 11 F2 ....51.35N 0.29E
agstoke England 10 D2 ....51.16N 1.06W
Iraq 95 G6 ....30.29N 47.48E
ein Myanmar 97 H4 ....16.45N 94.44E
enthwaite Lake England 14 D3 .....54.40N 3.14W
e-Terre Guadeloupe 71 L4 ....16.01N 61.44W
Rock i. Scotland 17 G4 ......56.05N 2.38W
Strait Australia 110 D3 ......39.43S 146.11E
k Iran 95 H5 ....27.12N 54.21E
France 44 H3 ....42.42N 9.27E
gne Belgium 42 E3 ....50.00N 5.43E
Equat. Guinea 84 E2 ....1.50N 9.48E
anó, Golfo de b. Cuba 71 H5 .....22.16N 82.38W
g China 103 H4 ....30.01N 99.08E
g Indonesia 97 I6 ....6.57S 109.43E
ngas Phil. 105 G6 ....13.46N 121.01E
ambâng Cambodia 104 C6 .....13.06N 103.14E
England 10 C2 ....51.23N 2.22W
and North East Somerset d. England 9 D2
.................51.21N 2.28W
gate Scotland 17 F3 ....55.54N 3.39W
urst Australia 110 D3 ....33.25S 149.38E
urst Canada 63 L2 ....47.36N 65.39W
urst Inlet Canada 62 H4 .....66.50N 108.10W
urst Island Australia 110 C5 .....11.29S 130.11E
urst Island Canada 63 I5 .....75.49N 98.59W
y England 15 F2 ....53.43N 1.38W
Algeria 84 E5 ....35.32N 6.13E
Rouge U.S.A. 65 H3 ....30.27N 91.11W
caloa Sri Lanka 96 F2 ....7.42N 81.39E
Ireland 11 F1 ....50.55N 0.29E
mt. Ethiopia 87 B4 ....6.51N 39.50E
Pulau-pulau is Indonesia 104 B3 .....0.14S 98.16E
mi Georgia 58 F2 ....41.39N 41.38E
au Indonesia 105 G2 ....5.29S 122.37E
hi Nigeria 84 E3 ....10.19N 9.50E
u Brazil 77 K3 ....22.20S 49.05W
ka Latvia 55 K7 ....56.25N 24.13E
zen Germany 54 E4 ....51.11N 14.26E
ean i. Indonesia 104 E2 .....5.48S 112.34E
mo Cuba 71 I5 ....20.22N 76.38W
nhongor Mongolia 103 I7 .....46.09N 100.41E
urt Turkey 57 N5 ....40.15N 40.14E
City Mich. U.S.A. 65 J5 .....43.35N 83.53W
City Tex. U.S.A. 64 G5 ......28.59N 96.07W
aratskaya Guba Rus. Fed. 58 H4 .....69.29N 66.01E
nne France 44 C5 ....43.29N 1.29W
euth Germany 54 D3 ....49.56N 11.36E
al Kabīr, Wādī watercourse Libya 52 G3 .....31.11N 15.53E
Spain 48 D2 ....37.30N 2.46W
hy Head England 11 F1 ......50.44N 0.15E
onsfield England 10 E2 ......51.36N 0.39W
gle Gulf Australia 105 H1 .....12.04S 129.55E
minster England 10 C1 ......50.46N 2.45W
dmore Canada 65 I6 ....49.36N 87.58W
a, Cabo c. Dom. Rep. 71 J4 .....17.38N 71.23W
a, Isla i. Dom. Rep. 71 J4 .....17.36N 71.30W
ufort Sea Canada/U.S.A. 62 F5 .....73.19N 129.52W
ufort West S. Africa 86 B1 ......32.20S 22.36E
uly Scotland 19 E2 ....57.29N 4.28W
uly i. Scotland 19 E2 ......57.29N 4.27W
uly Firth est. Scotland 19 E2 .....57.29N 4.23W
umaris Wales 12 C5 ....53.16N 4.05W
umont i. Dom. 73 Z9 ....49.40N 1.50W
umont U.S.A. 65 H3 ....30.05N 94.09W
une France 44 F5 ....47.01N 4.50E
uvais France 44 E6 ....49.26N 2.05E
ver Creek town Canada 62 D4 .....62.23N 140.49W
ington England 14 D2 ......53.21N 3.00W
les England 13 D3 ....52.28N 1.34E
erreá Spain 48 B5 ....42.51N 7.09W
nar Algeria 84 D5 ....31.36N 2.13W
kingham England 15 G2 .....53.24N 0.49W
cley U.S.A. 65 J4 ....37.47N 81.11W
ale England 15 F3 ....54.17N 1.35W
ford England 14 D2 ....52.03N 0.24W
ington England 15 F4 ......55.08N 1.36W
worth England 10 D3 ....52.29N 1.28W
rsheba Israel 53 J3 ....31.15N 34.48E
ville U.S.A. 64 G2 ....28.25N 97.45W
Lough l. Northern Ireland 16 C2 .....54.47N 6.27W
an China 103 N7 ....48.11N 126.31E
ai China 103 J2 ....21.27N 109.08E
China 103 L5 ....39.52N 116.27E
an an Oir hill Scotland 16 D3 ......55.54N 5.59W
an Dearg mt. High. Scotland 18 E2 .....57.47N 4.56W
an Dearg mt. P. and K. Scotland 19 F1 .....56.53N 3.53W
an Heasgarnich mt. Scotland 16 E4 .....56.31N 4.35W
am Mozambique 86 C3 ......19.50S 34.52E
ut Lebanon 53 K3 ....33.52N 35.30E
h Scotland 16 E3 ....55.45N 4.38W
s Romania 55 J2 ....46.40N 22.23E
d Portugal 48 B3 ....38.01N 7.52W
ria Algeria 84 E5 ....36.44N 5.03E
r Spain 48 C4 ....40.24N 5.46W
és Hungary 46 E1 ....46.46N 21.07E
éscsaba Hungary 54 I2 .....46.41N 21.05E
Pakistan 96 C5 ....26.12N 66.21E
rus Europe 55 L5 ....54.01N 28.39E
aya r. Rus. Fed. 59 S4 .....65.32N 173.15E
hatów Poland 46 D3 ....51.22N 19.22E
ther Islands Canada 63 K3 .....56.10N 78.47W
dwyne Somalia 85 I2 ......4.44N 45.13E
m Brazil 77 K7 ....1.26S 48.29W
v Rus. Fed. 55 Q5 ....53.48N 36.10E
ast Northern Ireland 16 D2 .....54.36N 5.55W
ast d. Northern Ireland 9 C4 .....54.36N 5.55W
ast Lough inlet Northern Ireland 16 D2 .....54.40N 5.52W
ford England 15 F4 ....55.36N 1.50W
gium Europe 42 D3 ....50.55N 4.14E
gorod Rus. Fed. 58 E3 .....50.35N 36.37E
grade Serbia 56 D7 ....44.48N 20.29E
tung i. Indonesia 104 D3 .....2.47S 108.14E
ze town Belize 70 G4 ......17.31N 88.14W
e Central America 70 G4 .....17.10N 88.18W
e France 44 D5 ....46.08N 1.03E

Bellary India 96 E4 ....15.10N 76.53E
Belle-Île i. France 44 B5 ......47.19N 3.15W
Belle Isle, Strait of Canada 63 M3 .....51.16N 56.57W
Bellingham England 15 E4 ......55.09N 2.15W
Bellingham U.S.A. 64 B6 ....48.45N 122.28E
Bellinzona Switz. 50 C7 ....46.12N 9.01E
Belluno Italy 50 E7 ....46.08N 12.13E
Belmopan Belize 70 G4 ....17.14N 88.46W
Belmullet Ireland 41 B4 ......54.14N 9.57W
Belo Horizonte Brazil 77 L4 .....19.55S 43.56W
Belper England 15 F2 ....53.02N 1.29W
Belukha, Gora mt. Kazakhstan/Rus. Fed. 58 J2 .....49.50N 86.41E
Belyy Rus. Fed. 55 O6 ....55.50N 32.57E
Bembridge England 10 D1 ......50.41N 1.05W
Ben Alder mt. Scotland 19 E1 .....56.49N 4.28W
Benavente Spain 48 C4 ....42.00N 5.40W
Benbane Head Northern Ireland 16 C3 .....55.15N 6.30W
Benbecula i. Scotland 18 B2 .....57.27N 7.23W
Ben Cleuch hill Scotland 17 F4 .....56.11N 3.46W
Ben Cruachan mt. Scotland 16 D4 .....56.25N 5.08W
Bend U.S.A. 64 B5 ....44.04N 121.17W
Bendigo Australia 110 D3 .....36.46S 144.18E
Benešov Czech Rep. 54 F3 .....49.47N 14.42E
Bengal, Bay of sea Indian Oc. 96 G4 .....17.51N 88.40E
Bengbu China 103 L4 ....32.54N 117.23E
Benghazi Libya 85 G5 ....32.06N 20.04E
Bengkulu Indonesia 104 C3 .....3.45S 102.18E
Benguela Angola 86 A3 ....12.36S 13.21E
Ben Hope hill Scotland 19 E3 .....58.25N 4.36W
Beni r. Bolivia 76 G5 ....11.01S 66.07W
Benidorm Spain 48 E3 ....38.32N 0.08W
Beni Mellal Morocco 84 D5 .....32.17N 6.25W
Benin Africa 84 E3 ....8.26N 2.11E
Benin, Bight of g. Africa 84 E2 .....5.17N 3.27E
Beni-Saf Algeria 52 C4 ....35.20N 1.21W
Benjamim Constant Brazil 76 G7 .....4.23S 69.58W
Ben Klibreck hill Scotland 19 E3 .....58.15N 4.24W
Ben Lawers mt. Scotland 16 E4 .....56.33N 4.13W
Ben Lomond hill Scotland 16 E4 .....56.11N 4.38W
Ben Loyal hill Scotland 19 E3 .....58.24N 4.27W
Ben Lui mt. Scotland 16 E4 .....56.24N 4.49W
Ben Macdui mt. Scotland 19 F2 .....57.05N 3.40W
Ben More mt. Scotland 16 C4 .....56.25N 6.00W
Ben More mt. Scotland 16 E4 .....56.23N 4.32W
Ben More Assynt hill Scotland 18 E3 .....58.08N 4.51W
Ben Nevis mt. Scotland 18 D1 .....56.48N 5.00W
Bentley England 15 F2 ....53.33N 1.09W
Benue r. Nigeria 84 E2 ....7.49N 6.48E
Ben Vorlich hill Scotland 16 E4 .....56.21N 4.13W
Ben Wyvis mt. Scotland 19 E2 .....57.41N 4.35W
Benxi China 103 M6 ....41.16N 123.45E
Beoraid, Loch l. Scotland 18 D1 .....56.54N 5.36W
Berat Albania 56 C5 ....40.42N 19.58E
Berau, Teluk b. Indonesia 105 I3 .....2.28S 132.36E
Berber Sudan 94 D3 ....18.00N 34.02E
Berbera Somalia 85 I3 ....10.24N 45.02E
Berbérati C.A.R. 84 F2 ....4.14N 15.47E
Berck France 44 D6 ....50.25N 1.35E
Berdyans'k Ukraine 53 K6 .....46.46N 36.48E
Berdychiv Ukraine 55 M3 .....49.53N 28.36E
Berehove Ukraine 46 F2 ......48.13N 22.38E
Berens River town Canada 62 I3 .....52.21N 97.01W
Berezhany Ukraine 46 G2 .....49.27N 24.56E
Berezivka Ukraine 55 N2 ......47.12N 30.55E
Berezniki Rus. Fed. 58 G3 .....59.25N 56.48E
Bergama Turkey 56 G4 ....39.07N 27.11E
Bergamo Italy 50 D6 ....45.42N 9.41E
Bergen Norway 40 A3 ....60.23N 5.22E
Bergerac France 44 D4 ....44.51N 0.29E
Bergisch Gladbach Germany 54 B4 .....50.58N 7.08E
Bering Sea N. Pacific Oc. 60 A7 .....60.00N 170.00E
Bering Strait Rus. Fed./U.S.A. 59 U4 .....66.18N 168.40W
Berkel r. Neth. 42 F5 ....52.08N 6.11E
Berkeley England 10 C2 ......51.41N 2.27W
Berkshire Downs hills England 10 D2 .....51.30N 1.20W
Berlin Germany 54 E5 ....52.31N 13.23E
Bermuda i. N. Atlantic Oc. 71 L7 .....32.24N 64.56W
Bern Switz. 50 B7 ....46.57N 7.27E
Berneray i. W. Isles Scotland 18 B1 .....56.47N 7.38W
Berneray i. W. Isles Scotland 18 B2 .....57.44N 7.18W
Beroun Czech Rep. 46 B2 .....49.58N 14.04E
Berounka r. Czech Rep. 46 B2 .....49.59N 14.22E
Berry Head England 13 D2 .....50.24N 3.29W
Bertoua Cameroon 84 F2 ......4.35N 13.41E
Beru atoll Kiribati 108 H5 .....1.17S 176.00E
Berwick-upon-Tweed England 15 E4 .....55.46N 2.00W
Besançon France 44 G5 ....47.15N 6.01E
Bessbrook Northern Ireland 16 C2 .....54.12N 6.23W
Betanzos Spain 48 A5 ....43.17N 8.12W
Beth, Oued r. Morocco 48 B1 .....34.25N 6.26W
Bethesda Wales 12 C5 ....53.11N 4.03W
Béthune France 42 B3 ....50.31N 2.38E
Betsiboka r. Madagascar 86 D3 .....15.58S 46.27E
Bettystown Ireland 12 A5 .....53.42N 6.15W
Betws-y-coed Wales 12 D5 .....53.05N 3.48W
Beult r. England 11 F2 ....51.13N 0.25E
Beverley England 15 G2 ......53.51N 0.26W
Bewdley England 10 C3 ....52.23N 2.19W
Bewl Water resr England 11 F2 .....51.04N 0.23E
Bexhill England 11 F1 ....50.50N 0.29E
Beykoz Turkey 57 H5 ....41.07N 29.05E
Beyla Guinea 84 D2 ....8.41N 8.41W
Beyneu Kazakhstan 58 G2 .....45.18N 55.11E
Beypazarı Turkey 57 I5 ......40.10N 31.56E
Beyşehir Turkey 57 I3 ....37.42N 31.43E
Beyşehir Gölü l. Turkey 57 I3 .....37.42N 31.33E
Béziers France 44 E3 ....43.21N 3.13E
Bhagalpur India 96 G6 ....25.15N 86.56E
Bhamo Myanmar 97 I5 ....24.18N 97.17E
Bhavnagar India 96 E5 ....21.46N 72.14E
Bhima r. India 96 E4 ....16.26N 77.13E
Bhopal India 96 E5 ....23.15N 77.23E
Bhubaneshwar India 96 G5 .....20.13N 85.53E
Bhuj India 96 D5 ....23.11N 69.44E
Bhutan Asia 97 H6 ....27.38N 90.33E
Biak Indonesia 105 J3 ....1.12S 136.05E
Biak i. Indonesia 105 J3 .....0.59S 135.59E
Biała Podlaska Poland 46 E4 .....52.02N 23.07E
Białogard Poland 46 B4 ......53.59N 15.59E
Białystok Poland 46 F4 ......53.08N 23.10E
Biarritz France 44 C3 ....43.18N 1.33W
Biberach an der Riß Germany 54 C2 .....48.06N 9.47E
Bicester England 10 D2 ......51.54N 1.09W
Bidar India 96 E4 ....17.54N 77.34E
Biddulph England 15 E2 ......53.07N 2.10W
Bidean nam Bian mt. Scotland 18 D1 .....56.39N 5.02W
Bideford England 13 C3 ......51.01N 4.12W
Biel Switz. 50 B7 ....47.09N 7.15E
Bielefeld Germany 54 C5 .....52.01N 8.32E
Biella Italy 50 C6 ....45.34N 8.04E
Bielsko-Biała Poland 46 D2 .....49.49N 19.03E

Bié Plateau f. Angola 82 E3 .....13.00S 16.00E
Bifoun Gabon 84 F1 ....0.15S 10.25E
Biga Turkey 56 G5 ....40.13N 27.13E
Bigbury Bay England 13 D2 .....50.15N 3.54W
Biggar Scotland 17 F3 ....55.37N 3.31W
Biggleswade England 11 E3 .....52.05N 0.16W
Bighorn r. U.S.A. 64 E6 ......46.10N 107.30W
Bighorn Mountains U.S.A. 64 E5 .....44.06N 106.55W
Big Spring U.S.A. 64 F3 ......32.16N 101.24W
Big Trout Lake town Canada 63 J3 .....53.49N 89.50W
Bihać Bos.-Herz. 56 A7 ....44.49N 15.53E
Bihar d. India 96 G6 ....24.13N 85.37E
Bihor, Vârful mt. Romania 55 J2 .....46.27N 22.44E
Bijapur India 96 E4 ....16.49N 75.48E
Bijar Iran 95 G7 ....35.51N 47.37E
Bijeljina Bos.-Herz. 56 C7 .....44.46N 19.14E
Bijelo Polje Montenegro 56 C6 .....43.02N 19.45E
Bikaner India 96 D6 ....28.00N 73.23E
Bilaspur India 102 E2 ....22.05N 82.09E
Bilaspur India 96 E7 ....31.17N 76.49E
Bila Tserkva Ukraine 55 N3 .....49.48N 30.07E
Bilecik Turkey 57 H5 ....40.09N 29.57E
Biłgoraj Poland 46 F3 ....50.33N 22.43E
Bilhorod-Dnistrovs'kyy Ukraine 53 J6 .....46.11N 30.20E
Billericay England 11 F2 .....51.38N 0.25E
Billingham England 15 F3 .....54.37N 1.17W
Billinghay England 15 G2 .....53.05N 0.17W
Billings U.S.A. 64 E6 ....45.48N 108.27W
Billingshurst England 11 E2 .....51.01N 0.27W
Bill of Portland hd England 10 C1 .....50.30N 2.30W
Bilopillya Ukraine 55 P4 .....51.09N 34.20E
Biloxi U.S.A. 65 I3 ....30.24N 88.57W
Bilston Scotland 17 F3 ....55.52N 3.11W
Bilton England 15 G2 ....53.47N 0.15W
Bimini Islands Bahamas 71 I6 .....25.46N 79.14W
Bindura Zimbabwe 86 C3 ......17.18S 31.19E
Bingham England 10 E3 ....52.57N 0.57W
Binghamton U.S.A. 65 K5 .....42.06N 75.55W
Bingley England 15 F2 ....53.51N 1.50W
Bintulu Malaysia 104 E4 .....3.12N 113.03E
Bioco i. Equat. Guinea 84 E2 .....3.16N 8.31E
Birāk Libya 52 F2 ....27.33N 14.16E
Birao C.A.R. 94 C3 ....10.15N 22.48E
Birecik Turkey 57 L3 ....37.01N 37.59E
Birhan mt. Ethiopia 85 H3 .....10.43N 37.57F
Birjand Iran 95 I6 ....32.53N 59.08E
Birkenhead England 14 D2 .....53.23N 3.01W
Birmingham England 10 D3 .....52.29N 1.53W
Birmingham U.S.A. 65 I3 ......33.32N 86.47W
Bîr Mogreïn Mauritania 84 C4 .....25.14N 11.34W
Birnin Konni Niger 84 E3 .....13.48N 5.14E
Birobidzhan Rus. Fed. 103 O7 .....48.45N 132.52E
Birr Ireland 41 D3 ....53.06N 7.55W
Birsay Scotland 19 F4 ....59.08N 3.18W
Birstall England 10 D3 ....52.41N 1.07W
Biržai Lithuania 46 G6 ....56.12N 24.45E
Biscay, Bay of sea France/Spain 48 C6 .....45.40N 5.07W
Bischofshofen Austria 54 E2 .....47.25N 13.13E
Bishkek Kyrgyzstan 102 C6 .....42.54N 74.32E
Bisho S. Africa 86 B1 ....32.51S 27.24E
Bishop Auckland England 15 F3 .....54.40N 1.41W
Bishop's Lydeard England 13 D3 .....51.04N 3.11W
Bishop's Stortford England 11 F2 .....51.52N 0.10E
Bishop's Waltham England 10 D1 .....50.57N 1.13W
Bisina, Lake Uganda 87 A3 .....1.38N 33.57E
Biskra Algeria 84 E5 ....34.51N 5.44E
Bismarck U.S.A. 64 F6 ....46.50N 100.46W
Bismarck Sea P.N.G. 110 D6 .....4.05S 149.01E
Bissau Guinea-Bissau 84 C3 .....11.53N 15.38W
Bistra r. Serbia 56 D6 ....42.09N 20.59E
Bistrița Romania 55 K2 ....47.09N 24.30E
Bistrița r. Romania 55 L2 .....46.30N 26.58E
Bitburg Germany 42 F2 ....49.58N 6.32E
Bitola Macedonia 56 D5 ......41.01N 21.20E
Bitterroot Range mts U.S.A. 64 D6 .....47.16N 115.41W
Biwa-ko l. Japan 106 C3 .....35.09N 135.59E
Biysk Rus. Fed. 58 J3 ....52.31N 85.17E
Bizerte Tunisia 52 E4 ....37.16N 9.52E
Bjørnøya i. Arctic Oc. 58 C5 .....74.24N 19.07E
Blackburn England 15 E2 .....53.45N 2.29W
Blackburn with Darwen d. England 9 D3 .....53.41N 2.27W
Black Combe hill England 14 D3 .....54.15N 3.20W
Blackfield England 10 D1 .....50.49N 1.22W
Black Forest mts Germany 54 C2 .....47.56N 8.08E
Black Head England 13 B2 .....50.00N 5.07W
Black Hill England 13 B2 .....53.32N 1.53W
Black Isle pen. Scotland 19 E2 .....57.35N 4.19W
Black Mountains hills Wales 12 D3 .....51.58N 3.08W
Blackpool England 14 D2 .....53.49N 3.03W
Blackpool d. England 9 D3 .....53.50N 3.01W
Black Sea Asia/Europe 57 M6 .....42.31N 38.22E
Blacksod Bay Ireland 41 A4 .....54.03N 10.03W
Black Volta r. Africa 84 D2 .....8.29N 0.51W
Blackwater r. England 11 F2 .....51.44N 0.41E
Blackwater r. Northern Ireland 16 C2 .....54.31N 6.34W
Blackwater r. Meath Ireland 41 E3 .....53.39N 6.41W
Blackwater r. Water. Ireland 41 D2 .....52.08N 7.51W
Blackwood Wales 12 D3 ....51.40N 3.12W
Blaenau Ffestiniog Wales 12 D4 .....52.59N 3.57W
Blaenau Gwent d. Wales 9 D2 .....51.46N 3.12W
Blaenavon Wales 12 D3 ....51.47N 3.06W
Blagdon England 10 C2 ....51.20N 2.43W
Blagoevgrad Bulgaria 56 D6 .....42.01N 23.06E
Blagoveshchensk Rus. Fed. 59 N3 .....50.17N 127.29E
Blair Atholl Scotland 19 F1 .....56.46N 3.51W
Blairgowrie Scotland 17 F4 .....56.35N 3.21W
Blanc, Mont mt. France/Italy 44 G4 .....45.50N 6.51E
Blanca, Bahía b. Argentina 73 C3 .....39.08S 61.47W
Blanche, Lake Australia 110 C3 .....29.15S 139.42E
Blanc Nez, Cap France 11 G1 .....50.56N 1.44E
Blanco, Cape U.S.A. 64 B5 .....42.51N 124.34W
Blandford Forum England 10 C1 .....50.51N 2.10W
Blanquilla, Isla i. Venezuela 71 L3 .....11.51N 64.35W
Blansko Czech Rep. 46 C2 .....49.21N 16.39E
Blantyre Malawi 86 C3 ....15.47S 35.02E
Bletchley England 10 E2 .....51.59N 0.45W
Blida Algeria 84 E5 ....36.33N 2.55E
Bloemfontein S. Africa 86 B2 .....29.07S 26.13E
Blois France 44 D5 ....47.35N 1.20E
Bloody Foreland pt Ireland 41 C5 .....55.10N 8.18W
Bloomington U.S.A. 65 I5 .....40.28N 89.00W
Blue Mountains U.S.A. 64 C6 .....45.27N 118.38W
Blue Nile r. Sudan 85 H3 .....15.38N 32.30E
Blue Stack hill Ireland 16 A2 .....54.45N 8.05W
Blue Stack Mountains hills Ireland 41 C4
.................54.42N 8.14W
Blumenau Brazil 77 K2 ....26.52S 49.04W
Blyth Northum. England 15 F4 .....55.08N 1.30W
Blyth Notts. England 15 F2 .....53.22N 1.04W
Blytheville U.S.A. 65 I4 .....35.56N 89.52W
Bo Sierra Leone 84 C2 ....7.55N 11.45W
Boa Esperança, Açude resr Brazil 77 L6 .....6.58S 43.47W

Boa Vista Brazil 77 H8 ....2.51N 60.43W
Boa Vista i. Cape Verde 84 B3 .....16.05N 22.40W
Bobaomby, Tanjona c. Madagascar 86 D3 .....11.57S 49.15E
Bobo-Dioulasso Burkina 84 D3 .....11.11N 4.18W
Bóbr r. Poland 46 B4 ....52.03N 15.04E
Boby mt. Madagascar 86 D2 .....22.13S 46.54E
Bochnia Poland 46 E2 ....49.58N 20.26E
Bocholt Germany 54 B4 ....51.50N 6.36E
Boddam Scotland 19 H2 ....57.28N 1.47W
Bodélé f. Chad 85 F3 ....16.12N 16.17E
Boden Sweden 40 E4 ....65.49N 21.41E
Bodenham England 10 C3 ......52.09N 2.41W
Bodmin England 13 C2 ....50.28N 4.43W
Bodmin Moor f. England 13 C2 .....50.34N 4.36W
Bodø Norway 40 C4 ....67.17N 14.23E
Bodrum Turkey 56 G3 ....37.02N 27.25E
Boğazlıyan Turkey 57 K4 .....39.11N 35.15E
Boggeragh Mountains hills Ireland 41 B2 .....52.01N 9.01E
Bogie r. Scotland 19 G2 ......57.27N 2.46W
Bognor Regis England 10 E1 .....50.47N 0.40W
Bogor Indonesia 104 D2 ....6.35S 106.49E
Bogotá Colombia 72 B7 ....4.35N 74.04W
Bo Hai g. China 103 L5 ......38.32N 119.14E
Bohain-en-Vermandois France 42 C2 .....49.59N 3.28E
Bohemian Forest mts Germany 54 E3 .....49.42N 12.27E
Bohol i. Phil. 105 G5 ....9.55N 124.16E
Bohu China 102 F6 ....41.57N 86.32E
Boise U.S.A. 64 C5 ....43.38N 116.11W
Bojnūrd Iran 95 I7 ....37.27N 57.19E
Bolhrad Ukraine 53 I6 ....45.41N 28.37E
Bolívar, Pico mt. Venezuela 71 J2 .....8.33N 70.59W
Bolivia S. America 76 H4 .....16.23S 64.00W
Bollnäs Sweden 40 D3 ....61.21N 16.24E
Bolmen l. Sweden 40 C2 ......56.52N 13.43E
Bologna Italy 50 D6 ....44.29N 11.22E
Bolsena, Lago di l. Italy 50 D5 .....42.36N 11.56E
Bol'shakovo Rus. Fed. 46 E5 .....54.53N 21.39E
Bol'shoy Aluy r. Rus. Fed. 59 Q4 .....68.29N 159.26E
Bol'shoy Lyakhovskiy, Ostrov i. Rus. Fed. 59 P5
.................73.26N 142.14E
Bolsover England 15 F2 ......53.14N 1.17W
Bolt Head England 13 D2 .....50.12N 3.47W
Bolton England 15 E2 ....53.35N 2.26W
Bolu Turkey 57 I5 ....40.44N 31.36E
Bolus Head England 41 A1 .....51.47N 10.20W
Bolzano Italy 50 D7 ....46.29N 11.21E
Boma Dem. Rep. Congo 86 A4 .....5.48S 13.03E
Bømlo i. Norway 40 A2 ....59.45N 5.13E
Bon, Cap c. Tunisia 52 F4 .....37.04N 11.04E
Bonaire i. Neth. Antilles 71 K3 .....12.02N 68.12W
Bonar Bridge Scotland 19 E2 .....57.54N 4.21W
Bonavista Canada 63 M2 ......48.33N 52.43W
Bondoukou Côte d'Ivoire 84 D2 .....8.03N 2.48W
Bo'ness Scotland 17 F4 ......56.01N 3.36W
Bonete, Cerro mt. Bolivia 76 G2 .....21.46S 66.29W
Bonifacio France 44 H2 ......41.23N 9.10E
Bonifacio, Strait of France/Italy 44 H2 .....41.15N 8.45E
Bonin Islands Japan 108 F7 .....27.13N 141.44E
Bonn Germany 54 B4 ....50.44N 7.04F
Bonnyrigg Scotland 17 F3 .....55.52N 3.06W
Bontosunggu Indonesia 104 F2 .....5.41S 119.43E
Boothby England 15 G2 ....53.51N 0.16W
Boothia, Gulf of Canada 63 J4 .....68.48N 86.41W
Boothia Peninsula Canada 63 I5 .....70.40N 94.39W
Bootle England 14 E2 ....53.27N 2.59W
Bor Turkey 57 K3 ....37.54N 34.33E
Borås Sweden 40 C2 ....57.44N 12.57E
Borazjan Iran 95 H5 ....29.16N 51.12E
Bordeaux France 44 C4 ....44.51N 0.34W
Borden Island Canada 62 G5 .....78.31N 111.01W
Borden Peninsula Canada 63 J5 .....72.45N 82.32W
Bordj Messaouda Algeria 52 E3 .....30.10N 9.25E
Bordj Omer Driss Algeria 84 E4 .....28.11N 6.47E
Boreray i. Scotland 18 B2 .....57.42N 7.16W
Borgarnes Iceland 40 X2 .....64.32N 21.55W
Borken Germany 42 F4 ....51.50N 6.51E
Borkum i. Germany 42 F6 .....53.37N 6.44E
Borlänge Sweden 40 C3 ....60.29N 15.26E
Borneo i. Asia 104 E4 ....0.08N 113.25E
Bornholm i. Denmark 40 C1 .....55.09N 14.38E
Bornova Turkey 56 G4 ....38.27N 27.11E
Borodyanka Ukraine 55 M4 .....50.39N 29.56E
Boroughbridge England 15 F3 .....54.06N 1.24W
Borüjerd Iran 95 G6 ....33.53N 48.43E
Boryspil' Ukraine 55 N4 ......50.21N 30.58E
Borzna Ukraine 55 O4 ....51.15N 32.26E
Borzya Rus. Fed. 59 M3 ......50.11N 116.31E
Bosanska Dubica Bos.-Herz. 56 B7 .....45.11N 16.48E
Bose China 103 J3 ....23.54N 106.37E
Bosna r. Bos.-Herz. 56 C7 .....45.04N 18.29E
Bosnia-Herzegovina Europe 56 B7 .....44.23N 17.40E
Bosobolo Dem. Rep. Congo 86 A5 .....4.10N 19.52E
Bosporus str. Turkey 57 H5 .....41.20N 29.06E
Bossembélé C.A.R. 85 F2 .....5.15N 17.38E
Bosten Hu l. China 102 F6 .....41.53N 87.24E
Boston England 11 E3 ....52.58N 0.01W
Boston U.S.A. 65 L5 ....42.23N 71.06W
Boston Spa England 15 F2 .....53.54N 1.20W
Botevgrad Bulgaria 56 E6 .....42.54N 23.47E
Bothnia, Gulf of Finland/Sweden 40 D3 .....61.09N 19.15E
Botoşani Romania 55 L2 ......47.45N 26.39E
Botswana Africa 86 B2 ....24.56S 22.47E
Botte Donato, Monte mt. Italy 50 G3 .....39.17N 16.28E
Bottesford England 15 G2 .....53.33N 0.38W
Bouaké Côte d'Ivoire 84 D2 .....7.42N 5.03W
Bouar C.A.R. 84 F2 ....5.56N 15.35E
Bouârfa Morocco 84 D5 ....32.34N 1.56W
Bougainville Island P.N.G. 110 E6 .....6.04S 154.53E
Bouillon Belgium 42 E2 ......49.48N 5.06E
Boujdour Western Sahara 84 C4 .....26.08N 14.28W
Boulder U.S.A. 64 E5 ....40.02N 105.16W
Boulogne-Billancourt France 44 E6 .....48.50N 2.15E
Boulogne-sur-Mer France 44 D7 .....50.43N 1.37E
Bounty Islands New Zealand 111 G2 .....47.40S 179.02E
Bourg-en-Bresse France 44 F5 .....46.12N 5.14E
Bourges France 44 E5 ....47.05N 2.24E
Bourke Australia 110 D3 .....30.07S 145.54E
Bourne England 11 E3 ....52.46N 0.23W
Bournemouth England 10 D1 .....50.43N 1.53W
Bournemouth d. England 9 E2 .....50.45N 1.50W
Bou Saâda Algeria 52 D4 .....35.13N 4.11E
Bow r. Canada 64 D6 ....49.58N 111.41W
Bowes England 15 E3 ....54.31N 2.00W
Bowland, Forest of England 14 E2 .....53.59N 2.33W
Boxtel Neth. 42 E4 ....51.35N 5.20E
Boyabat Turkey 57 K5 ....41.28N 34.46E
Boyle Ireland 41 C3 ....53.58N 8.18W
Boyne r. Ireland 41 E3 ....53.43N 6.18W
Boyuibe Bolivia 76 H3 ....20.27S 63.29W
Bozeman U.S.A. 64 D6 ....45.42N 111.02W
Bozüyük Turkey 57 I4 ....39.55N 30.01E
Braan r. Scotland 19 F1 ......56.34N 3.36W
Brabant Wallon d. Belgium 42 D3 .....50.39N 4.35E
Brač i. Croatia 56 B6 ....43.17N 16.31E

Bracadale, Loch b. Scotland 18 C2 ....57.21N 6.33W
Bräcke Sweden 40 C3 ....62.46N 15.26E
Brackley England 10 D3 ....52.02N 1.08W
Bracknell England 10 E2 ....51.25N 0.45W
Bracknell Forest d. England 9 E2 ....51.24N 0.45W
Brad Romania 56 E8 ....46.07N 22.48E
Bradano r. Italy 50 G4 ....40.23N 16.51E
Bradford England 15 F2 ....53.48N 1.45W
Bradford-on-Avon England 10 C2 ....51.21N 2.15W
Braemar Scotland 19 F2 ....57.00N 3.24W
Braga Portugal 48 A4 ....41.33N 8.26W
Bragança Brazil 77 K7 ....1.00S 46.49W
Bragança Portugal 48 B4 ....41.47N 6.45W
Brahmapur India 96 F4 ....19.21N 84.52E
Brahmaputra r. China/India 102 G2 ....23.36N 90.31E
Brăila Romania 56 G7 ....45.17N 27.58E
Braintree England 11 F2 ....51.53N 0.33E
Brämön i. Sweden 40 D3 ....62.13N 17.45E
Brampton England 14 E3 ....54.57N 2.44W
Branco r. Brazil 72 H7 ....1.18S 61.52W
Brandenburg Germany 54 E5 ....52.25N 12.34E
Brandesburton England 15 G2 ....53.55N 0.18W
Brandon Canada 62 I2 ....49.51N 99.57W
Brandon England 11 F3 ....52.27N 0.37E
Brandon Head Ireland 41 A2 ....52.17N 10.13W
Brandon Mountain hill Ireland 41 A2 ....52.14N 10.15W
Braniewo Poland 46 D5 ....54.23N 19.49E
Bransgore England 10 D1 ....50.47N 1.44W
Brasília Brazil 77 K4 ....15.49S 47.55W
Braşov Romania 56 F7 ....45.40N 25.36E
Bratislava Slovakia 54 G3 ....48.09N 17.06E
Bratsk Rus. Fed. 59 L3 ....56.16N 101.41E
Braunau am Inn Austria 54 E3 ....48.16N 13.02E
Braunschweig Germany 54 D5 ....52.17N 10.32E
Braunton England 13 C3 ....51.06N 4.10W
Brawley U.S.A. 64 C3 ....32.58N 115.32W
Brazos r. U.S.A. 64 G2 ....28.52N 95.29W
Brazzaville Congo 84 F1 ....4.17S 15.11E
Breamish r. England 15 E4 ....55.41N 2.13W
Brechin Scotland 19 G1 ....56.44N 2.39W
Breckland f. England 11 F3 ....52.28N 0.39E
Břeclav Czech Rep. 54 G3 ....48.46N 16.53E
Brecon Wales 12 D3 ....51.57N 3.24W
Brecon Beacons f. Wales 12 D3 ....51.53N 3.26W
Breda Neth. 42 D4 ....51.35N 4.46E
Breiðafjörður b. Iceland 40 W2 ....65.03N 24.07W
Breiðdalsvík Iceland 40 Z2 ....64.48N 14.02W
Bremen Germany 54 C5 ....53.05N 8.51E
Bremerhaven Germany 54 C5 ....53.33N 8.35E
Brenner Pass Austria/Italy 50 D7 ....46.59N 11.32E
Brentwood England 11 F2 ....51.37N 0.19E
Brescia Italy 50 D6 ....45.32N 10.13E
Bressanone Italy 50 D7 ....46.43N 11.40E
Bressay i. Scotland 19 H5 ....60.16N 1.18W
Bressuire France 44 C5 ....46.50N 0.30W
Brest Belarus 55 J5 ....52.05N 23.40E
Brest France 44 A6 ....48.24N 4.29W
Bretton Wales 12 E5 ....53.10N 2.58W
Bria C.A.R. 85 G2 ....6.32N 21.59E
Briançon France 44 G4 ....44.54N 6.38E
Brianne, Llyn resr Wales 12 D4 ....52.08N 3.45W
Bride r. Ireland 41 D2 ....52.04N 7.52W
Bridgend Wales 13 D3 ....51.30N 3.35W
Bridgend d. Wales 9 D2 ....51.34N 3.33W
Bridgeport U.S.A. 65 L5 ....41.12N 73.12W
Bridgetown Barbados 71 M3 ....13.05N 59.36W
Bridgnorth England 10 C3 ....52.32N 2.25W
Bridgwater England 13 D3 ....51.08N 3.00W
Bridgwater Bay England 13 D3 ....51.16N 3.19W
Bridlington England 15 G3 ....54.05N 0.12W
Bridlington Bay England 15 G3 ....54.03N 0.07W
Bridport England 10 C1 ....50.44N 2.45W
Brig Switz. 50 B7 ....46.19N 7.59E
Brigg England 15 G2 ....53.33N 0.29W
Brighstone England 10 D1 ....50.39N 1.23W
Brightlingsea England 11 G2 ....51.49N 1.01E
Brighton England 11 E1 ....50.49N 0.08W
Brighton and Hove d. England 9 E2 ....50.51N 0.08W
Brindisi Italy 50 G4 ....40.38N 17.56E
Brisbane Australia 110 E4 ....27.33S 153.03E
Bristol England 10 C2 ....51.27N 2.35W
Bristol d. England 9 D2 ....51.28N 2.36W
Bristol U.S.A. 65 J4 ....36.36N 82.10W
Bristol Bay U.S.A. 62 B3 ....57.22N 161.29W
Bristol Channel est. England 10 B2 ....51.20N 4.16W
British Columbia d. Canada 62 F3 ....51.49N 121.48W
British Empire Range mts Canada 63 J6 ....82.22N 80.08W
British Isles Europe 34 G3 ....54.00N 5.00W
Briton Ferry Wales 12 D3 ....51.38N 3.49W
Britstown S. Africa 86 B1 ....30.35S 23.30E
Brittany f. France 44 B6 ....48.10N 3.22W
Brittas Bay Ireland 12 A4 ....52.52N 6.03W
Brive-la-Gaillarde France 44 D4 ....45.10N 1.32E
Brixham England 13 D2 ....50.24N 3.31W
Brno Czech Rep. 54 G3 ....49.11N 16.37E
Broad r. U.S.A. 65 J3 ....34.00N 81.04W
Broadback r. Canada 65 K7 ....51.21N 78.50W
Broad Bay Scotland 18 C3 ....58.15N 6.15W
Broad Law hill Scotland 17 F3 ....55.30N 3.21W
Broadstairs England 11 G2 ....51.22N 1.26E
Broadway England 10 D3 ....52.02N 1.51W
Broadwey England 10 C1 ....50.39N 2.28W
Broadwindsor England 10 C1 ....50.49N 2.48W
Brockenhurst England 10 D1 ....50.49N 1.34W
Brock Island Canada 62 G5 ....77.53N 114.21W
Brodeur Peninsula Canada 63 J5 ....71.50N 88.32W
Brodick Scotland 16 D3 ....55.35N 5.09W
Brodnica Poland 46 D4 ....53.16N 19.24E
Brody Ukraine 55 K4 ....50.05N 25.09E
Broken Hill town Australia 110 D3 ....31.55S 141.27E
Bromley England 11 F2 ....51.24N 0.01E
Bromsgrove England 10 C3 ....52.20N 2.04W
Bromyard England 10 C3 ....52.11N 2.30W
Brønderslev Denmark 40 B2 ....57.17N 9.58E
Brønnøysund Norway 40 C4 ....65.28N 12.12E
Brooke England 11 G3 ....52.33N 1.23E
Brooke's Point town Phil. 104 F5 ....8.50N 117.51E
Brookings U.S.A. 64 G5 ....44.19N 96.44W
Brooks Canada 62 G3 ....50.35N 111.54W
Brooks Range mts U.S.A. 62 D4 ....69.18N 144.41W
Broom, Loch inlet Scotland 18 D2 ....57.56N 5.19W
Broome Australia 110 B5 ....17.57S 122.14E
Brora Scotland 19 F3 ....58.01N 3.51W
Brora r. Scotland 19 F3 ....58.00N 3.51W
Brosna r. Ireland 41 D3 ....53.13N 7.57W
Brotton England 15 G3 ....54.34N 0.56W
Brough Cumb. England 15 E3 ....54.32N 2.19W
Brough E. Yorks. England 15 G2 ....53.44N 0.34W
Brough Head Scotland 19 F4 ....59.08N 3.21W

Brough Ness pt Scotland 19 G3 ....58.44N 2.58W
Broughshane Northern Ireland 16 C2 ....54.54N 6.12W
Brownhills England 10 D3 ....52.39N 1.56W
Broxburn Scotland 17 F3 ....55.56N 3.28W
Bruay-la-Bussière France 42 B3 ....50.29N 2.33E
Brue r. England 10 C2 ....51.13N 2.59W
Brugge Belgium 42 C4 ....51.12N 3.15E
Brumado Brazil 77 L5 ....14.12S 41.34W
Brunei Asia 104 E4 ....5.06N 114.18E
Brunflo Sweden 40 C3 ....63.05N 14.51E
Brunswick U.S.A. 65 J3 ....31.09N 81.30W
Bruntál Czech Rep. 46 C2 ....49.59N 17.28E
Brussels Belgium 42 D3 ....50.50N 4.21E
Bruton England 10 C2 ....51.07N 2.27W
Bryansk Rus. Fed. 58 E3 ....53.15N 34.23E
Bryher i. Scotland 13 A1 ....49.57N 6.23W
Brynamman Wales 12 D3 ....51.49N 3.52W
Brynmawr Wales 12 D3 ....51.48N 3.10W
Brzeg Poland 46 C3 ....50.51N 17.28E
Buca Turkey 56 G4 ....38.22N 27.11E
Bucaramanga Colombia 72 B7 ....7.05N 73.09W
Bucharest Romania 56 G7 ....44.26N 26.06E
Buckhaven Scotland 17 F4 ....56.11N 3.02W
Buckie Scotland 19 G2 ....57.41N 2.58W
Buckingham England 10 E2 ....51.59N 0.59W
Buckinghamshire d. England 9 E2 ....51.47N 0.56W
Buckley Wales 12 D5 ....53.10N 3.05W
Budapest Hungary 54 H2 ....47.30N 19.04E
Buddon Ness pt Scotland 17 G4 ....56.28N 2.43W
Bude England 13 C2 ....50.50N 4.32W
Bude Bay England 13 C2 ....50.50N 4.38W
Buenaventura Colombia 72 B7 ....3.52N 77.00W
Buenos Aires Argentina 73 D3 ....34.36S 58.24W
Buenos Aires, Lago l. Argentina/Chile 73 B2 .46.31S 72.13W
Buffalo N. Y. U.S.A. 65 K5 ....42.53N 78.52W
Buffalo Wyo. U.S.A. 64 E5 ....44.20N 106.41W
Bug r. Poland 46 E4 ....51.30N 23.39E
Buhu r. Tanzania 87 A1 ....6.03S 35.20E
Builth Wells Wales 12 D4 ....52.09N 3.24W
Buir Nur l. Mongolia 103 L7 ....47.47N 117.53E
Bujumbura Burundi 85 G1 ....3.24S 29.22E
Bukavu Dem. Rep. Congo 86 B4 ....2.30S 28.49E
Bukittinggi Indonesia 104 C3 ....0.15S 100.20E
Bukoba Tanzania 86 C4 ....1.18S 31.48E
Bula Indonesia 105 I3 ....3.06S 130.28E
Bulawayo Zimbabwe 86 B2 ....20.09S 28.36E
Bulgan Mongolia 103 I7 ....48.48N 103.28E
Bulgaria Europe 56 F6 ....42.51N 25.15E
Bulun Rus. Fed. 59 N5 ....70.59N 127.16E
Buna Kenya 87 B2 ....2.47N 39.31E
Bunbury Australia 110 A3 ....33.20S 115.36E
Bunclody Ireland 41 E2 ....52.39N 6.39W
Buncrana Ireland 41 D5 ....55.09N 7.27W
Bunda Tanzania 87 A2 ....2.04S 33.56E
Bundaberg Australia 110 E4 ....24.52S 152.22E
Bundoran Ireland 41 C4 ....54.28N 8.18W
Bungay England 11 G3 ....52.27N 1.27E
Bungoma Kenya 87 A3 ....0.34N 34.34E
Buôn Ma Thuột Vietnam 104 D6 ....12.38N 108.05E
Bura Kenya 87 B2 ....1.06S 39.57E
Buraydah Saudi Arabia 94 F5 ....26.20N 43.57E
Burbage England 10 D2 ....51.21N 1.40W
Burdur Turkey 57 I3 ....37.43N 30.17E
Bure r. England 11 G3 ....52.37N 1.43E
Burë Ethiopia 85 H3 ....10.50N 36.57E
Burford England 10 D2 ....51.48N 1.38W
Burgas Bulgaria 56 G6 ....42.30N 27.28E
Burgess Hill town England 11 E1 ....50.57N 0.08W
Burghausen Germany 54 E3 ....48.10N 12.50E
Burghead Scotland 19 F2 ....57.42N 3.29W
Burgh le Marsh England 15 H2 ....53.10N 0.14E
Burgos Spain 48 D5 ....42.21N 3.41W
Burhanpur India 96 E5 ....21.18N 76.14E
Burkina Africa 84 D3 ....11.39N 1.18W
Burlington Colo. U.S.A. 64 F4 ....39.19N 102.17W
Burlington Iowa U.S.A. 65 H5 ....40.49N 91.06W
Burlington Vt. U.S.A. 65 L5 ....44.28N 73.13W
Burma see Myanmar
Burnham England 10 E2 ....51.32N 0.39W
Burnham Market England 11 F3 ....52.57N 0.44E
Burnham-on-Crouch England 11 F2 ....51.38N 0.49E
Burnham-on-Sea England 10 C2 ....51.14N 2.59W
Burnie Australia 110 D2 ....41.03S 145.57E
Burniston England 15 G3 ....54.19N 0.27W
Burnley England 15 E2 ....53.47N 2.15W
Burns U.S.A. 64 C5 ....43.36N 119.01W
Burns Lake town Canada 62 F3 ....54.15N 125.46W
Burntisland Scotland 17 F4 ....56.04N 3.14W
Burntwood Green England 10 D3 ....52.41N 1.54W
Burray i. Scotland 19 H5 ....60.05N 1.22W
Burray i. Scotland 19 G3 ....58.51N 2.53W
Burro, Serranías del mts Mexico 70 D6 ....29.02N 102.00W
Burrow Head Scotland 16 E2 ....54.41N 4.23W
Burry Inlet Wales 12 C3 ....51.38N 4.18W
Burry Port Wales 12 C3 ....51.41N 4.16W
Bursa Turkey 57 H5 ....40.14N 29.03E
Būr Safājah Egypt 53 J2 ....26.45N 33.55E
Burscough Bridge England 14 E2 ....53.36N 2.51W
Burton-in-Kendal England 14 E3 ....54.11N 2.43W
Burton Latimer England 10 E3 ....52.22N 0.41W
Burton upon Trent England 10 D3 ....52.48N 1.39W
Buru i. Indonesia 105 H3 ....3.24S 126.35E
Burundi Africa 85 H1 ....3.36S 30.03E
Burwash Landing Canada 62 E4 ....61.21N 138.58W
Burwell England 11 F3 ....52.16N 0.20E
Burwick Scotland 19 G3 ....58.45N 2.58W
Bury England 15 E2 ....53.36N 2.18W
Bury St Edmunds England 11 F3 ....52.15N 0.44E
Bush r. Northern Ireland 16 C3 ....55.13N 6.31W
Bushbush r. Kenya/Somalia 87 C2 ....1.11S 41.49E
Bushehr Iran 95 H5 ....28.58N 50.51E
Bushmills Northern Ireland 16 C3 ....55.12N 6.31W
Buta Dem. Rep. Congo 86 B5 ....2.49N 24.45E
Bute i. Scotland 16 D3 ....55.49N 5.06W
Bute, Sound of str. Scotland 16 D3 ....55.44N 5.19W
Buton i. Indonesia 105 G3 ....4.57S 123.00E
Butte U.S.A. 64 D6 ....46.01N 112.32W
Butterworth Malaysia 104 C5 ....5.22N 100.22E
Buttevant Ireland 41 C2 ....52.14N 8.40W
Butt of Lewis hd Scotland 18 C3 ....58.32N 6.17W
Butuan Phil. 105 H5 ....8.56N 125.32E
Buur Gaabo Somalia 87 C2 ....1.15S 41.49E
Buvuma Island Uganda 87 A3 ....0.10N 33.18E
Buxoro Uzbekistan 58 H1 ....39.46N 64.25E
Buxton England 15 F2 ....53.16N 1.55W
Büyük Ağrı Dağı mt. Turkey 94 F7 ....39.44N 44.15E
Büyükmenderes r. Turkey 57 G3 ....37.28N 27.11E
Buzău Romania 56 G7 ....45.09N 26.48E
Byarezina r. Belarus 55 K5 ....53.48N 25.58E
Byaroza Belarus 55 K5 ....52.32N 24.59E
Bydgoszcz Poland 46 D4 ....53.08N 18.02E
Byfield England 10 D3 ....52.11N 1.14W
Bylot Island Canada 63 K5 ....73.07N 79.01W
Byrranga, Gory mts Rus. Fed. 59 K5 ....74.25N 99.53E

Bytom Poland 46 D3 ....50.21N 18.55E

C

Caacupé Paraguay 77 I2 ....25.20S 57.05W
Cabanatuan Phil. 105 G7 ....15.31N 120.58E
Caban Coch Reservoir Wales 12 D4 ....52.15N 3.35W
Cabezas Bolivia 76 H4 ....18.46S 63.23W
Cabimas Venezuela 72 B8 ....10.23N 71.26W
Cabinda Angola 84 F1 ....5.33S 12.15E
Cabo Frio Brazil 73 E4 ....22.51S 42.02W
Cabonga, Réservoir Canada 65 K6 ....47.21N 76.32W
Cabo Pantoja Peru 76 E7 ....0.58S 75.13W
Cabora Bassa, Lake resr Mozambique 86 C3 ...15.46S 31.11E
Caborca Mexico 70 B7 ....30.44N 112.09W
Cabot Strait Canada 63 L2 ....47.39N 60.16W
Cabrera, Sierra de la mts Spain 48 B5 ....42.13N 6.51W
Cabriel r. Spain 48 E3 ....39.16N 1.04W
Cáceres Brazil 77 I4 ....16.03S 57.41W
Cáceres Spain 48 B3 ....39.29N 6.21W
Cachi, Nevados de mts Argentina 76 G3 ....24.48S 66.25W
Cachimbo, Serra do hills Brazil 77 J6 ....9.18S 54.11W
Cachoeiro de Itapemirim Brazil 77 L3 ....20.51S 41.08W
Čadca Slovakia 46 D2 ....49.26N 18.48E
Cadillac U.S.A. 65 I5 ....44.14N 85.23W
Cádiz Spain 48 B2 ....36.32N 6.17W
Cádiz, Golfo de g. Spain 48 B2 ....36.44N 7.14W
Caen France 44 C6 ....49.11N 0.21W
Caerleon Wales 12 E3 ....51.37N 2.57W
Caernarfon Wales 12 C5 ....53.08N 4.16W
Caernarfon Bay Wales 12 C5 ....53.06N 4.34W
Caerphilly Wales 12 D3 ....51.35N 3.13W
Caerphilly d. Wales 9 D2 ....51.38N 3.11W
Caerwent Wales 12 E3 ....51.37N 2.46W
Cagayan de Oro Phil. 105 G5 ....8.29N 124.39E
Cagliari Italy 50 C3 ....39.13N 9.08E
Cagliari, Golfo di b. Italy 50 C3 ....39.07N 9.13E
Caha Mountains hills Ireland 41 B1 ....51.41N 9.44W
Cahirciveen Ireland 41 A1 ....51.57N 10.13W
Cahore Point Ireland 41 E2 ....52.33N 6.11W
Cahors France 44 D4 ....44.28N 1.26E
Cahul Moldova 57 H7 ....45.54N 28.12E
Caia Mozambique 86 C3 ....17.50S 35.19E
Caiabis, Serra dos hills Brazil 77 I5 ....12.46S 56.21W
Caiapó, Serra do mts Brazil 77 J4 ....17.19S 52.31W
Caicos Islands Turks and Caicos Is 71 J5 ....21.45N 71.53W
Caimodorro mt. Spain 48 E4 ....40.32N 1.40W
Cairn Gorm mt. Scotland 19 F2 ....57.07N 3.39W
Cairngorm Mountains Scotland 19 F2 ....57.08N 3.45W
Cairnryan Scotland 16 D2 ....54.59N 5.02W
Cairns Australia 110 D5 ....16.54S 145.45E
Cairn Toul mt. Scotland 19 F2 ....57.03N 3.43W
Cairo Egypt 85 H5 ....30.01N 31.15E
Caister-on-Sea England 11 G3 ....52.39N 1.44E
Caistor England 15 G2 ....53.30N 0.19W
Caithness f. Scotland 19 F3 ....58.25N 3.22W
Cajamarca Peru 76 E6 ....7.11S 78.31W
Calabar Nigeria 84 E2 ....4.59N 8.19E
Calafat Romania 56 E6 ....43.59N 22.57E
Calais France 44 D7 ....50.57N 1.51E
Calais U.S.A. 65 M6 ....45.10N 67.18W
Calama Chile 73 C4 ....22.29S 68.56W
Calamian Group is Phil. 104 F6 ....11.59N 119.29E
Calamocha Spain 48 E4 ....40.56N 1.17W
Calanscio Sand Sea des. Libya 53 H3 ....30.11N 22.22E
Calapan Phil. 105 G6 ....13.24N 121.11E
Călăraşi Romania 56 G7 ....44.12N 27.19E
Calatayud Spain 48 E4 ....41.22N 1.37W
Calbayog Phil. 105 G6 ....12.05N 124.37E
Calcanhar, Ponta do pt Brazil 77 M6 ....5.07S 35.34W
Caldas da Rainha Portugal 48 A3 ....39.24N 9.08W
Caldey Island Wales 12 C3 ....51.38N 4.40W
Calf of Man i. Isle of Man 14 C3 ....54.04N 4.50W
Calgary Canada 62 G3 ....51.02N 114.04W
Cali Colombia 72 B7 ....3.22N 76.28W
Caliente U.S.A. 64 D4 ....37.37N 114.31W
California d. U.S.A. 64 B5 ....41.35N 122.50W
California, Gulf of Mexico 70 B7 ....30.51N 113.58W
Callan Ireland 41 D2 ....52.32N 7.24W
Callander Scotland 16 E4 ....56.15N 4.13W
Callanish Scotland 18 C3 ....58.12N 6.45W
Callao Peru 76 E5 ....12.04S 77.08W
Callington England 13 C2 ....50.30N 4.19W
Calne England 10 D2 ....51.26N 2.00W
Caltanissetta Italy 50 F2 ....37.30N 14.03E
Calvi France 44 H3 ....42.34N 8.45E
Cam r. England 11 F3 ....52.20N 0.15E
Camaçari Brazil 77 M5 ....12.43S 38.15W
Camagüey Cuba 71 I5 ....21.23N 77.54W
Camagüey, Archipiélago de is Cuba 71 I5 .....22.44N 78.34W
Ca Mau, Mui c. Vietnam 104 C5 ....8.35N 104.45E
Camberley England 10 E2 ....51.20N 0.44W
Cambodia Asia 104 D6 ....13.05N 105.10E
Camborne England 13 B2 ....50.13N 5.18W
Cambrai France 42 C3 ....50.10N 3.14E
Cambrian Mountains Wales 12 D4 ....52.37N 3.40W
Cambridge England 11 F3 ....52.12N 0.07E
Cambridge Bay town Canada 62 H4 ....69.02N 105.14W
Cambridgeshire d. England 9 F3 ....52.25N 0.02E
Camelford England 13 C2 ....50.37N 4.41W
Cameroon Africa 84 F2 ....5.45N 12.41E
Cameroun, Mont vol. Cameroon 84 E2 ....4.12N 9.12E
Cametá Brazil 77 K6 ....2.13S 49.30W
Campbell Island New Zealand 108 H2 ....52.31S 169.01E
Campbell Plateau f. S. Pacific Oc. 108 H2 ...49.32S 170.53E
Campbell River town Canada 62 F3 ....50.01N 125.14W
Campbeltown Scotland 16 D3 ....55.25N 5.36W
Campeche Mexico 70 F4 ....19.51N 90.30W
Campeche d. Mexico 70 F4 ....18.53N 90.28W
Campeche, Bahía de g. Mexico 70 F4 ....19.30N 93.30W
Campina Grande Brazil 77 M6 ....7.14S 35.49W
Campinas Brazil 77 K3 ....22.55S 47.04W
Campobasso Italy 50 F4 ....41.34N 14.39E
Campo Grande Brazil 77 J3 ....20.24S 54.34W
Campos Brazil 77 L3 ....21.45S 41.20W
Câmpulung Moldovenesc Romania 55 K2 ....47.32N 25.30E
Camrose Canada 62 G3 ....53.01N 112.49W
Çan Turkey 56 G5 ....40.02N 27.02E
Canada N. America 62 F4 ....46.44N 81.59W
Canadian r. U.S.A. 64 G4 ....35.11N 95.52W
Canadian Shield f. N. America 60 K7 ....50.00N 80.00W
Çanakkale Turkey 56 G5 ....40.09N 26.23E
Canarreos, Archipiélago de los is Cuba 71 H5 .21.44N 82.12W
Canary Islands N. Atlantic Oc. 48 X2 ....30.08N 18.27W
Canaveral, Cape U.S.A. 65 J2 ....28.33N 80.32W
Canberra Australia 110 D3 ....35.19S 149.09E
Cancún Mexico 70 G5 ....21.10N 86.50W
Canelones Uruguay 77 I1 ....34.32S 56.17W
Caniapiscau r. Canada 63 L3 ....56.19N 69.25W
Caniapiscau, Lac l. Canada 63 K3 ....54.21N 70.31W
Canindé r. Brazil 77 L6 ....6.17S 42.49W
Canisp hill Scotland 18 D3 ....58.07N 5.03W

Çankaya Turkey 57 J4 ....39.53N 3...
Çankırı Turkey 57 J5 ....40.36N 3...
Canna i. Scotland 18 C2 ....57.04N ...
Cannes France 44 G3 ....43.33N
Cannock England 10 C3 ....52.41N
Canoas Brazil 77 J2 ....29.54S 5...
Canora Canada 64 F7 ....51.39N 10...
Cantabrian Mountains Spain 48 C5 ....43.07N ...
Canterbury England 11 G2 ....51.17N
Cần Thơ Vietnam 104 D6 ....10.01N 10...
Canvey Island England 11 F2 ....51.31N
Cao Bằng Vietnam 104 D8 ....22.41N 10...
Capbreton France 44 C3 ....43.39N ...
Cape Breton Island Canada 63 L2 ....46.45N 60...
Cape Johnson Depth f. N. Pacific Oc. 108 E6 .10.26N 12...
Capel St Mary England 11 G3 ....52.00N
Cape Town S. Africa 86 A1 ....33.57S 1...
Cape Verde N. Atlantic Oc. 84 B3 ....15.47N 24...
Cape York Peninsula Australia 110 D5 ....12.33S 14...
Cap-Haïtien Haiti 71 J4 ....19.46N 72...
Capim r. Brazil 77 K7 ....1.30S 4...
Capitol Hill town N. Mariana Is 108 F7 ......15.12N 14...
Capraia, Isola di i. Italy 50 C5 ....43.04N ...
Caprera, Isola i. Italy 50 C4 ....41.13N
Capri, Isola di i. Italy 50 F4 ....40.32N 1...
Capricorn Channel Australia 110 E4 ....22.20S 15...
Caprivi Strip f. Namibia 86 B3 ....18.11S 2...
Caquetá r. Colombia 72 C6 ....1.27S 69...
Carabaya, Cordillera de mts Peru 76 F5 ......13.27S 71...
Caracal Romania 56 F7 ....44.07N 2...
Caracas Venezuela 72 C8 ....10.28N 66...
Carajás, Serra dos hills Brazil 77 J6 ....5.43S 51...
Caransebeş Romania 56 E7 ....45.25N 2...
Caratasca, Laguna de lagoon Honduras 71 H4 ..15.20N 83...
Caratinga Brazil 77 L4 ....19.45S 42...
Caravaca de la Cruz Spain 48 E3 ....38.07N 1...
Carbonara, Capo c. Italy 50 C3 ....39.06N ...
Carcassonne France 44 E3 ....43.13N
Cardiff Wales 13 D3 ....51.29N 3...
Cardiff d. Wales 9 D2 ....51.30N 3...
Cardigan Wales 12 C4 ....52.05N 4...
Cardigan Bay Wales 12 C4 ....52.33N 4...
Carei Romania 55 J2 ....47.41N 2...
Carey, Lake Australia 110 B4 ....28.57S 12...
Caribbean Sea N. Atlantic Oc. 71 H4 ....19.03N 83...
Caribou Mountains Canada 62 G3 ....59.02N 11...
Cark Mountain hill Ireland 16 B2 ....54.53N 7...
Carletonville S. Africa 86 B2 ....26.21S 2...
Carlingford Lough inlet Ireland/U.K. 41 E4 ..54.05N 6...
Carlisle England 14 E3 ....54.54N 2...
Carlow Ireland 41 E2 ....52.50N 6...
Carlow d. Ireland 41 E2 ....52.47N 6...
Carluke Scotland 17 F3 ....55.44N 3...
Carmacks Canada 62 E4 ....62.05N 136...
Carmarthen Wales 12 C3 ....51.51N 4...
Carmarthen Bay Wales 12 C3 ....51.38N 4...
Carmarthenshire d. Wales 9 C2 ....51.57N 4...
Carmel Head Wales 12 C5 ....53.25N 4...
Carmen, Isla i. Mexico 70 B6 ....25.59N 111...
Carnac France 44 B5 ....47.35N 3...
Carn Dearg hill Scotland 19 E2 ....57.06N 4...
Carndonagh Ireland 16 B3 ....55.15N 7...
Carnedd Llywelyn mt. Wales 12 D5 ....53.10N 3...
Carnedd y Filiast hill Wales 12 D4 ....52.59N 3...
Carnegie, Lake Australia 110 B4 ....26.10S 12...
Carn Eighe mt. Scotland 18 D2 ....57.17N 5...
Carnforth England 14 E3 ....54.08N 2...
Carnic Alps mts Italy 50 E7 ....46.40N 12...
Car Nicobar i. India 97 H2 ....9.10N 92...
Carnlough Northern Ireland 16 D2 ....54.59N 5...
Carn Mòr hill Scotland 19 F2 ....57.15N 3...
Carn nan Gabhar mt. Scotland 19 F1 ....56.50N 3...
Carnot, Cape Australia 110 C3 ....34.55S 135...
Carnoustie Scotland 17 G4 ....56.30N 2...
Carnsore Point Ireland 41 E2 ....52.10N 6...
Caroline Island atoll Kiribati 109 J5 ....9.58S 150...
Caroline Islands N. Pacific Oc. 108 F6 ......6.35N 144...
Carpathian Mountains Europe 55 J3 ....48.45N 23...
Carpentaria, Gulf of Australia 110 C5 ....14.06S 139...
Carpentras France 44 F4 ....44.04N 5...
Carra, Lough l. Ireland 41 B3 ....53.44N 9...
Carrantuohill mt. Ireland 41 B1 ....51.59N 9...
Carrara Italy 50 D6 ....44.04N 10...
Carrickfergus Northern Ireland 16 D2 ....54.43N 5...
Carrickfergus d. Northern Ireland 9 C4 ......54.44N 5...
Carrickmacross Ireland 41 E3 ....53.59N 6...
Carrick-on-Shannon Ireland 41 C3 ....53.56N 8...
Carrick-on-Suir Ireland 41 D2 ....52.21N 7...
Carron r. Falk. Scotland 17 F4 ....56.02N 3...
Carron r. High. Scotland 18 E2 ....57.53N 4...
Carrowmore Lake Ireland 41 B4 ....54.11N 9...
Carson City U.S.A. 64 C4 ....39.10N 119...
Carsphairn Scotland 16 E3 ....55.13N 4...
Cartagena Colombia 72 B8 ....10.23N 75...
Cartagena Spain 48 E2 ....37.36N 0...
Carteret France 13 Z9 ....49.23N 1...
Carteret, Cap de c. France 13 Z9 ....49.22N 1...
Carterton England 10 D2 ....51.46N 1...
Cartmel England 14 E3 ....54.12N 2...
Caruaru Brazil 77 M6 ....8.13S 35...
Carvin France 42 B3 ....50.29N 2...
Casablanca Morocco 84 D5 ....33.35N 7...
Casa Grande U.S.A. 64 D3 ....32.53N 111...
Cascade Range mts Canada/U.S.A. 62 F2 ....41.49N 122...
Cascavel Brazil 77 J3 ....24.55S 53...
Caserta Italy 50 F4 ....41.04N 14...
Cashel Ireland 41 D2 ....52.31N 7...
Casper U.S.A. 64 E5 ....42.52N 106...
Caspian Lowland f. Kazakhstan/Rus. Fed. 58 F2
....44.15N 45...
Caspian Sea l. Asia/Europe 58 G2 ....42.00N 51...
Cassiar Mountains Canada 62 E3 ....59.40N 130...
Cassley r. Scotland 18 E2 ....57.58N 4...
Castanhal Brazil 77 K7 ....1.18S 47...
Castelló de la Plana Spain 48 E3 ....39.59N 0...
Castlebar Ireland 41 B3 ....53.51N 9...
Castlebay Scotland 18 B1 ....56.57N 7...
Castleblayney Ireland 41 E4 ....54.07N 6...
Castle Cary England 10 C2 ....51.05N 2...
Castlecomer Ireland 41 D2 ....52.48N 7...
Castleconnell Ireland 41 C2 ....52.43N 8...
Castlederg Northern Ireland 16 B2 ....54.42N 7...
Castle Donington England 10 D3 ....52.50N 1...
Castle Douglas Scotland 17 F2 ....54.56N 3...
Castleford England 15 F2 ....53.43N 1...
Castleisland Ireland 41 B2 ....52.14N 9...
Castlereagh d. Northern Ireland 9 C4 ....54.33N 5...
Castletown Isle of Man 14 C3 ....54.05N 4...
Castres France 44 E3 ....43.36N 2...
Castries St Lucia 71 L3 ....14.00N 60...
Castro Verde Portugal 48 A2 ....37.42N 8...
Catacaos Peru 76 D6 ....5.18S 80...
Catamarca Argentina 73 C4 ....28.26S 65...
Catanduanes i. Phil. 105 G6 ....13.46N 124...

ia Italy 50 F2 .....37.30N 15.05E
zaro Italy 50 G3 .....38.55N 16.36E
man Phil. 105 G6 .....12.29N 124.38E
ham England 11 E2 .....51.17N 0.05W
land Bahamas 71 I5 .....24.28N 75.30W
he, Cabo c. Mexico 70 G5 .....21.37N 87.06W
rick England 15 F3 .....54.23N 1.38W
r. Colombia 71 J2 .....8.54N 74.29W
sia Brazil 77 M7 .....3.42S 38.42W
sus mts Asia/Europe 58 F2 .....43.53N 40.00E
ry France 42 C3 .....50.07N 3.25E
Ireland 41 I3 .....53.59N 7.22W
ton England 11 G3 .....52.46N 1.10E
a d. Ireland 41 D3 .....53.57N 7.15W
s Brazil 77 L7 .....4.54S 43.19W
do Sul Brazil 77 J2 .....29.13S 51.11W
ne French Guiana 72 D7 .....4.53N 52.21W
an Brac i. Cayman Is 71 I4 .....19.43N 79.48W
an Islands Central America 71 H4 .....19.31N 81.15W
d. Brazil 77 M7 .....4.51S 39.03W
i. Italy 50 F3 .....38.02N 14.02E
d Hungary 54 H2 .....47.10N 19.48E
bes i. Indonesia 104 G3 .....2.01S 120.29E
bes Sea Indonesia/Phil. 104 G4 .....3.03N 121.10E
Slovenia 54 F2 .....46.14N 15.15E
Germany 54 D5 .....52.38N 10.05E
Sea Ireland/U.K. 13 A2 .....50.54N 6.33W
, Llyn i. Wales 12 D3 .....52.57N 3.43W
erawasih, Teluk b. Indonesia 105 J3 .....2.05S 135.33E
ral d. Kenya 87 B2 .....0.42S 36.55E
ral, Cordillera mts Bolivia 76 G4 .....18.27S 66.22W
ral, Cordillera mts Colombia 72 B7 .....1.38N 76.51W
ral, Cordillera mts Peru 76 E5 .....10.02S 76.25W
ral African Republic Africa 85 G2 .....6.25N 20.12E
ral Pacific Basin f. Pacific Oc. 108 H6 .....3.53N 179.43E
ral Range mts P.N.G. 105 K3 .....4.57S 142.36E
ral Russian Upland hills Rus. Fed. 55 Q6 .....54.27N 36.28E
ral Siberian Plateau f. Rus. Fed. 59 M4 .....67.03N 110.35E
alonia i. Greece 56 D4 .....38.14N 20.21E
m Sea Indonesia 105 I3 .....2.33S 130.11E
digion d. Wales 9 D3 .....52.19N 3.58W
avodă Romania 57 H7 .....44.21N 28.02E
alvo, Isla i. Mexico 70 C5 .....24.10N 109.48W
de Pasco Peru 76 E5 .....10.42S 76.14W
Spain 48 B5 .....43.41N 7.26W
é Budějovice Czech Rep. 54 F3 .....48.59N 14.29E
nje Montenegro 56 C6 .....42.23N 18.55E
a N. Africa 52 B4 .....35.53N 5.20W
ennes France 44 E3 .....43.50N 3.17E
an Turkey 57 K3 .....37.01N 35.47E
an r. Turkey 57 K3 .....36.42N 35.37E
ahār Iran 95 J5 .....25.18N 60.38E
d Africa 85 F3 .....15.07N 18.13E
d, Lake Africa 84 F3 .....13.27N 14.24E
dan Rus. Fed. 102 G8 .....51.18N 91.31E
dron U.S.A. 64 F5 .....42.50N 102.57W
gai Hills Afgh./Pakistan 96 B6 .....29.17N 63.23E
ghcharān Afgh. 95 K6 .....34.28N 65.03E
gos Archipelago is. Indian Oc. 90 F2 .....7.00S 72.00E
ke Chake Tanzania 87 B1 .....5.15S 39.47E
a Peru 76 F4 .....15.49S 74.12W
bi Desert Kenya 87 B3 .....3.13N 37.14E
le England 10 D3 .....50.36N 1.19W
kida Greece 56 E4 .....38.27N 23.37E
llenger Deep f. N. Pacific Oc. 117 Q6 .....11.17N 142.30E
llenger Fracture Zone f. S. Pacific Oc. 108 M3
.....34.26S 113.31W
ons-en-Champagne France 44 F6 .....48.58N 4.22E
lon-sur-Saône France 44 F5 .....46.48N 4.51E
lus Iran 95 J3 .....36.37N 51.26E
n Pakistan 96 C7 .....30.55N 66.28E
mbéry France 44 F4 .....45.34N 5.55E
mo Häyk' l. Ethiopia 87 B4 .....5.49N 37.32E
monix-Mont-Blanc France 44 G4 .....45.55N 6.52E
mpagne-Ardenne d. France 42 D1 .....48.43N 4.15E
mpaign U.S.A. 65 I5 .....40.06N 88.17W
mpaqui, Cerro mt. Argentina 76 H1 .....31.59S 64.56W
mplain, Lake Canada/U.S.A. 65 L5 .....44.23N 73.22W
ñaral Chile 76 F2 .....26.19S 70.41W
ndalar r. India 62 D4 .....66.36N 145.51W
ndigarh India 96 E7 .....30.42N 76.48E
ndigarh India 102 D4 .....30.43N 76.52E
ndrapur India 96 E4 .....19.57N 79.21E
ngbai China 106 A4 .....
ngchun China 103 N6 .....43.53N 125.20E
ngde China 103 J3 .....29.03N 111.42E
ng Jiang r. China 103 M4 .....31.24N 121.48E
ngsha China 103 K3 .....28.10N 112.59E
ngzhi China 103 K5 .....36.06N 113.09E
ngzhou China 103 L4 .....31.47N 119.59E
nia Greece 56 F2 .....35.30N 24.02E
nnel Islands English Channel 13 Z9 .....49.20N 2.37W
nnel Islands U.S.A. 64 C3 .....33.41N 119.26W
nnel-Port-aux-Basques Canada 63 M2 .....47.33N 59.01W
nnel Tunnel France/U.K. 11 G2 .....51.04N 1.24E
nthaburi Thailand 104 C6 .....12.37N 102.08E
ntilly France 42 B2 .....49.12N 2.28E
o Phraya r. Thailand 104 C6 .....13.40N 100.36E
ouèn Morocco 52 B4 .....35.11N 5.16W
apala, Laguna de l. Mexico 70 D5 .....20.15N 103.04W
apecó Brazil 77 J2 .....27.09S 52.39W
apel-en-le-Frith England 15 F2 .....53.20N 1.54W
apeltown England 15 F2 .....53.28N 1.28W
apleau Canada 63 J2 .....47.51N 83.24W
ard England 10 C1 .....50.52N 2.58W
ari r. Chad 82 E6 .....13.00N 14.30E
arikār Afgh. 95 K7 .....35.02N 69.15E
arlbury England 10 D2 .....51.52N 1.29W
arleroi Belgium 42 D3 .....50.25N 4.27E
arles, Cape U.S.A. 65 K4 .....37.10N 75.58W
arleston S. C. U.S.A. 65 K3 .....32.48N 79.58W
arleston W. Va. U.S.A. 65 J4 .....38.21N 81.39W
arlestown Ireland 41 C3 .....53.57N 8.47W
arleville-Mézières France 44 F6 .....49.46N 4.44E
arlotte U.S.A. 65 J4 .....35.14N 80.50W
arlottesville U.S.A. 65 K4 .....38.02N 78.30W
arlottetown Canada 63 L2 .....46.16N 63.09W
artres France 44 D6 .....48.27N 1.30E
assiron, Pointe de pt France 44 C5 .....46.03N 1.24W
âteaubriant France 44 C5 .....47.43N 1.22W
âteaudun France 44 D6 .....48.04N 1.20E
âteauroux France 44 D5 .....46.48N 1.41E
âteau-Thierry France 44 E6 .....49.03N 3.25E
âtellerault France 44 D5 .....46.49N 0.33E
atham England 11 F2 .....51.23N 0.31E
atham Islands New Zealand 111 H3 .....43.24S 176.11E
atham Rise f. S. Pacific Oc. 108 I3 .....42.18S 176.14W
attahoochee r. U.S.A. 65 J3 .....30.55N 84.58W

Chattanooga U.S.A. 65 I4 .....35.02N 85.21W
Chatteris England 11 F3 .....52.27N 0.03E
Chaumont France 44 F6 .....48.07N 5.08E
Chauny France 44 E6 .....49.37N 3.13E
Chaves Brazil 77 K7 .....0.11S 49.58W
Cheadle England 10 D3 .....52.59N 1.59W
Cheb Czech Rep. 54 E4 .....50.05N 12.23E
Cheboksary Rus. Fed. 58 F3 .....56.09N 47.13E
Cheboygan U.S.A. 65 J6 .....45.39N 84.28W
Cheddar England 10 C2 .....51.17N 2.47W
Cheju-do i. S. Korea 103 N4 .....33.34N 126.43E
Chekhov Rus. Fed. 55 Q6 .....55.09N 37.28E
Cheleken Turkmenistan 95 H7 .....39.25N 53.01E
Chełm Poland 46 F3 .....51.08N 23.29E
Chelmer r. England 11 F2 .....51.45N 0.40E
Chelmno Poland 46 D4 .....53.21N 18.26E
Chelmsford England 11 F2 .....51.44N 0.29E
Cheltenham England 10 C2 .....51.54N 2.04W
Chelyabinsk Rus. Fed. 58 H3 .....55.11N 61.24E
Chemnitz Germany 54 E4 .....50.50N 12.56E
Ch'ench'a Ethiopia 87 B4 .....6.17N 37.38E
Chengde China 103 L6 .....40.52N 117.58E
Chengdu China 103 I4 .....30.43N 104.04E
Chennai India 96 F3 .....13.06N 80.16E
Chenzhou China 103 K3 .....25.44N 113.00E
Chepstow Wales 12 E3 .....51.38N 2.40W
Cher r. France 44 D5 .....47.20N 0.29E
Cherbourg France 44 C6 .....49.38N 1.37W
Cherchell Algeria 48 G2 .....36.32N 2.06E
Cherepovets Rus. Fed. 58 E3 .....59.08N 37.55E
Chergui, Chott ech l. Algeria 52 C3 .....34.03N 0.16W
Cherkasy Ukraine 55 O3 .....49.26N 32.05E
Cherkessk Rus. Fed. 53 L5 .....44.13N 42.03E
Chernihiv Ukraine 55 N4 .....51.29N 31.19E
Chernivtsi Ukraine 55 K3 .....48.19N 25.56E
Chernyakhovsk Rus. Fed. 46 E5 .....54.38N 21.49E
Chernyshevskiy Rus. Fed. 59 M4 .....62.56N 112.36E
Chervonohrad Ukraine 55 K4 .....50.23N 24.14E
Cherwell r. England 10 D2 .....51.44N 1.15W
Chesapeake Bay U.S.A. 65 K4 .....38.05N 76.14W
Chesham England 11 E2 .....51.43N 0.37W
Cheshire d. England 9 D3 .....53.13N 2.26W
Cheshskaya Guba b. Russian Fed. 35 I4 .....67.20N 46.30E
Cheshunt England 11 E2 .....51.42N 0.02W
Chesil Beach f. England 10 C1 .....50.38N 2.36W
Chester England 14 E2 .....53.12N 2.54W
Chesterfield England 15 F2 .....53.14N 1.25W
Chester-le-Street England 15 F3 .....54.52N 1.34W
Chetumal Mexico 70 G4 .....18.30N 88.18W
Cheviot Hills England 15 E4 .....55.12N 2.39W
Chew Bahir l. Ethiopia 87 B4 .....4.40N 36.56E
Chew Bahir Wildlife Reserve Ethiopia 87 B4 .....4.51N 36.51E
Chew Magna England 10 C2 .....51.22N 2.37W
Chew Valley Lake resr England 10 C2 .....51.21N 2.37W
Cheyenne U.S.A. 64 F5 .....41.09N 104.49W
Cheyenne r. U.S.A. 64 F5 .....44.44N 101.09W
Chhattisgarh d. India 96 F5 .....21.29N 81.46E
Chiai Taiwan 103 M2 .....23.29N 120.27E
Chiang Mai Thailand 104 B7 .....18.47N 98.59E
Chiang Rai Thailand 104 B7 .....19.55N 99.53E
Chiapas d. Mexico 70 F4 .....16.23N 92.17W
Chiba Japan 106 D3 .....35.37N 140.07E
Chibougamau Canada 63 K2 .....49.55N 74.22W
Chicago U.S.A. 65 I5 .....41.55N 87.38W
Chichester England 10 E1 .....50.50N 0.46W
Chiclayo Peru 76 E6 .....6.44S 79.51W
Chicoutimi Canada 63 K2 .....48.26N 71.03W
Chidley, Cape Canada 63 L4 .....60.26N 64.20W
Chiemsee l. Germany 54 E2 .....47.52N 12.28E
Chieti Italy 50 F5 .....42.21N 14.10E
Chifeng China 103 L6 .....42.11N 119.02E
Chiganak Kazakhstan 58 I2 .....45.10N 73.57E
Chihuahua Mexico 70 C6 .....28.38N 106.07W
Chihuahua d. Mexico 70 C6 .....29.10N 106.11W
Chile S. America 73 B3 .....34.06S 71.23W
Chile Basin f. S. Pacific Oc. 109 O3 .....31.51S 80.03W
Chile Rise f. S. Pacific Oc. 109 O3 .....41.37S 89.56W
Chilham England 11 F2 .....51.15N 0.58E
Chillán Chile 73 B3 .....36.37S 72.07W
Chiloé, Isla de i. Chile 73 B2 .....42.26S 74.29W
Chilpancingo Mexico 70 E4 .....17.33N 99.30W
Chiltern Hills England 10 E2 .....51.39N 0.50W
Chilung Taiwan 103 M3 .....25.07N 121.43E
Chimborazo mt. Ecuador 76 E7 .....1.27S 78.50W
Chimbote Peru 76 E6 .....9.03S 78.35W
Chimoio Mozambique 86 C3 .....19.07S 33.28E
China Asia 102 H3 .....38.39N 78.40E
Chindwin r. Myanmar 97 I5 .....21.27N 95.15E
Chingola Zambia 86 B3 .....12.33S 27.54E
Chinhoyi Zimbabwe 86 C3 .....17.21S 30.11E
Chinju S. Korea 106 A3 .....35.10N 128.05E
Chinook Trough f. N. Pacific Oc. 108 I8 .....41.53N 179.40W
Chioggia Italy 50 E6 .....45.12N 12.16E
Chios Greece 56 F4 .....38.22N 26.08E
Chios i. Greece 56 F4 .....38.24N 25.58E
Chipata Zambia 86 C3 .....13.37S 32.38E
Chippenham England 10 C2 .....51.27N 2.07W
Chipping Campden England 10 D3 .....52.03N 1.47W
Chipping Norton England 10 D2 .....51.57N 1.32W
Chipping Ongar England 11 F2 .....51.42N 0.15E
Chipping Sodbury England 10 C2 .....51.32N 2.23W
Chiriquí, Golfo de b. Panama 71 H2 .....8.02N 82.04W
Chirk Wales 12 D3 .....52.56N 3.03W
Chirnside Scotland 17 G3 .....55.48N 2.12W
Chirripo mt. Costa Rica 71 H2 .....9.30N 83.30W
Chisasibi Canada 63 K3 .....53.49N 78.59W
Chişinău Moldova 53 I6 .....47.02N 28.50E
Chita Rus. Fed. 59 M3 .....51.54N 113.27E
Chitambo Zambia 86 C3 .....12.54S 30.37E
Chitradurga India 96 E3 .....14.14N 76.22E
Chitral Pakistan 96 D8 .....35.53N 71.47E
Chittagong Bangl. 97 H5 .....22.20N 91.49E
Chittoor India 96 E3 .....13.12N 79.05E
Chitungwiza Zimbabwe 86 C3 .....18.01S 31.04E
Chojnice Poland 46 C4 .....53.42N 17.34E
Cholet France 44 C5 .....47.04N 0.53W
Chomutov Czech Rep. 54 E4 .....50.28N 13.24E
Chon Buri Thailand 104 C6 .....13.22N 101.02E
Ch'ŏngjin N. Korea 103 N6 .....41.46N 129.45E
Chongqing China 103 J3 .....29.34N 106.32E
Chongqing d. China 103 J3 .....30.04N 107.39E
Chŏnju S. Korea 103 N5 .....35.51N 127.09E
Chonos, Archipiélago de los is Chile 73 B2 .....44.59S 75.31W
Chorley England 14 E2 .....53.39N 2.38W
Chornobyl' Ukraine 55 N4 .....51.16N 30.14E
Chornomors'ke Ukraine 57 J7 .....45.30N 32.43E
Chortkiv Ukraine 55 K3 .....49.01N 25.47E
Chōshi Japan 106 D3 .....35.44N 140.49E
Choszczno Poland 46 B4 .....53.10N 15.26E
Choûm Mauritania 84 C4 .....21.20N 12.59W
Choybalsan Mongolia 103 K7 .....47.51N 114.34E
Chřiby hills Czech Rep. 46 C3 .....49.05N 17.11E
Christchurch England 10 D1 .....50.44N 1.47W

Christchurch New Zealand 111 G2 .....43.31S 172.37E
Christmas Island Indian Oc. 104 D1 .....10.30S 105.44E
Chūgoku-sanchi mts Japan 106 B2 .....34.45N 132.19E
Chukchi Sea Rus. Fed./U.S.A. 59 T4 .....69.12N 171.31W
Chukotskiy Poluostrov pen. Rus. Fed. 59 T4 .....65.58N 175.16W
Chulmleigh England 13 D2 .....50.55N 3.52W
Chumba Ethiopia 87 B4 .....4.30N 38.15E
Chumphon Thailand 104 B6 .....10.31N 99.13E
Ch'unch'ŏn S. Korea 103 N5 .....37.52N 127.46E
Chunya r. Rus. Fed. 59 K4 .....61.36N 96.31E
Chur Switz. 50 C7 .....46.51N 9.32E
Churchill Canada 63 I3 .....58.44N 94.05W
Churchill r. Man. Canada 63 I3 .....58.11N 94.23W
Churchill r. Nfld. and Lab. Canada 63 L3 .....53.16N 60.14W
Churchill, Cape Canada 63 I3 .....58.45N 93.16W
Church Stretton England 10 C3 .....52.32N 2.48W
Chuuk is Micronesia 108 G5 .....7.22N 151.37E
Chuxiong China 103 I3 .....25.02N 101.32E
Chyulu Range mts Kenya 87 B2 .....2.34S 37.41E
Ciechanów Poland 46 E4 .....52.53N 20.38E
Ciego de Ávila Cuba 71 I5 .....21.50N 78.45W
Cienfuegos Cuba 71 H5 .....22.10N 80.25W
Cigüela r. Spain 48 D3 .....39.08N 3.43W
Cihanbeyli Turkey 57 J4 .....38.40N 32.56E
Cilacap Indonesia 104 D2 .....7.41S 109.00E
Cimone, Monte mt. Italy 50 D6 .....44.11N 10.42E
Cinca r. Spain 48 F4 .....41.26N 0.21E
Cincinnati U.S.A. 65 J4 .....39.06N 84.32W
Cinderford England 10 C2 .....51.49N 2.30W
Ciney Belgium 42 E3 .....50.18N 5.06E
Cinto, Monte mt. France 44 H3 .....42.23N 8.56E
Cirebon Indonesia 104 D2 .....6.45S 108.34E
Cirencester England 10 D2 .....51.43N 1.58W
Ciudad Bolívar Venezuela 72 C7 .....8.01N 63.35W
Ciudad del Carmen Mexico 70 F4 .....18.39N 91.51W
Ciudad Delicias Mexico 70 C6 .....28.10N 105.30W
Ciudad de Valles Mexico 70 E5 .....21.59N 99.00W
Ciudad Guayana Venezuela 72 C7 .....8.20N 62.37W
Ciudad Ixtepec Mexico 70 E4 .....16.35N 95.06W
Ciudad Juárez Mexico 70 C7 .....31.44N 106.28W
Ciudad Madero Mexico 70 E5 .....22.19N 97.51W
Ciudad Obregón Mexico 70 C6 .....27.28N 109.57W
Ciudad Real Spain 48 D3 .....38.59N 3.54W
Ciudad Rodrigo Spain 48 B4 .....40.36N 6.31W
Ciudad Victoria Mexico 70 E5 .....23.45N 99.08W
Ciutadella de Menorca Spain 48 G4 .....40.00N 3.52E
Civitavecchia Italy 50 D5 .....42.05N 11.48E
Çivril Turkey 57 H4 .....38.18N 29.43E
Clackmannanshire d. Scotland 8 D5 .....56.09N 3.45W
Clacton-on-Sea England 11 G2 .....51.47N 1.09E
Claonaig Scotland 16 D3 .....55.45N 5.24W
Clara Ireland 41 D3 .....53.20N 7.37W
Clare d. Ireland 41 C2 .....52.53N 8.50W
Clare r. Ireland 41 B3 .....53.19N 9.03W
Clare Island Ireland 41 A3 .....53.49N 10.01W
Claremorris Ireland 41 C3 .....53.44N 8.59W
Clarksville U.S.A. 65 I4 .....36.32N 87.20W
Claro r. Brazil 77 J4 .....19.07S 50.39W
Clay Cross England 15 F2 .....53.10N 1.25W
Claydon England 11 G3 .....52.06N 1.07E
Clay Head Isle of Man 14 C3 .....54.12N 4.23W
Clayton U.S.A. 64 F4 .....36.28N 103.12W
Clear, Cape Ireland 41 B1 .....51.26N 9.31W
Clear Island Ireland 41 B1 .....51.26N 9.28W
Cleator Moor England 14 D3 .....54.31N 3.31W
Cleethorpes England 15 G2 .....53.33N 0.02W
Cleobury Mortimer England 10 C3 .....52.23N 2.29W
Clermont France 42 B2 .....49.23N 2.25E
Clermont-Ferrand France 44 E4 .....45.46N 3.05E
Clevedon England 10 C2 .....51.26N 2.51W
Cleveland U.S.A. 65 J5 .....41.30N 81.41W
Cleveland Hills England 15 F3 .....54.22N 1.13W
Cleveleys England 14 D2 .....53.53N 3.02W
Clew Bay Ireland 41 B3 .....53.48N 9.47W
Cliffe England 11 F2 .....51.28N 0.30E
Clinton U.S.A. 64 G4 .....35.32N 98.58W
Clipperton, Île N. Pacific Oc. 109 M6 .....10.21N 109.19W
Clisham hill Scotland 18 C2 .....57.58N 6.49W
Clitheroe England 15 E2 .....53.52N 2.23W
Clogher Head Ireland 41 E3 .....53.48N 6.13W
Clonakilty Ireland 41 C1 .....51.37N 8.53W
Clones Ireland 41 D4 .....54.10N 7.13W
Clonmel Ireland 41 D2 .....52.21N 7.43W
Cloud Peak U.S.A. 64 E5 .....44.24N 107.01W
Clovis U.S.A. 64 F3 .....34.27N 103.12W
Cluanie, Loch l. Scotland 18 D2 .....57.09N 5.07W
Cluj-Napoca Romania 55 J2 .....46.46N 23.36E
Clun England 10 B3 .....52.25N 3.02W
Clydach Wales 12 D3 .....51.42N 3.54W
Clyde r. Scotland 16 F3 .....55.55N 4.29W
Clyde, Firth of est. Scotland 16 E3 .....55.25N 4.59W
Clydebank Scotland 16 E3 .....55.54N 4.24W
Clyde River town Canada 63 L5 .....70.23N 68.31W
Coahuila d. Mexico 70 D6 .....27.30N 102.24W
Coalville England 10 D3 .....52.43N 1.22W
Coari Brazil 76 H7 .....4.08S 63.07W
Coari r. Brazil 76 H7 .....4.26S 63.30W
Coast d. Kenya 87 C2 .....2.40S 40.07E
Coastal Plain f. U.S.A. 65 H3 .....30.25N 94.23W
Coast Mountains Canada 62 D3 .....52.40N 127.48W
Coast Ranges mts U.S.A. 64 B5 .....40.40N 123.39W
Coatbridge Scotland 17 F3 .....55.52N 4.01W
Coats Island Canada 63 J4 .....62.41N 82.53W
Coatzacoalcos Mexico 70 F4 .....18.08N 94.26W
Cobh Ireland 41 C1 .....51.51N 8.18W
Cobija Bolivia 76 G6 .....11.03S 68.47W
Cochabamba Bolivia 76 G4 .....17.25S 66.11W
Cochin India 96 E2 .....9.55N 76.14E
Cochrane Canada 65 J6 .....49.04N 81.03W
Cockburnspath Scotland 17 G3 .....55.56N 2.22W
Cockermouth England 14 D3 .....54.40N 3.22W
Coco r. Honduras/Nicaragua 71 H3 .....14.59N 83.15W
Coco, Isla de i. N. Pacific Oc. 60 K2 .....5.32N 87.04W
Cocos Basin f. Indian Oc. 108 C6 .....0.02N 91.02E
Cocos Islands Indian Oc. 104 B1 .....11.56S 96.54E
Cocos Ridge f. N. Pacific Oc. 109 O6 .....0.42N 89.55W
Cocuy, Sierra Nevada del mt. Colombia 71 J2 .....6.28N 72.19W
Cod, Cape U.S.A. 65 L5 .....41.58N 70.01W
Coddington England 15 G2 .....53.05N 0.45W
Codó Brazil 77 L7 .....4.28S 43.50W
Codsall England 10 C3 .....52.38N 2.11W
Coeur d'Alene U.S.A. 64 C6 .....47.41N 116.47W
Coffs Harbour Australia 110 E3 .....30.19S 153.06E
Coggeshall England 11 F2 .....51.52N 0.42E
Coiba, Isla de i. Panama 71 H2 .....7.27N 81.51W
Coigeach, Rubha pt Scotland 18 D3 .....58.06N 5.28W
Coihaique Chile 73 B2 .....45.36S 72.05W
Coimbatore India 96 E3 .....10.59N 76.57E
Coimbra Portugal 48 A4 .....40.13N 8.25W
Coipasa, Salar de f. Bolivia 76 G4 .....19.26S 68.07W
Colatina Brazil 77 L4 .....19.35S 40.38W
Colchester England 11 F2 .....51.53N 0.54E
Coldstream Scotland 17 G3 .....55.39N 2.15W
Coleford England 10 C2 .....51.48N 2.37W

Coleraine Northern Ireland 16 C3 .....55.08N 6.40W
Coleraine d. Northern Ireland 8 B4 .....54.58N 6.41W
Colima Mexico 70 D4 .....19.14N 103.45W
Colima d. Mexico 70 D4 .....19.03N 103.59W
Colima, Nevado de vol. Mexico 70 D4 .....19.33N 103.37W
Coll i. Scotland 18 C1 .....56.36N 6.36W
Collier Bay Australia 110 B5 .....16.15S 124.15E
Colmar France 44 G6 .....48.05N 7.21E
Colne England 15 E2 .....53.51N 2.11W
Colne r. England 11 F2 .....51.51N 0.57E
Cologne Germany 54 B4 .....50.56N 6.57E
Colombia S. America 72 B7 .....3.45N 72.22W
Colombo Sri Lanka 96 E2 .....6.56N 79.50E
Colón Panama 71 I2 .....9.22N 79.55W
Colonsay i. Scotland 16 C4 .....56.05N 6.15W
Colorado r. Argentina 73 C3 .....39.42S 62.07W
Colorado r. Mexico/U.S.A. 64 C3 .....31.56N 115.01W
Colorado d. U.S.A. 64 E4 .....39.02N 105.31W
Colorado r. U.S.A. 64 G2 .....28.40N 96.01W
Colorado Plateau f. U.S.A. 64 E4 .....37.27N 109.54W
Colorado Springs town U.S.A. 64 F4 .....38.52N 104.47W
Coltishall England 11 G3 .....52.44N 1.22E
Columbia r. U.S.A. 65 J3 .....33.59N 81.01W
Columbia r. U.S.A. 64 B6 .....46.11N 123.23W
Columbia, Mount Canada 62 G3 .....52.08N 117.25W
Columbus Ga. U.S.A. 65 J3 .....32.32N 84.59W
Columbus Miss. U.S.A. 65 I3 .....33.33N 88.25W
Columbus Oh. U.S.A. 65 J4 .....39.58N 83.00W
Colville r. U.S.A. 60 C4 .....70.20N 150.32W
Colwyn Bay town Wales 12 D5 .....53.18N 3.43W
Comacchio Italy 50 E6 .....44.41N 12.11E
Combe Martin England 13 C3 .....51.12N 4.01W
Comber Northern Ireland 16 D2 .....54.33N 5.44W
Comeragh Mountains Ireland 41 D2 .....52.18N 7.39W
Como Italy 50 C6 .....45.48N 9.05E
Como, Lake Italy 50 C6 .....45.57N 9.11E
Comodoro Rivadavia Argentina 73 C2 .....45.56S 67.30W
Comorin, Cape India 90 G3 .....8.04N 77.35E
Comoros Africa 86 D3 .....11.50S 44.17E
Compiègne France 42 B2 .....49.25N 2.50E
Comrat Moldova 57 H8 .....46.18N 28.40E
Comrie Scotland 17 F4 .....56.23N 3.59W
Conakry Guinea 84 C2 .....9.31N 13.42W
Concarneau France 44 B5 .....47.53N 3.55W
Concepción Argentina 76 G2 .....27.18S 65.38W
Concepción Chile 73 B3 .....36.50S 73.04W
Conception, Point U.S.A. 64 B3 .....34.27N 120.26W
Conchos r. Mexico 70 D6 .....29.35N 104.29W
Concord U.S.A. 65 L5 .....43.12N 71.33W
Concordia Argentina 73 D3 .....31.24S 57.59W
Condor, Cordillera del mts Ecuador/Peru 76 E7 .....4.17S 78.34W
Congleton England 15 E2 .....53.10N 2.13W
Congo Africa 84 F1 .....2.24S 15.10E
Congo r. Congo/Dem. Rep. Congo 86 A4 .....6.05S 12.26E
Congo, Democratic Republic of the Africa 86 B4 .....3.43S 22.17E
Congo Basin f. Africa 80 E5 .....1.00S 20.00E
Coningsby England 15 G2 .....53.06N 0.10W
Coniston England 14 D3 .....54.22N 3.05W
Coniston Water l. England 14 D3 .....54.19N 3.04W
Conn, Lough l. Ireland 41 B4 .....54.01N 9.16W
Connah's Quay Wales 12 D5 .....53.13N 3.04W
Connecticut d. U.S.A. 65 L5 .....41.41N 72.36W
Connecticut r. U.S.A. 65 L5 .....41.16N 72.22W
Connemara f. Ireland 41 B3 .....53.28N 9.52W
Conon Bridge Scotland 19 E2 .....57.34N 4.26W
Consett England 15 F3 .....54.51N 1.50W
Con Son i. Vietnam 104 D5 .....8.42N 106.40E
Constance, Lake Germany/Switz. 54 C2 .....47.40N 9.17E
Constanţa Romania 57 H7 .....44.11N 28.37E
Constantine Algeria 84 E5 .....36.23N 6.38E
Conwy Wales 12 D5 .....53.17N 3.50W
Conwy d. Wales 9 D3 .....53.10N 3.37W
Conwy r. Wales 12 D5 .....53.14N 3.48W
Conwy Bay Wales 12 C5 .....53.16N 4.02W
Cook, Mount New Zealand 111 G2 .....43.37S 170.08E
Cook Islands S. Pacific Oc. 108 J4 .....20.05S 160.06W
Cookstown Northern Ireland 16 C2 .....54.39N 6.44W
Cookstown d. Northern Ireland 9 B4 .....54.39N 6.44W
Cook Strait New Zealand 111 G2 .....40.32S 174.01E
Cooktown Australia 110 D5 .....15.28S 145.17E
Coolangatta Australia 110 E4 .....28.10S 153.31E
Cooper Creek watercourse Australia 110 C4 .....28.29S 137.43E
Coos Bay town U.S.A. 64 B5 .....43.21N 124.12W
Copenhagen Denmark 40 C1 .....55.40N 12.34E
Copiapó Chile 73 B3 .....27.18S 70.23W
Copinsay i. Scotland 19 G3 .....58.54N 2.40W
Coquimbo Chile 76 F2 .....29.58S 71.20W
Corabia Romania 56 F6 .....43.47N 24.29E
Coral Harbour Canada 63 J4 .....64.12N 83.19W
Coral Sea S. Pacific Oc. 110 E5 .....13.27S 151.06E
Coral Sea Basin f. S. Pacific Oc. 108 G5 .....13.23S 152.14E
Coral Sea Islands Territory Australia 110 E5 .....15.01S 150.43E
Corbie France 42 B2 .....49.55N 2.31E
Corbridge England 15 E3 .....54.58N 2.01W
Corby England 10 E3 .....52.29N 0.41W
Córdoba Argentina 73 C3 .....31.24S 64.11W
Córdoba Mexico 70 E4 .....18.55N 96.53W
Córdoba Spain 48 C2 .....37.53N 4.46W
Córdoba, Sierras de mts Argentina 73 C3 .....32.55S 64.22W
Corfe Castle England 10 C1 .....50.38N 2.03W
Corfu i. Greece 56 C4 .....39.36N 19.47E
Corigliano Calabro Italy 50 G3 .....39.35N 16.32E
Corinth Greece 56 E3 .....37.56N 22.55E
Corixa Grande r. Bolivia/Brazil 77 I4 .....17.30S 57.56W
Cork Ireland 41 C1 .....51.54N 8.28W
Cork d. Ireland 41 C2 .....52.01N 8.39W
Çorlu Turkey 57 G5 .....41.09N 27.48E
Corner Brook Canada 63 M2 .....48.54N 57.47W
Corno, Monte mt. Italy 50 E5 .....42.28N 13.34E
Cornwall d. England 9 C1 .....50.32N 4.33W
Cornwall, Cape England 13 B2 .....50.08N 5.47W
Cornwallis Island Canada 63 I5 .....75.08N 94.56W
Coro Venezuela 72 C8 .....11.23N 69.40W
Coronado, Bahía de b. Costa Rica 71 H2 .....8.55N 83.48W
Coronation Gulf Canada 62 G4 .....68.08N 112.32W
Coronel Oviedo Paraguay 77 I2 .....25.21S 56.27W
Corpus Christi U.S.A. 64 G2 .....27.44N 97.27W
Corral de Cantos mt. Spain 48 C3 .....39.34N 4.27W
Corrente Brazil 77 K5 .....10.28S 45.07W
Corrib, Lough l. Ireland 41 B3 .....53.27N 9.19W
Corrientes Argentina 73 D3 .....27.27S 58.46W
Corrientes r. Argentina 77 I1 .....30.25S 59.35W
Corrientes, Cabo c. Mexico 70 C5 .....20.26N 105.42W
Corse, Cap c. France 44 H3 .....43.02N 9.22E
Corserine hill Scotland 16 E3 .....55.09N 4.21W
Corsham England 10 C2 .....51.26N 2.11W
Corsica i. France 44 H3 .....42.20N 8.29E
Corte France 44 H3 .....42.18N 9.09E
Cortegana Spain 48 B2 .....37.55N 6.49W
Cortina d'Ampezzo Italy 50 E7 .....46.32N 12.09E
Corton England 11 G3 .....52.31N 1.45E
Çorum Turkey 57 K5 .....40.33N 34.57E
Corumbá Brazil 77 I4 .....19.00S 57.37W
Corwen Wales 12 D4 .....52.59N 3.22W

Cosenza Italy 50 G3 ....39.18N 16.15E
Cosmoledo Islands Seychelles 86 D4 ....9.30S 49.00E
Cosne-Cours-sur-Loire France 44 E5 ....47.25N 2.56E
Costa Blanca f. Spain 48 E3 ....38.03N 0.20W
Costa Brava f. Spain 48 G4 ....41.28N 3.05E
Costa del Sol f. Spain 48 C2 ....36.25N 5.06W
Costa de Mosquitos f. Nicaragua 71 H3 ...12.08N 83.52W
Costa Rica Central America 71 H3 ....10.08N 84.19W
Cotabato Phil. 105 G5 ....7.13N 124.14E
Côte d'Azur f. France 44 G3 ....43.33N 7.13E
Côte d'Ivoire Africa 84 D2 ....7.35N 4.22W
Cothi r. Wales 12 C3 ....51.52N 4.10W
Cotonou Benin 84 E2 ....6.21N 2.27E
Cotopaxi, Volcán vol. Ecuador 76 E7 ....0.39S 78.26W
Cotswold Hills England 10 C2 ....51.36N 2.15W
Cottbus Germany 54 F4 ....51.45N 14.21E
Cottenham England 11 F3 ....52.17N 0.08E
Cottesmore England 10 E3 ....52.43N 0.40W
Coulogne France 42 A3 ....50.55N 1.53E
Coupar Angus Scotland 17 F4 ....56.33N 3.16W
Courland Lagoon b. Lithuania/Rus. Fed. 40 E1 ..55.16N 21.06E
Coutances France 44 C6 ....49.03N 1.27W
Coventry England 10 D3 ....52.24N 1.31W
Covilhã Portugal 48 B4 ....40.17N 7.29W
Cowan, Lake Australia 110 B3 ....31.45S 121.59E
Cowbridge Wales 13 D3 ....51.28N 3.27W
Cowdenbeath Scotland 17 F4 ....56.07N 3.20W
Cowes England 10 D1 ....50.46N 1.18W
Cowfold England 11 E1 ....50.59N 0.16W
Cow Green Reservoir England 15 E3 ....54.40N 2.20W
Coxim Brazil 77 J4 ....18.30S 54.44W
Cox's Bazar Bangl. 97 H5 ....21.27N 91.59E
Cozumel, Isla de i. Mexico 70 G5 ....20.22N 86.53W
Craig U.S.A. 64 E5 ....40.31N 107.32W
Craigavon Northern Ireland 16 C2 ....54.26N 6.21W
Craigavon d. Northern Ireland 9 B4 ....54.29N 6.22W
Craig Goch Reservoir Wales 12 D4 ....52.19N 3.37W
Craignure Scotland 16 D4 ....56.28N 5.43W
Crail Scotland 17 G4 ....56.16N 2.38W
Craiova Romania 56 E7 ....44.19N 23.48E
Cramlington England 15 F4 ....55.05N 1.35W
Cranbrook Canada 62 G2 ....49.32N 115.45W
Cranleigh England 11 E2 ....51.08N 0.29W
Crawley England 11 E2 ....51.07N 0.11W
Creag Meagaidh mt. Scotland 19 E1 ......56.57N 4.36W
Credenhill England 10 C3 ....52.05N 2.48W
Crediton England 13 D2 ....50.48N 3.39W
Cree r. Scotland 16 D2 ....54.52N 4.21W
Cree Lake Canada 62 H3 ....57.31N 106.29W
Creil France 42 B2 ....49.16N 2.29E
Cremona Italy 50 D6 ....45.08N 10.01E
Crépy-en-Valois France 42 B2 ....49.14N 2.53E
Cres i. Croatia 56 A7 ....44.51N 14.28E
Crescent City U.S.A. 64 B5 ....41.47N 124.09W
Creston U.S.A. 65 H5 ....41.03N 94.22W
Creswell England 15 F2 ....53.16N 1.13W
Crete i. Greece 56 F2 ....35.28N 24.41E
Creuse r. France 44 D5 ....47.00N 0.34E
Crewe England 15 E2 ....53.06N 2.26W
Crewkerne England 10 C1 ....50.53N 2.48W
Crianlarich Scotland 16 E4 ....56.24N 4.37W
Criccieth Wales 12 C4 ....52.55N 4.14W
Criciúma Brazil 77 K2 ....28.45S 49.25W
Crickhowell Wales 12 D3 ....51.51N 3.08W
Crieff Scotland 17 F4 ....56.23N 3.50W
Criffel hill Scotland 17 F2 ....54.57N 3.38W
Crimea pen. Ukraine 53 J6 ....45.20N 34.05E
Crimond Scotland 19 H2 ....57.36N 1.55W
Croatia Europe 56 B7 ....45.02N 15.14E
Croisilles France 11 H1 ....50.12N 2.53E
Croker Island Australia 105 I1 ....11.04S 132.38E
Cromarty Scotland 19 E2 ....57.41N 4.02W
Cromarty Firth est. Scotland 19 E2 ....57.38N 4.19W
Cromdale, Hills of Scotland 19 F2 ....57.19N 3.31W
Cromer England 11 G3 ....52.56N 1.18E
Cronamuck Mountain hill Ireland 16 B2 ...54.54N 7.51W
Crook England 15 F3 ....54.43N 1.45W
Crooked Island Bahamas 71 J5 ....22.48N 74.14W
Crooked Island Passage str. Bahamas 71 J5 ..22.29N 74.55W
Croom Ireland 41 C2 ....52.31N 8.43W
Crosby England 14 D2 ....53.29N 3.02W
Cross Fell hill England 15 E3 ....54.42N 2.29W
Crossgar Northern Ireland 16 D2 ....54.24N 5.45W
Crossmaglen Northern Ireland 16 C2 .....54.04N 6.36W
Crotone Italy 50 G3 ....39.05N 17.08E
Crouch r. England 11 F2 ....51.38N 0.36E
Crowborough England 11 F2 ....51.04N 0.10E
Crowland England 11 E3 ....52.41N 0.10W
Crowle England 15 G2 ....53.37N 0.50W
Crowthorne England 10 E2 ....51.22N 0.48W
Croyde England 13 C3 ....51.08N 4.13W
Croydon England 11 E2 ....51.23N 0.06W
Crozet Islands Indian Oc. 117 L3 ....47.00S 52.00E
Cruden Bay town Scotland 19 H2 ....57.25N 1.51W
Crumlin Northern Ireland 16 C2 ....54.38N 6.13W
Cruz, Cabo c. Cuba 71 I4 ....19.51N 77.43W
Cruzeiro do Sul Brazil 76 F6 ....7.41S 72.40W
Cuando r. Angola/Zambia 86 B3 ....17.39S 23.24E
Cuanza r. Angola 86 A4 ....9.21S 13.08E
Cuauhtémoc Mexico 70 C6 ....28.24N 106.53W
Cuba Central America 71 H5 ....21.18N 80.06W
Cubango r. Angola/Namibia 86 B3 ....18.01S 21.26E
Cuckfield England 11 E2 ....51.00N 0.09W
Cúcuta Colombia 72 B7 ....7.53N 72.31W
Cuddalore India 96 E3 ....11.42N 79.43E
Cuddapah India 96 E3 ....14.29N 78.48E
Cuenca Ecuador 76 E7 ....2.53S 79.00W
Cuenca Spain 48 D4 ....40.04N 2.08W
Cuenca, Serranía de mts Spain 48 D4 ....40.38N 2.08W
Cuernavaca Mexico 70 E4 ....18.56N 99.11W
Cuiabá Brazil 77 I4 ....15.33S 56.04W
Cuiabá r. Brazil 77 I4 ....17.19S 56.41W
Cuilcagh hill Ireland/U.K. 16 B2 ....54.12N 7.49W
Cuillin Hills Scotland 18 C2 ....57.14N 6.17W
Cuillin Sound str. Scotland 18 C2 ....57.08N 6.21W
Culiacán Mexico 70 C5 ....24.47N 107.24W
Cullen Scotland 19 G2 ....57.41N 2.49W
Cullera Spain 48 E3 ....39.10N 0.13W
Cullompton England 13 D2 ....50.51N 3.23W
Cullybackey Northern Ireland 16 C2 ......54.53N 6.21W
Cul Mòr hill Scotland 18 D3 ....58.03N 5.07W
Culuene r. Brazil 77 J5 ....11.11S 53.09W
Culzean Bay Scotland 16 E3 ....55.22N 4.49W
Cumaná Venezuela 72 C8 ....10.24N 64.09W
Cumbal, Nevado de vol. Colombia 76 E8 ...0.57N 77.51W
Cumberland r. U.S.A. 65 I4 ....36.30N 87.49W
Cumberland Sound str. Canada 63 L4 ....64.08N 63.14W
Cumbernauld Scotland 17 F3 ....55.57N 3.59W
Cumbria d. England 9 D4 ....54.42N 3.17W
Cumnock Scotland 16 E3 ....55.27N 4.16W
Cunene r. Angola 86 A3 ....17.15S 11.46E
Cuneo Italy 50 B6 ....44.24N 7.33E
Cupar Scotland 17 F4 ....56.19N 3.01W
Cupica, Golfo de b. Colombia 71 I2 ....06.35N 77.46W
Curaçao i. Neth. Antilles 71 K3 ....12.12N 69.04W

Curaray r. Ecuador 76 F7 ....2.25S 74.06W
Curitiba Brazil 77 K2 ....25.28S 49.17W
Curuá r. Brazil 77 J6 ....5.25S 54.21W
Cusco Peru 76 F5 ....13.31S 71.59W
Cushendall Northern Ireland 16 C3 ....55.05N 6.04W
Cuttack India 96 G5 ....20.27N 85.55E
Cuxhaven Germany 54 C5 ....53.52N 8.42E
Cuyo Islands Phil. 105 G6 ....11.11N 121.10E
Cwmbrân Wales 13 D3 ....51.39N 3.02W
Cyclades is Greece 56 F3 ....37.14N 24.37E
Cyprus Asia 57 J2 ....35.38N 33.17E
Cyrenaica f. Libya 53 H3 ....31.06N 22.24E
Czech Republic Europe 54 F3 ....49.38N 15.37E
Czersk Poland 46 C4 ....53.48N 17.59E
Częstochowa Poland 46 D3 ....50.48N 19.07E

D

Dąbrowa Górnicza Poland 46 D3 ....50.21N 19.15E
Dachau Germany 54 D3 ....48.15N 11.27E
Dagupan Phil. 104 G7 ....16.04N 120.21E
Da Hinggan Ling mts China 103 L6 ....43.33N 117.52E
Dahlak Archipelago is Eritrea 94 F3 ....15.58N 40.04E
Dahm, Ramlat des. Saudi Arabia/Yemen 94 G3 ...17.09N 45.00E
Dailly Scotland 16 E3 ....55.17N 4.43W
Dakar Senegal 84 C3 ....14.43N 17.28W
Dakhla Oasis Egypt 94 C5 ....25.25N 28.53E
Dakol'ka r. Belarus 55 M5 ....52.08N 28.52E
Dalaman Turkey 57 H3 ....36.47N 28.48E
Đa Lat Vietnam 104 D6 ....11.56N 108.26E
Dalbandin Pakistan 95 J5 ....28.56N 64.30E
Dalbeattie Scotland 17 F2 ....54.56N 3.49W
Dali China 103 I3 ....25.33N 100.13E
Dalian China 103 M5 ....38.51N 121.37E
Dalkeith Scotland 17 F3 ....55.54N 3.04W
Dallas U.S.A. 64 G3 ....32.46N 96.48W
Dalmally Scotland 16 E4 ....56.24N 4.58W
Dalmatia f. Bos.-Herz./Croatia 56 A7 ....44.01N 15.30E
Dalmellington Scotland 16 E3 ....55.19N 4.24W
Dal'negorsk Rus. Fed. 106 C4 ....44.28N 135.30E
Daloa Côte d'Ivoire 84 D2 ....6.54N 6.28W
Dalry Scotland 16 E3 ....55.43N 4.43W
Dalrymple Scotland 16 E3 ....55.24N 4.35W
Dalrymple, Mount Australia 110 D4 ....20.59S 148.37E
Dalton U.S.A. 65 J3 ....34.49N 84.56W
Dalton-in-Furness England 14 D3 ....54.09N 3.11W
Daly r. Australia 110 C5 ....13.31S 130.28E
Daman India 96 D5 ....20.24N 72.58E
Damanhûr Egypt 53 J3 ....31.02N 30.28E
Damar i. Indonesia 105 H2 ....7.08S 128.32E
Damaraland f. Namibia 86 A2 ....21.58S 17.06E
Damascus Syria 94 E6 ....33.30N 36.20E
Damāvand, Qolleh-ye mt. Iran 95 H7 ....35.58N 52.07E
Damghan Iran 95 H7 ....36.09N 54.19E
Dammam Saudi Arabia 95 H5 ....26.24N 50.10E
Dampier Australia 110 A4 ....20.41S 116.47E
Dampir, Selat str. Indonesia 105 I3 ....0.40S 130.43E
Đa Năng Vietnam 104 D7 ....16.01N 108.12E
Dande Ethiopia 87 B4 ....4.44N 36.25E
Dandong China 103 M6 ....40.06N 124.22E
Dane r. England 15 E2 ....53.15N 2.31W
Danger Island Indian Oc. 108 A5 ....6.24S 71.17E
Danube r. Bulgaria/Croatia/Serbia 53 I6 ..45.26N 29.38E
Danube Delta Romania/Ukraine 57 H7 ...45.11N 29.13E
Danville U.S.A. 65 K4 ....36.35N 79.24W
Dapaong Togo 84 E3 ....10.53N 0.15E
Da Qaidam Zhen China 102 H5 ....37.49N 95.18E
Daqing China 103 N7 ....46.28N 125.01E
Dar'ā Syria 94 E6 ....32.38N 36.07E
Dārāb Iran 95 H5 ....28.45N 54.32E
Darabani Romania 55 L3 ....48.11N 26.36E
Daraj Libya 84 F5 ....30.10N 10.29E
Darbhanga India 96 G6 ....26.10N 85.57E
Dardanelles str. Turkey 56 G5 ....40.12N 26.25E
Dar es Salaam Tanzania 86 C4 ....6.48S 39.16E
Darhan Mongolia 103 J7 ....49.23N 105.49E
Darién, Golfo del g. Colombia 72 B7 .....8.56N 77.01W
Darjiling India 96 G6 ....27.02N 88.19E
Darling r. Australia 110 D3 ....34.05S 141.56E
Darling Downs hills Australia 110 D4 ....27.58S 149.54E
Darlington England 15 F3 ....54.31N 1.33W
Darlington d. England 9 E4 ....54.33N 1.34W
Darmstadt Germany 44 H6 ....49.52N 8.38E
Darnah Libya 85 G5 ....32.42N 22.40E
Dart r. England 13 D2 ....50.25N 3.39W
Dartford England 11 F2 ....51.27N 0.13E
Dartmoor hills England 13 C2 ....50.36N 4.01W
Dartmouth Canada 65 N5 ....44.41N 63.35W
Dartmouth England 13 D2 ....50.21N 3.35W
Darton England 15 F2 ....53.35N 1.31W
Daru P.N.G. 105 K2 ....9.03S 143.12E
Darwen England 15 E2 ....53.42N 2.28W
Darwin Australia 110 C5 ....12.27S 130.51E
Datong China 103 K6 ....40.03N 113.20E
Daud Khel Pakistan 95 L6 ....32.51N 71.37E
Daugava r. Latvia 40 F2 ....57.03N 24.04E
Daugavpils Latvia 40 F1 ....55.53N 26.31E
Dauphin Canada 62 H3 ....51.09N 100.02W
Dauphiné f. France 44 F4 ....45.22N 5.07E
Davangere India 96 E3 ....14.27N 75.51E
Davao Phil. 105 H5 ....6.57N 125.34E
Davao Gulf Phil. 105 H5 ....6.22N 125.49E
Davenport U.S.A. 65 H5 ....41.32N 90.33W
Daventry England 10 D3 ....52.15N 1.10W
David Panama 71 H2 ....8.27N 82.25W
Davis Strait Canada/Greenland 63 M4 ...63.48N 56.19W
Davos Switz. 50 C7 ....46.48N 9.49E
Dawa Wenz r. Ethiopia 87 C4 ....4.11N 42.08E
Dawlish England 13 D2 ....50.35N 3.28W
Dawqah Oman 95 H3 ....18.37N 54.04E
Dawson Canada 62 E4 ....64.04N 139.24W
Daxian China 103 J4 ....31.05N 107.26E
Dayr az Zawr Syria 94 F7 ....35.19N 40.06E
Dayton U.S.A. 65 J4 ....39.45N 84.11W
Daytona Beach town U.S.A. 65 J2 ....29.08N 81.05W
Dazhou China 103 J4 ....31.12N 107.28E
Dead Sea l. Asia 94 E6 ....31.08N 35.27E
Deal England 11 G2 ....51.13N 1.24E
Dean, Forest of England 10 C2 ....51.48N 2.32W
Dearne r. England 15 F2 ....53.29N 1.14W
Death Valley U.S.A. 64 C4 ....36.34N 117.01W
Debak Malaysia 104 E4 ....1.31N 111.29E
Debar Macedonia 56 D5 ....41.31N 20.31E
Debenham England 11 G3 ....52.14N 1.11E
Debrecen Hungary 55 I2 ....47.32N 21.37E
Debre Zeyit Ethiopia 85 H2 ....8.45N 38.57E
Decatur U.S.A. 65 I3 ....34.37N 86.59W
Deccan f. India 96 E4 ....18.40N 77.65E
Děčín Czech Rep. 54 F4 ....50.47N 14.13E
Dee r. Scotland 19 G2 ....57.09N 2.05W
Dee r. Wales 12 D5 ....53.13N 3.01W

Dee est. Wales 12 D5 ....53.18N 3.09W
Deele r. Ireland 16 B2 ....54.51N 7.28W
Degodia f. Ethiopia 87 C4 ....4.13N 41.24E
De Grey r. Australia 110 A4 ....20.19S 119.14E
Dehra Dun India 96 E7 ....30.20N 78.05E
Dej Romania 55 J2 ....47.09N 23.53E
Delano Peak U.S.A. 64 D4 ....38.23N 112.21W
Delap-Uliga-Djarrit Marshall Is 108 H6 ...7.07N 171.22E
Delārām Afgh. 95 J6 ....32.11N 63.28E
Delaware d. U.S.A. 65 K4 ....38.58N 75.28W
Delft Neth. 42 D5 ....52.01N 4.21E
Delfzijl Neth. 42 F6 ....53.20N 6.55E
Delgado, Cabo c. Mozambique 86 D3 ....10.41S 40.36E
Delhi India 96 E6 ....28.38N 77.17E
Delhi d. India 102 D3 ....28.38N 77.08E
Delice r. Turkey 57 K5 ....40.31N 34.13E
Del Rio U.S.A. 64 F2 ....29.21N 100.54W
Demanda, Sierra de la mts Spain 48 D5 ...42.13N 3.27W
Deming U.S.A. 64 E3 ....32.16N 107.45W
Demirci Turkey 57 H4 ....39.02N 28.39E
Demirkazık Tepe mt. Turkey 57 K3 ....37.48N 35.09E
Demmin Germany 46 A4 ....53.54N 13.03E
Dempo, Gunung vol. Indonesia 104 C3 ...4.02S 103.06E
Denakil f. Africa 85 I3 ....14.27N 40.44E
Denbigh Wales 12 D5 ....53.11N 3.25W
Denbighshire d. Wales 9 D3 ....53.06N 3.20W
Den Burg Neth. 42 D6 ....53.03N 4.49E
Dendermonde Belgium 42 D4 ....51.01N 4.07E
Den Helder Neth. 42 D5 ....52.58N 4.46E
Denizli Turkey 57 H3 ....37.45N 29.05E
Denmark Europe 40 B2 ....56.13N 10.09E
Denmark Strait Greenland/Iceland 63 P4 ...66.11N 28.09W
Denny Scotland 17 F4 ....56.01N 3.54W
Denpasar Indonesia 104 F2 ....8.39S 115.14E
Denton U.S.A. 64 G3 ....33.15N 97.08W
D'Entrecasteaux Islands P.N.G. 110 E6 ...9.38S 151.02E
Denver U.S.A. 64 E4 ....39.45N 105.02W
Dêqên China 103 H3 ....28.26N 98.50E
Dera Ghazi Khan Pakistan 96 D7 ....30.05N 70.44E
Dera Ismail Khan Pakistan 96 D7 ....31.51N 70.56E
Derby Australia 110 B5 ....17.19S 123.38E
Derby England 10 D3 ....52.55N 1.28W
Derby d. England 9 E3 ....52.55N 1.28W
Derbyshire d. England 9 E3 ....53.11N 1.36W
Dereham England 11 F3 ....52.41N 0.56E
Derg r. Ireland/U.K. 41 D4 ....54.44N 7.26W
Derg, Lough l. Don. Ireland 41 D4 ....54.37N 7.51W
Derg, Lough l. Tipp. Ireland 41 C3 ....52.54N 8.28W
Derry d. Northern Ireland 8 B4 ....54.56N 7.10W
Derry r. Ireland 41 E2 ....52.41N 6.40W
Derryveagh Mountains Ireland 41 C4 ....54.56N 8.14W
Dersingham England 11 F3 ....52.51N 0.31E
Dêrub China 102 D4 ....33.25N 79.46E
Derudeb Sudan 94 E3 ....17.38N 36.05E
Derwent r. England 15 F2 ....53.45N 0.58W
Derwent Reservoir Derbys. England 15 F2 ...53.25N 1.44W
Derwent Reservoir Dur. England 15 F3 ...54.52N 1.58W
Derwent Water l. England 14 D3 ....54.34N 3.10W
Desaguadero r. Argentina 73 C3 ....34.03S 66.43W
Desaguadero r. Bolivia 76 G4 ....16.40S 69.01W
Désappointement, Îles du is French Polynesia 109 K5 ...13.59S 141.06W
Desē Ethiopia 85 H3 ....11.07N 39.38E
Deseado Argentina 73 C2 ....47.45S 65.55W
Des Moines U.S.A. 65 H5 ....41.36N 93.37W
Des Moines r. U.S.A. 65 H5 ....40.23N 91.28W
Desna r. Rus. Fed./Ukraine 55 M3 ....49.19N 28.31E
Desna r. Rus. Fed./Ukraine 55 N4 ....50.32N 30.33E
Dessau Germany 54 E4 ....51.50N 12.15E
Detroit U.S.A. 65 J5 ....42.19N 83.04W
Deva Romania 56 E7 ....45.54N 22.55E
Deveron r. Scotland 19 G2 ....57.40N 2.31W
Devét Skal hill Czech Rep. 46 C2 ....49.40N 16.02E
Devil's Bit Mountain hill Ireland 41 D2 ...52.49N 7.55W
Devil's Bridge Wales 12 D4 ....52.23N 3.51W
Devil's Lake town U.S.A. 64 G6 ....48.02N 98.46W
Devizes England 10 D2 ....51.21N 1.59W
Devon d. England 9 D2 ....50.32N 3.51W
Devon r. England 15 G2 ....53.04N 0.50W
Devon r. Scotland 17 F4 ....56.07N 3.51W
Devon Island Canada 63 I5 ....75.20N 91.06W
Devonport Australia 110 D2 ....41.11S 146.20E
Devrez r. Turkey 57 K5 ....41.27N 35.01E
Dewsbury England 15 F2 ....53.41N 1.38W
Dezfûl Iran 95 G6 ....32.22N 48.24E
Dezhou China 103 L5 ....37.25N 116.19E
Dhahran Saudi Arabia 95 H5 ....26.19N 50.07E
Dhaka Bangl. 97 H5 ....23.43N 90.24E
Dhamār Yemen 94 F2 ....14.34N 44.26E
Dhanbad India 96 G5 ....23.47N 86.25E
Dharwad India 96 E4 ....15.27N 75.04E
Dhaulagiri mt. Nepal 96 F6 ....28.40N 83.28E
Dhule India 96 D5 ....20.53N 74.52E
Diablo, Picacho del mt. Mexico 70 A7 ...30.59N 115.24W
Diamantina watercourse Australia 110 C4 ...26.30S 139.22E
Diamantina, Chapada f. Brazil 77 L5 ....14.21S 43.09W
Diamantina Deep f. Indian Oc. 108 C3 ...35.42S 104.20E
Dibrugarh India 97 H6 ....27.27N 94.55E
Dickinson U.S.A. 64 F6 ....46.53N 102.48W
Dida Galgalu f. Kenya 87 B3 ....3.11N 38.06E
Didcot England 10 D2 ....51.36N 1.15W
Diekirch d. Lux. 42 E2 ....49.59N 5.59E
Dieppe France 44 D6 ....49.55N 1.05E
Diest Belgium 42 E4 ....50.59N 5.03E
Digne-les-Bains France 44 G4 ....44.06N 6.15E
Dijon France 44 F5 ....47.20N 5.03E
Diksmuide Belgium 42 B4 ....51.02N 2.52E
Dili East Timor 105 H2 ....8.35S 125.36E
Dillon U.S.A. 64 D6 ....45.13N 112.37W
Dimapur India 97 H6 ....25.54N 93.47E
Dimitrovgrad Bulgaria 56 F6 ....42.03N 25.35E
Dinajpur Bangl. 97 G6 ....25.38N 88.39E
Dinan France 44 B6 ....48.27N 2.03W
Dinant Belgium 42 D3 ....50.16N 4.56E
Dinar Turkey 57 I4 ....38.04N 30.10E
Dīnār, Kūh-e mt. Iran 95 H6 ....30.49N 51.32E
Dinaric Alps mts Bos.-Herz./Croatia 56 B7 ...44.13N 16.16E
Dindigul India 96 E3 ....10.22N 77.59E
Dingle Ireland 41 A2 ....52.08N 10.16W
Dingle Bay Ireland 41 A2 ....52.00N 10.22W
Dingwall Scotland 19 E2 ....57.36N 4.26W
Dipolog Phil. 105 G5 ....8.39N 123.26E
Dir Pakistan 95 L7 ....35.11N 71.57E
Dirē Dawa Ethiopia 85 I2 ....9.34N 41.53E
Dirranbandi Australia 110 D4 ....28.40S 148.14E
Disappointment, Cape S. Atlantic Oc. 73 F1 ...54.51S 36.07W
Disappointment, Lake Australia 110 B4 ...23.30S 122.40E
Disko I. Greenland 83 M4 ....69.44N 53.33W
Diss England 11 G3 ....52.23N 1.07E
Distington England 14 D3 ....54.36N 3.32W
Distrito Federal d. Brazil 77 K4 ....15.56S 47.39W
Distrito Federal d. Mexico 70 E4 ....19.15N 99.08W
Diu India 96 D5 ....20.40N 71.03E

Divinópolis Brazil 77 L3 ....20.09S
Divnoye Rus. Fed. 53 L6 ....45.55N
Divriği Turkey 57 M4 ....39.22N
Dixon Entrance str. Canada/U.S.A. 62 E3 ...54.18N 13
Diyarbakir Turkey 53 L4 ....37.55N
Djado, Plateau du f. Niger 84 F4 ....21.30N
Djelfa Algeria 84 E5 ....34.38N
Djibouti Africa 85 I3 ....11.34N
Djibouti town Djibouti 85 I3 ....11.34N
Djouce Mountain hill Ireland 12 A5 ......53.08N
Dnieper r. Belarus 55 N4 ....51.16N
Dnieper r. Ukraine 55 O2 ....46.30N
Dniester r. Moldova 55 N2 ....46.25N
Dniester r. Ukraine 55 M3 ....48.06N
Dniprodzerzhyns'k Ukraine 55 P3 ....48.30N
Dnipropetrovs'k Ukraine 55 P3 ....48.30N
Dniprorudne Ukraine 55 P2 ....47.23N
Doba Chad 85 F2 ....8.40N
Doberai Peninsula Indonesia 105 I3 ......1.40S
Doboj Bos.-Herz. 56 C7 ....44.45N
Dobrich Bulgaria 57 G6 ....43.33N
Dobskie, Jezioro l. Poland 46 E5 ....54.04N
Dochart r. Scotland 16 E4 ....56.28N
Docking England 11 F3 ....52.54N
Dodecanese is Greece 56 G2 ....35.57N
Dodge City U.S.A. 64 F4 ....37.46N 100
Dodman Point England 13 C2 ....50.13N
Dodoma Tanzania 86 C4 ....6.10S
Doetinchem Neth. 42 F4 ....51.58N
Doha Qatar 95 H5 ....25.17N
Dokkum Neth. 42 E6 ....53.19N
Dolbenmaen Wales 12 C4 ....52.58N
Dole France 44 F5 ....47.06N
Dolgellau Wales 12 D4 ....52.45N
Dolomites mts Italy 50 D6 ....45.42N
Dolo Odo Ethiopia 87 C4 ....4.09N
Dolyna Ukraine 55 J3 ....48.58N
Dolyns'ka Ukraine 55 O3 ....48.07N
Dominica Central America 71 L4 ....15.18N
Dominican Republic Central America 71 J4 ...18.57N 70
Don r. Rus. Fed. 35 H2 ....47.06N
Don r. Scotland 19 G2 ....57.10N
Donaghadee Northern Ireland 16 D2 .....54.38N
Don Benito Spain 48 C3 ....38.58N
Doncaster England 15 F2 ....53.31N
Dondo Angola 86 A4 ....9.41S
Donegal Ireland 41 C4 ....54.39N
Donegal d. Ireland 41 C4 ....54.56N
Donegal Bay Ireland 41 C4 ....54.31N
Donegal Point Ireland 41 B2 ....52.43N
Donets'k Ukraine 53 K6 ....47.59N
Dongara Australia 110 A4 ....29.17S 11
Dongfang China 103 J1 ....19.03N 10
Dongfanghong China 106 B5 ....46.10N 13
Đông Hới Vietnam 104 D7 ....17.26N 10
Dongotona Mountains Sudan 87 A4 ......4.12N
Dongting Hu l. China 103 K3 ....29.20N 11
Donostia-San Sebastián Spain 48 E5 ....43.19N
Doon r. Scotland 16 E3 ....55.26N
Doon, Loch l. Scotland 16 E3 ....55.15N
Dorchester England 10 C1 ....50.43N
Dordogne r. France 44 C4 ....45.00N
Dordrecht Neth. 42 D4 ....51.48N
Dorking England 11 E2 ....51.14N
Dornbirn Austria 54 C2 ....47.26N
Dornoch Scotland 19 E2 ....57.53N
Dornoch Firth est. Scotland 19 E2 ....57.51N
Döröö Nuur l. Mongolia 102 G7 ....47.33N 93
Dorsale Camerounaise f. Cameroon/Nigeria 84 F2 ...5.59N 10
Dorset d. England 9 D2 ....50.53N
Dortmund Germany 54 B4 ....51.30N
Dos Bahías, Cabo c. Argentina 73 C2 ...44.56S 65.
Dosso Niger 84 E3 ....13.03N
Dothan U.S.A. 65 I3 ....31.14N 85.
Douai France 44 E7 ....50.22N
Douala Cameroon 84 F2 ....4.03N
Douglas Isle of Man 14 C3 ....54.09N
Douglas Scotland 17 F3 ....55.33N
Douglas U.S.A. 64 E3 ....31.20N 109.
Doullens France 42 B3 ....50.09N
Doune Scotland 17 E4 ....56.11N
Dounreay Scotland 19 F3 ....58.35N
Dourados Brazil 77 J3 ....22.13S 54.
Douro r. Portugal 48 A4 ....41.09N 8.
Dove r. Derbys. England 10 D4 ....52.50N
Dove r. Suff. England 11 G3 ....52.21N
Dover England 11 G2 ....51.08N
Dover U.S.A. 65 K4 ....39.09N 75.
Dover, Strait of France/U.K. 11 G1 ....50.53N
Down d. Northern Ireland 9 C4 ....54.17N
Down r. Northern Ireland 41 F4 ....54.20N
Downham Market England 11 F3 ....52.36N
Downpatrick Northern Ireland 16 D2 .....54.19N
Downpatrick Head Ireland 41 B4 ....54.20N
Downton England 10 D1 ....50.59N
Dowshī Afgh. 95 K7 ....35.38N
Drâa, Hammada du f. Algeria 52 B2 .....28.29N 8.
Drachten Neth. 42 F6 ....53.06N
Draguignan France 44 G3 ....43.32N
Drahichyn Belarus 55 K5 ....52.11N
Drakensberg mts Lesotho/S. Africa 86 B2 ...29.59S 28.
Drama Greece 56 F5 ....41.09N
Drammen Norway 40 B2 ....59.45N 1
Draperstown Northern Ireland 16 C2 .....54.48N 6.
Drava r. Austria 54 F2 ....46.38N 1
Drenthe d. Neth. 42 F5 ....52.53N
Dresden Germany 54 E4 ....51.03N 1
Dreux France 44 D6 ....48.44N
Drina r. Bos.-Herz./Serbia 56 C7 ....44.55N 1
Drobeta-Turnu Severin Romania 56 E7 ...44.37N 2
Drogheda Ireland 41 E3 ....53.43N 6
Drohobych Ukraine 55 J3 ....49.22N 2
Droitwich Spa England 10 C3 ....52.16N 2
Dronfield England 15 F2 ....53.18N
Drosh Pakistan 95 L7 ....35.33N 7
Drumheller Canada 62 G3 ....51.27N 112.
Drummore Scotland 16 E2 ....54.41N 4.
Druts' r. Belarus 55 N5 ....53.03N 3
Drygarn Fawr hill Wales 12 D4 ....52.13N 3.
Drymen Scotland 16 E4 ....56.04N
Duarte, Pico mt. Dom. Rep. 71 J4 ....19.03N 70.
Dubā Saudi Arabia 94 E5 ....27.20N
Dubai U.A.E. 95 I5 ....25.14N 55.
Dubawnt Lake Canada 62 H4 ....63.05N 101.
Dubbo Australia 110 D3 ....32.16S 148.
Dublin Ireland 41 E3 ....53.20N 6.
Dublin d. Ireland 41 E3 ....53.24N 6.
Dublin Bay Ireland 41 E3 ....53.21N 6.
Dubno Ukraine 55 K4 ....50.25N 25.
Dubrovnik Croatia 56 C6 ....42.39N 18.

vytsya Ukraine 55 L4 ....51.34N 26.34E
sa r. Lithuania 46 F5 ....55.04N 23.25E
Island atoll S. Pacific Oc. 109 L4 ...24.40S 124.48W
ka Rus. Fed. 59 J4 ....69.22N 86.11E
y England 10 C3 ....52.31N 2.05W
r. Spain 48 B4 ....41.02N 6.56W
Otok i. Croatia 56 A7 ....44.01N 15.01E
urg Germany 54 B4 ....51.28N 6.47E
än Qatar 95 H5 ....25.25N 50.47E
r. Argentina 76 H1 ....30.33S 62.34W
h U.S.A. 65 H6 ....46.45N 92.07W
rton England 13 D3 ....51.02N 3.33W
s U.S.A. 64 F4 ....35.53N 101.59W
arton Scotland 16 E3 ....55.57N 4.34W
ier mt. Slovakia 46 D2 ....48.57N 19.39E
ries Scotland 17 E3 ....55.04N 3.36W
ries and Galloway d. Scotland 8 D4 ...55.09N 3.46W
ät Egypt 53 J3 ....31.25N 31.49E
ff Head Ireland 16 B3 ....55.18N 7.31W
ny Point Ireland 41 E3 ....53.52N 6.14W
újváros Hungary 54 H2 ....46.59N 18.56E
ar Scotland 17 G4 ....56.00N 2.31W
ane Scotland 17 F4 ....56.11N 3.58W
ansby Head Scotland 19 F3 ....58.39N 3.01W
hurch England 10 D3 ....52.00N 1.17W
alk Ireland 41 E4 ....54.00N 6.24W
alk Bay Ireland 41 E3 ....53.57N 6.13W
ee Scotland 17 G4 ....56.28N 2.58W
ee d. Scotland 8 D5 ....56.29N 2.59W
onald Northern Ireland 16 D2 ....54.36N 5.48W
rum Bay Northern Ireland 16 D2 ...54.13N 5.46W
din New Zealand 111 G2 ....45.53S 170.30E
ermline Scotland 17 F4 ....56.04N 3.27W
annon Northern Ireland 16 D2 ....54.30N 6.46W
annon d. Northern Ireland 9 B4 ....54.28N 6.52W
arvan Ireland 41 D2 ....52.05N 7.38W
eness hd England 11 F1 ....50.55N 0.59E
iven Northern Ireland 16 C2 ....54.55N 6.55W
un Malaysia 104 C4 ....4.46N 103.23E
unab Sudan 94 E4 ....21.04N 37.04E
olme England 15 G2 ....53.18N 0.28W
ua China 106 A4 ....43.22N 128.14E
uang China 102 G6 ....40.07N 94.40E
erque France 44 E7 ....51.02N 2.22E
ery Beacon hill England 13 D3 ...51.10N 3.35W
irk France 44 E7 ....51.02N 2.22E
aoghaire Ireland 41 E3 ....53.17N 6.08W
eer Ireland 41 E3 ....53.50N 6.23W
oy Northern Ireland 16 C3 ....55.00N 6.24W
hore East Scotland 17 G4 ....52.09N 6.59W
nurry Northern Ireland 16 D2 ...54.33N 5.59W
et Bay Scotland 19 F3 ....58.37N 3.24W
et Head Scotland 19 F3 ....58.41N 3.23W
on Scotland 16 E3 ....55.57N 4.56W
Scotland 17 G3 ....55.47N 2.21W
table England 11 E2 ....51.53N 0.31W
egan, Loch b. Scotland 18 C2 ....57.31N 6.41W
nce r. France 44 F3 ....43.55N 4.45E
ngo Mexico 70 D5 ....24.02N 104.43W
ngo d. Mexico 70 D5 ....24.44N 104.59W
ngo U.S.A. 64 E4 ....37.16N 107.52W
zno Uruguay 77 I1 ....33.23S 58.04W
an S. Africa 86 C2 ....29.51S 31.02E
n Germany 44 F2 ....50.48N 6.29E
am England 15 F3 ....54.47N 1.35W
am d. England 9 D4 ....54.42N 2.05W
am S. Africa 65 K4 ....35.59N 78.54W
nitor mt. Montenegro 56 C6 ....43.07N 19.03E
ess Scotland 18 E3 ....58.34N 4.45W
ess, Kyle of inlet Scotland 18 E3 ...58.34N 4.49W
ës Albania 56 C5 ....41.19N 19.27E
ey Head Ireland 41 A1 ....51.34N 10.13W
ley England 10 C2 ....51.41N 2.21W
nanbe Tajikistan 96 C8 ....38.38N 68.51E
eldorf Germany 54 B4 ....51.13N 6.47E
in China 103 J3 ....26.13N 107.82E
ce Turkey 57 I5 ....40.50N 31.09E
kovo Rus. Fed. 55 P5 ....53.36N 34.21E
Scotland 19 G2 ....57.12N 2.11W
Cape Canada 63 L4 ....66.39N 61.16W
r. Wales 12 D3 ....52.33N 3.56W
wska Góra hill Poland 46 D4 ...53.34N 19.57E
church England 11 F2 ....51.01N 0.59E
ock England 10 C2 ....51.59N 2.26W
zhinsk Rus. Fed. 58 F3 ....56.14N 43.28E
ankoy Ukraine 53 J6 ....45.43N 34.24E
igdzhur, Khrebet mts Rus. Fed. 59 O3 ...55.53N 135.07E
dowo Poland 46 E4 ....53.15N 20.11E
na r. Belarus 55 M6 ....55.33N 28.13E

g England 11 E2 ....51.31N 0.18W
ston Scotland 17 G3 ....55.38N 2.41W
r. Loch l. Scotland 16 E4 ....56.23N 4.15W
gton England 15 F3 ....54.47N 1.21W
ngwold England 15 F3 ....54.07N 1.11W
Anglian Heights hills England 11 F3 ...52.03N 0.15E
Ayrshire d. Scotland 8 C4 ....55.29N 4.15W
bourne England 11 F1 ....50.46N 0.18E
Cape New Zealand 111 G3 ....37.40S 178.33E
Caroline Basin f. N. Pacific Oc. 108 F6 ...2.08N 148.16E
China Sea N. Pacific Oc. 103 N4 ...31.00N 127.22E
Dunbartonshire d. Scotland 8 C4 ...55.58N 4.12W
er Island S. Pacific Oc. 109 M4 ...27.05S 109.17W
ern d. Kenya 87 B3 ....0.23S 37.55E
ern Desert Egypt 53 J2 ....26.39N 32.50E
ern Equatoria d. Sudan 87 A4 ....5.00N 33.00E
ern Ghats mts India 96 E3 ....11.54N 77.22E
er Ross T. ....
Falkland i. Falkland Is 73 D1 ....52.11S 57.55W
Fen r. England 15 H2 ....53.05N 0.04E
field England 15 H3 ....54.15N 0.14W
Frisian Islands Germany 54 B5 ...53.45N 7.00E
Grinstead England 11 F2 ....51.08N 0.01E
Indiaman Ridge f. Indian Oc. 108 C4 ...23.28S 91.17E
Kilbride Scotland 16 E3 ....55.46N 4.10W
leigh England 10 D1 ....50.58N 1.22W
Linton Scotland 17 G3 ....55.59N 2.39W
Loch Tarbert inlet Scotland 18 C2 ...57.51N 6.46W
London S. Africa 86 B1 ....33.01S 27.56E
Looe England 13 C2 ....50.21N 4.27W
Lothian d. Scotland 8 D4 ....55.57N 2.45W
main Canada 63 K3 ....52.14N 78.24W
main r. Canada 63 K3 ....52.14N 78.24W
Mariana Basin f. N. Pacific Oc. 108 G6 ...14.07N 152.36E
on England 10 C1 ....50.33N 2.26W
Pacific Rise f. N. Pacific Oc. 109 M4 ...18.04N 107.07W
Renfrewshire d. Scotland 8 C4 ....55.46N 4.21W

East Riding of Yorkshire d. England 9 E3 ...53.55N 0.19W
Eastry England 11 G2 ....51.15N 1.18E
East Sea N. Pacific Oc. 106 B3 ....39.13N 133.37E
East Siberian Sea Rus. Fed. 59 P5 ...72.59N 148.21E
East Sussex d. England 9 F2 ....50.53N 0.17E
East Timor Asia 105 H2 ....8.57S 125.59E
Eastwood England 15 F2 ....53.01N 1.18W
Eaton Socon England 11 E3 ....52.13N 0.17W
Eau Claire U.S.A. 65 H5 ....44.49N 91.30W
Eau Claire, Lac à l' l. Canada 63 K3 ...56.13N 74.07W
Eauripik atoll Micronesia 105 K5 ...6.43N 143.04E
Eauripik Rise-New Guinea Rise f. N. Pacific Oc. 108 F6 ...8.13N 141.00E
Ebbw Vale Wales 12 D3 ....51.47N 3.12W
Eberswalde-Finow Germany 54 E5 ...52.50N 13.49E
Ebinur Hu l. China 102 E6 ....44.46N 82.51E
Ebro r. Spain 48 F4 ....40.43N 0.51E
Ecclefechan Scotland 17 F3 ....55.04N 3.16W
Eccleshall England 10 C3 ....52.52N 2.15W
Ech Chélif Algeria 84 E5 ....36.09N 1.17E
Écija Spain 48 C2 ....37.33N 5.04W
Eck, Loch l. Scotland 16 E4 ....56.04N 4.59W
Eckington England 10 C3 ....52.04N 2.07W
Ecuador S. America 76 E7 ....1.08S 78.05W
Eday i. Scotland 19 G4 ....59.11N 2.50W
Ed Da'ein Sudan 94 C2 ....11.27N 26.09E
Ed Damazin Sudan 85 H3 ....11.47N 34.20E
Ed Damer Sudan 94 D3 ....17.26N 33.58E
Ed Debba Sudan 94 D3 ....18.00N 30.55E
Ed Dueim Sudan 94 D2 ....13.57N 32.17E
Eden r. England 14 D3 ....54.57N 3.01W
Edessa Greece 56 E5 ....40.48N 22.04E
Edgeøya i. Arctic Oc. 58 D5 ....77.32N 22.45E
Edinburgh Scotland 17 F3 ....55.57N 3.11W
Edinburgh d. Scotland 8 D4 ....55.56N 3.17W
Edirne Turkey 56 G5 ....41.39N 26.34E
Edmonton Canada 62 G3 ....53.33N 113.33W
Edmundston Canada 63 L2 ....47.23N 68.20W
Edremit Turkey 56 G4 ....39.35N 27.00E
Edson Canada 62 G3 ....53.35N 116.25W
Edward, Lake Dem. Rep. Congo/Uganda 86 B4 ...0.17S 29.40E
Edwards Plateau f. U.S.A. 64 F3 ...30.28N 100.22W
Éfaté i. Vanuatu 111 F5 ....17.38S 168.30E
Effingham U.S.A. 65 I4 ....39.07N 88.33W
Eger Hungary 54 I2 ....47.54N 20.22E
Egilsay i. Scotland 19 G4 ....59.09N 2.55W
Egilsstaðir Iceland 40 Z2 ....65.16N 14.25W
Eğirdir Turkey 57 I3 ....37.51N 30.51E
Eğirdir Gölü l. Turkey 57 I3 ....37.59N 30.53E
Eglinton Northern Ireland 16 B3 ...55.02N 7.11W
Egremont England 14 D3 ....54.29N 3.32W
Egvekinot Rus. Fed. 59 T4 ....66.20N 179.17W
Egypt Africa 85 G4 ....29.53N 31.16E
Eifel hills Germany 54 B4 ....50.10N 6.39E
Eigg i. Scotland 18 C1 ....56.54N 6.10W
Eighty Mile Beach f. Australia 110 B5 ...19.54S 120.10E
Eilat Israel 53 J2 ....29.33N 34.56E
Eindhoven Neth. 42 E4 ....51.26N 5.29E
Eisenhüttenstadt Germany 54 F5 ...52.09N 14.38E
Eishort, Loch inlet Scotland 18 D2 ...57.09N 5.59W
Ekibastuz Kazakhstan 102 D8 ....51.46N 75.27E
Ekostrovskaya Imandra, Ozero l. Rus. Fed. 40 H4 ...67.29N 32.23E
Eksjö Sweden 40 C2 ....57.40N 14.59E
Elazığ Turkey 57 M4 ....38.39N 39.15E
Elba, Isola d' i. Italy 50 D5 ....42.46N 10.16E
El'ban Rus. Fed. 103 P8 ....50.03N 136.26E
Elbasan Albania 56 D5 ....41.07N 20.05E
El Bayadh Algeria 52 D5 ....33.41N 0.56E
Elbe r. Germany 54 C5 ....53.53N 9.05E
Elbert, Mount U.S.A. 64 E4 ....39.05N 106.25W
Elbistan Turkey 57 I4 ....38.12N 37.11F
Elbląg Poland 46 H5 ....54.10N 19.24E
El'brus mt. Rus. Fed. 58 F2 ....43.22N 42.25E
Elburz Mountains Iran 95 G7 ....36.52N 49.43E
El Callao Venezuela 71 L2 ....7.17N 61.47W
El Cerro Bolivia 77 I4 ....17.32S 61.36W
Elche-Elx Spain 48 E3 ....38.16N 0.41W
Elda Spain 48 E3 ....38.29N 0.47W
Eldama Ravine Kenya 87 A3 ....0.05N 35.44E
El Dera Kenya 87 B3 ....0.39N 38.43E
El Djouf des. Africa 82 C7 ....21.00N 8.00W
El Dorado U.S.A. 65 H3 ....33.13N 92.36W
Eldoret Kenya 87 A3 ....0.31N 35.15E
Elemi Triangle Africa 87 A4 ....4.53N 35.11E
El Eulma Algeria 52 E4 ....36.07N 5.48E
Eleuthera i. Bahamas 71 I6 ....25.21N 76.22W
El Fasher Sudan 85 G3 ....13.36N 25.20E
El Geneina Sudan 85 G3 ....13.26N 22.26E
Elgin Scotland 19 F2 ....57.39N 3.19W
El'ginskiy Rus. Fed. 59 P4 ....64.32N 141.40E
El Goléa Algeria 84 E5 ....30.34N 2.58E
Elgon, Mount Kenya/Uganda 87 A3 ...1.08N 34.34E
El Hierro i. Canary Islands 48 X1 ...27.40N 17.56W
El Jadida Morocco 84 D5 ....33.12N 8.27W
Ełk Poland 46 I4 ....53.50N 22.22E
Elkhovo Bulgaria 56 G6 ....42.11N 26.34E
Elko U.S.A. 64 C5 ....40.51N 115.46W
Ellef Ringnes Island Canada 63 H5 ...78.38N 101.56W
Él Lëh Ethiopia 87 B3 ....3.45N 39.14E
Ellensburg U.S.A. 64 B6 ....46.59N 120.32W
Ellesmere England 10 C3 ....52.54N 2.54W
Ellesmere Island Canada 63 J5 ...77.10N 83.03W
Ellesmere Port England 14 E2 ....53.17N 2.54W
Ellice r. Canada 62 H4 ....67.56N 103.59W
Ellon Scotland 19 G2 ....57.22N 2.04W
Elmalı Turkey 57 H3 ....36.44N 29.55E
El Meghaïer Algeria 52 E3 ....33.56N 5.56E
El Muglad Sudan 85 G3 ....11.01N 27.44E
El Obeid Sudan 85 H3 ....13.10N 30.11E
El Oued Algeria 52 E3 ....33.21N 6.54E
El Paso U.S.A. 64 E3 ....31.46N 106.24W
El Puerto de Santa María Spain 48 B2 ...36.36N 6.14W
El Salvador Central America 70 G3 ...13.22N 88.59W
El Tigre Venezuela 71 L2 ....8.52N 64.16W
Elvas Portugal 48 B3 ....38.53N 7.10W
Elverum Norway 40 B3 ....60.53N 11.33E
El Wak Kenya 87 C3 ....2.47N 40.56E
Ely England 11 F3 ....52.24N 0.15E
Ely U.S.A. 64 D4 ....39.15N 114.53W
Ely, Isle of f. England 11 F3 ....52.27N 0.14E
Emämrüd Iran 95 H7 ....36.24N 54.56E
Embu Kenya 87 B2 ....0.31S 37.26E
Emden Germany 54 B5 ....53.22N 7.13E
Emerson Canada 64 G6 ....49.02N 97.11W
Emi Koussi mt. Chad 85 F3 ....19.46N 18.34E
Emirdağ Turkey 57 I4 ....39.01N 31.09E
Emmeloord Neth. 42 E5 ....52.43N 5.45E
Emmen Neth. 42 F5 ....52.47N 6.54E
Emory Peak U.S.A. 64 F2 ....29.15N 103.18W
Emperor Seamount Chain f. N. Pacific Oc. 108 H9 ...52.16N 167.06E
Emperor Trough f. N. Pacific Oc. 108 H9 ...46.06N 173.14E

Ems r. Germany 54 B5 ....53.18N 7.22E
Encarnación Paraguay 77 I2 ....27.17S 55.49W
Endeh Indonesia 105 G2 ....8.47S 121.38E
Endicott Mountains U.S.A. 62 C4 ...67.50N 152.33W
Enfield England 11 E2 ....51.39N 0.05W
Engel's Rus. Fed. 58 F3 ....51.29N 46.06E
Enggano i. Indonesia 104 C2 ....5.25S 102.20E
England d. U.K. 9 E3 ....52.48N 1.24W
English Channel France/U.K. 11 E1 ...49.59N 1.24W
Enköping Sweden 40 D2 ....59.38N 17.06E
En Nahud Sudan 85 G3 ....12.42N 28.25E
Ennedi, Massif mts Chad 94 B3 ...16.59N 22.58E
Ennerdale Water l. England 14 D3 ...54.30N 3.22W
Ennis Ireland 41 C2 ....52.51N 8.59W
Enniscorthy Ireland 41 E2 ....52.30N 6.34W
Enniskerry Ireland 12 A5 ....53.11N 6.10W
Enniskillen Northern Ireland 16 B2 ...54.20N 7.37W
Ennistymon Ireland 41 B2 ....52.56N 9.17W
Enns r. Austria 54 F3 ....48.14N 14.31E
Enschede Neth. 42 F5 ....52.13N 6.54E
Ensenada Mexico 70 A7 ....31.52N 116.37W
Enshi China 103 J4 ....30.13N 109.28E
Enugu Nigeria 84 E2 ....6.24N 7.31E
Envira r. Brazil 76 F6 ....7.31S 70.14W
Épernay France 42 C2 ....49.03N 3.58E
Épinal France 44 G6 ....48.11N 6.27E
Epomeo, Monte vol. Italy 50 E4 ...40.44N 13.53E
Epping England 11 F2 ....51.42N 0.07E
Eppynt, Mynydd hills Wales 12 D4 ...52.05N 3.28W
Epsom England 11 E2 ....51.20N 0.16W
Epworth England 15 G2 ....53.32N 0.49W
Eqlīd Iran 95 H6 ....30.53N 52.42E
Equatorial Guinea Africa 84 E2 ...3.00N 8.36E
Équeurdreville-Hainneville France 13 Z9 ...49.39N 1.39W
Erbeskopf hill Germany 42 G2 ....49.43N 7.04E
Erciyes Dağı mt. Turkey 57 K4 ...38.32N 35.27E
Erdemli Turkey 57 K3 ....36.36N 34.19E
Erdi f. Chad 94 B3 ....19.02N 21.36E
Ereğli Konya Turkey 57 K3 ....37.30N 34.03E
Ereğli Zonguldak Turkey 57 I5 ...41.17N 31.25E
Erfurt Germany 54 D4 ....50.59N 11.02E
Ergani Turkey 57 M4 ....38.15N 39.46E
Ergene r. Turkey 56 G5 ....40.59N 26.22E
Ericht l. Scotland 17 F4 ....56.34N 3.15W
Ericht, Loch l. Scotland 19 E1 ...56.48N 4.25W
Erie U.S.A. 65 J5 ....42.07N 80.06W
Erie, Lake Canada/U.S.A. 63 J2 ...42.14N 80.53W
Eriskay i. Scotland 18 B2 ....57.04N 7.16W
Eritrea Africa 85 H3 ....15.57N 37.33E
Erlangen Germany 54 D3 ....49.35N 11.01E
Ermenek Turkey 57 J3 ....36.37N 32.54E
Ermoupoli Greece 56 F3 ....37.26N 24.56E
Erode India 96 E3 ....11.21N 77.43E
Er Rachidia Morocco 84 D5 ....31.54N 4.29W
Er Rahad Sudan 85 H3 ....12.44N 30.38E
Errigal hill Ireland 41 C5 ....55.02N 8.07W
Erris Head Ireland 41 A4 ....54.19N 10.01W
Errochty, Loch l. Scotland 19 E1 ...56.45N 4.11W
Erromango i. Vanuatu 111 F5 ...18.49S 168.58E
Erzgebirge mts Czech Rep./Germany 54 E4 ...50.33N 13.07E
Erzincan Turkey 57 M4 ....39.45N 39.29E
Erzurum Turkey 57 N4 ....39.53N 41.17E
Esbjerg Denmark 40 B1 ....55.28N 8.27E
Escanaba U.S.A. 65 I6 ....45.45N 87.03W
Escárcega Mexico 70 F4 ....18.39N 90.43W
Esch-sur-Alzette Lux. 42 E2 ....49.30N 5.59E
Eschweiler Germany 42 F3 ....50.49N 6.18E
Esfahān Iran 95 H6 ....32.41N 51.39E
Esha Ness hd Scotland 19 H5 ...60.30N 1.37W
Esk r. Scotland 17 F3 ....55.56N 3.04W
Eske, Lough l. Ireland 16 A2 ...54.42N 8.04W
Eski Gediz Turkey 57 I4 ....39.03N 29.25E
Eskilstuna Sweden 40 D2 ....59.22N 16.32E
Eskişehir Turkey 57 I4 ....39.47N 30.31E
Esla r. Spain 48 C4 ....41.30N 6.01W
Eslāmābād-e Gharb Iran 95 G6 ...34.06N 46.31E
Esmeraldas Ecuador 76 E8 ....0.55N 79.41W
Esperance Australia 110 B3 ....33.49S 121.52E
Espigüete mt. Spain 48 C5 ....42.57N 4.47W
Espinhaço, Serra do mts Brazil 77 L4 ...17.59S 43.59W
Espinosa Brazil 77 L5 ....14.54S 42.46W
Espírito Santo d. Brazil 77 L4 ...19.31S 40.33W
Espíritu Santo i. Vanuatu 111 F5 ...15.16S 166.35E
Espoo Finland 40 F3 ....60.12N 24.40E
Esquel Argentina 73 B2 ....42.55S 71.20W
Essen Germany 54 B4 ....51.27N 7.03E
Essequibo r. Guyana 72 D7 ....6.23N 58.36W
Essex d. England 9 F2 ....51.51N 0.42E
Estados, Isla de los i. Argentina 73 C1 ...54.44S 64.16W
Estats, Pic d' mt. France/Spain 48 F5 ...42.40N 1.24E
Estevan Canada 62 H2 ....49.08N 102.59W
Estonia Europe 40 F2 ....58.44N 25.26E
Estrela, Serra da mts Portugal 48 B4 ...40.11N 7.57W
Estrella mt. Spain 48 D3 ....38.24N 3.36W
Estrondo, Serra hills Brazil 77 K6 ...9.08S 48.42W
Étaples France 44 D7 ....50.31N 1.39E
Ethiopia Africa 85 H2 ....6.30N 39.41E
Ethiopian Highlands f. Ethiopia 85 H2 ...8.49N 36.39E
Etimesğut Turkey 57 J4 ....39.56N 32.39E
Etive, Loch inlet Scotland 16 D4 ...56.27N 5.12W
Etna, Mount vol. Italy 50 F2 ....37.45N 15.00E
Etosha Pan f. Namibia 86 A3 ....18.52S 16.19E
Ettelbruck Lux. 42 F2 ....49.51N 6.06E
Ettrick Forest f. Scotland 17 F3 ...55.31N 3.05W
Ettrick Water r. Scotland 17 G3 ...55.34N 2.49W
Etwall England 10 D2 ....52.53N 1.36W
Eugene U.S.A. 64 B5 ....44.04N 123.05W
Eugenia, Punta c. Mexico 70 A6 ...27.51N 115.04W
Euphrates r. Asia 94 F5 ....30.59N 47.24E
Eureka U.S.A. 64 B5 ....40.48N 124.09W
Europa, Picos de mts Spain 48 C5 ...43.07N 5.01W
Europe 34
Evans, Lac l. Canada 63 K3 ....50.49N 77.07W
Evanston U.S.A. 64 D5 ....41.17N 110.56W
Evansville U.S.A. 65 I4 ....37.59N 87.32W
Evaton S. Africa 86 B2 ....26.32S 27.49E
Everest, Mount China/Nepal 102 F3 ...27.59N 86.55E
Everglades U.S.A. 65 J2 ....26.15N 81.02W
Evesham England 10 D3 ....52.06N 1.57W
Evesham, Vale of f. England 10 D3 ...52.05N 1.57W
Évora Portugal 48 B3 ....38.34N 7.54W
Évreux France 44 D6 ....49.01N 1.09E
Evvoia i. Greece 56 F4 ....38.39N 24.14E
Ewaso Ngiro r. North Eastern Kenya 87 B3 ...0.31N 41.04E
Ewaso Ngiro r. Rift Valley Kenya 87 B2 ...2.02S 36.07E
Ewe, Loch b. Scotland 18 D2 ...57.50N 5.40W
Exe r. England 13 D2 ....50.41N 3.29W
Exeter England 13 D2 ....50.43N 3.32W
Exminster England 13 D2 ....50.41N 3.30W
Exmoor hills England 13 D3 ...51.10N 3.46W
Exmouth England 13 D2 ....50.37N 3.25W
Exuma Cays is Bahamas 71 I5 ...24.35N 76.34W
Exuma Sound str. Bahamas 71 I5 ...24.17N 75.59W
Eyasi, Lake Tanzania 86 C4 ....3.38S 35.05E

Eye P'boro. England 11 E3 ....52.37N 0.11W
Eye Suff. England 11 G3 ....52.19N 1.09E
Eyemouth Scotland 17 G3 ....55.52N 2.05W
Eye Peninsula f. Scotland 18 C3 ...58.14N 6.14W
Eyre, Lake (North) Australia 110 C4 ...28.24S 137.16E
Eyre, Lake (South) Australia 110 C4 ...28.30S 137.25E
Ezine Turkey 56 G4 ....39.46N 26.19E

F

Faafxadhuun Somalia 87 C3 ....2.11N 41.37E
Faenza Italy 50 D6 ....44.17N 11.53E
Făgăraş Romania 56 F7 ....45.50N 24.59E
Fagatogo American Samoa 108 I5 ...14.17S 170.41W
Fagersta Sweden 40 C2 ....59.59N 15.49E
Fairbanks U.S.A. 62 D4 ....64.50N 147.47W
Fair Head Northern Ireland 16 C3 ...55.14N 6.08W
Fair Isle i. Scotland 19 H4 ....59.34N 1.38W
Fairmont U.S.A. 65 H5 ....43.39N 94.28W
Fairweather, Mount Canada/U.S.A. 62 E3 ...58.54N 137.29W
Fais i. Micronesia 105 K5 ....9.45N 140.33E
Faisalabad Pakistan 96 D7 ....31.24N 73.09E
Fakaofo atoll Tokelau 108 I5 ....9.23S 171.08W
Fakenham England 11 F3 ....52.50N 0.51E
Fakfak Indonesia 105 I3 ....2.55S 132.17E
Fal r. England 13 C2 ....50.14N 4.58W
Falcon Lake Mexico/U.S.A. 70 E6 ...26.53N 99.20W
Falkenberg Sweden 40 C2 ....56.55N 12.31E
Falkirk Scotland 17 F4 ....56.00N 3.47W
Falkirk d. Scotland 8 D4 ....55.59N 3.48W
Falkland Islands S. Atlantic Oc. 73 D1 ...50.55S 59.36W
Falköping Sweden 40 C2 ....58.10N 13.33E
Falmouth England 13 B2 ....50.09N 5.04W
Falmouth Bay England 13 B2 ...50.07N 5.04W
Falso, Cabo c. Mexico 70 C5 ...22.53N 109.59W
Falster i. Denmark 40 B1 ....54.49N 11.58E
Falun Sweden 40 C3 ....60.36N 15.38E
Famagusta Cyprus 57 J2 ....35.06N 33.57E
Famatina, Sierra de mts Argentina 76 G2 ...28.03S 68.06W
Fanad Head Ireland 16 B3 ....55.17N 7.38W
Fane r. Ireland 41 E3 ....53.57N 6.22W
Fannich, Loch l. Scotland 18 D2 ...57.39N 5.03W
Farafra Oasis Egypt 94 C5 ....26.43N 28.09E
Farāh Afgh. 95 J6 ....32.23N 62.07E
Farallon de Pajaros vol. N. Mariana Is 105 K8 ...20.32N 144.55E
Farasān, Jazā'ir is Saudi Arabia 94 F3 ...16.48N 41.41E
Fareham England 10 D1 ....50.51N 1.11W
Farewell, Cape New Zealand 111 G2 ...40.29S 172.40E
Fargo U.S.A. 64 G6 ....46.52N 96.49W
Farnborough England 10 E2 ....51.17N 0.45W
Farndon England 14 E2 ....53.05N 2.53W
Farne Islands England 15 F4 ....55.38N 1.37W
Farnham England 10 E2 ....51.13N 0.48W
Faro Portugal 48 B2 ....37.01N 7.56W
Fårö i. Sweden 40 D2 ....57.58N 19.22E
Faroe Islands Europe 34 D4 ....62.00N 7.00W
Farrāshband Iran 95 H5 ....28.52S 52.05E
Fasā Iran 95 H5 ....28.56N 53.38E
Fastiv Ukraine 55 M4 ....50.04N 29.55E
Fatehgarh India 96 E6 ....27.22N 79.36E
Faulquemont France 42 F2 ....49.03N 6.36E
Faversham England 11 F2 ....51.19N 0.53E
Faxaflói b. Iceland 40 X2 ....64.27N 22.58W
Fayetteville U.S.A. 65 H4 ....35.02N 78.53W
Fdérik Mauritania 84 C4 ....22.42N 12.44W
Feale r. Ireland 41 B2 ....52.28N 9.38W
Fear, Cape U.S.A. 65 K3 ....33.51N 77.58W
Fehmarn i. Germany 54 D6 ....54.29N 11.07E
Feira de Santana Brazil 77 M5 ...12.12S 38.57W
Feldkirch Austria 54 C2 ....47.15N 9.36E
Felixstowe England 11 G2 ....51.58N 1.21E
Femunden l. Norway 40 B3 ....62.05N 11.48E
Feniton England 13 D2 ....50.47N 3.16W
Feodosiya Ukraine 53 K6 ....45.02N 35.22E
Ferdows Iran 95 I6 ....33.59N 58.10E
Fergus Falls town U.S.A. 64 G6 ...46.17N 96.07W
Ferkessédougou Côte d'Ivoire 84 D2 ...9.35N 5.13W
Fermanagh d. Northern Ireland 9 A4 ...54.27N 8.04W
Fermanagh f. Northern Ireland 41 D4 ...54.16N 7.35W
Fermoy Ireland 41 C2 ....52.08N 8.17W
Ferndown England 10 D1 ....50.48N 1.54W
Ferrara Italy 50 D6 ....44.50N 11.38E
Ferrol Spain 48 A5 ....43.29N 8.13W
Ferryhill England 15 F3 ....54.41N 1.33W
Fès Morocco 84 D5 ....34.04N 4.57W
Fethaland, Point of Scotland 19 H5 ...60.39N 1.18W
Fethard Ireland 41 D2 ....52.28N 7.42W
Fethiye Turkey 57 H3 ....36.37N 29.06E
Fetlar i. Scotland 19 I5 ....60.38N 0.49W
Feuilles, Rivière aux r. Canada 63 K3 ...58.46N 70.13W
Feyzābād Afgh. 95 L7 ....37.05N 70.41E
Fez Morocco 84 D5 ....34.04N 4.57W
Ffestiniog Wales 12 D4 ....52.58N 3.56W
Fianarantsoa Madagascar 86 D2 ...21.27S 47.07E
Fife d. Scotland 8 D4 ....56.16N 2.58W
Fife Ness pt Scotland 17 G4 ...56.16N 2.35W
Figeac France 44 E4 ....44.37N 2.01E
Figueira da Foz Portugal 48 A4 ...40.10N 8.51W
Figueres Spain 48 G5 ....42.16N 2.58E
Figuig Morocco 52 D5 ....32.09N 1.17W
Fiji S. Pacific Oc. 111 G5 ....17.51S 177.08E
Filadelfia Paraguay 77 H3 ....22.22S 60.03W
Filey England 15 G3 ....54.13N 0.18W
Filton England 10 C2 ....51.30N 2.35W
Filtu Ethiopia 87 C4 ....5.06N 40.38E
Findhorn r. Scotland 19 F2 ....57.38N 3.38W
Finisterre, Cape Spain 48 A5 ....42.53N 9.15W
Finland Europe 40 F3 ....63.43N 26.54E
Finland, Gulf of Europe 40 E2 ...59.31N 22.42E
Finlay r. Canada 62 F3 ....56.41N 124.49W
Finn r. Ireland 41 D4 ....54.50N 7.28W
Finspång Sweden 40 C2 ....58.42N 15.46E
Finstown Scotland 19 F4 ....59.00N 3.07W
Fintona Northern Ireland 16 B2 ...54.29N 7.19W
Fionn Loch l. Scotland 18 D2 ...57.46N 5.28W
Fionnphort Scotland 16 C4 ....56.19N 6.22W
Fisher Strait Canada 63 J4 ....63.14N 83.06W
Fishguard Wales 12 C3 ....51.59N 4.58W
Fishguard Bay Wales 12 C4 ....52.01N 4.58W
Fismes France 42 C2 ....49.18N 3.42E
Flagstaff U.S.A. 64 D4 ....35.12N 111.39W
Flamborough England 15 G3 ....54.07N 0.03W
Flamborough Head England 15 G3 ...54.07N 0.03W
Flannan Isles Scotland 18 B3 ....58.18N 7.39W
Flåsjön l. Sweden 40 C4 ....64.06N 15.53E
Flathead Lake U.S.A. 64 D6 ....47.52N 114.03W
Flat Holm i. Wales 13 D3 ....51.23N 3.07W
Fleet England 10 E2 ....51.17N 0.50W
Fleetwood England 14 D2 ....53.55N 3.02W
Flensburg Germany 54 C6 ....54.47N 9.25E
Flevoland d. Neth. 42 E5 ....52.17N 5.07E
Flinders r. Australia 110 D5 ....17.37S 140.35E

Flinders Island Australia 110 D3 ....39.56S 148.04E
Flinders Ranges mts Australia 110 C3 ......32.24S 137.57E
Flin Flon Canada 62 H3 ....54.46N 101.51W
Flint U.S.A. 65 J5 ....43.01N 83.42W
Flint Wales 12 D5 ....53.15N 3.08W
Flintshire d. Wales 9 D3 ....53.11N 3.07W
Florence Italy 50 D5 ....43.46N 11.16E
Florence U.S.A. 65 K3 ....34.11N 79.45W
Florencia Colombia 72 B7 ....1.36N 75.36W
Flores i. Indonesia 105 G2 ....8.29S 121.14E
Flores Sea Indonesia 104 F2 ....7.41S 119.59E
Floresta Brazil 77 M6 ....8.31S 38.32W
Florianópolis Brazil 77 K2 ....27.32S 48.32W
Florida d. U.S.A. 65 J3 ....30.12N 83.39W
Florida, Straits of Bahamas/U.S.A. 71 H5 ......23.59N 81.35W
Florida Keys is U.S.A. 65 J1 ....24.41N 81.38W
Florina Greece 56 D5 ....40.46N 21.24E
Florø Norway 40 A3 ....61.36N 5.01E
Flotta i. Scotland 19 F3 ....58.50N 3.05W
Fly r. P.N.G. 105 K2 ....8.18S 142.36E
Foča Bos.-Herz. 56 C6 ....43.29N 18.45E
Fochabers Scotland 19 F2 ....57.37N 3.06W
Focşani Romania 56 G7 ....45.42N 27.11E
Foggia Italy 50 F4 ....41.28N 15.33E
Fogo i. Cape Verde 84 B3 ....14.59N 24.18W
Foinaven hill Scotland 18 E3 ....58.25N 4.53W
Foix France 44 E3 ....42.58N 1.36E
Foligno Italy 50 E5 ....42.57N 12.42E
Folkestone England 11 G2 ....51.05N 1.10E
Fonseca, Golfo de b. Central America 70 G3 ....13.03N 88.12W
Fontainebleau France 44 E6 ....48.25N 2.43E
Fontur pt Iceland 40 Z2 ....66.23N 14.32W
Førde Norway 40 A3 ....61.27N 5.52E
Fordingbridge England 10 D1 ....50.56N 1.47W
Foreland hd England 10 D1 ....50.41N 1.04W
Foreland Point England 13 D3 ....51.15N 3.47W
Forfar Scotland 19 G1 ....56.39N 2.53W
Forlì Italy 50 E6 ....44.14N 12.02E
Formby England 14 D2 ....53.34N 3.04W
Formentera i. Spain 48 F3 ....38.40N 1.24E
Formosa Argentina 73 D4 ....26.07S 58.12W
Formosa, Serra hills Brazil 77 I5 ....12.31S 55.28W
Forres Scotland 19 F2 ....57.37N 3.37W
Forssa Finland 40 E3 ....60.49N 23.39E
Fort Albany Canada 63 J3 ....52.13N 81.41W
Fortaleza Brazil 77 M7 ....3.43S 38.32W
Fort Augustus Scotland 18 E2 ....57.09N 4.41W
Fort Chipewyan Canada 62 G3 ....58.42N 111.07W
Fort Collins U.S.A. 64 E5 ....40.35N 105.05W
Fort-de-France Martinique 71 L3 ....14.37N 61.05W
Fortescue r. Australia 110 A4 ....21.02S 116.06E
Fort Frances Canada 63 I2 ....48.37N 93.24W
Fort Good Hope Canada 62 F4 ....66.16N 128.39W
Forth r. Scotland 16 F4 ....56.07N 3.52W
Forth, Firth of est. Scotland 17 F4 ....56.01N 3.13W
Fort Lauderdale U.S.A. 65 J2 ....26.04N 80.11W
Fort Liard Canada 62 F4 ....60.14N 123.24W
Fort McMurray Canada 62 G3 ....56.43N 111.21W
Fort McPherson Canada 62 E4 ....67.33N 134.44W
Fort Nelson Canada 62 F3 ....58.45N 122.39W
Fort Peck Reservoir U.S.A. 64 E6 ....47.47N 106.55W
Fort Pierce U.S.A. 65 J2 ....27.18N 80.24W
Fortrose Scotland 19 E2 ....57.35N 4.08W
Fort St John Canada 62 F3 ....56.15N 120.49W
Fort Severn Canada 63 J3 ....56.00N 87.39W
Fort-Shevchenko Kazakhstan 58 G2 ....44.29N 50.17E
Fort Simpson Canada 62 F4 ....61.52N 121.22W
Fort Smith Canada 62 G4 ....60.00N 112.13W
Fort Smith U.S.A. 65 H4 ....35.26N 94.24W
Fortuneswell England 10 C1 ....50.34N 2.27W
Fort Wayne U.S.A. 65 I5 ....41.04N 85.08W
Fort William Scotland 18 D1 ....56.49N 5.06W
Fort Worth U.S.A. 65 G3 ....32.46N 97.19W
Fort Yukon U.S.A. 62 D4 ....66.35N 145.13W
Foshan China 103 K2 ....23.03N 113.06E
Fossano Italy 50 B6 ....44.33N 7.43E
Fougères France 44 C6 ....48.21N 1.12W
Foula i. Scotland 19 G5 ....60.10N 2.10W
Foulness Point England 11 F2 ....51.37N 0.57E
Fouta Djallon f. Guinea 84 C3 ....11.26N 12.34W
Fowey r. England 13 C2 ....50.26N 4.41W
Foxe Basin g. Canada 63 K4 ....66.53N 78.58W
Foxe Channel Canada 63 J4 ....64.56N 81.03W
Foxe Peninsula Canada 63 K4 ....64.48N 77.03W
Foxford Ireland 41 B3 ....53.58N 9.07W
Fox Islands U.S.A. 62 B3 ....52.45N 168.53W
Foyle r. Ireland/U.K. 41 D4 ....54.53N 7.26W
Foyle, Lough inlet Ireland/U.K. 41 D5 ....55.07N 7.07W
Foz do Iguaçu Brazil 77 J2 ....25.30S 54.32W
Framlingham England 11 G3 ....52.13N 1.21E
Franca Brazil 77 K3 ....20.32S 47.23W
France Europe 44 E5 ....46.57N 2.11E
Franceville Gabon 84 F1 ....1.37S 13.37E
Francistown Botswana 86 B2 ....21.10S 27.29E
Frankfort U.S.A. 65 J4 ....38.12N 84.53W
Frankfurt am Main Germany 54 C4 ....50.07N 8.41E
Frankfurt an der Oder Germany 54 F5 ....52.21N 14.33E
Franklin D. Roosevelt Lake resr U.S.A. 64 C6 ..48.16N 118.09W
Frantsa-Iosifa, Zemlya is Rus. Fed. 58 G5 .....79.40N 58.29E
Frasca, Capo della c. Italy 50 C3 ....39.46N 8.26E
Fraser r. Canada 62 F2 ....49.19N 121.38W
Fraserburgh Scotland 19 G2 ....57.42N 2.01W
Fraser Island Australia 110 E4 ....25.12S 153.11E
Freckleton England 14 E2 ....53.45N 2.52W
Fredericia Denmark 40 B1 ....55.34N 9.45E
Fredericton Canada 63 L2 ....45.57N 66.39W
Frederikshavn Denmark 40 B2 ....57.27N 10.32E
Fredrikstad Norway 40 B2 ....59.13N 10.56E
Freeport City Bahamas 71 I6 ....26.30N 78.45W
Freetown Sierra Leone 84 C2 ....8.28N 13.12W
Freiburg im Breisgau Germany 54 B3 ....48.00N 7.50E
Fréjus France 44 G3 ....43.26N 6.45E
Fremantle Australia 110 A3 ....32.05S 115.42E
French Guiana S. America 109 Q6 ....3.56N 53.03W
French Polynesia is S. Pacific Oc. 109 K4 ....18.43S 147.32W
Freshwater England 10 D1 ....50.41N 1.31W
Fresno U.S.A. 64 C4 ....36.46N 119.46W
Frévent France 11 H1 ....50.16N 2.17E
Freyming-Merlebach France 42 F2 ....49.09N 6.48E
Fria Guinea 84 C3 ....10.24N 13.35W
Friedrichshafen Germany 54 C2 ....47.39N 9.31E
Friesland d. Neth. 42 E6 ....53.08N 5.48E
Frinton-on-Sea England 11 G2 ....51.50N 1.15E
Frisa, Loch l. Scotland 16 C4 ....56.34N 6.06W
Frisian Islands Europe 34 E3 ....54.00N 7.00E
Frizington England 14 D3 ....54.32N 3.30W
Frobisher Bay Canada 63 L4 ....63.18N 67.31W
Frodsham England 14 E2 ....53.18N 2.44W
Frohavet b. Norway 40 B3 ....63.52N 9.12E
Frome England 10 C2 ....51.14N 2.19W
Frome r. England 10 C1 ....50.41N 2.05W
Frome, Lake Australia 110 C3 ....30.43S 139.48E
Frosinone Italy 50 E4 ....41.39N 13.21E
Frøya i. Norway 40 B3 ....63.41N 8.39E

Fruges France 11 H1 ....50.31N 2.08E
Frýdek-Místek Czech Rep. 54 H3 ....49.41N 18.21E
Fuenlabrada Spain 48 D4 ....40.17N 3.47W
Fuerteventura i. Canary Islands 48 Y2 ....28.36N 14.04W
Fujairah U.A.E. 95 I5 ....25.06N 56.21E
Fujian d. China 103 L3 ....25.52N 117.59E
Fuji-san vol. Japan 106 C3 ....35.22N 138.43E
Fukui Japan 106 C3 ....36.04N 136.13E
Fukuoka Japan 106 B2 ....33.35N 130.24E
Fukushima Japan 106 D3 ....37.45N 140.28E
Fulda Germany 54 C4 ....50.33N 9.41E
Fulford England 15 F2 ....53.56N 1.04W
Fulham England 11 E2 ....51.29N 0.13W
Fumay France 42 D2 ....49.59N 4.42E
Funafuti atoll Tuvalu 111 G6 ....8.25S 179.13E
Funchal Atlantic Oc. 84 C5 ....32.39N 16.54W
Fundy, Bay of Canada 63 L2 ....44.06N 67.03W
Fürth Germany 54 D3 ....49.29N 10.57E
Fushun China 103 M6 ....41.51N 123.50E
Fusong China 106 A4 ....42.20N 127.17E
Fuxin China 103 M6 ....42.02N 121.41E
Fuyu China 103 M7 ....47.44N 124.26E
Fuzhou Fujian China 103 L3 ....26.07N 119.21E
Fuzhou Jiangxi China 103 L3 ....27.58N 116.17E
Fyn i. Denmark 40 B1 ....55.38N 10.17E

G

Gaalkacyo Somalia 85 I2 ....6.46N 47.25E
Gabès Tunisia 52 F3 ....33.53N 10.07E
Gabès, Golfe de g. Tunisia 52 F3 ....34.08N 10.40E
Gabon Africa 84 F1 ....0.56S 11.32E
Gaborone Botswana 86 B2 ....24.38S 25.56E
Gabrovo Bulgaria 56 F6 ....42.53N 25.20E
Gadsden U.S.A. 65 I3 ....34.03N 86.04W
Gaer Wales 12 D3 ....51.53N 3.12W
Gaeta Italy 50 E4 ....41.13N 13.34E
Gaeta, Golfo di g. Italy 50 E4 ....41.06N 13.33E
Gaferut i. Micronesia 108 F6 ....9.15N 145.25E
Gafsa Tunisia 52 E3 ....34.26N 8.51E
Gagarin Rus. Fed. 55 P6 ....55.33N 35.01E
Gagnon Canada 63 L3 ....51.52N 68.07W
Gagra Georgia 57 N6 ....43.18N 40.16E
Gainesville U.S.A. 65 J2 ....29.36N 82.20W
Gainsborough England 15 G2 ....53.24N 0.46W
Gairdner, Lake Australia 110 C3 ....31.17S 135.38E
Gairloch Scotland 18 D2 ....57.44N 5.42W
Gair Loch b. Scotland 18 D2 ....57.43N 5.44W
Galana r. Kenya 87 C2 ....3.10S 40.08E
Galapagos Islands Ecuador 76 C7 ....0.03S 89.05W
Galapagos Rise f. Pacific Oc. 109 N5 ....8.25S 96.06W
Galashiels Scotland 17 G3 ....55.37N 2.49W
Galaţi Romania 57 H7 ....45.27N 28.03E
Gala Water r. Scotland 17 G3 ....55.36N 2.47W
Galdhøpiggen mt. Norway 40 B3 ....61.38N 8.19E
Galilee, Sea of l. Israel 53 K3 ....32.49N 35.37E
Gallabat Sudan 94 E2 ....12.57N 36.06E
Galle Sri Lanka 96 F2 ....6.04N 80.09E
Gallego Rise f. Pacific Oc. 109 M5 ....2.20S 117.59W
Galley Head Ireland 41 C1 ....51.32N 8.57W
Gallinas, Punta pt Colombia 71 J3 ....12.27N 71.42W
Gallipoli Italy 50 H4 ....40.03N 18.00E
Gallipoli Turkey 56 G5 ....40.25N 26.39E
Gällivare Sweden 40 E4 ....67.08N 20.40E
Gallup U.S.A. 64 E4 ....35.32N 108.45W
Galole Kenya 87 C2 ....1.34S 40.01E
Galston Scotland 16 E3 ....55.36N 4.23W
Galtat Zemmour Western Sahara 84 C4 ......25.08N 12.24W
Galtee Mountains hills Ireland 41 C2 ....52.19N 8.16W
Galveston U.S.A. 65 H2 ....29.15N 94.54W
Galveston Bay U.S.A. 65 H2 ....29.19N 94.46W
Galway Ireland 41 B3 ....53.16N 9.03W
Galway d. Ireland 41 B3 ....53.22N 9.16W
Galway Bay Ireland 41 B3 ....53.12N 9.16W
Gambia r. Gambia 84 C3 ....13.28N 16.35W
Gambier, Îles is French Polynesia 109 L4 ....22.56S 134.51W
Gamud mt. Ethiopia 87 B4 ....4.08N 38.07E
Gäncä Azerbaijan 58 F2 ....40.41N 46.22E
Gandadiwata, Bukit mt. Indonesia 104 F3 ....2.43S 119.25E
Gander Canada 63 M2 ....48.54N 54.17W
Gandhidham India 96 D5 ....23.06N 70.08E
Gandhinagar India 96 D5 ....23.14N 72.44E
Gandía Spain 48 E3 ....38.58N 0.10W
Ganges r. Bangl./India 96 H5 ....23.32N 90.08E
Ganges, Mouths of the Bangl./India 96 G5 ....21.17N 88.23E
Gannett Peak U.S.A. 64 E5 ....43.12N 109.39W
Gansu d. China 102 H6 ....40.01N 97.56E
Gantamaa Somalia 87 C3 ....2.25N 41.50E
Ganzhou China 103 K3 ....25.50N 114.53E
Gao Mali 84 D3 ....16.16N 0.02W
Gap France 44 G4 ....44.34N 6.05E
Gar China 102 E4 ....32.33N 80.05E
Gara, Lough l. Ireland 41 C3 ....53.57N 8.28W
Garanhuns Brazil 77 M6 ....8.52S 36.22W
Garbahaarey Somalia 87 C3 ....3.14N 42.16E
Garba Tula Kenya 87 B3 ....0.30N 38.31E
Garcia Sola, Embalse de resr Spain 48 C3 ....39.14N 5.02W
Gard r. France 44 F3 ....43.51N 4.37E
Garda, Lake Italy 50 D6 ....45.28N 10.33E
Garden City U.S.A. 64 F4 ....37.59N 100.53W
Gardēz Afgh. 95 K6 ....33.38N 69.09E
Garelochhead Scotland 16 E4 ....56.05N 4.50W
Garforth England 15 F2 ....53.48N 1.23W
Gargždai Lithuania 40 E1 ....55.43N 21.24E
Garissa Kenya 87 B2 ....0.25S 39.40E
Garmisch-Partenkirchen Germany 54 D2 .....47.30N 11.06E
Garonne r. France 44 C4 ....44.53N 0.32W
Garoowe Somalia 85 I2 ....8.23N 48.28E
Garoua Cameroon 84 F2 ....9.19N 13.23E
Garron Point Northern Ireland 16 D3 ....55.03N 5.57W
Garry r. Scotland 18 E2 ....57.04N 4.46W
Garry, Loch l. Scotland 19 E1 ....56.48N 4.15W
Garsen Kenya 87 C2 ....2.16S 40.06E
Garstang England 14 E2 ....53.54N 2.46W
Garvagh Northern Ireland 16 C2 ....54.59N 6.41W
Gary U.S.A. 65 I5 ....41.35N 87.20W
Gascony, Gulf of France 44 B3 ....43.43N 2.00W
Gascoyne r. Australia 110 A4 ....24.44S 114.03E
Gashua Nigeria 84 F3 ....12.51N 11.04E
Gaspé Canada 63 L2 ....48.48N 64.32W
Gaspé, Péninsule de pen. Canada 63 L2 ......48.35N 65.31W
Gastonia U.S.A. 65 J4 ....35.17N 81.11W
Gata, Cabo de c. Spain 48 D2 ....36.43N 2.11W
Gatehouse of Fleet Scotland 16 E2 ....54.53N 4.11W
Gateshead England 15 F3 ....54.57N 1.36W
Gatineau r. Canada 65 K6 ....45.27N 75.42W
Gävle Sweden 40 D3 ....60.41N 17.08E
Gaya India 96 G5 ....24.48N 85.00E
Gaya Niger 84 E3 ....11.54N 3.27E
Gaza Asia 53 J3 ....31.29N 34.19E
Gaza town Gaza 94 D6 ....31.31N 34.26E
Gaziantep Turkey 57 L3 ....37.03N 37.21E

Gdańsk Poland 46 D5 ....54.21N 18.39E
Gdańsk, Gulf of Poland/Rus. Fed. 46 D5 ......54.32N 19.12E
Gdynia Poland 46 D5 ....54.31N 18.33E
Geal Charn hill Scotland 19 F2 ....57.12N 3.30W
Gedaref Sudan 85 H3 ....14.02N 35.23E
Gediz r. Turkey 57 G4 ....38.35N 26.48E
Gedo r. Somalia 87 B3 ....2.52N 41.47E
Geel Belgium 42 E4 ....51.09N 5.00E
Geelong Australia 110 D3 ....38.08S 144.21E
Gejiu China 103 I2 ....23.22N 103.09E
Gela Italy 50 F2 ....37.04N 14.15E
Gelderland d. Neth. 42 F5 ....52.04N 6.08E
Gelincik Dağı mt. Turkey 57 I4 ....38.03N 30.42E
Gelligaer Wales 12 D3 ....51.40N 3.15W
Gelsenkirchen Germany 54 B4 ....51.33N 7.06E
Gemlik Turkey 57 H5 ....40.25N 29.09E
Genalē Wenz r. Ethiopia 87 C4 ....4.10N 42.05E
General Santos Phil. 105 H5 ....6.08N 125.15E
Geneva Switz. 50 B7 ....46.13N 6.09E
Geneva, Lake France/Switz. 44 G5 ....46.22N 6.16E
Genil r. Spain 48 C2 ....37.42N 5.18W
Genk Belgium 42 E3 ....50.57N 5.31E
Genoa Italy 50 C6 ....44.25N 8.56E
Genoa, Gulf of Italy 50 C6 ....44.08N 8.57E
George r. Canada 63 L3 ....58.19N 65.55W
Georgetown Guyana 72 D7 ....6.49N 58.09W
George Town Malaysia 104 C5 ....5.26N 100.17E
Georgia Asia 58 F2 ....41.49N 43.59E
Georgia d. U.S.A. 65 J3 ....32.35N 83.28W
Georgian Bay Canada 63 J2 ....45.17N 80.51W
Georgina watercourse Australia 110 C4 ......24.54S 139.35E
Georgiyevka Kazakhstan 102 E7 ....49.16N 81.34E
Gera Germany 54 E4 ....50.53N 12.06E
Geral de Goiás, Serra hills Brazil 77 K5 .....11.38S 46.01W
Geraldton Australia 110 A4 ....28.46S 114.37E
Gerede Turkey 57 J5 ....40.48N 32.12E
Gereshk Afgh. 95 J6 ....31.51N 64.37E
Gerlachovský štít mt. Slovakia 54 I3 ....49.10N 20.07E
Germany Europe 54 D4 ....51.18N 10.22E
Gevgelija Macedonia 56 E5 ....41.09N 22.30E
Geyik Dağı mt. Turkey 57 J3 ....36.52N 32.11E
Geyve Turkey 57 I5 ....40.30N 30.15E
Gezira f. Sudan 82 G6 ....14.30N 33.00E
Ghadāmis Libya 84 E5 ....30.05N 9.34E
Ghaem Shahr Iran 95 H7 ....36.32N 52.39E
Ghaghara r. India 96 F6 ....25.42N 84.51E
Ghana Africa 84 D2 ....8.23N 0.47W
Ghardaïa Algeria 84 E5 ....32.26N 3.49E
Gharyān Libya 52 F3 ....32.11N 13.01E
Ghāt Libya 84 F4 ....25.10N 10.13E
Ghazaouet Algeria 52 C4 ....35.06N 1.51W
Ghaziabad India 96 E6 ....28.40N 77.25E
Ghazni Afgh. 95 K6 ....33.33N 68.27E
Ghent Belgium 42 C4 ....51.03N 3.43E
Gherla Romania 46 F1 ....47.03N 23.55E
Giant's Causeway f. Northern Ireland 16 C3 ...55.14N 6.31W
Gibraltar Gibraltar 48 C2 ....36.08N 5.21W
Gibraltar, Strait of Morocco/Spain 48 B1 ....35.50N 6.05W
Gibson Desert Australia 110 B4 ....24.46S 123.25E
Gīdolē Ethiopia 87 B4 ....5.38N 37.25E
Gien France 44 E5 ....47.41N 2.38E
Gießen Germany 54 C4 ....50.35N 8.41E
Gifu Japan 106 C3 ....35.25N 136.46E
Gigha i. Scotland 16 D3 ....55.41N 5.46W
Gijón-Xixón Spain 48 C5 ....43.32N 5.39W
Gila r. U.S.A. 64 D3 ....32.45N 114.31W
Gilbert Islands Kiribati 108 H6 ....1.31N 170.43E
Gilbert Ridge f. Pacific Oc. 108 H5 ....0.07S 172.43E
Gilgil Kenya 87 B2 ....0.29S 36.21E
Gilgit Jammu and Kashmir 96 D8 ....35.54N 74.21E
Gill, Lough l. Ireland 41 C4 ....54.15N 8.25W
Gillette U.S.A. 64 E5 ....44.18N 105.29W
Gillingham Dor. England 10 C2 ....51.02N 2.17W
Gillingham Medway England 11 F2 ....51.23N 0.33E
Gilwern Wales 12 D3 ....51.49N 3.06W
Gimbala, Jebel mt. Sudan 94 B2 ....13.00N 24.20E
Giresun Turkey 57 M5 ....40.55N 38.23E
Girona Spain 48 G4 ....41.58N 2.49E
Gironde est. France 44 C4 ....45.31N 0.59W
Girvan Scotland 16 E3 ....55.15N 4.51W
Gisborne New Zealand 111 G3 ....38.39S 178.01E
Giurgiu Romania 56 F6 ....43.54N 25.57E
Giza Egypt 85 H4 ....29.59N 31.12E
Gizhiga Rus. Fed. 59 R4 ....62.01N 160.28E
Gjirokastër Albania 56 D5 ....40.07N 20.09E
Gjøvik Norway 40 B3 ....60.48N 10.41E
Gladstone Australia 110 E4 ....23.51S 151.18E
Glan r. Germany 42 G2 ....49.47N 7.42E
Glanton England 15 F4 ....55.25N 1.53W
Glasgow Scotland 16 E3 ....55.52N 4.15W
Glasgow d. Scotland 8 C4 ....55.52N 4.15W
Glasgow U.S.A. 64 E6 ....48.10N 106.34W
Glass, Loch l. Scotland 19 E2 ....57.44N 4.31W
Glastonbury England 10 C2 ....51.09N 2.43W
Glenarm Northern Ireland 16 D2 ....54.58N 5.56W
Glen Coe f. Scotland 18 D1 ....56.41N 5.05W
Glendale U.S.A. 64 D3 ....33.30N 112.12W
Glen Garry f. Scotland 18 D2 ....57.03N 5.05W
Glenluce Scotland 16 E2 ....54.53N 4.49W
Glen More f. Scotland 19 E2 ....57.09N 4.44W
Glen Moriston f. Scotland 18 E2 ....57.09N 4.52W
Glennallen U.S.A. 62 D4 ....62.09N 145.32W
Glenrothes Scotland 17 F4 ....56.12N 3.10W
Glen Shee f. Scotland 19 F1 ....56.48N 3.29W
Glinton England 11 E3 ....52.38N 0.18W
Gliwice Poland 46 D3 ....50.18N 18.40E
Głogów Poland 46 C3 ....51.40N 16.05E
Glomfjord Norway 40 C4 ....66.49N 13.57E
Glorieuses, Îles is Indian Oc. 86 D3 ....11.34S 47.18E
Glossop England 15 F2 ....53.27N 1.57W
Gloucester England 10 C2 ....51.52N 2.14W
Gloucestershire d. England 9 D2 ....51.49N 2.11W
Glusburn England 15 F2 ....53.54N 1.59W
Glyder Fawr hill Wales 12 C5 ....53.06N 4.02W
Glynneath Wales 12 D3 ....51.45N 3.37W
Gmünd Austria 54 F3 ....48.47N 14.59E
Gniezno Poland 46 C4 ....52.32N 17.36E
Goa d. India 96 D4 ....15.24N 74.11E
Goat Fell hill Scotland 16 D3 ....55.37N 5.11W
Gobabis Namibia 86 A2 ....22.27S 18.58E
Gobi des. China/Mongolia 103 J6 ....44.59N 107.19E
Gobowen England 10 B3 ....52.54N 3.02W
Goch Germany 42 F4 ....51.40N 6.09E
Godalming England 11 E2 ....51.11N 0.37W
Godavari r. India 96 F4 ....16.57N 81.49E
Godmanchester England 11 E3 ....52.19N 0.10W
Goes Neth. 42 C4 ....51.30N 3.54E
Goiânia Brazil 77 K4 ....16.41S 49.16W
Goiás Brazil 77 J4 ....15.54S 50.04W
Goiás d. Brazil 77 J4 ....16.15S 50.03W
Gökçeada i. Turkey 56 F5 ....40.12N 25.48E
Göksun Turkey 57 L4 ....38.02N 36.30E
Gölcük Turkey 57 H5 ....40.43N 29.49E

Gołdap Poland 46 F5 ....54.18N ...
Gold Coast town Australia 110 E4 ....28.03S 15...
Golmud China 102 G5 ....36.21N 9...
Golpāyegān Iran 95 H6 ....33.23N 5...
Golspie Scotland 19 F2 ....57.58N ...
Gómez Palacio Mexico 70 D6 ....25.35N 10...
Gonaïves Haiti 71 J4 ....19.27N 7...
Gonbad-e Kavus Iran 95 I7 ....37.14N 5...
Gonder Ethiopia 85 H3 ....12.39N ...
Gondia India 96 F5 ....21.28N 8...
Gongga Shan mt. China 103 I3 ....29.57N 10...
Good Hope, Cape of S. Africa 86 A1 ....34.22S ...
Goodwick Wales 12 C4 ....52.00N ...
Goole England 15 G2 ....53.42N ...
Göppingen Germany 54 C3 ....48.43N 9...
Gora mt. Rus. Fed. 58 H4 ....64.59N 6...
Góra Kalwaria Poland 46 E3 ....51.59N 2...
Gorakhpur India 96 F6 ....26.45N 8...
Gorebridge Scotland 17 F3 ....55.50N ...
Gorey Ireland 41 E2 ....52.40N 6...
Gorgān Iran 95 H7 ....36.50N 5...
Goris Armenia 95 G7 ....39.30N 4...
Gorizia Italy 50 E6 ....45.57N 1...
Gorlice Poland 46 E2 ....49.40N 2...
Görlitz Germany 54 F4 ....51.09N 1...
Gornji Vakuf Bos.-Herz. 56 B6 ....43.55N 1...
Gorno-Altaysk Rus. Fed. 102 F8 ....51.59N 8...
Gornyak Rus. Fed. 102 E8 ....50.59N 8...
Gorontalo Indonesia 105 G4 ....0.34N 12...
Gort Ireland 41 C3 ....53.04N ...
Gory mts Rus. Fed. 59 K4 ....69.06N 9...
Gorzów Wielkopolski Poland 46 B4 ....52.44N 1...
Gosberton England 11 E3 ....52.52N 0...
Gosford Australia 110 E3 ....33.25S 15...
Gosforth Cumb. England 14 D3 ....54.25N 3...
Gosforth T. and W. England 15 F4 ....55.00N 1...
Goshogawara Japan 106 D4 ....40.48N 14...
Gospić Croatia 56 A7 ....44.33N 1...
Gosport England 10 D1 ....50.48N 1...
Gostivar Macedonia 56 D5 ....41.47N 2...
Gotha Germany 54 D4 ....50.57N 1...
Gothenburg Sweden 40 B2 ....57.43N 1...
Gotland i. Sweden 40 D2 ....57.36N 1...
Göttingen Germany 54 C4 ....51.32N ...
Gouda Neth. 42 D5 ....52.00N ...
Gouin, Réservoir resr Canada 63 K2 ....48.39N 74...
Goulburn Australia 110 D3 ....34.47S 14...
Gourdon France 44 D4 ....44.45N ...
Governador Valadares Brazil 77 L4 ....18.49S 41...
Gower pen. Wales 12 C3 ....51.36N ...
Gowna, Lough l. Ireland 41 D3 ....53.53N 7...
Goya Argentina 77 I2 ....29.08S 59...
Göynük Turkey 57 I5 ....40.24N 3...
Gozo i. Malta 50 F2 ....36.05N 1...
Gradaús, Serra dos hills Brazil 77 J6 ....8.30S 50...
Grafham Water resr England 11 E3 ....52.18N 0...
Grafton Australia 110 E4 ....29.41S 15...
Grafton U.S.A. 64 G6 ....48.24N 97...
Grahamstown S. Africa 86 B1 ....33.19S 2...
Grain England 11 F2 ....51.27N ...
Grampian Mountains Scotland 19 E1 ....56.47N 4...
Granada Spain 48 D2 ....37.11N 3...
Gran Canaria i. Canary Islands 48 Y1 ....27.47N 15...
Gran Chaco f. Argentina/Paraguay 73 C4 .....27.08S 62...
Grand Canyon f. U.S.A. 64 D4 ....36.03N 112...
Grand Canyon town U.S.A. 64 D4 ....36.03N 112...
Grand Cayman i. Cayman Is 71 H4 ....19.23N 81...
Grande r. Brazil 77 K3 ....11.08S 43...
Grande, Bahía b. Argentina 73 C1 ....50.40S 68...
Grande Prairie Canada 62 G3 ....55.11N 118...
Grandes, Salinas f. Argentina 73 C3 ....30.24S 65...
Grand Falls - Windsor Canada 63 M2 ....48.53S 55...
Grand Forks U.S.A. 64 G6 ....47.55N 97...
Grand Island U.S.A. 64 G5 ....40.56N 98...
Grand Junction U.S.A. 64 E4 ....39.04N 108...
Grand Rapids town U.S.A. 65 I5 ....42.57N 85...
Grand Turk Turks and Caicos Is 71 J5 ....21.28N 71...
Grangemouth Scotland 17 F4 ....56.01N 3...
Grange-over-Sands England 14 E3 ....54.11N 2...
Gran Paradiso mt. Italy 50 B6 ....45.31N 7...
Gran Tarajal Canary Islands 48 Y2 ....28.12N 14...
Grantham England 10 E3 ....52.55N 0...
Grantown-on-Spey Scotland 19 F2 ....57.20N 3...
Grants Pass U.S.A. 64 B5 ....42.29N 123...
Grasse France 44 G3 ....43.39N 6...
Grassington England 15 F3 ....54.04N 1...
Grave, Pointe de pt France 44 C4 ....45.35N 1...
Gravelines France 11 H1 ....50.59N 2...
Gravesend England 11 F2 ....51.26N 0...
Grays England 11 F2 ....51.28N 0...
Graz Austria 54 F2 ....47.04N 15...
Great Abaco i. Bahamas 71 I6 ....26.08N 77...
Great Australian Bight g. Australia 110 B3 ....33.06S 129...
Great Baddow England 11 F2 ....51.43N 0...
Great Barrier Reef Australia 110 D5 ....11.25S 144...
Great Basin U.S.A. 64 C4 ....39.25N 116...
Great Bear Lake Canada 62 G4 ....66.03N 119...
Great Belt str. Denmark 54 D6 ....55.34N 10...
Great Bend U.S.A. 64 G4 ....38.23N 98...
Great Bernera i. Scotland 18 C3 ....58.14N 6...
Great Blasket Island Ireland 41 A2 ....52.06N 10...
Great Clifton England 14 D3 ....54.39N 3...
Great Cumbrae i. Scotland 16 E3 ....55.47N 4...
Great Dividing Range mts Australia 110 D3 ...37.30S 144...
Great Driffield England 15 G3 ....54.00N 0...
Great Dunmow England 11 F2 ....51.52N 0...
Greater Antilles is Caribbean Sea 71 H5 ......21.05N 81...
Greater London d. England 9 E2 ....51.30N 0...
Greater Manchester d. England 9 D3 ....53.31N 2...
Great Exuma i. Bahamas 71 I5 ....23.35N 75...
Great Falls town U.S.A. 64 D6 ....47.30N 111...
Great Gonerby England 10 E3 ....52.56N 0...
Greatham England 15 F3 ....54.38N 1...
Great Harwood England 15 E2 ....53.47N 2...
Great Inagua i. Bahamas 71 J5 ....21.13N 73...
Great Karoo f. S. Africa 86 B1 ....32.29S 23...
Great Linford England 10 E3 ....52.04N 0...
Great Malvern England 10 C3 ....52.07N 2...
Great Namaqualand f. Namibia 86 A2 ....26.29S 16...
Great Nicobar i. India 97 H2 ....7.06N 94...
Great Ormes Head Wales 12 D5 ....53.21N 3...
Great Ouse r. England 11 F3 ....52.46N 0...
Great Plains f. N. America 60 I7 ....45.00N 100...
Great Rhos hill Wales 12 D4 ....52.16N 3...
Great Rift Valley f. Africa 82 G4 ....7.00S 33...
Great St Bernard Pass Italy/Switz. 50 B6 ....45.53N 7...
Great Salt Lake U.S.A. 64 D5 ....40.58N 112...
Great Sand Sea des. Egypt/Libya 53 H2 ......28.55N 24...
Great Sandy Desert Australia 110 B4 ....20.35S 123...
Great Shelford England 11 F3 ....52.09N 0...
Great Slave Lake Canada 62 G4 ....61.26N 114...
Great Stour r. England 11 G2 ....51.18N 1...

Torrington England 13 C2 ....50.57N 4.08W
Victoria Desert Australia 110 B4 ....28.43S 128.38E
Whernside hill England 15 F3 ....54.10N 1.59W
Yarmouth England 11 G3 ....52.36N 1.44E
Monte Italy 50 E4 ....41.48N 13.59E
s, Sierra de mts Spain 48 C4 ....40.08N 5.43W
e Europe 56 D4 ....39.03N 21.56E
ey U.S.A. 64 F5 ....40.25N 104.41W
r. U.S.A. 64 F5 ....38.12N 109.53W
Bay town U.S.A. 65 I5 ....44.30N 88.02W
land i. N. America 63 N5 ....72.21N 41.01W
law Scotland 17 G3 ....55.42N 2.28W
ore Point Ireland 12 A4 ....52.14N 6.18W
River town U.S.A. 64 E5 ....41.36N 109.29W
sboro U.S.A. 64 A4 ....36.04N 79.48W
stone Point Scotland 18 D2 ....57.56N 5.40W
ville Liberia 84 D2 ....5.01N 9.02W
ville Miss. U.S.A. 65 H3 ....33.22N 91.01W
ville S. C. U.S.A. 65 J3 ....34.50N 82.27W
wich England 11 E2 ....51.29N 0.00W
wald Germany 54 E6 ....54.05N 13.24E
n Denmark 40 B2 ....56.24N 10.54E
da Central America 71 L3 ....12.03N 61.38W
de France 44 D3 ....43.46N 1.18E
ble France 44 F4 ....45.11N 5.44E
r. England 15 E3 ....54.09N 2.37W
Scotland 17 F2 ....54.59N 3.04W
n Germany 42 G5 ....52.06N 7.38E
na Greece 56 D5 ....40.05N 21.25E
nmacher d. Lux. 42 F2 ....49.42N 6.21E
Range hills Australia 110 D4 ....28.13S 142.33E
nen Germany 46 A5 ....54.07N 13.02E
sby England 15 G2 ....53.34N 0.04W
sey i. Iceland 40 Y2 ....66.32N 17.59W
dez, Cap c. France 11 G1 ....50.52N 1.36E
Scotland 19 G3 ....58.56N 2.45W
risk Wielkopolski Poland 46 C4 ....52.13N 16.22E
ngen Neth. 42 F6 ....53.13N 6.34E
ngen i. Neth. 42 F6 ....53.16N 6.40E
e Eylandt i. Australia 110 C5 .....13.58S 137.09E
er Speikkogel mt. Austria 54 F2 ....46.48N 14.58E
eto Italy 50 D5 ....42.45N 11.07E
glockner mt. Austria 54 E2 ......47.05N 12.41E
dhog r. Canada 63 J2 ....49.40N 81.56W
yy Rus. Fed. 58 J2 ....43.19N 45.42E
ziądz Poland 46 D4 ....53.30N 18.46E
ard Bay Scotland 18 D2 ....57.53N 5.32W
e Poland 46 B4 ....53.54N 15.12E
o Poland 46 B4 ....53.15N 14.29E
w Śląski Poland 46 B3 ....51.01N 15.25E
nayabo, Golfo de b. Cuba 71 I5 ...20.31N 77.38W
ajoz r. Spain 48 C2 ....37.51N 4.51W
alajara Mexico 70 D5 ....20.40N 103.24W
alajara Spain 48 D4 ....40.38N 3.09W
alcanal i. Solomon Is 111 F6 ....9.38S 160.05E
alete r. Spain 48 B2 ....36.32N 6.14W
alupe r. Spain 48 E4 ....41.15N 0.02W
alquivir r. Spain 48 B2 ....36.48N 6.21W
alupe i. Mexico 64 E2 ....29.09N 118.23W
alupe, Sierra de mts Spain 48 C3 ..39.20N 5.49W
arrama, Sierra de mts Spain 48 C4 ..40.40N 4.10W
eloupe i. Central America 71 L4 ...16.30N 61.29W
iana r. Portugal/Spain 48 B2 .....37.11N 7.24W
ix Spain 48 D2 ....37.18N 3.07W
ra, Península de la pen. Colombia 72 B8 .11.59N 71.45W
i i. N. Pacific Oc. 105 K6 ....13.29N 144.46E
ajuato Mexico 70 D5 ....21.01N 101.15W
ajuato d. Mexico 70 D5 ....21.16N 100.47W
are Venezuela 71 K2 ....9.03N 69.44W
e Cuba 71 H5 ....22.13N 84.05W
gdong d. China 103 K2 ....23.49N 114.45E
gxi Zhuangzu Zizhiqu d. China 103 J2 ..23.52N 108.27E
gyuan China 103 J4 ....32.24N 105.51E
gzhou China 103 K2 ....23.09N 113.21E
ipa r. Venezuela 71 L2 ....9.53N 62.26W
tánamo Cuba 71 I5 ....20.07N 75.13W
oré r. Bolivia/Brazil 76 E6 .....11.57S 65.04W
a, Sierra de mts Spain 48 E5 ...42.15N 0.20W
apuava Brazil 77 J2 ....25.24S 51.29W
da Portugal 48 B4 ....40.33N 7.16W
ave Mexico 70 C6 ....25.33N 108.30W
emala Central America 70 F4 ....15.43N 90.16W
emala City Guatemala 70 F3 ....14.37N 90.31W
iare r. Colombia 72 C7 ....4.02N 67.45W
aquil Ecuador 76 E7 ....2.10S 79.56W
aquil, Golfo de g. Ecuador 76 D7 ..3.10S 80.53W
mas Mexico 70 B6 ....27.57N 110.53W
Ethiopia 85 H3 ....11.16N 35.17E
randsdalen f. Norway 40 B3 ....61.58N 9.20E
ng r. China 106 A4 ....42.31N 128.03E
kédou Guinea 84 C2 ....8.33N 10.11W
na Algeria 52 E4 ....36.27N 7.29E
mine Morocco 84 C4 ....28.59N 10.02W
t France 44 D5 ....46.10N 1.53E
nsey i. Channel Is 13 Y9 ....49.29N 2.36W
rero Mexico 70 D4 ....17.41N 100.48W
s mt. Ethiopia 87 B4 ....6.08N 37.20E
na Highlands mts Guyana/Venezuela 72 C7 .6.18N 63.41W
ford England 15 E2 ....51.14N 0.34W
n China 103 K3 ....25.17N 110.19E
ea Africa 84 C3 ....10.50N 11.28W
ea, Gulf of Africa 84 E2 ....2.31N 4.26E
ea-Bissau Africa 84 C3 ....11.54N 14.45W
es France 42 A3 ....50.52N 1.52E
a Venezuela 71 L3 ....10.33N 62.19W
borough England 15 F3 ....54.32N 1.03W
e France 42 C2 ....49.54N 3.38E
China 103 J3 ....26.33N 106.39E
hou d. China 103 J3 ....26.59N 106.45E
rat d. India 96 D5 ....22.51N 72.32E
nwala Pakistan 96 D7 ....32.07N 74.13E
arga India 96 E4 ....17.20N 76.47E
ane Scotland 17 G4 ....56.02N 2.50W
Uganda 85 H3 ....2.45N 32.17E
dag Turkmenistan 95 H7 ....39.11N 54.29E
üşhane Turkey 57 M5 ....40.29N 39.28E
tur India 96 F4 ....16.19N 80.26E
r. Brazil 77 L6 ....6.51S 43.23W
rueia r. Brazil 77 K7 ....9.18S 46.11W
api r. Brazil 77 K7 ....4.15S 46.11W
au Nigeria 84 E3 ....12.15N 6.03E
Rus. Fed. 46 F5 ....54.36N 22.12E
ng Turkmenistan 95 J7 ....35.15N 62.13E
row Germany 54 E5 ....53.48N 12.11E
ahati India 97 H6 ....26.09N 91.46E
na Pakistan 96 B6 ....25.09N 62.23E
na S. America 72 D7 ....5.59N 59.59W
ahi Ethiopia 85 H2 ....11.49N 51.16E
rdafuy, Gees c. Somalia 85 J3 ...11.49N 51.16E
ebarra Bay Ireland 41 C4 ......54.53N 8.30W
ru Zimbabwe 86 B3 ....19.27S 29.50E
nedd r. Wales 9 C3 ....53.00N 4.02W

Gydan Peninsula Rus. Fed. 58 I5 ....70.08N 77.30E
Gyöngyös Hungary 54 H2 ....47.46N 19.56E
Győr Hungary 54 G2 ....47.41N 17.39E
Gypsumville Canada 62 I3 ....51.47N 98.37W
Gyula Hungary 46 E1 ....46.39N 21.16E
Gyumri Armenia 94 F8 ....40.47N 43.51E
Gyzylarbat Turkmenistan 58 G1 ....38.59N 56.17E

H

Haapajärvi Finland 40 F3 ....63.45N 25.20E
Haapsalu Estonia 40 E2 ....58.56N 23.33E
Haarlem Neth. 42 D5 ....52.22N 4.38E
Habaswein Kenya 87 B3 ....1.01N 39.56E
Habbān Yemen 95 G2 ....14.20N 47.05F
Hachijo-jima i. Japan 106 C2 ....33.07N 139.50E
Hachinohe Japan 106 D4 ....40.32N 141.31E
Hadd, Ra's al pt Oman 95 I4 ....22.30N 59.50E
Haddington Scotland 17 G3 ....55.58N 2.46W
Haderslev Denmark 40 B1 ....55.15N 9.29E
Had Kourt Morocco 48 C1 ....34.31N 5.48W
Hadleigh England 11 F3 ....52.03N 0.57E
Haḍramawt f. Yemen 95 G3 ....15.07N 47.48E
Hadyach Ukraine 55 O4 ....50.22N 33.59E
Haeju N. Korea 103 N5 ....38.02N 125.45E
Hagadera Kenya 87 C3 ....0.02N 40.22E
Hagar Nish Plateau f. Eritrea 94 E3 .....17.03N 37.58E
Hagåtña Guam 108 F6 ....13.29N 144.45E
Hagen Germany 54 B4 ....51.22N 7.28E
Hag's Head Ireland 41 B2 ....52.56N 9.29W
Hague, Cap de la c. France 13 Z9 ....49.44N 1.55E
Hai Tanzania 87 B2 ....3.37S 37.06E
Haifa Israel 53 J3 ....32.50N 34.58E
Haikou China 103 K2 ....20.01N 110.18E
Ḥā'il Saudi Arabia 94 F5 ....27.33N 41.41E
Hailsham England 11 F1 ....50.52N 0.15E
Hainan d. China 103 J1 ....19.00N 109.33E
Hainan i. China 108 D7 ....18.51N 110.29E
Hainaut d. Belgium 42 D3 ....50.31N 3.54W
Haines U.S.A. 62 E3 ....59.13N 135.25W
Hai Phong Vietnam 104 D8 ....20.48N 106.43E
Haiti Central America 71 J4 ....19.19N 73.30W
Haiya Sudan 85 H3 ....18.20N 36.23E
Hakodate Japan 106 D4 ....41.47N 140.44E
Halabja Iraq 95 G7 ....35.11N 45.56E
Ḥalānīyāt, Juzur al is Oman 95 I3 ....17.30N 56.11E
Halden Norway 40 B2 ....59.07N 11.25E
Halesowen England 10 C3 ....52.27N 2.03W
Halesworth England 11 G3 ....52.21N 1.30E
Halifax Canada 63 L2 ....44.39N 63.36W
Halifax England 15 F2 ....53.44N 1.51W
Halkirk Scotland 19 F3 ....58.31N 3.29W
Halladale r. Scotland 19 F3 ....58.34N 3.54W
Hall Beach town Canada 63 J4 ....68.42N 81.17W
Halle Belgium 42 D3 ....50.44N 4.14E
Halle Germany 54 D4 ....51.29N 11.59E
Hall Islands Micronesia 108 G6 ....8.55N 151.52E
Halls Creek town Australia 110 B5 ......18.17S 127.40E
Halmahera i. Indonesia 105 H4 ....1.06N 128.32E
Halmstad Sweden 40 C2 ....56.40N 12.52E
Halstead England 11 F2 ....51.57N 0.39E
Halton d. England 9 D3 ....53.20N 2.43W
Haltwhistle England 15 E3 ....54.58N 2.27W
Ham France 42 C2 ....49.45N 3.04E
Hamadān Iran 95 G6 ....34.46N 48.30E
Hamāh Syria 94 E7 ....35.08N 36.45E
Hamamatsu Japan 106 C2 ....34.42N 137.44E
Hamar Norway 40 B3 ....60.48N 11.05E
Hambleton Hills England 15 F3 ....54.19N 1.14W
Hamburg Germany 54 C5 ....53.34N 9.59E
Hämeenlinna Finland 40 F3 ....60.59N 24.27E
Hamersley Range mts Australia 110 A4 ...22.11S 116.31E
Hamhŭng N. Korea 103 N5 ....39.55N 127.33E
Hami China 102 G6 ....42.48N 93.27E
Hamilton Bermuda 71 L7 ....32.18N 64.46W
Hamilton Canada 63 K2 ....43.15N 79.51W
Hamilton New Zealand 111 G3 ....37.48S 175.16E
Hamilton Scotland 17 E3 ....55.47N 4.03W
Hamīm, Wādī al watercourse Libya 53 H3 ..30.04N 21.35E
Hamina Finland 40 F3 ....60.34N 27.12E
Hammamet, Golfe de g. Tunisia 52 F4 ....36.09N 10.50E
Hammerdal Sweden 40 C3 ....63.35N 15.21E
Hammerfest Norway 40 E5 ....70.40N 23.40E
Hampshire d. England 9 E2 ....51.10N 1.13W
Hampshire Downs hills England 10 D2 ....51.20N 1.35W
Ḥamrā', Al Ḥamādah al f. Libya 52 F2 ....29.40N 11.48E
Hamstreet England 11 F2 ....51.04N 0.54E
Hanamaki Japan 106 D3 ....39.23N 141.07E
Hanang mt. Tanzania 87 A1 ....4.26S 35.24E
Hancock U.S.A. 65 I6 ....47.08N 88.36W
Handa Island Scotland 18 D3 ....58.23N 5.13W
Handan China 103 K5 ....36.35N 114.32E
Handeni Tanzania 87 B2 ....5.25S 38.02E
Hangzhou China 103 M4 ....30.15N 120.10E
Hanna Canada 64 D7 ....51.38N 111.56W
Hannover Germany 54 C5 ....52.23N 9.44E
Hanöbukten b. Sweden 54 F6 ....55.48N 14.17E
Ha Nôi Vietnam 104 D8 ....21.01N 105.51E
Hantsavichy Belarus 55 L5 ....52.46N 26.27E
Hanzhong China 103 J4 ....33.04N 107.03E
Haparanda Sweden 40 F4 ....65.50N 24.08E
Happy Valley-Goose Bay town Canada 63 L3 ..53.19N 60.07W
Harare Zimbabwe 86 C3 ....17.49S 31.04E
Ḥarāsīs, Jiddat al des. Oman 95 I3 ......19.58N 55.33E
Harbin China 103 N7 ....45.40N 126.37E
Harderwijk Neth. 42 E5 ....52.21N 5.38E
Haren Germany 42 G5 ....52.48N 7.15E
Harer Ethiopia 85 I2 ....5.11N 42.10E
Hargeysa Somalia 85 I2 ....9.32N 44.05E
Hari Rūd r. Afgh./Iran 95 J7 ....36.50N 60.58E
Ḥā Hu r. China 102 H5 ....38.18N 97.23E
Harleston England 11 G3 ....52.24N 1.18E
Harlingen Neth. 42 E6 ....53.10N 5.25E
Harlow England 11 F2 ....51.47N 0.06E
Harney Basin U.S.A. 64 C5 ....43.23N 119.55W
Härnösand Sweden 40 D3 ....62.38N 17.56E
Har Nuur l. Mongolia 102 G7 ....48.02N 93.23E
Harpenden England 11 E2 ....51.49N 0.21W
Harray, Loch of l. Scotland 19 F4 ....59.01N 3.13W
Harricanaw r. Canada 63 K3 ....50.58N 79.33W
Harris, Sound of str. Scotland 18 B2 ....57.46N 7.10W
Harrisburg U.S.A. 65 K5 ....40.17N 76.54W
Harrison, Cape Canada 63 M3 ....54.56N 57.42W
Harrogate England 15 F2 ....53.59N 1.32W
Ḥârşova Romania 57 M7 ....44.41N 27.57E
Harstad Norway 40 D5 ....68.47N 16.32E
Harter Fell hill England 14 D3 ....54.29N 2.54W
Hart Fell hill Scotland 17 F3 ....55.24N 3.24W
Hartford U.S.A. 65 L5 ....41.46N 72.42W

Hartland England 13 C2 ....50.59N 4.29W
Hartland Point England 13 C3 ....51.01N 4.33W
Hartlepool England 15 F3 ....54.41N 1.13W
Hartlepool d. England 9 E4 ....54.40N 1.15W
Har Us Nuur l. Mongolia 102 G7 ....47.53N 92.19E
Harwich England 11 G2 ....51.56N 1.16E
Haryana d. India 96 E6 ....29.11N 76.12E
Haslemere England 10 E2 ....51.05N 0.43W
Hasselt Belgium 42 E3 ....50.56N 5.20E
Hassi Messaoud Algeria 84 E5 ....31.41N 6.10E
Hässleholm Sweden 40 C2 ....56.10N 13.46E
Hastings England 11 F1 ....50.51N 0.35E
Ha Tinh Vietnam 104 D7 ....18.18N 105.55E
Hatteras, Cape U.S.A. 65 K4 ....35.14N 75.34W
Hattiesburg U.S.A. 65 I3 ....31.23N 89.19W
Hat Yai Thailand 104 C5 ....7.01N 100.26F
Haud f. Ethiopia 85 I2 ....8.37N 44.15E
Haugesund Norway 40 A2 ....59.24N 5.18E
Haukivesi l. Finland 40 G3 ....62.06N 28.28E
Haut Atlas mts Morocco 84 D5 ....30.51N 8.03W
Haut-Folin hill France 44 F5 ....46.59N 4.01E
Hauts Plateaux f. Algeria 52 C3 ....33.42N 0.42W
Havana Cuba 71 H5 ....23.07N 82.22W
Havant England 10 E1 ....50.52N 0.59W
Haverfordwest Wales 12 C3 ....51.48N 4.58W
Haverhill England 11 F3 ....52.05N 0.26E
Havlíčkův Brod Czech Rep. 46 B2 ......49.36N 15.34E
Havre U.S.A. 64 E6 ....48.32N 109.41W
Havre-St-Pierre Canada 63 L3 ....50.14N 63.28W
Hawaii i. U.S.A. 109 J7 ....20.02N 155.17W
Hawaiian Islands N. Pacific Oc. 108 I7 ...28.26N 174.25W
Hawaiian Ridge f. N. Pacific Oc. 108 I7 ..26.19N 178.56W
Hawarden Wales 12 D5 ....53.11N 3.02W
Hawes England 15 E3 ....54.18N 2.12W
Haweswater Reservoir England 14 E3 ....54.30N 2.48W
Hawick Scotland 17 G3 ....55.26N 2.47W
Hawke Bay New Zealand 111 G3 ....39.24S 177.23E
Hawkhurst England 11 F2 ....51.03N 0.31E
Haxby England 15 F3 ....54.01N 1.04W
Hay Australia 110 D3 ....34.31S 144.48E
Hay r. Canada 62 G4 ....60.48N 115.47W
Haydarābad Iran 94 G7 ....37.04N 45.05E
Haydon Bridge England 15 E3 ....54.59N 2.15W
Hayle England 13 B2 ....50.11N 5.25W
Haymā' Oman 95 I3 ....19.54N 56.13F
Hay-on-Wye Wales 12 D3 ....52.05N 3.07W
Hay River town Canada 62 G4 ....60.51N 115.40W
Hayshab, Sabkhat al f. Libya 53 G3 .....31.55N 15.19E
Haywards Heath England 11 E1 ....50.59N 0.06W
Hazarajat f. Afgh. 95 K6 ....32.29N 65.07E
Hazebrouck France 42 B3 ....50.43N 2.32E
Heacham England 11 F3 ....52.54N 0.30E
Headcorn England 11 F2 ....51.10N 0.38E
Heanor England 11 F2 ....53.01N 1.21W
Hearst Canada 65 J6 ....49.41N 83.41W
Heathfield England 11 F1 ....50.58N 0.16E
Hebei d. China 103 L5 ....38.33N 115.49E
Hebron Israel 53 J3 ....31.53N 34.49E
Hecate Strait Canada 62 E3 ....52.36N 130.77W
Hechi China 103 J2 ....24.38N 108.04E
Heckington England 11 E3 ....52.59N 0.18W
Hede Sweden 40 C3 ....62.25N 13.32E
Heerenveen Neth. 42 E5 ....52.58N 5.56E
Heerlen Neth. 42 E3 ....50.53N 5.59E
Hefei China 103 L4 ....31.51N 117.19E
Hegang China 103 O7 ....47.13N 130.13E
Heidelberg Germany 54 C3 ....49.24N 8.41E
Heighington England 15 F2 ....53.13N 0.27W
Heilbronn Germany 54 C3 ....49.08N 9.12E
Heilen, Loch l. Scotland 19 F3 ....58.36N 3.17W
Heilongjiang d. China 103 N7 ....46.55N 128.30E
Heilong Jiang r. China 103 O7 ....48.25N 134.59E
Heinola Finland 40 F3 ....61.12N 26.02E
Hekla vol. Iceland 40 Y1 ....63.59N 19.41W
Helena U.S.A. 64 D6 ....46.36N 112.01W
Helensburgh Scotland 16 E4 ....56.00N 4.44W
Helgoländer Bucht g. Germany 54 C6 ....54.10N 8.14E
Hellín Spain 48 D3 ....38.31N 1.41W
Helmand r. Afgh. 95 J6 ....31.13N 61.35E
Helmond Neth. 42 E4 ....51.28N 5.40E
Helmsdale Scotland 19 F3 ....58.07N 3.39W
Helmsdale r. Scotland 19 F3 ....58.07N 3.38W
Helmsley England 15 F3 ....54.15N 1.04W
Helong China 106 A4 ....42.38N 128.59E
Helsingborg Sweden 40 C2 ....56.03N 12.42E
Helsingør Denmark 54 E7 ....56.02N 12.36E
Helsinki Finland 40 F3 ....60.10N 24.57E
Helston England 13 B2 ....50.06N 5.16W
Helvellyn hill England 14 D3 ....54.32N 3.01W
Hemel Hempstead England 11 E2 ....51.45N 0.27W
Henan d. China 103 K4 ....33.59N 112.54E
Henares r. Spain 48 D4 ....40.25N 3.29W
Henderson Island S. Pacific Oc. 109 L4 ..24.20S 128.20W
Hendon England 11 E2 ....51.35N 0.13W
Henfield England 11 E1 ....50.56N 0.16W
Hengelo Neth. 42 F5 ....52.16N 6.48E
Hengoed Wales 12 D3 ....51.39N 3.14W
Hengyang China 103 K3 ....26.53N 112.32E
Henichesʼk Ukraine 53 J6 ....46.10N 34.48E
Henley-on-Thames England 10 E2 ....51.32N 0.54W
Hennef Germany 42 G3 ....50.47N 7.18E
Henrietta Maria, Cape Canada 63 J3 ....55.21N 82.13W
Henzada Myanmar 97 I4 ....17.36N 95.26E
Herāt Afgh. 95 J6 ....34.22N 62.11E
Hereford England 13 C2 ....52.03N 2.43W
Herefordshire d. England 9 D3 ....52.07N 2.40W
Herm i. Channel Is 13 Y9 ....49.28N 2.26W
Herma Ness hd Scotland 19 I5 ....60.51N 0.54W
Hermosillo Mexico 70 B6 ....29.04N 110.58W
Herne Germany 42 G4 ....51.32N 7.13E
Herne Bay town England 11 G2 ....51.22N 1.08E
Hørning Denmark 40 B2 ....56.08N 8.58E
Hertford England 11 E2 ....51.48N 0.05W
Hertfordshire d. England 9 F2 ....51.55N 0.09E
Hesdin France 11 H1 ....50.22N 2.03E
Heswall England 14 D2 ....53.20N 3.06W
Hetton England 15 E3 ....54.01N 2.03W
Hexham England 15 E3 ....54.58N 2.07W
Heysham England 14 D3 ....54.02N 2.54W
Heywood England 14 E2 ....53.36N 2.13W
Hidaka-sanmyaku mts Japan 106 D4 ....42.49N 142.38E
Hidalgo d. Mexico 70 E5 ....20.35N 99.07W
Hidalgo del Parral Mexico 70 C6 ....26.56N 105.41W
Higham Ferrers England 11 E3 ....52.18N 0.36W
Highbridge England 10 C2 ....51.13N 2.59W
Highclere England 10 D2 ....51.20N 1.22W
Highland d. Scotland 8 C5 ....57.38N 4.59W
High Peak hills England 15 F2 ....53.23N 1.54W
High Seat hill England 15 E3 ....54.24N 2.18W
Highworth England 10 D2 ....51.38N 1.43W
High Wycombe England 10 E2 ....51.38N 0.45W
Hiiumaa i. Estonia 40 E2 ....58.50N 22.45E

Hijaz f. Saudi Arabia 94 E5 ....26.08N 37.01E
Hilāl, Ra's al pt Libya 53 H3 ....32.54N 22.09E
Hildesheim Germany 54 C5 ....52.09N 9.57E
Hillah Iraq 94 F6 ....32.27N 44.24E
Hillerød Denmark 40 C1 ....55.56N 12.18E
Hillside Scotland 19 G1 ....56.45N 2.29W
Hillswick Scotland 19 H5 ....60.29N 1.29W
Hilpsford Point England 14 D3 ....54.02N 3.12W
Hilversum Neth. 42 E5 ....52.13N 5.11E
Himachal Pradesh d. India 96 E7 ......31.59N 77.23E
Himalaya mts Asia 96 E7 ....33.06N 76.46E
Hinckley England 10 D3 ....52.33N 1.23W
Hinderwell England 15 G3 ....54.32N 0.46W
Hindhead England 10 E2 ....51.07N 0.44W
Hindley England 14 E2 ....53.32N 2.35W
Hindu Kush mts Afgh./Pakistan 95 K6 ...34.58N 67.52E
Hinnøya i. Norway 40 D5 ....68.37N 15.58F
Hiraman watercourse Kenya 87 B2 ......1.08S 39.54E
Hirosaki Japan 106 D4 ....40.36N 140.28E
Hiroshima Japan 106 B2 ....34.22N 132.27E
Hirson France 42 D2 ....49.55N 4.05E
Hirwaun Wales 12 D3 ....51.44N 3.31W
Hispaniola i. Caribbean Sea 71 J5 .....20.18N 72.57W
Hitachi Japan 106 D3 ....36.35N 140.39E
Hitchin England 11 E2 ....51.57N 0.17W
Hitra i. Norway 40 B3 ....63.31N 8.49E
Hiva Oa i. French Polynesia 109 K5 ....9.47S 138.57W
Hjälmaren l. Sweden 40 C2 ....59.14N 15.51E
Hjørring Denmark 40 B2 ....57.28N 10.01E
Hlybokaye Belarus 55 L6 ....55.08N 27.40E
Hobart Australia 110 D2 ....42.52S 147.19E
Hobro Denmark 40 B2 ....56.38N 9.48E
Ho Chi Minh City Vietnam 104 D6 ......10.45N 106.42E
Hochschwab mt. Austria 54 F2 ....47.38N 15.09E
Hoddesdon England 11 E2 ....51.46N 0.01W
Hodeidah Yemen 94 F2 ....14.50N 42.54E
Hódmezővásárhely Hungary 54 I2 ......46.25N 20.21E
Hodna, Chott el f. Algeria 52 D4 ....35.27N 4.55E
Hodnet England 10 C3 ....52.51N 2.35W
Hoek van Holland Neth. 42 D4 ....51.58N 4.08E
Hof Germany 54 D4 ....50.19N 11.55E
Höfn Iceland 40 Z2 ....64.16N 15.13W
Hofsjökull ice cap Iceland 40 Y2 ......64.49N 18.52W
Hoggar f. Algeria 84 E4 ....23.10N 4.23E
Hohhot China 103 K6 ....40.43N 111.44E
Hokkaidō i. Japan 106 D4 ....43.33N 143.77F
Holbæk Denmark 40 B1 ....55.43N 11.44E
Holbeach England 11 F3 ....52.48N 0.01E
Holbeach Marsh England 11 F3 ....52.51N 0.02E
Holderness pen. England 15 G2 ....53.52N 0.18W
Holguín Cuba 71 I5 ....20.54N 76.14W
Hollabrunn Austria 54 G3 ....48.34N 16.05E
Holland Fen f. England 11 E3 ....52.59N 0.11W
Hollesley Bay England 11 G3 ....52.02N 1.28E
Hollington England 11 F1 ....50.53N 0.33E
Hollingworth England 15 F2 ....53.28N 1.59W
Holme-on-Spalding-Moor England 15 G2 ..53.50N 0.47W
Holmfirth England 15 F2 ....53.34N 1.47W
Holstebro Denmark 40 B2 ....56.21N 8.37E
Holsworthy England 13 C2 ....50.49N 4.21W
Holt England 11 G3 ....52.55N 1.05E
Holyhead Wales 12 C5 ....53.19N 4.38W
Holyhead Bay Wales 12 C5 ....53.22N 4.40W
Holy Island England 15 F4 ....55.41N 1.47W
Holy Island Wales 12 C5 ....53.15N 4.41W
Holywell Wales 12 D5 ....53.17N 3.13W
Homa Bay town Kenya 87 A2 ....0.32S 34.27E
Homayunshahr Iran 95 H6 ....32.59N 50.23E
Homburg Germany 42 G2 ....49.19N 7.20E
Home Bay Canada 63 L4 ....68.52N 67.27W
Homs Syria 94 E6 ....34.44N 36.44E
Homyel' Belarus 55 N5 ....52.25N 31.01E
Honduras Central America 70 G3 ....14.47N 86.43W
Honduras, Gulf of Belize/Honduras 60 K3 ..16.20N 87.30W
Hønefoss Norway 40 B3 ....60.10N 10.14E
Hong Kong China 103 K2 ....22.16N 114.11E
Hong Kong d. China 103 K2 ....22.21N 114.19E
Honiara Solomon Is 111 E6 ....9.26S 159.57E
Honiton England 13 D2 ....50.48N 3.11W
Honley England 15 F2 ....53.36N 1.48W
Honolulu U.S.A. 109 J7 ....21.19N 157.52W
Honshū i. Japan 106 B3 ....35.42N 133.20E
Hood, Mount vol. U.S.A. 64 B6 ....45.23N 121.42W
Hood Point Australia 110 A3 ....34.19S 119.33E
Hoogeveen Neth. 42 F5 ....52.43N 6.30E
Hook England 10 E2 ....51.17N 0.58W
Hook Head England 41 E2 ....52.07N 6.56W
Hoorn Neth. 42 E5 ....52.39N 5.04E
Hope, Loch l. Scotland 19 E3 ....58.27N 4.39W
Hope, Point U.S.A. 62 B4 ....68.21N 166.49W
Hopedale Canada 63 L3 ....55.27N 60.00W
Hörby Sweden 54 E6 ....55.51N 13.40E
Horizon Deep f. S. Pacific Oc. 108 I4 ..23.23S 174.48W
Horley England 11 E2 ....51.10N 0.10W
Hormuz, Strait of Iran/Oman 95 I5 .....26.35N 56.59E
Horn Austria 46 B2 ....48.40N 15.40E
Horn c. Iceland 40 X2 ....66.28N 22.29W
Horn, Cape Chile 73 C1 ....56.04S 67.17W
Hornavan l. Sweden 40 D4 ....66.11N 17.44E
Horncastle England 15 G2 ....53.12N 0.07W
Hornepayne Canada 65 J6 ....49.13N 84.47W
Hornsea England 15 G2 ....53.55N 0.10W
Horodnya Ukraine 55 N4 ....51.53N 31.36E
Horodok Ukraine 55 J3 ....49.47N 23.39E
Horokhiv Ukraine 46 G3 ....50.30N 24.46E
Horrabridge England 13 C2 ....50.31N 4.06W
Horsens Denmark 40 B1 ....55.52N 9.51E
Horsham Australia 110 D3 ....36.43S 142.13E
Horsham England 11 E2 ....51.04N 0.19W
Horten Norway 40 B2 ....59.25N 10.28E
Horwich England 15 E2 ....53.36N 2.33W
Hotan China 102 E5 ....37.07N 80.02E
Houffalize Belgium 42 E3 ....50.08N 5.48E
Houghton le Spring England 15 F3 .....54.50N 1.28W
Houghton Regis England 11 E2 ....51.54N 0.31W
Hourn, Loch inlet Scotland 18 D2 ......57.08N 5.42W
Houston U.S.A. 65 G2 ....29.43N 95.19W
Hovd Mongolia 102 G7 ....47.59N 91.41E
Hove England 11 E1 ....50.50N 0.10W
Hoveton England 11 G3 ....52.43N 1.25E
Hövsgöl Nuur l. Mongolia 103 I8 ......50.59N 100.42E
Howden England 15 G2 ....53.45N 0.52W
Howland Island N. Pacific Oc. 108 I6 ...0.48N 176.38W
Hoy i. Scotland 19 F3 ....58.50N 3.16W
Høyanger Norway 40 A3 ....61.13N 6.04E
Hoyerswerda Germany 54 F4 ....51.27N 14.16E
Höytiäinen l. Finland 40 G3 ....62.46N 29.43E
Hradec Králové Czech Rep. 54 F4 ......50.13N 15.50E
Hrebinka Ukraine 55 O4 ....50.06N 32.26E
Hrodna Belarus 55 J5 ....53.41N 23.49E
Hsinchu Taiwan 103 M2 ....24.48N 120.58E
Huacho Peru 76 E5 ....11.09S 77.35W
Huaibei China 103 L4 ....33.57N 116.51E
Huainan China 103 L4 ....32.36N 117.02E

Huallaga r. Peru 76 E6 ....5.06S 75.40W
Huambo Angola 86 A3 ....12.46S 15.44E
Huancayo Peru 76 E5 ....12.03S 75.11W
Huang He r. China 103 L5 ....37.46N 118.57E
Huangshi China 103 L4 ....30.10N 115.08E
Huánuco Peru 76 E6 ....9.57S 76.14W
Huarmey Peru 76 E5 ....10.03S 78.11W
Huascarán, Nevado de mt. Peru 76 E6 ....9.09S 77.36W
Hubei d. China 103 K4 ....31.09N 113.06E
Hubli India 96 E4 ....15.18N 75.15E
Hucknall England 15 F2 ....53.02N 1.12W
Huddersfield England 15 F2 ....53.39N 1.47W
Hudiksvall Sweden 40 D3 ....61.43N 17.06E
Hudson r. U.S.A. 65 L5 ....40.54N 73.56W
Hudson Bay sea Canada 63 J3 ....59.05N 86.00W
Hudson Strait Canada 63 K4 ....63.31N 74.25W
Huê Vietnam 104 D7 ....16.26N 107.33E
Huelva Spain 48 B2 ....37.16N 6.55W
Huércal-Overa Spain 48 E2 ....37.23N 1.55W
Huesca Spain 48 E5 ....42.09N 0.25W
Huila, Nevado de vol. Colombia 76 E8 ....2.59N 75.57W
Hulin China 106 B5 ....45.42N 132.52E
Hull Canada 65 K6 ....45.27N 75.45W
Hulun Buir China 103 L7 ....49.04N 119.46E
Hulun Nur l. China 103 L7 ....48.32N 117.11E
Hulwān Egypt 53 J2 ....29.55N 31.18E
Humaitá Brazil 76 H6 ....7.33S 63.02W
Humber, Mouth of the England 15 H2 ....53.33N 0.06E
Humboldt r. U.S.A. 64 C5 ....40.04N 118.36W
Humenné Slovakia 46 E2 ....48.56N 21.54E
Humphreys Peak U.S.A. 64 D4 ....35.21N 111.40W
Húnaflói b. Iceland 40 X2 ....65.46N 20.50W
Hunan d. China 103 K3 ....27.26N 111.22E
Hunchun China 106 B4 ....42.52N 130.21E
Hunchun r. China 106 B4 ....42.38N 130.17E
Hungarian Plain f. Hungary 34 F2 ....46.30N 19.00E
Hungary Europe 54 H2 ....47.01N 18.59E
Hungerford England 10 D2 ....51.25N 1.31W
Hunish, Rubha pt Scotland 18 C2 ....57.42N 6.24W
Hunmanby England 15 G3 ....54.11N 0.19W
Hunsrück hills Germany 54 B3 ....49.47N 7.00E
Hunstanton England 11 F3 ....52.56N 0.30E
Huntingdon England 11 E3 ....52.20N 0.11W
Huntington U.S.A. 65 J4 ....38.25N 82.18W
Huntly Scotland 19 G2 ....57.27N 2.47W
Huntsville Ala. U.S.A. 65 I3 ....34.46N 86.34W
Huntsville Tex. U.S.A. 65 G3 ....30.42N 95.34W
Huri Hills Kenya 87 B3 ....3.23N 37.40E
Huron U.S.A. 64 G5 ....44.23N 98.13W
Huron, Lake Canada/U.S.A. 63 J2 ....44.39N 82.23W
Hurstpierpoint England 11 E1 ....50.56N 0.11W
Husum Germany 54 C6 ....54.29N 9.04E
Hutton Rudby England 15 F3 ....54.27N 1.17W
Huzhou China 103 M4 ....30.50N 120.08E
Hvannadalshnúkur vol. Iceland 40 Y2 ....64.01N 16.41W
Hvar i. Croatia 56 B6 ....43.08N 16.33E
Hyargas Nuur l. Mongolia 102 G7 ....49.02N 93.18E
Hyderabad India 96 E4 ....17.21N 78.25E
Hyderabad Pakistan 96 C6 ....25.21N 68.23E
Hyères France 44 G3 ....43.07N 6.08E
Hyesan N. Korea 106 A4 ....41.24N 128.11E
Hyrynsalmi Finland 40 G4 ....64.40N 28.29E
Hythe Hants. England 10 D1 ....50.52N 1.24W
Hythe Kent England 11 G2 ....51.04N 1.05E
Hyvinkää Finland 40 F3 ....60.38N 24.51E

I

Ialomiţa r. Romania 56 G7 ....44.43N 27.51E
Iar Connaught f. Ireland 41 B3 ....53.21N 9.19W
Iaşi Romania 53 I6 ....47.10N 27.35E
Ibadan Nigeria 84 E2 ....7.24N 3.55E
Ibagué Colombia 72 B7 ....4.24N 75.13W
Ibar r. Serbia 56 D6 ....43.43N 20.45E
Ibarra Ecuador 76 E8 ....0.23N 78.04W
Ibb Yemen 94 F2 ....14.03N 44.09E
Ibiapaba, Serra da hills Brazil 77 L7 ....3.38S 41.10W
Ibiza Spain 48 F3 ....38.54N 1.27E
Ibiza i. Spain 48 F3 ....39.10N 1.39E
Ibrā' Oman 95 I4 ....22.41N 58.33E
Ibstock England 10 D3 ....52.42N 1.24W
Ica Peru 76 E5 ....14.04S 75.43W
Iceland Europe 40 X2 ....64.42N 18.19W
Ichinoseki Japan 106 D3 ....38.55N 141.07E
Icklesham England 11 F1 ....50.55N 0.40E
Idaho d. U.S.A. 64 D5 ....44.08N 114.08W
Idaho Falls town U.S.A. 64 D5 ....43.32N 112.01W
Idar-Oberstein Germany 42 G2 ....49.42N 7.18E
Idfū Egypt 53 J1 ....24.55N 32.49E
Idhi mt. Greece 56 F2 ....35.13N 24.47E
Idlib Syria 57 L2 ....35.56N 36.38E
Ieper Belgium 42 B3 ....50.51N 2.53E
Iešjávri l. Norway 40 F5 ....69.39N 24.28E
Igan Malaysia 104 E4 ....2.51N 111.44E
Iganga Uganda 87 A3 ....0.37N 33.28E
Iggesund Sweden 40 D3 ....61.39N 17.05E
Iglesias Italy 50 C3 ....39.19N 8.32E
Iğneada Burnu pt Turkey 57 H5 ....41.53N 28.03E
Igoumenitsa Greece 56 D4 ....39.30N 20.17E
Iguaçu r. Brazil 77 J2 ....25.36S 54.35W
Iguaçu Falls Argentina/Brazil 77 J2 .....25.38S 54.26W
Iguatu Brazil 77 M6 ....6.22S 39.17W
Iisalmi Finland 40 F3 ....63.34N 27.11E
IJmuiden Neth. 42 D5 ....52.27N 4.37E
IJssel r. Neth. 42 E5 ....52.35N 5.50E
IJsselmeer l. Neth. 42 E5 ....52.48N 5.22E
IJzer r. Belgium 11 H2 ....51.09N 2.44E
Ikaahuk Canada 62 F5 ....71.55N 125.00W
Ikaria i. Greece 56 G3 ....37.39N 26.13E
Iki i. Japan 106 A2 ....33.45N 129.39E
Ilagan Phil. 105 G7 ....17.06N 121.53E
Ilaisamis Kenya 87 B3 ....1.36N 37.47E
Ilchester England 10 C2 ....51.00N 2.41W
Ilebo Dem. Rep. Congo 86 B4 ....4.21S 20.36E
Île-de-France f. France 42 B1 ....48.39N 2.63E
Ileret Kenya 87 B3 ....4.18N 36.14E
Ilford England 11 F2 ....51.33N 0.05E
Ilfracombe England 13 C3 ....51.12N 4.07W
Ilhéus Brazil 77 M5 ....14.46S 39.02W
Iligan Phil. 105 G5 ....8.13N 124.15E
Ilkeston England 10 D3 ....52.58N 1.18W
Ilkley England 15 F2 ....53.56N 1.49W
Illinois d. U.S.A. 65 I4 ....39.52N 89.07W
Illinois r. U.S.A. 65 H4 ....38.56N 90.30W
Illizi Algeria 84 E4 ....26.29N 8.30E
Ilminster England 10 C1 ....50.56N 2.54W
Iloilo Phil. 105 G6 ....10.41N 122.32E
Ilorin Nigeria 84 E2 ....8.30N 4.34E
Iman r. Rus. Fed. 106 B5 ....45.57N 133.45E
Imatra Finland 40 G3 ....61.11N 28.47E
Immingham England 15 G2 ....53.37N 0.13W
Imola Italy 50 D6 ....44.21N 11.42E

Imperatriz Brazil 77 K6 ....5.33S 47.26W
Imphal India 97 H5 ....24.46N 93.56E
Imroz Turkey 56 F5 ....40.10N 25.55E
Inambari r. Peru 76 G5 ....12.44S 69.47W
Inarijärvi l. Finland 40 F5 ....68.57N 27.37E
Inchard, Loch b. Scotland 18 D3 ....58.27N 5.04W
Inch'ini Terara mt. Ethiopia 87 B4 ....4.35N 37.07E
Inchkeith i. Scotland 17 F4 ....56.02N 3.08W
Inch'ŏn S. Korea 103 N5 ....37.28N 126.39E
Indalsälven r. Sweden 40 D3 ....62.32N 17.24E
Independence U.S.A. 65 H4 ....39.07N 94.26W
India Asia 96 E5 ....22.00N 79.00E
Indiana d. U.S.A. 65 I5 ....40.09N 86.01W
Indian-Antarctic Ridge f. Southern Oc. 108 D2 .49.49S 117.01E
Indianapolis U.S.A. 65 I4 ....39.46N 86.10W
Indian Ocean 117 M5
Indigirka r. Rus. Fed. 59 P5 ....71.28N 149.53E
Indonesia Asia 104 E2 ....4.12S 112.02E
Indore India 96 E5 ....22.40N 75.53E
Indre r. France 44 D5 ....47.14N 0.12E
Indus r. China/Pakistan 102 B3 ....23.56N 67.38E
Indus, Mouths of the Pakistan 96 C5 ..24.36N 66.36E
Inebolu Turkey 57 J5 ....41.58N 33.45E
İnegöl Turkey 57 H5 ....40.04N 29.30E
Infiernillo, Presa resr Mexico 70 D4 ..18.41N 101.57W
Infiesto Spain 48 C5 ....43.21N 5.20W
Ingatestone England 11 F2 ....51.40N 0.23E
Ingleborough hill England 15 E3 ....54.10N 2.24W
Ingleton England 15 E3 ....54.09N 2.28W
Ingoldmells England 15 H2 ....53.12N 0.20E
Ingolstadt Germany 54 D3 ....48.46N 11.27E
Inhambane Mozambique 86 C2 ....23.47S 35.31E
Inhul r. Ukraine 55 N2 ....46.58N 31.58E
Inhulets' r. Ukraine 55 O2 ....46.41N 32.49E
Inishbofin i. Ireland 41 A3 ....53.38N 10.14W
Inisheer i. Ireland 41 B3 ....53.04N 9.30W
Inishmaan i. Ireland 41 B3 ....53.05N 9.33W
Inishmore i. Ireland 41 B3 ....53.09N 9.47W
Inishmurray i. Ireland 41 C4 ....54.26N 8.40W
Inishowen pen. Ireland 41 D5 ....55.13N 7.17W
Inishowen Head Ireland 16 C3 ....55.14N 6.55W
Inishtrahull i. Ireland 41 D5 ....55.28N 7.13W
Inishtrahull Sound str. Ireland 16 B3 ..55.27N 7.28W
Inishturk i. Ireland 41 A3 ....53.42N 10.08W
Inn r. Europe 50 D7 ....46.55N 10.29E
Inner Mongolia d. China 103 I6 ....40.12N 103.26E
Inner Sound str. Scotland 18 D2 ....57.21N 5.57W
Innsbruck Austria 54 D2 ....47.16N 11.24E
Inny r. Ireland 41 D3 ....53.33N 7.50W
Inowrocław Poland 46 D4 ....52.48N 18.16E
In Salah Algeria 84 E4 ....27.13N 2.25E
Insch Scotland 19 G2 ....57.20N 2.37W
International Falls town U.S.A. 65 H6 ..48.36N 93.25W
Inukjuak Canada 63 K3 ....58.28N 78.04W
Inuvik Canada 62 F4 ....68.24N 133.43W
Inveraray Scotland 16 D4 ....56.14N 5.04W
Inverbervie Scotland 19 G1 ....56.51N 2.17W
Invercargill New Zealand 111 F2 ......46.25S 168.22E
Inverclyde d. Scotland 8 C4 ....55.54N 4.44W
Invergordon Scotland 19 E2 ....57.42N 4.10W
Inverkeithing Scotland 17 F4 ....56.02N 3.24W
Inverness Scotland 19 E2 ....57.29N 4.13W
Inverurie Scotland 19 G2 ....57.17N 2.22W
Investigator Ridge f. Indian Oc. 108 C5 .7.10S 98.15E
Ioannina Greece 56 D4 ....39.40N 20.51E
Iona i. Scotland 16 C4 ....56.19N 6.25W
Ionian Islands Greece 56 C4 ....39.26N 19.33E
Ionian Sea Greece/Italy 56 C4 ....38.11N 18.29E
Ios i. Greece 56 F3 ....36.44N 25.22E
Iowa d. U.S.A. 65 H5 ....42.12N 92.47W
Iowa City U.S.A. 65 H5 ....41.40N 91.32W
Ipatinga Brazil 77 L4 ....19.29S 42.28W
Ipoh Malaysia 104 C4 ....4.40N 101.04E
Ipswich England 11 G3 ....52.03N 1.09E
Iput' r. Rus. Fed. 55 N5 ....52.30N 31.37E
Iput' r. Belarus 55 N5 ....52.26N 31.04E
Iqaluit Canada 63 L4 ....63.45N 68.36W
Iquique Chile 73 B4 ....20.14S 70.07W
Iquitos Peru 76 F7 ....3.50S 73.13W
Iráklion Greece 56 F2 ....35.19N 25.08E
Iran Asia 95 H6 ....31.28N 55.05E
Iran, Pegunungan mts Indonesia 104 E4 .1.47N 114.46E
Iranian Plateau f. Iran 90 E5 ....32.00N 55.00E
Īrānshahr Iran 95 J5 ....27.13N 60.42E
Irapuato Mexico 70 D5 ....20.41N 101.23W
Iraq Asia 94 F6 ....32.50N 42.21E
Irbid Jordan 94 E6 ....32.34N 35.51E
Irbit r. Brazil 76 H7 ....3.06S 64.45W
Ireland Europe 41 D3 ....53.33N 7.43W
Ireland's Eye i. Ireland 41 E3 ....53.24N 6.03W
Irgiz Kazakhstan 58 H2 ....48.36N 61.18E
Iringa Tanzania 86 C4 ....7.48S 35.43E
Iriri r. Brazil 77 J7 ....3.52S 52.37W
Irish Sea Ireland/U.K. 41 F3 ....53.40N 5.11W
Irkutsk Rus. Fed. 59 L3 ....52.11N 104.09E
Iron Mountain U.S.A. 65 I6 ....45.49N 88.04W
Ironwood U.S.A. 65 H6 ....46.28N 90.09W
Irosin Phil. 105 G6 ....12.42N 124.00E
Irrawaddy r. Myanmar 97 I4 ....15.48N 95.05E
Irrawaddy, Mouths of the Myanmar 97 H4 .15.35N 94.02E
Irsha r. Ukraine 55 M4 ....50.46N 29.35E
Irthing r. England 14 E3 ....54.55N 2.49W
Irtysh r. Kazakhstan/Rus. Fed. 58 H4 .61.07N 68.50E
Irún Spain 48 E5 ....43.20N 1.48W
Irvine Scotland 16 E3 ....55.37N 4.40W
Isabela Phil. 105 G5 ....6.40N 121.59E
Isabela, Isla i. Ecuador 76 B7 ....0.41S 91.03W
Isabelia, Cordillera mts Nicaragua 71 G3 .13.13N 85.59W
Ísafjörður Iceland 40 X2 ....66.05N 23.10W
Isar r. Germany 54 E3 ....48.49N 12.59E
Isbister Scotland 19 H5 ....60.36N 1.05W
Ischia, Isola d' i. Italy 50 E4 ....40.42N 13.51E
Ise Japan 106 C2 ....34.29N 136.43E
Isère, Pointe pt French Guiana 72 D7 .5.47N 53.57W
Ishikari-wan b. Japan 106 D4 ....43.17N 140.58E
Ishim r. Kazakhstan/Rus. Fed. 58 I3 .57.43N 71.18E
Ishinomaki Japan 106 D3 ....38.25N 141.17E
Isiolo Kenya 87 B3 ....0.22N 37.38E
Isiro Dem. Rep. Congo 86 B5 ....2.46N 27.36E
İskenderun Turkey 57 L3 ....36.34N 36.08E
İskenderun Körfezi b. Turkey 57 K3 .36.38N 35.54E
Iskŭr r. Bulgaria 56 F6 ....43.44N 24.27E
Isla r. Ang. Scotland 19 F1 ....56.32N 3.22W
Isla r. Mor. Scotland 19 G2 ....57.31N 2.47W
Islamabad Pakistan 96 D7 ....33.42N 73.08E
Island Magee pen. Northern Ireland 16 D2 .54.50N 5.41W
Isle of Anglesey d. Wales 9 C3 ....53.18N 4.23W
Isle of Wight d. England 9 E2 ....50.41N 1.16W
Isles of Scilly d. England 9 B1 ....49.55N 6.17W
Isnā Egypt 53 J2 ....25.16N 32.30E
Isparta Turkey 57 I3 ....37.46N 30.32E
Israel Asia 53 J3 ....32.12N 34.48E
İstanbul Turkey 57 H5 ....41.07N 28.58E
Istria pen. Croatia 54 E1 ....45.12N 13.53E

Itaberaba Brazil 77 L5 ....12.31S 40.17W
Itabuna Brazil 77 M5 ....14.47S 39.17W
Itaituba Brazil 77 I7 ....4.16S 56.00W
Itajaí Brazil 77 K2 ....26.52S 48.41W
Italy Europe 50 D6 ....41.46N 14.35E
Itambé, Pico de mt. Brazil 77 L4 .....18.23S 43.20W
Itapetininga Brazil 73 E4 ....23.36S 48.03W
Itapicuru r. Maranhão Brazil 77 L7 ...2.55S 44.16W
Itapicuru r. Sergipe Brazil 77 M5 .....11.48S 37.30W
Itapicuru Mirim Brazil 77 L7 ....3.24S 44.21W
Itiquira r. Brazil 77 I4 ....17.18S 56.20W
Itui r. Brazil 76 F7 ....4.23S 70.13W
Ituxi r. Brazil 76 H6 ....7.21S 64.52W
Iul'tin Rus. Fed. 59 T4 ....67.51N 178.47W
Ivalo Finland 40 F5 ....68.39N 27.32E
Ivanava Belarus 46 G4 ....52.09N 25.32E
Ivano-Frankivs'k Ukraine 55 K3 .....48.55N 24.43E
Ivanovo Rus. Fed. 58 F3 ....56.59N 40.59E
Ivatsevichy Belarus 55 K5 ....52.43N 25.21E
Ivittuut Greenland 63 N4 ....61.13N 48.10W
Ivybridge England 13 D2 ....50.23N 3.55W
Iwaki Japan 106 D3 ....37.03N 140.53E
Iwo Nigeria 84 E2 ....7.38N 4.10E
Iwye Belarus 46 G4 ....53.55N 25.47E
Ixworth England 11 F3 ....52.18N 0.50E
Izabal, Lago de l. Guatemala 70 G4 .15.36N 89.08W
Izhevsk Rus. Fed. 58 G3 ....56.48N 53.10E
Izmayil Ukraine 53 I6 ....45.21N 28.51E
İzmir Turkey 56 G4 ....38.24N 27.10E
İzmir Körfezi g. Turkey 56 G4 ......38.30N 26.44E
İzmit Turkey 57 H5 ....40.46N 29.56E
Izu-Ogasawara Trench f. N. Pacific Oc. 108 F8 .34.34N 141.53E
Izu-shotō is Japan 106 C2 ....34.24N 139.14E

J

Jabalón r. Spain 48 C3 ....38.53N 4.05W
Jabalpur India 96 E5 ....23.10N 79.57E
Jablah Syria 57 K2 ....35.21N 35.56E
Jaboatão Brazil 77 N6 ....8.03S 34.55W
Jaca Spain 48 E5 ....42.34N 0.34W
Jacareacanga Brazil 77 I6 ....5.59S 57.33W
Jackson U.S.A. 65 H3 ....32.19N 90.12W
Jacksonville U.S.A. 65 J3 ....30.18N 81.42W
Jacmel Haiti 71 J4 ....18.16N 72.32W
Jacobabad Pakistan 96 C6 ....28.15N 68.29E
Jacuí r. Brazil 77 J1 ....30.03S 51.15W
Jacuípe r. Brazil 77 M5 ....12.33S 39.04W
Jādū Libya 52 F3 ....31.58N 12.04E
Jaén Spain 48 D2 ....37.46N 3.47W
Jaffna Sri Lanka 96 E2 ....9.41N 79.59E
Jagdalpur India 96 F4 ....19.04N 82.07E
Jahrom Iran 95 H5 ....28.31N 53.33E
Jaipur India 96 E6 ....26.51N 75.50E
Jaisalmer India 96 D6 ....26.52N 70.56E
Jajce Bos.-Herz. 56 B7 ....44.21N 17.16E
Jakarta Indonesia 104 D2 ....6.07S 106.48E
Jakobstad Finland 40 E3 ....63.40N 22.42E
Jalālābād Afgh. 95 L6 ....34.26N 70.28E
Jalgaon India 96 E5 ....21.01N 75.41E
Jalisco d. Mexico 70 D4 ....19.59N 104.18W
Jalna India 96 E4 ....19.49N 75.57E
Jalón r. Spain 48 E4 ....41.47N 1.02W
Jālū Libya 85 G4 ....29.03N 21.33E
Jamaica Central America 71 I4 .....17.30N 77.19W
Jamaica Channel Haiti/Jamaica 71 I4 .18.29N 75.24W
Jamanxim r. Brazil 77 I7 ....4.43S 56.24W
Jambi Indonesia 104 C3 ....1.37S 103.37E
James r. U.S.A. 64 G5 ....42.53N 97.17W
James Bay Canada 63 J3 ....53.23N 80.25W
Jamestown U.S.A. 64 G6 ....46.53N 98.43W
Jammu India 96 D7 ....32.42N 74.56E
Jammu and Kashmir Asia 96 E7 ...34.06N 76.59E
Jamnagar India 96 D5 ....22.26N 70.06E
Jampur Pakistan 96 D6 ....29.37N 70.41E
Jämsänkoski Finland 40 F3 ....61.56N 25.11E
Jamshedpur India 96 G5 ....22.46N 86.12E
Jandía hill Canary Islands 48 Y2 ..28.06N 14.21W
Jan Mayen i. Arctic Oc. 34 D5 .....72.00N 8.00W
Januária Brazil 77 L4 ....15.26S 44.20W
Japan Asia 106 C3 ....34.48N 133.17E
Japan, Sea of N. Pacific Oc. 106 B3 .39.13N 133.37E
Japan Trench f. N. Pacific Oc. 108 F8 .34.52N 143.17E
Japurá r. Brazil 76 H7 ....3.06S 64.45W
Jardines de la Reina, Archipiélago de los is Cuba 71 I5
                                        20.46N 79.01W
Jarocin Poland 46 C3 ....51.58N 17.31E
Jarosław Poland 46 F3 ....50.01N 22.40E
Järpen Sweden 40 C3 ....63.22N 13.28E
Järvenpää Finland 40 F3 ....60.29N 25.06E
Jarvis Island S. Pacific Oc. 108 J5 .0.26S 160.02W
Jäsk Iran 95 I5 ....25.40N 57.47E
Jasło Poland 46 E2 ....49.45N 21.28E
Jasper Canada 62 G3 ....52.53N 118.05W
Jastrzębie-Zdrój Poland 46 D2 ....49.57N 18.35E
Jataí Brazil 77 J4 ....17.53S 51.44W
Jatapu r. Brazil 77 I7 ....2.22S 58.11W
Jaú Brazil 77 K3 ....22.16S 48.33W
Java i. Indonesia 104 D2 ....8.12S 107.16E
Java Ridge f. Indian Oc. 108 D5 ....8.53S 107.00E
Javarthushuu Mongolia 103 K7 ....48.55N 112.44E
Java Sea Indonesia 104 E3 ....4.56S 110.49E
Java Trench f. Indian Oc. 108 C5 ...8.48S 104.02E
Jawhar Somalia 85 I2 ....2.43N 45.27E
Jawor Poland 46 C3 ....51.03N 16.12E
Jayapura Indonesia 105 K3 ....2.34S 140.42E
Jaz Mūriān, Hāmūn-e l. Iran 95 I5 .27.32N 58.47E
Jebel Abyad Plateau f. Sudan 94 C3 .19.25N 28.59E
Jedburgh Scotland 17 G3 ....55.29N 2.33W
Jeddah Saudi Arabia 94 E4 ....21.30N 39.08E
Jefferson City U.S.A. 65 H4 ....38.37N 92.11W
Jelenia Góra Poland 46 B3 ....50.55N 15.44E
Jelgava Latvia 40 E2 ....56.39N 23.44E
Jember Indonesia 104 E2 ....8.05S 113.45E
Jena Germany 54 D4 ....50.56N 11.36E
Jendouba Tunisia 52 E4 ....36.28N 8.47E
Jequié Brazil 77 L5 ....13.48S 40.00W
Jequitinhonha r. Brazil 77 M4 ......15.51S 38.52W
Jérémie Haiti 71 J4 ....18.38N 74.09W
Jerez de la Frontera Spain 48 B2 .36.41N 6.08W
Jerid, Chott el f. Tunisia 52 E4 .....33.38N 8.28E
Jersey i. Channel Is 13 Z8 ....49.16N 2.10W
Jerusalem Israel/West Bank 53 K3 .31.47N 35.13E
Jesi Italy 50 E5 ....43.31N 13.15E
Jesup U.S.A. 65 J3 ....31.34N 81.59W
Jhang Pakistan 95 L6 ....31.17N 72.23E
Jhansi India 96 E6 ....25.27N 78.37E
Jharkhand d. India 96 G5 ....23.36N 85.06E
Jiamusi China 103 O7 ....46.47N 130.15E
Ji'an China 103 K3 ....27.09N 114.56E

Jiangsu d. China 103 L4 ....33.10N 11[...]
Jiangxi d. China 103 L3 ....27.21N 11[...]
Jiaohe China 106 A4 ....43.43N 12[...]
Jiehkkevárri mt. Norway 40 D5 .....69.28N 1[...]
Jieznas Lithuania 46 G5 ....54.36N 2[...]
Jihlava Czech Rep. 54 F3 ....49.24N 1[...]
Jilf al Kabīr, Ḥaḍabat al f. Egypt 94 C4 .23.12N 2[...]
Jilib Somalia 85 I2 ....0.30N 4[...]
Jilin China 103 N6 ....43.53N 12[...]
Jilin d. China 103 N6 ....43.33N 12[...]
Jīma Ethiopia 85 H2 ....7.40N 3[...]
Jiménez Mexico 70 D6 ....27.08N 10[...]
Jinan China 103 L5 ....36.38N 11[...]
Jindřichův Hradec Czech Rep. 46 B2 .49.09N 1[...]
Jingdezhen China 103 L3 ....29.21N 11[...]
Jinghong China 103 I2 ....21.57N 10[...]
Jingmen China 103 K4 ....30.58N 11[...]
Jingzhou China 103 K4 ....30.17N 11[...]
Jinhua China 103 L3 ....29.10N 11[...]
Jining Nei Mongol China 103 K6 ...40.54N 11[...]
Jining Shandong China 103 L5 .....35.22N 11[...]
Jinja Uganda 85 H2 ....0.28N 3[...]
Jinka Ethiopia 87 B4 ....5.40N 3[...]
Jinzhou China 103 M6 ....41.02N 12[...]
Jiparaná r. Brazil 77 H6 ....8.09S 6[...]
Jipe, Lake Kenya/Tanzania 87 B2 ....3.35S 3[...]
Jiu r. Romania 56 E6 ....43.47N 2[...]
Jiujiang China 103 L3 ....29.43N 11[...]
Jiwani Pakistan 95 J5 ....25.07N 6[...]
Jixi China 103 O7 ....45.13N 13[...]
Jīzān Saudi Arabia 94 F3 ....16.56N 4[...]
João Pessoa Brazil 77 N6 ....7.05S 34[...]
Jodhpur India 96 D6 ....26.16N 7[...]
Joensuu Finland 40 G3 ....62.36N 2[...]
Jōetsu Japan 106 C3 ....37.10N 13[...]
Johannesburg S. Africa 86 B2 ......26.09S 2[...]
John o'Groats Scotland 19 F3 ......58.38N 3[...]
Johnston Wales 12 C3 ....51.45N 4[...]
Johnston Atoll N. Pacific Oc. 108 I7 .16.42N 169[...]
Johnstone Scotland 16 E3 ....55.50N 4[...]
Johor Bahru Malaysia 104 C4 ....1.29N 10[...]
Joinville Brazil 77 K2 ....26.17S 48[...]
Jokkmokk Sweden 40 D4 ....66.37N 1[...]
Jolo i. Phil. 105 G5 ....5.57N 12[...]
Jonava Lithuania 46 G5 ....55.04N 2[...]
Jones Sound str. Canada 63 J5 .....75.58N 88[...]
Jonglei d. Sudan 87 A4 ....7.17N 3[...]
Jönköping Sweden 40 C2 ....57.46N 1[...]
Jonquière Canada 63 K2 ....48.25N 71[...]
Joplin U.S.A. 65 H4 ....37.12N 94[...]
Jordan Asia 94 E6 ....31.17N 3[...]
Jörn Sweden 40 E4 ....65.03N 2[...]
Jos Nigeria 84 E2 ....9.55N[...]
Joseph Bonaparte Gulf Australia 110 B5 .14.08S 12[...]
Jos Plateau f. Nigeria 82 D5 ....9.50N 8[...]
Juan Fernández, Archipiélago is S. Pacific Oc. 109 O3
                                      33.24S 80[...]
Juàzeiro Brazil 77 L6 ....9.25S 40[...]
Juàzeiro do Norte Brazil 77 M6 ....7.11S 39[...]
Juba Sudan 85 H2 ....4.53N 3[...]
Jubba r. Somalia 85 I1 ....0.15S 4[...]
Jubbada Hoose d. Somalia 87 C3 ..0.16N 4[...]
Júcar r. Spain 48 E3 ....39.09N 0[...]
Juchitán Mexico 70 E4 ....16.29N 95[...]
Judenburg Austria 54 F2 ....47.11N 1[...]
Juist i. Germany 42 G6 ....53.40N[...]
Juiz de Fora Brazil 77 L3 ....21.46S 43[...]
Juliaca Peru 76 F4 ....15.28S 70[...]
Junction City U.S.A. 64 G4 ....39.03N 96[...]
Juneau U.S.A. 62 F3 ....58.19N 134[...]
Jungfrau mt. Switz. 50 B7 ....46.33N[...]
Junggar Pendi basin China 102 F7 .45.02N 87[...]
Jura mts France/Switz. 44 F4 ......45.38N[...]
Jura i. Scotland 16 D4 ....56.02N 5[...]
Jura, Sound of str. Scotland 16 D3 .55.51N 5[...]
Jurbarkas Lithuania 46 F5 ....55.05N 2[...]
Jūrmala Latvia 55 J7 ....56.57N 23[...]
Juruá r. Brazil 76 F7 ....2.39S 65[...]
Juruena r. Brazil 77 I6 ....7.21S 58[...]
Jutaí r. Brazil 76 G7 ....2.45S 66[...]
Jutland pen. Denmark 40 B2 ......56.13N 9[...]
Juventud, Isla de la i. Cuba 71 H5 .21.27N 82[...]
Jyväskylä Finland 40 F3 ....62.14N 25[...]

K

K2 mt. China/Jammu and Kashmir 102 D5 .35.52N 7[...]
Kaambooni Somalia 87 C2 ....1.41S 41[...]
Kaambooni, Raas pt Somalia 87 C2 .1.34S 41[...]
Kabaena i. Indonesia 105 G2 ....5.15S 121[...]
Kabalo Dem. Rep. Congo 86 B4 ....6.02S 26[...]
Kabarnet Kenya 87 A3 ....0.31N 35[...]
Kābul Afgh. 95 K6 ....34.30N 69[...]
Kabwe Zambia 86 B3 ....14.27S 28[...]
Kachagalau mt. Kenya 87 A3 ....2.20N 35[...]
Kachchh, Gulf of India 96 C5 .....22.35N 68[...]
Kachug Rus. Fed. 59 L3 ....53.54N 105[...]
Kadam mt. Uganda 87 A3 ....1.47N 34[...]
Kadavu i. Fiji 111 G5 ....19.00S 178[...]
Kadıköy Turkey 57 H5 ....40.59N 29[...]
Kadirli Turkey 57 L3 ....37.22N 36[...]
Kadugli Sudan 85 G3 ....11.01N 29[...]
Kaduna Nigeria 84 E3 ....10.30N 7[...]
Kaesŏng N. Korea 103 N5 ....37.58N 126[...]
Kafireas, Akra c. Greece 56 F4 ....38.10N 24[...]
Kaga Bandoro C.A.R. 85 F2 ....6.57N 19[...]
Kagoshima Japan 106 B2 ....31.34N 130[...]
Kahramanmaraş Turkey 57 L3 .....37.35N 36[...]
Kai, Kepulauan is Indonesia 105 I2 .5.26S 132[...]
Kaifeng China 103 K4 ....34.43N 114[...]
Kaimana Indonesia 105 I3 ....3.42S 133[...]
Kairouan Tunisia 52 F4 ....35.41N 10[...]
Kaiserslautern Germany 54 B3 .....49.27N 7[...]
Kaiyuan China 103 I2 ....23.40N 103[...]
Kajaani Finland 40 F4 ....64.13N 27[...]
Kajiado Kenya 87 B2 ....1.50S 36[...]
Kakamega Kenya 87 A3 ....0.17N 34[...]
Kakhovs'ke Vodoskhovyshche resr Ukraine 55 O2
                                     47.00N 33[...]
Kakinada India 96 F4 ....16.57N 82[...]
Kaktovik U.S.A. 62 D5 ....70.04N 143[...]
Kakuma Kenya 87 A3 ....3.40N 34[...]
Kalacha Dida Kenya 87 B3 ....3.07N 37[...]
Kalahari Desert Africa 86 B2 .....23.28S 22[...]
Kalajoki Finland 40 E4 ....64.15N 23[...]
Kalamaria Greece 56 E5 ....40.36N 22[...]
Kalamata Greece 56 E3 ....37.02N 22[...]
Kalāt Afgh. 95 K6 ....32.05N 66[...]
Kalecik Turkey 57 J5 ....40.05N 33[...]
Kalemie Dem. Rep. Congo 86 B4 ..5.56S 29[...]
Kalgoorlie Australia 110 B3 ....30.50S 121[...]
Kaliakra, Nos pt Bulgaria 57 H6 ..43.22N 28[...]

antan f. Indonesia 104 E3 ....2.10S 111.35E
ingrad Rus. Fed. 46 E5 ....54.42N 20.31E
kavichy Belarus 55 M5 ....52.08N 29.15E
bell U.S.A. 64 D6 ....48.11N 114.19W
c Poland 46 D3 ....51.46N 18.05E
ilven r. Sweden 40 E4 ....65.51N 23.08E
vesi l. Finland 40 F3 ....62.47N 27.47E
ön l. Sweden 40 C3 ....63.37N 13.00E
ar Sweden 40 D2 ....56.40N 16.22E
g U.S.A. 62 C4 ....64.20N 158.52W
a Rus. Fed. 58 E3 ....54.31N 36.16E
dborg Denmark 40 B1 ....55.41N 10.68E
h Ukraine 55 K3 ....49.02N 24.22E
r. Rus. Fed. 58 G3 ....56.01N 53.46E
iishi Japan 106 D3 ....39.16N 141.53E
n Turkey 57 J4 ....39.22N 33.43E
hatka Basin f. Bering Sea 108 H9 ....57.09N 166.28E
hatka Peninsula Rus. Fed. 59 Q3 ....56.10N 159.12E
nskoye Rus. Fed. 59 R4 ....62.33N 166.10E
nsk-Ural'skiy Rus. Fed. 58 H3 ....56.28N 61.48E
na Rus. Fed. 58 E3 ....8.44S 24.57E
n'-Kashyrs'kyy Ukraine 55 K4 ....51.37N 24.58E
oops Canada 62 F3 ....50.41N 120.21W
aala Uganda 85 H2 ....0.20N 32.34E
nen Neth. 42 E5 ....52.33N 5.55E
óng Cham Cambodia 104 D6 ....11.59N 105.26E
pôt Cambodia 104 C6 ....10.36N 104.12E
uli Uganda 87 A3 ....0.54N 33.06E
'yanets'-Podil's'kyy Ukraine 55 L3 ....48.41N 26.35E
'yanka-Buz'ka Ukraine 46 G3 ....50.06N 24.21E
yshin Rus. Fed. 58 F3 ....50.06N 45.25E
nga Dem. Rep. Congo 86 B4 ....5.51S 22.22E
zawa Japan 106 C3 ....36.34N 136.39E
nipuram India 96 E3 ....12.51N 79.43E
ahār Afgh. 95 K6 ....31.37N 65.47E
alaksha Rus. Fed. 40 H4 ....67.10N 32.23E
alakshskiy Zaliv g. Rus. Fed. 40 H4 ....66.38N 33.25E
ura Turkey 57 15 ....41.04N 30.08E
y Sri Lanka 96 F2 ....7.19N 80.34E
al Turkey 57 L4 ....39.14N 37.23E
än Iran 95 H5 ....27.50N 52.05E
aroo Island Australia 110 C3 ....35.48S 137.11E
avar Iran 95 G6 ....34.29N 47.51E
chenjunga mt. India/Nepal 96 G6 ....27.41N 88.12E
ding China 97 J7 ....30.03N 101.56E
ean, Kepulauan is Indonesia 104 F2 ....6.56S 115.13E
ertittivaq str. Greenland 63 P5 ....70.31N 24.44W
etet Kenya 87 B3 ....1.58N 36.03E
iqsualuijjuaq Canada 63 L3 ....58.35N 65.45W
iqsujuaq Canada 63 K4 ....61.34N 71.56W
mar China 102 F3 ....28.30N 89.33E
nüng S. Korea 106 A3 ....37.46N 128.52E
n, Poluostrov pen. Rus. Fed. 58 F4 ....66.50N 44.50E
aanpää Finland 40 E3 ....61.49N 22.25E
akee U.S.A. 65 I5 ....41.07N 87.51W
an Guinea 84 D3 ....10.23N 9.19W
er India 96 F5 ....20.16N 81.32E
Nigeria 84 E3 ....12.01N 8.31E
ur India 96 F5 ....26.27N 80.24E
as d. U.S.A. 64 G4 ....38.35N 98.34W
as r. U.S.A. 64 H4 ....39.07N 94.40W
as City U.S.A. 65 H4 ....39.11N 94.45W
k Rus. Fed. 59 K3 ....56.10N 95.43E
a mt. Ethiopia 87 A4 ....6.10N 35.35E
chari Burkina 84 E3 ....12.29N 1.30E
on atoll Kiribati 108 I5 ....2.44S 171.42W
e Botswana 86 B2 ....24.58S 25.21E
siung Taiwan 103 M2 ....22.39N 120.20E
oveld f. Namibia 86 A3 ....17.41S 12.33E
ack Senegal 84 C3 ....14.09N 16.04W
horwa Uganda 87 A3 ....1.27N 34.29E
nguria Kenya 87 A3 ....1.21N 35.07E
ngamarangi Rise f. N. Pacific Oc. 108 G6 ....6.41N 150.16E
eta Sudan 87 A4 ....4.47N 33.35E
svár Hungary 54 G2 ....46.22N 17.48E
abet Kenya 87 A3 ....0.13N 35.08E
skasing Canada 63 J2 ....49.26N 82.26W
tir U.S.A. 64 G3 ....2.05N 35.28E
-Bogaz-Gol, Zaliv b. Turkmenistan 58 G2 ....41.24N 53.32E
bük Turkey 57 J5 ....41.11N 32.38E
butak Kazakhstan 58 H2 ....49.55N 60.09E
chi Pakistan 96 C2 ....24.51N 67.03E
ganda Kazakhstan 58 I2 ....49.52N 73.04E
ginskiy Zaliv b. Rus. Fed. 59 R3 ....59.32N 164.48E
Iran 95 H7 ....35.45N 50.54E
kelong i. Indonesia 105 H4 ....4.22N 126.43E
koram Range mts Asia 96 D8 ....36.18N 74.54E
kum Desert Turkmenistan 58 G2 ....38.58N 60.05E
man Turkey 57 J3 ....37.11N 33.13E
may China 102 E7 ....45.31N 84.54E
nd Iran 95 G6 ....34.14N 46.16E
pinar Turkey 57 J3 ....37.43N 33.33E
sburg Namibia 86 A2 ....28.01S 18.45E
Sea Rus. Fed. 58 I5 ....74.13N 71.44E
suk Rus. Fed. 58 I3 ....53.43N 78.03E
alā' Iraq 94 F4 ....32.36N 44.01E
ag Hungary 54 I2 ....47.19N 20.55E
itsa Greece 56 D4 ....39.21N 21.55E
la Estonia 40 E2 ....58.59N 22.65E
ima Sudan 85 H3 ....18.31N 31.49E
ba, Lake Zambia/Zimbabwe 86 B3 ....17.37S 27.17E
mata, Selat str. Indonesia 104 D3 ....1.50S 108.08E
inits'ka Zatoka g. Ukraine 53 J6 ....45.27N 32.11E
ovac Croatia 56 A7 ....45.29N 15.33E
vo Bulgaria 56 F6 ....42.39N 24.48E
vy Vary Czech Rep. 54 E4 ....50.14N 12.53E
shamn Sweden 40 C2 ....56.11N 14.52E
koga Sweden 40 C2 ....59.20N 14.33E
skrona Sweden 40 C2 ....56.12N 15.38E
ruhe Germany 54 C3 ....49.01N 8.24E
stad Sweden 40 C2 ....56.23N 13.31E
nøy i. Norway 40 A2 ....59.11N 5.15E
ataka d. India 96 E2 ....13.57N 75.29E
obat Bulgaria 56 G6 ....42.38N 26.59E
ra Eritrea 85 H3 ....17.41N 38.23E
athos i. Greece 56 G2 ....35.36N 27.10E
enisi Greece 56 D4 ....35.30N 21.48E
ava Latvia 55 L7 ....56.47N 27.41E
yaka Turkey 56 G4 ....38.27N 27.08E
tula Finland 40 F3 ....62.53N 24.48E
al Turkey 57 H5 ....40.54N 29.11E
ngu Bay Kenya 87 A2 ....2.01S 40.06E
mskoye Rus. Fed. 59 M3 ....51.30N 114.25E
ma Turkey 57 H5 ....36.12N 29.37E
i r. Dem. Rep. Congo 86 A4 ....3.02S 16.58E
ma Zambia 86 C3 ....10.12S 31.12E
se Uganda 85 H2 ....3.10N 30.05E
än Iran 95 H6 ....33.58N 51.30E
i China 102 D5 ....39.29N 76.08E
iwazaki Japan 106 C3 ....37.22N 138.34E
ma Greece 56 G2 ....35.23N 26.52E
ala Sudan 85 H3 ....15.24N 36.20E

Kassel Germany 54 C4 ....51.19N 9.30E
Kasserine Tunisia 52 E4 ....35.11N 8.50E
Kastamonu Turkey 57 J5 ....41.22N 33.46E
Kastelli Greece 56 E2 ....35.30N 23.38E
Kastoria Greece 56 D5 ....40.31N 21.16E
Kastsyukovichy Belarus 55 O5 ....53.21N 32.09E
Katakwi Uganda 87 A3 ....1.54N 33.56E
Katerini Greece 56 E5 ....40.16N 22.31E
Katesh Tanzania 87 A1 ....4.32S 35.20E
Kate's Needle mt. Canada/U.S.A. 62 E3 ....57.02N 132.02W
Katha Myanmar 97 I5 ....24.11N 96.20E
Katherine Australia 110 C5 ....14.28S 132.18E
Kathmandu Nepal 96 G6 ....27.42N 85.18E
Kathua watercourse Kenya 87 B2 ....1.23S 39.09E
Katima Mulilo Namibia 86 B3 ....17.32S 24.15E
Katowice Poland 46 D3 ....50.16N 19.01E
Katrine, Loch l. Scotland 16 E4 ....56.15N 4.34W
Katrineholm Sweden 40 D2 ....58.59N 16.14E
Katsina Nigeria 84 E3 ....12.59N 7.36E
Kattegat str. Denmark/Sweden 40 B2 ....56.59N 11.21E
Kauai i. U.S.A. 109 J7 ....22.10N 159.43W
Kauhajoki Finland 40 E3 ....62.25N 22.11E
Kaunas Lithuania 40 E1 ....54.54N 23.55E
Kaura-Namoda Nigeria 84 E3 ....12.37N 6.35E
Kavala Greece 56 F5 ....40.56N 24.23E
Kavarna Bulgaria 57 H6 ....43.26N 28.19E
Kavīr, Dasht-e des. Iran 95 H6 ....34.36N 54.41E
Kawasaki Japan 106 C3 ....35.32N 139.43E
Kawm Umbū Egypt 53 J1 ....24.28N 32.55E
Kayes Mali 84 C3 ....14.26N 11.27W
Kayseri Turkey 57 K4 ....38.43N 35.29E
Kazach'ye Rus. Fed. 59 O5 ....70.45N 136.09E
Kazakhstan Asia 58 H2 ....49.18N 82.53E
Kazan' Rus. Fed. 58 F3 ....55.47N 49.07E
Kazanlŭk Bulgaria 56 F6 ....42.37N 25.23E
Kazerūn Iran 95 H5 ....29.37N 51.39E
Kazincbarcika Hungary 46 E1 ....48.16N 20.39E
Kea i. Greece 56 F3 ....37.38N 24.24E
Keady Northern Ireland 16 C2 ....54.15N 6.42W
Kearney U.S.A. 64 G5 ....40.43N 99.05W
Keban Baraji resr Turkey 57 M4 ....38.53N 38.55E
Kebkabiya Sudan 94 B2 ....13.37N 24.06E
Kebnekaise mt. Sweden 40 D4 ....67.55N 18.31E
Kebock Head Scotland 18 C3 ....58.03N 6.21W
Keçiören Turkey 57 J5 ....40.00N 32.50E
Kecskemét Hungary 54 H2 ....46.55N 19.42E
Kėdainiai Lithuania 40 E1 ....55.17N 23.59E
Kędzierzyn-Koźle Poland 46 D3 ....50.20N 18.13E
Keen, Mount hill Scotland 19 G1 ....56.58N 2.59W
Keetmanshoop Namibia 86 A2 ....26.35S 18.07E
Keewatin Canada 65 H6 ....49.46N 94.34W
Keflavík Iceland 40 X2 ....64.00N 22.34W
Kegworth England 10 D3 ....52.50N 1.17W
Keighley England 15 F2 ....53.52N 1.55W
Keitele l. Finland 40 F3 ....62.52N 26.00E
Keith Scotland 19 G2 ....57.33N 2.57W
Kelibia Tunisia 50 D2 ....36.51N 11.04E
Kelkit r. Turkey 57 L4 ....40.51N 36.26E
Kellett, Cape Canada 62 F5 ....71.59N 125.59W
Kells Ireland 41 E3 ....53.44N 6.52W
Kelmė Lithuania 46 F5 ....55.38N 22.56E
Kelo Chad 84 F2 ....9.18N 15.49E
Kelowna Canada 62 G2 ....49.53N 119.29W
Kelso Scotland 17 G3 ....55.36N 2.26W
Keluang Malaysia 104 C4 ....1.59N 103.19E
Kelvedon England 11 F2 ....51.50N 0.42E
Kem' Rus. Fed. 58 E4 ....64.57N 34.34E
Kemerovo Rus. Fed. 58 J3 ....55.23N 86.01E
Kemi Finland 40 F4 ....65.46N 24.33E
Kemijärvi Finland 40 F4 ....66.43N 27.23E
Kemijärvi l. Finland 40 F4 ....66.35N 27.25E
Kemijoki r. Finland 40 F4 ....65.47N 24.32E
Kemnay Scotland 19 G2 ....57.14N 2.27W
Kempston England 11 E3 ....52.07N 0.30W
Kempten Germany 54 D2 ....47.43N 10.18E
Kenai U.S.A. 62 C4 ....60.35N 151.16W
Kenamuke Swamp f. Sudan 87 A4 ....5.25N 34.00E
Kendal England 14 E3 ....54.20N 2.45W
Kendari Indonesia 105 G3 ....3.59S 122.35E
Kendawangan Indonesia 104 E3 ....2.30S 110.14E
Kengtung Myanmar 97 I5 ....21.18N 99.38E
Kenilworth England 10 D3 ....52.21N 1.35W
Kénitra Morocco 84 D5 ....34.16N 6.33W
Kenmare Ireland 41 B1 ....51.53N 9.35W
Kenmare River inlet Ireland 41 A1 ....51.43N 10.03W
Kennet r. England 10 E2 ....51.27N 0.57W
Kenora Canada 63 I2 ....49.47N 94.30W
Kent d. England 9 F2 ....51.12N 0.37E
Kent r. England 14 E3 ....54.15N 2.48W
Kentucky d. U.S.A. 65 J4 ....37.24N 84.54W
Kentucky r. U.S.A. 65 I4 ....38.41N 85.10W
Kenya Africa 87 B3 ....0.59N 37.32E
Kenya, Mount Kenya 87 B2 ....0.08S 37.18E
Kępno Poland 46 C3 ....51.17N 17.59E
Kerala d. India 96 E3 ....11.31N 75.51E
Kerch Ukraine 53 K6 ....45.22N 36.29E
Kerema P.N.G. 110 D6 ....7.56S 145.48E
Keren Eritrea 94 E3 ....15.46N 38.28E
Kericho Kenya 87 A2 ....0.22S 35.15E
Kerinci, Gunung vol. Indonesia 104 C3 ....1.42S 101.15E
Kerio watercourse Kenya 87 B3 ....2.56N 36.11E
Kerio Valley f. Kenya 87 A3 ....1.10N 35.45E
Kerki Turkmenistan 95 K7 ....37.51N 65.13E
Kerkyra Greece 56 C4 ....39.37N 19.55E
Kerma Sudan 94 D3 ....19.37N 30.26E
Kermadec Islands S. Pacific Oc. 108 I3 ....30.19S 178.19W
Kermadec Trench f. S. Pacific Oc. 108 I3 ....34.29S 177.56W
Kermān Iran 95 I6 ....30.17N 57.04E
Kermān Desert Iran 95 I5 ....28.27N 59.19E
Kermānshāh Iran 95 G6 ....34.19N 47.02E
Kerry d. Ireland 41 B2 ....52.09N 9.28W
Kerry Head Ireland 41 B2 ....52.09N 9.57W
Keşan Turkey 56 G5 ....40.51N 26.37E
Kessennuma Japan 106 D3 ....38.54N 141.33E
Kessingland England 11 G3 ....52.25N 1.43E
Keswick England 14 D3 ....54.36N 3.07W
Ketapang Indonesia 104 E3 ....1.50S 110.00E
Ketchikan U.S.A. 62 E3 ....55.20N 131.38W
Kettering England 10 E3 ....52.24N 0.44W
Keweenaw Bay U.S.A. 65 I6 ....46.52N 88.26W
Key, Lough l. Ireland 41 C4 ....54.01N 8.15W
Keyala Sudan 87 A4 ....4.29N 32.51E
Keynsham England 10 C2 ....51.25N 2.30W
Kežmarok Slovakia 46 E2 ....49.08N 20.26E
Khabarovsk Rus. Fed. 59 O2 ....48.30N 135.08E
Khadyzhensk Rus. Fed. 57 M7 ....44.25N 39.32E
Khairpur Pakistan 102 B3 ....27.31N 68.49E
Khambhat, Gulf of India 96 D4 ....19.59N 71.29E
Khānābād Afgh. 95 K7 ....36.42N 69.09E
Khandwa India 96 E5 ....21.49N 76.21E
Khanewal Pakistan 95 L6 ....30.19N 71.59E
Khanka, Lake China/Rus. Fed. 103 O6 ....44.54N 132.45E

Khanpur Pakistan 96 D6 ....28.37N 70.41E
Khantayskoye, Ozero l. Rus. Fed. 59 K4 ....68.25N 91.57E
Khanty-Mansiysk Rus. Fed. 58 H4 ....61.05N 69.01E
Kharagpur India 96 G5 ....22.20N 87.20E
Kharkiv Ukraine 55 O3 ....49.59N 36.16E
Khartoum Sudan 85 H3 ....15.32N 32.32E
Khāsh Iran 95 J5 ....28.12N 61.14E
Khashm el Girba Sudan 94 E2 ....14.56N 35.51E
Khaskovo Bulgaria 56 F5 ....41.56N 25.32E
Khatanga Rus. Fed. 59 L5 ....71.57N 102.24E
Khatangskiy Zaliv b. Rus. Fed. 59 L5 ....73.19N 107.17E
Khayelitsha S. Africa 86 A1 ....34.05S 18.39E
Khenchela Algeria 52 E4 ....35.26N 7.10E
Khenifra Morocco 52 B3 ....32.58N 5.37W
Kherson Ukraine 53 J6 ....46.39N 32.37E
Kheta r. Rus. Fed. 59 L5 ....71.55N 102.04E
Khimki Rus. Fed. 55 Q6 ....55.53N 37.26E
Khmel'nyts'kyy Ukraine 55 L3 ....49.25N 26.59E
Khon Kaen Thailand 104 C7 ....16.27N 102.52E
Khorinsk Rus. Fed. 103 J8 ....52.09N 109.48E
Khorramābād Iran 95 G6 ....33.27N 48.19E
Khorugh Tajikistan 95 L7 ....37.29N 71.35E
Khouribga Morocco 52 B3 ....32.53N 6.55W
Khowst Afgh. 95 K6 ....33.21N 69.59E
Khŭjand Tajikistan 102 B6 ....40.15N 69.38E
Khulna Bangl. 97 G5 ....22.50N 89.33E
Khunsar Iran 95 H6 ....33.10N 50.17E
Khust Ukraine 55 J3 ....48.10N 23.18E
Khvoy Iran 94 F7 ....38.33N 44.58E
Khyber Pass Afgh./Pakistan 95 L6 ....34.08N 71.12E
Kiambu Kenya 87 B2 ....1.13S 36.45E
Kiantajärvi l. Finland 40 G4 ....64.58N 29.06E
Kibaya Tanzania 87 B1 ....5.17S 36.33E
Kibre Mengist Ethiopia 87 B4 ....5.52N 38.57E
Kičevo Macedonia 56 D5 ....41.30N 20.58E
Kidderminster England 10 C3 ....52.23N 2.15W
Kidepo Valley National Park Uganda 87 A3 ....3.51N 33.48E
Kidsgrove England 15 E2 ....53.05N 2.14W
Kidwelly Wales 12 C3 ....51.44N 4.18W
Kiel Germany 54 D6 ....54.19N 10.08E
Kiel Canal Germany 40 B1 ....54.10N 9.27E
Kielce Poland 46 E3 ....50.51N 20.37E
Kielder Water resr England 15 E4 ....55.12N 2.34W
Kieler Bucht b. Germany 54 D6 ....54.27N 10.41E
Kiev Ukraine 55 N4 ....50.26N 30.34E
Kigali Rwanda 85 H1 ....1.59S 30.05E
Kigoma Tanzania 86 B4 ....4.51S 29.40E
Kii-suidō str. Japan 106 B2 ....33.57N 134.49E
Kikinda Serbia 56 D7 ....45.50N 20.28E
Kikori r. P.N.G. 110 D6 ....7.22S 144.14E
Kikwit Dem. Rep. Congo 86 A4 ....5.03S 18.50E
Kilbrannan Sound str. Scotland 16 D3 ....55.25N 5.27W
Kilcoole Ireland 12 A5 ....53.06N 6.03W
Kilcormac Ireland 41 D3 ....53.10N 7.44W
Kilcullen Ireland 41 E3 ....53.08N 6.45W
Kildare Ireland 41 E3 ....53.09N 6.55W
Kildare d. Ireland 41 E3 ....53.17N 6.47W
Kilifi Kenya 87 B2 ....3.36S 39.51E
Kilimanjaro d. Tanzania 87 B2 ....3.15S 37.23E
Kilimanjaro vol. Tanzania 86 C4 ....3.03S 37.21E
Kilimanjaro National Park Tanzania 87 B2 ....3.01S 37.13E
Kilis Turkey 57 L3 ....36.43N 37.07E
Kilkee Ireland 41 B2 ....52.41N 9.38W
Kilkeel Northern Ireland 16 D2 ....54.04N 5.59W
Kilkenny Ireland 41 D2 ....52.39N 7.15W
Kilkenny d. Ireland 41 D2 ....52.41N 7.14W
Kilkis Greece 56 E5 ....40.59N 22.52E
Killala Bay Ireland 41 B4 ....54.16N 9.08W
Killarney Ireland 41 B2 ....52.03N 9.30W
Killeen U.S.A. 64 G3 ....31.08N 97.44W
Killin Scotland 16 E4 ....56.28N 4.19W
Killorglin Ireland 41 B2 ....52.06N 9.47W
Killybegs Ireland 41 C4 ....54.38N 8.27W
Kilmallock Ireland 41 C2 ....52.24N 8.35W
Kilmarnock Ireland 16 E3 ....55.37N 4.30W
Kilmelford Scotland 16 D4 ....56.16N 5.28W
Kilmichael Point Ireland 41 E2 ....52.44N 6.08W
Kilrea Northern Ireland 16 C2 ....54.57N 6.33W
Kilrush Ireland 41 B2 ....52.38N 9.29W
Kilsyth Scotland 17 E3 ....55.59N 4.03W
Kilwinning Scotland 16 E3 ....55.39N 4.42W
Kimberley S. Africa 86 B2 ....28.44S 24.46E
Kimberley Plateau f. Australia 110 B5 ....17.26S 127.05E
Kimch'aek N. Korea 103 N6 ....40.41N 129.12E
Kinabalu, Gunung mt. Malaysia 104 F5 ....6.04N 116.33E
Kinango Kenya 87 B1 ....4.08S 39.20E
Kinder Scout hill England 15 F2 ....53.23N 1.52W
Kindersley Canada 62 H2 ....51.28N 109.10W
Kindu Dem. Rep. Congo 86 B4 ....2.57S 25.53E
King Island Australia 110 D3 ....39.50S 143.58E
Kingman U.S.A. 64 D4 ....35.14N 114.02W
Kingsbridge England 13 D2 ....50.17N 3.47W
Kingsclere England 10 D2 ....51.19N 1.14W
Kingscourt Ireland 41 E3 ....53.54N 6.48W
King's Lynn England 11 F3 ....52.45N 0.24E
Kingsmill Group is Kiribati 111 G6 ....1.37S 175.52E
Kingsnorth England 11 F2 ....51.07N 0.52E
Kingston Canada 63 K2 ....44.14N 76.30W
Kingston Jamaica 67 J4 ....18.00N 76.47W
Kingston upon Hull England 15 G2 ....53.45N 0.20W
Kingston upon Hull d. England 9 E3 ....53.46N 0.19W
Kingston upon Thames England 11 E2 ....51.25N 0.18W
Kingstown St Vincent 71 L3 ....13.10N 61.15W
Kingsville U.S.A. 64 G2 ....27.27N 97.47W
Kingswood England 10 C2 ....51.28N 2.30W
Kings Worthy England 10 D2 ....51.06N 1.18W
Kington England 10 B3 ....52.12N 3.02W
Kingussie Scotland 19 E2 ....57.05N 4.03W
King William Island Canada 63 I4 ....69.10N 97.45W
Kinlochbervie Scotland 18 D3 ....58.28N 5.03W
Kinlochleven Scotland 18 E1 ....56.43N 4.58W
Kinloss Scotland 19 F2 ....57.38N 3.34W
Kinna Sweden 40 C2 ....57.31N 12.40E
Kinnegad Ireland 41 D3 ....53.27N 7.06W
Kinross Scotland 17 F4 ....56.12N 3.25W
Kinsale Ireland 41 C1 ....51.42N 8.31W
Kinshasa Dem. Rep. Congo 86 A4 ....4.22S 15.23E
Kintore Scotland 19 G2 ....57.14N 2.21W
Kintyre pen. Scotland 16 D3 ....55.30N 5.39W
Kipini Kenya 87 B2 ....2.30S 40.32E
Kiribati Pacific Oc. 108 I5 ....6.00S 164.59W
Kırıkhan Turkey 57 L3 ....36.29N 36.22E
Kırıkkale Turkey 57 J4 ....39.50N 33.32E
Kiritimati atoll Kiribati 109 J6 ....1.44N 157.13W
Kirkbean Scotland 17 F2 ....54.55N 3.36W
Kirkby England 14 E2 ....53.29N 2.53W
Kirkby in Ashfield England 15 F2 ....53.06N 1.16W
Kirkby Lonsdale England 14 E3 ....54.12N 2.36W
Kirkbymoorside England 15 G3 ....54.16N 0.56W
Kirkby Stephen England 14 E3 ....54.29N 2.21W
Kirkcaldy Scotland 17 F4 ....56.07N 3.09W
Kirkcolm Scotland 16 D2 ....54.58N 5.05W

Kirkconnel Scotland 17 E3 ....55.23N 4.00W
Kirkcudbright Scotland 17 E2 ....54.50N 4.03W
Kirkenes Norway 40 G5 ....69.43N 30.01E
Kirkham England 14 E2 ....53.47N 2.52W
Kirkintilloch Scotland 16 E3 ....55.56N 4.09W
Kirkkonummi Finland 40 F3 ....60.07N 24.27E
Kirkland Lake town Canada 63 J2 ....48.10N 80.02W
Kırklareli Turkey 56 G5 ....41.44N 27.13E
Kirk Michael Isle of Man 14 C3 ....54.17N 4.35W
Kirkūk Iraq 94 F7 ....35.24N 44.24E
Kirkwall Scotland 19 G3 ....58.59N 2.58W
Kirov Rus. Fed. 55 P6 ....54.04N 34.20E
Kirovohrad Ukraine 55 O3 ....48.30N 32.16E
Kirovsk Rus. Fed. 40 G2 ....59.52N 30.59E
Kirovsk Rus. Fed. 40 H4 ....67.37N 33.40E
Kirriemuir Scotland 19 F1 ....56.41N 3.00W
Kırşehir Turkey 57 K4 ....39.09N 34.09E
Kirtlington England 10 D2 ....51.52N 1.16W
Kirton in Lindsey England 15 G2 ....53.29N 0.35W
Kiruna Sweden 40 E4 ....67.51N 20.14E
Kisangani Dem. Rep. Congo 86 B5 ....0.34N 25.11E
Kisii Kenya 87 A2 ....0.42S 34.46E
Kislovodsk Rus. Fed. 53 L5 ....43.55N 42.44E
Kismaayo Somalia 85 I1 ....0.19S 42.31E
Kisoro Uganda 85 G1 ....1.17S 29.45E
Kisumu Kenya 87 A2 ....0.04S 34.47E
Kita-Kyūshū Japan 106 B2 ....33.52N 130.50E
Kitale Kenya 87 A3 ....1.01N 35.00E
Kitami Japan 106 D4 ....43.49N 143.53E
Kitgum Uganda 87 A3 ....3.18N 32.53E
Kitimat Canada 62 F3 ....54.03N 128.39W
Kittilä Finland 40 F4 ....67.38N 24.54E
Kitui Kenya 87 B2 ....1.22S 38.00E
Kitwe Zambia 86 B3 ....12.48S 28.12E
Kiuruvesi Finland 40 F3 ....63.38N 26.37E
Kızıl Dağı mt. Turkey 57 M4 ....39.57N 38.12E
Kızılırmak r. Turkey 57 K5 ....41.49N 35.54E
Kladno Czech Rep. 54 F4 ....50.09N 14.08E
Klagenfurt Austria 54 F2 ....46.38N 14.19E
Klaipėda Lithuania 40 E1 ....55.43N 21.09E
Klamath r. U.S.A. 64 B5 ....41.27N 124.02W
Klamath Falls town U.S.A. 64 B5 ....42.15N 121.46W
Klazienaveen Neth. 42 F5 ....52.44N 6.59E
Kleve Germany 42 F5 ....51.47N 6.08E
Klimovo Rus. Fed. 55 O5 ....52.23N 32.12E
Klintsy Rus. Fed. 55 O5 ....52.45N 32.15E
Kłodzko Poland 46 C3 ....50.26N 16.39E
Kluczbork Poland 46 D3 ....50.58N 18.13E
Klyuchevskaya, Sopka vol. Rus. Fed. 59 R3 ....56.01N 160.41E
Knaresborough England 15 F3 ....54.01N 1.28W
Knighton Wales 12 D4 ....52.20N 3.03W
Knin Croatia 56 B7 ....44.03N 16.12E
Knockaboy hill Ireland 41 B1 ....51.48N 9.26W
Knockadoon Head Ireland 41 D1 ....51.53N 7.52W
Knockalongy hill Ireland 41 C4 ....54.12N 8.46W
Knock Hill Scotland 19 G2 ....57.35N 2.46W
Knocklayd hill Northern Ireland 16 C3 ....55.10N 6.15W
Knockmealdown Mountains hills Ireland 41 C2
...............52.14N 8.04W
Knottingley England 15 F2 ....53.42N 1.15W
Knowle England 10 D3 ....52.23N 1.44W
Knoxville U.S.A. 65 J4 ....35.59N 83.56W
Knutsford England 15 E2 ....53.18N 2.22W
Köbe Japan 106 C2 ....34.41N 135.11E
Koblenz Germany 54 B4 ....50.21N 7.35E
Kobroör i. Indonesia 105 I2 ....6.07S 134.30E
Kobryn Belarus 55 K5 ....52.12N 24.20E
Kočani Macedonia 56 E5 ....41.55N 22.23E
Kōchi Japan 106 B2 ....33.33N 133.32E
Kodiak U.S.A. 62 C3 ....57.46N 152.30W
Kodiak Island U.S.A. 62 C3 ....57.26N 153.20W
Kōfu Japan 106 C3 ....35.39N 138.34E
Køge Denmark 40 C1 ....55.27N 12.11E
Kohat Pakistan 95 L6 ....33.37N 71.30E
Kokand Uzbekistan 102 C6 ....40.31N 70.57E
Kokkola Finland 40 E3 ....63.51N 23.08E
Kokpekti Kazakhstan 102 E7 ....48.46N 82.21E
Kokshetau Kazakhstan 58 H3 ....53.17N 69.23E
Kola Rus. Fed. 40 H5 ....68.52N 33.03E
Kolaka Indonesia 105 G3 ....4.03S 121.38E
Kola Peninsula Rus. Fed. 58 E4 ....67.29N 34.49E
Kolding Denmark 40 B1 ....55.30N 9.28E
Kolguyev, Ostrov i. Rus. Fed. 58 F4 ....69.07N 49.03E
Kolhapur India 96 D4 ....16.40N 74.19E
Kolkata India 96 G5 ....22.32N 88.21E
Kołobrzeg Poland 46 B5 ....54.11N 15.35E
Kolomyya Ukraine 55 K3 ....48.32N 25.02E
Koluli Eritrea 94 F2 ....14.24N 40.20E
Kolvitskoye, Ozero l. Rus. Fed. 40 H4 ....67.04N 33.36E
Kolwezi Dem. Rep. Congo 86 B3 ....10.42S 25.28E
Kolyma r. Rus. Fed. 59 R4 ....69.22N 161.24E
Kolymskiy, Khrebet mts Rus. Fed. 59 R4 ....66.50N 167.12E
Komatsu Japan 106 C3 ....36.23N 136.28E
Kome Island Uganda 87 A2 ....0.06S 32.49E
Komotini Greece 56 F5 ....41.07N 25.24E
Komsomolets, Ostrov i. Rus. Fed. 59 K6 ....80.42N 94.20E
Komsomol's'k Ukraine 55 O3 ....49.01N 33.39E
Komsomol'sk-na-Amure Rus. Fed. 59 O3 ....50.36N 136.55E
Kondoa Tanzania 87 B1 ....4.55S 35.47E
Kong Christian IX Land f. Greenland 63 O4 ....66.49N 37.44W
Kongsberg Norway 40 B2 ....59.40N 9.39E
Kongsvinger Norway 40 C3 ....60.12N 12.01E
Konin Poland 46 D4 ....52.14N 18.15E
Konotop Ukraine 55 O4 ....51.14N 33.12E
Konso Ethiopia 87 B4 ....5.17N 37.29E
Konstanz Germany 54 C2 ....47.40N 9.10E
Konya Turkey 57 J3 ....37.52N 32.29E
Köping Sweden 40 D2 ....59.31N 16.00E
Koprivnica Croatia 54 G2 ....46.10N 16.50E
Kora National Park Kenya 87 B2 ....0.30S 39.00E
Korçë Albania 56 D5 ....40.37N 20.47E
Korčula i. Croatia 56 B6 ....42.54N 16.56E
Korea Bay China/N. Korea 103 M5 ....39.05N 124.20E
Korea Strait Japan/S. Korea 106 A2 ....34.12N 128.36E
Körfez Turkey 57 H5 ....40.47N 29.42E
Korinthiakos Kolpos str. Greece 56 E4 ....38.16N 22.11E
Kōriyama Japan 106 D3 ....37.24N 140.22E
Korkuteli Turkey 57 I3 ....37.04N 30.11E
Köroğlu Tepesi mt. Turkey 57 J5 ....40.30N 32.01E
Korogwe Tanzania 87 B1 ....5.09S 38.30E
Körös r. Hungary 46 E1 ....46.42N 20.11E
Korosten' Ukraine 55 M4 ....50.57N 28.39E
Koro Toro Chad 85 F3 ....16.05N 18.30E
Korsakov Rus. Fed. 59 P2 ....46.38N 142.45E
Korsze Poland 46 E5 ....54.11N 21.08E
Kortrijk Belgium 42 C3 ....50.49N 3.16E
Koryakskiy Khrebet mts Rus. Fed. 59 S4 ....62.59N 177.49E
Kos i. Greece 56 G3 ....36.46N 27.07E
Kościan Poland 46 C4 ....52.05N 16.39E
Kościerzyna Poland 46 C5 ....54.07N 17.59E
Kosciuszko, Mount Australia 110 D3 ....36.28S 148.15E
Košice Slovakia 46 E2 ....48.43N 21.16E
Kosovska Mitrovica Serbia 56 D6 ....42.52N 20.52E

Kosrae *atoll* Micronesia 108 G6 ....5.19N 163.04E
Kostanay Kazakhstan 58 H3 ....53.12N 63.40E
Kosti Sudan 85 H3 ....13.09N 32.38E
Kostroma Rus. Fed. 58 F3 ....57.46N 40.58E
Kostrzyn Poland 46 B4 ....52.35N 14.39E
Koszalin Poland 46 C5 ....54.11N 16.11E
Kota India 96 E6 ....25.10N 75.57E
Kota Bharu Malaysia 104 C5 ....6.08N 102.16E
Kotabumi Indonesia 104 C3 ....4.51S 104.55E
Kota Kinabalu Malaysia 104 F5 ....5.58N 116.05E
Kotel'nyy Rus. Fed. 59 O5 ....76.00N 137.59E
Kotel'nyy, Ostrov *i.* Rus. Fed. 59 O5 ...75.07N 139.31E
Kotido Uganda 87 A3 ....2.59N 34.06E
Kotlas Rus. Fed. 58 F4 ....61.16N 46.38E
Kötlutangi *pt* Iceland 40 Y1 ....63.24N 18.45W
Kotuy *r.* Rus. Fed. 59 L5 ....71.55N 102.06E
Kotzebue U.S.A. 62 B4 ....66.53N 162.32W
Kotzebue Sound *str.* U.S.A. 62 B4 ......66.33N 163.11W
Koundâra Guinea 84 C3 ....12.30N 13.19W
Kouvola Finland 40 F3 ....60.52N 26.42E
Kovel' Ukraine 55 N4 ....51.13N 24.43E
Kowloon China 104 E8 ....22.20N 114.13E
Kozan Turkey 57 K3 ....37.28N 35.48E
Kozani Greece 56 D5 ....40.18N 21.48E
Kozelets' Ukraine 55 N4 ....50.55N 31.07E
Kozhikode India 96 E3 ....11.15N 75.45E
Kozyatyn Ukraine 55 M3 ....49.42N 28.49E
Krabi Thailand 104 B5 ....8.05N 98.56E
Krâchéh Cambodia 104 D6 ....12.27N 106.03E
Kragujevac Serbia 56 D6 ....44.01N 20.55E
Kraków Poland 46 D7 ....50.03N 19.56E
Kraljevo Serbia 56 D6 ....43.43N 20.41E
Kramfors Sweden 40 D3 ....62.56N 17.46E
Kranj Slovenia 54 F2 ....46.15N 14.21E
Krasino Rus. Fed. 58 G5 ....70.44N 54.28E
Krasnoarmiys'k Ukraine 53 K6 ....48.17N 37.10E
Krasnodar Rus. Fed. 58 E2 ....45.02N 38.98E
Krasnohrad Ukraine 55 P3 ....49.22N 35.28E
Krasnoperekops'k Ukraine 55 J7 ....45.57N 33.49E
Krasnoyarsk Rus. Fed. 59 K3 ....56.03N 92.50E
Krefeld Germany 54 B4 ....51.20N 6.33E
Kremenchuk Ukraine 55 O3 ....49.04N 33.25E
Kremenchuts'ka Vodoskhovyshche *resr* Ukraine 55 O3
                                                49.18N 32.42E
Křemešník *hill* Czech Rep. 46 B2 ....49.24N 15.20E
Kretinga Lithuania 46 E5 ....55.53N 21.14E
Krishna *r.* India 96 E4 ....16.01N 80.53E
Kristiansand Norway 40 A2 ....58.08N 7.59E
Kristianstad Sweden 40 C2 ....56.02N 14.10E
Kristiansund Norway 40 A3 ....63.07N 7.45E
Kristinehamn Sweden 40 C2 ....59.19N 14.07E
Krk *i.* Croatia 56 A7 ....45.02N 14.47E
Kropotkin Rus. Fed. 53 L6 ....45.26N 40.41E
Krosno Poland 46 E2 ....49.41N 21.46E
Krotoszyn Poland 46 C3 ....51.42N 17.27E
Kruševac Serbia 56 D6 ....43.35N 21.19E
Krychaw Belarus 55 N5 ....53.44N 31.43E
Krymsk Rus. Fed. 57 L7 ....44.55N 37.58E
Krytiko Pelagos *sea* Greece 56 F3 ....36.11N 25.24E
Kryvyy Rih Ukraine 55 O2 ....47.54N 33.21E
Ksabi Algeria 84 D4 ....28.54N 0.47W
Ksar el Boukhari Algeria 52 D4 ....35.52N 2.45E
Ksar el Kebir Morocco 52 B4 ....35.01N 5.54W
Kuala Lumpur Malaysia 104 C4 ....3.06N 101.42E
Kuala Terengganu Malaysia 104 C5 ..5.19N 103.07E
Kuantan Malaysia 104 C4 ....3.50N 103.21E
Kuban' *r.* Rus. Fed. 57 L7 ....45.19N 37.22E
Kuching Malaysia 104 E4 ....1.32N 110.20E
Kugluktuk Canada 62 G4 ....67.46N 115.07W
Kuhmo Finland 40 G4 ....64.07N 29.30E
Kuito Angola 86 A3 ....12.23S 16.57E
Kujū-san *vol.* Japan 106 B2 ....33.05N 131.16E
Kūl *r.* Iran 95 I5 ....27.04N 55.44E
Kulal, Mount Kenya 87 B3 ....2.42N 36.58E
Kuldīga Latvia 40 E2 ....56.58N 21.59E
Külob Tajikistan 95 K7 ....37.54N 69.51E
Kulunda Rus. Fed. 102 D8 ....52.33N 78.56E
Kulundinskoye, Ozero *l.* Rus. Fed. 102 D8 ...53.04N 79.46E
Kumamoto Japan 106 B2 ....32.47N 130.43E
Kumanovo Macedonia 56 D6 ....42.08N 21.43E
Kumasi Ghana 84 D2 ....6.42N 1.38W
Kumbakonam India 96 E3 ....10.58N 79.23E
Kumertau Rus. Fed. 58 G3 ....52.44N 55.46E
Kumla Sweden 40 C2 ....59.07N 15.10E
Kumo Nigeria 84 F3 ....10.06N 11.11E
Kunashir, Ostrov *i.* Rus. Fed. 106 E4 ...44.13N 146.23E
Kunlun Shan *mts* China 102 D5 ....36.11N 78.10E
Kunming China 103 I3 ....25.02N 102.48E
Kuohijärvi *l.* Finland 40 F3 ....61.12N 24.59E
Kuopio Finland 40 F3 ....62.53N 27.41E
Kupa *r.* Croatia/Slovenia 56 B7 ...45.28N 16.25E
Kupang Indonesia 105 G1 ....10.12S 123.35E
Kupiškis Lithuania 40 F1 ....55.49N 24.59E
Kuqa China 102 E6 ....41.38N 83.01E
Kürdzhali Bulgaria 56 F5 ....41.39N 25.22E
Kure Atoll U.S.A. 108 I7 ....28.20N 178.17W
Kuressaare Estonia 40 E2 ....58.16N 22.29E
Kurgan Rus. Fed. 58 H3 ....55.28N 65.23E
Kurikka Finland 40 E3 ....62.37N 22.25E
Kuril Basin *f.* N. Pacific Oc. 108 F9 ...45.53N 145.16E
Kuril Islands Rus. Fed. 59 P2 ......46.04N 148.33E
Kuril'sk Rus. Fed. 59 P2 ....45.13N 147.57E
Kuril Trench *f.* N. Pacific Oc. 117 Q8 ...41.44N 146.31E
Kurmuk Sudan 85 H3 ....10.31N 34.16E
Kurnool India 96 E4 ....15.49N 77.59E
Kursk Rus. Fed. 55 P4 ....51.45N 36.12E
Kuršumlija Serbia 56 D6 ....43.08N 21.17E
Kurume Japan 106 B2 ....33.18N 130.31E
Kurun *r.* Sudan 87 A4 ....5.37N 34.33E
Kurunegala Sri Lanka 96 F2 ....7.30N 80.19E
Kuşadası Turkey 56 G3 ....37.52N 27.15E
Kushiro Japan 106 D4 ....42.59N 144.23E
Kuskokwim Mountains U.S.A. 62 C4 ...64.24N 155.17W
Kütahya Turkey 57 H4 ....39.25N 29.59E
Kutno Poland 46 D4 ....52.14N 19.22E
Kuujjuaq Canada 63 L3 ....58.10N 68.13W
Kuusamo Finland 40 G4 ....65.58N 29.09E
Kuwait Asia 95 G5 ....29.22N 47.08E
Kuwait *town* Kuwait 95 G5 ....29.18N 47.55E
Kuytun China 102 E6 ....44.20N 84.55E
Kuznetsk Rus. Fed. 58 F3 ....53.07N 46.37E
Kvaløya *i.* Norway 40 D5 ....70.04N 19.30E
Kwale Kenya 87 B1 ....4.12S 39.27E
KwaMashu S. Africa 86 C2 ....29.44S 30.59E
Kwa Mtoro Tanzania 87 A1 ....5.13S 35.26E
Kwangju S. Korea 103 N5 ....35.09N 126.54E
Kwania, Lake Uganda 87 A3 ....1.46N 32.42E
Kwanobuhle S. Africa 86 B1 ......33.48S 25.24E
Kwilu *r.* Angola/Dem. Rep. Congo 86 A4 ...3.23S 17.22E
Kwoka *mt.* Indonesia 105 I3 ......0.38S 132.28E
Kyakhta Rus. Fed. 59 L3 ....50.21N 106.30E
Kybartai Lithuania 46 F5 ....54.38N 22.46E
Kyle of Lochalsh Scotland 18 D2 ...57.17N 5.43W
Kyle of Tongue *inlet* Scotland 19 E3 ...58.28N 4.27W

Kyllini *mt.* Greece 56 E3 ....37.56N 22.24E
Kyoga, Lake Uganda 85 H2 ....1.28N 32.53E
Kyōto Japan 106 C2 ....34.59N 135.46E
Kyparissia Greece 56 D3 ....37.15N 21.41E
Kypshak, Ozero *l.* Kazakhstan 58 H3 ...50.09N 68.23E
Kyrenia Cyprus 57 J2 ....35.20N 33.19E
Kyrgyzstan Asia 102 C6 ....41.47N 74.37E
Kythira *i.* Greece 56 E3 ....36.16N 22.55E
Kythnos *i.* Greece 56 F3 ....37.26N 24.27E
Kyūshū *i.* Japan 106 B2 ....31.30N 131.45E
Kyushu-Palau Ridge *f.* N. Pacific Oc. 108 F7 ...27.44N 135.16E
Kyustendil Bulgaria 56 E6 ....42.17N 22.41E
Kyyivs'ke Vodoskhovyshche *resr* Ukraine 55 N4 ...50.54N 30.30E
Kyzyl Rus. Fed. 59 K3 ....51.43N 94.24E
Kyzylorda Kazakhstan 58 H2 .....44.51N 65.30E

L

Laâyoune Western Sahara 84 C4 ...27.09N 13.12W
La Banda Argentina 76 H2 ....27.41S 64.15W
Labé Guinea 84 C3 ....11.20N 12.18W
Labrador *f.* Canada 63 L3 ....54.04N 62.29W
Labrador City Canada 63 L3 ......52.59N 66.54W
Labrador Sea Canada/Greenland 63 M4 ...60.07N 56.06W
Laccadive Islands India 96 D3 ....10.59N 72.11E
Laceby England 15 G2 ....53.32N 0.10W
Lachlan *r.* Australia 110 D3 ......34.21S 143.57E
La Crosse U.S.A. 65 H5 ....43.48N 91.12W
Ladhar Bheinn *mt.* Scotland 18 D2 ...57.05N 5.35W
Lādīz Iran 95 J5 ....28.55N 61.18E
Ladoga, Lake Rus. Fed. 58 E4 ....60.48N 31.37E
Ladybank Scotland 17 F4 ....56.17N 3.08W
Ladybower Reservoir England 15 F2 ...53.23N 1.45W
Ladysmith S. Africa 86 B2 ....28.34S 29.47E
Lae P.N.G. 110 D6 ....6.43S 147.00E
Læsø *i.* Denmark 40 B2 ....57.15N 11.05E
Lafayette U.S.A. 65 H3 ....30.14N 92.03W
Lagan *r.* Northern Ireland 16 D2 ...54.37N 5.54W
Laggan, Loch *l.* Scotland 19 E1 ...56.56N 4.31W
Lagh Bogal *watercourse* Kenya/Somalia 87 C3 ...0.42N 40.57E
Lagh Bor *watercourse* Kenya/Somalia 87 C3 ...0.31N 42.04E
Lagh Dima *watercourse* Kenya/Somalia 87 C3 ...0.31N 41.03E
Lagh Kutulo *watercourse* Kenya/Somalia 87 C3 ...2.04N 40.58E
Laghouat Algeria 84 E5 ....33.42N 2.53E
Lagh Walde *watercourse* Ethiopia/Kenya 87 B3 ...2.38N 38.53E
La Gomera *i.* Canary Islands 48 X2 ...28.14N 17.18W
Lagos Nigeria 84 E2 ....6.26N 3.20E
Lagos Portugal 48 A2 ....37.06N 8.41W
La Grande U.S.A. 64 C6 ....45.19N 118.02W
La Grande 2, Réservoir Canada 63 K3 ...53.52N 76.54W
La Grande 3, Réservoir Canada 63 K3 ...53.36N 75.18W
La Grande 4, Réservoir Canada 63 K3 ...54.13N 73.17W
La Gran Sabana *f.* Venezuela 71 L2 ...5.13N 61.40W
Lahad Datu Malaysia 104 F5 ......5.02N 118.20E
Lahat Indonesia 104 C3 ....3.46S 103.34E
Lahij Yemen 94 F2 ....13.02N 44.50E
Lāhījān Iran 95 G7 ....37.11N 49.56E
Lahore Pakistan 96 D7 ....31.33N 74.22E
Lahti Finland 40 F3 ....60.59N 25.41E
Laidon, Loch *l.* Scotland 19 E1 ...56.39N 4.39W
Laihia Finland 40 E3 ....62.58N 22.01E
Lainioälven *r.* Sweden 40 E4 ...67.22N 22.39E
Lairg Scotland 19 E3 ....58.01N 4.24W
Lajes Brazil 77 J2 ....27.44S 50.19W
Lake City U.S.A. 65 J3 ....30.10N 82.39W
Lake District *f.* England 14 D3 ...54.30N 3.10W
Lakeland U.S.A. 65 J2 ....27.59N 81.58W
Lakki Pakistan 95 L6 ....32.35N 70.58E
Lakonikos Kolpos *b.* Greece 56 E3 ...36.32N 22.42E
Laksefjorden *str.* Norway 40 F5 ...70.52N 27.00E
Lakshadweep *d.* India 96 D3 ...10.35N 73.13E
La Línea de la Concepción Spain 48 C2 ...36.10N 5.21W
La Louvière Belgium 42 D3 ......50.28N 4.11E
La Mancha *f.* Spain 48 D3 ......39.15N 2.58W
Lamar U.S.A. 64 F4 ....38.06N 102.38W
Lamard Iran 95 H5 ....27.22N 53.08E
La Marmora, Punta *mt.* Italy 50 C3 ...39.59N 9.20E
La Martre, Lac *l.* Canada 62 G4 ...63.19N 118.02W
Lambay Island Ireland 41 F3 ....53.29N 5.59W
Lambourn England 10 D2 ....51.30N 1.32W
Lambourn Downs *hills* England 10 D2 ...51.32N 1.32W
Lamego Portugal 48 B4 ....41.06N 7.48W
Lamia Greece 56 E4 ....38.54N 22.25E
Lamlash Scotland 16 D3 ....55.32N 5.08W
Lammermuir Hills Scotland 17 G3 ...55.49N 2.50W
Lampang Thailand 104 B7 ....18.16N 99.32E
Lampeter Wales 12 C4 ....52.07N 4.05W
Lamu Kenya 87 C2 ....2.18S 40.52E
Lamu Island Kenya 87 C2 ....2.19S 40.50E
Lanark Scotland 17 F3 ....55.40N 3.47W
Lancashire *d.* England 9 D3 ....53.57N 2.51W
Lancaster England 14 E3 ....54.03N 2.48W
Lancaster Canal England 14 E2 ...53.59N 2.48W
Lancaster Sound *str.* Canada 63 J5 ...74.15N 89.18W
Landeck Austria 54 D2 ....47.08N 10.34E
Lander U.S.A. 64 E5 ....42.50N 108.42W
Landes *f.* France 44 C4 ....44.48N 0.55W
Landguard Point England 11 G2 ...51.56N 1.19E
Land's End *pt* England 13 B2 ...50.03N 5.46W
Landshut Germany 54 E2 ....48.33N 12.10E
Landskrona Sweden 54 E6 ......55.52N 12.50E
Lanesborough Ireland 41 D3 ...53.40N 7.59W
Langavat, Loch *l.* W. Isles Scotland 18 C2 ...57.48N 6.59W
Langavat, Loch *l.* W. Isles Scotland 18 C3 ...58.02N 6.49W
Langeland *i.* Denmark 40 B1 ...55.02N 10.55E
Langeoog *i.* Germany 42 G6 ...53.46N 7.36E
Langholm Scotland 17 G3 ......55.09N 2.59W
Langøya *i.* Norway 40 C5 ......68.44N 14.27E
Langres France 44 F5 ....47.52N 5.20E
Langstrothdale Chase *hills* England 15 E3 ...54.13N 2.18W
Languedoc *f.* France 44 D3 ....43.58N 1.57E
Lanivet England 13 C2 ....50.26N 4.46W
Länkäran Azerbaijan 95 G7 .....38.45N 48.51E
Lannion France 44 B6 ....48.44N 3.27W
Lanzarote *i.* Canary Islands 48 Z2 ...29.00N 13.35W
Lao Cai Vietnam 104 C8 ....22.30N 103.59E
Laois *d.* Ireland 41 D2 ....52.57N 7.23W
Laon France 44 E6 ....49.34N 3.38E
Laos Asia 104 C7 ....19.30N 103.01E
La Palma *i.* Canary Islands 48 X2 ...28.33N 17.44W
La Palma Panama 71 I2 ....8.24N 78.09W
La Palma del Condado Spain 48 B2 ...37.23N 6.33W
La Paragua Venezuela 71 L2 .....6.50N 63.19W
La Paz Bolivia 76 G4 ....16.30S 68.10W
La Paz Mexico 70 B5 ....24.08N 110.17W
La Pérouse Strait Japan/Rus. Fed. 106 D5 ...45.35N 141.33E
La Plata Argentina 73 D3 ......34.55S 57.58W
La Plata, Río de *str.* Argentina/Uruguay 73 D3 ...34.39S 57.53W

Lappajärvi *l.* Finland 40 E3 ....63.07N 23.41E
Lappeenranta Finland 40 G3 ....61.03N 28.11E
Lappland *f.* Europe 40 D4 .....67.12N 18.37E
Laptev Sea Rus. Fed. 59 N5 ....76.05N 125.40E
Lapua Finland 40 E3 ....62.58N 23.00E
L'Aquila Italy 50 E5 ....42.22N 13.24E
Larache Morocco 52 B4 ....35.12N 6.09W
Laramie U.S.A. 64 E5 ....41.20N 105.36W
Laredo U.S.A. 64 G2 ....27.30N 99.30W
Largs Scotland 16 E3 ....55.48N 4.52W
La Rioja Argentina 73 C4 ......29.25S 66.51W
Larisa Greece 56 E4 ....39.38N 22.25E
Larkana Pakistan 96 C6 ....27.31N 68.15E
Larnaca Cyprus 57 J2 ....34.55N 33.38E
Larne Northern Ireland 16 D2 ...54.51N 5.49W
Larne Lough *inlet* Northern Ireland 16 D2 ...54.49N 5.47W
La Rochelle France 44 C5 ......46.10N 1.09W
La Roche-sur-Yon France 44 C5 ...46.40N 1.25W
La Ronge Canada 62 H3 ....55.06N 105.17W
Larvik Norway 40 B2 ....59.03N 10.05E
La Sagra *f.* Spain 48 D4 ......40.05N 3.56W
La Sagra *mt.* Spain 48 D2 ....37.58N 2.35W
Las Cruces U.S.A. 64 E3 ....32.19N 106.47W
La Serena Chile 73 B4 ....29.53S 71.16W
Lashio Myanmar 97 I5 ....22.57N 97.44E
Las Marismas *marsh* Spain 48 B2 ...37.07N 6.35W
Las Palmas de Gran Canaria Canary Islands 48 Y2
                                              28.06N 15.26W
La Spezia Italy 50 C6 ....44.07N 9.49E
Las Tórtolas, Cerro *mt.* Chile 73 C4 ...29.56S 69.52W
Las Tunas Cuba 71 I5 ....20.57N 76.57W
Las Vegas U.S.A. 64 C4 ....36.10N 115.09W
Las Villuercas *mt.* Spain 48 C3 ...39.29N 5.23W
Latacunga Ecuador 76 E7 ......0.58S 78.37W
Latakia Syria 94 E7 ....35.31N 35.47E
Latheron Scotland 19 F3 ....58.17N 3.22W
Latina Italy 50 E4 ....41.28N 12.54E
La Tortuga, Isla *i.* Venezuela 71 K3 ...10.55N 65.22W
La Tuque Canada 65 L6 ....47.27N 72.47W
Latvia Europe 40 E2 ....56.47N 23.49E
Lauchhammer Germany 54 E4 ...51.30N 13.46E
Launceston Australia 110 D2 ...41.27S 147.09E
Launceston England 13 C2 .....50.38N 4.21W
Laurencekirk Scotland 19 G1 ...56.50N 2.28W
Laurinburg U.S.A. 65 K4 ......34.46N 79.28W
Laut *i.* Indonesia 104 F3 ......3.39S 116.18E
Laval France 44 C6 ....48.04N 0.46W
Lavenham England 11 F3 ......52.06N 0.48E
Lawton U.S.A. 64 G3 ....34.37N 98.24W
Lawz, Jabal al *mt.* Saudi Arabia 53 K2 ...28.39N 35.18E
Laxey Isle of Man 14 C3 ......54.14N 4.24W
Laxford, Loch *inlet* Scotland 18 D3 ...58.25N 5.06W
Laysan Island U.S.A. 108 I7 ...25.47N 171.43W
Lázaro Cárdenas Baja Calif. Mexico 70 A7 ...30.30N 115.56W
Lázaro Cárdenas Michoacán Mexico 70 D4 ...17.57N 102.12W
Leader Water *r.* Scotland 17 G3 ...55.36N 2.40W
Leane, Lough *l.* Ireland 41 B2 ...52.02N 9.34W
Leatherhead England 11 E2 ...51.17N 0.19W
Lebanon Asia 53 K3 ....33.17N 35.20E
Łebork Poland 46 C5 ....54.32N 17.45E
Łebsko, Jezioro *lagoon* Poland 46 C5 ...54.43N 17.30E
Lecce Italy 50 H4 ....40.20N 18.11E
Lechlade England 10 D2 ......51.42N 1.41W
Lech *r.* Austria/Germany 54 D2 ...47.32N 10.40E
Le Crotoy France 11 G1 ......50.13N 1.38E
Ledbury England 10 C3 ....52.02N 2.25W
Lee *r.* Ireland 41 C1 ....51.54N 8.25W
Leeds England 15 F2 ....53.48N 1.33W
Leek England 15 E2 ....53.07N 2.01W
Leeming England 15 F3 ....54.18N 1.33W
Lee Moor England 13 C2 .....50.26N 4.01W
Leer Germany 42 G6 ....53.15N 7.28E
Leeuwarden Neth. 42 E6 ......53.12N 5.48E
Leeuwin, Cape Australia 110 A3 ...34.23S 115.09E
Leeward Islands Caribbean Sea 71 L4 ...18.59N 64.04W
Lefkada *i.* Greece 56 D4 ......38.45N 20.35E
Legaspi Phil. 105 G6 ....13.08N 123.44E
Legionowo Poland 46 E4 ....52.25N 20.58E
Legnica Poland 46 C3 ....51.13N 16.10E
Leh India 96 E7 ....34.09N 77.36E
Le Havre France 44 D6 ....49.30N 0.08E
Leiah Pakistan 95 L6 ....30.58N 70.58E
Leicester England 10 D3 ......52.38N 1.08W
Leicester *d.* England 9 E3 ....52.39N 1.07W
Leicestershire *d.* England 9 E3 ...52.37N 0.59W
Leichhardt *r.* Australia 110 C5 ...17.35S 139.44E
Leiden Neth. 42 D5 ....52.10N 4.30E
Leigh England 15 E2 ....53.30N 2.31W
Leighton Buzzard England 10 E2 ...51.55N 0.40W
Leine *r.* Germany 54 D4 .....51.48N 9.58E
Leipzig Germany 54 E4 ....51.21N 12.23E
Leiston England 11 G3 ....52.13N 1.35E
Leith Scotland 17 F3 ....55.59N 3.10W
Leith Hill England 11 E2 .....51.11N 0.22W
Leitrim *d.* Ireland 41 C4 .....54.19N 8.13W
Leixlip Ireland 41 E3 ....53.22N 6.30W
Leizhou Bandao *pen.* China 103 J2 ...21.03N 109.41E
Lek *r.* Neth. 42 D4 ....51.54N 4.34E
Leka Norway 40 B4 ....65.05N 11.44E
Leksozero, Ozero *l.* Rus. Fed. 40 G3 ...63.51N 30.48E
Lelystad Neth. 42 E5 ....52.32N 5.29E
Le Mans France 44 D6 ....48.00N 0.12E
Lena *r.* Rus. Fed. 59 N5 ....72.20N 126.37E
Lens France 44 E7 ....50.26N 2.50E
Lensk Rus. Fed. 59 M4 ......60.44N 114.53E
Leoben Austria 54 F2 ....47.23N 15.06E
Leominster England 10 C3 ....52.14N 2.44W
León Mexico 70 D5 ....21.07N 101.44W
León Spain 48 C5 ....42.36N 5.34W
Le Puy-en-Velay France 44 E4 ...45.03N 3.53E
Lerum Sweden 40 C2 ....57.46N 12.17E
Lerwick Scotland 19 H5 ......60.09N 1.09W
Lesatima *mt.* Kenya 87 B2 ...0.21S 36.37E
Leshan China 103 I3 ....29.37N 103.44E
Leskovac Serbia 56 D6 ....42.59N 21.56E
Lesozavodsk Rus. Fed. 106 B5 ...45.23N 133.23E
Les Pieux France 13 Z9 ......49.31N 1.48W
Les Sables-d'Olonne France 44 C5 ...46.30N 1.47W
Lesser Antilles *is* Caribbean Sea 71 K3 ...12.28N 67.56W
Lesser Slave Lake Canada 62 G3 ...55.28N 115.29W
Lestijärvi *l.* Finland 40 F3 ...63.30N 24.47E
Leszno Poland 46 C3 ....51.51N 16.35E
Letchworth Garden City England 11 E2 ...51.58N 0.13W
Lethbridge Canada 62 G2 .....49.41N 112.49W
Leti, Kepulauan *is* Indonesia 105 H2 ...8.18S 127.58E
Letterkenny Ireland 41 D4 ....54.57N 7.43W
Leuchars Scotland 17 F4 ......56.23N 2.53W
Leuser, Gunung *mt.* Indonesia 104 B4 ...3.46N 97.11E
Leuven Belgium 42 D3 ....50.52N 4.43E
Levadeia Greece 56 E4 ....38.26N 22.53E

Leven England 15 G2 ....53.54N
Leven Scotland 17 G4 ....56.12N
Leven, Loch *inlet* Scotland 18 D1 ...56.41N
Leven, Loch *l.* Scotland 17 F4 ...56.12N
Levens England 14 E3 ....54.16N
Leverkusen Germany 54 B4 ....51.03N
Lewes England 11 F1 ....50.52N
Lewis, Isle of *i.* Scotland 18 C3 ...58.09N
Lexington U.S.A. 65 J4 ....38.02N
Leyburn England 15 F3 ....54.19N
Leyland England 14 E2 ....53.42N
Leyte *i.* Phil. 105 G6 ....11.05N
Lezhë Albania 56 C5 ....41.46N
L'gov Rus. Fed. 55 P4 ....51.39N
Lhargarbo China 102 G4 ......32.15N
Lhasa China 102 G3 ....29.39N
Lhazê China 102 F3 ....29.08N
Lhokseumawe Indonesia 104 B5 ...5.09N
L'Hospitalet de Llobregat Spain 48 G4 ...41.21N
Lianyungang China 103 L4 ....34.37N
Liaoning *d.* China 103 M6 ...41.30N
Liaoyuan China 103 N6 ....42.54N
Liard *r.* Canada 62 F4 ....61.51N
Libenge Dem. Rep. Congo 86 A5 ...3.37N
Liberal U.S.A. 64 F4 ....37.03N
Liberec Czech Rep. 54 F4 .....50.45N
Liberia Africa 84 D2 ....6.52N
Libin Belgium 42 E2 ....49.59N
Libourne France 44 C4 ....44.55N
Libreville Gabon 84 E2 ....0.28N
Libya Africa 84 F4 ....26.07N
Libyan Desert Egypt/Libya 85 G4 ...24.51N
Libyan Plateau *f.* Egypt/Libya 53 I3 ...30.59N
Lichfield England 10 D3 ......52.41N
Lichinga Mozambique 86 C3 ...13.17S
Lida Belarus 55 K5 ....53.53N
Liddel *r.* Scotland 17 G3 ....55.04N
Lidköping Sweden 40 C2 ......58.30N
Liechtenstein Europe 44 H5 ...47.07N
Liège Belgium 42 E3 ....50.38N
Liège *d.* Belgium 42 E3 .....50.29N
Lieksa Finland 40 G3 ....63.19N
Lienz Austria 54 E2 ....46.50N
Liepāja Latvia 40 E2 ....56.31N
Liévin France 42 B3 ....50.25N
Liezen Austria 50 F7 ....47.35N
Liffey *r.* Ireland 41 E3 .....53.21N
Lifford Ireland 41 D4 ....54.50N
Ligurian Sea France/Italy 44 H3 ...43.30N
Likasi Dem. Rep. Congo 86 B3 ...10.58S
Lilla Edet Sweden 40 C2 ......58.08N
Lille Belgium 42 D4 ....51.14N
Lille France 44 E7 ....50.38N
Lillehammer Norway 40 B3 ....61.06N
Lilleshall England 10 C3 .....52.44N
Lillestrøm Norway 40 B2 .....59.59N
Lilongwe Malawi 86 C3 ....13.57S
Lima Peru 76 E5 ....12.04S
Limassol Cyprus 57 J2 ....34.41N
Limavady Northern Ireland 16 C3 ...55.03N
Limavady *d.* Northern Ireland 8 B4 ...54.57N
Limburg *d.* Belgium 42 E3 ...51.04N
Limburg *d.* Neth. 42 E4 .....51.15N
Limerick Ireland 41 C2 ......52.40N
Limerick *d.* Ireland 41 C2 ...52.29N
Limingen *r.* Norway 40 C4 ...64.48N
Limnos *i.* Greece 56 F4 .....39.51N
Limoges France 44 D4 ....45.50N
Limousin *f.* France 44 D4 ...45.34N
Limoux France 44 E3 ....43.04N
Limpopo *r.* S. Africa/Zimbabwe 86 C2 ...25.13S
Linares Spain 48 D3 ....38.06N
Lincoln England 15 G2 ....53.14N
Lincoln U.S.A. 64 G5 ....40.51N
Lincolnshire *d.* England 9 E3 ...53.07N
Lincolnshire Wolds *hills* England 15 G2 ...53.30N
Lindesnes *c.* Norway 40 A2 ...58.00N
Lindfield England 11 E2 ......51.01N
Lindi Tanzania 86 C4 ....9.59S
Lindos Greece 57 H3 ....36.05N
Linfen China 103 K5 ....36.05N
Lingen Germany 54 B5 ......52.32N
Lingfield England 11 E2 .....51.11N
Lingga, Kepulauan *is* Indonesia 104 D3 ...0.02S
Linhares Brazil 77 L4 ....19.27S
Linköping Sweden 40 C2 .....58.25N
Linkou China 106 B5 ....45.11N
Linlithgow Scotland 17 F3 ...55.58N
Linney Head Wales 12 B3 ...51.37N
Linnhe, Loch *inlet* Scotland 16 D4 ...56.31N
Linosa, Isola di *i.* Italy 50 E1 ...35.51N
Linxia China 103 I5 ....35.31N
Linz Austria 54 F3 ....48.19N
Lions, Gulf of France 44 E3 ...43.00N
Lipari, Isole *is* Italy 50 F3 ...38.39N
Lipetsk Rus. Fed. 58 E3 .....52.37N
Liphook England 10 E2 ......51.04N
Lipova Romania 56 D8 ....46.05N
Lippe *r.* Germany 42 F4 ....51.39N
Lisala Dem. Rep. Congo 86 B5 ...2.10N
Lisbon Portugal 48 A3 ....38.44N
Lisburn Northern Ireland 16 C2 ...54.31N
Lisburn *d.* Northern Ireland 9 B4 ...54.31N
Liscannor Bay Ireland 41 B2 ...52.55N
Liskeard England 13 C2 ......50.27N
Lismore Australia 110 E4 ....28.47S
Lismore Ireland 41 D2 ....52.08N
Lisnaskea Northern Ireland 16 B2 ...54.15N
Liss England 10 E2 ....51.03N
Listowel Ireland 41 B2 ......52.26N
Lithuania Europe 55 J6 ......55.05N
Little Abaco *i.* Bahamas 71 I6 ...26.54N
Little Andaman *i.* India 97 H3 ...10.38N
Little Belt *str.* Denmark 40 B1 ...55.15N
Littleborough England 15 E2 ...53.39N
Little Cayman *i.* Cayman Is 71 H4 ...19.42N
Littlehampton England 11 E1 ...50.49N
Little Inagua Island Bahamas 71 J5 ...21.31N
Little Karoo *f.* S. Africa 86 B1 ...33.43S
Little Minch *str.* Scotland 18 C2 ...57.32N
Little Ouse *r.* England 11 F3 ...52.30N
Littleport England 11 F3 .....52.27N
Little Rock *town* U.S.A. 65 H3 ...34.46N
Liuzhou China 103 J2 ....24.21N
Liverpool England 14 E2 .....53.25N
Liverpool Canada 63 N5 .....44.02N
Livingston Scotland 17 F3 ...55.54N
Livingstone Zambia 86 B3 ...17.52S
Livorno Italy 50 D5 ....43.32N
Lizard England 13 B1 ....49.58N
Lizard Point England 13 B1 ...49.57N
Ljubljana Slovenia 54 F2 .....46.03N

gan r. Sweden 40 D3 ....62.18N 17.23E
gby Sweden 40 D3 ....56.51N 13.59E
al Sweden 40 D3 ....61.50N 16.06E
rth Wales 12 C4 ....52.12N 4.18W
adarn Fawr Wales 12 C4 ....52.24N 4.04W
eris Wales 12 C5 ....53.07N 4.08W
leilo Wales 12 D3 ....51.53N 3.59W
lovery Wales 12 D3 ....51.59N 3.48W
rindod Wells Wales 12 D4 ....52.14N 3.23W
ludno Wales 12 D5 ....53.19N 3.50W
lwrog Wales 12 C5 ....53.05N 4.19W
lysul Wales 12 C4 ....52.03N 4.18W
gwad Wales 12 C3 ....51.52N 4.09W
lli Wales 12 C3 ....51.41N 4.10W
s Spain 48 C5 ....43.25N 4.44W
air Caereinion Wales 12 D4 ....52.39N 3.20W
airfechan Wales 12 D5 ....53.15N 3.58W
airpwllgwyngyll Wales 12 C5 ....53.13N 4.12W
air-yn-neubwll Wales 12 C5 ....53.16N 4.33W
yllin Wales 12 D4 ....52.46N 3.16W
gadog Wales 12 D3 ....51.56N 3.53W
gefni Wales 12 C5 ....53.15N 4.19W
geler Wales 12 C4 ....52.02N 4.22W
gelynin Wales 12 C4 ....52.39N 4.07W
goed Wales 12 D4 ....53.18N 4.05W
gurig Wales 12 D4 ....52.58N 3.10W
dloes Wales 12 D4 ....52.27N 3.32W
lwchiarn Wales 12 D4 ....52.32N 3.17W
lyfni Wales 12 C4 ....53.03N 4.17W
os f. Col./Venez. 72 C7 ....5.54N 69.50W
rumney Wales 13 D3 ....51.31N 3.07W
rwst Wales 12 D5 ....53.08N 3.48W
sannan Wales 12 D4 ....53.11N 3.36W
crisant Wales 12 D3 ....51.33N 3.22W
twit Major Wales 13 D3 ....51.25N 3.29W
wnda Wales 12 C5 ....53.05N 4.17W
wnog Wales 12 D4 ....52.32N 3.27W
ybydder Wales 12 C4 ....52.04N 4.09W
Wales 12 D5 ....53.06N 3.00W
a Spain 48 F4 ....41.36N 0.38E
ena Spain 48 B3 ....38.15N 6.01W
Peninsula Wales 12 C4 ....52.51N 4.34W
d George, Mount Canada 62 F3 ....57.50N 124.57W
dminster Canada 62 G3 ....53.17N 110.00W
to Angola 86 A3 ....12.24S 13.32E
aaline Scotland 16 D4 ....56.32N 5.47W
boisdale Scotland 18 B2 ....57.09N 7.19W
gelly Scotland 17 F4 ....56.08N 3.18W
gilphead Scotland 16 D4 ....56.02N 5.26W
inver Scotland 18 D3 ....58.09N 5.14W
amaben Scotland 17 F3 ....55.08N 3.26W
maddy Scotland 18 B2 ....57.36N 7.10W
nagar Scotland 19 F1 ....56.58N 3.15W
ranza Scotland 16 D3 ....55.42N 5.17W
y, Loch l. Scotland 18 E1 ....56.56N 4.58W
erbie Scotland 17 F3 ....55.07N 3.21W
don England 11 G3 ....52.32N 1.29E
war Kenya 87 A3 ....3.06N 35.34E
Poland 46 D3 ....51.46N 19.27E
sten is Norway 40 C5 ....68.06N 12.44E
sa Sudan 87 A3 ....3.50N 33.10E
an, Mount Canada 62 D4 ....60.40N 140.02W
gerheads England 10 C3 ....52.55N 2.23W
one r. Cameroon/Chad 82 E6 ....12.10N 15.00E
roño Spain 48 D5 ....42.28N 2.26W
e r. France 44 B5 ....47.17N 2.07W
Ecuador 76 E7 ....4.00S 79.14W
Spain 48 C2 ....37.10N 4.09W
an tekojärvi resr Finland 40 F4 ....67.56N 27.35E
eren Belgium 42 D4 ....51.06N 4.00E
char Kenya 87 A3 ....2.22N 35.37E
chokio Kenya 87 A4 ....4.14N 34.21E
ken Norway 40 B3 ....63.07N 9.42E
oja Nigeria 84 E2 ....7.49N 6.44E
wa Kangole Kenya 87 A3 ....3.32N 35.50E
and l. Denmark 40 B1 ....54.47N 11.21E
ondo Tanzania 87 A2 ....2.01S 35.38E
n Bulgaria 56 E6 ....43.49N 23.14E
nami r. Dem. Rep. Congo 86 B5 ......0.47N 24.17E
nbok i. Indonesia 104 F2 ....9.07S 116.13E
né Togo 84 E2 ....6.09N 1.13E
nmel Belgium 42 E4 ....51.14N 5.19E
nond, Loch l. Scotland 16 E4 ....56.04N 4.37W
za Poland 46 F4 ....53.11N 22.05E
don Canada 63 J2 ....42.59N 81.14W
don England 11 E2 ....51.30N 0.07W
donderry Northern Ireland 16 B2 ....54.59N 7.20W
donderry f. Northern Ireland 16 E4 .54.59N 6.51W
donderry, Cape Australia 110 B5 ....13.47S 126.53E
g, Loch inlet Scotland 16 C1 ....56.06N 4.51W
ga, Proliv str. Rus. Fed. 59 S5 ....70.10N 178.17E
g Ashton England 10 C2 ....51.26N 2.39W
g Beach town U.S.A. 64 C3 ....33.47N 118.20W
g Bennington England 10 E3 ....52.59N 0.46W
g Eaton England 10 D3 ....52.54N 1.16W
gford England 10 D3 ....52.54N 7.48W
gford l. Ireland 41 D3 ....53.45N 7.41W
ghorsley England 15 F4 ....55.15N 1.46W
ghoughton England 15 F4 ....55.26N 1.37W
gido Tanzania 87 B2 ....2.47S 36.42E
g Island Bahamas 71 I5 ....23.18N 75.06W
g Island 65 L5 ....40.49N 72.36W
glac Canada 63 J2 ....49.47N 86.33W
gridge England 14 B2 ....53.50N 2.36W
g Stratton England 11 G3 ....52.29N 1.14E
gton England 14 E2 ....53.44N 2.48W
gtown England 14 E4 ....55.00N 2.58W
guyon France 42 E2 ....49.27N 5.37E
gview U.S.A. 65 H3 ....32.32N 94.44W
g Xuyên Vietnam 104 D6 ....10.20N 105.25E
gyearbyen Arctic Oc. 58 C5 ....77.59N 15.44E
s-le-Saunier France 44 F4 ....46.41N 5.33E
kout, Cape U.S.A. 65 K3 ....34.37N 76.33W
lmalasin vol. Tanzania 87 A2 ....3.02S 35.48E
p Head England 14 B2 ....54.23N 9.56W
Nur r. China 102 G6 ....40.28N 90.20E
phavet b. Norway 40 E5 ....70.21N 21.03E
ca Pakistan 95 K6 ....30.21N 68.43E
ca Spain 48 E2 ....37.41N 1.41W
d Howe Island Australia 111 ....31.26S 158.57E
d Howe Rise f. S. Pacific Oc. 108 G4 ..27.06S 160.37E
ient France 44 B5 ....47.45N 3.22W
, Firth of est. Scotland 16 D4 .....56.15N 5.54W
raine d. France 42 F1 ....48.48N 6.06E
ai National Reserve Kenya 87 B3 ....1.33N 37.39E
Angeles Chile 73 B3 ....37.28S 72.21W
Angeles U.S.A. 64 C3 ....34.01N 118.15W
Mochis Mexico 70 C6 ....25.48N 108.59W
Roques, Islas is Venezuela 71 K3 ...11.55N 66.39W
sie r. Scotland 19 F2 ....57.43N 3.17W
siemouth Scotland 19 F2 ....57.43N 3.17W
twithiel England 13 C2 ....50.24N 4.40W

Los Vilos Chile 76 F1 ....31.56S 71.29W
Lot r. France 44 D4 ....44.19N 0.20E
Lotagipi Swamp f. Kenya/Sudan 87 A4 ...4.44N 34.42E
Loth Scotland 19 G4 ....59.12N 2.41W
Lotikipi Plain f. Kenya/Sudan 87 A4 ....4.36N 34.38E
Lotta r. Finland/Rus. Fed. 40 G5 .68.40N 30.14E
Lotuke mt. Sudan 87 A4 ....4.08N 33.51E
Louangnamtha Laos 104 C8 ....21.03N 101.29E
Louangphabang Laos 104 C7 ....19.54N 102.10E
Loughborough England 10 D3 ....52.46N 1.12W
Loughor r. Wales 12 C3 ....51.42N 4.03W
Loughrea Ireland 41 C3 ....53.12N 8.35W
Loughton England 11 F2 ....51.39N 0.04E
Louisiana d. U.S.A. 65 H3 ....30.40N 91.56W
Louisville U.S.A. 65 I4 ....38.15N 85.46W
Louisville Ridge f. S. Pacific Oc. 108 I3 ..30.29S 173.10W
Loukhi Rus. Fed. 40 H4 ....66.04N 33.03E
Louny Czech Rep. 46 A3 ....50.21N 13.49E
Lourdes France 44 C3 ....43.06N 0.02W
Louth England 15 G2 ....53.22N 0.01W
Louth d. Ireland 41 E3 ....53.53N 6.31W
Lovech Bulgaria 56 F6 ....43.09N 24.42E
Lovozero Rus. Fed. 40 H5 ....68.01N 34.59E
Lowell U.S.A. 65 L5 ....42.39N 71.19W
Lower Lough Erne l. Northern Ireland 16 B2 ..54.29N 7.51W
Lowestoft England 11 G3 ....52.29N 1.45E
Łowicz Poland 46 D4 ....52.07N 19.57E
Loyal, Loch l. Scotland 19 E3 .....58.25N 4.22W
Loyauté, Îles is New Caledonia 111 F4 ..20.23S 167.17E
Loyne, Loch l. Scotland 18 D2 .....57.06N 5.05W
Loznica Serbia 56 C7 ....44.33N 19.15E
Luanda Angola 86 A4 ....8.50S 13.14E
Luarca Spain 48 B5 ....43.32N 6.31W
Luau Angola 86 B3 ....10.42S 22.15E
Lubaczów Poland 46 F3 ....50.10N 23.08E
Lubango Angola 86 A3 ....14.55S 13.30E
Lubartów Poland 46 F3 ....51.28N 22.37E
Lubbock U.S.A. 64 F3 ....33.38N 101.51W
Lübeck Germany 54 D5 ....53.52N 10.42E
Lübecker Bucht b. Germany 54 D6 ...54.03N 10.47E
Lubin Poland 46 C3 ....51.24N 16.13E
Lublin Poland 46 F3 ....51.14N 22.35E
Lubnaig, Loch l. Scotland 16 E4 ...56.18N 4.19W
Lubny Ukraine 55 O4 ....50.01N 33.00E
Lubuklinggau Indonesia 104 C3 .....3.23S 102.56E
Lumumbashi Dem. Rep. Congo 86 B3 ..11.40S 27.29E
Lubutu Dem. Rep. Congo 86 B4 ......0.44S 26.35E
Lucan Ireland 12 A5 ....53.21N 6.27W
Lucena Phil. 105 G6 ....13.56N 121.36E
Lucena Spain 48 C2 ....37.25N 4.29W
Lučenec Slovakia 54 H3 ....48.21N 19.41E
Lucerne Switz. 50 C7 ....47.03N 8.18E
Lucknow India 96 F6 ....26.51N 80.58E
Lüderitz Namibia 86 A2 ....26.40S 15.09E
Ludgershall England 10 D2 ....51.15N 1.37W
Ludhiana India 96 E7 ....30.54N 75.53E
Ludlow England 10 C3 ....52.22N 2.43W
Ludvika Sweden 40 C3 ....60.09N 15.12E
Ludwigsburg Germany 54 C3 ....48.54N 9.12E
Ludwigshafen am Rhein Germany 54 C3 ..49.28N 8.26E
Ludwigslust Germany 54 D5 ....53.20N 11.30E
Luena Angola 86 A3 ....11.47S 19.54E
Lufkin U.S.A. 65 H3 ....31.21N 94.44W
Luga Rus. Fed. 40 G2 ....58.43N 29.51E
Luga r. Rus. Fed. 40 G2 ....59.40N 28.18E
Lugano Switz. 50 C7 ....46.01N 8.57E
Lugg r. Wales 12 E4 ....52.02N 2.38W
Lugo Spain 48 B5 ....43.01N 7.33W
Lugoj Romania 56 D7 ....45.42N 21.55E
Luichart, Loch l. Scotland 18 E2 ..57.37N 4.48W
Luing i. Scotland 16 D4 ....56.14N 5.39W
Łuków Poland 46 F3 ....51.56N 22.24E
Luleå Sweden 40 E4 ....65.35N 22.10E
Luleälven r. Sweden 40 E4 ....65.35N 22.03E
Lüleburgaz Turkey 56 G5 ....41.25N 27.21E
Lumberton U.S.A. 65 K3 ....34.36N 79.05W
Lunan Bay Scotland 19 G1 ....56.39N 2.30W
Lund Sweden 40 C1 ....55.42N 13.12E
Lundy i. England 13 C3 ....51.11N 4.39W
Lune r. England 14 E3 ....54.03N 2.49W
Lüneburg Germany 54 D5 ....53.15N 10.25E
Lunéville France 44 G6 ....48.36N 6.30E
Luninyets Belarus 55 L5 ....52.14N 26.48E
Luoyang China 103 K4 ....34.38N 112.27E
Lupanshui China 103 I4 ....26.40N 104.48E
Lure France 44 G5 ....47.41N 6.30E
Lurgainn, Loch l. Scotland 18 D3 ..58.02N 5.14W
Lurgan Northern Ireland 16 C2 .....54.27N 6.19W
Lusaka Zambia 86 B3 ....15.23S 28.16E
Lushnjë Albania 56 C5 ....40.57N 19.42E
Lushoto Tanzania 87 B2 ....4.47S 38.18E
Lut, Dasht-e des. Iran 95 I6 ......30.47N 58.45E
Lutherstadt Wittenberg Germany 54 E4 ..51.52N 12.39E
Luton England 11 E2 ....51.53N 0.25W
Luton d. England 9 E2 ....51.54N 0.25W
Luts'k Ukraine 55 K4 ....50.45N 25.21E
Lutterworth England 10 D3 ....52.27N 1.12W
Luxembourg d. Belgium 42 E3 ....50.03N 5.27E
Luxembourg Europe 42 E2 ....49.49N 6.01E
Luxembourg town Lux. 42 F2 ....49.36N 6.08E
Luxor Egypt 85 H4 ....25.43N 32.39E
Luziânia Brazil 77 K4 ....16.17S 47.53W
Luzon i. Phil. 105 G7 ....15.24N 122.02E
Luzon Strait Phil. 104 G8 ....20.19N 121.07E
L'viv Ukraine 55 K3 ....49.50N 24.02E
Lycksele Sweden 40 D4 ....64.36N 18.41E
Lydd England 11 F1 ....50.57N 0.55E
Lydford England 13 C2 ....50.39N 4.06W
Lydney England 10 C2 ....51.44N 2.32W
Lyepyel' Belarus 55 M6 ....54.53N 28.42E
Lyme Bay England 10 C1 ....50.39N 2.59W
Lyme Regis England 10 C1 ....50.43N 2.56W
Lymington England 10 D1 ....50.45N 1.33W
Lynchburg U.S.A. 65 K4 ....37.24N 79.09W
Lyndhurst England 10 D1 ....50.52N 1.35W
Lynmouth England 13 D3 ....51.14N 3.50W
Lynn Lake town Canada 62 H3 ....56.51N 101.03W
Lynton England 13 D3 ....51.14N 3.50W
Lyon France 44 F4 ....45.45N 4.52E
Lyon r. Scotland 19 F1 ....56.37N 3.58W
Lytchett Minster England 10 C1 ....50.44N 2.03W
Lytham St Anne's England 14 D2 ....53.45N 3.02W
Lyubeshiv Ukraine 46 G3 ....51.46N 25.31E

M

Ma'ān Jordan 94 E6 ....30.12N 35.43E
Ma'arrat an Nu'mān Syria 57 L2 ....35.39N 36.40E
Maas r. Neth. 42 D4 ....51.43N 4.53E
Maaseik Belgium 42 E4 ....51.05N 5.48E
Maastricht Neth. 42 E3 ....50.51N 5.42E

Mabalane Mozambique 86 C2 ....23.50S 32.37E
Mablethorpe England 15 H2 ....53.20N 0.16E
Macaé Brazil 77 L3 ....22.22S 41.50W
Macao China 103 K2 ....22.15N 113.34E
Macará Ecuador 76 E7 ....4.24S 79.58W
Macas Ecuador 76 E7 ....2.19S 78.10W
Macassar Strait Indonesia 104 F3 ..3.55S 117.24E
Macclesfield England 15 E2 ....53.16N 2.07W
Macdonnell Ranges mts Australia 110 C4 ..23.33S 131.18E
Macduff Scotland 19 G2 ....57.40N 2.30W
Macedo de Cavaleiros Portugal 48 B4 ..41.32N 6.57W
Macedonia Europe 56 D5 ....41.31N 21.46E
Maceió Brazil 77 M6 ....9.36S 35.40W
Macgillycuddy's Reeks mts Ireland 41 B1 ..51.57N 9.52W
Mach Pakistan 96 C6 ....29.52N 67.20E
Machakos Kenya 87 B2 ....1.31S 37.16E
Machala Ecuador 76 E7 ....3.17S 79.57W
Machilipatnam India 96 F4 ....16.11N 81.10E
Machrihanish Scotland 16 D4 ....55.25N 5.44W
Machynlleth Wales 12 D4 ....52.35N 3.51W
Mackay Australia 110 D4 ....21.10S 149.11E
Mackay, Lake Australia 110 B4 .....22.36S 128.28E
Mackenzie r. Canada 62 E4 ....69.15N 134.11W
Mackenzie King Island Canada 62 G5 ..77.42N 111.56W
Mackenzie Mountains Canada 62 E4 ..65.04N 133.03W
MacLeod, Lake Australia 110 A4 ....24.08S 113.43E
Macomer Italy 50 C4 ....40.16N 8.47E
Mâcon France 44 F5 ....46.19N 4.50E
Macon U.S.A. 65 J3 ....32.53N 83.37W
Macquarie Island S. Pacific Oc. 108 G2 ..54.36S 158.58E
Macquarie Ridge f. S. Pacific Oc. 108 G2 ..55.50S 157.21E
Macroom Ireland 41 C1 ....51.54N 8.58W
Madadeni S. Africa 86 C2 ....27.45S 30.02E
Madagascar Africa 86 D3 ....19.57S 46.27E
Madeira r. Brazil 77 I7 ....3.23S 58.47W
Madeira is N. Atlantic Oc. 84 C5 ..33.15N 16.57W
Madeley England 10 C3 ....52.38N 2.26W
Madera Mexico 70 C6 ....29.11N 108.11W
Madhya Pradesh d. India 96 E5 ....23.32N 78.56E
Madidi r. Bolivia 76 G5 ....12.34S 66.54W
Madīnat ath Thawrah Syria 57 M2 ...35.51N 38.33E
Madison U.S.A. 65 I5 ....43.04N 89.23W
Mado Gashi Kenya 87 B3 ....0.42N 39.09E
Madona Latvia 55 L7 ....56.51N 26.13E
Madrakah, Ra's c. Oman 95 I3 ......19.01N 57.51E
Madre, Laguna lagoon Mexico 70 E6 ..25.06N 97.37W
Madre, Sierra mts C. America 60 J4 ..15.00N 90.00W
Madre de Dios Peru 76 F5 ....12.34S 70.05W
Madre de Dios r. Peru 72 C5 ......10.59S 66.07W
Madre del Sur, Sierra mts Mexico 70 D4 ..18.07N 101.24W
Madre Occidental, Sierra mts Mexico 70 C6 ..28.46N 108.51W
Madre Oriental, Sierra mts Mexico 70 D6 ..26.41N 101.44W
Madrid Spain 48 D4 ....40.26N 3.40W
Madura i. Indonesia 104 E2 ....7.02S 113.11E
Madurai India 96 E2 ....9.55N 78.07E
Maebashi Japan 106 C3 ....36.23N 139.04E
Maesteg Wales 12 D3 ....51.36N 3.40W
Maestra, Sierra mts Cuba 71 I4 ....19.54N 77.33W
Mafia Island Tanzania 86 C4 ....7.48S 39.52E
Mafraq Jordan 94 E6 ....32.20N 36.13E
Magadan Rus. Fed. 59 Q3 ....59.38N 151.00E
Magadi Kenya 87 B2 ....1.52S 36.19E
Magdalena r. Colombia 72 B8 ......11.06N 74.52W
Magdalena Mexico 70 B7 ....30.38N 110.59W
Magdeburg Germany 54 D5 ....52.07N 11.38E
Magellan, Strait of Chile 73 B1 ...53.42S 71.59W
Magerøya i. Norway 40 F5 ....70.59N 25.40E
Maggiorasca, Monte mt. Italy 50 C6 ..44.33N 9.30E
Maggiore, Lake Italy 50 C6 ....45.56N 8.36E
Maghera Northern Ireland 16 C2 ....54.50N 6.40W
Magherafelt Northern Ireland 16 C2 ..54.45N 6.36W
Magherafelt d. Northern Ireland 9 B4 ..54.49N 6.39W
Maghull England 14 E2 ....53.31N 2.57W
Magilligan Point Northern Ireland 16 C3 ..55.12N 6.56W
Magnitogorsk Rus. Fed. 58 G3 .....53.24N 59.08E
Mago National Park Ethiopia 87 B4 ..5.29N 36.17E
Maguarinho, Cabo c. Brazil 77 K7 ..0.19S 48.27W
Magwe Myanmar 97 H5 ....20.09N 94.56E
Mahābād Iran 95 G7 ....36.44N 45.41E
Mahagi Dem. Rep. Congo 86 B5 .....2.16N 30.55E
Mahajanga Madagascar 86 D3 ....15.41S 46.21E
Mahalevona Madagascar 86 D3 ......15.24S 49.53E
Maharashtra d. India 96 E4 ....19.24N 75.18E
Mahé i. Seychelles 85 J1 ....4.36S 55.24E
Mahilyow Belarus 55 N5 ....53.55N 30.20E
Mahón Spain 48 H3 ....39.53N 4.17E
Mahrāt, Jabal mt. Yemen 95 H3 ....17.07N 51.07E
Maicao Colombia 71 J3 ....11.25N 72.23W
Maidenhead England 10 E2 ....51.31N 0.43W
Maidstone England 11 F2 ....51.16N 0.31E
Maiduguri Nigeria 84 F3 ....11.50N 13.08E
Main r. Northern Ireland 16 C2 ....54.43N 6.18W
Mai-Ndombe, Lac l. Dem. Rep. Congo 86 A4 ..2.15S 18.22E
Maine d. U.S.A. 65 M6 ....45.20N 69.21W
Mainland i. Orkn. Scotland 19 F4 ..59.04N 3.15W
Mainland i. Shetl. Scotland 19 H5 ..60.21N 1.17W
Mainz Germany 54 C4 ....50.00N 8.16E
Maiquetía Venezuela 71 K3 ....10.32N 66.56W
Maisons-Laffitte France 42 B1 .....48.57N 2.09E
Maíz, Islas del is Nicaragua 71 H3 ..12.10N 83.02W
Maizuru Japan 106 C3 ....35.28N 135.24E
Maja Jezercë mt. Albania 56 C6 ....42.26N 19.50E
Majene Indonesia 104 F3 ....3.30S 118.54E
Majī Ethiopia 87 A4 ....6.08N 35.37E
Major, Puig mt. Spain 48 G3 ......39.48N 2.49E
Majorca i. Spain 48 G3 ....39.57N 2.43E
Makale Indonesia 104 F3 ....3.06S 119.52E
Makarska Croatia 56 B6 ....43.18N 17.02E
Makassar Indonesia 104 F2 ....5.06S 119.27E
Makat Kazakhstan 58 G2 ....47.37N 53.14E
Makgadikgadi f. Botswana 86 B2 ...20.45S 25.35E
Makhachkala Rus. Fed. 58 F2 ......42.59N 47.30E
Makindu Kenya 87 B2 ....2.18S 37.50E
Makran f. Iran/Pakistan 95 J5 ....26.29N 60.27E
Makurdi Nigeria 84 E2 ....7.43N 8.33E
Makuyuni Tanzania 87 B2 ....3.33S 36.05E
Mala, Punta pt Panama 71 H2 ......7.27N 80.00W
Malabar Coast f. India 96 D2 .....12.16N 74.30E
Malabo Equat. Guinea 84 E2 ....3.45N 8.46E
Malacca, Strait of Indonesia/Malaysia 104 B5 ..5.41N 98.38E
Maladzyechna Belarus 55 L6 ....54.18N 26.52E
Málaga Spain 48 C2 ....36.43N 4.25W
Malahide Ireland 41 E3 ....53.27N 6.09W
Malaita i. Solomon Is 111 F6 .....8.58S 161.09E
Malakal Sudan 85 H2 ....9.30N 31.40E
Malakula i. Vanuatu 111 F5 ....16.16S 167.19E
Malang Indonesia 104 E2 ....7.56S 112.46E
Malanje Angola 86 A4 ....9.33S 16.23E
Mälaren l. Sweden 40 D2 ....59.27N 17.18E
Malatya Turkey 57 M4 ....38.20N 38.20E
Malawi Africa 86 C3 ....11.32S 33.43E
Malāyer Iran 95 G6 ....34.17N 48.48E
Malaysia Asia 104 D4 ....3.39N 108.45E
Malbork Poland 46 D5 ....54.02N 19.02E

Malden Island Kiribati 109 J5 .....4.02S 154.57W
Maldives Indian Oc. 96 D2 ....6.09N 72.23E
Maldon England 11 F2 ....51.44N 0.40E
Male Maldives 96 D1 ....4.18N 73.29E
Maleas, Akra pt Greece 56 E3 .....36.26N 23.12E
Malgomaj l. Sweden 40 D4 ....64.44N 16.15E
Mali Africa 84 D3 ....13.54N 5.34W
Malili Indonesia 105 G3 ....2.37S 121.07E
Malindi Kenya 87 C2 ....3.14S 40.06E
Malin Head Ireland 41 D5 ....55.23N 7.24W
Malka Mari Kenya 87 C4 ....4.13N 40.47E
Mallaig Scotland 18 D2 ....57.00N 5.50W
Mallawī Egypt 53 J2 ....27.43N 30.50E
Mallow Ireland 41 C2 ....52.08N 8.39W
Malmédy Belgium 42 F3 ....50.26N 6.02E
Malmesbury England 10 C2 ....51.35N 2.06W
Malmö Sweden 40 C1 ....55.36N 13.01E
Måløy Norway 40 A3 ....61.56N 5.07E
Malpas England 14 E2 ....53.01N 2.46W
Malpaso mt. Canary Islands 48 W1 ..27.44N 18.01W
Malpelo, Isla de i. N. Pacific Oc. 109 O6 ..3.59N 81.34W
Malta Europe 50 F1 ....35.49N 14.18E
Maltby England 15 F2 ....53.25N 1.12W
Malton England 15 G3 ....54.08N 0.48W
Malvern Hills England 10 C3 ......52.04N 2.20W
Malyy Anyuy r. Rus. Fed. 59 R4 ...68.27N 161.01E
Mama r. Rus. Fed. 59 P4 ....66.28N 143.13E
Mamelodi S. Africa 86 B2 ....25.42S 28.23E
Mamoré r. Bolivia/Brazil 76 G5 ...10.23S 65.21W
Mamuju Indonesia 104 F3 ....2.40S 118.51E
Man, Isle of i. Irish Sea 9 C4 ...54.15N 4.39W
Man, Isle of i. Irish Sea 16 C2 ...54.16N 4.41W
Manacapuru Brazil 77 H7 ....3.14S 60.35W
Manacor Spain 48 G3 ....39.34N 3.14E
Manado Indonesia 105 G4 ....1.33N 124.52E
Managua Nicaragua 71 G3 ....12.07N 86.17W
Manama Bahrain 95 H5 ....26.12N 50.35E
Mananjary Madagascar 86 D2 ......21.14S 48.20E
Manaus Brazil 77 H7 ....3.04S 60.00W
Manavgat Turkey 57 I3 ....36.48N 31.26E
Manchester England 15 E2 ....53.29N 2.15W
Manchuria f. China 103 M7 ....46.27N 123.48E
Mand r. India 95 H5 ....21.42N 83.15E
Mandala, Puncak mt. Indonesia 105 K3 ..4.43S 140.21E
Mandalay Myanmar 97 I5 ....21.59N 96.06E
Mandalgovĭ Mongolia 103 J7 ......45.42N 106.19E
Mandera Kenya 87 C3 ....3.53N 41.50E
Mandioré, Lagoa l. Bolivia/Brazil 77 I4 ..18.08S 57.32W
Manevychi Ukraine 46 G3 ....51.17N 25.32E
Manfredonia Italy 50 F4 ....41.38N 15.55E
Manfredonia, Golfo di g. Italy 56 B5 ..41.31N 16.05E
Mangaia i. Cook Is 109 J4 ....21.52S 157.52W
Mangalia Romania 57 H6 ....43.49N 28.34E
Mangalore India 96 D3 ....12.53N 74.51E
Mangaung S. Africa 86 B2 ....29.09S 26.16E
Mangoky r. Madagascar 86 D2 ....23.25S 45.25E
Mangole i. Indonesia 105 H3 ....1.51S 125.49E
Mangotsfield England 10 C2 .....51.29N 2.31W
Mangu Kenya 87 B2 ....0.59S 36.57E
Manicouagan, Réservoir Canada 63 L3 ..51.18N 68.18W
Manihiki atoll Cook Is 108 J5 ...10.30S 160.55W
Maniitsoq Greenland 63 M4 ......65.26N 52.55W
Manila Phil. 105 G6 ....14.34N 120.59E
Manipur d. India 97 H5 ....24.53N 93.56E
Manisa Turkey 56 G4 ....38.36N 27.25E
Manitoba d. Canada 62 I3 ......53.40N 98.06W
Manitoba, Lake Canada 62 I3 ...51.34N 99.04W
Manizales Colombia 72 B7 ......5.00N 75.30W
Manmad India 96 D5 ....20.15N 74.30E
Mannheim Germany 54 C3 ....49.29N 8.28E
Manningtree England 11 G2 .....51.57N 1.04E
Manokwari Indonesia 105 I3 ....0.52S 134.06E
Manorbier Wales 12 C3 ....51.39N 4.48W
Manorhamilton Ireland 41 C4 ...54.18N 8.11W
Manra i. Kiribati 108 I5 ....4.26S 171.13W
Manresa Spain 48 F4 ....41.43N 1.50E
Mansa Zambia 86 B3 ....11.11S 28.53E
Mansel Island Canada 63 K4 ....62.05N 79.35W
Mansfield England 15 F2 ....53.09N 1.12W
Mansfield U.S.A. 65 J5 ....40.45N 82.32W
Manston England 10 C1 ....50.56N 2.16W
Manta Ecuador 76 D7 ....0.59S 80.42W
Mantua Italy 50 D6 ....45.09N 10.47E
Manukau New Zealand 111 G3 ....36.58S 174.50E
Manyara, Lake Tanzania 87 A2 ..3.42S 35.47E
Manzanares Spain 48 D3 ....39.00N 3.21W
Manzhouli China 103 L7 ....49.20N 117.29E
Maoke, Pegunungan mts Indonesia 105 J3 ..3.34S 135.25E
Mapinhane Mozambique 86 C2 ....22.17S 35.06E
Mapmakers Seamounts f. N. Pacific Oc. 108 H7 ..23.40N 165.39E
Mapuera r. Brazil 77 I7 ....1.05S 57.06W
Maputo Mozambique 86 C2 ....25.56S 32.34E
Mar, Serra do mts Brazil 77 J2 ..29.20S 50.12W
Mara d. Tanzania 87 A2 ....1.44S 34.21E
Maraba Brazil 77 K6 ....5.23S 49.08W
Maracá, Ilha de i. Brazil 77 J8 ..1.59N 50.22W
Maracaibo Venezuela 72 B8 .....10.40N 71.38W
Maracaibo, Lake inlet Venezuela 72 B7 ..9.45N 71.36W
Maracaju, Serra de hills Brazil 77 I3 ..21.59S 55.53W
Maracás, Chapada de hills Brazil 77 L5 ..13.22S 40.28W
Maracay Venezuela 72 C8 ....10.16N 67.35W
Marādah Libya 85 F4 ....29.12N 19.12E
Maradi Niger 84 E3 ....13.31N 7.07E
Marāgheh Iran 95 G7 ....37.23N 46.14E
Marajó, Ilha de i. Brazil 77 J7 ..0.45S 50.38W
Maralal Kenya 87 B3 ....1.06N 36.42E
Marand Iran 95 G7 ....38.26N 45.46E
Maranhão d. Brazil 77 K6 ......5.06S 45.19W
Marañón r. Peru 76 F7 ....4.27S 73.30W
Marathon Canada 63 I6 ....48.43N 86.23W
Marathonas Greece 56 E4 ......38.09N 23.58E
Marazion England 13 B2 ....50.07N 5.28W
Marbella Spain 48 C2 ....36.31N 4.52W
Marburg S. Africa 86 C1 ......30.43S 30.26E
Marburg an der Lahn Germany 54 C4 ..50.48N 8.46E
March England 11 F3 ....52.33N 0.05E
Marche-en-Famenne Belgium 42 E3 ..50.14N 5.21E
Mar Chiquita, Laguna l. Argentina 77 H1 ..30.43S 62.38W
Marchtrenk Austria 54 F3 .....48.12N 14.07E
Mardan Pakistan 96 D7 ....34.14N 72.04E
Mar del Plata Argentina 73 D3 ..37.59S 57.35W
Mardin Turkey 94 F7 ....37.18N 40.46E
Maree, Loch l. Scotland 18 D2 ..57.38N 5.21W
Maresfield England 11 F1 .....50.59N 0.05E
Margarita, Isla de i. Venezuela 72 C8 ..11.06N 63.53W
Margate England 11 G2 ....51.23N 1.23E
Margery Hill England 15 F2 ...53.28N 1.43W
Margherita Peak Dem. Rep. Congo/Uganda 86 B5 ..0.25N 29.56E
Märgow, Dasht-e des. Afgh. 95 J6 ..30.27N 62.22E
Marhanets' Ukraine 55 P2 .....47.40N 34.37E
Mariana Ridge f. N. Pacific Oc. 108 F7 ..20.44N 144.30E
Mariana Trench f. N. Pacific Oc. 108 F6 ..10.35N 141.08E
Marías, Islas is Mexico 70 C5 ..21.25N 106.33W
Maria van Diemen, Cape New Zealand 111 G3 ..34.29S 172.38E

Ma'rib Yemen 95 G3 ....15.32N 45.26E
Maribor Slovenia 54 F2 ....46.32N 15.40E
Marie-Galante i. Guadeloupe 71 L4 ....15.56N 61.14W
Mariehamn Finland 40 D3 ....60.06N 19.57E
Mariental Namibia 86 A2 ....24.39S 17.58E
Mariestad Sweden 40 C2 ....58.43N 13.50E
Marijampolė Lithuania 46 F5 ....54.33N 23.22E
Marília Brazil 77 K3 ....22.13S 49.57W
Mar"ina Horka Belarus 55 M5 ....53.31N 28.08E
Maringá Brazil 77 J3 ....23.27S 51.59W
Maritime Alps mts France/Italy 44 G4 ....44.16N 6.58E
Maritsa r. Bulgaria 56 G5 ....41.43N 26.20E
Mariupol' Ukraine 53 K6 ....47.06N 37.33E
Marka Somalia 85 I2 ....1.43N 44.44E
Markermeer r. Neth. 42 E5 ....52.34N 5.14E
Market Deeping England 11 E3 ....52.41N 0.19W
Market Drayton England 10 C3 ....52.54N 2.29W
Market Harborough England 10 E3 .....52.29N 0.55W
Markethill Northern Ireland 16 C2 ......54.17N 6.31W
Market Rasen England 15 G2 ....53.23N 0.20W
Market Warsop England 15 F2 ....53.12N 1.09W
Market Weighton England 15 G2 ....53.52N 0.40W
Markha r. Rus. Fed. 59 M4 ....63.29N 118.52E
Marlborough England 10 D2 ....51.25N 1.44W
Marlborough Downs hills England 10 D2 ...51.29N 1.48W
Marlow England 10 E2 ....51.34N 0.46W
Marmande France 44 D4 ....44.31N 0.10E
Marmara, Sea of g. Turkey 57 H5 ....40.43N 28.26E
Marmaris Turkey 57 H3 ....36.50N 28.15E
Marmolada mt. Italy 50 D7 ....46.26N 11.51E
Marne r. France 44 E6 ....48.49N 2.25E
Marne-la-Vallée France 44 E6 ....48.51N 2.36E
Maromokotro mt. Madagascar 86 D3 ....14.01S 48.58E
Marondera Zimbabwe 86 C3 ....18.13S 31.34E
Maroni r. French Guiana 72 D7 ....5.44N 54.01W
Maroua Cameroon 84 F3 ....10.37N 14.19E
Marple England 15 E2 ....53.24N 2.04W
Marquesas Islands French Polynesia 109 K5 ...8.39S 139.15W
Marquette U.S.A. 65 I6 ....46.32N 87.25W
Marra, Jebel mt. Sudan 85 G3 ....12.54N 24.11E
Marrakesh Morocco 84 D5 ....31.39N 7.58W
Marra Plateau f. Sudan 94 B2 ....13.24N 24.25E
Marsá al 'Alam Egypt 52 D1 ....25.04N 34.53E
Marsa al Burayqah Libya 85 F5 ....30.22N 19.35E
Marsabit Kenya 87 B3 ....2.20N 37.59E
Marsabit National Reserve Kenya 87 B3 ...2.11N 37.58E
Marsala Italy 50 E3 ....37.48N 12.26E
Marsá Maṭrūḥ Egypt 85 G5 ....31.20N 27.16E
Marseille France 44 F3 ....43.18N 5.23E
Marsfjället mt. Sweden 40 C4 ....65.06N 15.23E
Marshall Islands N. Pacific Oc. 108 H6 ...13.59N 164.53E
Märsta Sweden 40 D2 ....59.37N 17.53E
Martaban Myanmar 97 I4 ....16.34N 97.34E
Martaban, Gulf of Myanmar 97 I4 .....16.20N 96.57E
Martapura Indonesia 104 C3 ....4.20S 104.21E
Martin Slovakia 54 H3 ....49.04N 18.55E
Martinique i. Central America 71 L3 ....14.36N 60.56W
Martock England 10 C1 ....50.58N 2.46W
Mary Turkmenistan 95 J7 ....37.34N 61.52E
Maryborough Australia 110 E4 ....25.32S 152.41E
Maryland d. U.S.A. 65 K4 ....38.39N 76.30W
Maryport England 14 D3 ....54.43N 3.30W
Masai Mara National Reserve Kenya 87 A2 ...1.20S 35.04E
Masai Steppe f. Tanzania 87 B1 ....4.47S 36.53E
Masan S. Korea 103 N5 ....35.14N 128.36E
Masbate Phil. 105 G6 ....12.20N 123.37E
Masbate i. Phil. 105 G6 ....12.20N 123.36E
Mascara Algeria 52 D4 ....35.23N 0.08E
Maseno Kenya 87 A3 ....0.01N 34.36E
Maseru Lesotho 86 B2 ....29.19S 27.29E
Mashhad Iran 95 I7 ....36.18N 59.35E
Mashkel, Hamun-i- f. Pakistan 96 B6 ....28.15N 63.02E
Masinga Reservoir Kenya 87 B2 ....0.54S 37.26E
Maşīrah, Jazīrat i. Oman 95 I4 ....20.16N 58.58E
Maşīrah, Khalīj b. Oman 95 I3 ....19.47N 58.22E
Masjed Soleymān Iran 95 G6 ....31.57N 49.17E
Mask, Lough l. Ireland 41 B3 ....53.37N 9.21W
Mason City U.S.A. 65 H5 ....43.09N 93.12W
Massachusetts d. U.S.A. 65 L5 ....42.23N 72.18W
Massachusetts Bay U.S.A. 65 L5 .....42.25N 70.51W
Massakory Chad 84 F3 ....12.59N 15.43E
Massawa Eritrea 85 H3 ....15.36N 39.27E
Massif Central mts France 44 E4 ......45.16N 3.25E
Mastung Pakistan 95 K5 ....29.45N 66.56E
Masty Belarus 46 G4 ....53.25N 24.31E
Masuda Japan 106 B2 ....34.40N 131.50E
Masvingo Zimbabwe 86 C2 ....20.04S 30.48E
Matadi Dem. Rep. Congo 86 A4 ....5.49S 13.29E
Matagami Canada 65 K6 ....49.46N 77.38W
Matam Senegal 84 C3 ....15.40N 13.16W
Matamoros Mexico 70 E6 ....25.53N 97.34W
Matanzas Cuba 71 H5 ....23.04N 81.34W
Matara Sri Lanka 96 F2 ....5.58N 80.29E
Mataram Indonesia 104 F2 ....8.35S 116.10E
Mataró Spain 48 G4 ....41.33N 2.26E
Matā'utu Wallis and Futuna Is 108 I5 ....13.17S 176.07W
Matehuala Mexico 64 F1 ....23.40N 100.38W
Matera Italy 50 G4 ....40.40N 16.37E
Mathura India 96 E6 ....27.26N 77.43E
Matlock England 15 F2 ....53.08N 1.33W
Mato Grosso d. Brazil 77 J5 ....12.17S 54.47W
Mato Grosso, Planalto do f. Brazil 77 J4 ...15.05S 54.12W
Mato Grosso do Sul d. Brazil 77 J3 ....20.42S 53.59W
Maṭraḥ Oman 95 I4 ....23.37N 58.32E
Matsue Japan 106 B3 ....35.28N 133.03E
Matsumoto Japan 106 C3 ....36.15N 137.58E
Matsusaka Japan 106 C2 ....34.34N 136.33E
Matsu Tao i. Taiwan 103 M3 ....26.13N 120.03E
Matsuyama Japan 106 B2 ....33.49N 132.46E
Matterhorn mt. Italy/Switz. 50 B6 ...45.59N 7.40E
Maturín Venezuela 72 C7 ....9.44N 63.09W
Mau r. Kenya 87 A2 ....0.29S 35.52E
Maubeuge France 42 C3 ....50.17N 3.58E
Mauchline Scotland 16 E3 ....55.31N 4.23W
Maughold Head Isle of Man 14 C3 ....54.18N 4.18W
Maug Islands N. Mariana Is 105 L8 ....20.02N 145.16E
Maui i. U.S.A. 109 J7 ....20.48N 156.00W
Mauke i. Cook Is 109 J4 ....20.11S 157.18W
Maumere Indonesia 105 G2 ....8.40S 122.13E
Maun Botswana 86 B3 ....19.57S 23.25E
Mauritania Africa 84 C3 ....19.51N 11.35W
Mauritius country Indian Oc. 115 L4 ....20.10S 58.00E
May, Isle of i. Scotland 17 G4 ....56.11N 2.33W
Maya r. Rus. Fed. 59 O4 ....60.26N 134.33E
Mayaguana i. Bahamas 71 J5 ....22.23N 72.56W
Mayagüez Puerto Rico 71 K4 ....18.12N 67.08W
Mayamey Iran 95 I7 ....36.27N 55.40E
Mayar hill Scotland 19 F1 ....56.51N 3.15W
Maybole Scotland 16 E3 ....55.21N 4.41W
Mayen Germany 42 G3 ....50.19N 7.13E
Mayenne r. France 44 C5 ....47.30N 0.32W
Mayo Canada 62 E4 ....63.37N 135.54W
Mayo d. Ireland 41 B3 ....53.46N 9.13W

Mayotte i. Africa 86 D3 ....12.59S 45.09E
Mazār-e Sharīf Afgh. 95 K7 ....36.43N 67.07E
Mazatlán Mexico 70 C5 ....23.14N 106.27W
Mažeikiai Lithuania 40 E2 ....56.18N 22.22E
Mazyr Belarus 55 M5 ....52.03N 29.15E
Mbabane Swaziland 86 C2 ....26.20S 31.09E
Mbale Uganda 87 A3 ....1.05N 34.08E
Mbandaka Dem. Rep. Congo 86 A4 ...0.00S 18.17E
M'banza Congo Angola 86 A4 ....6.14S 14.15E
Mbarara Uganda 85 H1 ....0.35S 30.37E
Mbeya Tanzania 86 C4 ....8.53S 33.26E
Mbuji-Mayi Dem. Rep. Congo 86 B4 ...6.06S 23.36E
Mbulu Tanzania 87 A2 ....3.50S 35.31E
McClintock Channel Canada 62 I15 ....71.10N 101.39W
McClure Strait Canada 62 G5 ....74.09N 114.57W
McCook U.S.A. 64 F5 ....40.14N 100.39W
McGrath U.S.A. 62 C4 ....62.52N 155.37W
McKinley, Mount U.S.A. 62 C4 ......63.05N 150.20W
Mdantsane S. Africa 86 B1 ....32.58S 27.48E
Mead, Lake resr U.S.A. 64 D4 ....36.12N 114.24W
Mealasta Island Scotland 18 B3 .....58.05N 7.10W
Meall a' Bhuiridh mt. Scotland 18 E1 ....56.37N 4.51W
Meath d. Ireland 41 E3 ....53.41N 6.35W
Meaux France 44 E6 ....48.58N 2.53E
Mecca Saudi Arabia 94 E4 ....21.25N 39.47E
Mechelen Belgium 42 D4 ....51.01N 4.29E
Mecheria Algeria 52 C3 ....33.33N 0.19W
Meckenheim Germany 42 G3 ....50.37N 7.02E
Meden Indonesia 104 B4 ....3.38N 98.40E
Meden r. England 15 G2 ....53.25N 0.59W
Medenine Tunisia 52 F3 ....33.21N 10.31E
Medetsiz Tepe mt. Turkey 57 K3 ....37.24N 34.37E
Mediaş Romania 56 F7 ....46.10N 24.22E
Medicine Hat Canada 62 G3 ....50.03N 110.41W
Medina Saudi Arabia 94 E4 ....24.31N 39.32E
Medina del Campo Spain 48 C4 .....41.19N 4.54W
Mediterranean Sea World 52 E4 .....33.25N 32.44E
Medvezh'yegorsk Rus. Fed. 58 E4 ....62.55N 34.29E
Medway d. England 9 F2 ....51.22N 0.34E
Medway r. England 11 F2 ....51.21N 0.27E
Meerut India 96 E6 ....29.02N 77.45E
Mega Ethiopia 87 B4 ....4.01N 38.20E
Mega Escarpment f. Ethiopia/Kenya 87 B4 ...4.21N 37.20E
Megara Greece 56 E4 ....38.00N 23.21E
Meghalaya d. India 97 H6 ....25.36N 91.22E
Meiktila Myanmar 97 I5 ....20.50N 95.53E
Meiningen Germany 54 D4 ....50.34N 10.25E
Meißen Germany 54 E4 ....51.10N 13.28E
Meizhou China 103 L2 ....24.17N 116.09E
Mejicana mt. Argentina 76 G2 ......29.01S 67.50W
Mek'elē Ethiopia 94 E3 ....13.31N 39.28E
Meknès Morocco 84 D5 ....33.53N 5.30W
Mekong r. Asia 97 K3 ....10.53N 105.14E
Mekong, Mouths of the Vietnam 104 D5 ...9.03N 106.31E
Melaka Malaysia 104 C4 ....2.09N 102.17E
Melanesia is Pacific Oc. 108 G5 .....10.00S 165.00E
Melanesian Basin f. Pacific Oc. 108 G6 ...0.19N 164.50E
Melbourn England 11 F3 ....52.05N 0.01E
Melbourne Australia 110 D3 ....37.49S 144.59E
Melbourne U.S.A. 65 J2 ....28.01N 80.43W
Melby Scotland 19 H5 ....60.18N 1.40W
Melekeok Palau 105 I5 ....7.30N 134.39E
Melilla N. Africa 52 C4 ....35.18N 2.57W
Melitopol' Ukraine 55 P2 ....46.51N 35.22E
Melka Guba Ethiopia 87 B4 ....4.41N 39.13E
Melksham England 10 C2 ....51.22N 2.08W
Melo Uruguay 77 J1 ....32.22S 54.10W
Melrhir, Chott f. Algeria 84 E5 .....34.15N 6.23E
Melrose Scotland 17 G3 ....55.36N 2.43W
Meltham England 15 F2 ....53.36N 1.51W
Melton Mowbray England 10 E3 ....52.46N 0.53W
Melun France 44 E6 ....48.32N 2.39E
Melvich Scotland 19 F3 ....58.33N 3.55W
Melville Canada 62 H3 ....50.56N 102.49W
Melville Bay Greenland 63 L4 ......76.00N 64.00W
Melville Island Australia 110 C5 ....11.37S 130.55E
Melville Island Canada 62 H5 ......75.14N 109.26W
Melville Peninsula Canada 63 J4 ....68.09N 84.12W
Melvin, Lough l. Ireland/U.K. 41 C4 ...54.25N 8.09W
Memberamo r. Indonesia 105 J3 ....1.32S 137.52E
Memmingen Germany 54 D2 ....47.59N 10.11E
Memphis U.S.A. 65 H4 ....35.09N 90.04W
Mena Ukraine 55 O4 ....51.31N 32.14E
Menai Bridge Wales 12 C5 ....53.13N 4.10W
Menai Strait Wales 12 C5 ....53.09N 4.17W
Mende France 44 E4 ....44.31N 3.30E
Mendebo mts Ethiopia 87 B4 ....5.50N 38.39E
Mendī Ethiopia 85 H2 ....9.49N 35.03E
Mendip Hills England 10 C2 ....51.19N 2.46W
Mendoza Argentina 73 C3 ....32.53S 68.50W
Menongue Angola 86 A3 ....14.38S 17.42E
Mentawai, Kepulauan is Indonesia 104 B3 ...3.17S 99.55E
Mentok Indonesia 104 D3 ....2.05S 105.12E
Menzel Bourguiba Tunisia 52 E4 ....37.09N 9.46E
Meppel Neth. 42 F5 ....52.42N 6.11E
Meppen Germany 42 G5 ....52.41N 7.18E
Merano Italy 50 D7 ....46.41N 11.10E
Merauke Indonesia 105 K2 ....8.31S 140.25E
Mercedes Uruguay 77 I1 ....33.16S 58.01W
Mere England 10 C2 ....51.05N 2.16W
Merefa Ukraine 55 Q3 ....49.49N 36.04E
Mergui Myanmar 97 I3 ....12.27N 98.37E
Mergui Archipelago is Myanmar 97 I3 ...11.38N 97.41E
Mérida Mexico 70 G5 ....20.59N 89.37W
Mérida Spain 48 B3 ....38.56N 6.20W
Mérida Venezuela 72 B7 ....8.36N 71.07W
Mérida, Cordillera de mts Venezuela 71 J2 ...7.59N 71.35W
Meridian U.S.A. 65 I3 ....32.23N 88.40W
Merkys r. Lithuania 46 F5 ....54.08N 24.12E
Merowe Sudan 85 H3 ....18.27N 31.51E
Merrick hill Scotland 16 E3 ....55.08N 4.28W
Mersch Lux. 42 F2 ....49.45N 6.07E
Mersey est. England 14 E2 ....53.21N 2.56W
Merseyside d. England 9 D3 ....53.32N 3.06W
Mersin Turkey 57 K3 ....36.49N 34.37E
Merthyr Tydfil Wales 12 D3 ....51.45N 3.23W
Merthyr Tydfil d. Wales 9 D2 ....51.44N 3.20W
Merti Kenya 87 B3 ....1.02N 38.39E
Mértola Portugal 48 B2 ....37.38N 7.39W
Méru France 42 B2 ....49.14N 2.08E
Meru Kenya 87 B3 ....0.05N 37.38E
Meru vol. Tanzania 87 B2 ....3.15S 36.44E
Merzifon Turkey 57 K5 ....40.52N 35.27E
Merzig Germany 42 F2 ....49.27N 6.39E
Mesolongi Greece 56 D4 ....38.22N 21.26E
Mesopotamia f. Iraq 85 I5 ....35.42N 42.19E
Messina Italy 50 F4 ....38.11N 15.34E
Messiniakos Kolpos b. Greece 56 E3 ...36.51N 22.03E
Meta r. Col./Venez. 72 C7 ....6.10N 67.24W
Metheringham England 15 G2 ......53.08N 0.24W
Methwold England 11 F3 ....52.31N 0.33E
Metković Croatia 56 B6 ....43.03N 17.40E

Metlika Slovenia 54 F1 ....45.39N 15.19E
Metz France 42 G2 ....49.07N 6.11E
Meuse r. Belgium/France 42 E4 ....51.08N 5.51E
Mevagissey England 13 C2 ....50.16N 4.47W
Mexborough England 15 F2 ....53.30N 1.17W
Mexicali Mexico 70 A7 ....32.39N 115.28W
Mexico Central America 70 C5 ......31.47N 114.01W
México d. Mexico 70 E4 ....19.38N 99.46W
Mexico, Gulf of Mexico/U.S.A. 70 F5 ...22.09N 95.51W
Mexico City Mexico 70 E4 ....19.24N 99.12W
Meymaneh Afgh. 95 J7 ....35.56N 64.45E
Mezen' Rus. Fed. 58 F4 ....65.50N 44.18E
Mezha r. Rus. Fed. 55 N6 ....55.43N 31.30E
Mezőtúr Hungary 46 I3 ....46.59N 20.39E
Mezquital r. Mexico 70 C5 ....21.52N 105.29W
Mfangani Island Uganda 87 A2 .....0.37S 34.00E
Miami U.S.A. 65 J2 ....25.41N 80.18W
Miandowāb Iran 95 G7 ....36.58N 46.07E
Miandrivazo Madagascar 86 D3 ....19.30S 45.29E
Mīāneh Iran 95 G7 ....37.24N 47.40E
Mianwali Pakistan 95 L6 ....32.32N 71.34E
Miass Rus. Fed. 58 H3 ....54.58N 60.05E
Michalovce Slovakia 46 I3 ....48.45N 21.55E
Michigan d. U.S.A. 65 I6 ....46.12N 88.00W
Michigan, Lake U.S.A. 65 I5 ....43.02N 87.18W
Michipicoten Island Canada 65 I6 ...47.41N 85.48W
Michipicoten River town Canada 65 J6 ...47.57N 84.50W
Michoacán d. Mexico 70 D4 ....18.21N 102.59W
Michurinsk Rus. Fed. 58 F3 ....52.55N 40.30E
Micronesia is Pacific Oc. 108 F6 ....11.40N 147.31E
Micronesia, Federated States of N. Pacific Oc. 105 K5
  ....3.37N 153.49E
Mid-Atlantic Ridge f. Atlantic Ocean 109 Q7 ...16.18N 49.57W
Middlesbrough England 15 F3 ......54.34N 1.14W
Middlesbrough d. England 9 E4 ....54.33N 1.14W
Middleton England 15 E2 ....53.33N 2.12W
Middleton in Teesdale England 15 E3 ...54.38N 2.05W
Middleton St George England 15 F3 ....54.31N 1.28W
Middlewich England 15 E2 ....53.12N 2.27W
Midhurst England 10 E1 ....50.59N 0.44W
Midi, Canal du France 44 E3 ....43.14N 2.22E
Midland U.S.A. 64 F3 ....32.01N 101.58W
Midleton Ireland 41 C1 ....51.55N 8.10W
Midlothian d. Scotland 8 D4 ....55.50N 3.06W
Mid-Pacific Mountains f. N. Pacific Oc. 108 G7 ...23.27N 150.34E
Midway Islands N. Pacific Oc. 108 I7 ...28.18N 177.17W
Miekojärvi l. Finland 40 F4 ....66.34N 24.25E
Mielec Poland 46 I4 ....50.17N 21.26E
Miercurea-Ciuc Romania 56 F8 ....46.22N 25.48E
Mikhaylovskiy Rus. Fed. 102 D8 ...51.40N 79.45E
Mikkeli Finland 40 F3 ....61.41N 27.17E
Milan Italy 50 C6 ....45.28N 9.11E
Milborne Port England 10 C1 ....50.58N 2.28W
Mildenhall England 11 F3 ....52.21N 0.31E
Mildura Australia 110 D3 ....34.12S 142.11E
Miles City U.S.A. 64 E6 ....46.25N 105.47W
Milford Haven Wales 12 B3 ....51.43N 5.02W
Milk r. U.S.A. 64 E6 ....48.03N 106.19W
Millárs r. Spain 48 E3 ....39.57N 0.04W
Millau France 44 E4 ....44.06N 3.05E
Mille Lacs lakes U.S.A. 65 H6 ......46.14N 93.39W
Milleur Point Scotland 16 D3 ......55.01N 5.07W
Millom England 14 D3 ....54.13N 3.16W
Millport Scotland 16 E3 ....55.45N 4.56W
Milnthorpe England 14 E3 ....54.14N 2.46W
Milos i. Greece 56 F3 ....36.39N 24.25E
Milton Keynes England 10 E3 ......52.01N 0.44W
Milton Keynes d. England 9 E3 ....52.05N 0.44W
Milwaukee U.S.A. 65 I5 ....43.01N 87.55W
Mimizan France 44 C4 ....44.12N 1.14W
Mīnāb Iran 95 I5 ....27.09N 57.04E
Minas Indonesia 104 C4 ....0.52N 101.30E
Minas Gerais d. Brazil 77 L4 ....18.31S 44.00W
Minatitlán Mexico 70 F4 ....18.01N 94.33W
Mindanao i. Phil. 105 H5 ....7.48N 125.06E
Mindelo Cape Verde 84 B3 ....16.54N 24.59W
Mindoro i. Phil. 105 G6 ....13.05N 120.52E
Mindoro Strait Phil. 104 F6 ....12.41N 119.59E
Minehead England 13 D3 ....51.12N 3.29W
Mingulay i. Scotland 18 B1 ....56.49N 7.37W
Minna Nigeria 84 E2 ....9.38N 6.32E
Minneapolis U.S.A. 65 H5 ....44.55N 93.18W
Minnesota d. U.S.A. 65 H6 ....47.08N 92.44W
Minnesota r. U.S.A. 65 H5 ....44.55N 93.11W
Miño r. Portugal/Spain 48 A4 ......41.56N 8.45W
Minorca i. Spain 48 G4 ....40.06N 3.51E
Minot U.S.A. 64 F6 ....48.13N 101.18W
Minsk Belarus 55 L5 ....53.53N 27.34E
Mińsk Mazowiecki Poland 46 I4 ...52.11N 21.34E
Minsterley England 10 C3 ....52.38N 2.55W
Mintlaw Scotland 19 H2 ....57.31N 1.59W
Miranda Brazil 77 I3 ....20.11S 56.21W
Miranda de Ebro Spain 48 D5 .....42.42N 2.56W
Mirandela Portugal 48 B4 ....41.29N 7.10W
Mirbāṭ Oman 95 H3 ....17.02N 54.43E
Miri Malaysia 104 E4 ....4.27N 114.01E
Mirim, Lagoa l. Brazil/Uruguay 77 J1 ...32.40S 52.59W
Mirnyy Rus. Fed. 59 M4 ....62.25N 114.10E
Mirpur Khas Pakistan 96 C6 ....25.32N 69.04E
Mirzapur India 96 F6 ....25.09N 82.39E
Miskitos, Cayos is Nicaragua 71 H3 ...14.24N 82.44W
Miskolc Hungary 54 I3 ....48.06N 20.48E
Misoöl i. Indonesia 105 I3 ....1.53S 130.08E
Miṣrātah Libya 84 F5 ....32.21N 15.04E
Missinaibi r. Canada 63 J3 ....50.45N 81.31W
Mississippi d. U.S.A. 65 I3 ....32.33N 89.45W
Mississippi r. U.S.A. 65 H2 ....38.50N 90.09W
Mississippi Delta U.S.A. 65 I2 ......29.05N 89.06W
Missoula U.S.A. 64 D6 ....46.53N 113.58W
Missouri d. U.S.A. 65 H4 ....38.27N 92.10W
Missouri r. U.S.A. 65 H4 ....38.50N 90.09W
Mistassini Canada 65 K3 ....50.13N 73.48W
Mistassini, Lac l. Canada 63 K3 ...50.47N 73.34W
Mitchell U.S.A. 64 G5 ....43.42N 98.02W
Mitchell, Mount U.S.A. 65 J4 ......35.46N 82.15W
Mitchelstown Ireland 41 C2 ....52.16N 8.16W
Mito Japan 106 D3 ....36.23N 140.28E
Mittimatalik Canada 63 K5 ....72.35N 77.46W
Mitumba, Chaîne des mts Dem. Rep. Congo 86 B3
  ....11.46S 26.06E
Miyako Japan 106 D3 ....39.38N 141.57E
Miyazaki Japan 106 B2 ....31.54N 131.25E
Mizdah Libya 52 F3 ....31.25N 12.59E
Mizen Head Cork Ireland 41 B1 ....51.26N 9.49W
Mizen Head Wick. Ireland 41 E2 ...52.51N 6.03W
Mizhhir"ya Ukraine 46 F2 ....48.31N 23.31E
Mizoram d. India 97 H5 ....23.22N 92.57E
Mjölby Sweden 40 C2 ....58.20N 15.08E
Mkoani Tanzania 87 B1 ....5.23S 39.39E
Mkomazi Tanzania 87 B1 ....4.40S 38.06E

Mkomazi Game Reserve Tanzania 87 B2 ...3.53S 3
Mladá Boleslav Czech Rep. 46 B3 ...50.25N 1
Mława Poland 46 E4 ....53.07N 2
Mljet i. Croatia 56 B6 ....42.44N 1
Mmabatho S. Africa 86 B2 ....25.47S 2
Mobile U.S.A. 65 I3 ....30.40N 88
Mobile Bay U.S.A. 65 I3 ....30.24N 88
Mobridge U.S.A. 64 F6 ....45.32N 100
Moçambique Mozambique 86 D3 ...15.05S 4
Mocha Yemen 94 F2 ....13.20N 4
Mochudi Botswana 86 B2 ....24.25S 2
Mocuba Mozambique 86 D3 ....16.53S 3
Modbury England 13 D2 ....50.21N 3
Modena Italy 50 D6 ....44.39N 1
Moelfre Wales 12 C5 ....53.21N 4
Moel Sych hill Wales 12 D4 ....52.53N 3
Moffat Scotland 17 F3 ....55.20N 3
Mogadishu Somalia 85 I2 ....2.04N 4
Mohawk r. U.S.A. 65 L5 ....42.46N 73
Mohyliv Podil's'kyy Ukraine 55 L3 ...48.27N 2
Mo i Rana Norway 40 C4 ....66.19N 1
Moji das Cruzes Brazil 77 K3 ......23.32S 46
Mojos, Llanos de f. Bolivia 76 G5 ...14.42S 66
Mold Wales 12 D5 ....53.10N 3
Molde Norway 40 A3 ....62.44N 7
Moldova Europe 53 I6 ....46.59N 28
Moldoveanu, Vârful mt. Romania 56 F7 ...45.36N 24
Molėtai Lithuania 46 G5 ....55.14N 25
Molfetta Italy 56 B5 ....41.12N 16
Molopo watercourse Botswana/S. Africa 86 B2 ...28.32S 20
Moluccas is Indonesia 108 ......0.30S 12
Molucca Sea Indonesia 105 H3 ...1.08S 125
Mombasa Kenya 87 B2 ....3.59S 3
Møn i. Denmark 40 C1 ....55.00N 12
Mona, Isla i. Puerto Rico 71 K4 ...18.04N 67
Monach, Sound of str. Scotland 18 B2 ...57.33N 7
Monach Islands Scotland 18 B2 ...57.32N 7
Monaco Europe 44 G3 ....43.44N 7
Monadhliath Mountains Scotland 19 E2 ...57.04N 4
Monaghan Ireland 41 E4 ....54.15N 6
Monaghan d. Ireland 41 E4 ....54.10N 6
Mona Passage str. Dom. Rep./Puerto Rico 71 K4 ...18.01N 68
Monar, Loch l. Scotland 18 D2 ....57.25N 5
Monbetsu Japan 106 D4 ....44.21N 143
Monchegorsk Rus. Fed. 40 H4 ....67.57N 32
Mönchengladbach Germany 42 F4 ...51.12N 6
Monclova Mexico 70 D6 ....26.53N 101.
Moncton Canada 63 L2 ....46.04N 64.
Mondego r. Portugal 48 A4 ....40.10N 8.
Mondovì Italy 50 B6 ....44.23N 7
Moneymore Northern Ireland 16 C2 ...54.41N 6.
Monforte de Lemos Spain 48 B5 ...42.32N 7.
Monga Dem. Rep. Congo 86 B5 ...4.10N 22.
Mongolia Asia 103 I7 ....46.59N 103
Mongora Pakistan 95 L6 ....34.46N 72
Mongu Zambia 86 B3 ....15.15S 23
Moniaive Scotland 17 F3 ....55.12N 3.
Monmouth Wales 12 C3 ....51.49N 2.
Monmouthshire d. Wales 9 D2 ....51.47N 2.
Monnow r. U.K. 10 C2 ....51.49N 2.
Monroe La. U.S.A. 65 H3 ....32.30N 92.
Monrovia Liberia 84 C2 ....6.20N 10.
Mons Belgium 42 C3 ....50.27N 3
Montana Bulgaria 56 E6 ....43.25N 23.
Montana d. U.S.A. 64 E6 ....46.44N 109.
Montargis France 44 E5 ....47.59N 2
Montauban France 44 D4 ....44.01N 1.
Montbéliard France 44 G5 ....47.30N 6
Mont-de-Marsan France 44 C3 ....43.53N 0.
Montdidier France 42 B2 ....49.39N 2.
Monte Alegre Brazil 77 J7 ....1.58S 54.0
Monte-Carlo Monaco 44 G3 ......43.44N 7.
Montecristo, Isola di i. Italy 50 D5 ...42.19N 10.
Montego Bay town Jamaica 71 I4 ...18.28N 77.5
Montélimar France 44 F4 ....44.33N 4.
Monte Lindo r. Paraguay 77 I3 ....23.57S 57.1
Montemorelos Mexico 70 E6 ......25.11N 99.4
Montenegro Europe 56 C6 ....43.01N 19.
Montería Colombia 72 B7 ....8.43N 75.5
Monterrey Mexico 70 D6 ....25.42N 100.1
Monte Santu, Capo di c. Italy 50 C4 ...40.04N 9.
Montes Claros Brazil 77 L4 ....16.42S 43.4
Montevideo Uruguay 73 D3 ....34.52S 56.1
Monte Vista U.S.A. 64 E4 ....37.36N 106.0
Montgomery U.S.A. 65 I3 ....32.23N 86.3
Montgomery Wales 12 D4 ....52.34N 3.0
Mont-Joli Canada 65 M6 ....48.35N 68.1
Montluçon France 44 E5 ....46.21N 2.
Montmagny Canada 65 L6 ....46.59N 70.3
Montpelier U.S.A. 65 L5 ....44.16N 72.3
Montpellier France 44 E3 ....43.37N 3.
Montréal Canada 63 K2 ....45.32N 73.3
Montreuil France 11 G1 ....50.28N 1.
Montrose Scotland 19 G1 ....56.42N 2.2
Montserrat i. Central America 71 L4 ...16.44N 62.1
Monywa Myanmar 97 I5 ....22.05N 95.
Monza Italy 50 C6 ....45.35N 9.
Monzón Spain 48 F4 ....41.55N 0.
Moore, Lake Australia 110 A4 .....29.43S 117.
Moose r. Canada 63 J3 ....51.20N 80.3
Moose Jaw Canada 62 H3 ....50.26N 105.3
Moosomin Canada 64 F7 ....50.09N 101.4
Moosonee Canada 63 J3 ....51.16N 80.4
Mopti Mali 84 D3 ....14.30N 4.1
Moquegua Peru 76 F4 ....17.09S 70.5
Mora Sweden 40 C3 ....61.00N 14.3
Morar, Loch l. Scotland 18 D1 .....56.57N 5.4
Moray d. Scotland 8 D5 ....57.30N 3.1
Moray Firth b. Scotland 19 E2 ....57.31N 4.1
Morbach Germany 42 G2 ....49.48N 7.
Morden Canada 62 I2 ....49.12N 98.0
More, Loch l. Scotland 18 E3 ......58.18N 4.5
Morecambe England 14 E3 ....54.04N 2.5
Morecambe Bay England 14 D3 ...54.07N 3.0
Moree Australia 110 D4 ....29.28S 149.5
Morehead P.N.G. 105 K2 ....8.44S 141.3
Morelia Mexico 70 D4 ....19.39N 101.1
Morelos d. Mexico 70 E4 ....18.47N 98.5
Morena, Sierra mts Spain 48 B2 ...37.57N 6.0
Moretonhampstead England 13 D2 ...50.40N 3.4
Morgan City U.S.A. 65 H2 ....29.43N 91.2
Mori Japan 106 D4 ....42.06N 140.3
Morioka Japan 106 D3 ....39.42N 141.0
Moriston r. Scotland 18 E2 ....57.13N 4.8
Morlaix France 44 B6 ....48.35N 3.5
Morley England 15 F2 ....53.45N 1.3
Mornington Abyssal Plain f. S. Atlantic Oc. 109 O2
  ....50.59S 89.1
Morocco Africa 84 D5 ....31.57N 5.0
Morogoro Tanzania 86 C4 ....6.47S 37.4
Moro Gulf Phil. 105 G5 ....6.51N 123.2
Morombe Madagascar 86 D2 .....21.46S 43.2
Mörön Mongolia 103 I7 ....49.28N 100.0
Morondava Madagascar 86 D2 ....20.18S 44.1

n de la Frontera Spain 48 C2 ....37.08N 5.27W
n Comoros 86 D3 ....11.39S 43.14E
tai i. Indonesia 105 H4 ....2.23N 128.27E
to, Mount Uganda 87 A3 ....2.30N 34.47E
eth England 15 F4 ....55.10N 1.41W
ston Wales 12 D3 ....51.40N 3.56W
, Punta pt Chile 73 B4 ....27.07S 70.59W
Bay England 13 C3 ....51.10N 4.14W
ehoe England 13 C3 ....51.11N 4.12W
es, Rio das r. Brazil 77 J5 ....11.49S 50.37W
ock Islands Micronesia 108 G6 ....5.07N 153.11E
ngole mt. Uganda 87 A3 ....3.48N 34.02E
roa atoll French Polynesia 109 K4 ....21.50S 138.44W
ern r. Scotland 18 D1 ....56.36N 5.53W
orough England 15 F2 ....53.20N 1.22W
ow Rus. Fed. 58 E3 ....55.45N 37.38E
ow U.S.A. 64 C6 ....46.44N 116.58W
r. Germany 42 G3 ....50.22N 7.36E
lle r. France 44 G6 ....49.27N 6.42E
i Tanzania 86 C4 ....3.23S 37.20E
na Poland 46 C4 ....52.14N 16.51E
en Norway 40 C4 ....65.51N 13.12E
quitos, Golfo de los b. Panama 71 H2 ...8.56N 81.17W
Norway 40 B2 ....59.26N 10.39E
el Bay town S. Africa 86 B1 ....34.11S 22.08E
oró Brazil 77 M6 ....5.08S 37.15W
Czech Rep. 46 A3 ....50.32N 13.39E
aganem Algeria 52 D4 ....35.55N 0.06E
ar Bos.-Herz. 56 B6 ....43.20N 17.49E
l Iraq 94 F7 ....36.39N 43.05E
atnet l. Norway 40 B2 ....59.51N 8.06E
la Sweden 40 C2 ....58.32N 15.02E
erwell Scotland 17 F3 ....55.48N 3.59W
l Spain 48 D2 ....36.45N 3.31W
ins France 44 E5 ....46.34N 3.20E
mein Myanmar 97 I4 ....16.30N 97.40E
ndou Chad 84 F2 ....8.36N 16.05E
t Gambier town Australia 110 D3 ....37.52S 140.48E
t Isa town Australia 110 C4 ....20.45S 139.29E
ntmellick Ireland 41 D3 ....53.07N 7.20W
ntrath Ireland 41 D3 ....53.00N 7.28W
t's Bay England 13 B2 ....50.05N 5.29W
ntsorrel England 10 D3 ....52.44N 1.08W
rdi, Dépression du r. Chad 94 B3 ....18.01N 21.00E
ne r. Northern Ireland 16 B2 ....54.50N 7.28W
ne Mountains Northern Ireland 16 C2 ...54.06N 6.11W
sa i. Scotland 19 H5 ....60.00N 1.11W
scron Belgium 42 C3 ....50.44N 3.13E
on France 42 E2 ....49.37N 5.05E
r. Ireland 41 B4 ....54.07N 9.08W
ls England 85 H2 ....3.32N 39.03E
n Atlas mts Morocco 52 B3 ....32.25N 5.37W
e d. Northern Ireland 8 B4 ....54.59N 6.06W
ambique Africa 86 C2 ....20.09S 34.14E
ambique Channel Africa 86 D2 ....20.15S 40.16E
ken Tunisia 52 F4 ....35.43N 10.35E
nbweni Kenya 87 B1 ....4.25S 39.31E
o Kenya 87 A3 ....1.41N 35.22E
nsk Rus. Fed. 55 Q5 ....53.17N 36.36E
ara Tanzania 86 D3 ....10.19S 40.09E
a Malaysia 104 C4 ....2.02N 102.34E
abungo Indonesia 104 C3 ....1.27S 102.08E
ninga Mountains Zambia 82 G3 ...12.00S 31.00E
Wenlock England 10 C3 ....52.36N 2.33W
kle Roe r. Scotland 19 H5 ....60.21N 1.25W
kish Mountain hill Ireland 16 A3 ...55.06N 8.00W
an r. China 106 A5 ....46.15N 129.31E
anjiang China 103 N6 ....44.32N 129.34E
ukani Tanzania 87 A2 ....3.54S 35.48E
urnu Turkey 57 I5 ....40.27N 31.13E
da Mozambique 86 C3 ....11.38S 39.54E
a Turkey 57 H3 ....37.12N 28.21E
ammad Qol Sudan 94 E4 ....20.54N 37.07E
hausen Germany 54 D4 ....51.13N 10.27E
os Finland 40 F4 ....64.48N 25.58E
Ethiopia 87 A4 ....5.59N 35.33E
e Bheag Ireland 41 E2 ....52.42N 6.58W
kirk Scotland 17 E3 ....55.31N 4.04W
neag hill Scotland 18 C3 ....58.22N 6.18W
acheve Ukraine 55 J3 ....48.27N 22.43E
alla Yemen 95 G2 ....14.34N 49.06E
ono Uganda 87 A3 ....0.21N 32.45E
nje, Mount India 86 C3 ....15.54S 35.35E
le r. Germany 54 E4 ....51.52N 12.15E
ouse France 44 G5 ....47.45N 7.20E
r. China 106 B5 ....45.51N 133.26E
i. Scotland 16 D4 ....56.27N 5.58W
, Sound of str. Scotland 16 C4 ....56.37N 6.01W
aghareirk Mountains Ireland 41 B2 ...52.22N 9.17W
aghcleevaun hill Ireland 12 A5 ....53.06N 6.24W
Head Ireland 19 G4 ....59.23N 5.33W
ngar Ireland 41 D3 ....53.31N 7.20W
of Galloway d. Scotland 16 E2 ....54.38N 4.52W
of Kintyre hd Scotland 16 D3 ....55.17N 5.50W
of Oa hd Scotland 16 C3 ....55.35N 6.20W
an Pakistan 96 D7 ....30.12N 71.35E
abai India 96 D4 ....18.56N 72.51E
s Indonesia 105 G2 ....5.02S 122.30E
a r. Rus. Fed. 59 N4 ....67.51N 123.04E
desley England 11 G3 ....52.53N 1.26E
dford England 11 F3 ....52.31N 0.39E
ger India 96 G6 ....25.22N 86.28E
m r. Brazil 77 L7 ....2.49S 44.04W
ster Germany 54 B4 ....51.57N 7.38E
järvi l. Finland 40 G4 ....65.55N 29.38E
nioälven r. Finland/Sweden 40 E4 ...67.10N 23.33E
allón, Cerro mt. Chile 73 B2 ....49.50S 73.27W
ar Kenya 87 B2 ....0.43S 37.09E
chison watercourse Australia 110 A4 ...27.39S 114.09E
zia Spain 48 D2 ....43.19N 1.06W
eşul r. Romania 56 D8 ....46.11N 20.29E
et Chad 84 E3 ....43.28N 1.20E
aé Brazil 77 L3 ....21.08S 42.23W
tz l. France 44 F5 ....53.25N 12.43E
mansk Rus. Fed. 58 E4 ....68.57N 33.07E
ran Japan 106 D4 ....42.19N 140.58E
ay r. Australia 110 C3 ....35.22S 139.18E
ay Bridge Australia 110 C3 ...35.07S 139.17E
rumbidgee r. Australia 110 D3 ...34.42S 143.13E
wara India 96 F5 ....23.50N 80.23E
küÿ Libya 84 F4 ....25.54N 13.55E
ezuschlag Austria 54 F2 ....47.37N 15.41E
ala mt. Bulgaria 56 E6 ....42.11N 23.35E
grave Ranges mts Australia 110 C4 ...26.17S 131.01E
kogee U.S.A. 65 G4 ....35.47N 95.23W
mar Sudan 94 D3 ....18.13N 35.40E
ma Tanzania 86 C4 ....1.32S 33.47E

Musselburgh Scotland 17 F3 ....55.57N 3.03W
Mustafakemalpaşa Turkey 57 H5 ....40.02N 28.23E
Müt Egypt 85 G4 ....25.28N 28.58E
Mut Turkey 57 J3 ....36.39N 33.26E
Mutare Zimbabwe 86 C3 ....18.58S 32.39E
Mutis, Gunung mt. Indonesia 105 G2 ...9.35S 124.14E
Mutsu Japan 106 D4 ....41.17N 141.10E
Mutuali Mozambique 86 C3 ....14.52S 37.01E
Muzaffargarh Pakistan 95 L6 ....30.03N 71.11E
Muzaffarpur India 96 G5 ....26.05N 85.28E
Mwanza Tanzania 86 C4 ....2.30S 32.56E
Mwene-Ditu Dem. Rep. Congo 86 B4 ...7.01S 23.27E
Mweru, Lake Dem. Rep. Congo/Zambia 86 B4 ...8.57S 28.46E
Myanmar Asia 97 I5 ....22.37N 95.02E
Mykolayiv Ukraine 53 J6 ....46.57N 32.02E
Myronivka Ukraine 55 N3 ....49.39N 30.59E
Myrtle Beach town U.S.A. 65 K3 ....33.43N 78.54W
Myślibórz Poland 46 B4 ....52.55N 14.52E
Mysore India 96 E2 ....12.16N 76.36E
My Tho Vietnam 104 D6 ....10.20N 106.23E
Mytilini Greece 56 G4 ....39.07N 26.33E
Mzuzu Malawi 86 C3 ....11.27S 34.00E

N

Naas Ireland 41 E3 ....53.13N 6.40W
Naberera Tanzania 87 B1 ....4.12S 36.55E
Naberezhnyye Chelny Rus. Fed. 58 G3 ...55.42N 52.21E
Nabeul Tunisia 52 F4 ....36.29N 10.45E
Nacala Mozambique 86 D3 ....14.34S 40.40E
Nador Morocco 52 C4 ....35.11N 2.56W
Nadvirna Ukraine 46 G2 ....48.38N 24.35E
Nadym Rus. Fed. 58 I4 ....65.29N 72.34E
Næstved Denmark 40 B1 ....55.14N 11.46E
Nafplio Greece 56 E3 ....37.34N 22.49E
Naga Phil. 105 G6 ....13.35N 123.11E
Nagaland d. India 97 H6 ....26.03N 94.37E
Nagano Japan 106 C3 ....36.38N 138.11E
Nagaoka Japan 106 C3 ....37.26N 138.51E
Nagaon India 97 H6 ....26.19N 92.42E
Nagasaki Japan 106 A2 ....32.46N 129.52E
Nagercoil India 96 E2 ....8.10N 77.28E
Nagha Kalat Pakistan 95 K5 ....27.23N 65.13E
Nagichot Sudan 87 A4 ....4.14N 33.37E
Nagoya Japan 106 C3 ....35.10N 136.53E
Nagpur India 96 E5 ....21.09N 79.05E
Nagurskoye Rus. Fed. 58 F6 ....80.31N 47.57E
Nagykanizsa Hungary 54 G2 ....46.28N 16.59E
Naha Japan 103 N3 ....26.12N 127.39E
Nahāvand Iran 95 G6 ....34.12N 48.22E
Nailsworth England 10 C2 ....51.42N 2.13W
Nain Canada 63 L3 ....56.31N 61.31W
Na'in Iran 95 H6 ....32.50N 53.03E
Nairn Scotland 19 F2 ....57.35N 3.52W
Nairn r. Scotland 19 F2 ....57.35N 3.52W
Nairobi Kenya 87 B2 ....1.17S 36.48E
Naivasha Kenya 87 B2 ....0.44S 36.27E
Naivasha, Lake Kenya 87 B2 ....0.45S 36.19E
Najafābād Iran 95 H6 ....32.37N 51.20E
Najd f. Saudi Arabia 94 F5 ....26.14N 40.21E
Najin N. Korea 106 B4 ....42.15N 130.18E
Najrān Saudi Arabia 94 F3 ....17.34N 44.17E
Nakhodka Rus. Fed. 59 O2 ....42.48N 132.54E
Nakhon Ratchasima Thailand 104 C6 ...14.57N 102.08E
Nakhon Sawan Thailand 104 C7 ....15.40N 100.06E
Nakhon Si Thammarat Thailand 104 B5 ...8.25N 99.58E
Nakina Canada 65 I7 ....50.10N 86.43W
Nakonde Zambia 86 C4 ....9.21S 32.42E
Nakskov Denmark 40 B1 ....54.49N 11.09E
Nakuru Kenya 87 B2 ....0.16S 36.05E
Nalubaale Dam Uganda 87 A3 ....0.29N 33.14E
Nālūt Libya 84 F5 ....31.49N 10.57E
Namak, Kavīr-e l. Iran 95 I6 ....34.26N 57.32E
Namakzar-e Shadad f. Iran 95 I6 ....30.44N 58.01E
Namanga Kenya 87 B2 ....2.31S 36.49E
Namangan Uzbekistan 102 C6 ....40.59N 71.38E
Nam Co l. China 102 G4 ....30.42N 90.35E
Nam Đinh Vietnam 104 D8 ....20.22N 106.11E
Namib Desert Namibia 86 A2 ....25.21S 15.06E
Namibe Angola 86 A3 ....15.11S 12.10E
Namibia Africa 86 A2 ....23.22S 15.55E
Namlea Indonesia 105 H3 ....3.14S 127.05E
Namp'o N. Korea 103 N5 ....38.43N 125.23E
Nampula Mozambique 86 C3 ....15.10S 39.13E
Namsos Norway 40 B4 ....64.28N 11.31E
Namur Belgium 42 D3 ....50.28N 4.52E
Namur d. Belgium 42 D3 ....50.16N 4.53E
Nan Thailand 104 C7 ....18.47N 100.47E
Nanaimo Canada 64 B6 ....49.10N 123.56W
Nanao Japan 106 C3 ....37.03N 136.58E
Nanchang China 103 L3 ....28.42N 115.58E
Nanchong China 103 J4 ....30.46N 106.04E
Nancy France 44 G6 ....48.42N 6.11E
Nanjing China 103 L4 ....32.04N 118.50E
Nan Ling mts China 103 K2 ....24.59N 111.08E
Nanning China 103 J2 ....22.49N 108.24E
Nanortalik Greenland 63 N4 ....60.09N 45.15W
Nanping China 103 L3 ....26.41N 118.09E
Nansio Tanzania 87 A2 ....2.06S 33.03E
Nantes France 44 C5 ....47.13N 1.33W
Nantes à Brest, Canal de France 44 B5 ...47.42N 2.07W
Nantong China 103 M4 ....31.59N 120.56E
Nantucket Island U.S.A. 65 M5 ....41.17N 69.59W
Nantwich England 15 E2 ....53.04N 2.31W
Nant-y-moch Reservoir Wales 12 D4 ...52.28N 3.54W
Nanumea atoll Tuvalu 108 H5 ....5.38S 176.08E
Nanyang China 103 K4 ....33.01N 112.35E
Nanyuki Kenya 87 B3 ....0.00S 37.04E
Nao, Cabo de la c. Spain 48 F3 ....38.44N 0.15E
Napaimiut U.S.A. 62 C4 ....61.38N 158.24W
Napier New Zealand 111 G3 ....39.30S 176.53E
Naples Italy 50 F4 ....40.51N 14.15E
Napo r. Ecuador 76 F7 ....3.18S 72.37W
Narberth Wales 12 C3 ....51.48N 4.45W
Narbonne France 44 E3 ....43.11N 3.01E
Narborough Leics. England 10 D3 ....52.34N 1.13W
Narborough Norf. England 11 F3 ....52.41N 0.35E
Nares Strait Canada/Greenland 63 K5 ...79.12N 71.28W
Narmada r. India 96 D5 ....21.43N 73.06E
Naro-Fominsk Rus. Fed. 55 Q6 ....55.22N 36.45E
Narok Kenya 87 A2 ....1.06S 35.51E
Närpes Finland 40 E3 ....62.29N 21.21E
Narva Estonia 40 G2 ....59.22N 28.11E
Narvik Norway 40 D5 ....68.26N 17.25E
Nar'yan-Mar Rus. Fed. 58 G4 ....67.40N 53.10E
Naryn Kyrgyzstan 102 D6 ....41.19N 75.56E
Nashik India 96 D5 ....20.00N 73.52E
Nashville U.S.A. 65 I4 ....36.11N 86.46W
Näsijärvi l. Finland 40 E3 ....61.35N 23.44E
Nassau Bahamas 71 I6 ....25.04N 77.20W
Nassau i. Cook Is 108 I5 ....11.32S 165.22W
Nasser, Lake resr Egypt 85 H4 ....23.09N 33.02E

Nässjö Sweden 40 C2 ....57.39N 14.43E
Nata Botswana 86 B2 ....20.12S 26.10E
Nata Tanzania 87 A2 ....2.01S 34.22E
Natal Brazil 77 M5 ....5.44S 35.10W
Natchez U.S.A. 65 H3 ....31.35N 91.24W
Natron, Lake Tanzania 86 C4 ....2.18S 36.02E
Natuna, Kepulauan is Indonesia 104 D4 ...4.12N 107.23E
Natuna Besar i. Indonesia 104 D4 ...4.04N 108.28E
Naturaliste Plateau f. Indian Oc. 108 D3 ...34.04S 111.21E
Nauru S. Pacific Oc. 108 H5 ....0.30S 166.56E
Navahrudak Belarus 46 G4 ....53.36N 25.50E
Navalmoral de la Mata Spain 48 C3 ...39.53N 5.32W
Navan Ireland 41 E3 ....53.39N 6.41W
Navapolatsk Belarus 55 M6 ....55.32N 28.40E
Naver r. Scotland 19 E3 ....58.31N 4.13W
Naver, Loch l. Scotland 19 E3 ....58.17N 4.24W
Navlya Rus. Fed. 55 P5 ....52.49N 34.31E
Navojoa Mexico 70 C6 ....27.04N 109.32W
Nawabshah Pakistan 96 C6 ....26.13N 68.25E
Naxçivan Azerbaijan 95 G7 ....39.13N 45.24E
Naxos i. Greece 56 F3 ....37.02N 25.35E
Nayarit d. Mexico 70 D5 ....22.07N 104.45W
Naypyidaw Myanmar 97 I4 ....19.44N 96.13E
Nazareth Israel 53 K3 ....32.40N 35.18E
Nazas r. Mexico 70 D6 ....25.34N 104.55W
Nazca Peru 76 F5 ....14.51S 74.54W
Nazca Ridge f. S. Pacific Oc. 109 O4 ...22.54S 83.41W
Nazilli Turkey 57 H3 ....37.55N 28.19E
Nazrēt Ethiopia 85 H2 ....8.32N 39.15E
Nazwá Oman 95 I4 ....22.56N 57.31E
N'dalatando Angola 86 A4 ....9.18S 14.56E
Ndélé C.A.R. 85 G2 ....8.24N 20.38E
Ndeni i. Solomon Is 111 F5 ....10.41S 166.07E
Ndjamena Chad 84 F3 ....12.08N 15.03E
Ndola Zambia 86 B3 ....12.57S 28.39E
Ndoto mt. Kenya 87 B3 ....1.46N 37.09E
Neagh, Lough l. Northern Ireland 16 C2 ...54.40N 6.24W
Nea Liosia Greece 56 E4 ....38.04N 23.42E
Neapoli Greece 56 E3 ....36.31N 23.04E
Neath Wales 12 D3 ....51.39N 3.48W
Neath r. Wales 12 D3 ....51.39N 3.49W
Neath Port Talbot d. Wales 9 D2 ....51.43N 3.49W
Nebitdag Turkmenistan 95 H7 ....39.27N 54.17E
Neblina, Pico da mt. Brazil 76 G8 ....0.49N 66.13W
Nebraska d. U.S.A. 64 F5 ....41.30N 100.06W
Nebrodi, Monti mts Italy 50 F2 ....37.43N 14.02E
Nechisar National Park Ethiopia 87 B4 ...5.58N 37.45E
Neckar r. Germany 44 H6 ....49.31N 8.27E
Necker Island U.S.A. 108 J7 ....23.34N 164.42W
Needham Market England 11 G3 ....52.09N 1.03E
Needles U.S.A. 64 D3 ....34.50N 114.36W
Nefyn Wales 12 C4 ....52.56N 4.31W
Negēlē Ethiopia 87 B4 ....5.20N 39.34E
Negotin Serbia 56 E7 ....44.13N 22.33E
Negra, Cordillera mts Peru 76 E6 ....9.19S 78.15W
Negra, Punta c. Peru 76 D6 ....6.05S 81.21W
Negro r. Argentina 73 C2 ....41.01S 62.48W
Negro r. Brazil 77 I4 ....19.17S 57.15W
Negro r. S. America 77 H7 ....3.08S 59.57W
Negro r. Uruguay 73 D3 ....33.24S 58.21W
Negro, Cabo c. Morocco 48 C1 ....35.41N 5.17W
Negros i. Phil. 105 G5 ....9.43N 122.56E
Neijiang China 103 J3 ....29.35N 105.04E
Nei Mongol Zizhiqu d. China 103 I6 ...40.12N 103.26E
Neiße r. Germany/Poland 54 F5 ....52.04N 14.46E
Neiva Colombia 72 B7 ....2.55N 75.15W
Nek'emtē Ethiopia 85 H2 ....9.06N 36.32E
Nekso Denmark 54 F4 ....55.03N 15.08E
Nelidovo Rus. Fed. 55 O7 ....56.14N 32.47E
Nellore India 96 E3 ....14.29N 79.59E
Nelson Canada 62 G2 ....49.29N 117.17W
Nelson r. Canada 63 I3 ....56.58N 92.45W
Nelson England 15 E2 ....53.50N 2.13W
Nelson New Zealand 111 G2 ....41.17S 173.15E
Nelspruit S. Africa 86 C2 ....25.28S 30.59E
Neman Rus. Fed. 46 F5 ....55.02N 22.02E
Neman r. Rus. Fed. 55 J6 ....55.03N 22.14E
Nementcha, Monts des mts Algeria 52 E3 ...34.48N 6.23E
Nemuro Japan 106 E4 ....43.17N 145.30E
Nenagh Ireland 41 C2 ....52.52N 8.12W
Nene r. England 11 G3 ....52.49N 0.13E
Nenjiang China 103 N7 ....49.04N 125.12E
Nepal Asia 96 F6 ....28.59N 82.06E
Nephin hill Ireland 41 B4 ....54.01N 9.22W
Neris r. Lithuania 40 F1 ....54.55N 23.53E
Ness r. Scotland 19 E2 ....57.29N 4.14W
Ness, Loch l. Scotland 19 E2 ....57.10N 4.37W
Neston England 14 D2 ....53.17N 3.04W
Nestos r. Greece 56 F5 ....40.51N 24.48E
Netherlands Europe 42 E5 ....52.35N 5.33E
Netherlands Antilles is Central America 71 K3 ...12.30N 68.43W
Netley England 10 D1 ....50.52N 1.19W
Nettilling Lake Canada 63 K4 ....66.30N 70.39W
Neubari r. Sudan 87 A4 ....7.05N 33.14E
Neubrandenburg Germany 54 E5 ....53.33N 13.15E
Neuchâtel Switz. 50 B7 ....46.59N 6.56E
Neuchâtel, Lac de l. Switz. 50 B7 ....46.51N 6.48E
Neufchâteau Belgium 42 E2 ....49.51N 5.27E
Neumünster Germany 54 C6 ....54.05N 9.59E
Neunkirchen Germany 42 G2 ....49.21N 7.10E
Neuquén Argentina 73 C3 ....38.57S 68.03W
Neuruppin Germany 54 E5 ....52.56N 12.48E
Neustrelitz Germany 54 E5 ....53.22N 13.04E
Neuwied Germany 54 B4 ....50.26N 7.28E
Nevada d. U.S.A. 64 C4 ....39.03N 117.06W
Nevada, Sierra mts Spain 48 D2 ....37.04N 3.20W
Nevada, Sierra mts U.S.A. 64 B5 ....40.07N 121.00W
Nevel' Rus. Fed. 55 M7 ....56.01N 29.55E
Nevers France 44 E5 ....47.00N 3.09E
Nevinnomyssk Rus. Fed. 53 L5 ....44.38N 41.56E
Nevis, Loch inlet Scotland 18 D2 ....57.00N 5.42W
Nevşehir Turkey 57 K4 ....38.37N 34.43E
New Addington England 11 E2 ....51.21N 0.01W
New Alresford England 10 D2 ....51.05N 1.10W
Newark U.S.A. 65 L5 ....40.44N 74.24W
Newark-on-Trent England 15 G2 ....53.05N 0.49W
New Bern U.S.A. 65 K4 ....35.05N 77.03W
Newbiggin-by-the-Sea England 15 F4 ...55.11N 1.31W
Newbridge Ireland 41 E3 ....53.11N 6.48W
Newbridge Wales 12 D3 ....51.40N 3.09W
New Britain P.N.G. 110 D6 ....5.42S 148.56E
New Britain Trench f. S. Pacific Oc. 108 G5 ...6.35S 150.51E
New Brunswick d. Canada 63 L2 ....46.41N 66.28W
Newburgh Scotland 17 F4 ....56.21N 3.14W
Newbury England 10 D2 ....51.24N 1.19W
New Caledonia i. S. Pacific Oc. 111 F4 ...21.41S 164.17E
New Caledonia Trough f. Tasman Sea 108 G4 ...22.53S 164.54E
Newcastle Australia 110 E3 ....32.56S 151.44E
Newcastle Northern Ireland 16 D2 ....54.13N 5.53W
Newcastle Emlyn Wales 12 C4 ....52.02N 4.28W
Newcastleton Scotland 17 G3 ....55.11N 2.49W
Newcastle-under-Lyme England 15 E2 ...53.01N 2.13W
Newcastle upon Tyne England 15 F3 ...54.59N 1.37W
Newcastle West Ireland 41 B2 ....52.27N 9.03W

New Cumnock Scotland 16 E3 ....55.23N 4.11W
New Delhi India 96 E6 ....28.36N 77.17E
Newent England 10 C2 ....51.56N 2.24W
New Forest nature res. England 10 D1 ...50.52N 1.37W
Newfoundland i. Canada 63 M2 ....48.30N 56.04W
Newfoundland and Labrador d. Canada 63 M3 ...53.44N 56.53W
New Galloway Scotland 16 E3 ....55.05N 4.08W
New Georgia Sound str. Solomon Is 110 E6 ...7.21S 156.36E
New Glasgow Canada 65 N6 ....45.35N 62.35W
New Guinea i. Indonesia/P.N.G. 105 K2 ...5.26S 140.49E
New Hampshire d. U.S.A. 65 L5 ....44.02N 71.34W
Newhaven England 11 F1 ....50.48N 0.03E
New Haven U.S.A. 65 L5 ....41.18N 72.56W
New Hebrides Trench f. S. Pacific Oc. 108 H4 ...22.43S 170.39E
New Ireland i. P.N.G. 110 E6 ....3.33S 152.14E
New Jersey d. U.S.A. 65 L4 ....39.57N 74.26W
New Liskeard Canada 65 K6 ....47.31N 79.41W
Newmarket England 11 F3 ....52.15N 0.25E
Newmarket-on-Fergus Ireland 41 C2 ...52.46N 8.53W
New Mexico d. U.S.A. 64 E3 ....34.32N 105.55W
New Milton England 10 D1 ....50.45N 1.40W
Newnham England 10 C2 ....51.48N 2.27W
New Orleans U.S.A. 65 H2 ....29.58N 90.03W
New Pitsligo Scotland 19 G2 ....57.36N 2.12W
Newport Ess. England 11 F2 ....51.59N 0.13E
Newport I. o. W. England 10 D1 ....50.42N 1.17W
Newport Tel. Wren. England 10 C3 ....52.46N 2.22W
Newport New. Wales 12 E3 ....51.35N 2.59W
Newport Pem. Wales 12 C4 ....52.01N 4.50W
Newport d. Wales 9 D2 ....51.35N 2.59W
Newport Bay Wales 12 C4 ....52.02N 4.53W
Newport News U.S.A. 65 K4 ....37.00N 76.26W
Newport Pagnell England 10 E3 ....52.05N 0.43W
New Providence i. Bahamas 71 I6 ....25.03N 77.25W
Newquay England 13 B2 ....50.25N 5.04W
New Quay Wales 12 C4 ....52.13N 4.22W
New Romney England 11 F1 ....50.59N 0.56E
New Ross Ireland 41 E2 ....52.23N 6.57W
Newry Northern Ireland 16 C2 ....54.10N 6.19W
Newry and Mourne d. Northern Ireland 9 B4 ...54.10N 6.18W
Newry Canal Northern Ireland 16 C2 ...54.16N 6.21W
New Siberia Islands Rus. Fed. 59 P5 ...76.08N 149.21E
New South Wales d. Australia 110 D3 ...32.42S 146.24E
Newton Abbot England 13 D2 ....50.32N 3.37W
Newton Aycliffe England 15 F3 ....54.37N 1.34W
Newtonhill Scotland 19 G2 ....57.02N 2.09W
Newton-le-Willows England 14 E2 ....53.27N 2.38W
Newton Mearns Scotland 16 E3 ....55.46N 4.20W
Newtonmore Scotland 19 E2 ....57.04N 4.07W
Newton St Cyres England 13 D2 ....50.46N 3.35W
Newton Stewart Scotland 16 E2 ....54.58N 4.29W
Newtown Wales 12 D4 ....52.31N 3.19W
Newtownabbey Northern Ireland 16 D2 ...54.39N 5.54W
Newtownabbey d. Northern Ireland 9 C4 ...54.44N 5.59W
Newtownards Northern Ireland 16 D2 ...54.35N 5.41W
Newtown St Boswells Scotland 17 G3 ...55.35N 2.40W
Newtownstewart Northern Ireland 16 B2 ...54.43N 7.22W
New York U.S.A. 65 L5 ....40.41N 73.59W
New York d. U.S.A. 65 K5 ....42.43N 75.14W
New Zealand Oceania 111 G2 ....42.54S 174.10E
Neyriz Iran 95 H5 ....29.12N 54.19E
Neyshābūr Iran 95 I7 ....36.12N 58.46E
Ngaoundéré Cameroon 84 F2 ....7.19N 13.34E
Ngorongoro Conservation Area Tanzania 87 A2 ...3.06S 35.20E
Nguigmi Niger 84 F3 ....14.14N 13.05E
Ngulu atoll Micronesia 105 J5 ....8.28N 137.37E
Nha Trang Vietnam 104 D6 ....12.11N 109.11E
Niamey Niger 84 E3 ....13.31N 2.07E
Niangara Dem. Rep. Congo 86 B5 ....3.40N 27.52E
Nias i. Indonesia 104 B4 ....1.11N 97.04E
Niça Latvia 46 E6 ....56.21N 21.04E
Nicaragua Central America 71 G3 ....13.13N 85.57W
Nicaragua, Lake Nicaragua 71 G3 ....11.31N 85.17W
Nice France 44 G3 ....43.42N 7.17E
Nicobar Islands India 97 H2 ....8.00N 93.59E
Nicosia Cyprus 57 J2 ....35.10N 33.22E
Nicoya, Golfo de b. Costa Rica 71 H2 ...9.42N 84.48W
Nidd r. England 15 F2 ....54.01N 1.13W
Nidzica Poland 46 I5 ....53.22N 20.26E
Niedersachsen d. Germany 42 G5 ....52.43N 8.53E
Nienburg Germany 54 C5 ....52.38N 9.13E
Niers r. Germany 42 E4 ....51.42N 5.57E
Nieuwpoort Belgium 42 B4 ....51.08N 2.45E
Nieves, Pico de las mt. Canary Islands 48 Y1 ...27.57N 15.34W
Niğde Turkey 57 K3 ....37.59N 34.41E
Niger Africa 84 E3 ....17.03N 10.05E
Niger r. Africa 84 E2 ....4.17N 6.05E
Nigeria Africa 84 E2 ....9.09N 7.54E
Nigg Bay Scotland 19 E2 ....57.43N 4.05W
Niigata Japan 106 C3 ....37.55N 139.03E
Nijmegen Neth. 42 E4 ....51.50N 5.52E
Nikel' Rus. Fed. 40 G5 ....69.24N 30.13E
Nikopol' Ukraine 55 P2 ....47.34N 34.24E
Niksar Turkey 57 L5 ....40.35N 36.57E
Nikšić Montenegro 56 C6 ....42.46N 18.56E
Nikumaroro atoll Kiribati 108 I5 ....4.43S 174.31W
Nile r. Africa 85 H5 ....30.11N 31.06E
Nilgiri Hills India 96 E3 ....11.08N 76.28E
Nîmes France 44 F3 ....43.51N 4.22E
Ninetyeast Ridge f. Indian Oc. 108 B3 ...34.14S 86.15E
Ningbo China 103 M3 ....29.54N 121.34E
Ningxia Huizu Zizhiqu d. China 103 J5 ...37.11N 105.28E
Niobrara r. U.S.A. 64 F5 ....42.46N 98.02W
Nioro Mali 84 D3 ....15.14N 9.36W
Niort France 44 C5 ....46.20N 0.28W
Nipigon Canada 63 J2 ....49.00N 88.17W
Nipigon, Lake Canada 63 J2 ....49.43N 88.33W
Nipissing, Lake Canada 65 K6 ....46.15N 79.39W
Niš Serbia 56 D6 ....43.19N 21.54E
Niterói Brazil 77 L3 ....22.54S 43.06W
Nith r. Scotland 17 F3 ....55.02N 3.36W
Nitra Slovakia 54 H3 ....48.19N 18.05E
Niue i. S. Pacific Oc. 108 I4 ....19.03S 169.45W
Nivelles Belgium 42 D3 ....50.36N 4.20E
Nizamabad India 96 E4 ....18.40N 78.07E
Nizhneudinsk Rus. Fed. 59 K3 ....54.55N 98.58E
Nizhnevartovsk Rus. Fed. 58 I4 ....60.56N 76.38E
Nizhniy Novgorod Rus. Fed. 58 F3 ...56.17N 43.54E
Nizhnyaya Tunguska r. Rus. Fed. 59 J4 ...65.47N 87.59E
Nizhyn Ukraine 55 N4 ....51.02N 31.53E
Nizip Turkey 57 L3 ....36.59N 37.48E
Nkongsamba Cameroon 84 E2 ....4.58N 9.57E
Nobeoka Japan 106 B2 ....32.34N 131.41E
Nogales Mexico 70 B7 ....31.19N 110.57W
Nogent-le-Rotrou France 44 D6 ....48.19N 0.49E
Nogent-sur-Oise France 42 B2 ....49.17N 2.28E
Nohfelden Germany 42 G2 ....49.35N 7.08E
Noirmoutier, Île de i. France 44 B5 ...46.58N 2.16W
Nok Kundi Pakistan 95 J5 ....28.49N 62.50E
Nome U.S.A. 62 B4 ....64.32N 165.28W
Nonthaburi Thailand 104 C6 ....13.51N 100.32E
Noord-Brabant d. Neth. 42 E4 ....51.32N 5.01E
Noord-Holland d. Neth. 42 D5 ....52.46N 4.54E
Nordaustlandet i. Arctic Oc. 58 D5 ...79.36N 22.37E

Norden Germany 42 G6 ....53.36N 7.12E
Norderney i. Germany 42 G6 ....53.44N 7.19E
Norderstedt Germany 54 D5 ....53.44N 10.00E
Nordhausen Germany 54 D4 ....51.30N 10.47E
Nordhorn Germany 42 G5 ....52.26N 7.05E
Nord-Pas-de-Calais d. France 42 B3 ....50.14N 2.43E
Nordrhein-Westfalen d. Germany 42 G4 ...51.04N 7.25E
Nordvik Rus. Fed. 59 M5 ....74.01N 111.20E
Nore r. Ireland 41 E2 ....52.25N 6.58W
Norfolk d. England 9 F3 ....52.44N 0.59E
Norfolk U.S.A. 65 K4 ....36.53N 76.16W
Norfolk Broads f. England 11 G3 ....52.43N 1.28E
Norfolk Island S. Pacific Oc. 111 F4 ......28.59S 167.59E
Norfolk Island Ridge f. Tasman Sea 108 H4 ..23.53S 167.20E
Noril'sk Rus. Fed. 59 J4 ....69.19N 88.08E
Normandy f. France 44 C6 ....48.53N 0.32W
Normanton Australia 110 D5 ....17.41S 141.05E
Norra Storfjället mts Sweden 40 C4 ....65.53N 15.07E
Norrköping Sweden 40 D2 ....58.36N 16.12E
Norrtälje Sweden 40 D2 ....59.45N 18.41E
Norseman Australia 110 B3 ....32.14S 121.47E
Norte, Cabo c. Brazil 77 K8 ....1.40N 49.59W
Northallerton England 15 F3 ....54.20N 1.26W
North America 60
North American Basin f. Atlantic Oc. 116 G7 ..30.00N 60.00W
Northampton England 10 E3 ....52.14N 0.54W
Northamptonshire d. England 9 E3 ....52.14N 0.54W
North Australian Basin f. Indian Oc. 108 D5 ..14.09S 114.44E
North Ayrshire d. Scotland 8 C4 ....55.44N 4.44W
North Battleford Canada 62 H3 ....52.46N 108.17W
North Bay town Canada 63 K2 ....46.19N 79.28W
North Berwick Scotland 17 G4 ....56.04N 2.43W
North Cape New Zealand 111 G3 ....34.25S 173.03E
North Cape Norway 40 F5 ....71.10N 25.47E
North Carolina d. U.S.A. 65 K4 ....36.13N 79.52W
North Cave England 15 G2 ....53.47N 0.39W
North Channel U.K. 16 C3 ....55.23N 6.13W
North China Plain f. China 90 I4 ....34.30N 117.00E
North Dakota d. U.S.A. 64 F6 ....47.19N 100.24W
North Dorset Downs hills England 10 C1 ...50.46N 2.32W
North Down d. Northern Ireland 9 C4 .....54.39N 5.43W
North Downs hills England 11 E2 ....51.14N 0.58W
North Eastern d. Kenya 87 C3 ....1.16N 40.02E
North East Lincolnshire d. England 9 E3 ...53.37N 0.13W
Northeast Pacific Basin f. N. Pacific Oc. 109 J7 ..27.45N 154.35W
Northern Dvina r. Rus. Fed. 58 F4 ....64.31N 40.33E
Northern Ireland d. U.K. 9 B4 ....54.38N 6.49W
Northern Mariana Islands N. Pacific Oc. 105 K7 ..17.15N 143.32E
Northern Territory d. Australia 110 C5 ....17.40S 133.30E
North Esk r. Scotland 19 G1 ....56.45N 2.26W
North European Plain f. Europe 34 G3 ....56.00N 27.00E
North Foreland c. England 11 G2 ....51.23N 1.27E
North Frisian Islands Germany 54 C6 .....54.52N 8.02E
North Harris f. Scotland 18 C2 ....57.59N 6.48W
North Hykeham England 15 G2 ....53.11N 0.35W
North Island New Zealand 111 G3 ......38.11S 173.23E
North Korea Asia 103 N6 ....40.01N 126.39E
North Lanarkshire d. Scotland 8 D4 .....55.53N 3.57W
North Lincolnshire d. England 9 E3 ......53.37N 0.35W
North Platte U.S.A. 64 F5 ....41.09N 100.46W
North Platte r. U.S.A. 64 F5 ....41.10N 100.48W
North Ronaldsay i. Scotland 19 G4 ......59.24N 2.26W
North Ronaldsay Firth str. Scotland 19 G4 ..59.20N 2.29W
North Saskatchewan r. Canada 62 H3 ....53.13N 105.11W
North Sea Europe 34 E3 ....56.00N 4.00E
North Shields England 15 F4 ....55.01N 1.27W
North Siberian Lowland f. Rus. Fed. 59 L5 ..73.26N 103.17E
North Somercotes England 15 H2 ....53.27N 0.08E
North Somerset d. England 9 D2 ....51.24N 2.48W
North Sunderland England 15 F4 ....55.35N 1.39W
North Tidworth England 10 D2 ....51.14N 1.40W
North Tyne r. England 15 E3 ....54.59N 2.08W
North Ugie r. Scotland 19 H2 ....57.32N 1.55W
North Uist i. Scotland 18 B2 ....57.37N 7.26W
Northumberland d. England 8 D4 ....55.09N 2.35W
Northumberland Strait Canada 65 N6 ...46.50N 64.43W
North Walsham England 11 G3 ....52.49N 1.23E
North West Cape Australia 110 A4 .....21.49S 114.12E
Northwest Pacific Basin f. N. Pacific Oc. 108 G8 ..35.59N 154.41E
Northwest Territories d. Canada 62 H4 ..63.48N 105.17W
Northwich England 15 E2 ....53.16N 2.31W
North York Moors f. England 15 G3 ....54.23N 0.50W
North Yorkshire d. England 9 E4 ....54.12N 1.59W
Norton England 15 G3 ....54.08N 0.47W
Norton Fitzwarren England 13 D3 .....51.02N 3.08W
Norton Sound str. U.S.A. 62 B3 ....63.58N 163.01W
Norway Europe 40 B3 ....62.46N 10.30E
Norway House Canada 62 I3 ....53.56N 97.52W
Norwegian Sea N. Atlantic Oc. 34 D4 ...66.00N 2.00E
Norwich England 11 G3 ....52.38N 1.18E
Noshiro Japan 106 D4 ....40.12N 140.01E
Noss, Isle of i. Scotland 19 H5 ....60.09N 1.00W
Noteć r. Poland 46 D3 ....52.43N 15.26E
Nottingham England 10 D3 ....52.57N 1.09W
Nottingham d. England 9 E3 ....52.58N 1.10W
Nottinghamshire d. England 9 E3 ......53.03N 0.59W
Nouâdhibou Mauritania 84 C4 ....21.04N 17.00W
Nouâdhibou, Râs c. Mauritania 84 C4 ..20.51N 17.04W
Nouakchott Mauritania 84 C3 ....18.06N 15.58W
Nouméa New Caledonia 111 F4 ....22.18S 166.26E
Noup Head Scotland 19 F4 ....59.20N 3.04W
Nova Friburgo Brazil 77 L3 ....22.18S 42.32W
Nova Gradiška Croatia 56 B7 ....45.16N 17.23E
Nova Iguaçu Brazil 77 L3 ....22.44S 43.29W
Novara Italy 50 C6 ....45.27N 8.37E
Nova Scotia d. Canada 63 L2 ....43.53N 65.45W
Novaya Sibir', Ostrov i. Rus. Fed. 59 P5 ..75.04N 148.22E
Novaya Zemlya is Rus. Fed. 58 G5 .....71.41N 55.45E
Nové Zámky Slovakia 54 H2 ....47.59N 18.09E
Novi Pazar Serbia 56 D6 ....43.08N 20.30E
Novi Sad Serbia 56 C7 ....45.16N 19.51E
Novo Aripuanã Brazil 77 H6 ....5.07S 60.20W
Novodvinsk Rus. Fed. 58 F4 ....64.25N 40.50E
Novo Hamburgo Brazil 77 J2 ....29.40S 51.09W
Novohrad-Volyns'kyy Ukraine 55 L4 ..50.36N 27.37E
Novokuznetsk Rus. Fed. 58 J3 ....53.45N 87.09E
Novo Mesto Slovenia 54 F1 ....45.48N 15.10E
Novomoskovsk Rus. Fed. 58 E3 ....54.01N 38.19E
Novomoskovs'k Ukraine 55 P3 ....48.38N 35.14E
Novooleksiyivka Ukraine 57 K8 ....46.14N 34.39E
Novorossiysk Rus. Fed. 58 E2 ....44.43N 37.47E
Novosibirsk Rus. Fed. 58 J3 ....55.03N 83.02E
Novovolyns'k Ukraine 55 K4 ....50.43N 24.11E
Nový Jičín Czech Rep. 46 C2 ....49.36N 17.59E
Novyy Port Rus. Fed. 58 I4 ....68.13N 73.02E
Nowogard Poland 46 E4 ....53.40N 15.07E
Nowshera Pakistan 95 L6 ....34.00N 72.01E
Nowy Sącz Poland 46 E2 ....49.38N 20.42E
Nowy Targ Poland 46 E2 ....49.29N 20.03E
Noyabr'sk Rus. Fed. 58 I4 ....63.13N 75.32E
Noyon France 42 B2 ....49.35N 2.59E
Npitamaiong mt. Kenya 87 A3 ....3.08N 35.01E
Nu'aym f. Oman 95 I4 ....23.14N 55.59E
Nuba Mountains Sudan 94 D2 ....11.28N 30.33E

Nubian Desert Sudan 85 H4 ....20.25N 34.58E
Nudo Coropuna mt. Peru 76 F4 ....15.29S 72.43W
Nuevo Casas Grandes Mexico 70 C7 ...30.23N 107.56W
Nuevo Laredo Mexico 70 E6 ....27.29N 99.31W
Nuevo León d. Mexico 70 E6 ....25.51N 99.56W
Nui atoll Tuvalu 111 G6 ....7.12S 177.12E
Nuku'alofa Tonga 108 I4 ....21.07S 175.12W
Nukufetau atoll Tuvalu 111 G6 ....8.03S 178.25E
Nuku Hiva i. French Polynesia 109 K5 ..8.52S 140.06W
Nukunonu atoll Tokelau 108 I5 ....9.05S 171.50W
Nukus Uzbekistan 58 G2 ....42.27N 59.36E
Nullarbor Plain f. Australia 110 B3 .....31.01S 129.03E
Numazu Japan 106 C3 ....35.05N 138.52E
Nunavut d. Canada 63 I4 ....66.30N 89.54W
Nuneaton England 10 D3 ....52.31N 1.28W
Nunivak Island U.S.A. 62 B3 ....59.58N 166.18W
Nuoro Italy 50 C4 ....40.19N 9.20E
Nuqrah Saudi Arabia 94 F5 ....25.36N 41.26E
Nuremberg Germany 54 D3 ....49.27N 11.06E
Nurmes Finland 40 G3 ....63.33N 29.07E
Nushki Pakistan 95 K5 ....29.34N 66.02E
Nuuk Greenland 63 M4 ....64.11N 51.45W
Nyahururu Kenya 87 B3 ....0.04N 36.23E
Nyala Sudan 85 G3 ....12.03N 24.55E
Nyambeni Hills Kenya 87 B3 ....0.18N 37.54E
Nyanza d. Kenya 87 A2 ....0.26S 34.29E
Nyasa, Lake Africa 86 C4 ....9.59S 34.05E
Nyborg Denmark 40 B1 ....55.19N 10.47E
Nybro Sweden 40 C2 ....56.44N 15.55E
Nyeri Kenya 87 B2 ....0.23S 36.57E
Nyíregyháza Hungary 55 I2 ....47.57N 21.43E
Nyiru, Mount Kenya 87 B3 ....2.09N 36.50E
Nykarleby Finland 40 E3 ....63.31N 22.33E
Nykøbing Denmark 40 B1 ....54.46N 11.53E
Nyköping Sweden 40 D2 ....58.45N 17.01E
Nynäshamn Sweden 40 D2 ....58.54N 17.57E
Nysa Poland 46 C3 ....50.29N 17.20E
Nyurba Rus. Fed. 59 M4 ....63.17N 118.17E
Nyzhn'ohirs'kyy Ukraine 57 K7 ......45.27N 34.45E
Nzoia r. Kenya 87 A3 ....0.05N 33.57E

O

Oadby England 10 D3 ....52.36N 1.05W
Oahe, Lake U.S.A. 64 F5 ....44.49N 100.32W
Oahu i. U.S.A. 109 J7 ....21.34N 157.54W
Oakengates England 10 C3 ....52.42N 2.26W
Oakham England 10 E3 ....52.40N 0.44W
Oakland U.S.A. 64 B4 ....37.50N 122.15W
Oaxaca Mexico 70 E4 ....17.05N 96.40W
Oaxaca d. Mexico 70 E4 ....17.22N 96.20W
Ob' r. Rus. Fed. 58 H4 ....66.47N 69.08E
Óbidos Brazil 77 I7 ....1.50S 55.32W
Obihiro Japan 106 D4 ....42.55N 143.11E
Obninsk Rus. Fed. 55 Q6 ....55.04N 36.38E
Oborniki Poland 46 C4 ....52.38N 16.49E
Oboyan' Rus. Fed. 55 Q4 ....51.13N 36.16E
Obskaya Guba str. Rus. Fed. 58 I4 ..67.13N 72.49E
Occidental, Cordillera mts Colombia 72 B7 ..1.36N 77.47W
Occidental, Cordillera mts Peru 76 F4 ..16.07S 71.46W
Ocean Falls town Canada 62 F3 ....52.21N 127.41W
Oceania 117
Oceanside U.S.A. 64 C3 ....33.12N 117.23W
Ochil Hills Scotland 17 F4 ....56.12N 3.49W
Oda, Jebel mt. Sudan 85 H4 ....20.20N 36.39E
Ódáðahraun f. Iceland 40 Y2 ......64.48N 17.37W
Ödate Japan 106 D4 ....40.16N 140.34E
Ödemiş Turkey 57 G4 ....38.13N 27.58E
Odense Denmark 40 B1 ....55.24N 10.23E
Oder r. Germany 54 C4 ....51.43N 9.56E
Odesa Ukraine 53 J6 ....46.28N 30.39E
Odessa U.S.A. 64 F3 ....31.50N 102.20W
Odintsovo Rus. Fed. 55 Q6 ....55.40N 37.18E
Odra r. Germany/Poland 54 H3 ....49.54N 18.19E
Ofanto r. Italy 50 G5 ....41.21N 16.13E
Offaly d. Ireland 41 D3 ....53.15N 7.35W
Offenbach am Main Germany 54 C4 ..50.06N 8.46E
Offenburg Germany 54 B3 ....48.29N 7.57E
Ogadēn f. Ethiopia 85 I2 ....7.09N 45.27E
Ōgaki Japan 106 C3 ....35.21N 136.37E
Ogbomosho Nigeria 84 E2 ....8.08N 4.14E
Ogden U.S.A. 64 D5 ....41.14N 111.57W
Ogilvie r. Canada 62 E4 ....65.50N 137.13W
Oglio r. Italy 50 D6 ....45.01N 10.40E
Ogoki r. Canada 63 I7 ....51.40N 85.58W
Ogulin Croatia 56 A7 ....45.16N 15.14E
Ohio d. U.S.A. 65 J5 ....40.27N 82.28W
Ohio r. U.S.A. 65 I4 ....37.05N 89.12W
Ohrid Macedonia 56 D5 ....41.07N 20.49E
Ohrid, Lake Albania/Macedonia 56 D5 ..41.02N 20.43E
Oich r. Scotland 18 E2 ....57.09N 4.40W
Oich, Loch l. Scotland 18 E2 ......57.04N 4.46W
Oise r. France 44 E6 ....48.59N 2.04E
Ōita Japan 106 B2 ....33.13N 131.37E
Oiti mt. Greece 56 E4 ....38.48N 22.16E
Ojinaga Mexico 70 D6 ....29.33N 104.25W
Ojos del Salado, Nevado mt. Argentina/Chile 73 C4
                                    27.06S 68.35W
Oka r. Rus. Fed. 55 Q5 ....56.20N 43.59E
Okanogan r. U.S.A. 64 C6 ....48.06N 119.41W
Okavango Delta f. Botswana 86 B3 ..19.42S 23.02E
Okaya Japan 106 C3 ....36.03N 138.04E
Okayama Japan 106 B2 ....34.39N 133.55E
Okeechobee, Lake U.S.A. 65 J2 ...26.56N 81.00W
Okehampton England 13 C2 ......50.44N 4.00W
Okha India 96 C5 ....22.26N 69.08E
Okha Rus. Fed. 59 P3 ....53.33N 143.01E
Okhotsk Rus. Fed. 59 P3 ....59.22N 143.22E
Okhotsk, Sea of Japan/Rus. Fed. 106 D4 ..44.58N 144.06E
Okhtyrka Ukraine 55 P4 ....50.19N 34.54E
Okinawa i. Japan 103 N3 ....26.27N 127.58E
Oki-shotō is Japan 106 B3 ....36.07N 133.26E
Oklahoma d. U.S.A. 64 G4 ....35.41N 97.24W
Oklahoma City U.S.A. 64 G4 ......35.31N 97.31W
Oksskolten mt. Norway 40 C4 ....66.01N 14.20E
Oktyabr'skoy Revolyutsii, Ostrov i. Rus. Fed. 59 K5
                                    79.09N 96.82E
Öland i. Sweden 40 D2 ....56.57N 17.02E
Oława Poland 46 C3 ....50.56N 17.17E
Olbia Italy 50 C4 ....40.55N 9.30E
Old Crow Canada 62 E4 ....67.36N 139.54W
Oldenburg Germany 54 C5 ....53.09N 8.14E
Oldenzaal Neth. 42 F5 ....52.19N 6.56E
Oldham England 15 E2 ....53.33N 2.07W
Old Head of Kinsale Ireland 41 C1 ..51.36N 8.31W
Old Leake England 15 H2 ....53.02N 0.06E
Oldmeldrum Scotland 19 G2 .....57.20N 2.19W
Olean U.S.A. 65 K5 ....42.05N 78.26W
Olecko Poland 46 F5 ....54.02N 22.31E
Olekma r. Rus. Fed. 59 N4 ....60.05N 121.07E

Olekminsk Rus. Fed. 59 N4 ......60.24N 120.21E
Oleksandriya Ukraine 55 O3 .....48.41N 33.07E
Olenek Rus. Fed. 59 M4 ....68.28N 112.26E
Olenek r. Rus. Fed. 59 M5 ....72.58N 119.45E
Olenekskiy Zaliv b. Rus. Fed. 59 N5 ..73.22N 121.09E
Oléron, Île d' i. France 44 C4 .....45.55N 1.20W
Olevs'k Ukraine 55 L4 ....51.13N 27.39E
Olinda Brazil 77 N6 ....7.58S 34.46W
Oliva, Cordillera de mts Argentina/Chile 76 G2 ..29.56S 69.57W
Olmos Peru 76 E6 ....5.59S 79.46W
Olney England 10 E3 ....52.09N 0.42W
Olomouc Czech Rep. 54 G3 ......49.35N 17.16E
Oloron-Ste-Marie France 44 C3 ..43.12N 0.36W
Olsztyn Poland 46 E4 ....53.47N 20.29E
Olteţ r. Romania 56 F7 ....44.22N 24.07E
Olympia U.S.A. 64 B6 ....47.02N 122.53W
Olympus, Mount Greece 56 E5 ...40.05N 22.21E
Olympus, Mount U.S.A. 64 B6 ...47.45N 123.47W
Olyutorskiy Zaliv b. Rus. Fed. 59 R3 ..59.51N 168.08E
Omagh Northern Ireland 16 B2 ...54.36N 7.17W
Omagh d. Northern Ireland 9 B4 ..54.37N 7.16W
Omaha U.S.A. 64 G5 ....41.17N 95.58W
Oman Asia 95 H3 ....18.15N 53.34E
Oman, Gulf of Asia 95 I5 ....25.37N 56.49E
Ombersley England 10 C3 ....52.16N 2.14W
Ombrone r. Italy 50 D5 ....42.39N 11.01E
Omdurman Sudan 85 H3 ....15.38N 32.28E
Ommen Neth. 42 F5 ....52.32N 6.25E
Omolon r. Rus. Fed. 59 Q4 ....68.44N 158.43E
Omo National Park Ethiopia 87 A4 ..5.42N 35.47E
Omono r. Japan 106 D3 ....39.41N 140.04E
Omo Wenz r. Ethiopia 87 B4 .....4.36N 36.01E
Omsk Rus. Fed. 58 I3 ....55.00N 73.22E
Omsukchan Rus. Fed. 59 Q4 .....62.25N 155.43E
Omulew r. Poland 46 E4 ....53.04N 21.33E
Ōmuta Japan 106 B2 ....33.02N 130.28E
Onchan Isle of Man 14 C3 ....54.11N 4.27W
Ondjiva Angola 86 A3 ....17.04S 15.44E
Onega, Lake Rus. Fed. 58 E4 .....62.05N 35.21E
Oneşti Romania 56 G8 ....46.16N 26.46E
Ongole India 96 F4 ....15.32N 80.02E
Onitsha Nigeria 84 E2 ....6.08N 6.48E
Ono-i-Lau i. Fiji 108 I4 ....20.39S 178.45W
Ontario d. Canada 63 I3 ....51.51N 91.22W
Ontario, Lake Canada/U.S.A. 63 K2 ..43.31N 77.57W
Ontong Java Atoll Solomon Is 111 E6 ..5.24S 159.34E
Oosterschelde est. Neth. 42 C4 ..51.38N 3.35E
Oost-Vlaanderen d. Belgium 42 C3 ..50.56N 3.44E
Opala Dem. Rep. Congo 86 B4 ...0.36S 24.22E
Opava Czech Rep. 54 G3 ....49.56N 17.54E
Opochka Rus. Fed. 40 G2 ....56.43N 28.41E
Opole Poland 46 C3 ....50.40N 17.56E
Oporto Portugal 48 A4 ....41.11N 8.36W
Oradea Romania 55 I2 ....47.04N 21.57E
Oran Algeria 84 D5 ....35.42N 0.38W
Orange France 44 F4 ....44.09N 4.49E
Orange r. Namibia/S. Africa 86 A2 ..28.36S 16.28E
Orange, Cabo c. Brazil 72 D7 ....4.22N 51.17W
Oranmore Ireland 41 C3 ....53.16N 8.55W
Orchila, Isla i. Venezuela 71 K3 ..11.45N 66.09W
Orchy r. Scotland 16 D4 ....56.24N 5.01W
Ord, Mount hill Australia 110 B5 ..17.19S 125.29E
Ordu Turkey 57 L5 ....40.59N 37.53E
Örebro Sweden 40 D2 ....59.16N 15.14E
Oregon d. U.S.A. 64 B5 ....43.43N 120.32W
Orel Rus. Fed. 58 E3 ....52.58N 36.05E
Orenburg Rus. Fed. 58 G3 ....51.46N 55.05E
Orford Ness hd England 11 G3 ...52.05N 1.35E
Orhei Moldova 55 M2 ....47.22N 28.50E
Oriental, Cordillera mts Bolivia 76 G4 ..16.47S 66.35W
Oriental, Cordillera mts Colombia 72 B7 ..7.42N 72.45W
Oriental, Cordillera mts Peru 76 F5 ..10.29S 74.41W
Orillia Canada 65 K5 ....44.36N 79.25W
Orinoco r. Col./Venez. 72 C7 .....8.35N 61.50W
Orinoco Delta Venezuela 72 C7 ..9.22N 60.44W
Orissa d. India 96 F5 ....20.57N 84.15E
Oristano Italy 50 C3 ....39.55N 8.35E
Oristano, Golfo di b. Italy 50 C3 ..39.49N 8.30E
Orivesi l. Finland 40 G3 ....62.14N 29.27E
Orizaba Mexico 70 E4 ....18.53N 97.06W
Örkelljunga Sweden 54 E7 ....56.17N 13.17E
Orkney d. Scotland 8 D6 ....58.59N 2.42W
Orkney Islands Scotland 19 F4 ...59.06N 3.20W
Orlando U.S.A. 65 J2 ....28.31N 81.21W
Orléans France 44 D5 ....47.55N 1.54E
Ormoc Phil. 105 G6 ....11.00N 124.37E
Ormskirk England 14 E2 ....53.34N 2.53W
Orne r. France 44 C5 ....49.16N 0.14W
Örnsköldsvik Sweden 40 D3 .....63.18N 18.43E
Oromīya d. Ethiopia 87 B5 ......9.03N 37.33E
Oronsay i. Scotland 16 C4 ....56.01N 6.12W
Orosei Italy 50 C4 ....40.23N 9.42E
Orosei, Golfo di b. Italy 50 C4 ...40.15N 9.44E
Orsha Belarus 55 N6 ....54.30N 30.26E
Orsk Rus. Fed. 58 G3 ....51.07N 58.33E
Orşova Romania 56 E7 ....44.42N 22.25E
Oruro Bolivia 76 G4 ....17.59S 67.09W
Osa, Península de pen. Costa Rica 71 H2 ..8.34N 83.32W
Ōsaka Japan 106 C2 ....34.42N 135.30E
Oshakati Namibia 86 A3 ....17.45S 15.43E
Oshawa Canada 63 K2 ....43.54N 78.51W
O-shima i. Japan 106 C2 ....34.44N 139.28E
Osijek Croatia 56 C7 ....45.35N 18.42E
Ösjön l. Sweden 40 C3 ....63.06N 13.04E
Oskarshamn Sweden 40 D2 .....57.16N 16.26E
Oslo Norway 40 B2 ....59.55N 10.45E
Osmancık Turkey 57 K5 ....40.58N 34.48E
Osmaniye Turkey 57 L3 ....37.04N 36.15E
Osnabrück Germany 54 C5 ......52.17N 8.04E
Osorno Chile 73 B2 ....40.35S 73.09W
Osorno Spain 48 C5 ....42.24N 4.21W
Oss Neth. 42 E4 ....51.45N 5.32E
Ossa, Mount Australia 110 D2 ...41.56S 146.12E
Ostend Belgium 42 B4 ....51.13N 2.55E
Österdalälven l. Sweden 40 C3 ..61.40N 13.15E
Österdalen r. Norway 40 B3 .....61.51N 11.20E
Östersund Sweden 40 C3 ....63.11N 14.39E
Ostrava Czech Rep. 54 H3 ......49.51N 18.17E
Ostróda Poland 46 D4 ....53.42N 19.59E
Ostrov Rus. Fed. 58 D3 ....57.21N 28.21E
Ostrowiec Świętokrzyski Poland 46 E3 ..50.57N 21.23E
Ostrów Mazowiecka Poland 46 E4 ..52.48N 21.53E
Ostrów Wielkopolski Poland 46 C3 ..51.39N 17.49E
Ostrzeszów Poland 54 G4 ......51.25N 17.56E
Osūm r. Bulgaria 56 F6 ....43.42N 24.50E
Osumi-kaikyo str. Japan 106 B2 ..30.50N 130.52E
Ōsumi-shotō is Japan 106 B2 ...30.32N 130.36E
Osuna Spain 48 C2 ....37.14N 5.06W
Oswestry England 10 B3 ....52.51N 3.03W
Otaru Japan 106 D4 ....43.12N 140.59E
Otjiwarongo Namibia 86 A2 ....20.28S 16.40E

Otley England 15 F2 ....53.54N 1.41W
Otranto Italy 50 H4 ....40.09N 18.29E
Otranto, Strait of Albania/Italy 56 C5 ..40.36N 18.45E
Otta Norway 40 B3 ....61.46N 9.32E
Ottawa Canada 63 K2 ....45.25N 75.43W
Ottawa r. Canada 63 K2 ....45.28N 74.11W
Ottawa Islands Canada 63 J3 ...59.57N 80.12W
Otter r. England 13 D2 ....50.38N 3.18W
Otterburn England 15 E4 ....55.14N 2.10W
Ottery r. England 13 C2 ....50.39N 4.20W
Ottignies Belgium 42 D3 ....50.39N 4.34E
Otukpo Nigeria 84 E2 ....7.13N 8.08E
Ouachita r. U.S.A. 65 H3 ....31.50N 91.49W
Ouagadougou Burkina 84 D3 ....12.22N 1.31W
Ouargla Algeria 84 E5 ....31.59N 5.20E
Ouarzazate Morocco 84 D5 .....30.56N 6.53W
Oudenaarde Belgium 42 C3 .....50.51N 3.36E
Ouessa Congo 84 F2 ....1.36N 16.03E
Ouezzane Morocco 52 B3 ....34.46N 5.35W
Oughter, Lough l. Ireland 41 D4 ..54.01N 7.28W
Ouistreham France 44 C6 ....49.17N 0.15W
Oujda Morocco 84 D5 ....34.44N 1.55W
Oulainen Finland 40 F4 ....64.16N 24.47E
Oulton England 11 G3 ....52.30N 1.41E
Oulu Finland 40 F4 ....65.01N 25.28E
Oulujärvi l. Finland 40 F4 ....64.17N 27.14E
Oundle England 11 E3 ....52.29N 0.28W
Oupeye Belgium 42 E3 ....50.42N 5.38E
Ourense Spain 48 B5 ....42.21N 7.52W
Ouse r. E. Sussex England 11 F1 ..50.48N 0.03E
Ouse r. E. Yorks. England 15 G2 ..53.44N 0.55W
Outer Hebrides is Scotland 18 B2 ..57.53N 7.15W
Outokumpu Finland 40 G3 .....62.43N 29.02E
Out Skerries is Scotland 19 I5 ...60.26N 0.46W
Ovamboland f. Namibia 86 A3 ..17.50S 17.32E
Overijssel d. Neth. 42 F5 ....52.25N 6.30E
Overton Wales 12 E4 ....52.58N 2.56W
Övertorneå Sweden 40 E4 .....66.24N 23.40E
Oviedo Spain 48 C5 ....43.22N 5.50W
Ovruch Ukraine 55 M4 ....51.20N 28.48E
Owando Congo 84 F1 ....0.29S 15.54E
Owen Stanley Range mts P.N.G. 110 D6 ..8.59S 147.30E
Owyhee r. U.S.A. 64 C5 ....43.48N 117.01W
Öxarfjörður b. Iceland 40 Y2 ...66.12N 16.50W
Oxelösund Sweden 40 D2 ......58.40N 17.10E
Oxford England 10 D2 ....51.45N 1.16W
Oxfordshire d. England 9 E2 ...51.54N 1.10W
Oxnard U.S.A. 64 C3 ....34.12N 119.11W
Oxted England 11 F2 ....51.16N 0.00
Oyama Japan 106 C3 ....36.18N 139.49E
Oykel r. Scotland 18 E2 ....57.55N 4.26W
Ozark Plateau f. U.S.A. 65 H4 ..36.58N 93.23W
Ozarks, Lake of the U.S.A. 65 H4 ..38.14N 93.23W
Ózd Hungary 54 I3 ....48.13N 20.18E
Ozernovskiy Rus. Fed. 59 Q3 ...51.30N 156.31E

P

Paamiut Greenland 63 N4 ......62.01N 49.39W
Pabbay i. W. Isles Scotland 18 B1 ..56.51N 7.35W
Pabbay i. W. Isles Scotland 18 B2 ..57.46N 7.14W
Pabianice Poland 46 D3 ....51.40N 19.22E
Pacasmayo Peru 76 E6 ....7.26S 79.33W
Pachuca Mexico 70 E5 ....20.09N 98.44W
Pacific Ocean 108
Paczków Poland 46 C3 ....50.28N 17.00E
Padang Indonesia 104 C3 ......0.58S 100.21E
Paderborn Germany 54 C4 .....51.43N 8.46E
Padiham England 15 E2 ....53.48N 2.19W
Padre Island U.S.A. 64 G2 .....26.57N 97.24W
Padstow England 13 C2 ....50.32N 4.55W
Padua Italy 50 D6 ....45.24N 11.53E
Pag i. Croatia 56 A7 ....44.31N 14.58E
Pagadian Phil. 105 G5 ....7.50N 123.29E
Pagai Selatan i. Indonesia 104 C3 ..2.58S 100.25E
Pagai Utara i. Indonesia 104 C3 ..2.36S 100.12E
Pagan i. N. Mariana Is 108 F7 ...18.08N 145.46E
Page U.S.A. 64 D4 ....36.55N 111.29W
Paget, Mount S. Atlantic Oc. 73 F1 ..54.23S 36.40W
Paignton England 13 D2 ....50.26N 3.33W
Päijänne l. Finland 40 F3 ......61.30N 25.32E
Painswick England 10 C2 ......51.47N 2.12W
Paisley Scotland 16 E3 ....55.51N 4.26W
Pakanbaru Indonesia 104 C4 ...0.34N 101.27E
Pakaraima Mountains S. America 71 L1 ..3.47N 63.42W
Pakistan Asia 96 C6 ....28.01N 64.47E
Pakokku Myanmar 97 I5 ....21.21N 95.06E
Pakxé Laos 104 D7 ....15.04N 105.50E
Palana Rus. Fed. 59 Q3 ....59.05N 159.55E
Palangkaraya Indonesia 104 E3 ..2.18S 113.56E
Palatka Rus. Fed. 59 Q4 ....60.08N 150.53E
Palau N. Pacific Oc. 105 I5 .....7.23N 134.32E
Palawan i. Phil. 104 F5 ....8.50N 117.40E
Palawan Trough f. N. Pacific Oc. 108 D6 ..7.53N 116.29E
Palembang Indonesia 104 C3 ..2.59S 104.45E
Palencia Spain 48 C5 ....42.01N 4.32W
Palermo Italy 50 E3 ....38.07N 13.22E
Pali India 96 D5 ....25.46N 73.19E
Palikir Micronesia 108 G6 ......6.55N 158.09E
Palk Strait India/Sri Lanka 96 E2 ..9.36N 79.29E
Pallisa Uganda 87 A3 ....1.10N 33.41E
Palma de Mallorca Spain 48 G3 ..39.35N 2.40E
Palmas, Cape Liberia 84 D2 ....4.22N 7.44W
Palmerston atoll Cook Is 108 J4 ..18.01S 163.02W
Palmerston North New Zealand 111 G2 ..40.22S 175.39E
Palmi Italy 50 F3 ....38.21N 15.51E
Palmira Colombia 72 B7 ......3.31N 76.19W
Palmyra Atoll N. Pacific Oc. 108 J6 ..5.51N 162.06W
Palopo Indonesia 104 G3 .....3.01S 120.11E
Palos, Cabo de c. Spain 48 E2 ..37.37N 0.42W
Palu Indonesia 104 F3 ....0.54S 119.51E
Pamiers France 44 D3 ....43.07N 1.36E
Pamir mts Asia 95 L7 ....38.39N 72.47E
Pampas f. Argentina 73 C3 .....36.23S 64.00W
Pamplona Spain 48 E5 ....42.49N 1.39W
Panagyurishte Bulgaria 56 F6 ...42.30N 24.11E
Panaji India 96 D4 ....15.30N 73.51E
Panama Central America 71 H2 ..8.22N 81.31W
Panama, Gulf of Panama 71 I2 ...7.38N 79.11W
Panama, Isthmus of f. C. America 60 K3 ..9.00N 80.00W
Panama Canal Panama 71 I2 ....9.07N 79.44W
Panamá City U.S.A. 65 I3 ......30.10N 85.44W
Panamá City Panama 71 I2 .....8.59N 79.32W
Panay i. Phil. 105 G6 ....11.10N 122.34E
Pančevo Serbia 56 D7 ....44.52N 20.38E
Panevėžys Lithuania 40 F1 .....55.44N 24.21E
Pangani Tanzania 87 B1 ....5.29S 38.59E
Pangkalanbuun Indonesia 104 E3 ..2.40S 111.37E
Pangkalpinang Indonesia 104 D3 ..2.05S 106.07E
Pangnirtung Canada 63 L4 .....66.03N 65.45W
Panjgur Pakistan 95 J5 ....26.58N 64.06E
Pantanal f. Brazil 77 I4 ....18.00S 57.04W

elleria, Isola di i. Italy 50 E2 ......36.47N 12.04E
hihua China 103 I3 ......26.35N 101.43E
a Italy 50 G3 ......39.21N 16.03E
Stour i. England 19 H5 ......60.21N 1.42W
Westray i. Scotland 19 G4 ......59.22N 2.52W
ete French Polynesia 109 K4 ......17.30S 149.31W
nburg Germany 42 G6 ......53.05N 7.24E
os Cyprus 57 J2 ......34.47N 32.25E
a, Gulf of P.N.G. 110 D6 ......8.34S 144.45E
a New Guinea Oceania 110 D6 ......6.05S 146.34E
England 13 C2 ......50.21N 4.42W
d. Brazil 77 J7 ......3.46S 51.57W
cel Islands S. China Sea 104 E7 ......16.46N 112.39E
gua r. Bolivia 77 I3 ......13.31S 61.50W
guai r. Brazil 77 I3 ......22.06S 57.57W
guay r. Argentina/Paraguay 73 D4 ......27.12S 58.39W
guay S. America 77 I3 ......22.45S 58.44W
íba d. Brazil 77 M6 ......7.06S 36.43W
kou Benin 84 E2 ......9.22N 2.36E
maribo Suriname 72 D7 ......5.51N 55.17W
ná r. Argentina 77 I3 ......31.44S 60.31W
ná d. Brazil 77 J3 ......24.50S 51.01W
ná r. Brazil 77 J3 ......12.31S 48.12W
ná r. S. America 77 I1 ......33.52S 59.12W
naguá Brazil 77 K2 ......25.32S 48.33W
naíba r. Brazil 77 K2 ......20.04S 51.00W
napanema r. Brazil 77 J3 ......22.36S 53.01W
napiacaba, Serra mts Brazil 77 J3 ......24.58S 50.21W
ngul Mare, Vârful mt. Romania 56 E7 ......45.21N 23.33E
to r. Bahia Brazil 77 M4 ......15.41S 38.59W
to r. Mato Grosso do Sul Brazil 77 J3 ......21.39S 52.14W
ubice Czech Rep. 54 F4 ......50.02N 15.47E
ecis, Serra dos hills Brazil 77 H5 ......11.28S 63.12W
epare Indonesia 40 F2 ......4.01S 119.40E
a, Península de pen. Venezuela 71 L3 ......10.43N 62.58W
ma, Serra mts Brazil 71 L1 ......2.57N 64.15W
ntins Brazil 77 I7 ......2.38S 56.46W
France 44 E6 ......48.52N 2.12E
na Italy 50 D6 ......44.48N 10.19E
naíba Brazil 77 L7 ......2.56S 41.45W
naíba r. Brazil 77 L7 ......3.02S 41.51W
Estonia 40 F2 ......58.23N 24.30E
pamisus mts Afgh. 95 J7 ......35.06N 61.20E
os i. Greece 56 F3 ......37.06N 25.08E
ett r. England 13 B2 ......50.18N 3.00W
y, Cape Canada 63 F5 ......70.12N 124.31W
y Islands Canada 62 G5 ......76.50N 111.03W
seta r. Poland 46 B5 ......54.11N 15.34E
chenay France 44 C5 ......46.39N 0.15W
try Mountains hills Ireland 41 B3 ......53.36N 9.39W
u r. Brazil 77 J7 ......1.31S 52.41W
adena U.S.A. 64 C3 ......34.11N 118.08W
ado, Cabo c. Ecuador 76 D7 ......0.22S 80.28W
cani Romania 55 L2 ......47.15N 26.44E
ewalk Germany 46 B4 ......53.30N 14.00E
eka r. Poland 46 E3 ......51.24N 19.46E
ni Pakistan 95 J5 ......25.13N 63.31E
sau Germany 54 E3 ......48.34N 13.25E
sero, Capo c. Italy 50 F2 ......36.40N 15.08E
so Fundo Brazil 77 J2 ......28.18S 52.24W
tavy Belarus 55 M6 ......55.07N 26.50E
taza r. Peru 76 E7 ......4.56S 76.24W
to Colombia 72 B7 ......1.11N 77.17W
valys Lithuania 46 G6 ......56.03N 24.25E
agonia f. Argentina 73 B1 ......51.44S 71.19W
chway England 10 C2 ......51.32N 2.34W
e Island Kenya 87 C2 ......2.06S 41.08W
erson U.S.A. 65 L5 ......40.54N 74.09W
na India 96 G6 ......25.35N 85.16E
os Albania 56 D5 ......40.40N 19.39E
os, Lagoa dos l. Brazil 77 J1 ......30.39S 50.58W
os de Minas Brazil 77 K4 ......18.36S 46.30W
quía Argentina 76 G1 ......30.03S 66.53W
raïkos Kolpos b. Greece 56 D4 ......38.15N 21.26E
ras Greece 56 D4 ......38.14N 21.45E
rington England 15 G2 ......53.41N 0.01W
u France 44 C3 ......43.18N 0.22W
ulo Afonso Brazil 77 M6 ......9.20S 38.13W
via Italy 50 C6 ......45.11N 9.09E
vlodar Kazakhstan 58 I3 ......52.18N 77.02E
vlohrad Ukraine 55 P3 ......48.31N 35.53E
vlovskaya Rus. Fed. 53 K6 ......46.09N 39.47E
vapon Myanmar 97 I4 ......16.16N 95.41E
ysandú Uruguay 73 D3 ......32.19S 58.05W
zardzhik Bulgaria 56 F6 ......42.12N 24.20E
ace r. Canada 62 G3 ......58.54N 111.50W
acehaven England 11 E1 ......50.48N 0.00W
ace River town Canada 62 G3 ......56.15N 117.17W
ak, Mount U.S.A. 64 E4 ......38.26N 109.13W
arl r. U.S.A. 65 I3 ......30.10N 89.37W
r Serbia 56 D6 ......42.39N 20.17E
chora r. Rus. Fed. 58 G4 ......68.13N 53.54E
cos U.S.A. 64 F3 ......31.23N 103.30W
cos U.S.A. 65 I3 ......29.50N 101.28W
cs Hungary 54 H2 ......46.05N 18.13E
dro Juan Caballero Paraguay 77 I3 ......22.29S 55.44W
ebles Scotland 17 F3 ......55.39N 3.12W
el r. Canada 62 E4 ......68.03N 134.26W
el Isle of Man 14 C3 ......54.13N 4.41W
gasus Bay New Zealand 111 G2 ......43.20S 172.49E
gu Myanmar 97 I4 ......17.18N 96.28E
gwell Bay England 11 G2 ......51.19N 1.21E
ipus, Lake Estonia/Rus. Fed. 40 F2 ......58.38N 27.28E
kalongan Indonesia 104 D2 ......6.54S 109.38E
lat, Mont mt. France 44 G4 ......44.16N 6.43E
leng i. Indonesia 105 G3 ......1.15S 123.29E
llo Finland 40 F4 ......66.47N 23.59E
lotas Brazil 77 J1 ......31.46S 52.19W
lotas, Rio das r. Brazil 73 D4 ......27.35S 51.24W
mba Mozambique 86 D3 ......12.59S 40.32E
mba Zambia 86 B3 ......16.33S 27.22E
mba Channel Tanzania 87 B1 ......5.33S 39.19E
mba Island Tanzania 86 C4 ......5.25S 39.46E
mbrey Wales 12 C3 ......51.41N 4.17W
mbroke Canada 65 K6 ......45.49N 77.06W
mbroke Wales 12 C3 ......51.40N 4.55W
mbroke Dock Wales 12 C3 ......51.41N 4.57W
mbrokeshire d. Wales 9 C2 ......51.55N 4.48W
mbury England 15 F2 ......51.01N 1.09W
ñalara mt. Spain 48 D4 ......40.51N 3.56W
ña Nevada, Cerro mt. Mexico 70 E5 ......23.46N 99.50W
ñaranda de Bracamonte Spain 48 C4 ......40.55N 5.11W
narth Wales 13 D3 ......51.26N 3.10W
nas, Golfo de g. Chile 73 B2 ......47.18S 75.35W
ndine Wales 12 C3 ......51.45N 4.34W
ndlebury England 10 C2 ......53.30N 2.19W
ndle Hill England 15 E2 ......53.52N 2.18W
ndleton U.S.A. 64 C6 ......45.39N 118.48W
nicuik Scotland 17 F3 ......55.50N 3.13W
ninsular Malaysia Malaysia 104 C4 ......3.59N 102.43E
nkridge England 10 C3 ......52.43N 2.07W
nnines hills England 15 E3 ......54.23N 2.18W

Pennsylvania d. U.S.A. 65 K5 ......41.18N 78.00W
Penny Icecap Canada 63 L4 ......67.10N 66.02W
Penrhyn atoll Cook Is 109 J5 ......8.58S 157.53W
Penrhyn Basin f. S. Pacific Oc. 109 J5 ......7.12S 157.13W
Penrhyn Mawr pt Wales 12 C4 ......52.51N 4.43W
Penrith England 14 E3 ......54.40N 2.45W
Penryn England 13 B2 ......50.10N 5.06W
Pensacola U.S.A. 65 I3 ......30.27N 87.13W
Penticton Canada 64 C6 ......49.30N 119.35W
Pentire Point England 13 B2 ......50.35N 5.00W
Pentland Firth str. Scotland 19 F3 ......58.43N 3.16W
Pentland Hills Scotland 17 F3 ......55.43N 3.30W
Pentland Skerries is Scotland 19 G3 ......58.41N 2.54W
Penygadair hill Wales 12 C4 ......52.42N 3.55W
Pen-y-Ghent hill England 15 E3 ......54.10N 2.15W
Penza Rus. Fed. 58 F3 ......53.12N 45.01E
Penzance England 13 B2 ......50.07N 5.32W
Penzhinskaya Guba b. Rus. Fed. 59 R4 ......62.05N 163.30E
Peoria U.S.A. 65 I5 ......40.41N 89.37W
Pereira Colombia 72 B7 ......4.45N 75.41W
Peremyshlyany Ukraine 46 G2 ......49.40N 24.34E
Périgueux France 44 D4 ......45.11N 0.43E
Perija, Sierra de mts Venezuela 71 J2 ......9.09N 73.12W
Perito Moreno Argentina 73 B2 ......46.36S 71.02W
Perlas, Punta de pt Nicaragua 71 H3 ......12.24N 83.31W
Perm' Rus. Fed. 58 G3 ......58.01N 56.14E
Pernambuco d. Brazil 77 M6 ......8.23S 37.51W
Pernik Bulgaria 56 E6 ......42.36N 23.02E
Péronne France 42 B2 ......49.56N 2.56E
Perpignan France 44 E3 ......42.42N 2.54E
Perranporth England 13 B2 ......50.21N 5.09W
Pershore England 10 C3 ......52.07N 2.04W
Perth Australia 110 A3 ......31.56S 115.47E
Perth Scotland 17 F4 ......56.24N 3.26W
Perth and Kinross d. Scotland 8 C5 ......56.37N 4.07W
Perth Basin f. Indian Oc. 108 D4 ......29.52S 109.00E
Peru S. America 76 E7 ......5.50S 77.14W
Peru-Chile Trench f. S. Pacific Oc. 109 O5 ......9.16S 81.56W
Perugia Italy 50 E5 ......43.07N 12.23E
Pervomays'k Ukraine 55 N3 ......48.03N 30.51E
Pesaro Italy 50 E5 ......43.55N 12.53E
Pescara Italy 50 F5 ......42.27N 14.12E
Pescara r. Italy 50 F5 ......42.28N 14.13E
Pesebre, Punta pt Canary Islands 48 Y2 ......28.07N 14.29W
Peshawar Pakistan 96 D7 ......34.01N 71.40E
Peshkopi Albania 56 D5 ......41.41N 20.26E
Peterborough Canada 63 K2 ......44.18N 78.20W
Peterborough England 11 E3 ......52.34N 0.14W
Peterborough d. England 9 E3 ......52.36N 0.16W
Peterhead Scotland 19 H2 ......57.31N 1.47W
Peterlee England 15 F3 ......54.46N 1.20W
Petersfield England 10 E2 ......51.00N 0.56W
Petersville U.S.A. 62 C4 ......62.33N 150.50W
Petit Mécatina r. Canada 63 M3 ......50.40N 59.25W
Petra Velikogo, Zaliv b. Rus. Fed. 106 B4 ......42.41N 131.50E
Petrich Bulgaria 56 E5 ......41.24N 23.12E
Petrolina Brazil 77 L6 ......9.22S 40.25W
Petropavlovsk Kazakhstan 58 H3 ......54.51N 69.06E
Petropavlovsk-Kamchatskiy Rus. Fed. 59 Q3 ......53.01N 158.44E
Petroşani Romania 56 E7 ......45.25N 23.23E
Petrozavodsk Rus. Fed. 58 E4 ......61.48N 34.19E
Petworth England 11 E1 ......50.59N 0.36W
Pevensey England 11 F1 ......50.49N 0.21E
Pewsey England 10 D2 ......51.20N 1.46W
Pforzheim Germany 54 C3 ......48.53N 8.42E
Phan Thiết Vietnam 104 D6 ......10.55N 108.06E
Phatthalung Thailand 104 C5 ......7.39N 100.06E
Phayao Thailand 104 B7 ......19.10N 99.57E
Phet Buri Thailand 104 B6 ......13.06N 99.56E
Philadelphia U.S.A. 65 K4 ......39.57N 75.10W
Philippeville Belgium 42 D3 ......50.12N 4.33E
Philippine Basin f. N. Pacific Oc. 108 E7 ......16.41N 126.12E
Philippines Asia 105 G6 ......15.36N 122.55E
Philippine Trench f. N. Pacific Oc. 108 E6 ......15.40N 123.45E
Phitsanulok Thailand 104 C7 ......16.50N 100.18E
Phnom Penh Cambodia 104 C6 ......11.33N 104.57E
Phoenix U.S.A. 64 D3 ......33.31N 112.07W
Phoenix Islands Kiribati 108 I5 ......2.43S 173.22W
Phôngsali Laos 104 C8 ......21.41N 102.08E
Phrae Thailand 104 C7 ......18.07N 100.12E
Phuket Thailand 104 B5 ......7.53N 98.23E
Piacenza Italy 50 C6 ......45.03N 9.42E
Pianosa, Isola i. Italy 50 D5 ......42.34N 10.06E
Piatra Neamţ Romania 55 L2 ......46.56N 26.22E
Piauí d. Brazil 77 L6 ......7.39S 42.52W
Piave r. Italy 50 E6 ......45.32N 12.44E
Picardie d. France 42 B2 ......49.42N 2.54E
Picardy f. France 44 D6 ......49.47N 1.35E
Pichanal Argentina 76 H3 ......23.18S 64.11W
Pickering England 15 G3 ......54.15N 0.47W
Pickering, Vale of f. England 15 G3 ......54.13N 0.45W
Piedras Negras Mexico 70 D6 ......28.40N 100.34W
Pieksämäki Finland 40 F3 ......62.18N 27.10E
Pielinen l. Finland 40 G3 ......63.14N 29.41E
Pierre U.S.A. 64 F5 ......44.23N 100.23W
Pietermaritzburg S. Africa 86 C2 ......29.36S 30.23E
Pietrosa mt. Romania 55 K2 ......47.34N 24.41E
Pihlajavesi l. Finland 40 G3 ......61.45N 28.46E
Pijijiapan Mexico 70 F4 ......15.46N 93.14W
Piła Poland 46 C4 ......53.09N 16.45E
Pilar Paraguay 77 I2 ......26.49S 58.19W
Pilcomayo r. Bolivia/Paraguay 77 I2 ......25.18S 57.43W
Pilica r. Poland 46 E3 ......51.52N 21.17E
Pimperne England 10 C1 ......50.53N 2.08W
Pinang i. Malaysia 104 C5 ......5.21N 100.11E
Pinar del Río Cuba 71 H5 ......22.25N 83.43W
Píncźow Poland 46 E3 ......50.31N 20.32E
Pindaré r. Brazil 77 L7 ......3.17S 44.50W
Pindus Mountains Greece 56 D4 ......39.56N 20.56E
Pine Bluff U.S.A. 65 H3 ......34.16N 92.02W
Pinega Rus. Fed. 58 F4 ......64.41N 43.24E
Pineios r. Greece 56 E4 ......39.53N 22.43E
Pinerolo Italy 50 B6 ......44.53N 7.20E
Pingdingshan China 103 K4 ......33.45N 113.18E
Pingxiang Guangxi China 103 J2 ......22.03N 106.50E
Pingxiang Jiangxi China 103 K3 ......27.42N 113.52E
Pinsk Belarus 55 L5 ......52.08N 26.06E
Pionki Poland 46 E3 ......51.29N 21.28E
Piotrków Trybunalski Poland 46 D3 ......51.25N 19.41E
Pipmuacan, Réservoir Canada 65 L6 ......49.37N 70.33W
Piracicaba Brazil 77 K3 ......22.44S 47.38W
Piraeus Greece 56 E3 ......37.56N 23.38E
Pirot Serbia 56 E6 ......43.09N 22.34E
Pisa Italy 50 D5 ......43.42N 10.24E
Pisco Peru 76 E5 ......13.43S 76.12W
Písek Czech Rep. 54 F3 ......49.19N 14.10E
Pisuerga r. Spain 48 C4 ......41.34N 4.50W
Pisz Poland 46 E4 ......53.38N 21.48E
Pitcairn Island S. Pacific Oc. 109 L4 ......25.03S 130.06W
Pitcairn Islands S. Pacific Oc. 109 L4 ......23.55S 126.51W
Piteå Sweden 40 E4 ......65.19N 21.30E
Piteşti Romania 56 F7 ......44.52N 24.53E
Pitlochry Scotland 19 F1 ......56.42N 3.44W

Pittsburgh U.S.A. 65 K5 ......40.26N 79.59W
Piz Bernina mt. Italy/Switz. 50 C7 ......46.23N 9.54E
Plasencia Spain 48 B4 ......40.02N 6.05W
Platinum U.S.A. 62 B3 ......58.59N 161.48W
Platte r. U.S.A. 64 G5 ......41.04N 95.53W
Plauen Germany 54 E4 ......50.30N 12.08E
Plavsk Rus. Fed. 55 Q5 ......53.42N 37.18E
Plenty, Bay of g. New Zealand 111 G3 ......37.37S 176.59E
Pleven Bulgaria 56 F6 ......43.25N 24.37E
Płock Poland 46 D4 ......52.33N 19.43E
Pločno mt. Bos.-Herz. 56 B6 ......43.36N 17.35E
Ploieşti Romania 56 G7 ......44.56N 26.02E
Plomb du Cantal mt. France 44 E4 ......45.03N 2.46E
Płoty Poland 46 B4 ......53.49N 15.16E
Plovdiv Bulgaria 56 F6 ......42.10N 24.44E
Plungė Lithuania 46 E5 ......55.55N 21.51E
Plymouth England 13 C2 ......50.22N 4.08W
Plymouth d. England 9 C2 ......50.24N 4.08W
Plympton England 13 C2 ......50.23N 4.03W
Plymstock England 13 C2 ......50.21N 4.06W
Plynlimon hill Wales 12 C4 ......52.28N 3.47W
Plzeň Czech Rep. 54 E3 ......49.45N 13.23E
Pô Burkina 84 D3 ......11.12N 1.08W
Po r. Italy 50 E6 ......45.02N 12.11E
Pobeda, Gora mt. Rus. Fed. 59 P4 ......65.12N 145.54E
Pocatello U.S.A. 64 D5 ......42.54N 112.25W
Pochep Rus. Fed. 55 O5 ......52.56N 33.27E
Pocklington England 15 G2 ......53.56N 0.47W
Poços de Caldas Brazil 77 K3 ......21.48S 46.31W
Podgorica Montenegro 56 C6 ......42.26N 19.16E
Podkamennaya Tunguska r. Rus. Fed. 59 K4 ......61.36N 90.08E
Podol'sk Rus. Fed. 55 Q6 ......55.25N 37.34E
P'ohang S. Korea 106 A3 ......36.01N 129.22E
Pohnpei atoll Micronesia 108 G6 ......6.53N 158.22E
Pointe-à-Pitre Guadeloupe 72 C8 ......16.15N 61.32W
Pointe-Noire Congo 84 F1 ......4.44S 11.53E
Poitiers France 44 D5 ......46.35N 0.20E
Pokaran India 96 D6 ......26.53N 71.57E
Poland Europe 46 D4 ......52.07N 19.27E
Polatlı Turkey 57 J4 ......39.35N 32.08E
Polatsk Belarus 55 M6 ......55.29N 28.47E
Polegate England 11 F1 ......50.49N 0.15E
Pol-e Khomrī Afgh. 95 K7 ......35.56N 68.46E
Policastro, Golfo di b. Italy 50 F4 ......39.57N 15.33E
Police Poland 46 B4 ......53.33N 14.35E
Polis Cyprus 57 J2 ......35.01N 32.25E
Polkowice Poland 46 C3 ......51.30N 16.04E
Pollaphuca Reservoir Ireland 41 E3 ......53.08N 6.30W
Pollino, Monte mt. Italy 50 G3 ......39.54N 16.12E
Polokwane S. Africa 86 B2 ......23.54S 29.27E
Polperro England 13 C2 ......50.20N 4.31W
Poltava Ukraine 55 P3 ......49.36N 34.34E
Polygyros Greece 56 E5 ......40.23N 23.27E
Polykastro Greece 56 E5 ......40.59N 22.34E
Polynesia is Pacific Oc. 108 I6 ......8.00S 170.00E
Pombal Portugal 48 A3 ......39.55N 8.37W
Ponce Puerto Rico 71 K4 ......18.00N 66.37W
Pondicherry India 96 E3 ......11.57N 79.48E
Ponferrada Spain 48 B5 ......42.33N 6.36W
Ponta do Sol Cape Verde 84 B3 ......17.10N 25.05W
Ponta Grossa Brazil 77 J2 ......25.03S 50.07W
Pont-à-Mousson France 42 F1 ......48.54N 6.03E
Pontardawe Wales 12 D3 ......51.43N 3.51W
Pontefract England 15 F2 ......53.41N 1.18W
Ponteland England 15 F4 ......55.03N 1.44W
Pontevedra Spain 48 A5 ......42.27N 8.37W
Pontianak Indonesia 104 D3 ......0.03S 109.18E
Pontine Islands Italy 50 E4 ......40.56N 12.59E
Pontoise France 44 E6 ......49.03N 2.06E
Pont-Ste-Maxence France 42 B2 ......49.18N 2.37E
Pontycymer Wales 12 D3 ......51.37N 3.35W
Pontypool Wales 12 D3 ......51.42N 3.02W
Pontypridd Wales 12 D3 ......51.36N 3.20W
Poole England 10 D1 ......50.43N 1.59W
Poole d. England 9 E2 ......50.44N 1.57W
Poole Bay England 10 D1 ......50.40N 1.55W
Pooley Bridge England 14 E3 ......54.37N 2.49W
Poopó, Lago de l. Bolivia 76 G4 ......18.50S 67.05W
Popayán Colombia 76 E8 ......2.24N 76.37W
Popigay r. Rus. Fed. 59 L5 ......72.56N 106.10E
Poplar Bluff U.S.A. 65 H4 ......36.47N 90.23W
Popocatépetl, Volcán vol. Mexico 70 E4 ......19.02N 98.38W
Poprad Slovakia 54 I3 ......49.04N 20.18E
Porbandar India 96 C5 ......21.39N 69.40E
Pori Finland 40 E3 ......61.29N 21.48E
Porlock England 13 D3 ......51.13N 3.36W
Poronaysk Rus. Fed. 59 P2 ......49.16N 143.03E
Porsangerfjorden str. Norway 40 F5 ......70.19N 25.18E
Porsangerhalvøya pen. Norway 40 F5 ......70.45N 25.01E
Porsgrunn Norway 40 B2 ......59.08N 9.39E
Porsuk r. Turkey 57 I4 ......39.41N 31.58E
Portadown Northern Ireland 16 C2 ......54.25N 6.26W
Portaferry Northern Ireland 16 D2 ......54.23N 5.32W
Portage la Prairie Canada 62 I2 ......49.58N 98.19W
Portalegre Portugal 48 B3 ......39.18N 7.25W
Port Angeles U.S.A. 64 B6 ......48.06N 123.25W
Port Arthur U.S.A. 65 H2 ......29.53N 93.58W
Port Askaig Scotland 16 C3 ......55.51N 6.06W
Port Augusta Australia 110 C3 ......32.29S 137.45E
Port-au-Prince Haiti 71 J4 ......18.33N 72.19W
Portavogie Northern Ireland 16 D2 ......54.27N 5.26W
Port Blair India 97 H3 ......11.41N 92.42E
Port-de-Paix Haiti 71 J4 ......19.57N 72.50W
Port Elizabeth S. Africa 86 B1 ......33.57S 25.37E
Port Ellen Scotland 16 C3 ......55.38N 6.11W
Port Erin Isle of Man 14 C3 ......54.05N 4.45W
Port-Gentil Gabon 84 E1 ......0.46S 8.49E
Port Glasgow Scotland 16 E3 ......55.56N 4.41W
Port Harcourt Nigeria 84 E2 ......4.46N 7.01E
Porthcawl Wales 13 D3 ......51.29N 3.42W
Port Hedland Australia 110 A4 ......20.23S 118.37E
Porthleven England 13 B2 ......50.05N 5.19W
Porthmadog Wales 12 C4 ......52.56N 4.08W
Portimão Portugal 48 A2 ......37.08N 8.32W
Port Isaac Bay England 13 C2 ......50.36N 4.50W
Portishead England 10 C2 ......51.29N 2.46W
Portknockie Scotland 19 G2 ......57.42N 2.51W
Portland Australia 110 D3 ......38.21S 141.34E
Portland Me. U.S.A. 65 L5 ......43.41N 70.17W
Portland Oreg. U.S.A. 64 B6 ......45.29N 122.38W
Portland, Isle of pen. England 10 C1 ......50.33N 2.25W
Portlaoise Ireland 41 D3 ......53.02N 7.17W
Portlethen Scotland 19 G2 ......57.04N 2.08W
Port Lincoln Australia 110 C3 ......34.43S 135.49E
Port Macquarie Australia 110 E3 ......31.25S 152.53E
Portnahaven Scotland 16 C3 ......55.40N 6.31W
Port Ness Scotland 18 C3 ......58.30N 6.14W
Porto Alegre Brazil 77 J1 ......30.03S 51.11W
Porto Esperidião Brazil 77 I4 ......15.50S 58.32W
Port of Spain Trinidad and Tobago 71 L3 ......10.37N 61.30W
Portogruaro Italy 50 E6 ......45.46N 12.50E

Porto-Novo Benin 84 E2 ......6.30N 2.40E
Porto Primavera, Represa resr Brazil 77 J3 ......21.27S 52.03W
Porto Santana Brazil 77 J7 ......0.01S 51.09W
Porto Torres Italy 50 C4 ......40.50N 8.25E
Porto-Vecchio France 44 H2 ......41.35N 9.16E
Porto Velho Brazil 76 H6 ......8.47S 63.54W
Portoviejo Ecuador 76 D7 ......1.06S 80.28W
Portpatrick Scotland 16 D2 ......54.51N 5.07W
Port Pirie Australia 110 C3 ......33.10S 138.02E
Portree Scotland 18 C2 ......57.25N 6.12W
Portrush Northern Ireland 16 C3 ......55.12N 6.39W
Port Said Egypt 85 H5 ......31.16N 32.18E
Portsmouth England 10 D1 ......50.48N 1.06W
Portsmouth d. England 9 E2 ......50.50N 1.04W
Portsmouth U.S.A. 65 J4 ......38.44N 82.59W
Portsoy Scotland 19 G2 ......57.41N 2.41W
Portstewart Northern Ireland 16 C3 ......55.11N 6.43W
Port Sudan Sudan 85 H3 ......19.36N 37.12E
Port Talbot Wales 12 D3 ......51.36N 3.48W
Portugal Europe 48 B3 ......39.41N 7.57W
Portumna Ireland 41 C3 ......53.06N 8.13W
Port Vila Vanuatu 108 H4 ......17.44S 168.17E
Port William Scotland 16 E2 ......54.46N 4.35W
Posadas Argentina 73 D4 ......27.23S 55.52W
Poso Indonesia 105 G3 ......1.24S 120.47E
Posse Brazil 77 K5 ......14.06S 46.22W
Potenza Italy 50 F4 ......40.38N 15.48E
P'ot'i Georgia 53 L5 ......42.09N 41.40E
Potiskum Nigeria 84 F3 ......11.42N 11.04E
Potosí Bolivia 76 G4 ......19.36S 65.47W
Potsdam Germany 54 E5 ......52.24N 13.04E
Poulton-le-Fylde England 14 E2 ......53.51N 2.59W
Poŭthisăt Cambodia 104 C6 ......12.32N 103.57E
Považská Bystrica Slovakia 46 D2 ......49.07N 18.27E
Powell, Lake resr U.S.A. 64 D4 ......37.34N 110.37W
Powick England 10 C3 ......52.10N 2.15W
Powys d. Wales 9 D3 ......52.23N 3.25W
Poyang Hu l. China 103 L3 ......29.05N 116.22E
Požarevac Serbia 56 D7 ......44.37N 21.11E
Poza Rica Mexico 70 E5 ......20.35N 97.26W
Poznań Poland 46 C4 ......52.25N 16.56E
Pozoblanco Spain 48 C3 ......38.23N 4.50W
Prabumulih Indonesia 104 C3 ......3.26S 104.13E
Prachatice Czech Rep. 46 B2 ......49.01N 14.00E
Prachuap Khiri Khan Thailand 104 B6 ......11.49N 99.49E
Prague Czech Rep. 54 F4 ......50.04N 14.26E
Praia Cape Verde 84 B3 ......14.55N 23.29W
Prapat Indonesia 104 B4 ......2.41N 98.57E
Prato Italy 50 D5 ......43.52N 11.06E
Pravdinsk Rus. Fed. 46 E5 ......54.27N 21.01E
Prawle Point England 13 D2 ......50.12N 3.44W
Pregolya r. Rus. Fed. 46 E5 ......54.41N 20.22E
Prenzlau Germany 46 A4 ......53.19N 13.52E
Preparis Island Cocos Is 97 H3 ......14.51N 93.39E
Přerov Czech Rep. 54 G3 ......49.27N 17.27E
Presidencia Roque Sáenz Peña Argentina 77 H2 ......26.44S 60.27W
Presidente Prudente Brazil 77 J3 ......22.10S 51.23W
Prešov Slovakia 54 I3 ......48.59N 21.16E
Prespa, Lake Europe 56 D5 ......40.52N 21.03E
Presque Isle town U.S.A. 65 M6 ......46.41N 68.01W
Prestatyn Wales 12 D5 ......53.20N 3.24W
Presteigne Wales 12 D4 ......52.16N 3.00W
Preston Dor. England 10 C1 ......50.39N 2.25W
Preston Lancs. England 14 E2 ......53.46N 2.42W
Prestonpans Scotland 17 G3 ......55.58N 2.59W
Prestwich England 15 E2 ......53.30N 2.17W
Prestwick Scotland 16 E3 ......55.30N 4.37W
Pretoria S. Africa 86 B2 ......25.44S 28.13E
Preveza Greece 56 D4 ......38.57N 20.46E
Prienai Lithuania 46 F5 ......54.38N 23.57E
Prievidza Slovakia 54 H3 ......48.47N 18.38E
Prijedor Bos.-Herz. 56 B6 ......44.59N 16.43E
Prijepolje Serbia 56 C6 ......43.23N 19.39E
Prilep Macedonia 56 D5 ......41.21N 21.33E
Primorsko-Akhtarsk Rus. Fed. 57 M8 ......46.03N 38.10E
Prince Albert Canada 62 H3 ......53.12N 105.44W
Prince Alfred, Cape Canada 62 F5 ......74.20N 124.47W
Prince Charles Island Canada 63 K4 ......67.48N 76.12W
Prince Edward Island d. Canada 63 L2 ......46.41N 63.09W
Prince Edward Islands Indian Oc. 117 K3 ......47.00S 37.00E
Prince George Canada 62 F3 ......53.55N 122.46W
Prince of Wales Island Australia 110 D5 ......10.43S 142.09E
Prince of Wales Island Canada 63 I5 ......72.27N 99.08W
Prince of Wales Island U.S.A. 62 E3 ......55.38N 132.45W
Prince Patrick Island Canada 62 G5 ......76.57N 118.47W
Prince Rupert Canada 62 E3 ......54.19N 130.19W
Princes Risborough England 10 E2 ......51.43N 0.50W
Príncipe i. São Tomé and Príncipe 84 E2 ......1.39N 7.22E
Pripet r. Ukraine 55 N4 ......51.16N 30.16E
Pripet Marshes Belarus/Ukraine 55 K4 ......51.39N 24.34E
Priština Serbia 56 D6 ......42.40N 21.10E
Privas France 44 F4 ......44.44N 4.36E
Prizren Serbia 56 D6 ......42.13N 20.43E
Probolinggo Indonesia 104 D2 ......7.47S 113.13E
Probus England 13 C2 ......50.18N 4.57W
Providence U.S.A. 65 L5 ......41.50N 71.25W
Providence, Cape New Zealand 111 F2 ......46.01S 166.28E
Providencia, Isla de i. Caribbean Sea 71 H3 ......13.21N 81.20W
Provins France 44 E6 ......48.34N 3.18E
Prudhoe Bay town U.S.A. 62 D5 ......70.18N 148.10W
Prüm Germany 42 F3 ......50.13N 6.25E
Pruszków Poland 46 E4 ......52.10N 20.49E
Prut r. Europe 55 M1 ......45.28N 28.12E
Pryluky Ukraine 55 O4 ......50.35N 32.24E
Przemyśl Poland 46 F2 ......49.47N 22.46E
Psara i. Greece 56 F4 ......38.37N 25.35E
Psebay Rus. Fed. 57 N7 ......44.07N 40.47E
Psel r. Rus. Fed./Ukraine 55 P4 ......51.05N 35.15E
Pskov Rus. Fed. 40 G2 ......57.49N 28.19E
Pskov, Lake Estonia/Rus. Fed. 40 F2 ......58.02N 27.56E
Pucallpa Peru 76 F6 ......8.22S 74.35W
Pudsey England 15 F2 ......53.48N 1.40W
Puebla Mexico 70 E4 ......19.02N 98.12W
Puebla d. Mexico 70 E4 ......18.04N 98.39W
Pueblo U.S.A. 64 F4 ......38.17N 104.38W
Puente-Genil Spain 48 C2 ......37.23N 4.46W
Puerto Ángel Mexico 70 E4 ......15.40N 96.29W
Puerto de la Estaca Canary Islands 48 X1 ......27.47N 17.54W
Puerto del Rosario Canary Islands 48 Z2 ......28.30N 13.52W
Puertollano Spain 48 C3 ......38.41N 4.06W
Puerto Maldonado Peru 76 G5 ......12.39S 69.14W
Puerto Montt Chile 73 B2 ......41.27S 72.58W
Puerto Natales Chile 73 B1 ......51.35S 72.24W
Puerto Peñasco Mexico 70 B7 ......31.19N 113.32W
Puerto Princesa Phil. 104 F5 ......9.45N 118.45E
Puerto Rico i. Central America 71 K4 ......17.45N 66.34W
Puerto Vallarta Mexico 70 C5 ......20.40N 105.14W
Pukch'ŏng N. Korea 106 A4 ......40.14N 128.19E
Puksubaek-san mt. N. Korea 106 A4 ......40.38N 127.47E
Pula Croatia 54 E1 ......44.53N 13.51E
Pulborough England 11 E1 ......50.57N 0.30W
Pułtusk Poland 54 I5 ......52.42N 21.05E
Pune India 96 D4 ......18.32N 73.57E
Punjab d. India 96 E7 ......30.17N 75.18E

Punta Arenas Chile 73 B1 ....53.09S 70.57W
Punto Fijo Venezuela 71 J3 ....11.39N 70.11W
Pur r. Rus. Fed. 58 I4 ....67.33N 77.53E
Purari r. P.N.G. 110 D6 ....7.46S 144.54E
Purbeck, Isle of pen. England 10 C1 ....50.39N 2.01W
Puri India 96 G4 ....19.48N 85.55E
Purmerend Neth. 42 D5 ....52.31N 4.57E
Purus r. Brazil/Peru 77 H7 ....3.42S 61.28W
Pusan S. Korea 103 N5 ....35.09N 129.03E
Pustoshka Rus. Fed. 55 M7 ....56.20N 29.22E
Puting, Tanjung pt Indonesia 104 E3 ....3.35S 111.50E
Putrajaya Malaysia 104 C4 ....2.55N 101.39E
Puttalam Sri Lanka 96 E2 ....8.01N 79.50E
Putumayo r. Colombia 72 B6 ....2.43S 70.03W
Puvurnituq Canada 63 K4 ....60.02N 77.17W
Puy de Dôme mt. France 44 E4 ....45.46N 2.58E
Puy de Sancy mt. France 44 E4 ....45.31N 2.49E
Pwllheli Wales 12 C4 ....52.53N 4.25W
Pyaozero, Ozero l. Rus. Fed. 40 G4 ....66.11N 30.47E
Pyasina r. Rus. Fed. 59 J5 ....73.35N 86.19E
Pyè Myanmar 97 I4 ....18.48N 95.13E
Pyhäjoki r. Finland 40 F4 ....64.28N 24.15E
Pyhäselkä l. Finland 40 G3 ....62.31N 29.41E
Pyinmana Myanmar 97 I4 ....19.44N 96.13E
Pyle Wales 13 D3 ....51.32N 3.42W
Pylos Greece 56 D3 ....36.55N 21.42E
P'yŏngyang N. Korea 103 N5 ....39.01N 125.44E
Pyramid Lake U.S.A. 64 C5 ....40.09N 119.37W
Pyrenees mts Europe 48 G5 ....42.30N 2.00E
Pyrgos Greece 56 D3 ....37.40N 21.27E
Pyryatyn Ukraine 55 O4 ....50.14N 32.30E
Pyrzyce Poland 46 B4 ....53.08N 14.54E

Q

Qamanittuaq Canada 63 I4 ....64.17N 95.43W
Qamdo China 102 H4 ....31.13N 97.08E
Qarshi Uzbekistan 95 K7 ....38.52N 65.48E
Qasigiannguit Greenland 63 M4 ....68.48N 51.11W
Qatar Asia 95 H5 ....25.25N 51.57E
Qattara Depression f. Egypt 85 G4 ....29.48N 27.06E
Qāyen Iran 95 I6 ....33.42N 59.05E
Qazvin Iran 95 G7 ....36.17N 49.58E
Qeshm Iran 95 I5 ....26.57N 56.15E
Qiemo China 102 F5 ....38.05N 85.33E
Qijiaojing China 102 G6 ....43.25N 91.38E
Qilian Shan mts China 102 H5 ....39.21N 97.06E
Qinā Egypt 85 H4 ....26.08N 32.45E
Qingdao China 103 M5 ....36.05N 120.24E
Qinghai d. China 102 H4 ....36.07N 96.31E
Qinghai Hu l. China 103 I5 ....36.49N 100.06E
Qinhuangdao China 103 L5 ....39.56N 119.38E
Qinzhou China 103 J2 ....21.57N 108.31E
Qionghai China 103 K1 ....19.13N 110.29E
Qiqihar China 103 M7 ....47.13N 123.58E
Qitaihe China 106 B5 ....45.41N 130.46E
Qom Iran 95 H6 ....34.38N 50.51E
Qornet es Saouda mt. Lebanon 57 L2 ....34.18N 36.06E
Quang Ngai Vietnam 104 D7 ....15.04N 108.50E
Quantock Hills England 13 D3 ....51.10N 3.15W
Quanzhou China 103 K3 ....25.57N 111.05E
Quchan Iran 95 I7 ....36.59N 58.29E
Québec Canada 63 K2 ....46.48N 71.15W
Québec d. Canada 63 K3 ....54.45N 74.31W
Queenborough England 11 F2 ....51.25N 0.45E
Queen Charlotte Islands Canada 62 E3 ....53.59N 133.20W
Queen Charlotte Sound str. Canada 62 F3 ..51.24N 129.09W
Queen Elizabeth Islands Canada 63 I4 ....76.31N 107.31W
Queen Maud Gulf Canada 62 H4 ....68.13N 102.08W
Queensland d. Australia 110 D4 ....22.37S 144.17E
Quelimane Mozambique 86 C3 ....17.53S 36.53E
Querétaro Mexico 70 D5 ....20.37N 100.22W
Querétaro d. Mexico 70 E5 ....20.51N 99.50W
Quetta Pakistan 96 C7 ....30.14N 67.03E
Quetzaltenango Guatemala 70 F3 ....14.50N 91.30W
Quezon City Phil. 105 G6 ....14.36N 121.01E
Quibala Angola 86 A3 ....10.44S 14.59E
Quibdó Colombia 72 B7 ....5.39N 76.38W
Quilon India 96 E2 ....8.53N 76.36E
Quimper France 44 A5 ....47.59N 4.06W
Quintana Roo d. Mexico 70 G4 ....18.44N 88.47W
Quito Ecuador 76 E7 ....0.14S 78.30W
Quixadá Brazil 77 M7 ....4.55S 38.59W
Quoich, Loch l. Scotland 18 D2 ....57.03N 5.18W
Quoile r. Northern Ireland 16 D2 ....54.21N 5.42W
Quy Nhơn Vietnam 104 D6 ....13.44N 109.13E
Quzhou China 103 L3 ....28.57N 118.52E

R

Raahe Finland 40 F4 ....64.41N 24.29E
Raalte Neth. 42 F5 ....52.23N 6.17E
Raasay i. Scotland 18 C2 ....57.23N 6.02W
Raasay, Sound of str. Scotland 18 C2 ....57.26N 6.06W
Raba Indonesia 104 F2 ....8.32S 118.46E
Rabat Morocco 84 D5 ....34.01N 6.47W
Rābigh Saudi Arabia 94 E4 ....22.50N 39.00E
Race, Cape Canada 63 M2 ....46.38N 53.09W
Rach Gia Vietnam 104 D5 ....9.59N 105.06E
Racibórz Poland 46 D3 ....50.06N 18.13E
Radom Poland 46 E3 ....51.24N 21.09E
Radomsko Poland 46 D3 ....51.04N 19.27E
Radstock England 10 C2 ....51.17N 2.27W
Radun' Belarus 46 G5 ....54.03N 24.59E
Radviliškis Lithuania 46 F5 ....55.49N 23.32E
Radyvyliv Ukraine 46 G3 ....50.08N 25.15E
Rafha' Saudi Arabia 94 F5 ....29.33N 43.25E
Rafsanjān 95 I6 ....30.24N 55.59E
Raglan Wales 12 E3 ....51.46N 2.51W
Ragusa Italy 50 F2 ....36.55N 14.44E
Rahachow Belarus 55 N5 ....53.05N 30.03E
Rahimyar Khan Pakistan 96 D6 ....28.22N 70.19E
Raichur India 96 E4 ....16.13N 77.18E
Rainier, Mount vol. U.S.A. 64 B6 ....46.54N 121.44W
Raipur India 96 F5 ....21.14N 81.39E
Raivavae i. French Polynesia 109 K4 ....23.51S 147.39W
Rajahmundry India 96 F4 ....17.00N 81.52E
Rajanpur Pakistan 95 L5 ....29.05N 70.24E
Rajasthan d. India 96 D6 ....26.40N 73.31E
Rajkot India 96 D5 ....22.14N 70.53E
Rakhiv Ukraine 55 K3 ....48.03N 24.12E
Rakitnoye Rus. Fed. 55 P4 ....50.50N 35.50E
Rakvere Estonia 40 F2 ....59.21N 26.22E
Raleigh U.S.A. 65 K4 ....35.47N 78.37W
Ramapo Deep f. N. Pacific Oc. 108 F8 ....30.59N 142.13E
Rame Head England 13 C2 ....50.19N 4.15W
Râmhormoz Iran 95 G6 ....31.10N 49.35E
Râmnicu Vâlcea Romania 56 F7 ....45.07N 24.22E
Ramsbottom England 15 E2 ....53.39N 2.19W
Ramsey England 11 E3 ....52.27N 0.06W
Ramsey Isle of Man 14 C3 ....54.19N 4.23W
Ramsey Bay Isle of Man 14 C3 ....54.20N 4.22W
Ramsey Island Wales 12 B3 ....51.51N 5.22W
Ramsgate England 11 G2 ....51.20N 1.25E
Ramu Kenya 87 C3 ....3.53N 41.14E
Rancagua Chile 73 B3 ....34.11S 70.44W
Ranchi India 96 G5 ....23.22N 85.20E
Randers Denmark 40 B2 ....56.27N 10.03E
Rangiroa atoll French Polynesia 109 K5 ....14.59S 147.42W
Rangoon Myanmar 97 I4 ....16.49N 96.08E
Rangpur Bangl. 97 G6 ....25.46N 89.16E
Rankin Inlet Canada 63 I4 ....62.52N 92.03W
Rannoch, Loch l. Scotland 19 E1 ....56.41N 4.23W
Rannoch Moor f. Scotland 18 E1 ....56.38N 4.46W
Ranong Thailand 104 B5 ....9.57N 98.38E
Rantauprapat Indonesia 104 B4 ....2.06N 99.47E
Raoul Island Indian Oc. 111 H4 ....29.16S 177.57W
Rapa r. French Polynesia 109 K4 ....27.35S 144.21W
Rapallo Italy 50 C6 ....44.21N 9.14E
Raphoe Ireland 16 B2 ....54.52N 7.35W
Rapid City U.S.A. 64 F5 ....44.04N 103.14W
Raroia atoll French Polynesia 109 K4 ....16.05S 142.23W
Rarotonga i. Cook Is 109 J4 ....21.12S 159.46W
Ras Dejen mt. Ethiopia 85 H3 ....13.12N 38.23E
Rasht Iran 95 G7 ....37.16N 49.34E
Raskoh mts Pakistan 95 K5 ....28.54N 65.26E
Ras Tannūrah Saudi Arabia 95 H5 ....26.38N 50.10E
Rat Buri Thailand 104 B6 ....13.31N 99.50E
Rathdrum Ireland 41 E2 ....52.56N 6.14W
Rathenow Germany 54 E5 ....52.37N 12.20E
Rathfriland Northern Ireland 16 C2 ....54.14N 6.09W
Rathkeale Ireland 41 C2 ....52.31N 8.56W
Rathlin Island Northern Ireland 16 C3 ....55.17N 6.10W
Rathluirc Ireland 41 C2 ....52.21N 8.41W
Ratne Ukraine 55 K4 ....51.40N 24.32E
Rattray Head Scotland 19 H2 ....57.37N 1.49W
Rättvik Sweden 40 C3 ....60.53N 15.08E
Rauma Finland 40 E3 ....61.08N 21.31E
Raunds England 11 E3 ....52.20N 0.32W
Ravenna Italy 50 E6 ....44.25N 12.13E
Ravensthorpe Australia 110 B3 ....33.34S 120.01E
Rawaki i. Kiribati 108 I5 ....3.42S 170.40W
Rawalpindi Pakistan 96 D7 ....33.38N 73.08E
Rawicz Poland 46 C3 ....51.37N 16.51E
Rawlins U.S.A. 64 E5 ....41.48N 107.13W
Rawson Argentina 73 C2 ....43.15S 65.06W
Rawtenstall England 15 E2 ....53.42N 2.17W
Rayleigh England 11 F2 ....51.35N 0.36E
Razgrad Bulgaria 56 G6 ....43.32N 26.30E
Ré, Île de i. France 44 C5 ....46.10N 1.22W
Reading England 10 E2 ....51.27N 0.58W
Reading d. England 9 E2 ....51.27N 0.59W
Rebiana Sand Sea des. Libya 94 B4 ....24.42N 21.18E
Reboly Rus. Fed. 40 G3 ....63.50N 30.48E
Rechytsa Belarus 55 N5 ....52.22N 30.26E
Recife Brazil 77 N6 ....8.02S 34.48W
Reconquista Argentina 77 I2 ....29.09S 59.38W
Red r. U.S.A. 65 H3 ....31.05N 91.44W
Red Bluff U.S.A. 64 B5 ....40.11N 122.14W
Redcar England 15 F3 ....54.37N 1.03W
Redcar and Cleveland d. England 9 E4 ....54.33N 1.02W
Red Deer Canada 62 G3 ....52.16N 113.49W
Redding U.S.A. 64 B5 ....40.36N 122.29W
Redditch England 10 D3 ....52.19N 1.56W
Red Lake town Canada 63 I3 ....51.01N 93.50W
Red Lakes U.S.A. 65 H6 ....48.03N 94.44W
Redruth England 13 B2 ....50.14N 5.14W
Red Sea Africa/Asia 94 E4 ....26.30N 34.42E
Red Wharf Bay Wales 12 C5 ....53.19N 4.11W
Ree, Lough l. Ireland 41 D3 ....53.32N 7.59W
Regensburg Germany 54 E3 ....49.01N 12.06E
Reggane Algeria 84 E4 ....26.46N 0.08E
Reggio di Calabria Italy 50 F3 ....38.06N 15.39E
Reggio nell'Emilia Italy 50 D6 ....44.41N 10.38E
Regina Canada 62 H3 ....50.27N 104.37W
Reidh, Rubha pt Scotland 18 D2 ....57.52N 5.51W
Reigate England 11 E2 ....51.14N 0.12W
Reims France 44 F6 ....49.15N 4.03E
Reindeer Lake Canada 62 H3 ....57.24N 102.23W
Reinosa Spain 48 C5 ....42.59N 4.07W
Reiphólsfjöll hill Iceland 40 X2 ....65.41N 22.20W
Reliance Canada 62 H4 ....62.43N 109.06W
Relizane Algeria 52 D4 ....35.44N 0.40E
Rena Norway 40 B3 ....61.08N 11.22E
Renfrewshire d. Scotland 8 C4 ....55.52N 4.31W
Reni Ukraine 57 H7 ....45.27N 28.18E
Rennell i. Solomon Is 111 F5 ....11.40S 160.18E
Rennes France 44 C6 ....48.07N 1.41W
Reno r. Italy 50 E6 ....44.35N 12.17E
Reno U.S.A. 64 C4 ....39.32N 119.48W
Republican r. U.S.A. 64 G4 ....39.06N 96.52W
Repulse Bay town Canada 63 J4 ....66.32N 86.08W
Resistencia Argentina 73 D4 ....27.24S 58.59W
Reşiţa Romania 56 D7 ....45.18N 21.53E
Resolute Canada 63 I5 ....74.41N 94.46W
Resolution Island Canada 63 L4 ....61.34N 64.52W
Retford England 15 G2 ....53.19N 0.57W
Rethel France 42 D2 ....49.31N 4.23E
Rethymno Greece 56 F2 ....35.21N 24.28E
Réunion i. Indian Oc. 117 L4 ....20.00S 55.00E
Reus Spain 48 F4 ....41.09N 1.06E
Reutlingen Germany 54 D2 ....48.30N 9.12E
Revillagigedo, Islas is Mexico 70 B4 ....18.34N 112.24W
Rewa India 96 F5 ....24.32N 81.18E
Reykjavík Iceland 40 X2 ....64.08N 21.55W
Reynosa Mexico 70 E6 ....26.04N 98.17W
Rēzekne Latvia 40 F2 ....56.31N 27.20E
Rhayader Wales 12 D4 ....52.18N 3.31W
Rheine Germany 42 G4 ....52.17N 7.28E
Rheinland-Pfalz d. Germany 42 G2 ....49.46N 7.27E
Rhine r. Germany 34 E3 ....51.58N 6.11E
Rhode Island d. U.S.A. 65 L5 ....41.40N 71.35W
Rhodes Greece 57 H3 ....36.26N 28.13E
Rhodes i. Greece 57 H3 ....36.15N 28.10E
Rhodope Mountains Bulgaria/Greece 56 E5 ..41.52N 23.41E
Rhondda Wales 12 D3 ....51.39N 3.30W
Rhondda Cynon Taff d. Wales 9 D2 ....51.36N 3.23W
Rhône r. France/Switz. 44 F3 ....43.37N 4.40E
Rhyl Wales 12 D5 ....53.19N 3.29W
Riau, Kepulauan is Indonesia 104 C4 ....0.34N 104.11E
Ribble r. England 15 E2 ....53.45N 2.45W
Ribe Denmark 40 B1 ....55.20N 8.46E
Ribeira r. Brazil 77 K3 ....24.39S 47.25W
Ribeirão Preto Brazil 77 K3 ....21.12S 47.48W
Riberalta Bolivia 76 G5 ....11.01S 66.05W
Ribniţa Moldova 55 M2 ....47.46N 29.00E
Říčany Czech Rep. 46 B2 ....49.59N 14.40E
Richfield U.S.A. 64 D4 ....38.47N 112.05W
Richland U.S.A. 64 C6 ....46.19N 119.17W
Richmond England 15 F3 ....54.24N 1.44W
Richmond U.S.A. 65 K4 ....37.34N 77.28W
Riesa Germany 54 E4 ....51.18N 13.17E
Rietavas Lithuania 46 E5 ....55.43N 21.56E
Rifstangi pt Iceland 40 Y2 ....66.33N 16.13W
Rift Valley f. Kenya 87 A3 ....0.50N 35.34E
Riga Latvia 40 F2 ....56.56N 24.07E
Riga, Gulf of Estonia/Latvia 40 E2 ....57.24N 23.45E
Riihimäki Finland 40 F3 ....60.44N 24.47E
Rijeka Croatia 56 A7 ....45.20N 14.26E
Rimini Italy 50 E6 ....44.04N 12.34E
Rimouski Canada 63 L2 ....48.27N 68.32W
Rimsdale, Loch l. Scotland 19 E3 ....58.17N 4.10W
Ringkøbing Denmark 40 B2 ....56.05N 8.15E
Ringvassøya i. Norway 40 D5 ....69.55N 18.56E
Ringwood England 10 D1 ....50.51N 1.47W
Riobamba Ecuador 76 E7 ....1.41S 78.42W
Río Branco Brazil 76 G5 ....10.01S 67.48W
Río Cuarto Argentina 73 C3 ....33.08S 64.21W
Rio de Janeiro Brazil 77 L3 ....22.55S 43.17W
Rio de Janeiro d. Brazil 77 J1 ....21.58S 42.12W
Rio Grande Brazil 77 J1 ....30.39S 54.07W
Río Grande r. Mexico/U.S.A. 71 J6 ....25.57N 97.10W
Rio Grande do Norte d. Brazil 77 M6 ....5.49S 36.21W
Rio Grande do Sul d. Brazil 77 J1 ....30.39S 54.07W
Ríohacha Colombia 72 B8 ....11.32N 72.58W
Rio Verde Brazil 77 J4 ....17.48S 50.55W
Ripley England 15 F2 ....53.03N 1.24W
Ripon England 15 F3 ....54.08N 1.32W
Risca Wales 12 D3 ....51.37N 3.06W
Rishton England 15 E2 ....53.46N 2.25W
Riva del Garda Italy 50 D6 ....45.53N 10.50E
Rivera Uruguay 77 I1 ....31.00S 55.33W
Riverside U.S.A. 64 C3 ....33.57N 117.24W
Rivne Ukraine 55 L4 ....50.37N 26.14E
Riyadh Saudi Arabia 95 G4 ....24.43N 46.41E
Rize Turkey 57 N5 ....41.02N 40.30E
Rjuvbrokkene mt. Norway 40 A2 ....59.11N 7.10E
Roadford Reservoir England 13 C2 ....50.42N 4.13W
Roanne France 44 F5 ....46.03N 4.05E
Roanoke U.S.A. 65 K4 ....37.16N 79.58W
Roanoke r. U.S.A. 65 K4 ....36.02N 76.22W
Robertsfors Sweden 40 E4 ....64.12N 20.52E
Roberval Canada 63 K2 ....48.31N 72.14W
Robson, Mount Canada 62 G3 ....53.07N 119.06W
Roca, Cabo da c. Portugal 48 A3 ....38.47N 9.29W
Rocca Busambra mt. Italy 50 E2 ....37.51N 13.24E
Rocha Uruguay 73 D3 ....34.30S 54.19W
Rochdale England 15 E2 ....53.37N 2.10W
Rochefort Belgium 42 E3 ....50.10N 5.13E
Rochefort France 44 C4 ....45.57N 0.58W
Rochester England 11 F2 ....51.23N 0.30E
Rochester Minn. U.S.A. 65 H5 ....44.02N 92.27W
Rochester N. Y. U.S.A. 65 K5 ....43.09N 77.38W
Rochford England 11 F2 ....51.35N 0.42E
Rockhampton Australia 110 E4 ....23.23S 150.34E
Rockingham Forest England 11 E3 ....52.31N 0.32W
Rocky Mountains Canada/U.S.A. 62 F3 ....40.57N 107.58W
Rodel Scotland 18 C2 ....57.45N 6.58W
Rodez France 44 E4 ....44.22N 2.34E
Rodrigues Island Mauritius 108 A4 ....19.37S 63.40E
Roe r. Northern Ireland 16 C3 ....55.06N 6.58W
Roermond Neth. 42 E4 ....51.12N 5.59E
Roeselare Belgium 42 C3 ....50.56N 3.08E
Rogagua, Laguna l. Bolivia 76 G5 ....14.03S 67.05W
Roggeveen Basin f. S. Pacific Oc. 109 O3 ....32.50S 89.54W
Rokiškis Lithuania 40 F1 ....55.57N 25.35E
Rolla U.S.A. 65 H4 ....37.56N 91.46W
Rom mt. Uganda 87 A3 ....3.23N 33.37E
Roma i. Indonesia 105 H2 ....7.31S 127.25E
Romain, Cape U.S.A. 65 K3 ....32.59N 79.27W
Roman Romania 55 L2 ....46.55N 26.55E
Romania Europe 53 H6 ....46.07N 24.36E
Romanzof, Cape U.S.A. 62 B4 ....61.49N 166.06W
Rombas France 42 F2 ....49.15N 6.05E
Rome Italy 50 E4 ....41.54N 12.28E
Romford England 11 F2 ....51.35N 0.11E
Romney Marsh f. England 11 F2 ....51.03N 0.54E
Romny Ukraine 55 O4 ....50.45N 33.28E
Romsey England 10 D1 ....50.59N 1.30W
Rona i. Scotland 18 D2 ....57.33N 5.57W
Ronas Hill Scotland 19 H5 ....60.32N 1.27W
Ronda Spain 48 C2 ....36.44N 5.10W
Rondônia d. Brazil 76 H5 ....11.18S 62.19W
Rondonópolis Brazil 77 J4 ....16.29S 54.38W
Rønne Denmark 40 C1 ....55.06N 14.43E
Ronse Belgium 42 C3 ....50.45N 3.36E
Roosendaal Neth. 42 D4 ....51.31N 4.28E
Roque de los Muchachos vol. Canary Islands 48 X2 ..28.45N 17.51W
Roquefort France 44 C4 ....44.02N 0.19W
Roraima d. Brazil 77 H8 ....1.27N 60.48W
Roraima, Mount Guyana 72 C7 ....5.15N 60.44W
Røros Norway 40 B3 ....62.34N 11.23E
Rosario Argentina 73 C3 ....32.56S 60.41W
Roscoff France 44 B6 ....48.43N 3.59W
Roscommon Ireland 41 C3 ....53.38N 8.11W
Roscommon d. Ireland 41 C3 ....53.49N 8.16W
Roscrea Ireland 41 D2 ....52.57N 7.48W
Roseau Dominica 71 L4 ....15.17N 61.23W
Roseburg U.S.A. 64 B5 ....43.13N 123.21W
Roseires Reservoir Sudan 94 D2 ....11.33N 34.31E
Rosenheim Germany 54 E2 ....47.51N 12.08E
Roşiori de Vede Romania 56 F7 ....44.07N 25.00E
Roslavl' Rus. Fed. 55 O5 ....53.57N 32.51E
Rossan Point Ireland 16 B2 ....54.42N 8.48W
Rossel Island P.N.G. 110 E5 ....11.24S 154.10E
Rossington England 15 F2 ....53.29N 1.03W
Rosslare Harbour Ireland 41 E2 ....52.15N 6.20W
Rosso Mauritania 84 C3 ....16.31N 15.49W
Ross of Mull pen. Scotland 16 C4 ....56.18N 6.19W
Ross-on-Wye England 10 C3 ....51.55N 2.35W
Røssvatnet l. Norway 40 C4 ....65.46N 14.19E
Rostock Germany 54 E6 ....54.05N 12.07E
Rostov-na-Donu Rus. Fed. 58 E2 ....47.13N 39.44E
Roswell U.S.A. 64 F3 ....33.21N 104.30W
Rota i. N. Mariana Is 105 L6 ....14.09N 145.17E
Rote i. Indonesia 105 G1 ....10.29S 123.24E
Rothbury England 15 F4 ....55.19N 1.54W
Rother r. England 10 E1 ....50.57N 0.32W
Rotherham England 15 F2 ....53.26N 1.20W
Rothes Scotland 19 F2 ....57.32N 3.12W
Rothesay Scotland 16 D3 ....55.50N 5.03W
Rothwell England 11 E3 ....52.25N 0.48W
Rotterdam Neth. 42 D4 ....51.55N 4.30E
Rotuma i. Fiji 111 G5 ....12.29S 177.05E
Roubaix France 44 E7 ....50.42N 3.10E
Rouen France 44 D6 ....49.26N 1.05E
Round Hill England 15 F3 ....54.24N 1.05W
Round Mountain Australia 110 E3 ....30.24S 152.15E
Rousay i. Scotland 19 F4 ....59.11N 3.08W
Rouyn-Noranda Canada 65 K6 ....48.14N 79.02W
Rovaniemi Finland 40 F4 ....66.29N 25.42E
Rovigo Italy 50 D6 ....45.04N 11.47E
Rovinj Croatia 54 E1 ....45.05N 13.39E
Royale, Isle i. U.S.A. 65 I6 ....48.02N 88.52W
Royal Leamington Spa England 10 D3 ....52.17N 1.31W
Royal Tunbridge Wells England 11 F2 ....51.08N 0.16E
Royan France 44 C4 ....45.38N 1.01W
Royston England 11 E3 ....52.03N 0.01W
Royton England 15 E2 ....53.34N 2.07W
Rub' al Khālī des. Saudi Arabia 95 G3 ....19.01N 46.53E
Rubtsovsk Rus. Fed. 58 J3 ....51.33N 81.11E
Rudnaya Pristan' Rus. Fed. 106 C4 ....43.43N 135.16E
Rudnya Rus. Fed. 55 N6 ....54.57N 31.07E
Rudnyy Kazakhstan 58 H3 ....52.57N 63.07E
Rufiji r. Tanzania 86 C4 ....8.02S 39.19E
Rugby England 10 D3 ....52.23N 1.15W
Rugby U.S.A. 64 F6 ....48.20N 100.00W
Rugeley England 10 D3 ....52.46N 1.56W
Rügen i. Germany 54 E6 ....54.23N 13.24E
Ruhr r. Germany 42 F4 ....51.26N 6.44E
Rukwa, Lake Tanzania 86 C4 ....8.09S 32.21E
Rum i. Scotland 18 C1 ....56.59N 6.18W
Ruma Serbia 56 C7 ....45.01N 19.49E
Rum Cay i. Bahamas 71 J5 ....23.42N 74.52W
Runcorn England 14 E2 ....53.20N 2.44W
Rundu Namibia 86 A3 ....17.54S 19.46E
Ruoqiang China 102 F5 ....38.58N 88.10E
Rurutu i. French Polynesia 109 J4 ....22.28S 151.21W
Ruse Bulgaria 56 F6 ....43.49N 25.58E
Rushden England 11 E3 ....52.17N 0.36W
Russian Federation Asia/Europe 58 I4 ....57.12N 40.00E
Ruteng Indonesia 104 G2 ....8.33S 120.28E
Ruthin Wales 12 D5 ....53.07N 3.18W
Rutland d. England 9 E3 ....52.42N 0.38W
Rutland Water resr England 10 E3 ....52.39N 0.37W
Ruza Rus. Fed. 55 O6 ....55.42N 36.12E
Ružomberok Slovakia 54 H3 ....49.05N 19.19E
Rwanda Africa 85 G1 ....2.16S 29.59E
Ryan, Loch b. Scotland 16 D3 ....55.01N 5.04W
Ryazan' Rus. Fed. 58 E3 ....54.37N 39.43E
Rybinsk Rus. Fed. 58 E3 ....58.03N 38.51E
Rybinskoye Vodokhranilishche resr Rus. Fed. 58 E3 ..58.21N 38.24E
Rybnik Poland 46 D3 ....50.06N 18.32E
Ryde England 10 D1 ....50.44N 1.10W
Rye England 11 F1 ....50.57N 0.44E
Rye r. England 15 G3 ....54.10N 0.44W
Rye Bay England 11 F1 ....50.55N 0.45E
Ryōtsu Japan 106 C3 ....38.04N 138.26E
Ryukyu Islands Japan 103 M2 ....24.13N 124.14E
Rzeszów Poland 46 F3 ....50.02N 22.00E
Rzhev Rus. Fed. 55 P7 ....56.16N 34.17E

S

Saale r. Germany 54 D4 ....51.57N 11.55E
Saarbrücken Germany 54 B3 ....49.15N 6.59E
Saaremaa i. Estonia 40 E2 ....58.14N 22.22E
Saarland d. Germany 42 F2 ....49.28N 6.53E
Saarlouis Germany 42 F2 ....49.20N 6.46E
Sab' Ābār Syria 57 L1 ....33.42N 37.12E
Šabac Serbia 56 C7 ....44.46N 19.42E
Sabadell Spain 48 G4 ....41.33N 2.07E
Sabah d. Malaysia 104 F5 ....5.27N 116.30E
Sabana, Archipiélago de is Cuba 71 H5 ......23.18N 80.49W
Sabhā Libya 84 F4 ....26.55N 14.29E
Sabinas Mexico 70 D6 ....27.52N 101.07W
Sable, Cape Canada 63 L2 ....43.25N 65.38W
Sable, Cape U.S.A. 65 J2 ....25.09N 81.10W
Sable Island Canada 63 M2 ....43.57N 59.55W
Şabyā Saudi Arabia 94 F3 ....17.07N 42.39E
Sabzevār Iran 95 I7 ....36.12N 57.41E
Sacramento U.S.A. 64 B4 ....38.34N 121.28W
Sacramento Mountains U.S.A. 64 E3 ....34.23N 106.05W
Sado r. Portugal 48 A3 ....38.25N 8.36W
Sadoga-shima i. Japan 106 C3 ....37.56N 138.26E
Säffle Sweden 40 C2 ....59.08N 12.56E
Saffron Walden England 11 F3 ....52.02N 0.15E
Safi Morocco 84 D5 ....32.22N 9.13W
Safonovo Rus. Fed. 55 O6 ....55.07N 33.12E
Sagar India 96 E5 ....23.50N 78.44E
Sagres Portugal 48 A2 ....37.01N 8.56W
Sahand, Kūh-e mt. Iran 95 G7 ....37.38N 46.27E
Sahara des. Africa 84 E4 ....19.01N 9.40E
Saidpur Bangl. 96 G6 ....25.46N 88.54E
Saimaa l. Finland 40 G3 ....61.15N 28.27E
St Abb's Head Scotland 17 G3 ....55.55N 2.08W
St Agnes England 13 B2 ....50.18N 5.13W
St Agnes i. England 13 A1 ....49.53N 6.20W
St Albans England 11 E2 ....51.45N 0.20W
St Alban's Head England 10 C1 ....50.35N 2.03W
St-Amand-les-Eaux France 42 C3 ....50.26N 3.26E
St-Amand-Montrond France 44 E5 ....46.44N 2.30E
St Andrews Scotland 17 G4 ....56.20N 2.48W
St Anne Channel Is 13 Z9 ....49.43N 2.12W
St Ann's Head Wales 12 B3 ....51.41N 5.12W
St Anthony Canada 63 M3 ....51.20N 55.35W
St Asaph Wales 12 D5 ....53.15N 3.27W
St Austell England 13 C2 ....50.20N 4.47W
St Austell Bay England 13 C2 ....50.19N 4.44W
St-Barthélemy i. Central America 71 L4 ....17.54N 62.49W
St Bees England 14 D3 ....54.30N 3.36W
St Bees Head England 14 D3 ....54.31N 3.38W
St Brelade Channel Is 13 Z8 ....49.11N 2.12W
St Bride's Bay Wales 12 B3 ....51.48N 5.18W
St-Brieuc France 44 B6 ....48.31N 2.45W
St Catherine's Point England 10 D1 ....50.34N 1.17W
St Clears Wales 12 C3 ....51.49N 4.30W
St Cloud U.S.A. 65 H6 ....45.34N 94.10W
St Columb Major England 13 C2 ....50.26N 4.56W
St David's Wales 12 B3 ....51.53N 5.16W
St David's Head Wales 12 B3 ....51.54N 5.20W
St-Denis France 42 B1 ....48.57N 2.22E
St-Dié France 44 G6 ....48.17N 6.57E
St-Dizier France 44 F6 ....48.39N 4.57E
Saintes France 44 C4 ....45.45N 0.37W
St-Étienne France 44 F4 ....45.26N 4.24E
Saintfield Northern Ireland 16 D2 ....54.27N 5.49W
St Gallen Switz. 50 C7 ....47.26N 9.22E
St-Gaudens France 44 D3 ....43.07N 0.43E
St George's Grenada 71 L3 ....12.04N 61.45W
St George's Channel Ireland/U.K. 41 E1 ......51.58N 6.08W
St Germans England 13 C2 ....50.24N 4.19W
St Govan's Head Wales 12 C2 ....51.36N 4.56W
St Helena i. Atlantic Oc. 116 I5 ....16.00S 6.00W
St Helena Bay S. Africa 86 A1 ....32.43S 18.07E
St Helens England 14 E2 ....53.27N 2.44W
St Helens, Mount vol. U.S.A. 64 B6 ....46.08N 122.13W
St Helier Channel Is 13 Z8 ....49.11N 2.07W
St Ives Cambs. England 11 E3 ....52.20N 0.04W
St Ives Corn. England 13 B2 ....50.13N 5.29W
St Ives Bay England 13 B2 ....50.13N 5.28W

an, Lac l. Canada 65 L6 ....48.37N 72.07W
e r. U.S.A. 66 C6 ....47.25N 116.45W
John Canada 63 L2 ....45.16N 66.04W
in Channel Is 13 Z8 ....49.15N 2.08W
in r. U.S.A. 65 M6 ....45.46N 66.12W
hn's Antigua 71 L4 ....17.05N 61.51W
hn's Canada 63 M2 ....48.28N 52.18W
hn's Point Northern Ireland 16 D2 ....54.13N 5.39W
hn's Town of Dalry Scotland 16 E3 ....55.06N 4.10W
seph U.S.A. 65 H4 ....39.48N 94.51W
seph, Lake Canada 65 H7 ....50.59N 90.57W
st England 13 B2 ....50.08N 5.41W
verne England 13 B2 ....50.03N 5.05W
da l. Scotland 18 A2 ....57.49N 8.33W
ts and Nevis Central America 71 L4 ....17.17N 62.35W
wrence inlet Canada 63 L2 ....48.18N 69.06W
wrence, Gulf of Canada 63 L2 ....48.20N 61.29W
wrence Island U.S.A. 62 B4 ....63.05N 169.50W
 France 44 C6 ....49.07N 1.05W
ouis Senegal 84 C3 ....16.00N 16.29W
uis U.S.A. 65 H4 ....38.43N 90.14W
cia Central America 71 L3 ....13.57N 60.53W
agnus Bay Scotland 19 H5 ....60.24N 1.37W
alo France 44 B6 ....48.39N 2.00W
ialo, Golfe de g. France 44 B6 ....48.48N 2.16W
argaret's Hope Scotland 19 G3 ....58.49N 2.57W
artin Channel Is 13 Y9 ....49.26N 2.33W
artin Channel Is 13 Z8 ....49.13N 2.03W
artin i. Central America 71 L4 ....18.08N 62.59W
artin's i. England 13 A1 ....49.58N 6.17W
ary's i. England 13 A1 ....49.56N 6.16W
atthew Island U.S.A. 62 A4 ....60.27N 172.49W
aurice r. Canada 65 L6 ....46.22N 72.32W
awes England 13 B2 ....50.09N 5.01W
oritz Switz. 50 C7 ....46.30N 9.50E
azaire France 44 B5 ....47.17N 2.13W
eots England 11 E3 ....52.14N 0.16W
iklaas Belgium 42 D4 ....51.10N 4.10E
mer France 42 B3 ....50.45N 2.16E
uen Channel Is 13 Z8 ....49.14N 2.12W
aul U.S.A. 65 H5 ....44.57N 93.05W
eter Port Channel Is 13 Y9 ....49.28N 2.32W
etersburg Rus. Fed. 58 E3 ....59.56N 30.18E
etersburg U.S.A. 65 J2 ....27.45N 82.42W
ierre and Miquelon is N. America 63 M2 ....46.42N 56.29W
ol-sur-Ternoise France 11 H1 ....50.23N 2.20E
ölten Austria 54 F3 ....48.12N 15.38E
uentin France 44 E6 ....49.51N 3.17E
ampson Channel Is 13 Y9 ....49.29N 2.31W
ncent and the Grenadines Central America 71 L3 ....12.50N 60.52W
th Belgium 42 F3 ....50.17N 6.07E
endel Germany 42 G2 ....49.28N 7.09E
an i. N. Mariana Is 108 F7 ....15.15N 145.49E
anulkki hill Finland 40 F4 ....66.57N 25.48E
ma, Nevado mt. Bolivia 76 G4 ....18.09S 68.52W
 Morocco 48 D1 ....34.37N 3.23W
ai Japan 106 C2 ....34.34N 135.29E
akah Saudi Arabia 94 F5 ....29.56N 40.05E
akawea, Lake Canada 65 H4 ....47.45N 102.15W
arya r. Turkey 57 I5 ....41.07N 30.38E
ata Japan 106 C3 ....38.54N 139.49E
nalin i. Rus. Fed. 59 P2 ....48.10N 142.40E
ura Japan 106 D3 ....35.44N 140.13E
v. Cape Verde 84 B3 ....16.49N 22.59W
 Sweden 40 D2 ....59.55N 16.36E
do r. Argentina 77 C3 ....32.27S 60.49W
do r. Mexico 70 C6 ....26.45N 99.26W
alah Oman 95 H4 ....17.02N 54.10E
amanca Spain 48 C4 ....40.58N 5.39W
antai Lithuania 46 F4 ....56.04N 21.35F
wati i. Indonesia 105 I3 ....1.05S 130.53E
yar i. Indonesia 105 G2 ....6.08S 120.30E
y Gómez, Isla i. S. Pacific Oc. 109 M4 ....26.31S 105.42W
iininkai Lithuania 46 G5 ....54.18N 25.23E
ombe England 13 D2 ....50.14N 3.46W
lanha S. Africa 86 A1 ....33.01S 17.57E
 Australia 110 D3 ....38.06S 147.06E
 England 15 E2 ....53.26N 2.19W
hurst England 11 F1 ....50.59N 0.30E
khard Rus. Fed. 58 H4 ....66.31N 66.43E
em India 96 E3 ....11.37N 78.08E
em U.S.A. 64 B5 ....44.54N 122.58W
rno Italy 50 F4 ....40.40N 14.47E
rno, Golfo di g. Italy 50 F4 ....40.25N 14.43E
ord England 15 E2 ....53.29N 2.18W
gado r. Brazil 77 M7 ....4.27S 37.46W
hli Turkey 57 H4 ....38.29N 28.08E
horsk Belarus 55 L5 ....52.47N 27.32E
nas Brazil 77 L4 ....16.10S 42.17W
nas U.S.A. 64 B4 ....36.41N 121.39W
sbury England 10 D2 ....51.04N 1.48W
sbury U.S.A. 65 K4 ....38.22N 75.36W
sbury Plain f. England 10 C2 ....51.15N 2.03W
tre r. Brazil 77 L6 ....9.30S 40.33W
uit Canada 63 K4 ....62.11N 75.42W
non r. U.S.A. 64 C3 ....45.52N 116.45W
non Arm Canada 64 C7 ....50.42N 119.17W
mon River Mountains U.S.A. 64 C5 ....44.46N 115.01W
 Finland 40 E3 ....60.23N 23.08E
sk Rus. Fed. 53 L6 ....51.32N 46.02E
a U.S.A. 64 D3 ....33.22N 112.17W
ta Argentina 73 C4 ....24.45S 65.25W
tash England 13 C2 ....50.24N 4.13W
tcoats Scotland 16 E3 ....55.38N 4.47W
tee Islands Ireland 41 E2 ....52.07N 6.36W
tillo Mexico 70 D6 ....25.25N 101.01W
t Lake City U.S.A. 64 D5 ....40.42N 111.54W
to Uruguay 77 I1 ....31.23S 57.57W
ton Sea l. U.S.A. 64 C3 ....33.28N 115.58W
vador Brazil 77 M6 ....12.57S 38.25W
yan Azerbaijan 95 G2 ....39.35N 48.58E
zburg Austria 54 E2 ....47.48N 13.03E
zgitter Germany 54 D5 ....52.10N 10.24E
mandağ Turkey 57 K3 ....36.04N 35.58E
mani Japan 106 D4 ....42.05N 142.45E
mar r. Phil. 105 H6 ....11.54N 125.43E
mara Rus. Fed. 58 G3 ....53.11N 50.09E
marinda Indonesia 104 F3 ....0.29S 117.11E
marrā' Iraq 94 F6 ....34.12N 43.54E
mba Dem. Rep. Congo 86 B4 ....4.38S 26.20E
mbalpur India 96 F5 ....21.27N 83.59E
mbir Ukraine 55 J3 ....49.31N 23.12E
mbre r. Belgium/France 42 D3 ....50.17N 4.06E
me Tanzania 87 B1 ....4.05S 37.45E
mer France 11 G3 ....50.38N 1.45E
moa S. Pacific Oc. 108 I5 ....13.58S 173.23W
moa Basin f. S. Pacific Oc. 108 I4 ....15.26S 165.38W
mos i. Greece 56 G3 ....37.49N 26.44E
mothraki i. Greece 56 F5 ....40.24N 25.34E
mpit Indonesia 104 E3 ....2.34S 112.55E
msun Turkey 57 L5 ....41.17N 36.19E

San Mali 84 D3 ....13.18N 4.54W
San'ā' Yemen 94 F3 ....15.23N 44.11E
Sanandaj Iran 95 G7 ....35.16N 46.58E
San Andrés, Isla de i. Caribbean Sea 71 H3 ....12.33N 81.41W
San Angelo U.S.A. 64 F3 ....31.28N 100.23W
San Antonio U.S.A. 64 G2 ....29.22N 98.27W
San Antonio, Cabo c. Cuba 71 H5 ....21.51N 84.55W
San Benedicto, Isla i. Mexico 70 B4 ....19.19N 110.47W
San Bernardo 78 F6 1 ....33.36S 70.41W
San Borja Bolivia 76 G5 ....14.49S 66.54W
San Cristóbal i. Solomon Is 111 F5 ....10.38S 161.38E
San Cristóbal Venezuela 72 B7 ....7.45N 72.15W
San Cristóbal, Isla i. Ecuador 76 B7 ....0.48S 89.20W
San Cristóbal de la Laguna Canary Islands 48 X2 ....28.28N 16.19W
Sancti Spíritus Cuba 71 I5 ....21.56N 79.26W
Sanda Island Scotland 16 D3 ....55.16N 5.35W
Sandakan Malaysia 104 F5 ....5.51N 118.05E
Sandane Norway 40 A3 ....61.47N 6.14E
Sandanski Bulgaria 56 E5 ....41.34N 23.16E
Sanday i. Scotland 19 G4 ....59.15N 2.29W
Sanday Sound str. Scotland 19 G4 ....59.12N 2.34W
Sandbach England 15 E2 ....53.09N 2.22W
Sandhurst England 10 E2 ....51.21N 0.48W
San Diego U.S.A. 64 C3 ....32.43N 117.05W
Sandıklı Turkey 57 I4 ....38.28N 30.16E
Sandnes Norway 40 A2 ....58.51N 5.44E
Sandnessjøen Norway 40 C4 ....66.01N 12.39E
Sandomierz Poland 46 E3 ....50.41N 21.45E
Sandoway Myanmar 97 H4 ....18.27N 94.22E
Sandown England 10 D1 ....50.40N 1.09W
Sandpoint U.S.A. 64 C6 ....48.16N 116.33W
Sandray i. Scotland 18 B1 ....56.54N 7.30W
Sandviken Sweden 40 D3 ....60.37N 16.46E
Sandwich England 11 G2 ....51.16N 1.20E
Sandy England 11 E3 ....52.08N 0.18W
Sandy Cape Australia 110 E4 ....24.42S 153.15E
Sandy Lake town Canada 63 I3 ....53.03N 93.18W
San Felipe Mexico 70 B7 ....31.02N 114.50W
San Félix Chile 109 Q4 ....28.54S 70.30W
San Fernando Argentina 77 I1 ....34.28S 58.31W
San Fernando Phil. 104 G7 ....16.38N 120.18E
San Fernando Spain 48 B2 ....36.28N 6.11W
San Fernando de Apure Venezuela 72 C7 ....7.49N 67.28W
San Francisco U.S.A. 64 B4 ....37.45N 122.25W
San Francisco, Cabo de c. Ecuador 76 D8 ....0.40N 80.03W
San Francisco de Paula, Cabo c. Argentina 73 C2 49.42S 67.40W
Sangha r. Congo 86 B4 ....1.10S 16.47E
Sangir, Kepulauan is Indonesia 105 G4 ....2.15N 124.57E
Sangkulirang Indonesia 104 F4 ....0.55N 117.58E
Sangli India 96 D4 ....16.53N 74.38E
Sangre de Cristo Range mts U.S.A. 64 E4 ....38.19N 106.01W
Sangue r. Brazil 77 I5 ....11.02S 58.32W
San Jorge, Golfo de g. Argentina 73 C2 ....45.57S 65.55W
San José Costa Rica 71 H2 ....9.57N 84.02W
San Jose U.S.A. 64 B4 ....37.18N 121.57W
San José, Isla i. Mexico 70 B5 ....24.54N 110.33W
San José del Cabo Mexico 70 C5 ....23.04N 109.44W
San Juan Argentina 73 C3 ....31.33S 68.31W
San Juan r. Costa Rica/Nicaragua 71 H1 ....10.47N 83.44W
San Juan Puerto Rico 71 K4 ....18.26N 66.04W
San Juan r. U.S.A. 64 D4 ....37.15N 110.30W
San Juan Bautista Paraguay 77 I2 ....26.34S 57.06W
San Juan Mountains U.S.A. 64 E4 ....37.35N 107.17W
Şanlıurfa Turkey 57 M3 ....37.09N 38.49E
San Lorenzo mt. Spain 48 D5 ....42.14N 2.58W
Sanlúcar de Barrameda Spain 48 B2 ....36.46N 6.21W
San Luis Argentina 76 G1 ....33.19S 66.21W
San Luis, Lago de l. Bolivia 76 H5 ....13.45S 64.00W
San Luis Obispo U.S.A. 64 B4 ....35.18N 120.40W
San Luis Potosí Mexico 70 D5 ....22.10N 100.57W
San Luis Potosí d. Mexico 70 D5 ....22.51N 100.48W
San Marcos U.S.A. 64 G2 ....29.51N 97.56W
San Marino Europe 50 E5 ....43.58N 12.27E
San Marino San Marino 50 E5 ....43.57N 12.27E
San Martín r. Bolivia 77 H5 ....13.05S 63.48W
San Matías, Golfo g. Argentina 73 C2 ....41.20S 64.35W
San Miguel r. Bolivia 76 H5 ....13.52S 63.54W
San Miguel El Salvador 70 G3 ....13.32N 88.08W
San Miguel de Tucumán Argentina 73 C4 ....26.48S 65.16W
Sanming China 103 L3 ....26.11N 117.39E
San Nicolás de los Arroyos Argentina 77 H1 ....33.20S 60.14W
Sanok Poland 46 F2 ....49.34N 22.11E
San Pablo Phil. 105 G6 ....14.04N 121.18E
San Pedro Paraguay 77 I3 ....24.08S 57.08W
San Pedro, Sierra de mts Spain 48 B3 ....39.31N 7.15W
San Pedro de Ycuamandyyú Paraguay 73 D4 ....24.07S 57.07W
San Pedro Sula Honduras 70 G4 ....15.28N 88.01W
San Pietro, Isola di i. Italy 50 C3 ....39.10N 8.14E
Sanquhar Scotland 17 F3 ....55.22N 3.56W
San Quintín, Cabo c. Mexico 64 C3 ....30.23N 116.01W
San Remo Italy 50 B5 ....43.49N 7.47E
San Salvador i. Bahamas 71 J5 ....24.07N 74.27W
San Salvador El Salvador 70 G3 ....13.43N 89.11W
San Salvador de Jujuy Argentina 73 C4 ....24.10S 65.20W
San Sebastián de la Gomera Canary Islands 48 X2 ....28.05N 17.06W
San Severo Italy 50 F4 ....41.41N 15.23E
Santa Ana El Salvador 70 G3 ....14.00N 89.31W
Santa Ana U.S.A. 64 C3 ....33.45N 117.56W
Santa Barbara U.S.A. 64 C3 ....34.27N 119.43W
Santa Catarina d. Brazil 77 J2 ....27.00S 50.57W
Santa Clara Cuba 71 I5 ....22.24N 79.56W
Santa Cruz Bolivia 76 H4 ....17.47S 63.12W
Santa Cruz, Isla i. Ecuador 76 B7 ....0.36S 90.10W
Santa Cruz de la Palma Canary Islands 48 X2 ....28.41N 17.46W
Santa Cruz de Tenerife Canary Islands 48 X2 ....28.27N 16.15W
Santa Cruz do Sul Brazil 77 J2 ....29.44S 52.25W
Santa Cruz Islands Solomon Is 111 F5 ....10.46S 167.21E
Santa Elena, Bahía de b. Ecuador 76 D7 ....2.07S 81.05W
Santa Fé Argentina 73 C3 ....31.37S 60.42W
Santa Fe U.S.A. 64 E4 ....35.42N 105.57W
Santa Isabel i. Solomon Is 111 E6 ....7.54S 159.11E
Santa Margarita, Isla i. Mexico 70 B5 ....24.25N 111.50W
Santa Maria Brazil 77 J2 ....29.41S 53.48W
Santa Maria U.S.A. 64 B3 ....34.58N 120.26W
Santa Maria di Leuca, Capo c. Italy 50 H3 ....39.47N 18.21E
Santa Marta Colombia 72 B8 ....11.16N 74.12W
Santander Spain 48 D5 ....43.28N 3.48W
Santarém Brazil 77 J7 ....2.25S 54.43W
Santarém Portugal 48 A3 ....39.15N 8.41W
Santa Rosa Argentina 73 C3 ....36.37S 64.17W
Santa Rosalía Mexico 70 B6 ....27.21N 112.18W
Santiago r. Cape Verde 84 B3 ....15.19N 23.45W
Santiago Chile 73 B3 ....33.28S 70.39W
Santiago Dom. Rep. 71 J4 ....19.29N 70.41W
Santiago de Compostela Spain 48 A5 ....42.53N 8.32W
Santiago de Cuba Cuba 71 I5 ....20.00N 75.49W
Sant Jordi, Golf de g. Spain 48 F4 ....40.49N 0.59E
Santo André Brazil 77 K3 ....23.38S 46.30W
Santo Antão i. Cape Verde 84 B3 ....17.01N 25.21W
Santo Domingo Dom. Rep. 71 K4 ....18.31N 69.52W
Santoña Spain 48 D5 ....43.27N 3.27W
Santos Brazil 77 K3 ....23.58S 46.20W

Santos Plateau f. S. Atlantic Oc. 109 Q4 ....27.20S 45.43W
Santo Tomé Argentina 77 I2 ....28.32S 56.05W
San Valentín, Cerro mt. Chile 73 B2 ....46.35S 73.27W
San Vincenzo Italy 50 D5 ....43.05N 10.32E
San Carlos Brazil 77 K3 ....22.02S 47.53W
São Francisco r. Brazil 77 M5 ....10.19S 36.31W
São José do Rio Preto Brazil 77 K3 ....20.49S 49.22W
São Luís Brazil 77 L7 ....2.35S 44.18W
São Marcos, Baía de b. Brazil 77 L7 ....2.31S 44.19W
São Mateus Brazil 77 M4 ....18.42S 39.51W
Saône r. France 44 F4 ....45.44N 4.49E
São Paulo Brazil 77 K3 ....23.35S 46.43W
São Paulo d. Brazil 77 K3 ....22.19S 48.23W
São Raimundo Nonato Brazil 77 L6 ....9.01S 42.37W
São Sebastião, Ilha do i. Brazil 77 K3 ....23.51S 45.17W
São Tomé São Tomé and Príncipe 84 E2 ....0.19N 6.44E
São Tomé i. São Tomé and Príncipe 84 E2 ....0.21N 6.35E
São Tomé and Príncipe Africa 84 E2 ....1.00N 7.04E
São Vicente Brazil 77 K3 ....23.58S 46.22W
São Vicente, Cabo de c. Portugal 48 A2 ....37.01N 8.59W
Sapporo Japan 106 D4 ....43.04N 141.20E
Sapri Italy 50 F4 ....40.04N 15.38E
Saqqaq Greenland 63 M5 ....70.01N 51.56W
Saqqez Iran 95 G7 ....36.12N 46.15E
Sarāb Iran 95 G7 ....37.55N 47.31E
Sara Buri Thailand 104 C6 ....14.29N 100.57E
Sarajevo Bos.-Herz. 56 C6 ....43.51N 18.25E
Sarandë Albania 56 D4 ....39.53N 20.01E
Saransk Rus. Fed. 58 F3 ....54.11N 45.12E
Sarasota U.S.A. 65 J2 ....27.19N 82.33W
Saratov Rus. Fed. 58 F3 ....51.34N 45.59E
Saravan Iran 95 J5 ....27.20N 62.25E
Sarawak d. Malaysia 104 E4 ....1.46N 111.55E
Saray Turkey 57 G5 ....41.26N 27.55E
Sardindida Plain f. Kenya 87 B3 ....2.41N 39.59E
Sardinia i. Italy 50 C4 ....40.16N 8.04E
Sarektjåkkå mt. Sweden 40 D4 ....67.27N 17.43E
Sar-e Pol Afgh. 95 K7 ....36.15N 65.57E
Sargodha Pakistan 96 D7 ....32.01N 72.41E
Sarh Chad 85 F2 ....9.07N 18.23E
Sārī Iran 95 H7 ....36.33N 53.03E
Sarigan i. N. Mariana Is 105 L7 ....16.42N 145.48E
Sarıyer Turkey 57 H5 ....41.10N 29.03E
Sark i. Channel Is 13 Y9 ....49.24N 2.24W
Şarkışla Turkey 57 L4 ....39.21N 36.25E
Şarköy Turkey 56 G5 ....40.37N 27.06E
Särna Sweden 40 C3 ....61.42N 13.08E
Sarny Ukraine 55 L4 ....51.20N 26.37E
Saros Körfezi b. Turkey 56 G5 ....40.34N 26.36E
Sarpsborg Norway 40 B2 ....59.17N 11.08E
Sarreborg France 44 G6 ....48.44N 7.03E
Sarreguemines France 42 G2 ....49.07N 7.04E
Sarria Spain 48 B5 ....42.47N 7.24W
Sarthe r. France 44 C5 ....47.34N 0.31W
Sasebo Japan 106 A2 ....33.09N 129.44E
Saskatchewan d. Canada 62 H3 ....53.08N 106.03W
Saskatchewan r. Canada 62 H3 ....53.40N 100.27W
Saskatoon Canada 62 H3 ....52.08N 106.39W
Sassandra Côte d'Ivoire 84 D2 ....4.57N 6.05W
Sassari Italy 50 C4 ....40.43N 8.34E
Sassnitz Germany 54 E6 ....54.31N 13.38E
Satpura Range mts India 96 D5 ....21.47N 74.23E
Satu Mare Romania 55 J2 ....47.47N 22.53E
Sauðárkrókur Iceland 40 Y2 ....65.45N 19.40W
Saudi Arabia Asia 94 F4 ....23.41N 44.13E
Sault Sainte Marie Canada 63 J2 ....46.31N 84.20W
Saumlakki Indonesia 105 I2 ....8.00S 131.20F
Saundersfoot Wales 12 C3 ....51.43N 4.42W
Saurimo Angola 86 B4 ....9.39S 20.25E
Sava r. Europe 56 D6 ....44.50N 20.28E
Savai'i i. Samoa 108 I5 ....13.25S 172.39W
Savannah U.S.A. 65 J3 ....32.04N 81.07W
Savannah r. U.S.A. 65 J3 ....32.02N 80.53W
Savannakhét Laos 104 C7 ....16.32N 104.46E
Save r. Mozambique/Zimbabwe 86 C2 ....20.56S 35.03E
Savona Italy 50 C6 ....44.19N 8.29E
Savu Sea Indonesia 105 G2 ....9.51S 121.22E
Sawel Mountain hill Northern Ireland 16 B2 ....54.49N 7.02W
Sawhāj Egypt 85 H4 ....26.31N 31.38E
Sawston England 11 F3 ....52.07N 0.10E
Sawtry England 11 E3 ....52.26N 0.17W
Sawu i. Indonesia 105 G1 ....10.32S 121.58E
Saxilby England 15 G2 ....53.16N 0.40W
Saxmundham England 11 G3 ....52.13N 1.29E
Sayhūt Yemen 95 H3 ....15.15N 51.19F
Saylac Somalia 85 I3 ....11.17N 43.28E
Saynshand Mongolia 103 K6 ....44.46N 110.12E
Scafell Pike hill England 14 D3 ....54.27N 3.13W
Scalasaig Scotland 16 C4 ....56.04N 6.11W
Scalby England 15 G3 ....54.18N 0.27W
Scalloway Scotland 19 H5 ....60.08N 1.17W
Scalp hill Ireland 41 C2 ....52.59N 8.29W
Scalpay i. High. Scotland 18 D2 ....57.18N 5.59W
Scalpay i. W. Isles Scotland 18 C2 ....57.52N 6.39W
Scalp Mountain hill Ireland 16 B3 ....55.06N 7.22W
Scampton England 15 G2 ....53.18N 0.34W
Scandinavia f. Europe 34 F4 ....65.00N 18.00E
Scapa Flow inlet Scotland 19 F3 ....58.54N 3.08W
Scarba i. Scotland 16 D4 ....56.10N 5.45W
Scarborough England 15 G3 ....54.17N 0.24W
Scarp i. Scotland 18 B3 ....58.01N 7.11W
Schaffhausen Switz. 50 C7 ....47.42N 8.38E
Schagen Neth. 42 D5 ....52.47N 4.48E
Schefferville Canada 63 L3 ....54.47N 66.48W
Scheldt r. Belgium 42 D4 ....51.21N 4.15E
Schiehallion mt. Scotland 19 E1 ....56.40N 4.06W
Schiermonnikoog i. Neth. 42 F6 ....53.31N 6.17E
Schleswig Germany 54 C6 ....54.31N 9.33E
Schwaner, Pegunungan mts Indonesia 104 E3 ....0.46S 112.26E
Schwarzer Mann hill Germany 42 F3 ....50.15N 6.21E
Schwedt an der Oder Germany 54 F5 ....53.04N 14.18E
Schweinfurt Germany 54 D4 ....50.03N 10.13E
Schwerin Germany 54 D5 ....53.38N 11.25E
Scilly, Isles of England 13 A1 ....49.53N 6.17W
Scioto r. U.S.A. 65 J4 ....38.44N 82.59W
Scole England 11 G3 ....52.22N 1.09E
Scone Scotland 17 F4 ....56.25N 3.24W
Scotland U.K. 8 D5 ....57.01N 3.53W
Scottish Borders d. Scotland 8 D4 ....55.40N 2.44W
Scottsbluff U.S.A. 64 F5 ....41.54N 103.41W
Scourie Scotland 18 D3 ....58.21N 5.09W
Scranton U.S.A. 65 K5 ....41.25N 75.39W
Scridain, Loch inlet Scotland 16 C4 ....56.21N 6.11W
Scunthorpe England 15 G2 ....53.35N 0.39W
Scuol Switz. 50 D7 ....46.48N 10.18E
Scutari, Lake Albania/Montenegro 56 C6 ....42.14N 19.12E
Seaford England 11 F1 ....50.46N 0.06E
Seaham England 15 F3 ....54.50N 1.20W
Seamer England 15 G3 ....54.14N 0.26W
Seascale England 14 D3 ....54.24N 3.29W
Seaton Cumb. England 14 D3 ....54.40N 3.31W
Seaton Dev. England 13 D2 ....50.42N 3.04W

Seaton Delaval England 15 F4 ....55.04N 1.31W
Seattle U.S.A. 64 B6 ....47.36N 122.20W
Sebastián Vizcaíno, Bahía b. Mexico 70 B6 ....28.08N 114.45W
Sebeş Romania 56 E7 ....45.58N 23.34E
Şebinkarahisar Turkey 57 M5 ....40.17N 38.25E
Sechura, Bahía de b. Peru 76 D6 ....5.42S 81.18W
Secunderabad India 96 E4 ....17.25N 78.27E
Sedan France 44 F6 ....49.42N 4.57E
Sedbergh England 15 E3 ....54.19N 2.31W
Sedlčany Czech Rep. 46 B2 ....49.39N 14.26E
Šeduva Lithuania 46 F5 ....55.46N 23.44E
Seefin hill Ireland 41 D2 ....52.14N 7.36W
Segen Wenz watercourse Ethiopia 87 B4 ....4.58N 36.54E
Segera Tanzania 87 B1 ....5.20S 38.34E
Segorbe Spain 48 E3 ....39.51N 0.28W
Segovia Spain 48 C4 ....40.57N 4.06W
Segura r. Spain 48 E3 ....38.06N 0.38W
Segura, Sierra de mts Spain 48 D2 ....37.59N 2.46W
Seiland i. Norway 40 E5 ....70.28N 23.18E
Seinäjoki Finland 40 E3 ....62.47N 22.50E
Seine r. France 44 D6 ....49.26N 0.15E
Seine, Baie de b. France 44 C6 ....49.29N 0.32W
Sejny Poland 46 F5 ....54.06N 23.21E
Sekondi Ghana 84 D2 ....4.58N 1.43W
Selaru i. Indonesia 105 I2 ....8.13S 130.55E
Selatan, Tanjung pt Indonesia 104 E3 ....4.09S 114.38E
Selattyn England 10 B3 ....52.54N 3.05W
Selawik U.S.A. 62 B4 ....66.36N 160.16W
Selby England 15 F2 ....53.47N 1.04W
Selkirk Canada 62 I3 ....50.09N 96.53W
Selkirk Scotland 17 G3 ....55.33N 2.50W
Sellindge England 11 F2 ....51.06N 0.59E
Selsey England 10 E1 ....50.44N 0.47W
Selsey Bill hd England 10 E1 ....50.43N 0.49W
Selvas f. Brazil 76 F6 ....6.29S 71.47W
Selwyn Mountains Canada 62 E4 ....64.16N 131.38W
Selwyn Range hills Australia 110 C4 ....21.14S 139.54E
Semarang Indonesia 104 E2 ....6.55S 110.29E
Semenivka Ukraine 55 O5 ....52.10N 32.35E
Seminoe Reservoir U.S.A. 64 E5 ....42.06N 106.51W
Semipalatinsk Kazakhstan 58 J3 ....50.25N 80.19E
Semnān Iran 95 H7 ....35.30N 53.21E
Semois r. Belgium/France 42 D2 ....49.53N 4.45E
Sena Madureira Brazil 76 G6 ....9.07S 68.42W
Sendai Japan 106 D3 ....38.15N 140.53E
Senegal Africa 84 C3 ....14.29N 14.41W
Sénégal r. Mauritania 84 C3 ....16.00N 16.31W
Senftenberg Germany 46 B3 ....51.31N 14.00E
Senja i. Norway 40 D5 ....69.20N 17.14E
Senlis France 42 B2 ....49.12N 2.36E
Sennar Sudan 85 H3 ....13.31N 33.36E
Sens France 44 E6 ....48.12N 3.17E
Seoul S. Korea 103 N5 ....37.32N 127.00E
Sepik r. P.N.G. 105 K3 ....3.53S 144.33E
Sept-Îles Canada 63 L3 ....50.13N 66.23W
Seram i. Indonesia 105 H3 ....3.03S 129.24E
Serang Indonesia 104 D2 ....6.04S 106.09E
Serbia Europe 56 D6 ....44.01N 20.55E
Şereflikoçhisar Turkey 57 J4 ....38.56N 33.33E
Seremban Malaysia 104 C4 ....2.41N 101.54E
Serengeti National Park Tanzania 87 A2 ....2.28S 34.46E
Serengeti Plains f. Kenya 87 B2 ....3.43S 38.05E
Serere Uganda 87 A3 ....1.31N 33.28E
Seret r. Ukraine 55 K3 ....48.36N 25.51E
Sergipe d. Brazil 77 M5 ....10.30S 37.14W
Serik Turkey 57 I3 ....36.57N 31.07E
Serov Rus. Fed. 58 H3 ....59.38N 60.34E
Serowe Botswana 86 B2 ....22.24S 26.42E
Serpukhov Rus. Fed. 58 E3 ....54.55N 37.25E
Serra da Mesa, Represa resr Brazil 77 K5 ....14.17S 48.30W
Serres Greece 56 E5 ....41.06N 23.33E
Serui Indonesia 105 J3 ....1.52S 136.17E
Sestroretsk Rus. Fed. 40 G3 ....60.05N 29.57E
Sète France 44 E3 ....43.24N 3.42E
Sete Lagoas Brazil 77 L4 ....19.28S 44.13W
Setesdal f. Norway 40 A2 ....59.15N 7.23E
Sétif Algeria 84 E5 ....36.11N 5.25E
Seto-naikai sea Japan 106 B2 ....33.38N 132.17E
Settat Morocco 84 D5 ....32.58N 7.36W
Settle England 15 E3 ....54.04N 2.17W
Setúbal Portugal 48 A3 ....38.32N 8.53W
Setúbal, Baía de b. Portugal 48 A3 ....38.20N 9.02W
Seul, Lac l. Canada 65 H7 ....50.21N 92.29W
Sevastopol' Ukraine 53 J5 ....44.36N 33.31E
Seven Heads Ireland 41 C1 ....51.34N 8.42W
Sevenoaks England 11 F2 ....51.16N 0.12E
Severn r. Canada 63 J3 ....55.59N 87.36W
Severn r. U.K. 10 C2 ....51.51N 2.21W
Severnaya Zemlya is Rus. Fed. 59 L6 ....80.09N 103.23E
Severo-Kuril'sk Rus. Fed. 59 Q3 ....50.40N 156.06E
Sevier Lake U.S.A. 64 D4 ....38.56N 113.09W
Seville Spain 48 C2 ....37.23N 5.59W
Seward U.S.A. 62 D4 ....60.09N 149.24W
Seward Peninsula U.S.A. 62 B4 ....65.29N 164.05W
Seychelles Indian Oc. 85 J1 ....4.40S 55.43E
Seydişehir Turkey 57 I3 ....37.25N 31.52E
Seyðisfjörður Iceland 40 Z2 ....65.16N 14.02W
Seyhan r. Turkey 57 K3 ....36.44N 34.54E
Seym r. Rus. Fed./Ukraine 55 P4 ....51.16N 34.16E
Seymchan Rus. Fed. 59 Q4 ....62.50N 152.20E
Sfântu Gheorghe Romania 56 F7 ....45.52N 25.48E
Sfax Tunisia 52 F3 ....34.45N 10.45E
Sgurr Alasdair hill Scotland 18 C2 ....57.12N 6.13W
Sgurr Dhomhnuill hill Scotland 18 D1 ....56.45N 5.27W
Sgurr Mòr mt. Scotland 18 D2 ....57.42N 5.01W
Shaanxi d. China 103 J4 ....34.43N 108.13E
Shaftesbury England 10 C2 ....51.00N 2.12W
Shahr-e Kord Iran 95 H6 ....32.19N 50.49E
Shahrezā Iran 95 H6 ....32.00N 51.52E
Shakhovskaya Rus. Fed. 55 P7 ....56.02N 35.30E
Shakhty Rus. Fed. 53 L6 ....47.42N 40.12E
Shalkar Kazakhstan 58 G2 ....47.47N 59.39E
Shandong d. China 103 L5 ....36.22N 117.45E
Shandong Bandao pen. China 103 M5 ....37.05N 121.02E
Shanghai China 103 M4 ....31.15N 121.29E
Shangqiu China 103 L4 ....34.24N 115.38E
Shanklin England 10 D1 ....50.38N 1.10W
Shannon r. Ireland 41 C2 ....52.40N 8.38W
Shannon, Mouth of the Ireland 41 B2 ....52.31N 9.51W
Shantarskiye Ostrova is Rus. Fed. 59 O3 ....55.20N 137.22E
Shantou China 103 L2 ....23.24N 116.42E
Shanxi d. China 103 K5 ....38.03N 111.48E
Shaoguan China 103 K2 ....24.48N 113.37E
Shaoxing China 103 M4 ....30.01N 120.38E
Shaoyang China 103 K3 ....27.14N 111.30E
Shap England 15 E3 ....54.32N 2.41W
Shapinsay i. Scotland 19 G4 ....59.02N 2.48W
Shaqrā' Saudi Arabia 94 G5 ....25.15N 45.16E
Sharjah U.A.E. 95 I5 ....25.21N 55.23E
Shark Bay Australia 110 A4 ....25.17S 113.32E
Shashemenē Ethiopia 85 H2 ....7.12N 38.36E
Shasta, Mount vol. U.S.A. 64 B5 ....41.23N 122.10W
Shchigry Rus. Fed. 55 Q4 ....51.52N 36.56E
Shchuchyn Belarus 46 G4 ....53.37N 24.44E

Sheberghān Afgh. 95 K7 ...36.42N 65.45E
Sheboygan U.S.A. 65 I5 ...43.45N 87.43W
Sheelin, Lough l. Ireland 41 D3 ...53.49N 7.19W
Sheep Haven b. Ireland 16 B3 ...55.12N 7.55W
Sheerness England 11 F2 ...51.26N 0.46E
Sheffield England 15 F2 ...53.23N 1.28W
Shelby U.S.A. 64 D6 ...48.29N 111.48W
Shelikhova, Zaliv g. Rus. Fed. 59 Q4 ...60.40N 157.23E
Shelikof Strait U.S.A. 62 C3 ...57.27N 155.17W
Shengena mt. Tanzania 87 B1 ...4.16S 37.56E
Shenyang China 103 M6 ...41.46N 123.24E
Shenzhen China 103 K2 ...22.33N 114.09E
Shepetivka Ukraine 55 L4 ...50.11N 27.04E
Sheppey, Isle of i. England 11 F2 ...51.24N 0.46E
Shepshed England 10 D3 ...52.46N 1.18W
Shepton Mallet England 10 C2 ...51.11N 2.33W
Sherborne England 10 C1 ...50.57N 2.31W
Sherbrooke Canada 63 K2 ...45.24N 71.54W
Shereiq Sudan 94 D3 ...18.42N 33.40E
Sheridan U.S.A. 64 E5 ...44.48N 106.55W
Sheringham England 11 G3 ...52.57N 1.13E
's-Hertogenbosch Neth. 42 E4 ...51.41N 5.19E
Sherwood Forest England 15 F2 ...53.04N 1.07W
Shetland d. Scotland 8 E7 ...60.14N 0.57W
Shetland Islands Scotland 19 I5 ...60.36N 0.47W
Sheyenne r. U.S.A. 64 G6 ...47.03N 96.50W
Shiant Islands Scotland 18 C2 ...57.53N 6.25W
Shibām Yemen 95 G3 ...15.59N 48.57E
Shiel, Loch l. Scotland 18 D1 ...56.47N 5.35W
Shieldaig Scotland 18 D2 ...57.31N 5.39W
Shifnal England 10 C3 ...52.40N 2.22W
Shihezi China 102 F6 ...44.14N 86.03E
Shijiazhuang China 103 K5 ...38.00N 114.30E
Shikarpur India 96 E3 ...14.14N 75.18E
Shikarpur Pakistan 95 K5 ...27.56N 68.42E
Shikoku i. Japan 106 B2 ...33.08N 133.49E
Shikoku-sanchi mts Japan 106 B2 ...33.26N 132.53E
Shildon England 15 F3 ...54.38N 1.39W
Shillong India 97 H6 ...25.33N 91.53E
Shimoga India 96 E3 ...13.54N 75.31E
Shimoni Kenya 87 B1 ...4.39S 39.22E
Shimonoseki Japan 106 B2 ...33.57N 130.57E
Shin, Loch l. Scotland 19 E3 ...58.09N 4.38W
Shingū Japan 106 C2 ...33.43N 136.00E
Shining Tor hill England 15 E2 ...53.16N 2.00W
Shipley England 15 F2 ...53.50N 1.47W
Shipston on Stour England 10 D3 ...52.04N 1.37W
Shirane-san mt. Japan 106 C3 ...35.40N 138.13E
Shīrāz Iran 95 H5 ...29.37N 52.31E
Shire r. Malawi 86 C3 ...17.41S 35.19E
Shizuishan China 103 J5 ...38.58N 106.27E
Shizuoka Japan 106 C2 ...34.58N 138.23E
Shklow Belarus 55 N6 ...54.13N 30.17E
Shkodër Albania 56 C6 ...42.04N 19.31E
Shona, Eilean i. Scotland 18 D1 ...56.48N 5.53W
Sho'rchi Uzbekistan 95 K7 ...37.59N 67.46E
Shostka Ukraine 55 O4 ...51.51N 33.29E
Shpola Ukraine 55 N3 ...49.01N 31.23E
Shreveport U.S.A. 65 H3 ...32.29N 93.46W
Shrewsbury England 10 C3 ...52.42N 2.45W
Shropshire d. England 9 D3 ...52.45N 2.38W
Shuangjiang China 103 H2 ...23.28N 99.49E
Shumagin Islands U.S.A. 62 C3 ...55.09N 161.01W
Shumen Bulgaria 56 G6 ...43.16N 26.56E
Shuqrah Yemen 95 G2 ...13.24N 45.40E
Shushtar Iran 95 G6 ...32.01N 48.49E
Shwebo Myanmar 97 I5 ...22.34N 95.43E
Shwegyin Myanmar 97 I4 ...17.56N 96.52E
Shymkent Kazakhstan 58 H2 ...42.19N 69.38E
Siahan Range mts Pakistan 95 J5 ...27.13N 63.38E
Šiauliai Lithuania 40 E1 ...55.56N 23.19E
Siaya Kenya 87 A3 ...0.02N 34.15E
Šibenik Croatia 56 A6 ...43.44N 15.54E
Siberia f. Rus. Fed. 59 M4 ...65.18N 115.57E
Siberut i. Indonesia 104 B3 ...1.23S 98.41E
Sibi Pakistan 95 K5 ...29.30N 67.55E
Sibiloi National Park Kenya 87 B3 ...3.59N 36.24E
Sibiu Romania 56 F7 ...45.48N 24.10E
Sibolga Indonesia 104 B4 ...1.40N 98.48E
Sibsey England 15 H2 ...53.02N 0.01E
Sibu Malaysia 104 E4 ...2.17N 111.51E
Sibut C.A.R. 85 F2 ...5.44N 19.05E
Sichuan d. China 103 I4 ...30.05N 103.11E
Sicily i. Italy 50 F3 ...38.21N 14.09E
Sidi Bel Abbès Algeria 84 D5 ...35.12N 0.38W
Sidi Kacem Morocco 52 B3 ...34.12N 5.39W
Sidlaw Hills Scotland 17 F4 ...56.26N 3.21W
Sidmouth England 13 D2 ...50.41N 3.14W
Sidney U.S.A. 64 F5 ...41.12N 103.09W
Sidon Lebanon 53 K3 ...33.33N 35.23E
Siedlce Poland 46 F4 ...52.10N 22.17E
Siegen Germany 54 C4 ...50.52N 8.01E
Siena Italy 50 D5 ...43.19N 11.20E
Sieradz Poland 46 D3 ...51.36N 18.44E
Sierra Leone Africa 84 C2 ...8.35N 11.58W
Sighetu Marmației Romania 55 J2 ...47.56N 23.54E
Sighișoara Romania 56 F8 ...46.14N 24.47E
Siglufjörður Iceland 40 Y2 ...66.08N 18.52W
Sigüenza Spain 48 D4 ...41.05N 2.37W
Siguiri Guinea 84 D3 ...11.28N 9.10W
Sihanoukville Cambodia 104 C6 ...10.38N 103.54E
Siilinjärvi Finland 40 F3 ...63.05N 27.40E
Siirt Turkey 94 F7 ...37.55N 41.58E
Sikar India 96 E6 ...27.31N 75.13E
Sikasso Mali 84 D3 ...11.19N 5.40W
Sikeston U.S.A. 65 I4 ...36.51N 89.34W
Sikhote-Alin' mts Rus. Fed. 59 O2 ...43.58N 133.53E
Sikkim d. India 96 G6 ...27.31N 88.27E
Sil r. Spain 48 B5 ...42.28N 7.42W
Šilalė Lithuania 46 E5 ...55.29N 22.11E
Silesia f. Europe 46 C3 ...50.45N 17.01E
Siletiteniz, Ozero l. Kazakhstan 102 C8 ...53.11N 72.53E
Silifke Turkey 57 J3 ...36.22N 33.56E
Siling Co l. China 102 F4 ...31.47N 88.61E
Silistra Bulgaria 56 G7 ...44.07N 27.16E
Silivri Turkey 57 H5 ...41.04N 28.16E
Siljan l. Sweden 40 C3 ...60.53N 14.44E
Šilutė Lithuania 46 E5 ...55.21N 21.28E
Silver City U.S.A. 64 E3 ...32.45N 108.19W
Silverstone England 10 D3 ...52.05N 1.02W
Silverton England 13 D2 ...50.49N 3.29W
Simav Turkey 57 H4 ...39.05N 28.58E
Simēn mts Ethiopia 94 E2 ...13.16N 37.50E
Simeulue i. Indonesia 104 B4 ...2.41N 96.08E
Simferopol' Ukraine 53 J5 ...44.57N 34.07E
Șimleu Silvaniei Romania 46 F1 ...47.14N 22.50E
Šimojärvi l. Finland 40 F4 ...66.01N 27.15E
Simplon Pass Switz. 50 C7 ...46.15N 8.02E
Simpson Desert Australia 110 C4 ...24.59S 136.50E
Simrishamn Sweden 54 F6 ...55.33N 14.21E
Sinai pen. Egypt 85 H4 ...29.13N 33.47E
Sinai, Mont hill France 42 D2 ...49.09N 4.08E
Sinaloa d. Mexico 70 C6 ...25.42N 108.11W
Sincelejo Colombia 72 B7 ...9.17N 75.24W

Sinclair's Bay Scotland 19 F3 ...58.30N 3.07W
Sines Portugal 48 A2 ...37.58N 8.52W
Singa Sudan 94 D2 ...13.09N 33.54E
Singapore Asia 104 C4 ...1.27N 104.32E
Singapore town Singapore 104 C4 ...1.19N 103.51E
Singaraja Indonesia 104 F2 ...8.06S 115.06E
Singida Tanzania 86 C4 ...4.50S 34.45E
Singkawang Indonesia 104 D4 ...0.57N 108.59E
Sinj Croatia 56 B6 ...43.42N 16.38E
Sinkat Sudan 94 E3 ...18.45N 36.49E
Sinop Turkey 57 K6 ...42.02N 35.08E
Sint Maarten i. Neth. Antilles 71 L4 ...18.02N 63.04W
Sion Mills Northern Ireland 16 B2 ...54.47N 7.28W
Sioux City U.S.A. 64 G5 ...42.32N 96.23W
Sioux Falls town U.S.A. 64 G5 ...43.32N 96.43W
Sioux Lookout Canada 63 I3 ...50.06N 91.56W
Sipacate Guatemala 70 F3 ...13.59N 91.08W
Siping China 103 M6 ...43.04N 124.24E
Sipura i. Indonesia 104 B3 ...2.12S 99.42E
Sira r. Norway 40 A2 ...58.16N 6.24E
Siret r. Romania 56 H7 ...45.25N 28.02E
Sīrjān Iran 95 I5 ...29.27N 55.40E
Sirrei Ethiopia 87 C4 ...6.43N 42.05E
Sirte Libya 85 F5 ...31.09N 16.40E
Sirte, Gulf of Libya 85 F5 ...31.11N 18.03E
Širvintos Lithuania 46 G5 ...55.02N 24.58E
Sisak Croatia 56 B7 ...45.29N 16.23E
Sisimiut Greenland 63 M4 ...66.56N 53.40W
Sisophon Cambodia 104 C6 ...13.34N 102.59E
Sistan, Daryācheh-ye marsh Afgh./Iran 95 J6 ...31.33N 61.10E
Sisteron France 44 F4 ...44.12N 5.57E
Siteia Greece 56 G2 ...35.12N 26.06E
Sitka U.S.A. 62 E3 ...57.03N 135.18W
Sittard Neth. 42 E3 ...50.59N 5.51E
Sittingbourne England 11 F2 ...51.20N 0.44E
Sittwe Myanmar 97 H5 ...20.08N 92.54E
Sivas Turkey 57 L4 ...39.43N 37.00E
Siverek Turkey 57 M3 ...37.44N 39.21E
Sivrihisar Turkey 57 I4 ...39.27N 31.32E
Sīwah Egypt 85 G4 ...29.09N 25.30E
Skadovs'k Ukraine 57 J8 ...46.07N 32.54E
Skaftárós r. mouth Iceland 40 Y1 ...63.41N 17.47W
Skagen Denmark 40 B2 ...57.43N 10.35E
Skagerrak str. Denmark/Norway 40 B2 ...57.27N 8.13E
Skagway U.S.A. 62 E3 ...59.29N 135.18W
Skara Sweden 40 C2 ...58.23N 13.26E
Skarżysko-Kamienna Poland 46 E3 ...51.07N 20.53E
Skegness England 15 H2 ...53.09N 0.20E
Skellefteå Sweden 40 E4 ...64.45N 20.58E
Skellefteälven r. Sweden 40 E4 ...64.42N 21.07E
Skelmersdale England 14 E2 ...53.33N 2.46W
Skerries Ireland 41 E3 ...53.35N 6.06W
Ski Norway 40 B2 ...59.43N 10.50E
Skibbereen Ireland 41 B1 ...51.33N 9.16W
Skiddaw hill England 14 D3 ...54.39N 3.09W
Skien Norway 40 B2 ...59.12N 9.36E
Skierniewice Poland 46 E3 ...51.57N 20.09E
Skikda Algeria 84 E5 ...36.54N 6.57E
Skipton England 15 E2 ...53.58N 2.01W
Skive Denmark 40 B2 ...56.34N 9.02E
Skokholm Island Wales 12 B3 ...51.41N 5.16W
Skomer Island Wales 12 B3 ...51.44N 5.20W
Skopje Macedonia 56 D5 ...41.59N 21.27E
Skövde Sweden 40 C2 ...58.23N 13.51E
Skovorodino Rus. Fed. 59 N3 ...54.05N 123.52E
Skuodas Lithuania 46 E6 ...56.16N 21.32E
Skwierzyna Poland 46 B4 ...52.36N 15.30E
Skye i. Scotland 18 C2 ...57.21N 6.20W
Skyros i. Greece 56 F4 ...38.53N 24.35E
Slagelse Denmark 40 B1 ...55.24N 11.22E
Slamet vol. Indonesia 104 D2 ...7.14S 109.10E
Slaney r. Ireland 41 E2 ...52.25N 6.34W
Slatina Romania 56 F7 ...44.26N 24.22E
Slave r. Canada 62 G4 ...61.17N 113.31W
Slave Lake town Canada 62 G3 ...55.17N 114.47W
Slavonski Brod Croatia 56 C7 ...45.10N 18.01E
Slavyansk-na-Kubani Rus. Fed. 57 M7 ...45.16N 38.08E
Slawharad Belarus 55 N5 ...53.27N 31.00E
Sławno Poland 46 C5 ...54.22N 16.41E
Sleaford England 11 E4 ...53.00N 0.24W
Sleat, Sound of str. Scotland 18 D2 ...57.02N 5.53W
Sleights England 15 G3 ...54.27N 0.40W
Slieve Anierin hill Ireland 16 B2 ...54.05N 7.59W
Slieve Beagh hill Ireland/U.K. 16 B2 ...54.20N 7.12W
Slievecallan hill Ireland 41 B2 ...52.51N 9.16W
Slieve Car hill Ireland 41 B4 ...54.04N 9.40W
Slieve Donard hill Northern Ireland 16 D2 ...54.11N 5.55W
Slievenamon hill Ireland 41 D2 ...52.26N 7.34W
Slieve Snaght hill Ireland 41 D5 ...55.12N 7.20W
Sligo Ireland 41 C4 ...54.17N 8.28W
Sligo d. Ireland 41 C4 ...54.07N 8.30W
Sligo Bay Ireland 41 C4 ...54.18N 8.55W
Sliven Bulgaria 56 G6 ...42.41N 26.19E
Slobozia Romania 56 G7 ...44.34N 27.23E
Slonim Belarus 55 K5 ...53.05N 25.19E
Slough England 11 E2 ...51.31N 0.36W
Slough d. England 9 E2 ...51.30N 0.35W
Slovakia Europe 54 H3 ...48.45N 19.35E
Slovenia Europe 54 F1 ...46.09N 14.37E
Slovyechna r. Belarus 55 M4 ...51.39N 29.43E
Sluch r. Ukraine 55 L4 ...51.37N 26.39E
Słupsk Poland 46 C5 ...54.27N 17.02E
Slutsk Belarus 55 L5 ...53.01N 27.32E
Slyne Head Ireland 41 A3 ...53.24N 10.14W
Slyudyanka Rus. Fed. 103 I8 ...51.28N 103.36E
Smallwood Reservoir Canada 63 L3 ...54.01N 64.50W
Smarhon' Belarus 55 L6 ...54.29N 26.25E
Smila Ukraine 55 N3 ...49.12N 31.54E
Smoky r. U.S.A. 62 G3 ...56.08N 117.20W
Smøla i. Norway 40 A3 ...63.24N 7.59E
Smolensk Rus. Fed. 58 E3 ...54.47N 32.04E
Smolikas mt. Greece 56 D5 ...40.05N 20.56E
Smolyan Bulgaria 56 F5 ...41.35N 24.41E
Snæfell hill Isle of Man 14 C3 ...54.16N 4.28W
Snaith England 15 F2 ...53.41N 1.01W
Snake r. U.S.A. 64 C6 ...46.13N 119.59W
Snares Islands New Zealand 108 H2 ...48.02S 166.37E
Snåsa Norway 40 C4 ...64.15N 12.23E
Sneek Neth. 42 E6 ...53.02N 5.40E
Snettisham England 11 F3 ...52.53N 0.30E
Snežnik mt. Slovenia 54 F1 ...45.35N 14.26E
Śniardwy, Jezioro l. Poland 46 E4 ...53.46N 21.42E
Snizort, Loch b. Scotland 18 C2 ...57.33N 6.28W
Snøtinden mt. Norway 40 C4 ...66.38N 13.57E
Snov r. Ukraine 55 N4 ...51.32N 31.32E
Snowdon mt. Wales 12 C5 ...53.04N 4.04W
Soay i. Scotland 18 C2 ...57.09N 6.15W
Sobradinho, Barragem de resr Brazil 77 L5 ...10.14S 42.24W
Sobral Brazil 77 L7 ...3.41S 40.19W
Sochi Rus. Fed. 58 E2 ...43.36N 39.44E
Société, Archipel de la is French Polynesia 109 J4
...17.22S 152.28W
Socorro, Isla i. Mexico 70 B4 ...18.51N 110.58W

Socotra i. Yemen 95 H2 ...12.34N 54.30E
Sodankylä Finland 40 F4 ...67.25N 26.34E
Söderhamn Sweden 40 D3 ...61.18N 17.04E
Södertälje Sweden 40 D2 ...59.12N 17.38E
Sodo Ethiopia 85 H2 ...6.49N 37.42E
Södra Kvarken str. Finland/Sweden 40 D3 ...60.19N 19.02E
Sofia Bulgaria 56 E6 ...42.41N 23.19E
Sognefjorden inlet Norway 40 A3 ...61.05N 5.33E
Soham England 11 F3 ...52.20N 0.20E
Soignies Belgium 42 D3 ...50.35N 4.04E
Soissons France 44 E6 ...49.23N 3.20E
Sokal' Ukraine 46 G3 ...50.29N 24.17E
Söke Turkey 56 G3 ...37.45N 27.23E
Sokhumi Georgia 58 F2 ...43.00N 41.02E
Sokółka Poland 46 F4 ...53.24N 23.31E
Sokoto Nigeria 84 E3 ...13.05N 5.15E
Sokoto r. Nigeria 84 E3 ...11.23N 4.09E
Solapur India 96 E4 ...17.41N 75.55E
Solihull England 10 D3 ...52.25N 1.47W
Solikamsk Rus. Fed. 58 G3 ...59.42N 56.44E
Sollefteå Sweden 40 D3 ...63.10N 17.17E
Solomon Islands S. Pacific Oc. 111 F6 ...7.13S 157.49E
Solomon Sea S. Pacific Oc. 110 E6 ...7.01S 152.18E
Solway Firth est. Scotland 17 F2 ...54.48N 3.33W
Solwezi Zambia 86 B3 ...12.10S 26.26E
Soma Turkey 56 G4 ...39.10N 27.36E
Somalia Africa 85 I2 ...3.56N 46.23E
Sombor Serbia 56 C7 ...45.47N 19.07E
Somerset d. England 9 D2 ...51.04N 2.56W
Somerset Island Canada 63 I5 ...73.19N 93.22W
Somerton England 10 C2 ...51.03N 2.44W
Somme r. France 44 D6 ...50.11N 1.39E
Sønderborg Denmark 54 C6 ...54.55N 9.48E
Sondrio Italy 50 C7 ...46.10N 9.52E
Songea Tanzania 86 C3 ...10.39S 35.38E
Songkhla Thailand 104 C5 ...7.10N 100.35E
Son La Vietnam 104 C8 ...21.20N 103.57E
Sono r. Brazil 77 K6 ...8.58S 48.07W
Sonora d. Mexico 70 B6 ...29.42N 110.36W
Sonora r. Mexico 70 B6 ...28.47N 111.54W
Soria Spain 48 D4 ...41.47N 2.26W
Soroca Moldova 53 I6 ...48.09N 28.17E
Sorocaba Brazil 77 K3 ...23.45S 47.30W
Sorol atoll Micronesia 105 K5 ...8.10N 140.22E
Sorong Indonesia 105 I3 ...0.54S 131.17E
Soroti Uganda 85 H2 ...1.42N 33.37E
Sørøya i. Norway 40 E5 ...70.34N 22.32E
Sorraia r. Portugal 48 A3 ...39.02N 8.50W
Sorsele Sweden 40 D4 ...65.31N 17.33E
Sortavala Rus. Fed. 40 G3 ...61.42N 30.41E
Soshanguve S. Africa 86 B2 ...25.31S 28.06E
Sosna r. Rus. Fed. 55 R5 ...52.41N 38.54E
Sosneado mt. Argentina 73 C3 ...34.44S 69.59W
Sosnowiec Poland 46 D3 ...50.17N 19.08E
Souk Ahras Algeria 52 E4 ...36.17N 7.59E
Souk el Arbaâ du Rharb Morocco 48 C1 ...34.40N 5.58W
Souris r. Canada 64 G6 ...49.41N 99.40W
Sousse Tunisia 52 F4 ...35.47N 10.39E
Soustons France 44 C3 ...43.45N 1.20W
South Africa, Republic of Africa 86 B1 ...30.06S 24.04E
Southam England 10 D3 ...52.15N 1.23W
South America 72-73
Southampton England 10 D1 ...50.55N 1.24W
Southampton d. England 9 E2 ...50.55N 1.24W
Southampton Island Canada 63 J4 ...64.31N 85.04W
South Anston England 15 F2 ...53.21N 1.13W
South Australia d. Australia 110 C3 ...30.27S 132.43E
South Australian Basin f. Indian Oc. 108 D3 ...37.58S 119.18E
South Ayrshire d. Scotland 8 C4 ...55.09N 4.47W
South Bank England 15 F3 ...54.35N 1.10W
South Bend U.S.A. 65 I5 ...41.40N 86.13W
Southborough England 11 F2 ...51.09N 0.16E
South Carolina d. U.S.A. 65 J3 ...34.02N 80.47W
South Cave England 15 G2 ...53.46N 0.36W
South China Sea N. Pacific Oc. 104 F6 ...12.00N 117.49E
South Dakota d. U.S.A. 64 F5 ...44.27N 100.14W
South Dorset Downs hills England 10 C1 ...50.42N 2.37W
South Downs hills England 10 E1 ...50.53N 0.28W
South East Cape Australia 110 D2 ...43.38S 146.55E
Southeast Indian Ridge f. Indian Oc. 108 A4 ...31.15S 76.54E
Southeast Pacific Basin f. S. Pacific Oc. 116 D2 .63.41S 112.50W
Southend d. England 9 F2 ...51.33N 0.42E
Southend-on-Sea England 11 F2 ...51.32N 0.43E
Southern Alps mts New Zealand 111 G2 ...43.26S 170.28E
Southern Ocean 116 H2
Southern Uplands hills Scotland 16 E3 ...55.14N 4.32W
Southery England 11 F3 ...52.32N 0.24E
South Esk r. Scotland 19 G1 ...56.43N 2.33W
South Fiji Basin f. S. Pacific Oc. 108 H4 ...25.53S 175.02E
South Georgia i. S. Atlantic Oc. 73 F1 ...53.50S 36.30W
South Gloucestershire d. England 9 D2 ...51.33N 2.27W
South Harris pen. Scotland 18 B2 ...57.49N 7.03W
South Honshu Ridge f. N. Pacific Oc. 108 F8 ...31.09N 138.30E
South Horr Kenya 87 B3 ...2.07N 36.56E
South Island New Zealand 111 G2 ...44.24S 172.31E
South Kirkby England 15 F2 ...53.36N 1.19W
South Kitui National Reserve Kenya 87 B2 ...1.35S 38.50E
South Korea Asia 103 N5 ...35.32N 128.04E
South Lanarkshire d. Scotland 8 D4 ...55.35N 3.56W
Southminster England 11 F2 ...51.40N 0.50E
South Molton England 13 D3 ...51.01N 3.50W
South Nahanni r. Canada 62 F4 ...61.03N 123.18W
South Ockendon England 11 F2 ...51.31N 0.18E
South Platte r. U.S.A. 64 F5 ...41.08N 100.47W
Southport Australia 110 E3 ...27.56S 153.23E
Southport England 14 D2 ...53.39N 3.00W
South Ronaldsay i. Scotland 19 G3 ...58.47N 2.54W
South Saskatchewan r. Canada 62 H3 ...53.09N 105.08W
South Shields England 15 F3 ...54.59N 1.26W
South Solomon Trench f. S. Pacific Oc. 108 G5 .11.28S 162.19E
South Tasman Rise f. Southern Oc. 108 F2 ...45.34S 146.08E
South Tyne r. England 15 E3 ...54.59N 2.08W
South Uist i. Scotland 18 B2 ...57.17N 7.22W
South Walls pen. Scotland 19 F3 ...58.47N 3.08W
Southwell England 15 G2 ...53.04N 0.57W
Southwest Pacific Basin f. S. Pacific Oc. 109 O4 ...22.54S 83.41W
Southwold England 11 G3 ...52.19N 1.41E
South Woodham Ferrers England 11 F2 ...51.39N 0.37E
South Wootton England 11 F3 ...52.46N 0.26E
South Yorkshire d. England 9 E3 ...53.28N 1.16W
Sovetsk Rus. Fed. 46 E5 ...55.05N 21.53E
Soweto S. Africa 86 B2 ...26.15S 27.50E
Sozh r. Europe 55 N4 ...51.57N 30.48E
Spain Europe 48 D4 ...40.26N 3.48W
Spalding England 11 E3 ...52.47N 0.09W
Span Head hill England 13 D3 ...51.07N 3.49W
Sparks U.S.A. 64 C4 ...39.32N 119.46W
Sparti Greece 56 E3 ...37.04N 22.26E
Spartivento, Capo c. Italy 50 G2 ...37.56N 16.05E
Spas-Demensk Rus. Fed. 55 P6 ...54.25N 34.03E
Spassk-Dal'niy Rus. Fed. 106 B4 ...44.32N 132.48E
Spatha, Akra pt Greece 56 E2 ...35.41N 23.44E
Speke Gulf Tanzania 87 A2 ...2.19S 32.57E

Spencer Gulf est. Australia 110 C3 ...34.54S 13
Spennymoor England 15 F3 ...54.42N 1
Sperrin Mountains hills Northern Ireland 16 B2 ...54.47N 7
Spey r. Scotland 19 F2 ...57.39N 3
Speyer Germany 44 H6 ...49.19N
Spijkenisse Neth. 42 D4 ...51.50N
Spilsby England 15 H2 ...53.10N
Spitsbergen i. Arctic Oc. 58 C5 ...78.37N 1
Split Croatia 56 B6 ...43.31N 1
Spofforth England 15 F2 ...53.57N 1
Spokane U.S.A. 64 C6 ...47.38N 117
Spratly Islands S. China Sea 104 E6 ...10.01N 11
Spree r. Germany 54 E5 ...52.32N 1
Springfield Ill. U.S.A. 65 I4 ...39.48N 89
Springfield Mass. U.S.A. 65 L5 ...42.05N 72
Springfield Mo. U.S.A. 65 H4 ...37.16N 93
Sprowston England 11 G3 ...52.39N
Spurn Head England 15 H2 ...53.34N 0
Srebrenica Bos.-Herz. 56 C7 ...44.07N 19
Srednekolymsk Rus. Fed. 59 M3 ...67.32N 15
Sretensk Rus. Fed. 59 M3 ...52.08N 117
Sri Aman Malaysia 104 E4 ...1.12N 11
Sri Jayewardenepura Kotte Sri Lanka 96 E2 ...6.56N 79
Sri Lanka Asia 96 F2 ...7.29N 80
Srinagar India 96 D7 ...34.08N 74
Stadskanaal Neth. 42 F5 ...52.59N
Staffa i. Scotland 16 C4 ...56.26N 6
Stafford England 10 C3 ...52.48N 2
Staffordshire d. England 9 D3 ...52.52N 2
Staines England 11 E2 ...51.26N 0.
Stalbridge England 10 C1 ...50.57N 2
Stalham England 11 G3 ...52.46N 1
Stalowa Wola Poland 46 F3 ...50.34N 22
Stamford England 11 E3 ...52.39N 0.
Stamford Bridge England 15 G2 ...53.59N 0.
Standish England 14 E2 ...53.35N 2.
Stanley England 15 F3 ...54.52N 1.
Stanley Falkland Is 73 D1 ...51.43S 57.
Stannington England 15 F4 ...55.06N 1.
Stanovoy Khrebet mts Rus. Fed. 59 N3 ...57.21N 120
Stansted Mountfitchet England 11 F2 ...51.54N 0
Stanton England 11 F3 ...52.19N 0
Starachowice Poland 46 E3 ...51.02N 21
Stara Zagora Bulgaria 56 F6 ...42.26N 25
Starbuck Island Kiribati 109 J5 ...5.36S 155.
Stargard Szczeciński Poland 46 B4 ...53.20N 15
Starogard Gdański Poland 46 D4 ...53.58N 18
Starokostyantyniv Ukraine 55 L3 ...49.45N 27
Start Bay England 13 D2 ...50.18N 3.
Start Point England 13 D2 ...50.13N 3.
Staryya Darohi Belarus 55 M5 ...53.02N 28
Staryy Oskol Rus. Fed. 58 E3 ...51.18N 37
Stavanger Norway 40 A2 ...58.58N 5
Staveley England 15 F2 ...53.16N 1.
Stavropol' Rus. Fed. 53 L6 ...45.03N 41
Stavropol'skaya Vozvyshennost' hills Rus. Fed. 58 F2
...45.05N 42
Steenwijk Neth. 42 F5 ...52.47N 6
Steep Holm i. England 10 B2 ...51.20N 3.
Stefansson Island Canada 62 H5 ...73.21N 105.
Steinfurt Germany 42 G5 ...52.09N 7.
Steinkjer Norway 40 B4 ...64.01N 11.
Stenness, Loch of l. Scotland 19 F4 ...59.00N 3.
Sterling U.S.A. 64 F5 ...40.39N 103.
Sterlitamak Rus. Fed. 58 G3 ...53.36N 55
Stevenage England 11 E2 ...51.54N 0.
Stewart Canada 62 F3 ...55.57N 129.
Stewart r. Canada 62 E4 ...63.18N 139.
Stewart Island New Zealand 111 F2 ...47.09S 167
Stewarton Scotland 16 E3 ...55.41N 4.3
Steyning England 11 E1 ...50.53N 0.2
Steyr Austria 54 F3 ...48.02N 14.
Stikine r. Canada 62 E3 ...56.41N 132.
Stilton England 11 E3 ...52.29N 0.3
Stinchar r. Scotland 16 D3 ...55.06N 5.0
Stirling Scotland 17 F4 ...56.07N 3.5
Stirling d. Scotland 8 C5 ...56.17N 4.2
Stjørdalshalsen Norway 40 B3 ...63.28N 10.
Stob Choire Claurigh mt. Scotland 18 E1 ...56.50N 4.5
Stockholm Sweden 40 D2 ...59.20N 18.
Stockport England 15 E2 ...53.24N 2.0
Stockton U.S.A. 64 B4 ...37.57N 121.1
Stockton-on-Tees England 15 F3 ...54.34N 1.1
Stockton-on-Tees d. England 9 E4 ...54.34N 1.2
Stœng Trêng Cambodia 104 D6 ...13.28N 105.
Stoer, Point of Scotland 18 D3 ...58.16N 5.2
Stoke-on-Trent England 15 E2 ...53.00N 2.1
Stoke-on-Trent d. England 9 D3 ...53.01N 2.1
Stokesay England 10 C3 ...52.26N 2.5
Stokesley England 15 F3 ...54.28N 1.1
Stolin Belarus 55 L4 ...51.53N 26.
Stone England 10 C3 ...52.54N 2.0
Stonehaven Scotland 19 G1 ...56.58N 2.1
Stony Rapids town Canada 62 H3 ...59.15N 105.5
Stora Lulevatten l. Sweden 40 D4 ...67.09N 19.
Storavan l. Sweden 40 D4 ...65.40N 18.
Støren Norway 40 B3 ...63.02N 10.
Stornoway Scotland 18 C3 ...58.13N 6.2
Storrington England 11 E1 ...50.55N 0.2
Storsjön l. Sweden 40 C3 ...63.13N 14.
Storskrymten mt. Norway 40 B3 ...62.22N 9.0
Storuman Sweden 40 D4 ...65.05N 17.0
Storuman l. Sweden 40 D4 ...65.11N 16.5
Stotfold England 11 E3 ...52.01N 0.1
Stour r. Dor. England 10 D1 ...50.44N 1.4
Stour r. Kent England 11 G2 ...51.18N 1.2
Stour r. Warwicks. England 10 D3 ...52.11N 1.4
Stourbridge England 10 C3 ...52.27N 2.0
Stourport-on-Severn England 10 C3 ...52.20N 2.1
Stowbtsy Belarus 55 L5 ...53.28N 26.
Stowmarket England 11 F3 ...52.11N 0.5
Stow-on-the-Wold England 10 D2 ...51.56N 1.4
Strabane Northern Ireland 16 B2 ...54.49N 7.2
Strabane d. Northern Ireland 9 B4 ...54.47N 7.2
Stradbroke England 11 G3 ...52.19N 1.1
Strakonice Czech Rep. 46 A2 ...49.15N 13.5
Stralsund Germany 54 E6 ...54.18N 13.
Stranda Norway 40 A3 ...62.18N 6.9
Strangford Lough inlet Northern Ireland 16 D2 ...54.28N 5.3
Stranraer Scotland 16 D2 ...54.54N 5.0
Strasbourg France 44 G6 ...48.35N 7.4
Stratford-upon-Avon England 10 D3 ...52.11N 1.4
Strathaven Scotland 17 E3 ...55.41N 4.0
Strathbogie, Loch of l. Scotland 19 H2 ...57.37N 1.5
Strathbogie f. Scotland 19 G2 ...57.26N 2.5
Strathmore f. Scotland 18 E3 ...58.25N 4.3
Strathspey f. Scotland 19 F2 ...57.11N 3.4
Strathy Point Scotland 19 E3 ...58.36N 4.0
Stratton England 13 C2 ...50.49N 4.5
Stratton St Margaret England 10 D2 ...51.35N 1.4
Straubing Germany 54 E3 ...48.54N 12.5
Straumnes pt Iceland 40 X2 ...66.26N 23.1
Streatley England 10 D2 ...51.32N 1.0
Street England 10 C2 ...51.07N 2.4

ka Rus. Fed. 59 Q4 .... 61.52N 152.11E
ham England 11 F3 .... 52.21N 0.13E
nonas r. Greece 56 E5 .... 40.48N 23.51E
na, Island of Scotland 19 F3 .... 58.42N 3.08W
inboli, Isola i. Italy 50 F3 .... 38.45N 15.14E
nness Scotland 19 F3 .... 58.58N 3.18W
insund Sweden 40 C3 .... 63.52N 15.34E
nsay i. Scotland 19 G4 .... 59.08N 2.13W
nsay Firth str. Scotland 19 G4 .... 59.06N 2.50W
id England 10 C2 .... 51.45N 2.13W
er Denmark 40 B2 .... 56.29N 8.36E
na r. Northern Ireland 16 B2 .... 54.43N 7.21W
na r. Bulgaria 56 E5 .... 41.23N 23.20E
nble Head Wales 12 B4 .... 51.42N 5.08W
nica Macedonia 56 E5 .... 41.26N 22.38E
Ukraine 55 J3 .... 49.15N 23.51E
r. Ukraine 46 G2 .... 49.23N 24.13E
ey England 10 D3 .... 52.16N 1.54W
ino Rus. Fed. 55 R6 .... 54.54N 38.05E
ry England 11 G2 .... 51.18N 1.07E
Stony Desert Australia 110 D4 .... 28.20S 141.15E
gart Germany 54 C3 .... 48.47N 9.10E
r. Belarus/Ukraine 55 L5 .... 52.08N 26.35E
in Sudan 85 H3 .... 19.06N 37.18E
otica Serbia 56 C8 .... 46.06N 19.41E
ava Romania 55 L2 .... 47.40N 26.16E
r. Ireland 41 C3 .... 53.16N 8.03W
e Bolivia 76 G4 .... 19.06S 65.18W
ik Ukraine 57 K7 .... 44.51N 34.59E
n Africa 85 G3 .... 13.34N 30.02E
oury Canada 63 J2 .... 46.29N 80.59W
oury England 11 D2 .... 52.03N 0.44E
d f. Sudan 85 G2 .... 7.43N 29.41E
ety mts Czech Rep./Poland 54 F4 .... 50.46N 15.50E
r. Egypt 85 H4 .... 29.58N 32.33E
, Gulf of Egypt 85 H4 .... 28.03N 33.33E
Canal Egypt 53 J3 .... 30.47N 32.19E
olk d. England 9 F3 .... 52.10N 0.52E
ata r. Kenya 87 B3 .... 2.01N 36.32E
uti Bay Tanzania 87 A2 .... 1.45S 33.33E
ar Oman 95 I4 .... 24.22N 56.44E
Germany 54 D4 .... 50.36N 10.42E
enhe China 106 B4 .... 44.20N 131.11E
r. Ireland 41 D2 .... 52.20N 7.23W
hou China 103 K4 .... 31.42N 113.20E
abumi Indonesia 104 D2 .... 6.58S 106.53E
adana Indonesia 104 D3 .... 1.12S 109.59E
hinichi Rus. Fed. 55 P6 .... 54.07N 35.22E
kur Pakistan 96 C4 .... 27.42N 68.55E
i. Norway 40 A3 .... 61.09N 4.55E
abesi i. Indonesia 105 H3 .... 2.12S 125.58E
iman Range mts Pakistan 90 F5 .... 30.00N 68.00E
na Romania 57 H7 .... 45.09N 29.39E
ana Peru 76 D7 .... 4.56S 80.41W
y Wales 13 D3 .... 51.24N 3.13W
nona Italy 50 E5 .... 42.02N 13.55S
Archipelago is Phil. 105 G5 .... 6.55N 123.10E
l Sea N. Pacific Oc. 104 F5 .... 8.20N 119.64S
halé d. Ethiopia 87 C4 .... 6.59N 43.45E
natra i. Indonesia 104 B4 .... 3.05N 98.12E
nba i. Indonesia 104 G2 .... 9.49S 120.11E
nbawa i. Indonesia 104 F2 .... 8.54S 118.45E
nburgh Scotland 19 H4 .... 59.52N 1.17W
nburgh Head Scotland 19 H4 .... 59.51N 1.16W
nmer Isles Scotland 18 D3 .... 58.01N 5.30W
ny Ukraine 55 P4 .... 50.55N 34.48E
art, Loch inlet Scotland 18 D1 .... 56.40N 5.51W
da, Selat str. Indonesia 104 C2 .... 6.32S 104.55E
da Trench f. Indian Oc. 108 C5 .... 8.48S 104.02E
iderland England 15 F3 .... 54.54N 1.23W
dsvall Sweden 40 D3 .... 62.24N 17.17E
aga Tanzania 87 B1 .... 4.27S 38.14E
igurlu Turkey 57 K5 .... 40.11N 34.22E
olijärvet l. Finland 40 G4 .... 66.14N 28.04E
onenjoki Finland 40 F3 .... 62.37N 27.07E
oerior U.S.A. 65 H6 .... 46.41N 92.01W
oerior, Lake Canada/U.S.A. 63 J2 .... 47.46N 87.14W
q ash Shuyükh Iraq 95 G6 .... 30.51N 46.20E
r Oman 95 I4 .... 22.34N 59.31E
ab Pakistan 95 K5 .... 28.29N 66.19E
abaya Indonesia 104 E2 .... 7.13S 112.45E
rakarta Indonesia 104 E2 .... 7.31S 110.52E
at India 96 D5 .... 21.11N 72.53E
endranagar India 96 D5 .... 22.42N 71.41E
gut Rus. Fed. 58 I4 .... 61.13N 73.22E
rigao Phil. 105 H5 .... 9.48N 125.29E
in Thailand 104 C6 .... 14.52N 103.32E
iname S. America 72 D7 .... 4.05N 56.22W
rey d. England 9 E2 .... 51.15N 0.29W
tsey i. Iceland 40 X1 .... 63.18N 20.36W
sangerd Iran 95 G4 .... 31.37N 48.04E
ehri Turkey 57 M5 .... 40.10N 38.04E
surluk Turkey 57 H4 .... 39.55N 28.09E
tak Jammu and Kashmir 96 E7 .... 33.07N 77.34E
therland f. Scotland 19 E3 .... 58.16N 4.24W
tlej r. India/Pakistan 96 D6 .... 29.24N 71.08E
tterton England 11 E3 .... 52.54N 0.06W
tton England 11 F3 .... 52.23N 0.07E
tton Bridge England 11 F3 .... 52.46N 0.11E
tton Coldfield England 10 D3 .... 52.34N 1.49W
tton in Ashfield England 15 F2 .... 53.08N 1.16W
va Fiji 111 G5 .... 18.07S 178.28E
vorov Rus. Fed. 55 Q6 .... 54.07N 36.11E
watki Poland 46 F5 .... 54.06N 22.56E
warrow atoll Cook Is 108 J5 .... 13.11S 162.57W
zhou Anhui China 103 L4 .... 33.34N 116.59E
zhou Jiangsu China 103 M4 .... 31.18N 120.40E
zuka Japan 106 C2 .... 34.53N 136.35E
albard is Arctic Oc. 58 C5 .... 79.47N 16.53E
apa r. Rus. Fed. 55 P4 .... 51.44N 34.57E
eg Sweden 40 C3 .... 62.02N 14.23E
endborg Denmark 40 B1 .... 55.04N 10.37E
etlograd Rus. Fed. 53 L6 .... 45.20N 42.51E
etogorsk Rus. Fed. 59 N3 .... 61.07N 28.51E
iahnúkur vol. Iceland 40 Y2 .... 64.25N 17.09W
itava r. Czech Rep. 46 C2 .... 48.54N 16.37E
itavy Czech Rep. 54 G3 .... 49.45N 16.28E
itlovods'k Ukraine 55 O3 .... 49.03N 33.15E
obodnyy Rus. Fed. 59 N3 .... 51.23N 128.04E
yetlahorsk Belarus 55 M5 .... 52.38N 29.46E
vadlincote England 10 D3 .... 52.46N 1.33W
vaffham England 11 F3 .... 52.39N 0.41E
vains Island atoll American Samoa 108 I5 .... 11.01S 171.03W
vakopmund Namibia 86 A2 .... 22.41S 14.32E
vale r. England 15 F3 .... 54.05N 1.21W
vanage England 10 D1 .... 50.36N 1.58W
vanley England 11 F2 .... 51.24N 0.11E
van River town Canada 64 F7 .... 52.06N 101.16W
vansea Wales 12 C3 .... 51.37N 3.57W
vansea i. Wales 9 D2 .... 51.39N 3.57W
vansea Bay Wales 12 C3 .... 51.34N 3.54W
vaziland Africa 86 C2 .... 26.29S 31.30E

Sweden Europe 40 C3 .... 61.48N 15.08E
Sweetwater r. U.S.A. 64 E5 .... 42.27N 106.55W
Świdnica Poland 46 C3 .... 50.50N 16.29E
Świdwin Poland 46 B4 .... 53.47N 15.47E
Świebodzin Poland 46 B4 .... 52.15N 15.32E
Świecie Poland 46 D4 .... 53.25N 18.27E
Swift Current Canada 62 H3 .... 50.17N 107.47W
Swilly, Lough inlet Ireland 41 D5 .... 55.15N 7.34W
Swindon England 10 D2 .... 51.33N 1.47W
Swindon d. England 9 E2 .... 51.35N 1.45W
Swineshead England 11 E3 .... 52.57N 0.10W
Świnoujście Poland 46 B4 .... 53.54N 14.15E
Swords Ireland 41 E3 .... 53.27N 6.13W
Sybil Point Ireland 41 A2 .... 52.11N 10.28W
Sychevka Rus. Fed. 55 P6 .... 55.49N 34.17E
Sydney Australia 110 E3 .... 33.54S 151.11E
Sydney Canada 63 L2 .... 46.06N 60.08W
Syktyvkar Rus. Fed. 58 G4 .... 61.41N 50.48E
Sylarna mt. Norway/Sweden 40 C3 .... 63.01N 12.12E
Sylt i. Germany 40 B1 .... 54.49N 8.15E
Syracuse Italy 50 F2 .... 37.04N 15.17E
Syracuse U.S.A. 65 K5 .... 43.04N 76.11W
Syr Darya r. Asia 102 A7 .... 46.05N 60.55E
Syria Asia 94 E6 .... 35.25N 39.17E
Syrian Desert Asia 94 E6 .... 32.02N 39.22E
Syros i. Greece 56 F3 .... 37.27N 24.53E
Syzran' Rus. Fed. 58 F3 .... 53.10N 48.29E
Szczecin Poland 46 B4 .... 53.26N 14.34E
Szczecinek Poland 46 C4 .... 53.42N 16.42E
Szczytno Poland 46 E4 .... 53.34N 20.59E
Szeged Hungary 54 I2 .... 46.15N 20.09E
Székesfehérvár Hungary 54 H2 .... 47.12N 18.25E
Szekszárd Hungary 54 H2 .... 46.22N 18.42E
Szolnok Hungary 54 I2 .... 47.10N 20.12E
Szombathely Hungary 54 G2 .... 47.15N 16.38E

T

Tabas Iran 95 I6 .... 33.35N 56.52E
Tabasco d. Mexico 70 F4 .... 18.03N 92.59W
Tabatinga, Serra da hills Brazil 77 L5 .... 10.56S 44.37W
Tábor Czech Rep. 54 F3 .... 49.24N 14.42E
Tabora Tanzania 86 C4 .... 5.00S 32.47E
Tabrīz Iran 95 G7 .... 38.04N 46.17E
Tabuaeran atoll Kiribati 109 J6 .... 3.49N 159.16W
Tabūk Saudi Arabia 94 E5 .... 28.22N 36.38E
Täby Sweden 40 D2 .... 59.27N 18.04E
Tacheng China 102 E7 .... 46.43N 83.01E
Tacloban Phil. 105 H6 .... 11.12N 125.01E
Tacna Peru 76 F4 .... 18.01S 70.15W
Tacoma U.S.A. 64 B6 .... 47.15N 122.27W
Tacuarembó Uruguay 73 D3 .... 31.42S 55.59W
Tadcaster England 15 F2 .... 53.53N 1.16W
Tadjoura Djibouti 94 F2 .... 11.46N 42.48E
Tadmur Syria 94 E6 .... 34.34N 38.17E
Taegu S. Korea 103 N5 .... 35.52N 128.35E
Taejŏn S. Korea 103 N5 .... 36.22N 127.24E
Taf r. Wales 12 C3 .... 51.47N 4.27W
Taganrog Rus. Fed. 53 K6 .... 47.14N 38.55E
Taganrog, Gulf of Rus. Fed./Ukraine 53 K6 .... 47.00N 38.31E
Tagbilaran Phil. 105 G5 .... 9.38N 123.53E
Tagula Island P.N.G. 110 E5 .... 11.33S 153.23E
Tagus r. Portugal 48 A3 .... 38.59N 8.56W
Tahat, Mont mt. Algeria 84 E4 .... 23.18N 5.32E
Tahiti i. French Polynesia 109 K4 .... 17.49S 149.15W
T'aichung Taiwan 103 M2 .... 24.09N 120.42E
Tain Scotland 19 E2 .... 57.49N 4.03W
T'ainan Taiwan 103 M2 .... 23.01N 120.13E
T'aipei Taiwan 103 M3 .... 25.04N 121.33E
Taiping Malaysia 104 C4 .... 4.55N 100.42E
Taita Hills Kenya 87 B2 .... 3.26S 38.21E
Taiti mt. Kenya 87 A3 .... 1.20N 35.57E
T'aitung Taiwan 103 M2 .... 22.45N 121.08E
Taivalkoski Finland 40 G4 .... 65.34N 28.14E
Taivaskero hill Finland 40 F5 .... 68.04N 24.02E
Taiwan Asia 103 M2 .... 23.34N 121.32E
Taiwan Strait China/Taiwan 103 L2 .... 23.49N 119.16E
Taiyuan China 103 K5 .... 37.48N 112.38E
Ta'izz Yemen 94 F2 .... 13.35N 43.59E
Tajikistan Asia 115 M7 .... 38.54N 71.08E
Tak Thailand 104 B7 .... 16.51N 99.08E
Takabba Kenya 87 C3 .... 3.21N 40.13E
Takamatsu Japan 106 B2 .... 34.19N 134.03E
Takaoka Japan 106 C3 .... 36.45N 137.01E
Takaungu Kenya 87 B2 .... 3.41S 39.50E
Taklimakan Desert China 102 E5 .... 38.25N 80.58E
Talagang Pakistan 95 L6 .... 32.55N 72.29E
Talara Peru 76 D7 .... 4.37S 81.18W
Talaud, Kepulauan is Indonesia 105 H4 .... 4.05N 127.24E
Talavera de la Reina Spain 48 C3 .... 39.58N 4.49W
Talca Chile 73 B3 .... 35.26S 71.39W
Talcahuano Chile 73 B3 .... 36.44S 73.07W
Taldykorgan Kazakhstan 58 I2 .... 44.59N 78.22E
Talgarth Wales 12 D3 .... 51.59N 3.14W
Taliabu i. Indonesia 105 G3 .... 1.47S 124.43E
Tallahassee U.S.A. 65 J3 .... 30.26N 84.17W
Tallinn Estonia 40 F2 .... 59.27N 24.45E
Taloyoak Canada 63 I4 .... 69.27N 93.22W
Talsi Latvia 40 E2 .... 57.15N 22.35E
Taltal Chile 76 F2 .... 25.24S 70.33W
Taltson r. Canada 62 G4 .... 61.24N 112.43W
Tamale Ghana 84 D2 .... 9.25N 0.51W
Tamanrasset Algeria 84 E4 .... 22.48N 5.33E
Tamar r. England 13 C2 .... 50.29N 4.13W
Tamaulipas d. Mexico 70 E5 .... 22.41N 99.13W
Tama Wildlife Reserve Ethiopia 87 B4 .... 6.02N 36.12E
Tambach Kenya 87 B3 .... 0.37N 35.31E
Tambacounda Senegal 84 C3 .... 13.47N 13.40W
Tambelan, Kepulauan is Indonesia 104 D4 .... 1.03N 107.03E
Tambov Rus. Fed. 58 F3 .... 52.43N 41.26E
Tambre r. Spain 48 A5 .... 42.49N 8.51W
Tâmega r. Portugal 48 A4 .... 41.05N 8.17W
Tamiahua, Laguna de lagoon Mexico 70 E5 .... 21.39N 97.36W
Tamil Nadu d. India 96 E3 .... 11.11N 78.08E
Tamiš r. Serbia 56 D7 .... 44.50N 20.39E
Tampa U.S.A. 65 J2 .... 27.57N 82.29W
Tampere Finland 40 E3 .... 61.30N 23.48E
Tampico Mexico 70 E5 .... 22.16N 97.52W
Tamsweg Austria 54 E2 .... 47.08N 13.47E
Tamworth Australia 110 E3 .... 31.06S 150.56E
Tamworth England 10 D3 .... 52.38N 1.41W
Tana r. Kenya 87 C2 .... 2.31S 40.30E
Tana, Lake Ethiopia 85 H3 .... 11.59N 37.16E
Tanafjorden inlet Norway 40 G5 .... 70.32N 28.13E
Tanami Desert Australia 110 C5 .... 19.26S 131.26E
Tanana U.S.A. 62 C4 .... 65.12N 152.04W
Tanaro r. Italy 50 C6 .... 45.01N 8.47E
Tando Adam Pakistan 96 C6 .... 25.43N 68.40E
Tandragee Northern Ireland 16 C2 .... 54.21N 6.24W
Tanega-shima i. Japan 106 B2 .... 30.28N 130.58E

Tanga Tanzania 86 C4 .... 5.06S 39.05E
Tanga d. Tanzania 87 B1 .... 5.59S 38.02E
Tanganyika, Lake Africa 86 B4 .... 5.00S 29.26E
Tangier Morocco 84 D5 .... 35.47N 5.49W
Tangshan China 103 L5 .... 39.34N 118.13E
Tanimbar, Kepulauan is Indonesia 105 I2 .... 7.29S 131.40E
Tanjay Phil. 105 G5 .... 9.29N 123.01E
Tanjungpandan Indonesia 104 D3 .... 2.46S 107.37E
Tanjungredeb Indonesia 104 F4 .... 2.09N 117.27E
Tank Pakistan 95 L6 .... 32.14N 70.29E
Tanna i. Vanuatu 111 F5 .... 19.32S 169.14E
Tanout Niger 84 E3 .... 14.56N 8.53E
Ţanţā Egypt 85 H5 .... 30.47N 31.00E
Tanzania Africa 86 C4 .... 6.14S 34.03E
Taonan China 103 M7 .... 45.12N 122.48E
Taourirt Morocco 52 C3 .... 34.25N 2.55W
Tapachula Mexico 70 F3 .... 14.56N 92.15W
Tapajós r. Brazil 77 J7 .... 2.23S 54.48W
Tapauá r. Brazil 76 H6 .... 5.52S 64.27W
Tapi r. India 96 D5 .... 21.13N 72.58E
Taquari r. Brazil 77 I4 .... 19.05S 57.22W
Tar r. Ireland 41 D2 .... 52.17N 7.50W
Tara r. Bos.-Herz./Montenegro 56 C6 .... 43.20N 18.53E
Tarakan Indonesia 104 F4 .... 3.20N 117.37E
Taran, Mys pt Rus. Fed. 46 D5 .... 54.58N 19.59E
Taranaki, Mount vol. New Zealand 111 G3 .... 39.18S 174.03E
Tarancón Spain 48 D4 .... 40.01N 3.00W
Tarangire National Park Tanzania 87 B1 .... 4.05S 36.04E
Taransay i. Scotland 18 B2 .... 57.55N 7.02W
Taranto Italy 50 G4 .... 40.28N 17.14E
Taranto, Gulf of Italy 50 G4 .... 40.07N 17.20E
Tarapoto Peru 76 E6 .... 6.31S 76.24W
Tarauacá Brazil 76 F6 .... 8.10S 70.43W
Tarbat Ness pt Scotland 19 F2 .... 57.52N 3.46W
Tarbert A. and B. Scotland 16 D3 .... 55.58N 5.50W
Tarbert A. and B. Scotland 16 D3 .... 55.52N 5.25W
Tarbert W. Isles Scotland 18 C2 .... 57.54N 6.48W
Tarbes France 44 D3 .... 43.14N 0.05E
Târgoviște Romania 56 F7 .... 44.56N 25.27E
Târgu Jiu Romania 56 E7 .... 45.03N 23.17E
Târgu Mureș Romania 55 K2 .... 46.32N 24.34E
Târgu Secuiesc Romania 56 G8 .... 46.00N 26.08E
Tarija Bolivia 76 H3 .... 21.36S 64.47W
Tarim Yemen 95 G3 .... 16.08N 49.23E
Tarim Basin China 102 E5 .... 39.41N 80.53E
Tarime Tanzania 87 A2 .... 1.21S 34.20E
Tarleton England 14 E2 .... 53.41N 2.50W
Tarn r. France 44 D4 .... 44.05N 1.03E
Tarnica mt. Poland 46 F2 .... 49.05N 22.46E
Tarnobrzeg Poland 46 E3 .... 50.34N 21.40E
Tarnów Poland 46 E3 .... 50.01N 20.59E
Tarnowskie Góry Poland 46 D3 .... 50.27N 18.52E
Tarragona Spain 48 F4 .... 41.07N 1.15E
Tarsus Turkey 57 K3 .... 36.54N 34.53E
Tartu Estonia 40 F2 .... 58.23N 26.43E
Ţarţūs Syria 57 K2 .... 34.54N 35.53E
Tashk, Daryācheh-ye l. Iran 95 H5 .... 29.42N 53.29E
Tashkent Uzbekistan 58 H2 .... 41.16N 69.15E
Tasiilaq Greenland 63 O4 .... 65.37N 37.42W
Tasikmalaya Indonesia 104 D2 .... 7.19S 108.17E
Tasman Abyssal Plain f. Tasman Sea 108 G3 .... 32.04S 154.38E
Tasman Basin f. Tasman Sea 108 G3 .... 41.29S 158.18E
Tasmania d. Australia 110 D2 .... 42.27S 145.20E
Tasman Sea S. Pacific Oc. 110 G2 .... 40.31S 170.54E
Tatabánya Hungary 54 H2 .... 47.34N 18.26E
Tatarbunary Ukraine 57 H7 .... 45.50N 29.37E
Tatarsk Rus. Fed. 58 I3 .... 55.13N 75.59E
Tatarskly Proliv str. Rus. Fed. 59 P3 .... 50.29N 141.05E
Tatvan Turkey 94 F7 .... 38.29N 42.17E
Taua Brazil 77 L6 .... 6.01S 40.23W
Taubaté Brazil 77 L3 .... 22.59S 45.32W
Taunggyi Myanmar 97 I5 .... 20.49N 97.05E
Taunton England 13 D3 .... 51.01N 3.06W
Taunus hills Germany 54 B4 .... 50.10N 7.59E
Taupo, Lake New Zealand 111 G3 .... 38.48S 175.55E
Tauragė Lithuania 46 F5 .... 55.15N 22.17E
Taurus Mountains Turkey 57 J3 .... 37.00N 32.09E
Taverham England 11 G3 .... 52.41N 1.12E
Tavira Portugal 48 B2 .... 37.08N 7.38W
Tavistock England 13 C2 .... 50.33N 4.08W
Tavoy Myanmar 97 I3 .... 14.06N 98.13E
Tavşanlı Turkey 57 H4 .... 39.32N 29.28E
Tavy r. England 13 C2 .... 50.27N 4.09W
Taw r. England 13 C3 .... 51.04N 4.03W
Tawau Malaysia 104 F4 .... 4.16N 117.54E
Tawe r. Wales 12 D3 .... 51.37N 3.55W
Tawitawi i. Phil. 105 G5 .... 5.14N 119.57E
Tay r. Scotland 17 F4 .... 56.23N 3.24W
Tay, Firth of est. Scotland 17 F4 .... 56.25N 3.07W
Tay, Loch l. Scotland 16 E4 .... 56.30N 4.11W
Tayma' Saudi Arabia 94 E5 .... 27.39N 38.28E
Taymura r. Rus. Fed. 59 K4 .... 63.43N 98.05E
Taymyr, Ozero l. Rus. Fed. 59 L5 .... 74.20N 101.51E
Taymyr Peninsula Rus. Fed. 59 J5 .... 73.54N 89.12E
Tây Ninh Vietnam 104 D6 .... 11.17N 106.07E
Tayport Scotland 17 G4 .... 56.27N 2.53W
Taytay Phil. 104 F6 .... 10.49N 119.30E
Taz r. Rus. Fed. 58 I4 .... 67.34N 78.36E
Taza Morocco 52 C3 .... 34.16N 3.56W
Tczew Poland 46 D5 .... 54.06N 18.48E
Te Anau, Lake New Zealand 111 F2 .... 45.18S 167.48E
Tébessa Algeria 52 E4 .... 35.23N 8.12E
Tebingtinggi Indonesia 104 B4 .... 3.19N 99.08E
Tecuci Romania 56 G7 .... 45.51N 27.26E
Tedzhen Turkmenistan 95 J7 .... 37.22N 60.25E
Tees r. England 15 F3 .... 54.35N 1.15W
Tees Bay England 15 F3 .... 54.41N 1.09W
Tefé r. Brazil 76 H7 .... 3.41S 64.52W
Tegucigalpa Honduras 70 G3 .... 14.05N 87.12W
Tehrān Iran 95 H7 .... 35.39N 51.23E
Tehuantepec, Gulf of Mexico 70 F4 .... 15.47N 94.53W
Teide, Pico del vol. Canary Islands 48 X2 .... 28.16N 16.37W
Teifi r. Wales 12 C4 .... 52.05N 4.40W
Teign r. England 13 D2 .... 50.32N 3.35W
Teignmouth England 13 D2 .... 50.33N 3.30W
Teith r. Scotland 16 E4 .... 56.09N 3.59W
Tekirdağ Turkey 56 G5 .... 40.59N 27.30E
Tel Aviv-Yafo Israel 53 J3 .... 32.04N 34.46E
Teles Pires r. Brazil 77 I6 .... 7.20S 58.03W
Telford England 10 C3 .... 52.41N 2.27W
Telford and Wrekin d. England 9 D3 .... 52.45N 2.28W
Telšiai Lithuania 46 F5 .... 55.59N 22.16E
Tembenchi r. Rus. Fed. 59 K4 .... 64.35N 99.48E
Teme r. England 10 C3 .... 52.10N 2.13W
Temirtau Kazakhstan 58 I3 .... 50.03N 72.57E
Temple Ewell England 11 G2 .... 51.09N 1.16E
Templemore Ireland 41 D2 .... 52.48N 7.50W
Temryuk Rus. Fed. 57 L7 .... 45.17N 37.23E
Temuco Chile 73 B3 .... 38.44S 72.35W
Tena Ecuador 76 E7 .... 0.59S 77.49W
Tenasserim Myanmar 97 I3 .... 12.02N 98.58E
Tenbury Wells England 10 C3 .... 52.18N 2.36W
Tenby Wales 12 C3 .... 51.40N 4.42W

Ten Degree Channel India 97 H2 .... 9.57N 92.51E
Tendö Japan 106 D3 .... 38.21N 140.22E
Tenerife i. Canary Islands 48 X2 .... 28.28N 16.39W
Tennessee d. U.S.A. 65 I4 .... 36.12N 85.01W
Tennessee r. U.S.A. 65 I4 .... 37.08N 88.25W
Tenterden England 11 F2 .... 51.04N 0.41E
Tentudia mt. Spain 48 B3 .... 38.03N 6.19W
Teófilo Otôni Brazil 77 L4 .... 17.52S 41.31W
Tepic Mexico 70 D5 .... 21.31N 104.55W
Teplice Czech Rep. 54 E4 .... 50.38N 13.50E
Teraina i. Kiribati 109 J6 .... 4.42N 160.24W
Teramo Italy 50 E5 .... 42.39N 13.42E
Terebovlya Ukraine 55 K3 .... 49.18N 25.42E
Teresina Brazil 77 L6 .... 5.07S 42.44W
Tergnier France 42 C2 .... 49.40N 3.18E
Terme Turkey 57 L5 .... 41.12N 36.59E
Terminillo, Monte mt. Italy 50 E5 .... 42.29N 12.59E
Términos, Laguna de lagoon Mexico 70 F4 .... 18.30N 91.37W
Termiz Uzbekistan 95 K7 .... 37.15N 67.17E
Termoli Italy 50 F5 .... 41.59N 14.59E
Tern r. England 10 C3 .... 52.40N 2.40W
Ternate Indonesia 105 H4 .... 0.49N 127.20E
Terneuzen Neth. 42 C4 .... 51.19N 3.50E
Terni Italy 50 E5 .... 42.33N 12.39E
Ternopil' Ukraine 55 K3 .... 49.33N 25.36E
Terrace Canada 62 F3 .... 54.32N 128.37W
Terrassa Spain 48 G4 .... 41.34N 2.00E
Terre Haute U.S.A. 65 I4 .... 39.28N 87.24W
Terrington Marsh England 11 F3 .... 52.47N 0.16E
Terschelling i. Neth. 42 E6 .... 53.27N 5.28E
Teseney Eritrea 94 E3 .... 15.07N 36.39E
Teslin Canada 62 E4 .... 60.12N 132.39W
Test r. England 10 D1 .... 50.56N 1.29W
Tetas, Punta pt Chile 73 B4 .... 23.28S 70.34W
Tetbury England 10 C2 .... 51.38N 2.09W
Tete Mozambique 86 C3 .... 16.10S 33.36E
Tetney England 15 G2 .... 53.29N 0.01W
Tétouan Morocco 84 D5 .... 35.34N 5.23W
Tetovo Macedonia 56 D6 .... 42.00N 20.58E
Teuco r. Argentina 73 C4 .... 25.39S 60.11W
Teviot r. Scotland 17 G3 .... 55.36N 2.26W
Teviothead Scotland 17 G3 .... 55.20N 2.56W
Tewkesbury England 10 C2 .... 51.59N 2.09W
Texarkana U.S.A. 65 H3 .... 33.25N 94.08W
Texas d. U.S.A. 64 G3 .... 31.58N 99.13W
Texel i. Neth. 42 D6 .... 53.09N 4.46E
Texoma, Lake U.S.A. 64 G3 .... 33.59N 96.53W
Tezpur India 97 H6 .... 26.36N 92.49E
Thabana-Ntlenyana mt. Lesotho 86 B2 .... 29.29S 29.16E
Thai Binh Vietnam 104 D8 .... 20.24N 106.19E
Thailand Asia 104 C7 .... 16.14N 101.59E
Thailand, Gulf of Asia 104 C6 .... 11.08N 101.16E
Thai Nguyên Vietnam 104 D8 .... 21.31N 105.52E
Thal Desert Pakistan 95 L6 .... 31.25N 71.33E
Thame England 10 E2 .... 51.45N 0.58W
Thame r. England 10 D2 .... 51.38N 1.10W
Thames est. England 11 F2 .... 51.30N 0.31E
Thames r. England 11 F2 .... 51.27N 0.21E
Thanet, Isle of pen. England 11 G2 .... 51.22N 1.17E
Thanh Hoa Vietnam 104 D7 .... 19.47N 105.49E
Thar Desert India/Pakistan 96 C6 .... 25.48N 69.50E
Thasos i. Greece 56 F5 .... 40.40N 24.31E
Thatcham England 10 D2 .... 51.24N 1.16W
Thaton Myanmar 97 I4 .... 16.54N 97.23E
Thaxted England 11 F2 .... 51.57N 0.21E
The Bahamas Central America 71 I6 .... 24.55N 77.44W
The Calf hill England 15 E3 .... 54.22N 2.31W
The Cheviot hill England 15 E4 .... 55.29N 2.09W
The Fens f. England 11 E3 .... 52.42N 0.08W
The Gambia Africa 84 C3 .... 13.22N 16.25W
The Great Oasis Egypt 94 D4 .... 24.52N 30.42E
The Gulf Asia 95 H5 .... 28.03N 50.06E
The Hague Neth. 42 D5 .... 52.04N 4.18E
Thelon r. Canada 62 I4 .... 64.17N 96.18W
The Marsh England 11 F3 .... 52.50N 0.10E
The Minch str. Scotland 18 C3 .... 58.02N 6.02W
The Mullet b. Ireland 41 A4 .... 54.10N 10.07W
The Mumbles Wales 12 C3 .... 51.34N 4.00W
The Naze pt England 11 G2 .... 51.52N 1.17E
The Needles f. England 10 D1 .... 50.40N 1.37W
The North Sound str. Scotland 19 G4 .... 59.17N 2.43W
Theodore Roosevelt r. Brazil 77 H6 .... 7.35S 60.21W
The Old Man of Coniston hill England 14 D3 .... 54.22N 3.07W
The Pas Canada 62 H3 .... 53.49N 101.16W
The Rinns of Galloway pen. Scotland 16 D2 .... 54.52N 5.02W
Thermaïkos Kolpos g. Greece 56 E5 .... 40.11N 22.54E
The Solent str. England 10 D1 .... 50.45N 1.23W
The Sound est. England 13 C2 .... 50.21N 4.09W
Thessaloniki Greece 56 E5 .... 40.38N 22.57E
The Storr hill Scotland 18 C2 .... 57.31N 6.11W
Thet r. England 11 F3 .... 52.24N 0.45E
Thetford England 11 F3 .... 52.24N 0.45E
The Trossachs hills Scotland 16 E4 .... 56.13N 4.26W
The Wash b. England 11 F3 .... 52.50N 0.11E
The Weald f. England 11 F2 .... 51.05N 0.18E
Thiers France 44 E4 .... 45.51N 3.33E
Thiès Senegal 84 C3 .... 14.48N 16.56W
Thika Kenya 87 B2 .... 1.03S 37.05E
Thimbu Bhutan 97 G6 .... 27.29N 89.42E
Thionville France 44 G6 .... 49.22N 6.10E
Thira i. Greece 56 F3 .... 36.27N 25.27E
Thirlmere resr England 14 D3 .... 54.33N 3.04W
Thirsk England 15 F3 .... 54.14N 1.20W
Thiruvananthapuram India 96 E2 .... 8.30N 76.57E
Thisted Denmark 40 B2 .... 56.57N 8.41E
Thomastown Ireland 41 D2 .... 52.31N 7.07W
Thompson Canada 62 I3 .... 55.48N 97.55W
Thornaby-on-Tees England 15 F3 .... 54.32N 1.17W
Thornbury England 10 C2 .... 51.36N 2.31W
Thorne England 15 G2 .... 53.37N 0.58W
Thornhill Scotland 17 F3 .... 55.15N 3.46W
Thornton England 14 D2 .... 53.52N 3.00W
Thrakiko Pelagos sea Greece 56 F5 .... 40.22N 24.46E
Thrapston England 11 E3 .... 52.24N 0.32W
Thuin Belgium 42 D3 .... 50.20N 4.17E
Thule Greenland 63 L5 .... 77.28N 69.11W
Thun Switz. 50 B7 .... 46.45N 7.38E
Thunder Bay town Canada 63 J2 .... 48.26N 89.15W
Thurles Ireland 41 D2 .... 52.41N 7.49W
Thurrock d. England 9 F2 .... 51.31N 0.22E
Thursby England 14 D3 .... 54.51N 3.03W
Thurso Scotland 19 F3 .... 58.36N 3.31W
Thurso r. Scotland 19 F3 .... 58.36N 3.31W
Thurso Bay Scotland 19 F3 .... 58.36N 3.31W
Tianjin China 103 L5 .... 39.04N 117.15E
Tianshui China 103 J4 .... 34.30N 105.37E
Tiaret Algeria 52 D4 .... 35.20N 1.19E
Tibagi r. Brazil 77 J3 .... 23.07S 50.57W
Tibati Cameroon 84 F2 .... 6.26N 12.35E
Tiber r. Italy 50 E4 .... 41.44N 12.14E
Tibesti mts Chad 85 F4 .... 21.00N 17.30E
Tibet, Plateau of f. China 102 E4 .... 33.48N 84.16E
Tiburón, Isla i. Mexico 70 B6 .... 29.08N 112.29W
Ticehurst England 11 F2 .... 51.03N 0.25E

Tidjikja Mauritania 84 C3 ....18.31N 11.26W
Tiel Neth. 42 E4 ....51.52N 5.25E
Tielt Belgium 42 C3 ....50.59N 3.20E
Tienen Belgium 42 D3 ....50.48N 4.56E
Tien Shan mts China/Kyrgyzstan 102 D6 ....40.48N 76.25E
Tierra del Fuego, Isla Grande de i. Argentina/Chile 73 C1
....54.11S 68.48W
Tiétar r. Spain 48 C3 ....39.56N 5.54W
Tighina Moldova 53 I6 ....46.49N 29.29E
Tigre r. Ecuador/Peru 76 F7 ....4.27S 74.06W
Tigre r. Venezuela 72 C7 ....9.26N 62.25W
Tigris r. Iraq/Syria 95 G6 ....30.59N 47.25E
Tihāmah f. Saudi Arabia 85 I3 ....17.18N 42.25E
Tijuana Mexico 70 A7 ....32.29N 117.02W
Tikhoretsk Rus. Fed. 57 N7 ....45.52N 40.06E
Tiki Basin f. S. Pacific Oc. 109 L4 ......18.48S 129.30W
Tikrīt Iraq 94 F6 ....34.33N 43.37E
Tiksi Rus. Fed. 59 N5 ....71.38N 128.36E
Tilburg Neth. 42 E4 ....51.33N 5.05E
Tilbury England 11 F2 ....51.28N 0.22E
Tilehurst England 10 D2 ....51.27N 1.02W
Tillabéri Niger 84 E3 ....14.13N 1.29E
Tillicoultry Scotland 17 F4 ....56.09N 3.44W
Ţimā Egypt 53 J2 ....26.53N 31.25E
Timashevsk Rus. Fed. 57 M7 ....45.37N 38.56E
Timbuktu Mali 84 D3 ....16.46N 2.59W
Timiş r. Romania 56 D7 ....45.27N 20.52E
Timişoara Romania 56 D7 ....45.46N 21.14E
Timmins Canada 63 J2 ....48.29N 81.21W
Timon Brazil 77 L6 ....5.08S 42.48W
Timor i. East Timor/Indonesia 105 H2 ....8.49S 126.02E
Timor Sea Australia/Indonesia 110 B5 ....11.23S 126.22E
Timrå Sweden 40 D3 ....62.30N 17.20E
Tindouf Algeria 84 D4 ....27.42N 8.07W
Tinian i. N. Mariana Is 108 F6 ....14.58N 145.41E
Tinos i. Greece 56 F3 ....37.40N 25.12E
Tintagel England 13 C2 ....50.40N 4.45W
Tinto hill Scotland 17 F3 ....55.36N 3.40W
Tipasa Algeria 48 G2 ....36.33N 2.28E
Tipperary Ireland 41 C2 ....52.28N 8.10W
Tipperary d. Ireland 41 D2 ....52.43N 7.54W
Tiptree England 11 F2 ....51.49N 0.45E
Tiracambu, Serra do hills Brazil 77 K7 ....4.46S 47.10W
Tirana Albania 56 C5 ....41.19N 19.49E
Tiraspol Moldova 53 I6 ....46.51N 29.37E
Tiree i. Scotland 16 C4 ....56.30N 6.57W
Tirga Mòr hill Scotland 18 C2 ....57.59N 6.59W
Tirso r. Italy 50 C3 ....39.53N 8.32E
Tiruchchirappalli India 96 E3 ....10.49N 78.41E
Tiruppur India 96 E3 ....11.06N 77.18E
Tisa r. Serbia 56 D7 ....45.08N 20.17E
Tisza r. Hungary 55 I2 ....46.09N 20.04E
Tiszafüred Hungary 46 E1 ....47.36N 20.46E
Titicaca, Lake Bolivia/Peru 76 G4 ....15.49S 69.40W
Tiverton England 13 D2 ....50.54N 3.29W
Tivoli Italy 50 E4 ....41.58N 12.49E
Tizi Ouzou Algeria 52 D4 ....36.41N 4.05E
Tiznit Morocco 84 D4 ....29.41N 9.43W
Tiztoutine Morocco 48 D1 ....34.58N 3.09W
Tlaxcala Mexico 70 E4 ....19.21N 98.13W
Tlaxcala d. Mexico 70 E4 ....19.35N 98.20W
Tlemcen Algeria 84 D5 ....34.54N 1.19W
Toamasina Madagascar 86 D3 ....18.09S 49.22E
Toba, Danau l. Indonesia 104 B4 ......2.32N 98.59E
Tobago i. Trinidad and Tobago 71 L3 ....11.17N 60.38W
Tobelo Indonesia 105 H4 ....1.44N 127.57E
Tobermory Scotland 18 C1 ....56.38N 6.04W
Toboali Indonesia 104 D3 ....2.59S 106.30E
Tobol r. Kazakhstan/Rus. Fed. 58 H3 ....58.10N 68.13E
Tobol'sk Rus. Fed. 58 H3 ....58.14N 68.16E
Tocantins d. Brazil 77 K5 ....11.15S 48.38W
Tocantins r. Brazil 77 K7 ....1.49S 49.13W
Tocopilla Chile 76 F3 ....22.04S 70.10W
Todmorden England 15 E2 ....53.43N 2.06W
Toft Scotland 19 H5 ....60.28N 1.13W
Togian, Kepulauan is Indonesia 105 G3 ....0.06S 121.53E
Togo Africa 84 E2 ....8.27N 1.11E
Tok U.S.A. 62 D4 ....63.21N 143.01W
Tokaj Hungary 46 E2 ....48.06N 21.25E
Tokara-rettō is Japan 106 A1 ....28.34N 129.00E
Tokat Turkey 57 L5 ....40.19N 36.32E
Tokelau is S. Pacific Oc. 108 I5 ....8.30S 171.28W
Tokushima Japan 106 B2 ....34.04N 134.34E
Tōkyō Japan 106 C3 ....35.40N 139.46E
Tōkyō d. Japan 106 C3 ....35.22N 139.03E
Tôlañaro Madagascar 86 D2 ....25.02S 46.58E
Toledo Spain 48 C3 ....39.52N 4.01W
Toledo U.S.A. 65 J5 ....41.39N 83.33W
Toledo, Montes de mts Spain 48 C3 ....39.39N 4.54W
Toledo Bend Reservoir U.S.A. 65 H3 ....31.38N 93.43W
Tolentino Italy 50 E5 ....43.13N 13.19E
Toliara Madagascar 86 D2 ....23.22S 43.39E
Tolitoli Indonesia 105 G4 ....1.05N 120.50E
Tollesbury England 11 F2 ....51.45N 0.50E
Tolsta Head Scotland 18 C3 ....58.21N 6.10W
Toluca Mexico 70 E4 ....19.18N 99.39W
Tol'yatti Rus. Fed. 58 F3 ....53.31N 49.26E
Tomakomai Japan 106 D4 ....42.38N 141.36E
Tomanivi mt. Fiji 111 G5 ....17.37S 178.00E
Tomaszów Lubelski Poland 46 F3 ....50.28N 23.25E
Tomaszów Mazowiecki Poland 46 E3 ....51.32N 20.01E
Tombigbee r. U.S.A. 65 I3 ....31.11N 87.57W
Tombua Angola 86 A3 ....15.50S 11.50E
Tomelloso Spain 48 D3 ....39.09N 3.00W
Tomini, Teluk g. Indonesia 104 G3 ....0.21S 120.54E
Tomsk Rus. Fed. 58 J3 ....56.30N 85.01E
Tomtabacken hill Sweden 40 C2 ......57.30N 14.29E
Tonbridge England 11 F2 ....51.12N 0.17E
Tondano Indonesia 105 G4 ....1.21N 124.56E
Tønder Denmark 40 B1 ....54.57N 8.52E
Tone r. England 10 C2 ....51.04N 2.56W
Tonelagee hill Ireland 12 A5 ....53.03N 6.23W
Tonga S. Pacific Oc. 108 I4 ....20.05S 173.45W
Tongatapu Group is Tonga 108 I4 ....21.07S 174.45W
Tonga Trench f. S. Pacific Oc. 108 I4 ....21.47S 173.51W
Tongeren Belgium 42 E3 ....50.47N 5.28E
Tonghua China 103 N6 ....41.43N 125.57E
Tongking, Gulf of China/Vietnam 103 J2 ....20.29N 108.15E
Tongliao China 103 M6 ....43.31N 122.14E
Tongling China 103 L4 ....30.55N 117.52E
Tongshan China 103 L4 ....34.12N 117.14E
Tongue Scotland 19 E3 ....58.29N 4.25W
Tonle Sap l. Cambodia 104 C6 ....13.04N 103.51E
Tonopah U.S.A. 64 C4 ....38.04N 117.14W
Tønsberg Norway 40 B2 ....59.17N 10.23E
Toowoomba Australia 110 E4 ....27.33S 151.58E
Topeka U.S.A. 65 G4 ....39.04N 95.36W
Topozero, Ozero l. Rus. Fed. 40 H4 ....65.42N 32.00E
Topsham England 13 D2 ....50.41N 3.28W
Torbat-e Heydariyeh Iran 95 I7 ......35.13N 59.06E
Torbat-e Jām Iran 95 J7 ....35.15N 60.34E
Torbay d. England 9 D2 ....50.26N 3.34W
Tor Bay England 13 D2 ....50.25N 3.32W
Tordesillas Spain 48 C4 ....41.31N 4.59W

Torenberg hill Neth. 42 E5 ....52.14N 5.52E
Torfaen d. Wales 9 D2 ....51.44N 3.05W
Tormes r. Spain 48 B4 ....41.18N 6.27W
Torneälven r. Sweden 40 F4 ....65.49N 24.09E
Torneträsk l. Sweden 40 D5 ....68.23N 18.56E
Tornio Finland 40 F4 ....65.50N 24.11E
Toronto Canada 63 K2 ....43.40N 79.23W
Toropets Rus. Fed. 55 N7 ....56.30N 31.38E
Tororo Uganda 87 A3 ....0.39N 34.10E
Torpoint England 13 C2 ....50.22N 4.12W
Torquay England 13 D2 ....50.28N 3.31W
Torre mt. Portugal 48 B4 ....40.20N 7.35W
Torrecerredo mt. Spain 48 C5 ....43.12N 4.49W
Torre del Greco Italy 50 F4 ....40.47N 14.23E
Torremolinos Spain 48 C2 ....36.36N 4.30W
Torrens, Lake Australia 110 C3 ....30.32S 137.28E
Torreón Mexico 70 D6 ....25.31N 103.27W
Torres Islands Vanuatu 111 F5 ....13.08S 166.17E
Torres Strait Australia 110 D6 ....9.50S 142.11E
Torres Vedras Portugal 48 A3 ....39.06N 9.15W
Torrevieja Spain 48 E2 ....37.59N 0.40W
Torridge r. England 13 C2 ....50.59N 4.11W
Torridon Scotland 18 D2 ....57.33N 5.31W
Torridon, Loch b. Scotland 18 D2 ....57.37N 5.50W
Tortosa Spain 48 F4 ....40.50N 0.32E
Toruń Poland 46 D4 ....53.01N 18.37E
Tory Island Ireland 41 C5 ....55.16N 8.13W
Tosno Rus. Fed. 40 G2 ....59.33N 30.54E
Tosya Turkey 57 K5 ....40.59N 34.04E
Totland England 10 D1 ....50.41N 1.32W
Totnes England 13 D2 ....50.26N 3.41W
Totton England 10 D1 ....50.55N 1.29W
Tottori Japan 106 B3 ....35.29N 134.14E
Toubkal, Jbel mt. Morocco 84 D5 ....31.03N 7.57W
Touggourt Algeria 84 E5 ....33.06N 6.04E
Toulon France 44 F3 ....43.08N 5.56E
Toulouse France 44 D3 ....43.37N 1.26E
Toungoo Myanmar 97 I4 ....18.55N 96.25E
Touraine f. France 44 D5 ....47.14N 0.21E
Tournai Belgium 42 C3 ....50.36N 3.24E
Tournon-sur-Rhône France 44 F4 ....45.04N 4.50E
Tours France 44 D5 ....47.23N 0.42E
Tove r. England 10 E3 ....52.05N 0.50W
Towada Japan 106 D4 ....40.36N 141.12E
Towcester England 10 E3 ....52.08N 0.59W
Townsville Australia 110 D5 ....19.15S 146.49E
Towori, Teluk b. Indonesia 105 G3 ....2.02S 121.57E
Towot Sudan 87 A4 ....6.10N 34.23E
Toyama Japan 106 C3 ....36.41N 137.13E
Toyama-wan b. Japan 106 C3 ....36.54N 137.14E
Toyota Japan 106 C3 ....35.05N 137.10E
Tozeur Tunisia 52 E3 ....33.55N 8.07E
Trabzon Turkey 57 M5 ....40.59N 39.44E
Trafalgar, Cabo c. Spain 48 B2 ....36.11N 6.02W
Trakai Lithuania 46 G5 ....54.38N 24.56E
Tralee Ireland 41 B2 ....52.16N 9.42W
Tralee Bay Ireland 41 B2 ....52.18N 9.57W
Tramore Ireland 41 D2 ....52.10N 7.09W
Tranås Sweden 40 C2 ....58.02N 14.59E
Trangan i. Indonesia 105 I2 ....6.35S 134.16E
Transylvanian Alps mts Romania 55 J1 ....45.35N 24.40E
Trapani Italy 50 E3 ....38.01N 12.31E
Trasimeno, Lago l. Italy 50 E5 ....43.08N 12.06E
Traunsee l. Austria 54 E2 ....47.54N 13.47E
Traverse City U.S.A. 65 I5 ....44.46N 85.37W
Travnik Bos.-Herz. 56 B7 ....44.14N 17.40E
Trawsfynydd, Llyn resr Wales 12 D4 ....52.55N 3.59W
Trebišov Slovakia 55 I3 ....48.39N 21.44E
Tredegar Wales 12 D3 ....51.46N 3.15W
Tregaron Wales 12 D4 ....52.13N 3.56W
Treig, Loch l. Scotland 18 E1 ....56.48N 4.44W
Trelleborg Sweden 40 C1 ....55.22N 13.10E
Tremadog Bay Wales 12 C4 ....52.52N 4.16W
Trenčín Slovakia 54 H3 ....48.53N 18.02E
Trent r. England 15 G2 ....53.38N 0.43W
Trento Italy 50 D7 ....46.04N 11.08E
Trenton U.S.A. 65 L5 ....40.13N 74.47W
Tresco i. England 13 A1 ....49.57N 6.19W
Tres Puntas, Cabo c. Argentina 73 C2 ....47.08S 65.53W
Treviso Italy 50 E6 ....45.40N 12.15E
Trevose Head England 13 B2 ....50.33N 5.06W
Trier Germany 54 B3 ....49.45N 6.38E
Trieste Italy 50 E6 ....45.39N 13.46E
Trikala Greece 56 D4 ....39.33N 21.46E
Trim Ireland 41 E3 ....53.33N 6.47W
Trincomalee Sri Lanka 96 F2 ....8.37N 81.13E
Tring England 10 E2 ....51.48N 0.39W
Trinidad Bolivia 76 H5 ....14.44S 64.51W
Trinidad i. Trinidad and Tobago 71 L3 ....10.27N 61.13W
Trinidad U.S.A. 64 F4 ....37.11N 104.30W
Trinidad and Tobago Central America 71 L3 ....10.49N 61.00W
Tripoli Greece 56 E3 ....37.31N 22.23E
Tripoli Lebanon 53 K3 ....34.26N 35.52E
Tripoli Libya 84 F5 ....32.52N 13.08E
Tripolitania f. Libya 52 F3 ....30.39N 13.17E
Tripura d. India 97 H5 ....23.36N 91.35E
Tristan da Cunha i. Atlantic Oc. 116 I4 ....38.00S 12.00W
Trnava Slovakia 54 G3 ....48.22N 17.36E
Trobriand Islands P.N.G. 110 E6 .....8.33S 151.05E
Troisdorf Germany 42 G3 ....50.49N 7.09E
Trois-Rivières Canada 63 K2 ....46.21N 72.35W
Trollhättan Sweden 40 C2 ....58.16N 12.18E
Trombetas r. Brazil 77 I7 ....1.31S 56.06W
Tromsø Norway 40 D5 ....69.39N 18.57E
Trondheim Norway 40 B3 ....63.25N 10.22E
Troödos, Mount Cyprus 57 J2 ....34.56N 32.51E
Troon Scotland 16 E3 ....55.32N 4.40W
Trostan hill Northern Ireland 16 C3 ....55.03N 6.09W
Troup Head Scotland 19 G2 ....57.42N 2.18W
Trout Lake Canada 65 H7 ....51.15N 93.06W
Trowbridge England 10 C2 ....51.19N 2.12W
Troyes France 44 F6 ....48.18N 4.05E
Trubchevsk Rus. Fed. 55 O5 ....52.35N 33.47E
Trujillo Peru 76 E6 ....8.07S 79.02W
Truro Canada 63 L2 ....45.22N 63.13W
Truro England 13 B2 ....50.16N 5.03W
Trutnov Czech Rep. 46 B3 ....50.33N 15.55E
Trzebiatów Poland 46 B5 ....54.04N 15.16E
Tsaratanana, Massif du mts Madagascar 86 D3 ....13.44S 48.59E
Tsavo r. Kenya 87 B2 ....2.58S 38.31E
Tsavo East National Park Kenya 87 B2 ....2.43S 38.45E
Tsavo West National Park Kenya 87 B2 ....3.18S 37.58E
Tsetserleg Mongolia 103 I7 ....47.19N 101.29E
Tshchikskoye Vodokhranilishche resr Rus. Fed. 57 M7
....45.07N 39.28E
Tshwane S. Africa 86 B2 ....25.44S 28.13E
Tsimlyanskoye Vodokhranilishche resr Russian Fed. 35 I2
....48.00N 43.00E
Tsna r. Belarus 55 L5 ....52.09N 27.01E
Tsu Japan 106 C2 ....34.43N 136.31E
Tsuchiura Japan 106 D3 ....36.05N 140.12E
Tsugarū-kaikyō str. Japan 106 D4 ....41.16N 140.21E
Tsumeb Namibia 86 A3 ....19.14S 17.43E
Tsumis Park Namibia 86 A2 ....23.47S 17.31E

Tsuruga Japan 106 C3 ....35.38N 136.04E
Tsushima is Japan 106 A2 ....34.24N 129.23E
Tuam Ireland 41 C3 ....53.31N 8.51W
Tuamotu, Archipel des is French Polynesia 109 K5
....14.29S 142.50W
Tuapse Rus. Fed. 57 M7 ....44.06N 39.04E
Tuban Indonesia 104 E2 ....6.55S 112.02E
Tubbercurry Ireland 41 C4 ....54.03N 8.43W
Tübingen Germany 54 C3 ....48.31N 9.04E
Tubruq Libya 85 G5 ....32.04N 23.57E
Tubuai i. French Polynesia 109 K4 ....23.21S 149.30W
Tubuai Islands French Polynesia 109 J4 ....23.34S 153.12W
Tucavaca Bolivia 77 I4 ....18.37S 58.56W
Tucson U.S.A. 64 D3 ....32.14N 110.54W
Tucumcari U.S.A. 64 F4 ....35.12N 103.44W
Tucuruí Brazil 77 K7 ....3.42S 49.44W
Tucuruí, Represa resr Brazil 77 K7 ....4.26S 49.07W
Tudela Spain 48 E5 ....42.04N 1.36W
Tuela r. Portugal 48 B4 ....41.38N 7.08W
Tufts Abyssal Plain f. N. Pacific Oc. 109 K9 ....49.37N 146.59W
Tuguegarao Phil. 105 G7 ....17.37N 121.43E
Tui Spain 48 A5 ....42.03N 8.38W
Tukangbesi, Kepulauan is Indonesia 105 G2 ....5.40S 123.55E
Tukums Latvia 40 E2 ....56.58N 23.10E
Tula watercourse Kenya 87 B2 ....0.50S 39.48E
Tula Rus. Fed. 58 E3 ....54.12N 37.37E
Tulcea Romania 57 H7 ....45.10N 28.48E
Tul'chyn Ukraine 55 M3 ....48.41N 28.50E
Tulít'a Canada 62 F4 ....64.55N 125.31W
Tullamore Ireland 41 D3 ....53.17N 7.30W
Tulle France 44 D4 ....45.16N 1.46E
Tullow Ireland 41 E2 ....52.48N 6.44W
Tully r. Australia 110 D5 ....18.03S 145.50E
Tullybrack hill Northern Ireland 16 B2 ....54.23N 7.52W
Tulsa U.S.A. 64 G4 ....36.09N 95.58W
Tumaco Colombia 72 B7 ....1.48N 78.49W
Tumba, Lac l. Dem. Rep. Congo 86 A4 ....0.52S 18.05E
Tumbes Peru 76 D7 ....3.35S 80.27W
Tumen r. Asia 106 A4 ....42.14N 130.41E
Tumen China 106 A4 ....42.59N 129.51E
Tumkur India 96 E3 ....13.19N 77.06E
Tummel r. Scotland 19 F1 ....56.39N 3.40W
Tummel, Loch l. Scotland 19 F1 ......56.42N 3.58W
Tump Pakistan 95 J5 ....26.06N 62.26E
Tumucumaque, Serra hills Brazil 77 I8 ....1.59N 56.09W
Tunceli Turkey 57 M4 ....39.06N 39.33E
Tundzha r. Bulgaria 56 G5 ....41.39N 26.33E
Tunis Tunisia 52 F4 ....36.46N 10.16E
Tunis, Golfe de g. Tunisia 50 D4 ....37.08N 10.31E
Tunisia Africa 52 E3 ....34.52N 9.24E
Tunja Colombia 72 B7 ....5.30N 73.22W
Tunnsjøen l. Norway 40 C4 ....64.42N 13.24E
Tuolumne r. U.S.A. 64 B4 ....37.36N 121.10W
Tupinambarana, Ilha i. Brazil 77 I7 ....3.50S 58.55W
Tupiza Bolivia 76 G3 ....21.27S 65.45W
Tura Rus. Fed. 59 L4 ....64.16N 100.15E
Turabah Saudi Arabia 94 F4 ....21.14N 41.37E
Turbat Pakistan 96 B6 ....26.01N 63.07E
Turbo Colombia 71 I2 ....8.05N 76.43W
Turda Romania 55 J2 ....46.34N 23.47E
Turgutlu Turkey 56 G4 ....38.29N 27.42E
Turhal Turkey 57 L5 ....40.23N 36.04E
Turia r. Spain 48 E3 ....39.26N 0.18W
Turin Italy 50 B6 ....45.04N 7.41E
Turiys'k Ukraine 46 G3 ....51.05N 24.32E
Turkana, Lake Ethiopia/Kenya 85 H2 ....3.59N 35.57E
Turkey Asia/Europe 57 I4 ....39.19N 34.21E
Turkmenabat Turkmenistan 58 H1 ....39.05N 63.34E
Turkmenbashi Turkmenistan 58 G2 ....40.02N 52.59E
Turkmenistan Asia 115 L7 ....40.00N 60.00E
Turks and Caicos Islands Central America 71 J5 ....21.59N 71.36W
Turks Islands Turks and Caicos Is 71 J5 ....21.25N 71.09W
Turku Finland 40 E3 ....60.27N 22.15E
Turkwel watercourse Kenya 87 B3 ....3.03N 36.08E
Turnhout Belgium 42 D4 ....51.19N 4.57E
Turnu Măgurele Romania 56 F6 ......43.45N 24.51E
Turpan China 102 F6 ....42.52N 89.12E
Turquino, Pico mt. Cuba 71 I5 ....20.02N 76.51W
Turriff Scotland 19 G2 ....57.32N 2.28W
Tuscaloosa U.S.A. 65 I3 ....33.11N 87.30W
Tutbury England 10 D3 ....52.51N 1.41W
Tuticorin India 96 E2 ....8.48N 78.08E
Tuttlingen Germany 54 C2 ....47.59N 8.49E
Tutuila i. American Samoa 108 I5 ....14.16S 170.33W
Tuvalu S. Pacific Oc. 111 G6 ....7.24S 178.20E
Tuxford England 15 G2 ....53.14N 0.54W
Tuxpan Mexico 70 E5 ....20.58N 97.22W
Tuxtla Gutiérrez Mexico 70 F4 ....16.46N 93.08W
Tuz, Lake Turkey 57 J4 ....38.42N 33.24E
Tuzla Bos.-Herz. 56 C7 ....44.33N 18.42E
Tver' Rus. Fed. 58 E3 ....56.50N 35.54E
Tweed r. U.K. 15 E4 ....55.45N 2.06W
Twin Falls town U.S.A. 64 D5 ....42.35N 114.27W
Twyford England 10 E2 ....51.29N 0.52W
Tyler U.S.A. 65 G3 ....32.22N 95.18W
Tynda Rus. Fed. 59 N3 ....55.07N 124.44E
Tyne r. Scotland 17 G4 ....56.00N 2.36W
Tyne and Wear d. England 8 E4 ......54.56N 1.16W
Tynemouth England 15 F4 ....55.01N 1.25W
Tynset Norway 40 B3 ....62.16N 10.47E
Tyre Lebanon 53 K3 ....33.15N 35.14E
Tyrrhenian Sea France/Italy 50 D4 ....40.13N 10.15E
Tyumen' Rus. Fed. 58 H3 ....57.09N 65.28E
Tywi r. Wales 12 C3 ....51.48N 4.20W

U

Uaupés Brazil 76 G7 ....0.06S 67.02W
Ubangi r. C.A.R./Dem. Rep. Congo 85 F1 ....0.25S 17.44E
Úbeda Spain 48 D3 ....38.01N 3.22W
Uberaba Brazil 77 K4 ....19.46S 47.53W
Uberlândia Brazil 77 K4 ....18.56S 48.14W
Ubon Ratchathani Thailand 104 C7 ....15.14N 104.53E
Ucayali r. Peru 76 F7 ....4.28S 73.29W
Uchur r. Rus. Fed. 59 O3 ....57.19N 131.17E
Uckfield England 11 F1 ....50.58N 0.06E
Uda r. Rus. Fed. 59 O3 ....54.41N 135.18E
Udaipur India 96 D5 ....24.35N 73.47E
Uddevalla Sweden 40 B2 ....58.21N 11.57E
Uddjaure l. Sweden 40 D4 ....65.56N 17.52E
Udine Italy 50 E7 ....46.04N 13.14E
Udon Thani Thailand 104 C7 ....17.22N 102.50E
Udupi India 96 D3 ....13.20N 74.46E
Ueda Japan 106 C3 ....36.24N 138.15E
Uele r. Dem. Rep. Congo 86 B5 ......3.32N 25.16E
Uelzen Germany 54 D5 ....52.58N 10.34E
Ufa Rus. Fed. 58 G3 ....54.44N 55.58E
Uganda Africa 85 H2 ....2.34N 32.37E
Uglegorsk Rus. Fed. 59 P2 ....49.02N 142.02E
Uherské Hradiště Czech Rep. 46 C2 ....49.04N 17.28E
Uig Scotland 18 C2 ....57.35N 6.21W
Uíge Angola 86 A4 ....7.36S 15.05E
Uinta Mountains U.S.A. 64 D5 ....40.36N 110.59W

Ukerewe Island Tanzania 87 A2 .....1.57S 32.
Ukhta Rus. Fed. 58 G4 ....63.33N 53.
Ukiah U.S.A. 64 B4 ....39.09N 123.
Ukmergė Lithuania 46 G5 ....55.15N 24.
Ukraine Europe 55 N3 ....49.23N 31.
Ulaangom Mongolia 102 G7 ....49.57N 92.
Ulan Bator Mongolia 103 J7 ....47.48N 106.
Ulanhot China 103 M7 ....46.04N 122.
Ulan-Ude Rus. Fed. 59 L3 ....51.49N 107.
Ulchin S. Korea 106 A3 ....36.59N 129.
Uliastay Mongolia 102 H7 ....47.36N 96.
Ulithi atoll Micronesia 105 J6 ....10.07N 139.
Ullapool Scotland 18 D2 ....57.54N 5.
Ullswater l. England 14 E3 ....54.34N 2.
Ullŭng-do i. S. Korea 106 B3 ....37.30N 130.
Ulm Germany 54 C3 ....48.25N 9.
Ulster Canal Ireland/U.K. 16 B2 ......54.14N 7.
Uludağ mt. Turkey 57 H5 ....40.06N 29.
Ulundi S. Africa 86 C2 ....28.19S 31.
Uluru hill Australia 110 C4 ....25.20S 131.
Ulva i. Scotland 16 C4 ....56.28N 6.
Ulverston England 14 D3 ....54.12N 3.
Ul'yanovsk Rus. Fed. 58 F3 ....54.18N 48.
Uman' Ukraine 55 N3 ....48.45N 30.
Umboi i. P.N.G. 110 D6 ....5.42S 147.
Umeå Sweden 40 E3 ....63.50N 20.
Umeälven r. Sweden 40 D4 ....63.46N 20.
Umm Keddada Sudan 94 C2 ....13.35N 26.
Umm Ruwaba Sudan 94 D2 ....12.52N 31.
Umm Sa'ad Libya 85 G5 ....31.34N 25.
Umtata S. Africa 86 B1 ....31.35S 28.
Umuarama Brazil 77 J3 ....23.46S 53.
Una r. Bos.-Herz./Croatia 56 B7 ......45.16N 16.
'Unayzah Saudi Arabia 94 F5 ....26.05N 43.
Unecha Rus. Fed. 55 O5 ....52.51N 32.
Ungava, Péninsule d' pen. Canada 63 K4 ....60.46N 74.
Ungava Bay Canada 63 L3 ....59.16N 67.
Unggi N. Korea 106 B4 ....42.21N 130.
Ungwana Bay Kenya 87 C2 ....2.47S 40.
Unimak Island U.S.A. 62 B3 ....54.58N 164.
Unini r. Brazil 76 H7 ....1.41S 61.
United Arab Emirates Asia 95 H4 ....23.30N 52.
United Kingdom Europe 8-19 ....54.35N 1.
United States of America N. America 64 G4 ....38.59N 99.
Unst i. Scotland 19 I5 ....60.46N 0.
Upa r. Rus. Fed. 55 Q6 ....54.01N 36.
Upavon England 10 D2 ....51.18N 1.4
Upemba, Lac l. Dem. Rep. Congo 86 B4 ....8.39S 26.
Upernavik Greenland 63 M5 ....72.48N 56.0
Upington S. Africa 86 B2 ....28.28S 21.
Upolu i. Samoa 108 I5 ....14.04S 171.
Upper Klamath Lake U.S.A. 64 B5 ....42.22N 121.5
Upper Lough Erne l. Northern Ireland 16 B2 ....54.15N 7.3
Upper Tean England 10 D3 ....52.57N 1.5
Uppingham England 10 E3 ....52.35N 0.4
Uppsala Sweden 40 D2 ....59.51N 17.
Upton upon Severn England 10 C3 ....52.04N 2.1
Ural r. Kazakhstan/Rus. Fed. 58 G2 ....46.65S 51.
Ural Mountains Rus. Fed. 58 H4 ......66.50N 63.
Ural'sk Kazakhstan 58 G3 ....51.11N 51.
Uranium City Canada 62 H3 ....59.31N 108.
Urawa Japan 106 C3 ....35.51N 139.
Ure r. England 15 F3 ....54.05N 1.2
Urengoy Rus. Fed. 58 I4 ....65.55N 78.
Urganch Uzbekistan 58 H2 ....41.32N 60.
Urie r. Scotland 19 G2 ....57.16N 2.2
Urla Turkey 56 G4 ....38.17N 26.
Urmia, Lake Iran 94 G7 ....37.57N 45.
Uruaçu Brazil 77 K5 ....14.31S 49.
Uruapan Mexico 70 D4 ....19.25N 102.0
Urubamba r. Peru 76 F5 ....10.46S 73.4
Urucara Brazil 77 I7 ....2.31S 57.4
Uruguaiana Brazil 77 I2 ....29.45S 57.0
Uruguay r. Argentina/Brazil/Uruguay 77 I1 ....33.52S 58.2
Uruguay S. America 73 D3 ....32.45S 55.5
Ürümqi China 102 F6 ....43.44N 87.3
Urziceni Romania 56 G7 ....44.43N 26.3
Uşak Turkey 57 I4 ....38.40N 29.
Ushuaia Argentina 73 C1 ....54.46S 68.1
Usk Wales 12 E3 ....51.42N 2.5
Usk r. Wales 12 E3 ....51.34N 2.5
Usk Reservoir Wales 12 D3 ....51.56N 3.4
Usol'ye-Sibirskoye Rus. Fed. 59 L3 ....52.40N 103.3
Ussuri r. China/Rus. Fed. 106 C5 ....48.24N 135.0
Ussuriysk Rus. Fed. 59 O2 ....43.48N 131.5
Ustica, Isola di i. Italy 50 E3 ....38.41N 13.1
Ust'-Ilimsk Rus. Fed. 59 L3 ....58.02N 102.4
Ústí nad Labem Czech Rep. 54 F4 ....50.40N 14.0
Ustka Poland 46 C5 ....54.35N 16.5
Ust'-Kamchatsk Rus. Fed. 59 R3 ....56.15N 162.3
Ust'-Kamenogorsk Kazakhstan 58 J2 ....49.52N 82.4
Ust'-Kut Rus. Fed. 59 L3 ....56.45N 105.4
Ust'-Maya Rus. Fed. 59 O4 ....60.27N 134.3
Ust'-Olenek Rus. Fed. 59 M5 ....72.55N 119.4
Ustyurt Plateau f. Kazakhstan/Uzbekistan 58 G2 ....43.29N 56.1
Utah d. U.S.A. 64 D4 ....39.34N 111.34
Utena Lithuania 46 G5 ....55.30N 25.3
Utica U.S.A. 65 K5 ....43.06N 75.15
Utiel Spain 48 E3 ....39.34N 1.11
Utrecht Neth. 42 E5 ....52.05N 5.0
Utrecht d. Neth. 42 E5 ....52.05N 5.1
Utrera Spain 48 C2 ....37.11N 5.46
Utsunomiya Japan 106 C3 ....36.34N 139.5
Uttaradit Thailand 104 C7 ....17.37N 100.0
Uttaranchal d. India 96 E7 ....30.11N 79.08
Uttar Pradesh d. India 96 E6 ....27.37N 79.17
Uttoxeter England 10 D3 ....52.54N 1.52
Uusikaupunki Finland 40 E3 ....60.48N 21.25
Uvs Nuur l. Mongolia 102 G8 ....50.20N 92.3
Uwajima Japan 106 B2 ....33.13N 132.34
Uxbridge England 11 E2 ....51.33N 0.29
Uyuni Bolivia 76 G3 ....20.30S 66.51
Uyuni, Salar de f. Bolivia 76 G3 .....20.13S 67.36
Uzbekistan Asia 115 M8 ....40.00N 60.00
Uzhhorod Ukraine 55 J3 ....48.37N 22.1
Užice Serbia 56 C6 ....43.51N 19.51
Uzunköprü Turkey 56 G5 ....41.15N 26.41

V

Vaal r. S. Africa 86 B2 ....29.05S 23.39
Vaasa Finland 40 E3 ....63.06N 21.38
Vác Hungary 54 H2 ....47.47N 19.09
Vadodara India 96 D5 ....22.16N 73.14
Vadsø Norway 40 G5 ....70.05N 29.44
Vaduz Liechtenstein 54 C2 ....47.08N 9.32
Værøy i. Norway 40 C4 ....67.39N 12.36
Vaganski Vrh mt. Croatia 56 A7 .....44.22N 15.30
Váh r. Slovakia 54 H2 ....47.46N 18.08
Vaiaku Tuvalu 108 H5 ....8.28S 179.10
Vaitupu i. Tuvalu 111 G6 ....7.27S 178.43
Valdai Hills Russian Fed. 34 H3 ......57.10N 33.00

peñas Spain 48 D3 .....38.46N 3.22W
s, Península pen. Argentina 73 C2 .....42.41S 63.25W
ez U.S.A. 62 D4 .....61.07N 146.16W
via Chile 73 B3 .....39.50S 73.13W
'Or Canada 63 K2 .....48.06N 77.47W
osta U.S.A. 65 J3 .....30.51N 83.18W
nes f. Norway 40 B3 .....60.56N 9.13E
acia Spain 48 E3 .....43.29N 0.21W
acia Venezuela 72 C8 .....10.10N 67.59W
acia, Golfo de g. Spain 48 F3 .....39.28N 0.02E
acia de Alcántara Spain 48 B3 .....39.25N 7.14W
aciennes France 44 E7 .....50.21N 3.32E
of Glamorgan d. Wales 9 D2 .....51.26N 3.21W
a Venezuela 72 D7 .....9.14N 70.35W
r, Mont mt. France 44 D3 .....42.48N 1.05E
co, Golfe de b. France 50 C4 .....41.40N 8.52E
co, Gulf of Italy 44 H2 .....41.40N 8.50E
vo Serbia 56 C7 .....44.17N 19.55E
n Latvia 40 F2 .....57.46N 26.00E
eakoski Finland 40 F3 .....61.15N 24.03E
enswaard Neth. 42 E4 .....51.21N 5.27E
dolid Spain 48 C4 .....41.39N 4.43W
de la Pascua Venezuela 71 K2 .....9.10N 65.57W
dupar Colombia 72 B8 .....10.30N 73.16W
tta Malta 50 F1 .....35.54N 14.30E
y Wales 12 C5 .....53.17N 4.34W
araíso Chile 73 B3 .....33.03S 71.36W
Tanjung c. Indonesia 105 J2 .....8.26S 137.40E
mala Finland 40 F3 .....61.20N 22.56E
Turkey 94 F7 .....38.30N 43.22E
Lake Turkey 94 F7 .....38.37N 42.47E
ouver Canada 62 F2 .....49.16N 123.08W
ouver Island Canada 62 F2 .....49.28N 125.39W
Diemen Gulf Australia 105 I1 .....11.54S 132.00E
ern l. Sweden 40 D2 .....59.05N 13.36E
ersborg Sweden 40 C2 .....58.23N 12.20E
drano Madagascar 86 D2 .....23.22S 47.34E
mo P.N.G. 105 K3 .....2.42S 141.20E
näs Sweden 40 D3 .....63.55N 19.46E
nes France 44 B5 .....47.39N 2.45W
aa Finland 40 F3 .....60.18N 24.57E
ua Levu i. Fiji 111 G5 .....16.10S 179.40E
atu S. Pacific Oc. 111 F5 .....16.05S 167.04E
nasi India 96 F6 .....25.20N 83.04E
ngerfjorden str. Norway 40 G5 .....70.04N 29.07E
ždin Croatia 56 G2 .....46.19N 16.22E
erg Sweden 40 C2 .....57.07N 12.16E
ar r. Macedonia 56 E5 .....41.07N 22.32E
na Lithuania 46 G5 .....54.13N 24.35E
se Italy 50 C6 .....45.49N 8.50E
aus Finland 40 F3 .....62.19N 27.54E
a Bulgaria 57 G6 .....43.12N 27.54E
amo Sweden 40 C2 .....57.11N 14.03E
alota Hungary 54 H2 .....47.12N 18.08E
Barris r. Brazil 77 M5 .....11.02S 37.11W
erás Sweden 40 D2 .....59.37N 16.33E
erdalälven r. Sweden 40 C3 .....60.32N 15.07E
ervik Sweden 40 D2 .....57.45N 16.39E
l'kiv Ukraine 55 N4 .....50.11N 30.19E
ersay i. Sweden 40 D4 .....53.06N 6.53E
najökull ice cap Iceland 40 Y2 .....64.28N 16.37W
tern l. Sweden 40 D2 .....58.05N 14.21E
u Group is Tonga 108 I4 .....18.24S 174.21W
kavysk Belarus 55 K5 .....53.09N 24.27E
ö Sweden 40 C2 .....56.53N 14.49E
hte r. Germany 42 F5 .....52.37N 6.43E
ndam Neth. 42 E5 .....53.06N 6.53E
nendaal Neth. 42 E5 .....52.01N 5.33E
a i. Norway 40 B4 .....65.39N 11.53E
e Denmark 40 B1 .....55.43N 9.32E
en Germany 42 F4 .....51.53N 6.59E
es Macedonia 56 E5 .....41.42N 21.47E
ez-Málaga Spain 48 C2 .....36.47N 4.06W
has r. Brazil 72 F5 .....17.13S 44.49W
ska Morava canal Serbia 56 D7 .....44.43N 21.03E
kaya r. Rus. Fed. 55 M7 .....57.50N 28.15E
kaya r. Rus. Fed. 59 S4 .....64.32N 176.06E
kiye Luki Rus. Fed. 58 E3 .....56.20N 30.31E
kiy Novgorod Rus. Fed. 58 E3 .....58.33N 31.16E
iko Türnovo Bulgaria 56 F6 .....43.05N 25.39E
ino, Monte mt. Italy 50 E5 .....42.09N 13.23E
izh Rus. Fed. 55 N6 .....55.36N 31.12E
ore India 96 E3 .....12.56N 79.07E
'sk Rus. Fed. 58 F4 .....61.03N 42.05E
ten Germany 46 A4 .....52.41N 13.11E
ndôme France 44 D5 .....47.48N 1.04E
nezuela S. America 71 K2 .....7.35N 66.30W
nezuela, Golfo de g. Venezuela 72 B8 .....11.32N 71.03W
nezuelan Basin f. Caribbean Sea 109 P7 .....15.44N 70.59W
nice Italy 50 E6 .....45.26N 12.20E
nice, Gulf of Europe 50 E6 .....45.19N 12.43E
nray Neth. 42 E4 .....51.31N 5.58E
nta r. Latvia/Lithuania 40 E2 .....56.24N 21.21E
ntspils Latvia 40 E2 .....57.23N 21.36E
a Spain 48 E2 .....37.15N 1.52W
acruz Mexico 70 E4 .....19.11N 96.09W
acruz d. Mexico 70 E5 .....20.54N 97.46W
rcelli Italy 50 C6 .....45.19N 8.26E
rdalsøra Norway 40 B3 .....63.47N 11.29E
rde r. Brazil 77 J3 .....21.10S 51.58W
rde r. Paraguay 77 I3 .....23.01S 57.46W
rde r. U.S.A. 64 D3 .....33.33N 111.39W
rdun France 44 F6 .....49.10N 5.24E
n Spain 48 B4 .....41.56N 7.25W
khnevilyuysk Rus. Fed. 59 N4 .....63.26N 120.12E
khoyansk Rus. Fed. 59 O4 .....67.32N 133.27E
khoyanskiy Khrebet mts Rus. Fed. 59 N5 .....70.07N 128.50E
roia Greece 56 E5 .....40.32N 22.13E
rmont d. U.S.A. 65 L5 .....44.03N 72.42W
rona Italy 50 D6 .....45.26N 10.59E
rsailles France 44 E6 .....48.48N 2.08E
rt, Cap c. Senegal 84 C3 .....14.44N 17.31W
rviers Belgium 42 E3 .....50.35N 5.52E
rvins France 42 C2 .....49.50N 3.54E
rwood England 10 D1 .....50.53N 1.52W
soul France 44 G5 .....47.38N 6.09E
sterålen is Norway 40 D5 .....68.43N 13.59E
stfjorden str. Norway 40 C4 .....67.40N 13.54E
stmannaeyjar is Iceland 40 X1 .....63.24N 20.13W
sturhorn hd Iceland 40 Z2 .....64.17N 14.59W
suvius vol. Italy 50 F4 .....40.50N 14.26E
szprém Hungary 54 G2 .....47.06N 17.54E
ttore, Monte mt. Italy 50 E5 .....42.49N 13.17E
urne Belgium 42 B4 .....51.04N 2.40E
zère r. France 44 D4 .....44.53N 0.53E
zirköprü Turkey 57 K5 .....41.09N 35.28E
ana do Castelo Portugal 48 A4 .....41.42N 8.49W
borg Denmark 40 B2 .....56.27N 9.24E
bo Valentia Italy 50 G3 .....38.40N 16.06E
Spain 48 G4 .....41.56N 2.15E
cenza Italy 50 D6 .....45.33N 11.33E

Vichy France 44 E5 .....46.08N 3.26E
Victoria d. Australia 110 D3 .....36.56S 144.52E
Victoria r. Australia 110 C5 .....15.23S 130.17E
Victoria Canada 62 F2 .....48.25N 123.22W
Victoria U.S.A. 64 G2 .....28.49N 96.59W
Victoria, Lake Africa 86 C4 .....0.59S 32.51E
Victoria, Mount Myanmar 97 H5 .....21.11N 93.56E
Victoria, Mount P.N.G. 110 D6 .....8.49S 147.30E
Victoria Falls Zambia/Zimbabwe 86 B3 .....17.49S 25.42E
Victoria Island Canada 62 H5 .....70.42N 106.38W
Victoria Nile r. Uganda 87 A3 .....2.15N 31.21E
Viedma Argentina 73 C2 .....40.50S 63.00W
Viedma, Lago l. Argentina 73 B2 .....49.35S 72.49W
Vienna Austria 54 G3 .....48.12N 16.23E
Vienne France 44 F4 .....45.31N 4.53E
Vienne r. France 44 D5 .....47.13N 0.05E
Vientiane Laos 104 C7 .....17.58N 102.37E
Vierzon France 44 E5 .....47.14N 2.04E
Vieste Italy 50 G4 .....41.53N 16.11E
Vietnam Asia 104 D7 .....19.20N 104.48E
Vignemale mt. France 44 C3 .....42.46N 0.09W
Vigo Spain 48 A5 .....42.14N 8.43W
Vijayawada India 96 F4 .....16.33N 80.39E
Vik Iceland 40 Y1 .....63.26N 19.02W
Vikna i. Norway 40 B4 .....64.53N 10.50E
Vilagarcía de Arousa Spain 48 A5 .....42.36N 8.45W
Vilaine r. France 44 B5 .....47.35N 2.16E
Vila Real Portugal 48 B4 .....41.18N 7.44W
Vila Velha Brazil 77 L4 .....20.22S 40.20W
Vilcabamba, Cordillera mts Peru 76 F5 .....12.30S 73.27W
Vilhelmina Sweden 40 D4 .....64.37N 16.41E
Vilhena Brazil 77 H5 .....12.42S 60.07W
Viljandi Estonia 40 F2 .....58.22N 25.35E
Vilkaviškis Lithuania 46 F5 .....54.39N 23.03E
Vilkija Lithuania 46 F5 .....55.03N 23.35E
Vil'kitskogo, Proliv str. Rus. Fed. 59 K5 .....77.30N 98.42E
Villach Austria 54 E2 .....46.37N 13.50E
Villahermosa Mexico 70 F4 .....18.00N 92.53W
Villa Insurgentes Mexico 70 B6 .....25.16N 111.47W
Villa Montes Bolivia 76 H3 .....21.14S 63.30W
Villaputzu Italy 50 C3 .....39.26N 9.35E
Villarrica Paraguay 77 I2 .....25.43S 56.25W
Villarrobledo Spain 48 D3 .....39.16N 2.36E
Villavicencio Colombia 72 B7 .....4.07N 73.36W
Villefranche-sur-Saône France 44 F4 .....45.59N 4.44E
Villena Spain 48 E3 .....38.38N 0.51W
Villeneuve-sur-Lot France 44 D4 .....44.25N 0.42E
Villers-Cotterêts France 42 C2 .....49.15N 3.06E
Villeurbanne France 44 F4 .....45.46N 4.54E
Vilnius Lithuania 40 F1 .....54.40N 25.16E
Vilvoorde Belgium 42 D3 .....50.55N 4.27E
Vilyuy r. Rus. Fed. 59 N4 .....64.24N 126.28E
Viña del Mar Chile 76 F1 .....33.02S 71.34W
Vindelälven r. Sweden 40 D3 .....63.56N 19.51E
Vinh Vietnam 104 D7 .....18.38N 105.42E
Vinkovci Croatia 56 C7 .....45.17N 18.49E
Vinnytsya Ukraine 55 M3 .....49.14N 28.30E
Viranşehir Turkey 57 M3 .....37.13N 39.47E
Vire France 44 C6 .....48.50N 0.53W
Virden Canada 64 F6 .....49.51N 100.56W
Virginia d. U.S.A. 65 K4 .....37.47N 78.19W
Virgin Islands (U.K.) Central America 71 L4 .....18.37N 64.37W
Virgin Islands (U.S.A.) Central America 71 L4 .....18.14N 64.53W
Virovitica Croatia 56 B7 .....45.50N 17.23E
Virton Belgium 42 E2 .....49.34N 5.33E
Vis i. Croatia 56 B6 .....43.05N 16.06E
Visaginas Lithuania 55 L6 .....55.36N 26.26E
Visby Sweden 40 D2 .....57.38N 18.18E
Viscount Melville Sound str. Canada 62 G5 .....73.50N 112.57W
Viseu Portugal 48 B4 .....40.40N 7.55W
Vishakhapatnam India 96 F4 .....17.42N 83.22E
Visu, Monte mt. Italy 50 B6 .....44.40N 7.06E
Vistula r. Poland 46 D5 .....54.18N 18.55E
Viterbo Italy 50 E5 .....42.24N 12.07E
Viti Levu i. Fiji 111 G5 .....18.05S 177.19E
Vitim r. Rus. Fed. 59 M3 .....59.26N 112.35E
Vitória Brazil 77 L3 .....20.19S 40.21W
Vitória da Conquista Brazil 77 L5 .....14.50S 40.47W
Vitoria-Gasteiz Spain 48 D5 .....42.51N 2.39W
Vitsyebsk Belarus 55 N6 .....55.12N 30.10E
Vittel France 44 F6 .....48.12N 5.57E
Vizianagaram India 96 F4 .....18.08N 83.31E
Vlaams-Brabant d. Belgium 42 D3 .....50.56N 4.36E
Vlaardingen Neth. 42 D4 .....51.54N 4.21E
Vlădeasa, Vârful mt. Romania 55 J2 .....46.45N 22.50E
Vladimir Rus. Fed. 58 F3 .....56.08N 40.24E
Vladivostok Rus. Fed. 59 O2 .....43.07N 131.56E
Vlieland i. Neth. 42 D6 .....53.16N 4.57E
Vlissingen Neth. 42 C4 .....51.27N 3.34E
Vlorë Albania 56 C5 .....40.28N 19.30E
Vltava r. Czech Rep. 54 F4 .....50.19N 14.29E
Voe Scotland 19 H5 .....60.21N 1.16W
Vohimena, Tanjona c. Madagascar 86 D2 .....25.36S 45.12E
Voi Kenya 87 B2 .....3.24S 38.35E
Volcano Islands Japan 108 F7 .....24.53N 140.34E
Volda Norway 40 A3 .....62.08N 6.05E
Volga r. Rus. Fed. 58 F2 .....45.47N 47.34E
Volga Uplands hills Russian Fed. 35 I3 .....53.15N 45.45E
Volgograd Rus. Fed. 58 F2 .....48.44N 44.30E
Völklingen Germany 42 F2 .....49.15N 6.51E
Volodymyr-Volyns'kyy Ukraine 55 K4 .....50.51N 24.20E
Vologda Rus. Fed. 58 E3 .....59.13N 39.54E
Volos Greece 56 E4 .....39.22N 22.57E
Volta, Lake resr Ghana 84 D2 .....6.23N 0.05E
Volta Redonda Brazil 77 L3 .....22.30S 44.07W
Volzhskiy Rus. Fed. 58 G3 .....53.24N 50.05E
Voreioi Sporades is Greece 56 E4 .....39.15N 23.27E
Vorkuta Rus. Fed. 58 H4 .....67.29N 64.05E
Voronezh Rus. Fed. 58 E3 .....51.38N 39.12E
Vorskla r. Rus. Fed. 55 P3 .....48.55N 34.08E
Vosges France 44 G5 .....48.12N 6.41E
Voss Norway 40 A3 .....60.38N 6.27E
Vostochnyy Sayan mts Rus. Fed. 59 K3 .....54.43N 94.48E
Vostok Island Kiribati 109 J5 .....10.04S 152.25W
Vouziers France 42 D2 .....49.24N 4.42E
Voznesens'k Ukraine 55 N2 .....47.33N 31.21E
Vranje Serbia 56 D6 .....42.33N 21.54E
Vratsa Bulgaria 56 E6 .....43.12N 23.33E
Vrbas r. Bos.-Herz. 56 B7 .....45.07N 17.31E
Vršac Serbia 56 D7 .....45.07N 21.17E
Vung Tau Vietnam 104 D6 .....10.22N 107.05E
Vuollerim Sweden 40 E4 .....66.26N 20.37E
Vyatka r. Rus. Fed. 58 F3 .....58.36N 49.41E
Vyaz'ma Rus. Fed. 55 P6 .....55.13N 34.18E
Vyborg Rus. Fed. 40 G3 .....60.42N 28.46E
Vychegda r. Russian Fed. 35 I4 .....61.15N 46.28E
Vyrnwy, Lake Wales 12 D4 .....52.46N 3.29E
Vyškov Czech Rep. 46 C2 .....49.16N 17.00E
Vyžuona r. Lithuania 46 G5 .....55.34N 25.31E

W

Wa Ghana 84 D3 .....10.04N 2.30W
Wabasca r. Canada 62 G3 .....58.18N 115.23W
Wabash r. U.S.A. 65 I4 .....37.50N 88.01W
Wabē Gestro r. Ethiopia 87 C4 .....4.19N 42.03E
Wabē Mena r. Ethiopia 87 C4 .....5.32N 41.12E
Wabush Canada 63 L3 .....52.51N 66.49W
Waco U.S.A. 64 G3 .....31.34N 97.08W
Wad Pakistan 96 C6 .....27.20N 66.30E
Waddān Libya 84 F4 .....29.09N 16.09E
Waddenzee str. Neth. 42 D5 .....52.51N 4.51E
Waddington England 15 G2 .....53.10N 0.32W
Waddington, Mount Canada 62 F3 .....51.21N 125.18W
Wadebridge England 13 C2 .....50.31N 4.50W
Wadhurst England 11 F2 .....51.04N 0.20E
Wadi Halfa Sudan 85 H4 .....21.48N 31.20E
Wad Medani Sudan 85 H3 .....14.22N 33.30E
Wagga Wagga Australia 110 D3 .....35.08S 147.23E
Wahpeton U.S.A. 64 G6 .....46.15N 96.50W
Waigeo i. Indonesia 105 I3 .....0.11S 130.59E
Wainfleet All Saints England 15 H2 .....53.06N 0.14E
Waingapu Indonesia 104 G2 .....9.38S 120.15E
Waini Point Guyana 72 D7 .....8.22N 59.44W
Wainwright U.S.A. 62 C5 .....70.39N 159.51W
Wajir Kenya 87 C3 .....1.44N 40.03E
Wakasa-wan b. Japan 106 C3 .....35.45N 135.36E
Wakayama Japan 106 C2 .....34.13N 135.10E
Wake Island N. Pacific Oc. 108 H7 .....19.18N 166.39E
Wakefield England 15 F2 .....53.41N 1.30W
Wakkanai Japan 106 D5 .....45.24N 141.40E
Wałbrzych Poland 46 C3 .....50.46N 16.18E
Wałcz Poland 46 C4 .....53.17N 16.29E
Wales d. U.K. 9 D3 .....52.04N 3.41W
Wallasey England 14 D2 .....53.26N 3.04W
Wallingford England 10 D2 .....51.36N 1.08W
Wallis and Futuna Islands S. Pacific Oc. 108 I5 .....13.24S 177.57W
Walls Scotland 19 H5 .....60.14N 1.33W
Walney, Isle of i. England 14 D3 .....54.04N 3.16W
Walsall England 10 D3 .....52.35N 1.59W
Waltham on the Wolds England 10 E3 .....52.49N 0.49W
Walton-on-Thames England 11 E2 .....51.23N 0.25W
Walvis Bay town Namibia 86 A2 .....22.58S 14.30E
Wandsworth England 11 E2 .....51.27N 0.12W
Wangqing China 106 A4 .....43.19N 129.44E
Wantage England 10 D2 .....51.35N 1.25W
Warangal India 96 E4 .....17.59N 79.35E
Warboys England 11 E3 .....52.24N 0.05W
Warburton watercourse Australia 110 C4 .....27.54S 137.19E
Ward Hill Scotland 19 F3 .....58.54N 3.22W
Ward's Stone hill England 14 E3 .....54.02N 2.38W
Wareham England 10 C1 .....50.41N 2.07W
Waremme Belgium 42 E3 .....50.42N 5.15E
Warka Poland 46 E3 .....51.47N 21.11E
Warlingham England 11 E2 .....51.19N 0.03W
Warminster England 10 C2 .....51.12N 2.11W
Warrego r. Australia 110 D3 .....30.24S 145.21E
Warrenpoint Northern Ireland 16 C2 .....54.06N 6.15W
Warri Nigeria 84 E2 .....5.35N 5.45E
Warrington England 14 E2 .....53.23N 2.36W
Warrington d. England 9 D3 .....53.24N 2.33W
Warsaw Poland 46 E4 .....52.15N 21.01E
Warta r. Poland 46 B4 .....52.35N 14.37E
Warwick England 10 D3 .....52.17N 1.35W
Warwickshire d. England 9 E3 .....52.19N 1.32W
Washington England 15 F3 .....54.54N 1.31W
Washington U.S.A. 65 K4 .....38.54N 77.01W
Washington d. U.S.A. 64 B6 .....47.36N 120.19W
Washington, Mount U.S.A. 65 L5 .....44.18N 71.18W
Waskaganish Canada 63 K3 .....51.28N 78.46W
Wast Water l. England 14 D3 .....54.26N 3.18W
Watampone Indonesia 104 G3 .....4.31S 120.21E
Watchet England 13 D3 .....51.11N 3.20W
Waterford Ireland 41 D2 .....52.10N 7.53W
Waterford d. Ireland 41 D2 .....52.10N 7.53W
Watergate Bay England 13 B2 .....50.27N 5.05W
Waterlooville England 10 D1 .....50.53N 1.02W
Water of Saughs r. Scotland 19 G1 .....56.47N 2.37W
Watertown U.S.A. 64 G5 .....44.53N 97.07W
Watford England 11 E2 .....51.39N 0.23W
Watlington England 10 D2 .....51.39N 1.00W
Watson Lake town Canada 62 F4 .....60.05N 128.42W
Watten, Loch l. Scotland 19 F3 .....58.29N 3.21W
Watton England 11 F3 .....52.34N 0.50E
Wau Sudan 85 G2 .....7.40N 27.59E
Wausau U.S.A. 65 I5 .....44.58N 89.37W
Waveney r. England 11 G3 .....52.29N 1.41E
Wear r. England 15 F3 .....54.54N 1.27W
Weber Basin f. Indonesia 108 E5 .....5.42S 130.54E
Webi Shabeelle r. Somalia 85 I2 .....0.10N 42.46E
Webuye Kenya 87 A3 .....0.37N 34.44E
Wedmore England 10 C2 .....51.14N 2.49W
Weener Germany 42 G6 .....53.10N 7.21E
Weert Neth. 42 E4 .....51.15N 5.43E
Wegorzewo Poland 46 E5 .....54.13N 21.44E
Weifang China 103 L5 .....36.42N 119.03E
Weihai China 103 M5 .....37.30N 122.07E
Weinan China 103 J4 .....34.27N 109.33E
Weipa Australia 105 K1 .....12.37S 141.55E
Wejherowo Poland 46 D5 .....54.36N 18.14E
Weldiya Ethiopia 85 H3 .....11.49N 39.36E
Welkom S. Africa 86 B2 .....27.59S 26.44E
Welland r. England 11 E3 .....52.52N 0.03W
Wellesley Islands Australia 110 C5 .....16.18S 139.33E
Wellingborough England 10 E3 .....52.18N 0.42W
Wellington Som. England 13 D2 .....50.59N 3.13W
Wellington Tel. Wre. England 10 C3 .....52.42N 2.31W
Wellington New Zealand 111 G2 .....41.18S 174.46E
Wells, Lake Australia 110 B4 .....26.40S 123.16E
Wells-next-the-Sea England 11 F3 .....52.57N 0.51E
Wels Austria 54 F3 .....48.10N 14.01E
Welshpool Wales 12 D4 .....52.40N 3.09W
Welwyn Garden City England 11 E2 .....51.48N 0.12W
Wem England 10 C3 .....52.51N 2.44W
Wembley England 11 E2 .....51.33N 0.18W
Wemindji Canada 63 K3 .....53.00N 78.49W
Wemyss Bay town Scotland 16 E3 .....55.53N 4.53W
Wenchi Ghana 84 D2 .....7.45N 2.07W
Wendo Ethiopia 85 H2 .....6.35N 38.25E
Wendover England 10 E2 .....51.46N 0.44W
Wenlock Edge f. England 10 C3 .....52.27N 2.49W
Wensleydale f. England 15 E3 .....54.09N 2.02W
Wensum r. England 11 G3 .....52.37N 1.20E
Wenzhou China 103 M3 .....27.59N 120.61E
Wesel Germany 42 F4 .....51.40N 6.38E
Weser r. Germany 54 C5 .....53.15N 8.29E
Wessel, Cape Australia 110 C5 .....11.03S 136.46E
Wessel Islands Australia 110 C5 .....11.19S 136.42E
West Australian Basin f. Indian Oc. 117 O5 .....17.42S 102.36E
West Bank Asia 53 K3 .....31.52N 35.19E
West Bengal d. India 96 G5 .....22.34N 87.20E

West Berkshire d. England 9 E2 .....51.28N 1.20W
West Bridgford England 10 D3 .....52.56N 1.08W
West Bromwich England 10 D3 .....52.31N 1.59W
Westbury England 10 C2 .....51.15N 2.11W
West Calder Scotland 17 F3 .....55.51N 3.34W
West Caroline Basin f. N. Pacific Oc. 108 F6 .....2.42N 136.26E
West Dunbartonshire d. Scotland 8 C4 .....55.59N 4.31W
Western d. Kenya 87 A3 .....0.22N 34.35E
Western Australia d. Australia 110 B4 .....24.24S 121.53E
Western Desert Egypt 53 I2 .....26.42N 29.45E
Western Dvina r. Europe 55 N6 .....55.28N 30.54E
Western Ghats mts India 96 D3 .....14.19N 74.54E
Western Isles d. Scotland 8 B6 .....58.15N 6.33W
Western Sahara Africa 84 C4 .....22.14N 15.05W
Wester Ross f. Scotland 18 D2 .....57.39N 5.20W
Westerschelde est. Neth. 42 C4 .....51.27N 3.27E
West Falkland i. Falkland Is 73 C1 .....51.16S 61.32W
West Fen f. Cambs. England 11 F3 .....52.45N 0.00E
West Fen f. Lincs. England 15 G2 .....53.04N 0.05W
West Frisian Islands Neth. 42 D6 .....53.24N 4.37E
Westhill Scotland 19 G2 .....57.09N 2.17W
West Kirby England 14 D2 .....53.22N 3.11W
West Lavington England 10 D2 .....51.17N 1.59W
West Linton Scotland 17 F3 .....55.45N 3.21W
West Loch Roag b. Scotland 18 C3 .....58.15N 6.57W
West Lothian d. Scotland 8 D4 .....55.54N 3.31W
West Malling England 11 F2 .....51.18N 0.25E
West Mariana Basin f. N. Pacific Oc. 108 F7 .....17.32N 140.09E
Westmeath d. Ireland 41 D3 .....53.34N 7.24W
West Mersea England 11 F2 .....51.47N 0.56E
West Midlands d. England 9 E3 .....52.28N 1.49W
Weston-super-Mare England 10 C2 .....51.21N 2.59W
Westport Ireland 41 B3 .....53.48N 9.31W
Westray i. Scotland 19 F4 .....59.18N 3.02W
Westray Firth str. Scotland 19 F4 .....59.16N 3.07W
West Siberian Plain f. Rus. Fed. 58 J4 .....62.39N 80.21E
West Sussex d. England 11 E1 .....51.00N 0.18W
West-Terschelling Neth. 42 E6 .....53.22N 5.13E
West Virginia d. U.S.A. 65 J4 .....38.45N 80.27W
West-Vlaanderen d. Belgium 42 B3 .....50.59N 2.56E
Westward Ho! England 13 C3 .....51.02N 4.14W
West Yorkshire d. England 9 D3 .....53.46N 2.04W
Wetar i. Indonesia 105 H2 .....7.49S 126.13E
Wete Tanzania 87 B1 .....5.04S 39.43E
Wetherby England 15 F2 .....53.56N 1.23W
Wetzlar Germany 44 H7 .....50.34N 8.30E
Wexford Ireland 41 E2 .....52.20N 6.28W
Wexford d. Ireland 41 E2 .....52.37N 6.32W
Wexford Bay Ireland 41 E2 .....52.25N 6.19W
Weybridge England 11 E2 .....51.22N 0.27W
Weyburn Canada 64 F6 .....49.40N 103.52W
Weymouth England 10 C1 .....50.37N 2.27W
Whalsay i. Scotland 19 I5 .....60.21N 0.57W
Whangarei New Zealand 111 G3 .....35.43S 174.19E
Wharfe r. England 15 F2 .....53.50N 1.08W
Wheeler Peak N. M. U.S.A. 64 E4 .....36.33N 105.24W
Wheeler Peak Nev. U.S.A. 64 D4 .....38.57N 114.17W
Whernside hill England 15 E3 .....54.14N 2.24W
Whitburn Scotland 17 F3 .....55.52N 3.41W
Whitby England 15 G3 .....54.29N 0.37W
Whitchurch England 14 E2 .....52.58N 2.41W
Whitchurch Wales 13 D3 .....51.31N 3.13W
White r. U.S.A. 65 I3 .....33.59N 91.09W
Whitecourt Canada 62 G3 .....54.08N 115.43W
Whitehaven England 14 D3 .....54.33N 3.35W
Whitehead Northern Ireland 16 D2 .....54.45N 5.42W
Whitehill England 10 E2 .....51.06N 0.52W
Whitehorse Canada 62 E4 .....60.44N 135.06W
White Nile r. Sudan/Uganda 85 H3 .....15.38N 32.30E
White Sea Rus. Fed. 58 E4 .....65.51N 36.58E
White Volta r. Burkina/Ghana 84 D2 .....9.07N 1.10W
Whitfield England 11 G2 .....51.09N 1.17E
Whithorn Scotland 16 E2 .....54.44N 4.25W
Whitland Wales 12 C3 .....51.49N 4.37W
Whitley Bay town England 15 F4 .....55.03N 1.27W
Whitney, Mount U.S.A. 64 C4 .....36.35N 118.16W
Whitsand Bay England 13 C2 .....50.20N 4.20W
Whitstable England 11 G2 .....51.22N 1.01E
Whittlesey England 11 E3 .....52.34N 0.08W
Whyalla Australia 110 C3 .....33.03S 137.31E
Wichita U.S.A. 64 G4 .....37.42N 97.20W
Wichita Falls town U.S.A. 64 G3 .....33.55N 98.29W
Wick Scotland 19 F3 .....58.26N 3.06W
Wick r. Scotland 19 F3 .....58.26N 3.05W
Wickford England 11 F2 .....51.37N 0.31E
Wickham England 10 D1 .....50.54N 1.11W
Wickham Market England 11 G3 .....52.09N 1.22E
Wicklow Ireland 41 E2 .....52.59N 6.02W
Wicklow d. Ireland 41 E3 .....53.02N 6.27W
Wicklow Head Ireland 41 E2 .....52.58N 5.59W
Wicklow Mountains Ireland 41 E2 .....52.53N 6.34W
Widecombe in the Moor England 13 D2 .....50.34N 3.49W
Wide Firth str. Scotland 19 F4 .....59.01N 3.02W
Widnes England 14 E2 .....53.21N 2.44W
Wielka Sowa mt. Poland 46 C3 .....50.40N 16.29E
Wieluń Poland 46 D3 .....51.13N 18.34E
Wiener Neustadt Austria 54 G2 .....47.49N 16.15E
Wieprz r. Poland 46 E3 .....51.32N 21.50E
Wiesbaden Germany 54 C4 .....50.05N 8.14E
Wiesmoor Germany 42 G6 .....53.25N 7.45E
Wieżyca hill Poland 46 D5 .....54.14N 18.08E
Wigan England 14 E2 .....53.33N 2.38W
Wight, Isle of i. England 10 D1 .....50.39N 1.07W
Wigston England 10 D3 .....52.35N 1.06W
Wigton England 14 D3 .....54.50N 3.10W
Wigtown Scotland 16 E2 .....54.52N 4.27W
Wigtown Bay Scotland 16 E2 .....54.48N 4.19W
Wijchen Neth. 42 E4 .....51.48N 5.43E
Wildhorn mt. Switz. 50 B7 .....46.21N 7.22E
Wilhelm, Mount P.N.G. 110 D6 .....5.46S 144.52E
Wilhelmshaven Germany 54 C5 .....53.32N 8.08E
Willemstad Neth. Antilles 109 M2 .....12.07N 68.56W
William, Mount Australia 110 D3 .....37.19S 142.35E
Williams Lake town Canada 62 F3 .....52.08N 122.09W
Willingdon England 11 F1 .....50.48N 0.15E
Williston U.S.A. 64 F6 .....48.10N 103.37W
Williston Lake Canada 62 F3 .....55.51N 123.43W
Williton England 13 D3 .....51.10N 3.19W
Wills, Lake Australia 110 B4 .....21.20S 128.37E
Wilmington Del. U.S.A. 65 K4 .....39.43N 75.38W
Wilmington N. C. U.S.A. 65 K3 .....34.13N 77.58W
Wilmslow England 15 E2 .....53.20N 2.14W
Wilson's Promontory pen. Australia 110 D3 .....38.55S 146.27E
Wilton England 10 D2 .....51.05N 1.52W
Wiltshire d. England 9 E2 .....51.24N 1.53W
Wiltz Lux. 42 E2 .....49.58N 5.56E
Wimblington England 11 F3 .....52.31N 0.05E
Wimborne Minster England 10 D1 .....50.48N 1.59W
Wimereux France 11 G1 .....50.46N 1.37E
Winam Gulf Kenya 87 A2 .....0.20S 34.24E
Wincanton England 10 C2 .....51.03N 2.25W
Winchester England 10 D2 .....51.04N 1.19W

Windermere England 14 E3 ....54.23N 2.54W
Windermere l. England 14 E3 ....54.18N 2.57W
Windhoek Namibia 86 A2 ....22.34S 17.04E
Windrush r. England 10 D2 ....51.43N 1.25W
Windsor Canada 65 J5 ....42.18N 83.01W
Windsor England 11 E2 ....51.29N 0.37W
Windsor and Maidenhead d. England 9 E2 ...51.28N 0.40W
Windward Islands Caribbean Sea 71 L4 ...15.42N 60.03W
Windward Passage str. Cuba/Haiti 71 J4 ...19.40N 74.11W
Wingate England 15 F3 ....54.44N 1.23W
Winisk r. Canada 63 J3 ....55.01N 85.22W
Winkleigh England 13 D2 ....50.51N 3.57W
Winnebago, Lake U.S.A. 65 I5 ....44.00N 88.28W
Winnemucca U.S.A. 64 C5 ....40.59N 117.44W
Winnipeg Canada 62 I2 ....49.53N 97.10W
Winnipeg, Lake Canada 62 I3 ....51.31N 96.40W
Winnipegosis, Lake Canada 62 H3 ....53.05N 100.40W
Winsford England 15 E2 ....53.12N 2.31W
Winslow England 10 E2 ....51.57N 0.53W
Winslow U.S.A. 64 D4 ....35.02N 110.42W
Winston-Salem U.S.A. 65 J4 ....36.07N 80.17W
Winterswijk Neth. 42 F4 ....51.58N 6.42E
Winterthur Switz. 50 C7 ....47.30N 8.43E
Winterton England 15 G2 ....53.39N 0.36W
Wirksworth England 15 F2 ....53.05N 1.34W
Wirral pen. England 14 D2 ....53.22N 3.07W
Wisbech England 11 F3 ....52.40N 0.10E
Wisconsin d. U.S.A. 65 I5 ....44.30N 89.32W
Wishaw Scotland 17 F3 ....55.46N 3.55W
Wismar Germany 54 D5 ....53.53N 11.28E
Witham England 11 F2 ....51.48N 0.38E
Witham r. England 11 F3 ....52.56N 0.05E
Witheridge England 13 D2 ....50.55N 3.42W
Withernsea England 15 H2 ....53.44N 0.02E
Witney England 10 D2 ....51.47N 1.29W
Wittenberge Germany 54 D5 ....52.59N 11.45E
Wittlich Germany 42 F2 ....49.59N 6.53E
Wittmund Germany 42 G6 ....53.35N 7.47E
Witu Kenya 87 C2 ....2.23S 40.27E
Wiveliscombe England 13 D3 ....51.03N 3.19W
Wivenhoe England 11 F2 ....51.51N 0.58E
Wkra r. Poland 46 E4 ....52.27N 20.45E
Władysławowo Poland 46 D5 ....54.47N 18.25E
Włocławek Poland 46 D4 ....52.39N 19.05E
Włodawa Poland 46 F3 ....51.33N 23.33E
Wokam i. Indonesia 105 I2 ....5.45S 134.31E
Woking England 11 E2 ....51.19N 0.34W
Wokingham England 10 E2 ....51.25N 0.50W
Wokingham d. England 9 E2 ....51.24N 0.53W
Wolfsberg Austria 54 F2 ....46.50N 14.51E
Wolfsburg Germany 54 D5 ....52.25N 10.48E
Wolgast Germany 46 A5 ....54.03N 13.47E
Wolin Poland 46 B4 ....53.51N 14.36E
Wollaston Lake Canada 62 H3 ....58.16N 103.22W
Wollongong Australia 110 E3 ....34.25S 150.51E
Wolsingham England 15 F3 ....54.44N 1.53W
Wolvega Neth. 42 F5 ....52.53N 6.00E
Wolverhampton England 10 C3 ....52.35N 2.08W
Wombwell England 15 F2 ....53.31N 1.24W
Wŏnsan N. Korea 103 N5 ....39.09N 127.27E
Woodbridge England 11 G3 ....52.06N 1.19E
Woodcote England 10 D2 ....51.32N 1.04W
Woodhall Spa England 15 G2 ....53.09N 0.13W
Woodlark Island P.N.G. 110 E6 ....8.58S 152.47E
Woods, Lake of the Canada/U.S.A. 63 I2 ...49.22N 94.50W
Woodstock England 10 D2 ....51.51N 1.21W
Wooler England 15 E4 ....55.33N 2.01W
Wootton Bassett England 10 D2 ....51.32N 1.54W
Worcester England 10 C3 ....52.12N 2.13W
Worcester S. Africa 86 A1 ....33.38S 19.27E
Worcester U.S.A. 65 L5 ....42.16N 71.48W
Worcestershire d. England 9 D3 ....52.12N 2.12W
Wörgl Austria 54 E2 ....47.29N 12.05E
Workington England 14 D3 ....54.39N 3.32W
Worksop England 15 F2 ....53.19N 1.07W
Worms Germany 44 H6 ....49.38N 8.21E
Worms Head Wales 12 C3 ....51.34N 4.21W
Worth England 11 E2 ....51.07N 0.09W
Worthing England 11 E1 ....50.49N 0.22W
Wowoni i. Indonesia 105 G3 ....4.09S 123.13E
Wragby England 15 G2 ....53.17N 0.18W
Wrangel Island Rus. Fed. 59 T5 ....71.07N 178.56W
Wrangell U.S.A. 62 E3 ....56.28N 132.22W
Wrangle England 15 H2 ....53.02N 0.07E
Wrath, Cape Scotland 18 D3 ....58.38N 5.00W
Wreake r. England 10 D3'.................52.42N 1.06W
Wrexham Wales 12 E5 ....53.03N 2.59W
Wrexham d. Wales 9 D3 ....53.01N 2.59W
Wrigley Canada 62 F4 ....63.12N 123.24W
Wrocław Poland 46 C3 ....51.06N 17.02E
Września Poland 46 C4 ....52.19N 17.34E
Wuhai China 103 J5 ....39.36N 106.53E
Wuhan China 103 K4 ....30.37N 114.18E
Wuhu China 103 L4 ....31.21N 118.25E

Wuppertal Germany 42 G4 ....51.16N 7.09E
Würzburg Germany 54 C3 ....49.48N 9.55E
Wuvulu Island P.N.G. 105 K3 ....1.43S 142.50E
Wuwei China 103 I5 ....37.52N 102.38E
Wuxi China 103 M4 ....31.31N 120.18E
Wuzhou China 103 K2 ....23.28N 111.22E
Wye England 11 F2 ....51.11N 0.56E
Wye r. Wales 12 E3 ....51.37N 2.40W
Wylye r. England 10 D2 ....51.04N 1.48W
Wymondham England 11 G3 ....52.34N 1.07E
Wyndham Australia 110 B5 ....15.29S 128.05E
Wynyard Canada 64 F7 ....51.46N 104.12W
Wyoming d. U.S.A. 64 E5 ....42.57N 107.30W
Wyszków Poland 46 E4 ....52.36N 21.28E
Wythall England 10 D3 ....52.23N 1.53W

X

Xai-Xai Mozambique 86 C2 ....25.02S 33.41E
Xankändi Azerbaijan 95 G7 ....39.49N 46.46E
Xanthi Greece 56 F5 ....41.09N 24.53E
Xavantes, Serra dos hills Brazil 77 K5 ...12.34S 49.14W
Xiamen China 103 L2 ....24.29N 118.11E
Xi'an China 103 J4 ....34.12N 108.59E
Xiangfan China 103 K4 ....32.03N 112.07E
Xiangkhoang Laos 104 C7 ....19.21N 103.25E
Xiangtan China 103 K3 ....27.52N 112.47E
Xichang China 103 I3 ....27.55N 102.11E
Xigazê China 102 F3 ....29.17N 88.45E
Xi Jiang r. China 90 I4 ....22.23N 113.20E
Xilinhot China 103 L6 ....43.54N 116.08E
Xingtai China 103 K5 ....37.01N 114.33E
Xingu r. Brazil 77 J7 ....1.37S 52.12W
Xining China 103 I5 ....36.35N 101.40E
Xinjiang Uygur Zizhiqu d. China 102 D6 ...40.15N 78.50E
Xintai China 103 L5 ....35.55N 117.45E
Xinxiang China 103 K5 ....35.14N 113.54E
Xizang Zizhiqu d. China 102 F4 ....31.26N 88.12E
Xun Jiang r. China 103 K2 ....23.27N 111.25E
Xuwen China 104 E8 ....20.18N 110.09E

Y

Yabēlo Ethiopia 87 B4 ....4.51N 38.08E
Yabēlo Wildlife Sanctuary nature res. Ethiopia 87 B4
.................4.56N 38.22E
Yablonovyy Khrebet mts Rus. Fed. 59 L3 ...50.48N 108.47E
Yacuma r. Bolivia 76 G5 ....13.39S 65.25W
Yakima U.S.A. 64 B6 ....46.36N 120.29W
Yakumo Japan 106 D4 ....42.15N 140.15E
Yaku-shima i. Japan 106 B2 ....30.15N 130.36E
Yakutsk Rus. Fed. 59 N4 ....61.59N 129.40E
Yala Thailand 104 C5 ....6.32N 101.17E
Yalova Turkey 57 H5 ....40.39N 29.17E
Yalta Ukraine 57 K7 ....44.30N 34.11E
Yamagata Japan 106 D3 ....38.15N 140.20E
Yamal Peninsula Rus. Fed. 58 H5 ....70.40N 69.23E
Yambol Bulgaria 56 G6 ....42.29N 26.30E
Yamoussoukro Côte d'Ivoire 84 D2 ....6.48N 5.15W
Yamuna r. India 96 F6 ....25.26N 81.57E
Yana r. Rus. Fed. 59 O5 ....71.09N 135.57E
Yanbu' al Baḩr Saudi Arabia 94 E4 ......24.05N 38.06E
Yangôn Myanmar 97 I4 ....16.49N 96.08E
Yangquan China 103 K5 ....37.52N 113.33E
Yanji China 103 N6 ....42.54N 129.31E
Yanskiy Zaliv g. Rus. Fed. 59 O5 ....71.55N 135.13E
Yantai China 103 M5 ....37.30N 121.21E
Yaoundé Cameroon 84 F2 ....3.51N 11.30E
Yap i. Micronesia 105 J5 ....9.30N 138.12E
Yapen i. Indonesia 105 J3 ....1.46S 136.12E
Yap Trench f. N. Pacific Oc. 108 F6 ....7.14N 136.38E
Yaqui r. Mexico 70 B6 ....27.36N 110.36W
Yare r. England 11 G3 ....52.35N 1.38E
Yaren Nauru 108 H5 ....0.33S 166.55E
Yarm England 15 F3 ....54.30N 1.21W
Yarmouth Canada 63 L2 ....43.50N 66.07W
Yarmouth England 10 D1 ....50.42N 1.30W
Yaroslavl' Rus. Fed. 58 E3 ....57.37N 39.53E
Yartsevo Rus. Fed. 55 O6 ....55.04N 32.41E
Yasawa Group is Fiji 111 G5 ....16.56S 177.18E
Yasyel'da r. Belarus 55 L5 ....52.08N 26.27E
Yatağan Turkey 57 H3 ....37.20N 28.09E
Yeta Plateau f. Kenya 87 B2 ....1.20S 37.42E
Yate England 10 C2 ....51.32N 2.25W
Yatton England 10 C2 ....51.23N 2.49W
Yavari r. Brazil/Peru 76 G7 ....4.18S 69.59W
Yaví, Cerro mt. Venezuela 72 C7 ....5.32N 65.58W
Yavoriv Ukraine 46 F2 ....49.57N 23.25E
Yawatahama Japan 106 B2 ....33.27N 132.26E
Yazd Iran 95 H6 ....31.53N 54.21E

Z

Zaandam Neth. 42 D5 ....52.26N 4.51E
Zabīd Yemen 94 F2 ....14.11N 43.15E
Zābol Iran 95 J6 ....30.59N 61.31E
Zacatecas Mexico 70 D5 ....22.46N 102.38W
Zacatecas d. Mexico 70 D5 ....23.56N 102.42W
Zadar Croatia 56 A7 ....44.07N 15.14E
Zafra Spain 48 B3 ....38.26N 6.25W
Zagreb Croatia 56 A7 ....45.48N 15.58E
Zagros Mountains Iran 95 G6 ....34.02N 47.10E
Zāhedān Iran 95 J5 ....29.30N 60.52E
Zahlé Lebanon 53 K3 ....33.50N 35.55E
Zaječar Serbia 56 E6 ....43.54N 22.16E
Zākhō Iraq 94 F7 ....37.08N 42.42E
Zakynthos Greece 56 D3 ....37.47N 20.54E
Zakynthos i. Greece 56 D3 ....37.45N 20.42E
Zalaegerszeg Hungary 54 G2 ....46.51N 16.53E
Zalău Romania 55 J2 ....47.11N 23.04E
Zambezi r. Africa 86 C3 ....15.41S 30.25E
Zambia Africa 86 B3 ....14.13S 27.30E
Zamboanga Phil. 105 G5 ....6.56N 122.05E
Zamora Spain 48 C4 ....41.31N 5.44W

Yealmpton England 13 D2 ....50.21N 3.59W
YeDebub Bihēroch Bihēreseboch na Hizboch d. Ethiopia 87 B4
.................6.14N 36.32E
Yekaterinburg Rus. Fed. 58 H3 ....56.53N 60.35E
Yell i. Scotland 19 H5 ....60.35N 1.06W
Yellowknife Canada 62 G4 ....62.29N 114.19W
Yellow Sea N. Pacific Oc. 103 N5 ....35.28N 125.29E
Yellowstone r. U.S.A. 64 F6 ....47.59N 103.59W
Yell Sound str. Scotland 19 H5 ....60.37N 1.15W
Yemen Asia 95 G3 ....14.48N 45.46E
Yenisey r. Rus. Fed. 59 J5 ....70.22N 82.59E
Yeniseysk Rus. Fed. 59 K3 ....58.27N 92.13E
Yeovil England 10 C1 ....50.56N 2.38W
Yerevan Armenia 58 F2 ....40.11N 44.32E
Yereymentau Kazakhstan 102 C8 ....51.36N 73.08E
Yeşilırmak r. Turkey 57 L5 ....41.27N 36.36E
Yes Tor hill England 13 C2 ....50.41N 4.01W
Yevpatoriya Ukraine 53 J6 ....45.12N 33.22E
Yeysk Rus. Fed. 53 K6 ....46.43N 38.17E
Yibin China 103 I3 ....28.46N 104.36E
Yichang China 103 K4 ....30.41N 111.19E
Yichun China 103 N7 ....47.37N 128.52E
Yıldızeli Turkey 57 L4 ....39.53N 36.35E
Yinchuan China 103 J5 ....38.26N 106.18E
Yingkou China 103 M6 ....40.40N 122.15E
Yining China 102 E6 ....43.54N 81.22E
Yirga Alem Ethiopia 87 B4 ....6.47N 38.22E
Yirga Ch'efē Ethiopia 87 B4 ....6.06N 38.11E
Yli-Kitka l. Finland 40 G4 ....66.10N 28.46E
Ylitornio Finland 40 E4 ....66.20N 23.41E
Y Llethr hill Wales 12 D4 ....52.49N 3.59W
Ylöjärvi Finland 41 D1 ....61.34N 23.36E
Yogyakarta Indonesia 104 E2 ....7.47S 110.23E
Yokohama Japan 106 C3 ....35.26N 139.37E
Yonne r. France 44 E6 ....48.23N 2.58E
York England 15 F2 ....53.58N 1.05W
York d. England 9 E3 ....53.57N 1.04W
York, Cape Australia 110 D5 ....10.41S 142.36E
York, Cape Canada 63 J5 ....73.47N 87.15W
York, Vale of f. England 15 F3 ....54.13N 1.32W
Yorkshire Wolds hills England 15 G2 ...53.53N 0.35W
Yorkton Canada 62 H3 ....51.12N 102.27W
Youghal Ireland 41 D1 ....51.58N 7.51W
Yozgat Turkey 57 K4 ....39.49N 34.47E
Yser r. France 11 H1 ....50.54N 2.37E
Ystad Sweden 40 C1 ....55.26N 13.49E
Ystalyfera Wales 12 D3 ....51.46N 3.47W
Ystwyth r. Wales 12 D4 ....52.24N 4.05W
Ysyk-Köl l. Kyrgyzstan 102 D6 ....42.25N 77.12E
Ythan r. Scotland 19 G2 ....57.22N 2.01W
Yūbari Japan 106 D4 ....43.04N 141.59E
Yucatán d. Mexico 70 G5 ....20.35N 89.05W
Yucatán pen. Mexico 70 F4 ....19.17N 90.15W
Yucatan Channel Cuba/Mexico 71 G5 ...22.16N 86.46W
Yueyang China 103 K3 ....29.23N 113.07E
Yukon r. Canada/U.S.A. 62 B4 ....62.44N 164.41W
Yukon Territory d. Canada 62 E4 ....63.23N 135.52W
Yulin China 103 K2 ....22.37N 110.12E
Yuma U.S.A. 64 D3 ....32.43N 114.38W
Yumen China 102 H5 ....39.46N 97.33E
Yunak Turkey 57 I4 ....38.48N 31.44E
Yungas f. Bolivia 76 G4 ....16.51S 65.20W
Yunnan d. China 103 I2 ....24.45N 101.07E
Yushu China 102 H4 ....32.59N 96.59E
Yuxi China 103 I2 ....24.20N 102.33E
Yuzhno-Kuril'sk Rus. Fed. 106 E4 ....44.04N 145.49E
Yuzhno-Sakhalinsk Rus. Fed. 59 P2 ...46.57N 142.39E
Yuzhnoukrayinsk Ukraine 55 N2 ....47.50N 31.11E

Zamość Poland 46 F3 ....50.43N 23
Zanjān Iran 95 G7 ....36.40N 48
Zanzibar Tanzania 86 C4 ....6.08S 39
Zanzibar Island Tanzania 86 C4 ....6.17S 39
Zaozhuang China 103 L4 ....34.52N 117
Zapadnaya Dvina Rus. Fed. 55 O7 ....56.16N 32
Zapadnyy Sayan f. Rus. Fed. 59 J3 .....51.41N 88
Zapolyarnyy Rus. Fed. 40 G5 ....69.26N 30
Zaporizhzhya Ukraine 55 P2 ....47.50N 35
Zara Turkey 57 L4 ....39.54N 37
Zaragoza Spain 48 E4 ....41.40N 0.
Zarand Iran 95 I6 ....30.49N 56
Zarasai Lithuania 46 H5 ....55.44N 26
Zaraza Venezuela 71 K2 ....9.21N 65.
Zaria Nigeria 84 E3 ....11.07N 7
Zarubino Rus. Fed. 106 B4 ....42.37N 131
Żary Poland 46 B3 ....51.38N 15
Zarzis Tunisia 52 F3 ....33.30N 11
Zawiercie Poland 46 D3 ....50.29N 19
Zawiłah Libya 52 G2 ....26.08N 15
Zaysan Kazakhstan 102 E7 ....47.27N 84
Zaysan, Lake Kazakhstan 58 J2 ....48.05N 83
Zealand i. Denmark 40 B1 ....55.23N 11
Zeebrugge Belgium 42 C4 ....51.20N 3
Zeeland d. Neth. 42 C4 ....51.31N 3
Zeil, Mount Australia 110 C4 ....23.24S 132
Zelenograd Rus. Fed. 55 Q7 ....56.00N 37
Zelenogradsk Rus. Fed. 46 E5 ....54.58N 20
Zémio C.A.R. 85 G2 ....5.00N 25.
Zenica Bos.-Herz. 56 B7 ....44.11N 17.
Zereh, Gowd-e f. Afgh. 95 J5 ....29.50N 62.
Zeya Rus. Fed. 59 N3 ....53.47N 126.
Zêzere r. Portugal 48 A3 ....39.28N 8.2
Zgierz Poland 46 D3 ....51.51N 19.
Zhabinka Belarus 46 G4 ....52.11N 24.
Zhambyl Kazakhstan 102 C6 ....42.50N 71.
Zhangjiakou China 103 K6 ....40.41N 114.
Zhangping China 103 L3 ....25.21N 117.
Zhangshu China 103 L3 ....28.04N 115.
Zhanjiang China 103 K2 ....21.10N 110.
Zhaotong China 103 I3 ....27.22N 103.
Zhashkiv Ukraine 55 N3 ....49.15N 30.
Zhejiang d. China 103 M3 ....29.21N 120.
Zheleznogorsk Rus. Fed. 55 P5 ....52.19N 35.
Zhengzhou China 103 K4 ....34.41N 113.
Zhezkazgan Kazakhstan 58 H2 ....47.45N 67.
Zhlobin Belarus 55 N5 ....52.54N 30.
Zhmerynka Ukraine 55 M3 ....49.03N 28.
Zhob Pakistan 95 K6 ....31.21N 69.
Zhovti Vody Ukraine 55 O3 ....48.21N 33.
Zhukovskiy Rus. Fed. 55 R6 ....55.35N 38.
Zhuzhou China 103 K3 ....27.49N 113.
Zhydachiv Ukraine 46 G2 ....49.23N 24.
Zhytkavichy Belarus 55 L5 ....52.13N 27.
Zhytomyr Ukraine 55 M4 ....50.15N 28.
Zibo China 103 L5 ....36.47N 118.
Zielona Góra Poland 46 B3 ....51.57N 15.
Zighan Libya 53 H2 ....25.27N 22.0
Zigong China 103 I3 ....29.24N 104.
Žilina Slovakia 54 H3 ....49.14N 18.4
Zillah Libya 53 G2 ....28.32N 17.3
Zima Rus. Fed. 103 I8 ....53.54N 101.5
Zimbabwe Africa 86 B3 ....22.06S 30.9
Zimmi Sierra Leone 84 C2 ....7.16N 11.1
Zimnicea Romania 56 F6 ....43.40N 25.
Zinder Niger 84 E3 ....13.48N 8.5
Zlín Czech Rep. 54 G3 ....49.13N 17.4
Złotów Poland 46 C4 ....53.22N 17.0
Zmiyevka Rus. Fed. 55 Q5 ....52.40N 36.2
Znam"yanka Ukraine 55 O3 ....48.43N 32.4
Znojmo Czech Rep. 54 G3 ....48.51N 16.0
Zolochiv Ukraine 55 K3 ....49.48N 24.5
Zolotonosha Ukraine 55 O3 ....49.42N 32.0
Zonguldak Turkey 57 I5 ....41.27N 31.4
Żory Poland 46 D3 ....50.03N 18.4
Zouar Chad 85 F4 ....20.27N 16.3
Zouérat Mauritania 84 C4 ....22.46N 12.29
Zrenjanin Serbia 56 D7 ....45.23N 20.2
Zugdidi Georgia 53 L5 ....42.30N 41.5
Zugspitze mt. Austria/Germany 54 D2 ...47.26N 10.5
Zuid-Holland d. Neth. 42 D4 ....51.57N 4.2
Zújar r. Spain 48 C3 ....39.01N 5.46
Zülpich Germany 42 F3 ....50.41N 6.4
Zunyi China 103 J3 ....27.40N 106.5
Zürich Switz. 50 C7 ....47.23N 8.3
Zutphen Neth. 42 F5 ....52.09N 6.1
Zuwārah Libya 52 F3 ....32.56N 12.0
Zvolen Slovakia 54 H3 ....48.35N 19.0
Zvornik Bos.-Herz. 56 C7 ....44.24N 19.0
Zwickau Germany 54 E4 ....50.43N 12.3
Zwolle Neth. 42 F5 ....52.30N 6.0
Zyryanovsk Kazakhstan 102 E7 ....49.46N 84.2

References

BP Statistical Review of World Energy
British Geological Survey
Census 2001
Dartmouth Flood Observatory
Department of Trade and Industry, UK
Department of Transport, UK
Met Office, UK
UK National Statistics
UN Commodity Trade Statistics

UNESCO World Heritage Sites
United Nations Population Information Network
US Census Bureau
USGS Earthquake Hazards Program
USGS Minerals Yearbook
World Bank Group
World Resources Institute
World Tourism Organization

Photo credits

MODIS Rapid Response Team, NASA/GSFC
p73 Argentina and Paraguay, p5 and p80 Rondônia, p118 Hurricane Katrina
NASA/GSFC/MITI/ERSDAC/JAROS, and U.S./Japan ASTER Science Team
p51 Vesuvius
NASA Johnson Space Center
p135 Dalla-Fort Worth Airport

Science Photo Library
p32 Manchester, p4, p5 and p43 Europoort CNES 1999 Distribution
Spot Image, p68 San Francisco, p101 Bangladesh
USGS Land Processes Data Center
p97 Kolkata

Acknowledgements

General Bathymetric Chart of the Oceans (GEBCO)
Ministry of Planning and National Development, Nairobi, Kenya
Rotterdam Municipal Port Management, Rotterdam, Netherlands

Instituto Geográfico e Cartográfico, São Paulo, Brazil
International Hydrographic Organisation, Monaco
National Atlas and Thematic Mapping Organisation, Kolkata, India

Maps on the pages listed below are derived in part from material originally published in the **Collins Longman Student Atlas.**
Pp20-21, p23, p24 (part), p27 (part), p28 (part), p29, p30, p36, p38, p39, p61, p67 (part), pp68-69, p74, p76 (inset), p78 (part), p79 (part),
p83, p88 (part), p89 (part), p92-93, p94 (inset), p97 (inset), p99 (part), p107 (part), p111 (part), p113, p114-115, p116-117, p118-119 (part)